BARRON'S

HOW TO PREPARE FOR THE

AP*

ENGLISH

ADVANCED PLACEMENT EXAMINATIONS

LITERATURE AND COMPOSITION
LANGUAGE AND COMPOSITION

7TH EDITION

George Ehrenhaft,
Max Nadel, and
Arthur Sherver, Jr.

DISCARD

*AP and Advanced Placement Program are registered
trademarks of the College Entrance Examination Board,
which was not involved with the production of and does
not endorse this book.

BARRON'S

All inquiries should be addressed to:
Barron's Educational Series, Inc.
250 Wireless Boulevard
Hauppauge, NY 11788
http://www.barronseduc.com

Library of Congress Catalog Card No. 99-58224

International Standard Book No. 0-7641-1230-9

Library of Congress Cataloging-in-Publication Data

Ehrenhaft, George.
    How to prepare for the advanced placement examination,
English : literature and composition, language and composition /
George Ehrenhaft, Max Nadel, Arthur Sherrer, Jr.—7th ed.
    p. cm.
        Rev. ed. of: How to prepare for the advanced placement exam-
    ination, English / Max Nadel. 6th ed. © 1997.
        Includes bibliographical references.
        ISBN 0-7641-1230-9
        1.   English   philology—Examinations—Study   guides.
    2. Advanced placement programs (Education) I. Nadel, Max.
    II. Sherrer, Arthur. III. How to prepare for the advanced place-
    ment examination, English. IV. Title. Ehrenhaft, George.

PE66.E38   2000
428'.0076—dc21   99-58224

PRINTED IN THE UNITED STATES OF AMERICA
9 8 7 6 5 4

Contents

Acknowledgments

The authors gratefully acknowledge the following copyright holders for permission to reprint material used.

Page 6: From "Milan," *The Innocents Abroad* by Mark Twain (1869). Anthologized in *Discovery of Europe,* ed. Philip Rahv, DoubledayAnchor, 1960.

Pages 18–19: Excerpt from "The Way to Rainy Mountain" by N. Scott Momaday. First published January 26, 1967 in *The Reporter.*

Pages 21–22: From *White Man, Listen!* by Richard Wright. Copyright © 1957 by Richard Wright. Reprinted by permission of John Hawkins & Associates, Inc.

Pages 26–27: From "Modern Architecture, Being the Kahn Lecture for 1930" by Frank Lloyd Wright, Princeton University Press, 1931. Printed in *Toward Liberal Education,* Louis G. Locke et al., eds. Holt, Rinehart and Winston, NY, 1962.

Pages 32–33: From "The Mystical West Puzzles the Practical East" by F. M. Esfandiary. *New York Times Magazine,* February 6, 1967. Reprinted in *Rhetoric* by Albert E. DiPippo. Glenco Press, 1971.

Page 34: From *For the New Intellectual* by Ayn Rand. New American Library, 1963. Printed in *The Rhetoric of Argumentation,* William J. Brandt. BobbsMerrill, 1970.

Page 34: From *Call to Greatness* by Adlai E. Stevenson. Atheneum, 1962. Printed in *The Rhetoric of Argumentation,* William J. Brandt. BobbsMerrill, 1970.

Pages 38–39: From "Winston Churchill in 1940" by Isaiah Berlin (1949). *Personal Impressions,* Viking Press, 1981.

Pages 51–52: From *The Bible,* translated by James Moffatt, Harper and Bros., 1950.

Page 52: From *Confessions of a Barbarian* by Edward Abbey. Little, Brown, 1994.

Page 61: From "Address at Pueblo, Colorado, September 25, 1919," *The Messages and Papers of Woodrow Wilson.* The Review of Reviews Corporation, 1924, II, 1129.

Pages 64–65: From *The Common Sense of Science* by J. Bronowski. Copyright © 1953 by the President and Fellows of Harvard College. With permission of Harvard University Press.

Pages 167–169: "Ode to the Americas," from *Selected Odes of Pablo Neruda* by Pablo Neruda. Translated and edited by Margaret Sayers Peden. Copyright © 1990 The University of California Press; reprinted with permission.

Page 171: "In Praise of Darkness," translated by Hoyt Rogers, copyright © 1999 by Hoyt Rogers, from *Selected Poems* by Jorge Luis Borges. Used by permission of Viking Penguin, a division of Penguin Putnam Inc.

Page 173: "Pushkin" from *Poems of Ahkmatova.* Translated by Stanley Kunitz with Max Hayward. Copyright © 1973 Little, Brown and Company, Inc.; reprinted with permission.

Pages 329–330: From *Religion and Science* by Bertrand Russell. Oxford University Press, 1935.

Pages 332–334: From *West with the Night* by Beryl Markham. North Point Press, 1942.

Pages 335–337: From "Reflections on Exile" by Edward Said. *Granta,* Autumn, 1984.

Pages 338–339: From *The Frontier in American History* by Frederick Jackson Turner. Holt, Rinehart and Winston, 1920.

Pages 341–342: From "The Corps" by Henry Allen. *The Washington Post,* March 5, 1972.

Pages 344–345: From *The Dark of the Moon* by Eric Severeid. Harold Matson Company, Inc., 1958.

Pages 345–346: From *Out of My Later Years* by Albert Einstein. NY: The Philosophical Library, Inc. 1950. A: pp. 42–43. B: pp. 130–131. As printed in *Rhetoric* by Albert E. DiPippo. Philosophical Library, New York.

Pages 360–361: From *Civilization on Trial* by Arnold J. Toynbee. Oxford University Press, 1948.

Pages 365–366: From *Introductory Lecture, Delivered . . . October 3, 1892* by A.E. Housman. Cambridge University Press, 1937. Reprinted by permission.

Page 373: From *Off Broadway* by Maxwell Anderson. William Sloane Associates, 1947.

Pages 373–374: From "The Cultural Importance of the Arts" by Susanne K. Langer. *Creation and Expression,* Scribner's, 1957.

Page 398: From "What Are Years?" in *Collected Poems* by Marianne Moore. Copyright © 1941, 1969 by Marianne Moore. With permission from Macmillan Publishing Company.

Page 419: From "Hampstead Revisited" by Alfred Levinson. *Travelogs,* Signford Press 1981.

Introducing the AP English Exams

The College Board offers two different Advanced Placement examinations in English:

1. Language and Composition
2. Literature and Composition

This book will help you prepare for one or both of these exams.

1. The Language and Composition exam tests your capacity to analyze a range of prose passages representing various historical periods, rhetorical styles, and disciplines. It also tests your ability to write a variety of analytical essays that show how authors use language to express their views, convey meaning, and create effects in their readers.
2. The Literature and Composition exam focuses on close reading of literary content. It tests your ability to comprehend and interpret the form and substance of poems and prose passages. In addition, it asks you write clear, concise, and persuasive interpretive essays in which you must demonstrate your understanding of the broad implications of particular works of literature.

Both examinations last three hours and consist of two sections. The first section, which takes one hour, consists of multiple-choice questions and counts for 45 percent of the total score. The second section, lasting two hours, requires you to write three essays and comprises 55 percent of your grade.

	Part I	Part II
Language and Composition	Fifty to sixty multiple-choice questions based on your reading of four or five prose passages from literature, history, science, art, language, and so on. (One hour)	Two essays analyzing the style, rhetoric, use of language (e.g., diction, imagery, sentence structure) of selected prose passages. Followed by a third essay, usually an argument, that responds to a passage or a given topic. (Two hours)
Literature and Composition	Fifty to sixty multiple-choice questions based on your reading of two or three prose fiction passages and two or three poems. (One hour)	Three essays, one on a given poem, one on a passage of prose fiction—each analyzing how form and content relate to the meaning—and a third essay on your choice of novel or play. (Two hours)

Like all other AP exams, scores are reported on a scale of 1–5. In general, scores are interpreted as follows:

5 extremely well-qualified
4 well-qualified
3 qualified
2 possibly qualified
1 not recommended for AP credit

A high score on either exam demonstrates a proficiency in English at least on a par with students who have successfully completed an introductory college level course in composition or literature. Recognizing this, many colleges and universities may waive your freshman English requirement, give you credit for the required course, or permit you to take a more advanced course in your first year. Since each college and university has its own policies regarding the awarding of credit for a good score, you should check with the admissions office of the institution you hope to attend.

This book will familiarize you with the multiple-choice questions and give you practical help in essay writing. In addition, the sections in this book that deal with the Literature exam will add to your knowledge of works of literature and sharpen your powers of critical evaluation. The sections on the Language exam offer a review of the required grammar, an introduction to rhetorical principles, and practice in analyzing a variety of short passages.

You can use this book to prepare on your own for either exam. In addition, the book can serve as a resource for AP English teachers. Its use will lighten the teacher's burden since most of the content of the course—selections of reading material, terminology, glossaries, analyses, sample essays with evaluations, exam questions, and sample tests—are included. The works discussed and analyzed can readily be incorporated into a course of study or used as a ready-made syllabus. Questions and exercises are intended to stimulate thinking and inspire the writing of in-depth analyses like those required on the AP exam.

Especially helpful are the two practice tests in Language and Composition and four practice tests in Literature and Composition. Answer keys and explanations of all multiple-choice questions allow you to evaluate your own performance. Suggested responses for all essay questions are also included.

To all students preparing to take an AP English exam, the authors wish the best of luck.

PART ONE

LANGUAGE AND COMPOSITION EXAM

1 Overview of the Test

The Language and Composition exam is a reading test. It obliges you not only to comprehend the selected passages but also to be aware of how authors manipulate language to create meaning and to evoke a response in the reader.

To do well on this test, therefore, you must be an active reader. Merely understanding the words will not be enough. Rather, you must be willing to extract the full meaning of prose passages by analyzing and defining the composing techniques that give a text its aesthetic character. To do that you must know about rhetoric. You need to know how sentence structure affects readers, how the choice of details contributes to meaning, and how form relates to content. You must also understand and be able to recognize (among other things) themes, tone, diction, syntactical patterns, allusions, imagery, paradox, irony, satire, and rhetorical devices. In short, you must be a dissector of passages—someone who can read a passage and figure out how all its components work together to convey meaning and create an effect on the reader.

To demonstrate your grasp of rhetoric during the three-hour exam, you will be given both short-answer and essay questions. For the first sixty minutes you will read a handful of relatively short nonfiction passages and be asked ten or so multiple-choice questions about each one. During the remaining time you will write three essays, each related to a short passage that you are asked to read and analyze. Typically, two of the essay questions pertain to the author's use of language—they ask for stylistic and rhetorical analyses. The third question often asks you to write an argument that defends or challenges a point of view expressed by the author. Not every exam follows this pattern, so be prepared to answer a different type of question. (See "Answering Essay Questions" (page 93) for examples of questions from previous exams.)

The multiple-choice section of the test is 45 percent of the total score and the essays are 55 percent.

The essays are scored holistically. That is, the essays will be read rather quickly for the overall impression they make. Readers are trained to look for clearly organized, well-developed, and forceful responses that reveal a depth of understanding and insight. Because AP students hope to earn college credit for their efforts, readers also look for prose that is worthy of a mature writer. Readers will be most impressed by clarity, coherence, good reasoning, and a writing style that demonstrates—by its diction, voice, syntax, rhythm, and tone—your command of a variety of effective writing techniques. (See "Answering Essay Questions" [page 93] for a discussion of effective writing.)

2 Multiple-Choice Questions

Multiple-choice questions test your ability to read critically and recognize rhetorical elements in individual passages. In general, the questions are meant to test your awareness of the techniques used by writers to create meaning and effect. You'll be asked to draw inferences about the surface and deeper-level meanings of all or parts of several passages. You'll be asked to analyze the language choices the writers have made and recognize features of style, organization, and aesthetic character.

To answer fifty or more questions, it helps to be aware of how structural patterns and grammatical and syntactic relationships contribute to meaning. Questions pertain to almost everything that the author has done to compose the passage. Thus, the list of what you need to know includes the functions of paragraphs and how paragraphs are used in developing ideas. You also must have a sense of sentences: how sentences function in a passage; how sentences of different lengths, structure, and type (simple, compound, complex, compound-complex) relate to tone and meaning. You must be aware of the uses of subordination, coordination, appositives, and parenthetical ideas.

You may also be asked about word order, tone, diction (word choice), transitions, repetition, parallelism, and use of alliteration, allusion, antithesis, apostrophe, and figurative language that includes metaphor, allusions, similes, hyperbole, paradox, and irony.

Questions about language may be worded as follows.

The second paragraph of the passage contains all of the following EXCEPT
(A) a simple sentence
(B) a compound sentence
(C) a complex sentence
(D) a declarative sentence
(E) an interrogative sentence

To answer this question you need to know the terminology and be able to pick out sentence types. The review of sentence types in this chapter will help you do just that.

Another type of grammar question is apt to be phrased like this.

Lines 12–18 contain which of the following?
(A) Subordinate clauses
(B) Hyperbole
(C) A single periodic sentence
(D) An allusion
(E) Parallel syntax

Strictly speaking, only choices (A), (C), and (E) relate to grammar. The others tend to be more rhetorical in nature. The nature of each choice, however, matters less than your ability to identify various examples of grammatical usage and rhetoric when you see them.

Typically, no more than two or three multiple-choice questions on the AP Literature exam pertain directly to English grammar. The preponderance of questions—other than literary interpretation—relate to rhetoric, particularly to what is called "rhetorical stance," a catch-all term loosely referring to the position of the author or speaker vis-à-vis the subject in the passage. Broadly speaking, rhetorical stance is much like tone and style of writing, as these sample questions show.

A tone question can be worded like this.

> The speaker's tone in the last two stanzas of the poem can best be described as which of the following?
> (A) Contemptuous
> (B) Satirical
> (C) Pretentious
> (D) Reproachful
> (E) Flippant

A rhetorical stance question can be worded like this.

> The change in the author's rhetorical stance that occurs between the third and fourth paragraphs can best be described as a shift from
> (A) figurative to literal
> (B) objective to subjective
> (C) laconic to energetic
> (D) critical to descriptive
> (E) assertive to tentative

A mood question can be worded like this.

> The mood of the second paragraph of the passage is best described as
> (A) quizzical
> (B) elegiac
> (C) whimsical
> (D) suspenseful
> (E) satiric

In literary criticism, the term *mood* refers to the feelings that a poem or prose piece arouses in the reader. Mood, therefore, is technically different from *tone,* which refers to the author's or speaker's feelings about the subject. Considering the foregoing questions, though, this subtle distinction is ignored on the AP exam, where the terms are used more or less interchangeably.

To prepare multiple-choice questions, AP test writers ordinarily choose passages written between the seventeenth and twenty-first century, although they might occasionally toss in a passage from the pen of an ancient Greek or Roman. In each exam, they attempt to balance genre, time period, and individual style. Passages are nonfiction and are composed by essayists, historians, journalists, diarists, autobiographers, political writers, philosophers, and critics. You won't find simple passages that leave little room for interpretation, nor will you find passages that are so ornate or ambiguous that they invite numerous interpretations.

On the multiple-choice portion of the exam, the authors and titles of the passages are not given. In effect, your sensitivity to the written word is on the line. You will be prepared if you have a great deal of reading experience, both from school and on your own. The kind of close textual analysis usually practiced in AP English classes will help you read the passages and answer the questions.

Sample Passage and Questions

"Do you wiz zo haut can be?"

That was what the guide asked, when we were looking up at the bronze horses on the Arch of Peace. It meant, Do you wish to go up there? I give it as a specimen of guide-English. These are the people
(5)   that make life a burden to the tourist. Their tongues are never still. They talk forever and forever, and that is the kind of billingsgate they use. Inspiration itself could hardly comprehend them. If they would only show you a masterpiece of art, or a venerable tomb, or a prison-house, or a battlefield, hallowed by touching memories, or historical reminiscences,
(10)   or grand traditions, and then step aside and hold still for ten minutes and let you think, it would not be so bad. But they interrupt every dream, every pleasant train of thought, with their tiresome cackling. Sometimes when I have been standing before some cherished old idol of mine that I remembered years and years ago in pictures in the geography at school, I
(15)   have thought I would give a whole world if the human parrot at my side would suddenly perish where he stood and leave me gaze, and ponder, and worship.

No, we did not "wiz zo haut can be." We wished to go to La Scala, the largest theater in the world, I think they call it. We did so. It was
(20)   a large place. Seven separate and distinct masses of humanity—six great circles and a monster parquette.[1]

We wished to go to the Ambrosian Library, and we did that also. We saw a manuscript of Virgil, with annotations in the handwriting of Petrarch, the gentleman who loved another man's Laura, and lavished
(25)   upon her all through life a love which was clear waste of the raw material. It was sound sentiment, but bad judgment. It brought both parties fame, and created a fountain of commiseration for them in sentimental breasts that is running yet. But who says a word in behalf of poor Mr. Laura? (I do not know his other name.) Who glorifies him? Who bedews him
(30)   with tears? Who writes poetry about him? Nobody. How do you suppose *he* liked the state of things that has given the world so much pleasure? How did he enjoy having another man following his wife everywhere and making her name a familiar word in every garlic-exterminating mouth in Italy with his sonnets to her preempted eyebrows? *They* got
(35)   fame and sympathy—he got neither. This is a peculiarly felicitous instance of what is called poetical justice. It is all very fine; but it does not chime with my notions of right. It is too one-sided—too ungenerous. Let the world go on fretting about Laura and Petrarch if it will; but as for me, my tears and lamentations shall be lavished upon the unsung defendant.

Line

_____

[1]the lowest floor of a theater; the orchestra section

1. The opening sentence of the first main paragraph (lines 2–3) contains all of the following EXCEPT
    (A) a proper noun
    (B) a transitional word or phrase
    (C) a dependent clause
    (D) prepositional phrases
    (E) parallelism

Comment: This is one of a relatively small percent of questions on the exam that pertain to the grammatical components of a sentence. To answer the question successfully you need to be familiar with sentence structure and with the concepts and terminology of traditional grammar.

In order to find the answer, you must examine the sentence, looking for the features listed in the five choices. The one feature that does not appear is the correct answer. (In any set of AP exam questions you are apt to find two or three items that ask you to identify the exception or to name which of several choices apply—as in questions 2 and 6 that follow.)

Choice (A) is not a good choice because the "Arch of Peace" is a proper noun. Choice (B) may seem like a possible answer because the sentence in question does not contain any of the common transitional words or phrases found in English. However, the word "that" functions as a transition, linking this sentence to the quotation with which the passage began. Because the sentence contains a subordinate clause ("when we were looking . . ."), Choice (C) is not a correct response. Nor is Choice (D) a valid answer because the sentence contains two prepositional phrases: "at the bronze horses" and "on the Arch of Peace." By the process of elimination, then, Choice (E) is the correct answer.

2. In line 12, the word "cackling" derives its effect from
        I. Its use as a description of human speech
       II. Its position as the last word in the sentence
      III. The sound of the word
    (A) I only
    (B) I and II only
    (C) I and II only
    (D) II and III only
    (E) I, II, and III

Comment: By singling out the word "cackling," the question implies that readers will find the word unusual in some way. Your job is to determine what gives the word its power in this particular context. It goes without saying that chickens, turkeys, and other fowl are known to cackle—not humans. Therefore, Roman numeral I is a good choice.

What about the position of "cackling" in the sentence? Beginnings and endings are often places of prominence in a sentence. Knowing that, writers make an impact on a reader by saving a catchy or unusual word for the end. Roman II, therefore, is also a valid answer. As for Roman III, you must ask yourself whether the sound of the word "cackling" has a particular force. It probably does because it is somewhat onomatopoeic—that is, it sounds like the action it describes. Because all three descriptions fit, (E) is the best answer to this question.

3.   The locution "Do you wiz zo haut can be?" (line 1) implies that the narrator
   (A)   disapproves of guides who talk too much
   (B)   does not speak Italian
   (C)   cannot understand the guide
   (D)   is annoyed by the guide
   (E)   would prefer that the guide keep his mouth shut

Comment: Look for the answer to this question in the first main paragraph of the passage (lines 2–17), which provides a context for the locution and reveals the narrator's state of mind. Choice (A) is a tempting answer because the narrator clearly disapproves of guides whose "tongues are never still." But don't answer too quickly. Remember that the question is about that opening locution. There is no clear link between the guide's words—or, more accurately, the words that the narrator hears—and the quantity of talking done by the guide. The same reasoning applies to Choice (E), which seems acceptable until you carefully examine the larger context of the passage. With Choice (B), it is possible that the author doesn't speak Italian. But again, that fact is not related to the opening locution, which is meant to be a phonetic transcription of what the author hears. Choice (D) may also be true, but the author's annoyance is only suggested by the quasi-English utterance with which the passage opens. We are left, therefore, with Choice (C). Because the narrator cannot understand the Italian's words, he mocks them. Indeed, later he adds, "Inspiration itself could hardly comprehend them" (line 7). Several of the choices in this question, although incorrect, seem to be potential answers because they accurately describe the narrator's opinions. Don't be misled by these so-called distractors. They are meant to draw unwary students away from the question being asked. Readers may confuse these facts with the truth of the statement in answering the question.

4.   The objects of the verb "show" in line 8 make up a list of places that
   (A)   tourists favor
   (B)   Italy has in great abundance
   (C)   inspire dreams
   (D)   demand visitors' respect
   (E)   provoke emotions

Comment: There is no reason for including the term "objects of the verb" in this question. The phrase is meant either to fool students into thinking that they face a grammar question or intimidate those with a shaky grasp of grammatical terminology. Whatever the purpose, the answer to the question is found in the overall context and tone of the passage. Choice (B) should be eliminated because the passage contains no evidence that Italy is abundantly endowed with masterpieces of art, venerable tombs, and so forth. (Italy, in fact, has plenty of art and tombs, but the passage doesn't imply that.) Choices (C), (D), and (E) are all partly true. But not all the places listed inspire dreams, demand respect, or provoke emotions. Some do, some don't. Therefore, Choice (A), being the most inclusive of the choices, is the best answer.

5. The tone in the clause "and we did that also" (line 22) suggests that the narrator
   (A) enjoys sightseeing
   (B) is tired of traveling in Italy
   (C) remembers seeing a photo of the Ambrosian Library in a geography schoolbook
   (D) is an indifferent tourist
   (E) dutifully follows the guide from place to place

Comment: To answer this question, you must know the definition of *tone*— the author's attitude toward his subject. In this case, the contents of the previous paragraph (lines 17–21) offer a good clue. Telling us about a wish to see La Scala, he writes, "We did so. It was a large place. Seven . . ." That taken care of, he moves on to the Ambrosian Library (". . . we did that also"). Between the lines, the author is conveying the idea that he is blasé about visiting these places. Indeed, going to the opera house and to the library means little to him— until he sees the Virgil manuscript. Choice (A) is highly unlikely considering the totality of the narrator's account of his time in Italy. Choice (B) may be valid to a point, although the narrator never states outright that he'd like to go home. Choice (C) has no basis in fact. Choice (D), the correct answer, is evident in the narrator's account of La Scala and of his visit to the Ambrosian Library—at least until he lays eyes on the Virgil manuscript. Choice (E) seems reasonable except that the narrator twice says "we wished to go to . . . ," implying an act of volition that is contrary to following the guide around from place to place.

6. Which of the following prepare the reader for the reference to "every garlic-exterminating mouth in Italy" (lines 33–34)?
   I. "waste of raw material" (line 25)
   II. "it brought both parties fame" (line 26)
   III. "a fountain of commiseration" (line 27)
   IV. "her name a familiar word" (line 33)
   (A) I and III only
   (B) II and IV only
   (C) I, III, and IV only
   (D) II, III, and IV only
   (E) I, II, III, and IV

Comment: This question pertains to the rhetorical unity inherent in well-written prose. A passage often achieves a kind of coherence by repeatedly echoing a certain idea, not phrased in the same words each time but in words that are related. The phrase in question suggests that Laura's name is famous throughout Italy. To prepare us for this fact, the author has included a number of phrases that indicate how well-known Laura has become. Each of the phrases marked Roman II, III, and IV alludes directly or indirectly to the magnitude of her renown. Only Roman I fails to allude to Laura's fame. Therefore, Choice (D) is the correct answer.

7. To the narrator, the Virgil manuscript is
    (A) a popular attraction for tourists
    (B) a historically significant document
    (C) a literary masterpiece
    (D) an example of bad judgment
    (E) a stimulus for reflection

Comment: In the last paragraph of the passage, the narrator focuses not on the Virgil manuscript *per se* but on Petrarch's annotations. Petrarch's handwritten notes inspire the narrator to reflect on Petrarch's relationship with Laura. Rather than sentimentalize Petrarch's love, however, the narrator thinks about "Mr. Laura," the "wronged" husband. In that sense, Choice (E) most accurately describes the narrator's attitude toward the Virgil manuscript.

8. In line 25, "a clear waste of raw material" is best interpreted to mean that
    (A) Petrarch's love of Laura was unrequited
    (B) Petrarch should have loved another woman
    (C) Petrarch's sonnets were of poor quality
    (D) Petrarch's annotations on Virgil's manuscript were pointless
    (E) Too many tears have been spilled over the sad story of Petrarch and Laura

Comment: Questions that ask you to interpret the meaning of a sample of figurative language are popular on AP exams. The metaphor "clear waste of raw material" refers to "a love" that evidently was unhappy, making Choice (A) the best answer. If you piece together the story from hints in the passage, it seems that Petrarch loved Laura, who was married to another man. His love lasted a long time ("lavished upon her all through life"), and brought the pair not only fame but sympathy ("created a fountain of commiseration"). Hindsight suggests that Petrarch might have been better off loving another woman—Choice (B)—but then his famous love sonnets might never have been written. Choice (C) and Choice (D) are not supported by material in the passage. Choice (E) is suggested by lines 37–39 ("Let the world go on fretting . . ."), but there is no obvious connection to the phrase "a clear waste of raw material."

9. In which of the following sentences does the narrator use hyperbole to convey the intensity of his feelings?
    (A) Line 4: "These are the people . . ."
    (B) Lines 12–13: "Sometimes when I . . ."
    (C) Line 18: "We wished to go . . ."
    (D) Line 28: "But who says a word . . ."
    (E) Line 36: "It is all very fine . . ."

Comment: To find the answer to this question you must recognize *hyperbole.* Read all the sentences indicated by Choices (A)–(E). Look for an exaggeration meant to achieve a rhetorical effect. Only (B) contains such an overstatement: "I would give the whole world if the human parrot at my side would suddenly perish . . . ." The "whole world" is a lot to give to be rid of the guide. Moreover, the author's wish that the guide "would suddenly perish" is an extreme measure that overstates his desire to be rid of the man.

10. Which of the following best describes the narrator's overall tone?
    (A) admiring and respectful
    (B) pugnacious and patronizing
    (C) contemptuous and hateful
    (D) satirical and ironic
    (E) moralistic and solemn

Comment: Choose an answer in which both adjectives accurately describe the narrator's tone. Choice (B) contains only one such adjective: *patronizing.* The author adopts an air of superiority and condescension toward the guide in the very first line of the passage. In spite of his haughtiness, though, he is never hostile. Thus, *pugnacious* is not a valid description. There is very little in the passage to suggest that Choice (A) is the correct answer. Choice (C) overstates the author's attitude. While he shows signs of contemptuousness, he never crosses the line to outright hatefulness. Because the humor in the passage eliminates Choice (E), we are left with Choice (D) as the correct answer. Indeed, throughout the passage the author holds up to derision not only the guide but his own situation as a tourist in Italy. What's more, in discussing Laura's husband, the author's tongue is lodged firmly in his cheek. In other words, the passage reeks of irony.

11. The structure of the sentences in lines 28–31 does all of the following EXCEPT
    (A) create suspense
    (B) express a mock indignation
    (C) provoke amusement
    (D) vary the rhythm of the prose
    (E) add a touch of playfulness

Comment: At issue in this question is the effect of sentence structure on a reader's response to a passage. By and large, the lines in question consist of a series of short interrogatives about "poor Mr. Laura." Also included is a parenthetical remark and a one-word answer—"Nobody"—to several of the questions. The writing in the passage is informal, its tone more lighthearted than ponderous. A series of staccato-like rhetorical questions might suggest anger, but the subject matter (the long-ignored husband of the famous Laura) is far from somber. Thus, Choices (B), (C), and (E) accurately describe the passage. Choice (D) is also valid because the rest of the passage is made up predominantly of longer, complex, and compound sentences. Only Choice (A) does not apply.

The foregoing questions represent a sample of the many types of questions included in the exam. The following list will give you an idea of numerous other types that that have recently appeared:

1. Identify the relation of a sentence in the first paragraph to the passage as a whole.
2. Name the rhetorical strategy or device used in a particular section of the passage.
3. Identify the function of a sentence within a paragraph, or a paragraph within the whole.
4. Choose the best title or main topic of a passage.

5. Compare two segments of the passage for their theme, tone, style, sentence structure, diction, syntax, effect, or rhetorical purpose.
6. Determine how unity (or point of view, emphasis, contrast, or other feature) is achieved in all or part of the passage.
7. Recognize the overall genre of the passage.
8. Identify the author's implied or actual purpose or the purpose of particular images, diction, organization, sentence structure, or other stylistic choice.

Techniques for Reading Passages

By this time in your school career you have taken numerous tests like the SATs or ACTs, for which you have read passages like those on the AP English exam and answered multiple-choice questions. No doubt you've developed certain techniques of test taking. You've probably also observed that there is no universal technique that serves everyone equally. What works for others may not work for you and vice versa.

Nevertheless, it is helpful to be aware of which techniques lead you to do your best. As you prepare for the AP exam, consider trying each of the alternatives discussed below. If time permits, you might try each one in turn as you work your way through the exercises that follow or take the practice exams in the last section of this book. Gradually you'll discover which technique—or combination of techniques—works best for you.

OPTION A

Read the passage carefully from start to finish with pencil in hand. As you read, keep in mind that on this test you will be asked questions primarily about the language and rhetoric of the passage, not about its meaning (although you may get a small number of comprehension questions). While reading, underline any unusual turns of phrase. Make a note of particularly vivid images and of figures of speech. Try also to figure out the tone of the passage. Ask yourself, "What is the author trying to say about the subject?" Then mark any words, phrases, or ideas that clearly contribute to the tone. Finally, observe how the passage is organized. Is there a progression of ideas? What does each paragraph contribute to the main point of the passage? Then turn to the questions, referring to the passage as necessary to find or check your answers.

OPTION B

Skim the passage for its general idea. Read faster than you normally would, trying only to ascertain the general topic and the approach used by the author: Is the passage formal or informal? Personal or objective? Is it mainly a narrative? A description? An argument for or against some issue? The answers to these questions will be fairly apparent during a quick read-through. Make a mental note of any unusual words and phrases. Read intently enough to get an impression of the content and writing style of the passage, but don't dawdle. Then, as you answer the questions, refer to the passage.

OPTION C

Skim the passage for a general impression; then go back and read it more thoroughly using your pencil to mark the passage and take notes. Two readings, one fast and one slow, allow you to pick out features of language and rhetoric that you might overlook during a single reading. Why? Because from the first reading you'll know what the passage is about, and during the second you'll be able to focus on the features that contribute to the overall meaning and effect of the passage. After the second reading proceed to the questions, referring to the passage to check your answers.

OPTION D

Read the passage only after you've read the questions. Because it's virtually impossible to remember ten or twelve questions about material you haven't read, review the questions quickly—only to become acquainted with the kinds of information you are expected to draw out of the passage. Identify each question with a brief notation: "MI" (main idea), "T" (tone), "POV" (point of view), "SS" (sentence structure), and so on. (You can devise your own system.) When you know the questions beforehand, you can read the passage more purposefully, taking into account the matters raised by the questions.

Whatever you do, don't even think of answering the questions without thoroughly reading the passage from start to finish. Misguided students sometimes read one question first, then start scouring the passage in search of an answer. Then they move to the second question and repeat their search. Before they know it, time runs out, and they are far from finishing. Moreover, such a fragmented approach reduces the likelihood of grasping the overall point of the passage.

Reading Practice

A good score on the exam may be linked directly to your power as a reader. Unlike the reading sections on the SAT or ACT, in which you read passages mainly for their content, the multiple-choice section of the AP exam requires you to answer more probing questions about the author's intent, tone, style, structure, and so forth. Therefore, you must know each passage intimately. You must grasp not only what it says but how the author composed it. In short, you must understand its anatomy—how it was built, the materials used, how the parts are related, and what holds it all together.

To be a strong reader, you should probably develop the habit of dissecting passages piece by piece, line by line. Keep in mind that nothing in a well-written passage exists by accident. Good authors make deliberate choices of every syllable they write. Nothing is left to chance—not the words, the sentences, the punctuation, the order and content of paragraphs, nor the overall structure of their work. Every bit of their prose has a point and purpose behind it. (That, incidentally, is one of the great differences between good prose and bad prose. The good writer works very hard to find the best words to put in the best order.) Your job on the AP test is to analyze just what the author did.

Many readers are aware of the components of writing. A strong reader, however, will be able to discern each component, not unlike the way an artist discerns each color in a swatch of paint or the gourmet detects the presence of an herb or spice in a fine sauce.

Fortunately, it is possible to train yourself to read with your antennae up—to read with perspicuity. By honing your reading skills, you may find that the structure and composition of whatever you read becomes increasingly transparent. By regularly practicing the following steps, you will, in effect, be preparing yourself for the AP exam.

1. Condense the main idea of whatever you read into a pithy sentence or two. (An ambitious student might even jot down a brief outline.) If you can clearly and accurately identify the thesis, you've come a long way. Sometimes the thesis will be stated outright. In that case, underline or highlight it is some way. If it is only implied by the evidence, however, put it into your own words. Writing it out on paper or on a computer screen is a sure sign that you are serious about finding the essence of a passage.

2. Look for clues to the author's attitude, purpose, and intent. Is the passage meant largely to entertain? To inform? To provoke controversy? To inspire or to enlighten the reader? Does the author have a bias, an ax to grind, an ulterior motive? It's hard to conceive of a piece of writing in which the author's attitude is totally hidden.

3. Analyze structure. Which ideas come first? Second? Third? Is there a reason for the sequence of ideas? How are ideas linked to each other? Does the end contain echoes of earlier ideas?

4. Examine how the author creates an effect on the reader. Study word choice, sentence structure and length, the order of ideas, figures of speech, use of rhythm and sound—all components of writing style. How does author keep you interested? Is the writing formal or informal? Is the author friendly or stand-offish, enthusiastic or cool?

5. Think about the author's qualifications to write on a topic. Details usually reveal the authority of the writer. Writing by someone who doesn't know the topic intimately is apt to be top-heavy with generalities.

6. Become an annotator. Mark up passages profusely, writing in margins and underlining noteworthy ideas and features.

What follows is a selection of two short passages that have been annotated for you. Although the notes are not exhaustive, they suggest what an alert reader might observe during a close reading of each passage.

PASSAGE 1

As soon as the Pigeons discover a
sufficiency of food to entice them to alight,
(Anthropomorphic view: (attributes human trait to birds' instinctive behavior))

they fly around in circles, reviewing the

Line   countryside below. During these evolutions
(Suggests progressive change)

(5)   the dense mass which they form presents a
beautiful spectacle, as it changes direction;

Sibilant sounds ("s," "sh," "z") suggest swoosh of birds' wings

turning from a glistening sheet of azure, as
the backs of the birds come simultaneously
(Visual images support "beautiful spectacle" (line 6))

into view, to a suddenly presented rich, deep

(10)   purple. After that they pass lower, over the
woods, and for a moment are lost among the
(Simple sentence structure contrasts with sentences 1 and 2 for variety and balance)

Passing in and out of view: evolutionary (line 4)

foliage. Again they emerge and glide aloft.

They may now alight, but the next moment take
to wing as if suddenly alarmed, the flapping of
(First half of passage concludes with sound imagery)

(15)   their wings producing a noise like the roar of
distant thunder, as they sweep through ^simile
the forests to see if danger is near. However,
(Turning point of passage Part 1: birds in air Part 2: birds on ground)

more anthropomorphism ←

hunger soon brings them to the ground. On
alighting they industriously throw aside the

(20) withered leaves in quest of the fallen mast.
The rear ranks continually rise, passing over

*unusual term for "nuts/
acorns on forest floor."
(see line 30)*

*Evolution of flock
(line 4) evident here
and throughout passage*

the main body and alighting in front, and in
such rapid succession that the whole flock
seems still on the wing. The quantity of ground

(25) swept in this way is astonishing. So completely
has it been cleared that the gleaner who might

*Observer's reaction . . .
again*

follow in the rear of the flock would find his
labor completely lost. While feeding, their
avidity is at times so great that, in attempting

(30) to swallow a large acorn or nut, they may be
seen to gasp for a long while as if in the
agonies of suffocation.

defines "mast" (line 20)

*comparison "gasp" is "seen"
instead of "heard" (?)*

— From "Passenger Pigeon"
by John James Audubon

Content of passage
  1. Somewhat anthropomorphic description of birds' behavior
  2. Observer's reaction

Overall purpose
  To describe a natural phenomenon: written with sense of wonder and admiration
  Tone: appreciative

PASSAGE 2

Imperative "must" repeated

Transition from previous ¶

Who is "us"?

Thus the biographer must go ahead of the
rest of us, like the miner's canary, detecting
falsity, unreality, and the presence of obsolete

*Simile raises sense
of alarm*

Line conventions. His sense of truth must be alive

(5) and on tiptoe. Then again, since we live in an

*Figure of speech
(personification)*

*Alliteration makes the
language memorable*

age when a thousand cameras are pointed, by
newspapers, letters, and diaries, at every character
from every angle, he must be prepared to admit
contradictory versions of the same face.

(10) Biography will enlarge its scope by hanging up
looking glasses at odd corners. And yet from all

*Echoes "from every
angle" (line 8): lends
unity to passage*

*Verbs in future tense:
author is making pitch for
biography in the future.*

this diversity it will bring out, not a riot of
confusion, but a richer unity. And again since

*Transition similar to
line 5: author piles up
and repeats ideas for
emphasis*

*Reiterates ideas
in lines 5–8; adds
unity to passage*

(15) (so much is known that used to be unknown), the
question now inevitably asks itself whether the
lives of great men only should be recorded. Is
not anyone who has lived a life and left a record
of that life worthy of biography—the failures

*Rhetorical questions
(statements in question
form assert ideas
forcefully.)*

*Explains the "us" in line 2: "we"
are the audience of writers, critics,
and other friends of literature*

as well as the successes, the humble as well

(20) as the illustrious? And what is greatness?
And what is smallness? We must revise our

*Last sentence expresses main idea of ¶:
Biographers of the future will
find rich source of subjects in
the lives of ordinary people*

standards of merit and set up new heroes for
our admiration.

Imperative . . . again

—From *The Death of the Moth and Other Essays* by Virginia Woolf

Tone of passage: earnest, confident, authoritative, hopeful

Others may have made different, yet equally valid, comments about each of the foregoing passages. What matters is not that the words you use may differ from those of other readers but that they accurately convey what the authors have done in writing the passages.

Now try your hand at annotating a sample passage written by John Livingston Lowes. Read the passage at least twice—first to see what the passage is about, and then, during the second reading, to jot down whatever you notice about its structure and composition. When you are done, write out a statement that summarizes the main idea of the passage and state your perception of the author's tone. Then compare your notes to those made by the authors of this book (below). No doubt you will record ideas that they missed and vice versa.

A passage for annotation:

There are two deep-seated idiosyncrasies
of human nature that bear on our acceptance
or rejection of what is offered us. We have, in
Line   the first place, an innate bias for the familiar.
(5)   Whatever we're thoroughly unfamiliar with is
apt to seem to us odd, or queer, or curious, or
bizarre. For it is no mere trick of speech, but
one of those appallingly veracious records of
human nature and experience in which the
(10)   history of words abounds, through which
"outlandish" and "crude" attained their present
meaning. For "outlandish" meant in the beginning
only what doesn't belong to our own land, and
"uncouth" was simply "unknown." The change in
(15)   meaning registers a universal trait. Whatever is
alien to our own ways—the costume, manners,
modes of speech of another race or of other
times—is strange; and "strange" itself, which
started out by meaning merely "foreign," is
(20)   only another record of the same idiosyncrasy.
But there is still another trait that is no less
broadly human. Whatever is too familiar wearies
us. Incessant recurrence without variety breeds
tedium; the overiterated becomes the monotonous,
(25)   and the monotonous irks and bores. And there we are.
Neither that which we do not know at all, nor that
which we know too well, is to our taste. We are
averse to shocks, and we go to sleep under narcotics.
Both the shock and the narcotic have, I grant, at
(30)   times their fascination. But they are apt to be
forward, not permanent, sweet, not lasting.
The source of more or less abiding satisfaction
for most normal human beings lies in a happy
merging of the two—in the twofold delight in
(35)   an old friend recognized as new, or a new friend
recognized as old. The experience and the
pleasure are universal. All the lovers who
have ever lived have made experiment of it;
a face that you have passed a hundred times,

(40)   nor cared to see, remains the face you've
always known, but becomes all at once the
most beautiful and thrilling object in the world;
the person you've never known before, you find
all at once you've known from all eternity. Now

(45)   art, like love, sends its roots deep into what we
are. And our most permanent aesthetic satisfaction
arises as a rule from things familiar enough to
give the pleasure of recognition, yet not so trite
as to rob us of the other pleasure of surprise.

(50)   We are keen for the new, but we insist that it
establish some connection with what is friendly
and our own; we want the old, but we want it
to seem somehow new. Things may recur as often
as they please, so long as they surprise us—like

(55)   the Ghost in Hamlet—each time they appear.

—From *Convention and Revolt in Poetry*

Here is the same passage annotated by the authors:

Passage must cover two idiosyncrasies, or human traits

Topic sentence of passage

There are two deep-seated idiosyncrasies
of human nature that bear on our acceptance
or rejection of what is offered us. We have, in

Line
(5)   the first place, an innate bias for the familiar.

Trait #1 (2nd trait in line 21)

Author defines "bias for the familiar" (line 5) by explaining our aversion to the unfamiliar

Whatever we're thoroughly unfamiliar with is
apt to seem to us odd, or queer, or curious, or
bizarre. For it is no mere trick of speech, but
one of those appallingly veracious records of

4 adjectives show subtle gradations of meaning

(10)   human nature and experience in which the
history of words abounds, through which
"outlandish" and "crude" attained their present
meaning. For "outlandish" meant in the beginning
only what doesn't belong to our own land, and
"uncouth" was simply "unknown." The change in

A digression into word origins. Purpose? — To show how deep-seated is our rejection of the unfamiliar (?)

(15)   meaning registers a universal trait. Whatever is
alien to our own ways—the costume, manners,
modes of speech of another race or of other
times—is strange; and "strange" itself, which
started out by meaning merely "foreign," is

Development of discussion of word origins. Several examples add up to convincing case.

(20)   only another record of the same idiosyncrasy.
But there is still another trait that is no less
broadly human. Whatever is too familiar wearies
us. Incessant recurrence without variety breeds
tedium; the overiterated becomes the monotonous,

2nd trait introduced

2nd trait defined Development of 2nd trait

(25)   and the monotonous irks and bores. And there we are.

An interim conclusion based on discussion in lines 1–25

Neither that which we do not know at all, nor that
which we know too well, is to our taste. We are
averse to shocks, and we go to sleep under narcotics.
Both the shock and the narcotic have, I grant, at

An interruption: gives the reader a chance to let ideas sink in.

(30)   times their fascination. But they are apt to be
forward, not permanent, sweet, not lasting.

Author introduces another way to look at the issue

Antitheses used for greater impact

The source of more or less abiding satisfaction

Uses qualifier "more or less" to avoid dogmatism

Parallelism: juxtaposition of phrases makes each trait more vivid.

Short, pithy sentence for variety and greater rhetorical impact between two long sentences

Author expands discussion to include abstract world of "art"

Having presented the 2 traits, author merges them and starts to explain their significance

Author uses comparisons (analogies) from everyday experience to heighten reader's understanding

Reveals point of whole discussion: to explain why we respond emotionally to the arts

Subtle idea phrased in down-to-earth language

Allusion makes readers assess their own responses to the ghost of Hamlet's father

(35) for most normal human beings lies in a happy merging of the two—in the twofold delight in an old friend recognized as new, or a new friend recognized as old. The experience and the pleasure are universal. All the lovers who have ever lived have made experiment of it;

(40) a face that you have passed a hundred times, nor cared to see, remains the face you've always known, but becomes all at once the most beautiful and thrilling object in the world; the person you've never known before, you find all at once you've known from all eternity. Now

(45) art, like love, sends its roots deep into what we are. And our most permanent aesthetic satisfaction arises as a rule from things familiar enough to give the pleasure of recognition, yet not so trite as to rob us of the other pleasure of surprise.

(50) We are keen for the new, but we insist that it establish some connection with what is friendly and our own; we want the old, but we want it to seem somehow new. Things may recur as often as they please, so long as they surprise us—like

(55) the Ghost in Hamlet—each time they appear.

Point of passage
to point out that two contradictory human traits—bias for the familiar and our delight in being surprised—enhance our responses to the arts.

Tone: urbane / learned / analytical / informative

Under the pressure of time on the AP exam, you can't do a complete annotation as illustrated above. However, if you get into the habit of writing comments, underlining, and generally scrawling notes all over the things you read, it's likely that you'll sail through the passages on the exam. Like most other skills, proficiency in annotation diminishes if you stop practicing. So, keep at it because it's easy to slip out of the groove if you stop for any length of time.

Techniques for Answering Questions

The multiple-choice questions on the exam have been carefully written to separate well-qualified students from those who are less qualified. To earn a "5" you must answer most of the questions correctly. To earn a grade of "3" on the whole exam, you need to get about 50 or 60 percent of the short-answer questions right—provided that your essays are generally acceptable. The questions are not arranged in order of difficulty as they are on some standardized tests. Usually, they follow the progress of the passage, but not always.

In the scoring, wrong answers are penalized to compensate for random guessing. Therefore, don't guess unless you can eliminate one or more of the five choices. Here's the rationale:

Each question is worth one point. For each correct answer, one point will be added to your raw score. For every wrong answer, however, a quarter of a point will be deducted. An item left blank will neither add nor take away from your score. So, if you haven't a clue about how to answer a question, leave it blank.

On the other hand, if you can confidently eliminate one of the five choices, it pays to guess. You have a 1 in 4 chance that you'll get it right. It's not certain that you'll answer correctly, but suppose that on four of the roughly fifty questions you can eliminate one wrong answer and guess four times. If you guess right just once, you will have earned a point and lost three-quarters of a point, a net gain of one quarter. If you leave all four blank, you will gain nothing. This method is risky because you could make four incorrect guesses, but the chances of an incorrect answer every time are only 1 in 4.

When a question gives you trouble, and you can't decide among three choices, common wisdom says that you should go with your first impulse. You may be right. Testing experts and psychologists agree that there's a better than average chance of success if you trust your intuition. There are no guarantees, however. Because the mind works in so many ways, relying on your initial choice may not always work for you.

Passages for Practice

Using the following passages and related questions, practice each of the suggested techniques. Your performance will help you determine which approach is likely to help you do your best on the AP exam.

PASSAGE 1

Yellowstone, it seemed to me, was the top of the world, a region of deep lakes and dark timber, canyons and waterfalls. But, beautiful as it is, one might have the sense of confinement there. The skyline in all directions is close at hand, the high wall of the woods and deep cleavages of shade. There is a perfect freedom in the mountains, but it belongs to the eagle and the elk, the badger and the bear. The Kiowas reckoned their stature by the distance they could see, and they were bent and blind in the wilderness.

Descending eastward, the highland meadows are a stairway to the plain. In July the inland slope of the Rockies is luxuriant with flax and buckwheat, stonecrop and larkspur. The earth unfolds and the limit of the land recedes. Clusters of trees, and animals grazing far in the distance, cause the vision to reach away and wonder to build upon the mind. The sun follows a longer course in the day, and the sky is immense beyond all comparison. The great billowing clouds that sail upon it are shadows that move upon the grain like water, dividing light. Farther down, in the land of the Crows and Blackfeet, the plain is yellow. Sweet clover takes hold of the hills and bends upon itself to cover and seal the soil. There the Kiowas paused on the way; they had come to the place where they must change their lives. The sun is at home on the plains. Precisely there does it have the certain character of a god. When the Kiowas came to the land of the Crows, they could see the dark lees of the hills at dawn across the Bighorn River, the profusion of light on the grain shelves, the oldest deity ranging after the solstices. Not yet would they veer southward to the caldron of the land that lay below; they must wean their blood from the northern winter and hold the mountains a while longer in their view. . . .

A dark mist lay over the Black Hills, and the land was like iron. At the top of a ridge I caught sight of Devil's Tower upthrust against the gray sky as if in the birth of time the core of the earth had broken through its crust and the motion of the world was begun.

Line
(5)

(10)

(15)

(20)

(25)

(30)

1. The writer adopts the point of view of
   (A) a tourist on an Indian reservation
   (B) a botanist studying plant life in Yellowstone
   (C) a Native American visiting the land of his ancestors
   (D) a student of Indian customs and traditions
   (E) a historian returning to a familiar place

The details about Indian tribes indicate the author's knowledge of the people who once inhabited the Yellowstone region. Therefore, the author is not a casual visitor to a reservation; eliminate Choice (A). The land and nature are described at length, but not with the eye of a botanist; eliminate (B). The awe that he evidently feels about the scenery suggests that the author has come into this country for the first time; eliminate (E). The passage contains no evidence that the speaker is a student of Indian customs; eliminate (D). The remaining answer, (C), is correct. The writer's obvious reverence for the land implies that he has strong ties to the Yellowstone. For him it is like sacred ground.

2. "Descending eastward" (line 9) is a participial phrase modifying
   (A) "slope"
   (B) "highland"
   (C) "meadows"
   (D) "stairway"
   (E) "plain"

A participial phrase is a group of words introduced by a verbal—here, "descending." It performs an adjective function and modifies the subject of the clause that follows it. In the given sentence, only the *meadows* descend. Therefore, the correct answer is (C).

3. The speaker's tone in the passage can best be described as
   (A) earnest and profound
   (B) reverent and poetic
   (C) sensible and scholarly
   (D) exotic and sentimental
   (E) sober and philosophic

The speaker's main purpose in the passage is to follow the march of the Kiowas down from the mountain eastward to the plain. While he is earnest, his thoughts are not noticeably profound; eliminate (A). Choice (B) accurately describes the speaker's wonder and the esthetic pleasure he derives from the changing beauty of the country across which the Kiowas once passed. His language is filled with poetic images. Choice (C) is not correct: the speaker's approach is not at all *scholarly* but rather impressionistic. Likewise, in (D) *exotic* does not accurately describe either the speaker's state of mind or the land he describes so reverently. (E) is not a good choice because the passage is not philosophical. Rather, much of the passage is down to earth—literally.

4. The power of the sun is perceived at its greatest
   (A) following the solstices
   (B) during spring, when the flowers start to bloom
   (C) at early morning, when the sun dries the grass for the grazing animals
   (D) just before the solstices
   (E) in the season between the summer and winter solstices

The sun, according to lines 20–24, is most noticeable "after the solstices," (A). None of the other choices is supported by material in the passage.

5. Lines 13–16 contain which of the following?
    (A) Onomatopoeia and hyperbole
    (B) Personification and conceit
    (C) Paradox and ambiguity
    (D) Synecdoche and internal rhyme
    (E) Metaphor and simile

Because the lines in question contain examples of metaphor—"clouds . . . are shadows," and of simile—"move upon the grain like water," the correct answer is (E). To eliminate the incorrect choices, you must be familiar with the definitions of several literary terms, all of which are explained in the Review of Literary and Rhetorical Words, pages 467–472.

6. The style of this passage can best be described as
    (A) wordy and pedantic
    (B) ornate and flowery
    (C) graphic and graceful
    (D) terse and didactic
    (E) severe and classic

The language is fluent, rhythmic, and poetic. The author portrays the land in vivid images, making (C) the best answer. None of the adjectives in the four other choices applies to the style of the passage.

7. The primary rhetorical function of the last sentence in paragraph 1 (lines 6–8) is to
    (A) provide a transition to the next paragraph
    (B) support the main idea of the passage
    (C) introduce a contradiction that needs to be explained later
    (D) illustrate an idea presented earlier in the paragraph
    (E) present a thesis that will be developed later in the passage

The sentence in question introduces the Kiowas into the passage. Because the discussion of the Kiowas is not immediately picked up in paragraph 2, the sentence does not serve as a transition, as suggested by (A). Eliminate (B) because the sentence merely adds detail to the portrayal of the Kiowas. Eliminate (C) because the sentence is not at all contradictory to material in the paragraph; rather, it serves as a specific example of "the sense of confinement" mentioned earlier in the paragraph (line 3). Therefore (D) is the correct answer. Because the notion of freedom/confinement is dropped after the first paragraph, (E) cannot be the correct answer to the question.

PASSAGE 2

Let's imagine a mammoth flying saucer from Mars landing, say, in a peasant Swiss village and debouching swarms of fierce-looking men whose skins are blue and whose red eyes flash lightning
Line   bolts that deal instant death. The inhabitants are all the more terri-
(5)   fied because the arrival of these men had been predicted. The religious myths of the Western world—the Second Coming of Christ, the Last Judgment, etc., have conditioned Europeans for just such

(10) an improbable event. Hence, those Swiss natives will feel that resistance is useless for a while. As long as the blue strangers are casually kind, they are obeyed and served. They become the Fathers of the people. Is this a fragment of paperback science fiction? No. It's more prosaic than that. The image I've sketched above is the manner, by and large, in which white Europe overran Asia and Africa.

(15)   But why did Europe do this? Did it only want gold, power, women, raw materials? It was more complicated than that.

The fifteenth-, sixteenth-, and seventeenth-century neurotic European, sick of his thwarted instincts, restless, filled with self-disgust, was looking for not only spices and gold and slaves when

(20) he set out; he was looking for an Arcadia, a Land's End, a Shangri-la, a world peopled by shadow men, a world that would permit free play for his repressed instincts. Stripped of tradition, these misfits, adventurers, indentured servants, convicts and freebooters were the most advanced individualists of their time. Rendered

(25) socially superfluous by the stifling weight of the Church and nobility, buttressed by the influence of the ideas of Hume and Descartes, they had been brutally molded toward attitudes of emotional independence and could doff the cloying ties of custom, tradition, and family. The Asian-African native, anchored in

(30) family-dependence systems of life, could not imagine why or how these men had left their homelands, could not conceive of the cold, arid emotions sustaining them. . . .

Living in a waking dream, generations of emotionally impoverished colonial European whites wallowed in the quick gratification

(35) of greed, reveled in the cheap superiority of racial domination, slaked their sensual thirst in illicit sexuality, draining off the dammed-up libido that European morality had condemned, amassing through trade a vast reservoir of economic fat, thereby establishing vast accumulations of capital which spurred the

(40) industrialization of the West. Asia and Africa thus became a neurotic habit that Europeans could forgo only at the cost of a powerful psychic wound, for this emotionally crippled Europe had, through the centuries, grown used to leaning upon this black crutch. But what of the impact of those white faces upon the personali-

(45) ties of the native? Steeped in dependence systems of family life and anchored in ancestor-worshiping religions, the native was prone to identify those powerful white faces falling athwart his existence with the potency of his dead father who has sustained him in the past. Temporarily accepting the invasion, he trans-

(50) ferred his loyalties to those white faces, but, because of the psychological, racial, and economic luxury which those faces derived from their denomination, the native was kept at bay.

Today, as the tide of white domination of the land mass of Asia and Africa recedes, there lies exposed to view a procession of shat-

(55) tered cultures, disintegrated societies, and a writhing sweep of more aggressive, irrational religion than the world has known for centuries. And, as scientific research, partially freed from the blight of colonial control, advances, we are witnessing the rise of a new genre of academic literature dealing with colonial and post-colo-

(60) nial facts from a wider angle of vision than ever possible before.

In this new literature one enters a universe of menacing shadows where disparate images coalesce—white turning into black,

the dead coming to life, the top becoming the bottom—until you
think you are seeing Biblical beasts with seven heads and ten
(65) horns rising out of the sea.

   An agony was induced into the native heart, rotting and pulver-
izing it as it tried to live under a white domination with which it
could not identify in any real sense, a white domination that
mocked it. The more Westernized that native heart became, the
(70) more anti-Western it had to be, for that heart was not weighing
itself in terms of white Western values that made it feel degraded.
Vainly attempting to embrace the world of white faces that rejected it, it recoiled and sought refuge in the ruins of moldering tradition. But it was too late; it was trapped; it found haven in neither.

8. The author introduces the subject of the passage in the first paragraph by
using
  (A) an exposé
  (B) an allusion
  (C) a parable
  (D) an exposition
  (E) a fable

   The imaginative account of the conquest of a Swiss village by Martians is a parable—a short, fictitious story that illustrates a moral attitude or religious principle,
in this case a series of historic events describing European takeovers of Asian and
African communities. (C) is the correct answer. An *exposé* is a factual revelation
of something discreditable. An *allusion* is a reference to a familiar person, place,
or thing. An *exposition* is an explanation of the background or situation in a story
or play. A *fable* is a tale that uses animals to point out a moral or truth.

9. The expression "advanced individualists" (line 24) is an example of
  (A) irony
  (B) hyperbole
  (C) an oxymoron
  (D) understatement
  (E) parody

   The tone of the sentence in which the expression appears is critical of the
people who initiated the colonial system. The term "advanced individualists" has positive connotations, but in this context is intended to be ironic,
for the author makes clear that the colonists had a destructive and corrosive
influence. The correct answer is (A). (B) may seem like a possible answer
because some of the impassioned prose in the passage may strike a reader as
overstatement. The phrase in question, however, is more ironic than exaggerated. One could argue for (C) as the answer because in the context the
phrase seems contrary to the truth. But to qualify as an oxymoron, the phrase
itself must contain contradictory terms. You can eliminate (D) because there
are no subtle understatements in the passage. And since there is nothing
about the phrase that suggests mockery for comic effect, (E) is not a reasonable answer.

10. The sentence in lines 44–45 serves all of the following rhetorical functions EXCEPT
    (A) to introduce the main topic of the paragraph that follows
    (B) to provide a transition between the previous and the following paragraphs
    (C) to draw the reader into the passage by asking a question
    (D) to act as a dividing line between the discussion of causes and the discussion of effects
    (E) to anticipate possible objections to ideas to be presented in the rest of passage

The question asked by the author initiates a discussion about the effects of colonization. Therefore, (A), (B), and (D) are not correct. By asking a question rather than making a statement, the author attempts to arouse the reader's curiosity. Hooked by the question, the reader won't be satisfied until he reads the remainder of the paragraph. Because (E) does not apply, it is the correct answer.

11. Which two adjectives best describe the prevailing tone of the passage?
    (A) Objective and impartial
    (B) Angry and contentious
    (C) Pedantic and scholarly
    (D) Restrained and philosophic
    (E) Thoughtful and moralistic

The passage is a vigorous indictment of the prolonged and cruel exploitation of lands and people for material gain. The language is intensely critical and impassioned. The correct answer is (B).

12. A metaphor used in paragraph 4 (lines 33–53) of the passage refers to the exploitation of Africans and Asians as
    (A) a storm descending upon helpless people
    (B) a cruel act by a malignant deity
    (C) an incursion of devils posing as saints
    (D) a remedy for a disabling illness
    (E) a transformation of heroes made villains by circumstances

In lines 42–43 the author describes Europe's dependence on Asia and Africa: an "emotionally crippled Europe . . . grown used to leaning upon this black crutch." The correct answer is (D). The other choices contain good ideas, but they don't appear in the passage.

13. The countries of Arcadia, Land's End, and Shangri-la (lines 20–21) are cited as metaphors for the goals of the freebooting Europeans. The author terms the inhabitants of these places "shadow men" because
    (A) the inhabitants of these utopias were like dreamers in a lotus land
    (B) the Europeans saw them as no hindrance to their power to exert control
    (C) the Europeans trusted the ideas of Hume and Descartes
    (D) shadow men have no power, no faith, no solid society
    (E) the Europeans feared becoming shadow men themselves in a new, unfamiliar world

The colonists had no clear idea of what the people in these far-off places were like, but they imagined the inhabitants as "shadow men" who would not oppose the settlers' freedom to do as they wished. In essence, the natives lacked substance. The correct answer is (B).

14. The dominant stylistic and grammatical structures used in this passage are
    (A) present and past participial phrases
    (B) simple declarative sentences for dramatic emphasis
    (C) rhetorical questions
    (D) sequences of compound sentences
    (E) complex sentences introduced by adverbial clauses

Reading the passage, you will find a plethora of verbals ending in "ing" and "ed," many in a compound series and almost all modifying nouns. The effect is to heighten emotion and to accumulate evidence to support the author's views. Although there are other grammatical structures, the participles predominate. (A) is the correct answer.

15. The best synonym for "cloying" as used in line 28 of the passage is
    (A) bitter
    (B) honeid
    (C) limiting
    (D) oppressive
    (E) slavish

The word "cloying" is used critically in the sense of too much of a good thing. Custom, tradition, and family, with their promises of some reward, had turned sour. The suggestion is that even a good thing, like sweetness, can oversatiate. The correct answer is (B).

16. The expression "slaked their sensual thirst in illicit sexuality" (lines 33–34) is an example of
    (A) onomatopoeia
    (B) a metaphor
    (C) assonance
    (D) allegory
    (E) alliteration

Onomatopoeia applies to words that imitate sounds. A *metaphor* is a figurative comparison without using "like" or "as." *Assonance* is the repetition of vowel sounds without the repetition of consonants. An *allegory* is a story in which people, things, and actions represent an idea or a generalization about life. *Alliteration* is the repetition of initial consonant sounds. Because the sound *s* is prevalent in this expression, (E) is the correct answer.

17. "Living in a waking dream" (line 33) is a participial phrase modifying
    (A) "generations" (line 33)
    (B) "whites" (line 34)
    (C) "gratification" (line 34)
    (D) "greed" (line 35)
    (E) "superiority" (line 35)

A participial phrase performs an adjective function. It usually modifies the subject of the sentence in which it appears. Here the subject of the sentence is "generations." The correct answer, therefore, is (A). (This sentence also contains three additional participial phrases introduced by "draining," "amassing," and "establishing." These, too, modify the subject, "generations.")

18.   The style of the passage can best be described as
    (A)   informal and colloquial
    (B)   graphic and trenchant
    (C)   long-winded and labored
    (D)   complex and formal
    (E)   polished and felicitous

The language in the passage is strong and vigorous in keeping with the indictment of the Europeans' treatment of native populations in Asia and Africa. (B) is the correct answer.

19.   Which of the following beliefs is held most strongly by the author of the passage?
    (A)   Whites brought some positive civilizing customs to Asian and African peoples.
    (B)   The religious beliefs of Africans and Asians were the source of their own undoing.
    (C)   The future of African and Asian populations looks promising.
    (D)   Europeans caused permanent damage to African and Asian ways of life.
    (E)   Not all colonialists were cruel and destructive.

The last paragraph of the passage emphasizes that once the damage had been done, "it was too late" to recover. (D) is the correct answer. There is nothing in the passage to suggest that (A), (C), or (E) is a valid choice. (B) has some merit as an answer because the author states (line 46) that the natives were "anchored in ancestor-worshiping religions." But the question asks you to identify the author's "most strongly" held belief. In choosing between (B) and (D), the latter must prevail because it states what the passage is all about.

PASSAGE 3

            Let us take for text on this, our fourth afternoon, the greatest of all references to simplicity, the inspired admonition: *"Consider the lilies of the field—they toil not, neither do they spin, yet verily I say unto*
Line   *thee—Solomon in all his glory was not arrayed like one of these."* An
(5)   inspired saying—attributed to an humble Architect in ancient times, called Carpenter, who gave up Architecture nearly two thousand years ago to go to work upon its Source.
        And if the text should seem to you too far away from our subject this afternoon—
(10)   "The Cardboard House"
    —consider that for that very reason the text has been chosen. The cardboard house needs an antidote. The antidote is far more important than the house. As antidote—and as practical example, too, of the working out of an ideal of organic simplicity that has taken
(15)   place here on American soil, step by step, under conditions that are

your own—could I do better than to take apart for your benefit the
buildings I have tried to build, to show you how they were, long ago,
dedicated to the Ideal of Organic Simplicity? It seems to me that
while another might do better than that, I certainly could not—for that

(20)   is, truest and best, what I know about the Subject. What a man *does,*
that he has.

When, "in the cause of Architecture," in 1893, I first began to build
the houses, sometimes referred to by the thoughtless as The New
School of the Middle West . . . , the only way to simplify the awful

(25)   building in vogue at the time was to conceive a finer entity—a better
building—and get it built. The buildings standing then were all tall and
all tight. Chimneys were lean and taller still, sooty fingers threatening
the sky. And beside them, sticking up by way of dormers through the
cruelly sharp, saw-tooth roofs, were the attics for "help" to swelter in.

(30)   Dormers were elaborate devices, cunning little buildings complete in
themselves, stuck to the main roof slopes to let "help" poke heads out
of the attic for air.

Invariably the damp sticky clay of the prairie was dug out for a
basement under the whole house, and the rubblestone walls of this

(35)   dank basement always stuck up above the ground a foot or more and
blinked, with half windows. So the universal "cellar" showed itself as
a bank of some kind of masonry running around the whole house, for
the house to sit up on—like a chair. The lean, upper house-walls of the
usual two floors above this stone or brick basement were wood, set

(40)   on top of this masonry-chair, clapboarded and painted, or else
shingled and stained, preferably shingled and mixed, up and down, all
together with mouldings crosswise. These overdressed wood
housewalls had, cut in them—or cut out of them, to be precise—big
holes for the big cat and little holes for the little cat to get in and out

(45)   or for ulterior purposes of light and air. The house-walls were
be-corniced or bracketed up at the top into the tall, purposely
profusely complicated roof, dormers plus. The whole roof, as well as
the roof as a whole, was scalloped and ridged and tipped and swanked
and gabled to madness before they would allow it to be either

(50)   shingled or slated. The whole exterior was be-deviled—that is to say,
mixed to puzzle-pieces, with corner boards, panel-boards,
window-frames, corner-blocks, plinth-blocks, rosettes, fantails,
ingenious and jigger work in general. This was the only way they
seemed to have, then, of "putting on style." The scroll-saw and

(55)   turning lathe were at the moment the honest means of this fashionable
mongering by the wood-butcher and to this entirely "moral" end.
Unless the householder of the period were poor indeed, usually an
ingenious corner-tower on his house eventuated into a candle-snuffer
dome, a spire, an inverted rutabega or radish or onion or—what is

(60)   your favorite vegetable? Always elaborate bay-windows and fancy
porches played "ring around a rosy" on this "imaginative" corner
feature. And all this the building of the period could do equally well in
brick or stone. It was an impartial society. All material looked pretty
much alike in that day.

20. Which of the following statements best describes the rhetorical purpose of the quotation in the first sentence of the passage?
    (A) It implies the importance of the message contained in the passage that follows.
    (B) It expresses the timelessness of the topic.
    (C) It alerts the reader to an idea that the remainder of the passage will refute.
    (D) It introduces a figure of speech that the speaker will analyze later in the passage.
    (E) It provides a specific example of a familiar saying.

Because quotations from the Bible carry considerable rhetorical weight, particularly among some audiences, (A) may be a somewhat valid answer, but the preponderance of evidence points to (B). The speaker begins with a Biblical quotation to suggest the timelessness of the topic. Indeed, in lines 8–11 he reminds his audience that the quote has been chosen because of its currency even two thousand years after it was written. (B) is the correct answer. (C) contradicts the contents of the passage. (D) is only partially true; while the quote contains personification, the speaker does not analyze it. (E) has little merit; although the quotation may be familiar, it is not used as an example of anything.

21. The speaker can be identified as all of the following EXCEPT
    (A) a cultural historian, specializing in architecture
    (B) a builder of private homes
    (C) an expert home designer
    (D) a creator of new techniques for constructing homes
    (E) a critic of building styles of the past

The speaker is an architectural specialist, to be sure, but his emphasis is home design, not cultural history. The contents of the passage indicate that he knows about construction of houses, that he has designed a new kind of house and that he rejects home designs of the past. Therefore, (A) is the correct answer.

22. In general, the speaker's tone in the passage progresses from
    (A) comical to grave
    (B) opinionated to factual
    (C) didactic to emotional
    (D) earnest to moralistic
    (E) high-principled to disparaging

As the speaker warms to the topic, he begins to insert humor into his remarks. The last two thirds of the passage, in fact, includes a rather witty description of houses that were "in vogue" in the 1890s. Consequently, (A) is not a good answer. Nor is (B) because, if anything, the speaker becomes more opinionated as the passage progresses. Eliminate (C), too, because at no point is the tone either didactic or emotional. While the speaker's intent may be earnest, he is never moralistic, which eliminates (D). Choice (E) most aptly describes the progress of the passage. At first the speaker cites the worthiness of his credentials and, by poking fun at the appearance of traditional Victorian homes, explains why he chose to design a new, organically simple style of house.

23. The idea of the phrase "cardboard house" (line 12) is echoed in the speaker's later reference to
     (A) "saw-tooth roofs" (line 29)
     (B) "clapboarded and painted" (line 40)
     (C) "big holes . . . little holes" (lines 43–44)
     (D) "puzzle pieces" (line 51)
     (E) "All material looked pretty much alike. . . " (lines 63–64)

The speaker states that the "cardboard house needs an antidote." The antidote proposed exemplifies the "ideal of organic simplicity" (line 14). Therefore, the answer to this question should reflect something antithetical to "organic simplicity." Of the choices, (D) comes closest. What the speaker calls "mixed puzzle pieces" are the "corner boards, plinth-blocks, rosettes" and other decorative features that characterize Victorian architecture.

24. Which of the following best describes the effect of the last sentence of the second paragraph: "What a man *does,* that he *has*" (lines 20–21)?
     (A) It reinforces the author's authority to speak on the topic.
     (B) It establishes rapport with the audience.
     (C) It endows the material that follows with greater significance.
     (D) It explains the task the speaker has undertaken.
     (E) It defines the speaker's point of view

The sentence in question succinctly states a principle of competence: what you *do* is what you *know.* Because the speaker designs organically simple houses, he claims to have a firm grasp of the "Ideal of Organic Simplicity." In effect, therefore, he is telling his listeners that he has the credentials to speak on the topic. (A) is the best answer.

25. The series of adjectives in lines 48–49 is meant specifically to illustrate
     (A) "sooty fingers threatening the sky" (lines 27–28)
     (B) "cruelly sharp saw-tooth roofs" (line 29)
     (C) "Dormers . . . stuck to the main roof " (lines 30–31)
     (D) "overdressed wood housewalls" (lines 42–43)
     (E) "purposely profusely complicated roof " (lines 47–48)

The piling up of colorful adjectives is meant to exaggerate the lavish attention paid to the design of excessively ornate Victorian roofs. Therefore, (E) is the correct answer. (A), (B), and (C) refer only to individual design features often found on old-fashioned roofs. (D) is not related to roofs at all.

26. Which of the following most accurately describes the function of first sentence of the fourth paragraph ("Invariably . . . with half windows")?
     (A) It describes a building technique the author once used.
     (B) It introduces details of the principle of Organic Simplicity mentioned earlier in the passage.
     (C) It particularizes elements of the "awful" buildings referred to earlier in the passage.
     (D) It discredits the "New School of the Middle West."
     (E) It reveals an error often made by thoughtless homebuilders.

The speaker makes clear that he originated a simple architectural style in response to the "awful" houses built at the end of the nineteenth century. By the fourth paragraph, he has begun to describe those houses. To emphasize their unsightliness, he cites numerous examples of poor design, one of them in this sentence. (C), then, is the correct answer. If you chose (E), consider that the speaker refrains from condemning homebuilders of the past. To his eye, the houses they designed were "awful," but he recognizes that they merely followed the conventions of their time.

27. All of the following phrases from the passage are examples of figurative language EXCEPT
   (A) "sooty fingers" (line 27)
   (B) "bank of some kind of masonry" (line 37)
   (C) "wood-butcher" (line 56)
   (D) "inverted rutabega" (line 59)
   (E) "porches played 'ring around a rosy' " (line 61)

   (A), (C), and (D) are metaphors. (E) is a personification. Only (B) is to be taken literally and, therefore, is the correct answer.

28. In context, the word "impartial" (line 63) is best interpreted to mean
   (A) indiscriminate
   (B) apathetic
   (C) reasonable
   (D) judicious
   (E) unbiased

   To explain his use of the word "impartial," the speaker says that "All material looked pretty much alike in that day" (lines 63–64). If that is the case, the people failed to discriminate between kinds of material. Brick or stone—it was all the same to them. In a larger sense, the design of one house was no better or worse than the design of another. Therefore (A) is the best answer.

3 Essay Questions

After an hour of multiple-choice questions, you have two hours left to write three essays; the suggested time for each is forty minutes.

For two of the essays you will be given a passage to read and analyze. (The author, date, and context of the passage are often identified.) Then you are asked to respond to the passage by writing a relatively brief essay that describes how the style and rhetoric of the passage enable the author to convey a particular view or achieve a particular goal. (Sometimes you'll be given two short passages instead of one, in which case you're asked to analyze and compare them.) The question may suggest that you consider such elements as tone, diction, and selection of detail. While these elements may give you a direction, they are sometimes meant only as suggestions. In such cases, the choice is yours. If the syntax, irony, and allusion in a passage strike you as more significant than the suggestions you are given, you may feel free to discuss them.

Sometimes the question will direct you to write about the specific elements of language mentioned in the question. Then you don't have a choice. You must deal with figures of speech, syntax—or whatever the instructions say. In either case, be sure to answer the question. Don't alter the question to suit yourself. If you don't write on the topic, your score will suffer.

The third question is usually more open ended than the others. Instead of being instructed to write an analysis of a passage, you are asked to read a quotation of one or more sentences, or perhaps a short paragraph or two, and then to write a well-organized, persuasive essay in which you argue for or against the validity of the ideas in the quote. As you write the essay, you are free to use supporting evidence from your observations, experience, or reading. In effect, this essay is the most personal of the three, but it still requires logical, well-reasoned argumentation. AP Exam readers won't be impressed by an essay full of unsupported generalizations that merely express your personal opinions, however sincere and heartfelt they may be.

To give you a more concrete idea of the essays you are expected to write on the exam, here are synopses of the three questions that students were given during each of the last several years:

1994

1. Write an essay "in which you define the attitude" that the writer of the given passage wants you to adopt toward his subject; then "analyze the rhetorical strategies" the writer uses to promote that attitude.
2. Write a "carefully reasoned persuasive essay that defends, challenges, or qualifies" the main idea in a short quotation. "Use evidence from your reading and/or observation to develop your position."
3. After reading a passage, write "an essay in which you characterize" the author's view of the subject and then analyze how the writer conveys this view, possibly using "such stylistic elements as diction, imagery, syntax, tone, and selection of detail."

1995

1. Write a "a carefully reasoned essay" evaluating the author's argument as presented in a short passage.
2. Write an essay on the given passage, analyzing the author's use of "rhetorical techniques."
3. Write "an essay that defends, challenges, or qualifies" the ideas contained in a short passage. Use "specific evidence from your observation, experience, or reading" to develop your position.

1996

1. In an essay, analyze how the author of a passage uses "rhetorical strategies and stylistic devices to convey her views."
2. After reading an autobiographical passage, "in a well-written essay, analyze some of the ways" in which the author recreates the experience. Consider using "such devices as contrast, repetition, pacing, diction, and imagery."
3. "Drawing on your own knowledge and experience, write a carefully reasoned essay defending, challenging, or qualifying" the views expressed in a given passage.

1997

1. Write a well-organized essay that analyzes how the author of an autobiographical passage uses language to explore and represent herself.
2. Read an autobiographical passage, noting the author's use of "such elements as syntax, figurative language, and selection of detail." Then write an essay in which you identify the stylistic elements in the third paragraph that distinguish it from the rest of the passage and how this difference reinforces the author's "rhetorical purpose in the passage as a whole."
3. "Using your own critical understanding of contemporary society as evidence, write a carefully argued essay that agrees or disagrees" with the views expressed in a given passage.

1998

1. After reading a passage from a letter, write an essay "in which you analyze the techniques" the author uses to achieve his purpose.
2. Write a carefully reasoned, persuasive essay that demonstrates which idea in an excerpt from a novel has greater validity. "Use specific evidence from your observation, experience, or reading to develop your position."
3. Read a given letter and the response it evoked. Then write "an essay analyzing the rhetorical strategies each writer uses to achieve his purpose and explaining which letter offers the more persuasive case."

1999

1. After reading two passages about Florida's Okefenokee Swamp, write an essay in which you analyze "how the distinctive style of each passage reveals the purpose of its writer."
2. Read a passage by Jamaica Kincaid. Then write an essay that analyzes the rhetorical strategies Kincaid uses to convey her attitude toward England.
3. Read a brief excerpt from Sophocles' *Antigone*. Then write a "carefully reasoned essay that explores the validity" of the character's words. Use examples from your reading, observation, or experience to develop your position.

Sample Questions

Question 1
(Suggested time—
40 minutes)

Read the following passage, written in 1967 and published in the Sunday magazine of the *New York Times.* Then write an essay in which you analyze how the structure of the passage and the use of language help convey the writer's views.

Americans and Western Europeans, in their sensitivity to lingering problems around them, tend to make science and progress their scapegoats. There is a belief that progress has precipitated

Line
(5)   widespread unhappiness, anxieties, and other social and emotional problems. Science is viewed as a cold mechanical discipline having nothing to do with human warmth and the human spirit.

But to many of us from the nonscientific East, science does not have such repugnant associations. We are not afraid of it, nor are we disappointed by it. We know all too painfully that our social and

(10) emotional problems festered long before the age of technology. To us, science is warm and reassuring. It promises hope. It is helping us at long last gain some control over our persecutory environments, alleviating age-old problems—not only physical but also, and especially, problems of the spirit.

(15)   Shiraz, for example, a city in southern Iran, has long been renowned for its rose gardens and nightingales; its poets, Sadi and Hafiz, and its mystical, ascetic philosophy, Sufism. Much poetry has been written in glorification of the spiritual attributes of this oasis city. And to be sure, Shiraz is a green, picturesque town, with a quaint bazaar and refreshing

(20) gardens. But in this "romantic" city thousands of emotionally disturbed and mentally retarded men, women, and children were, until recently, kept in chains in stifling prison cells and lunatic asylums.

Every now and again, some were dragged, screaming and pleading, to a courtyard and flogged for not behaving "normally." But for the

(25) most part, they were made to sit against damp walls, their hands and feet locked in chains, and thus immobilized, without even a modicum of affection from their helpless families and friends, they sat for weeks and months and years—often all their lives. Pictures of these wretched men, women, and children can still be seen in this "city of poetry," this

(30) "city with a spiritual way of life."

It was only recently that a wealthy young Shirazi who, against the admonitions of his family, had studied psychology at the University of Teheran and foreign universities, returned to Shiraz and after considerable struggle with city officials succeeded in opening a

(35) psychiatric clinic, the first in those regions. After still more struggle, he arranged to have the emotionally disturbed and the mentally retarded transferred from prison to their homes, to hospitals, and to his clinic, where he and his staff now attend them.

They are fortunate. All over Asia and other backward areas,

(40) emotionally disturbed men and women are still incarcerated in these medieval dungeons called lunatic asylums. The cruel rejection and punishment are intended to teach them a lesson or help exorcise evil spirits.

The West, still bogged down in its ridiculous romanticism, would

(45) like to believe that emotional disturbances, dope addiction, delinquency are all modern problems brought on by technological progress, and that backward societies are too spiritual and beautiful to need the

ministrations of science. But while the West can perhaps afford to
think this way, the people of backward lands cannot.

(50)   Young Middle Eastern men and women are daily flouting the
devitalizing repressions and fatalism of Islam. India is valiantly
straining to extricate itself from the dead weight of social traditions
whose corrosive nihilism and spiritualism the realist Nehru disdained.
Japan's new industrialism and pragmatism are obvious renunciations

(55)   of the debilitating influences of Zen. China's revolutionary leaders
are prodding their people to reject the ancient traditions and philosophies
[that] had helped perpetrate the country's backwardness and misery,
making it prey to incessant foreign rapacities.

If at times these struggles have been erratic and violent, it is only

(60)   because the obstacles are awesome, the inertia too entrenched, the
people's suffering too anguished, their impatience too eruptive.
Moreover, the total cultural reorganizations such as Asia and Africa
are undergoing inevitably engender their own temporary dislocations
and confusions. But their goals, the direction, remain constant.

(65)   We are on the move, however awkwardly at first, to a saner, better world.

Commentary

This question asks you to analyze two aspects of the passage: 1) its structure, or organization, and 2) its language. The first aspect is fairly specific. As you read the passage, you must observe what the author discusses first, second, third, and so on. The essay must explain not only the order of ideas but the reason the author may have chosen that order.

The second part of the question is more general. It invites you to analyze the use of language, which may include the author's choice of words (diction), syntax (word order), figures of speech, sentence structure, rhythm, sound, tone, or any other characteristics of style and rhetoric you choose.

Although the question directs you to write about two different aspects of the passage, the essay itself should be unified. That is, a good essay should not consist of, say, two disparate paragraphs, one exclusively devoted to structure and another to language. Rather, the essay should include material that shows the interrelationship of structure and language in the passage. This might be covered in a separate paragraph, or it could be woven into the overall fabric of the essay.

Before you begin to write, read the passage at least *twice:* once for an overview and once to begin your analysis. You may notice early on that the opening paragraph contains generalizations about Westerners' concepts of science and progress. Then the author contrasts the Western view of science and progress with the Eastern view. Immediately, you see that the author, by using the first person pronoun (as in "many of us") will be speaking from the perspective of an Easterner. Consequently, his discussion of Eastern views is apt to come across as more well-informed, more authoritative, perhaps more personal.

To support his position, the author gives an extended example—the city of Shiraz—to illustrate just how different the East is from the West. The description and vivid images of Shiraz memorably convey the idea that the "spiritual way of life" has a side to it that Westerners don't know about. This is the heart of the passage. The use of quotation marks around "romantic" and "city of poetry" is meant to point out the discrepancy between idealized and real versions of Shiraz.

As the passage draws to a close, the author reiterates the initial contrast between West and East, with the emphasis on the East. To show that Shiraz is not the only backward place in the East, the author lists the struggles faced by several Eastern countries—one sentence per country. The last paragraph offers a generalized statement about conditions in Asia and Africa, reminding the reader of the contrast made at the beginning of the passage.

Question 2
(Suggested time—
40 minutes)

The two passages below comment on the state of American society during the early 1960s. Read the passages carefully. Then, in a well-organized essay, analyze the specific stylistic and rhetorical differences between the two passages, paying particular attention to how the two authors present themselves to the reader.

PASSAGE A

When a man, a business corporation, or an entire society is
approaching bankruptcy, there are two courses that those involved
can follow: they can evade the reality of their situation and act on a
Line   frantic, blind, rage-of-the-moment expediency—not daring to look
(5)   ahead, wishing no one would name the truth, yet desperately hoping
that something will save them somehow—or they can identify with
the situation, check their premises, discover their hidden assets, and
start rebuilding.
   America, at present, is following the first course. The grayness,
(10)   the stale cynicism, the noncommittal cautiousness, the guilty
evasiveness of our public voices suggest the attitude of the courtiers
in the story "The Emperor's New Clothes" who have professed
admiration for the Emperor's nonexistent garments, having accepted
the assertion that anyone who failed to perceive them was morally
(15)   depraved at heart.
   Let me be the child in the story and declare that the Emperor is naked—
or that America is culturally bankrupt.

PASSAGE B

Great movements and forces, springing from deep wells, have
converged at this midcentury point, and I suspect we have barely
begun to comprehend what has happened and why. In the
Line   foreground is the mortal contest with world communism, which is
(5)   apparent, if the means of dealing with it are not always apparent.
But in the background are the opaque, moving forms and shadows
of a world revolution, of which communism is more the scavenger
than the inspiration; a world in transition from an age with which
we are familiar to an age shrouded in mist. We Americans have to
(10)   deal with both the foreground and the background of this troubled,
anxious age.
   It is easy to state our ends, our goals, but it is hard to fit them
to our means. Every day, for example, politicians, of which
there are plenty, swear eternal devotion to the ends of peace
(15)   and security. They always remind me of the elder Holmes'
apostrophe to a katydid: "Thou say'st an undisputed thing in such
a solemn way." And every day statesmen, of which there are a few,
must struggle with limited means to achieve these unlimited ends,
both in fact and in understanding. For the nation's purposes always
(20)   exceed its means, and it is finding a balance between means and the ends
that is the heart of foreign policy and that makes it such a
speculative, uncertain business.

Commentary   The question offers you the opportunity to write a comparison using virtually anything in the passages that you think is important. The phrase "stylistic and rhetorical differences" is a broad invitation for you to write about language, sentence structure, tone—whatever you choose, provided it is germane to style and rhetoric. In addition, the question suggests that you say something about how the author of each passage presents himself. That is, what does the passage reveal about each author's personality? Consider that as free advice handed to you by the test writers. By singling out the author's persona, they have called your attention to an issue that could quickly give your essay a ready-made focus—the author's voice. Your task then is to simply answer the question, "What does the style and rhetoric of each passage tell you about the person who wrote it?"

The author of the first passage comes across as someone who speaks with authority. To put it bluntly, the author (who happens to be Ayn Rand—although that information is not given) presents herself as a know-it-all, a forceful critic who confidently declares that she knows exactly what is wrong with America and is anything but timid about asserting her views. "America, at present, is following the first course," she says, referring to the course that is epitomized by the foolish, "morally depraved" courtiers in "The Emperor's New Clothes." The analogy is apt, for the widely known tale is a universally accepted allusion to stupidity and self-delusion. Then, assuming the mantle of the uncorrupted child in the story, the author declares "that America is culturally bankrupt."

Rand establishes the voice of a prophet early in the passage. In the first sentence she asserts that "there are two courses"—and only *two*—for a society to follow when it is approaching bankruptcy. (Whether she means a literal or figurative bankruptcy remains unclear until the end of the passage.) The first course is described with emotionally loaded language—"frantic, blind, rage-of-the-moment expediency," as if to say that no right-thinking person could subscribe to such a course. The second, by contrast, is laid out in 1-2-3 order with clipped phrases: "identify with the situation, check their premises, discover their hidden assets, and start rebuilding" (lines 6–8)—steps that are serious and precise and stand in stark contrast to the current wimpiness of an America "not daring to look ahead, wishing no one would name the truth, yet desperately hoping that something will save them somehow" (lines 4–6).

While Rand concludes that America is a defective country in need of major repair, the author of the second passage, Adlai E. Stevenson, takes a more circumspect view. Unlike Rand, Stevenson disclaims the role of expert by insisting on the complexity of the problems and conceding that neither he nor anyone else has any clear-cut solutions. He acknowledges that the country is troubled and anxious. But rather than identify causes and offer simple formulaic solutions, as Rand does, Stevenson tries to describe the forces at play in America. He cannot precisely pinpoint them, however. Having sprung mysteriously—and metaphorically—from "deep wells" (line 1), they defy definition. The author calls them "opaque, moving forms and shadows" (line 6), and—carrying the metaphor still further—says that our vision of the future is "shrouded in mist." In brief, his approach, unlike Rand's, is tentative, exploratory, and suggestive.

The phrase "We Americans" (line 9) stands for the author's attempt to maintain a dialogue-like relationship with the audience. A brief anecdote, in which politicians are compared to insects, is bound to appeal to readers (politicians are always easy to ridicule). The personal, colloquial language—"They always remind me of . . ."—makes the author sound like a friendly uncle rather than an intellect, yet his allusion to the discrepancy between ends and means is the product of considerable cerebral activity. The author describes the business of foreign policy as "speculative, uncertain." Considering the style and rhetoric of the passage, he might have well been describing his own approach to the subject of the passage.

Question 3
(Suggested time—
40 minutes)

In *A Time for Greatness,* the author Herbert Agar wrote

> A natural result of the belief that business is business is the belief that there is a special form of business morality, different from the morality that rules the rest of life. "This is business," says the man who is cutting a corner that he would not cut in private life. "This is business," says the man who is behaving cruelly and irresponsibly, or who is running his own business in a way that would wreck the entire system if his competitors did the same.

Some people would argue that what Agar calls a business morality plays a significant role not only in business but in all human endeavors.

Write a well-reasoned, persuasive essay that supports, challenges, or qualifies this idea about the pervasiveness of business morality in all human actions and decisions. To develop your argument, you may use evidence from your reading, your studies, and/or your observation and experience.

Commentary

This question has been worded in such a way to allow you the greatest possible freedom in writing a persuasive essay. Presumably, every student taking the AP exam will have an opinion about what has often been called situational ethics—that is, a code of morality founded not on a consistent set of rules but on the circumstances. Put another way, the situation—in business or elsewhere—governs what is wrong or right.

Whether you agree that circumstances determine moral behavior, whether you think of morality as an absolute regardless of the situation, or whether you come down somewhere between those two positions, your task is to write an essay that proves the validity of your point of view. Remember that a persuasive essay is meant to sway readers whose views are contrary to yours. Therefore, you must gather compelling evidence in support of your position. That the evidence may come from virtually any source is both a blessing and a curse—a blessing because of the many possibilities: the books you've read, the media, current events, what you've observed, heard, and experienced. But it is a curse because you have so much to choose from and you must be careful to select only the three or four most persuasive pieces of evidence.

In general, when making a persuasive case, it pays to develop at least three reasons in support of your position. The formulaic "five-paragraph essay," so often touted as a standard to follow, contains an introduction, three paragraphs of development, and a conclusion. Why *three* paragraphs of development? Mainly because three is a number that works. If you can come up with three different arguments, you create the impression that you have thought about the subject and now can speak with the voice of authority. One paragraph is too simple, two is better but still shallow. Three, however, is thoughtful. It suggests depth and insight. If you can't think of three, however, stick with two, but don't make up a third that is simply a rehash of the first two disguised as something new. Psychologically, three also creates a sense of wholeness for the reader, like the beginning, middle, and end of a story. It's no accident that the number three recurs in all literature, from *Goldilocks and the Three Bears* to *The Bible.*

In a persuasive essay, too, you can bolster your argument by refuting what you might expect your opponent to say. In making a case, therefore, anticipate the strongest opposing argument you can. Then point out its flaws. By doing so, you will not only weaken your opponent's case, you will be strengthening your own.

AP exam readers will not judge your essay based on the opinion you express. Even if they disagree with you, they are obliged to ignore their own biases and grade you according to criteria of good writing. They may consider you dead wrong, but if you write a cogent, forceful essay that demonstrates a mastery of the persuasive rhetoric, your essay will receive a high score. (One caveat, though: no matter how skillfully written your essay, if it contains faulty reasoning or misinformation, you will be penalized.)

Once you've collected your ideas for or against the issue proposed by the question, stop for a moment and figure out which idea to put first, which to put second, and so on. Order is important. The best order is the clearest order, the arrangement that readers can follow with the least effort. No plan is superior to another provided you have a valid reason for using it. The plan least likely to succeed is the aimless one, the one in which you state and develop ideas in the random order they happened to come to mind. It's better by far to rank your ideas in order of importance. Decide which provides the strongest support of your thesis. Although your best argument may be listed first in your notes, save it for last on the essay. Giving it away at the start is self-defeating because everything that follows will be anticlimactic. In other words, work towards your best point, not away from it. An excellent way to plot three good ideas is to lead with your second best, save your best for the end, and sandwich your least powerful idea between the others. This structure recognizes that the end and the beginning of an essay are its critical parts. A good opening draws the reader in and creates an all-important first impression, but a memorable ending, coming last, is what readers have fresh in their minds when they assign you a grade.

But, as always, you mustn't follow these guidelines slavishly. If you can justify another organization, by all means use it.

Question with Student Responses

Below is a typical AP exam question and two student responses written under examination conditions: a time limit, no access to a dictionary or other book, and a certain amount of tension. No doubt you will notice that one student, Lynn, wrote an essay that deserves a high score. Chris, the other student, more or less missed the boat. By reading Lynn's essay and the comments that follow, you will see what an above-average writer must do to earn an 8 or a 9, the highest scores. Chris's essay will alert you to some of the pitfalls to avoid when you write an essay of your own. For the descriptive criteria used to score AP essays, see pages 43–44.

The Question
(Suggested time—
40 minutes)

The following passage by Isaiah Berlin comes from "Winston Churchill in 1940," a review of the first volume of Churchill's World War II memoirs. After reading it carefully, write an essay in which you characterize Berlin's view of Churchill and analyze how Berlin conveys this view. Your analysis might consider such stylistic elements as structure, diction, syntax, tone, and selection of detail.

Churchill's dominant category, the single, central, organizing principle of his moral and intellectual universe, is a historical imagination so strong, so comprehensive, as to encase the whole of the present and the whole of the
Line
(5)
future in a framework of a rich and multicolored past. Such an approach is dominated by a desire—and a capacity—to find fixed moral and intellectual bearings, to give shape and character, colour and direction and coherence, to the stream of events. . .
  Churchill sees history—and life—as a great Renaissance pageant: when he thinks of France or Italy, Germany or the Low Countries, Russia,
(10)
India, Africa, the Arab lands, he sees vivid historical images—something between Victorian illustrations in a child's book of history and the great procession painted by Benozzo Gozzoli in the Riccardi Palace. His eye is never that of the neatly classifying sociologist, the careful psychological analyst, the plodding antiquary, the patient historical scholar. His poetry
(15)
has not that anatomical vision which sees the naked bone beneath the flesh, skulls, and skeletons and the omnipresence of decay and death beneath the flow of life. The units out of which his world is constructed are simpler and larger than life, the patterns vivid and repetitive like those of an epic poet, or at times like those of a dramatist who sees persons
(20)
and situations as timeless symbols and embodiments of eternal, shining principles. The whole is a series of symmetrically formed and somewhat stylized compositions, either suffused with bright light or cast in darkest shadow, like a legend by Carpaccio, with scarcely any nuance, painted in primary colors, with no half tones, nothing intangible, nothing impalpable,
(25)
nothing half spoken or hinted or whispered: the voice does not alter in pitch or timbre.
  The archaisms of style to which Churchill's wartime speeches accustomed us are indispensable ingredients of the heightened tone, the formal chronicler's attire, for which the solemnity of the occasion called.
(30)
Churchill is fully conscious of this: the style should adequately respond to the demands which history makes upon the actors from moment to moment. "Ideas set forth," he wrote in 1940 about a Foreign Office draft, "appeared to me to err in trying to be too clever, to enter into refinements of policy unsuited to the tragic simplicity and grandeur of the times and the issues at stake."
(35)
  His own narrative consciously mounts and swells until it reaches the great climax of the Battle of Britain. The texture and the tension are those of a tragic opera, where the very artificiality of the medium, both in the recitative and in the arias, serves to eliminate the irrelevant dead level of normal existence and to set off in high relief the deeds and sufferings of the principal characters.
(40)
The moments of comedy in such a work must necessarily conform to the style of the whole and be parodies of it; and this is Churchill's practice. When he says that he viewed this or that "with stern and tranquil gaze," or informs his officials that any "chortling" by them of the failure of a chosen scheme "will be viewed with great disfavor by me," or describes the "celestial grins" of his
(45)
collaborators over the development of a well-concealed conspiracy, he does precisely this; the mock-heroic tone—reminiscent of *Stalky & Co.*—does not break the operatic conventions. But conventions though they may be,

(50)

(55)

(60)

(65)

they are not donned and doffed by the author at will: by now they are his second nature, and have completely fused with the first; art and nature are no longer distinguishable. The rigid pattern of his prose is the normal medium of his ideas not merely when he sets himself to compose, but in the life of the imagination which permeates his daily existence.

Churchill's language is a medium which he invented because he needed it. It has a bold, ponderous, fairly uniform, easily recognizable rhythm which lends itself to parody (including his own) like all strongly individualized styles. A language is individual when its user is endowed with sharply marked characteristics and succeeds in creating a medium for their expression. The origins, the constituents, the classical echoes which can be found in Churchill's prose are obvious enough; the product, however, is unique. Whatever the attitude that may be taken towards it, it must be recognized as a large-scale phenomenon of our time. To ignore or deny this would be blind or frivolous or dishonest. The utterance is always, and not merely on special occasions, formal (though it alters in intensity and colour with the situation), always public, Ciceronian, addressed to the world, remote from the hesitancies and stresses of introspection and private life.

Lynn's Response
(Typed as it was written)

Mark Antony tells the citizens of Rome, "I've come to bury Caesar, not to praise him." Berlin tells us, his audience, in effect, "I've come to praise Churchill, not to bury him." From the opening paragraph to the last line, the passage portrays Churchill as some kind of larger than life genius. To Berlin, Churchill is a man of mythic proportions. Like a God, he has a "historical imagination so strong, so comprehensive, as to encase the whole of the present and the whole of the future in a framework of a rich and multicolored past." With these words Berlin introduces Churchill's omnipotence to the reader in the opening paragraph.

In the rest of the passage, he deals with a different aspect of Churchill's awesome powers, from his vision of history to the style of his writing to the language he used when he wrote speeches and books. The second paragraph calls Churchill's vision of history a "great Renaissance pageant," a metaphor that is carried through the end of the passage. Because the Renaissance was a period when the arts flourished and Europe emerged from the Dark Ages, to associate Churchill with the Renaissance is to imply that he possesses the qualities of a truly great and influential figure in the history of the world. In fact, Churchill's view of history is compared to a work of art—something between picture book illustrations and "the great procession painted by Benozzo Gozzoli in the Riccardi Palace." (To be honest, I don't know what that painting looks like, but can imagine it to be a rich, detailed tapestry of life in fifteenth-century Italy.)

From lines 12 to 17 Berlin catalogues what Churchill's vision is *not:* It is not that of a sociologist, a psychologist, a historical scholar, etc. Those categories are too ordinary, too common for a figure like Churchill. Instead, he sees the world through the eyes of an "epic poet" like Homer, perhaps, or with the insight of a "dramatist who sees persons and situations as timeless symbols and embodiments of eternal, shining principles," a description that fits none other than Shakespeare himself. Berlin ends the paragraph with another comparison, pointing out that Churchill's vision of history resembles the legends of Carpaccio, another Italian artist, most likely from the Renaissance.

In the fourth paragraph. Berlin compares Churchill's writing to "tragic opera." Why he makes that analogy is clear when you think of opera as an art form that deals with intense issues of life and death, love and passion, all presented in a highly stylized manner. Like grand opera, where the music swells and melodrama prevails, Churchill's language transcends the normal use of words. Berlin quotes some of these uncommon phrases and words— "chortling" and "celestial grins," for example.

Berlin must know that exaggerated language is frowned upon by good writers and orators, but he adds toward the end of the passage that Churchill needed this kind of "mock-heroic" tone in order to convey to his audience the magnitude and the seriousness of the subject he was writing about. His tone was that of formal classical oration, like Cicero. This is another reference to the Renaissance because of the return to Classicism that occurred during that time. The style that he adopted was not fake or phony. As Berlin says, it was "second nature," a part of him and his "daily existence." Churchill was obliged to hide any "hesitancies and stresses of introspection and private life." As a leader in a time of great trouble, Churchill knew he had to rise above the masses, but when he did, he didn't just pretend to rise, which again may remind us of a famous God-like act.

Comment to Lynn

Your essay contains some stylistic weaknesses—wordiness, some awkward sentence structure, a conclusion that is slightly hyperbolic. But these are flaws that you'd expect to find in a hurriedly written essay, and they take very little away from your ability to analyze the passage and point out several of its rhetorical strategies and stylistic devices.

Your essay contains five paragraphs, including an introduction and a conclusion. The introduction, with its appealing and clever allusion to Shakespeare's *Julius Caesar,* is given a paragraph of its own and serves to show Berlin's admiration for Churchill. As you correctly point out, Berlin presents Churchill as a personage with God-like qualities. Your conclusion is an integral part of the final paragraph, and, as effective conclusions often do, it reminds the reader where the essay began—namely, with a reference to Churchill's transcendent qualities.

Much of your essay explains how the author develops the theme of Churchill as a Renaissance figure. Although you don't actually state that the passage achieves unity by repeatedly associating Churchill with the Renaissance, you astutely point out that the relationship is a major concern of the author. A generous assortment of apt quotations from the passage illustrate and support this point of view.

You took a risk at the end of the second paragraph by admitting a bit of ignorance. Your confession adds a charming, human touch to your essay and in no way interferes with the flow of ideas. In fact, your speculation about Gozzoli's painting shows that you understand the sort of painting that Berlin is most likely referring to in order to make his point.

The last piece of your essay is a little muddled. You may be trying to cover too much ground by discussing Churchill's language and his leadership style in the same paragraph. Also, your use of the term "mock-heroic" needs clarification. Your essay suggests that Churchill adopted a "mock-heroic" style because of the war. If the war was a real crisis, though, he would not have mocked it with fancy, overblown words.

Although your essay is not perfect, it is an excellent piece of work. Throughout, you refer directly or indirectly to the text. You answer the question thoroughly and accurately, and you demonstrate an ability to write clear and effective prose. This essay deserves a score of 8 or 9.

Chris's Response
(Typed as written)

Winston Churchill was one of the great leaders of the 20th century. He was the head of the English government during World War 2, and he said to the people, "Give me blood, toil and trouble, sweat and tears." Which made the British fight harder to overthrow Hitler. Churchill is also famous for inventing "The Iron Curtain." He used that expression at Westchester College in Missouri during a speech.

Since he was such a great man, Isaiah Berlin wrote a fantastic review of Churchill's memoir of World War 2. He said that Churchill's "dominant category, the single, central, organizing principle of his moral and intellectual universe, is a historical imagination." This shows he respects Churchill's imagination. It "give shape and character, colour and direction and coherence, to the stream of events," as Berlin said.

Berlin uses beautiful language, such as poetic alliteration, as an example, when he goes "skulls and skeletons" and "decay and death." He puts lots of t-sounds in lines 25-26 when he says, "the voice does not alter in pitch or timbre," and also in line 36 when he writes "texture and tension." He uses personification in line 35-36 when he goes "narrative consciously mounts and swells."

Berlin is one of the world's best users of allusion. Look at all the proper nouns in the passage. Line 8 has Renaissance. Line 9 has France, Italy, Germany, the Low Countries, Russia, etc. In line 12, he has put Benozzo Gozzoli and Riccardi Palace. Later he talks about "Stalky & Co." and Ciceronian. Allusions are references to things that readers understand and they enrich the meaning of a passage with their connotations.

In the last paragraph Berlin makes a hyperbole. In line 53, he says, "Churchill's language is a medium which he invented. That is overstating what Churchill did. No one knows who invented language. It goes back to the cave man. When he says that Churchill invented it, he exaggerates the truth to create the effect that Churchill is truly a giant statesman in the history of our time and will long be remembered by all men.

Comment to Chris

Your command of history is a little shaky. Churchill used slightly different words to inspire wartime Britain. It's not quite accurate to say that he also "invented" the Iron Curtain. Rather, he coined the phrase during a speech at West*minster* College. Regardless, the opening paragraph fails to contribute much to the analysis of the passage. It is more like prewriting—the writing that gets you loosened up before getting to the heart of the matter.

You've made a decent effort to explain the main idea of the passage. Quite correctly, you state that Berlin's choice of words shows a *respect*—one might even say *reverence*—for Churchill. But your essay is more descriptive than analytical. You quote from the passage at length in the second paragraph, but the purpose for doing so in unclear.

The next three paragraphs identify rhetorical devices that Berlin used. Your examples of alliteration are accurate. On the other hand, you seem to think that every proper noun is also an allusion. Technically, it is, of course, but literary allusions are meant primarily to enrich the meaning of a text. Most of the nouns in your list of allusions serve no such function. In your last paragraph you call one of Berlin's ideas a *hyperbole.* This represents a misreading of the text. Berlin does not say that Churchill invented language but that he invented a personal, individualized way of speaking and writing.

Regardless of how accurately you identified rhetorical and stylistic devices, however, be aware that simply identifying them is not enough. In addition, you must explain what each device contributes to the meaning and effect of the passage.

Notice that the second paragraph begins with an error in modification. What you've said is that Berlin, not Churchill, is a great man. This, along with several other errors in grammar and usage, weakens the overall effect of the essay. This essay deserves a score of 1 or 2.

How AP Essays Are Scored

Each year in early June, more than 1,000 college and secondary-school teachers gather in Princeton, New Jersey to read and evaluate AP essays written by students from across the country and overseas. Readers are chosen for their ability to make sound judgments about student writing and are trained to use a common set of scoring standards. Each essay is scored on a scale of 0 (low) to 9 (high) and is read by two different readers. If the scores assigned by the two readers differ by more than one grade, a third reader evaluates the essay.

A 9 ESSAY
Essays deserving a score of 9 demonstrate the writer's exceptional control of effective writing techniques. They are clear, interesting, and correct. They analyze rhetorical and stylistic devices with precision. They refer frequently to the text, directly or indirectly, and succinctly describe how such matters as tone, irony, diction, and use of examples contribute to the structure and meaning of a passage. Or they present a persuasive argument cogently and convincingly, using appropriate evidence to support a clearly articulated point of view. If errors exist, they are inconsequential.

AN 8 ESSAY
Essays earning an 8 are extremely well-written and demonstrate considerable mastery of written English. They meet all the criteria for essays earning 9, but fall just slightly short of distinction.

A 7 ESSAY
Essays scored 7 competently analyze rhetorical strategies and stylistic devices. They often use specific examples from the text and discuss, directly or indirectly, such matters as tone, irony, diction, and use of examples. They are reasonably well-developed and coherent. A few errors in word choice or sentence structure may exist, but no error is egregious enough to interfere with the clear expression of the writer's ideas.

A 6 ESSAY

Essays earning a 6 are generally the same as those receiving a 7 except that the prose style may be less mature, or the errors more serious.

A 5 ESSAY

Essays given a grade of 5 adequately answer the question but may lack full development. Ideas may be presented clearly but remain unsupported. The essay may be well organized and convey the writer's ideas, but lapses in diction or syntax weaken the impact of the essay and suggest that the writer is not fully in control of effective writing techniques.

A 4 ESSAY

An essay earning a 4 responds inadequately to the question. It may miss the point of the question or analyze secondary stylistic or rhetorical strategies. It may be superficial, or its ideas may be developed incoherently—jumping from topic to topic. Although the point of the essay may be clear, the prose is immature, showing the writer's lack of control over organization, word choice, or syntax.

A 3 ESSAY

Essays deserving a score of 3 are similar to essays scored 4 except the analysis is less astute or is seriously flawed. The prose demonstrates that the writer has difficulty controlling organization, choosing the correct words, or using standard English syntax to convey ideas.

A 2 ESSAY

An essay earning a score of 2 demonstrates the writer's inability to analyze the passage. It may wander off the topic or substitute a simpler task than that assigned by the question. The prose often reveals weaknesses in organizing material, in expressing ideas clearly, and in writing grammatically.

A 1 ESSAY

An essay deserving a 1 may be similar to an essay scored 2, but the ideas are more simplistic, and the expression flawed, perhaps bordering on the incomprehensible.

A 0 ESSAY

A 0 score indicates a blank paper, an essay not on the assigned topic, or a piece of writing that merely paraphrases the prompt.

You've no doubt noticed that the foregoing descriptions lack precision. It's no secret that grading essays is far from an exact science. But the readers are expected to be fair and to focus their attention on an essay's strengths rather than on its weaknesses.

Writing Essays: What You Need to Know About the Craft of Writing

On the AP exam you are expected to write analytical expository essays—the kind often required in English and other classes. An analytical essay is a form of discourse in which the writer attempts to explain a subject. It communicates ideas about people as individuals and as groups, about institutions, about the meaning of events, about values and dogmas of faith and culture, about relationships, and—what is relevant here—about the meaning of a work of art or literature.

Just as you won't learn to play the piano, twirl a baton, or swing dance by reading books on music, baton-twirling, or dancing, you are not likely to become a better writer of essays by reading a book on essay writing. The gains you make come about through practice, practice, practice. The best this book can do is to lay out some basic principles of essay writing for you to read, contemplate, and incorporate into the writing you do every day. The more experience you have, the more control you'll have, and ultimately, the better you will perform on the AP exam—as well as in future college courses and whatever work you do afterwards.

The first principle of good writing is *Know your subject.* You may be nimble-witted and intelligent beyond belief. You may have a wonderful way with words and a stylish way to express ideas, but without a solid grasp of the material, your essay may be nothing but ruffles and flourishes—pretty sounds with no substance. Knowing what you are talking about, then, is the paramount prerequisite of good writing.

With that in mind, let the following guidelines nag you into attending to the three most desirable essay writing goals: clarity, interest, and correctness.

1. *Clarity* because your ideas probably need to be clear to you before you can make them clear to others.
2. *Interest* because readers will desert you if you bore them.
3. *Correctness* because you and your work will inevitably be judged according to how well you demonstrate the conventions of writing.

If your good ideas are expressed clearly, interestingly, and correctly, there is no reason that you should not expect to write three winning essays on the AP exam.

The English language contains numerous adjectives that describe good writing: *effective, eloquent, well-written, lively, stylish, polished, descriptive, honed, vivid, engaging,* and countless others. The essay questions on the AP exam almost invariably tell you to write a "well-organized" or "carefully reasoned" or "focused" essay—directions that, in essence, say that it should be 1) clear, or easy to follow; 2) interesting, or expressed in economical, entertaining language; and 3) correct, or written in such a way that readers will not have to struggle to figure out what you are saying.

Frankly, the forty minutes suggested for each essay is not a great deal of time to read the question, plan what you will say, write several hundred words of analysis, edit and proofread your draft, and submit a finished piece of work. In effect, you are being forced to condense into a short time what would normally take far longer. A saving grace, however, is that the AP test readers don't expect three polished pieces of immortal prose, but just three competently written essays.

The number of words in each essay is up to you, but quality is far more important than quantity. On the AP test, length takes a back seat to answering the question and covering the subject. Be aware, however, that a single paragraph is not likely to give you the chance to develop your ideas sufficiently. A multiparagraph essay, on the other hand, offers you an opportunity to be expansive, to use a variety of details to support your main idea, and to show that you have the capacity to discuss a complex subject clearly and logically. In the end, though, the actual number of words is less crucial than what the words say.

Planning Time

Perhaps the key to making the most of your time lies in planning the essay. Allot yourself ten to fifteen minutes of the suggested forty minutes.

Start with the question. Read it twice or three times, underlining significant ideas and words until you are confident that you know *exactly* what you are being asked to write about. Then, with the task firmly in mind, read the passage at least twice—first for an overview, then for a more detailed study of its contents. During the second reading, underline key ideas and unusual words applicable to answering the question. Scribble notes in the margin. Jot down thoughts and ideas that occur to you as you read. Give the passage a third reading just to make sure you haven't missed anything important.

Then spend a few minutes writing an outline. Not a formal outline, but rather a list of ideas arranged in the order you'll use them in your essay. In general, a planned essay is likely to be clearer than one without a plan. It speaks well of you as a writer when you present ideas in a thought-out sequence instead of spilling them onto the page in the order they happened to pop into your mind. Since time is brief, outlining may consist of no more than scrawling a word or phrase to remind you of the gist of each paragraph, and then numbering the paragraphs in the order you expect to use them.

When you plan the essay that asks your opinion on an issue, it could work in your favor to figure out just what your position is. You won't be penalized for taking an unpopular or politically incorrect stance, but taking an unviable or illogical position will count against you. (Example: On the issue of whether pride—that is, *hubris*—is a destructive or a beneficial characteristic of man, you argue that all poverty-stricken people lack pride.) You could, of course, try straddling the fence on an issue with the "it-all-depends" argument. Such an approach is judicious and safe but not too interesting. It also could lead you to write an essay that merely describes or restates the question. If your judgment tells you that the question warrants a middle-of-the-road response, though, don't hesitate to write one. In the end, readers won't be impressed by your position but by the forcefulness of your presentation.

In the final analysis, the position to choose is the one about which you have the most compelling things to say. Unless you know your own mind well, simply make two lists. In the first list, jot down arguments in favor of the issue. Use the second list to record opposing arguments. Then decide which list holds the greater promise for an essay. From then on, focus on the issue. When you begin to write, state outright what you think. Let all the following paragraphs support your view in some fashion. Also consider devoting some or all of a paragraph to refuting the main argument that an opponent to your position might use.

Writing Time

When it comes time to make judgments about writing, the word *effectively* comes up repeatedly. It's a popular word because it's easy to use and hard to define. It means so much, and yet so little. Surely it connotes virtue, but virtues come in many stripes. You probably know effective writing when you see it, but what the AP folks have in mind is good organization, diction, syntax, sentence structure, a mature style of writing, paragraphing, development of ideas, logic, and correct mechanics (grammar, spelling, punctuation).

To write effectively, you must write clearly, which means choosing words that will convey exactly what you mean. Because thinking is the first step to clarity, if you don't fully grasp the meaning of your own words, think some more. Because you can't expect readers to think for you, unscramble everything that might interfere with clear meaning. Readers want to understand what you have to say. They need help, however, which only you can provide. Keep asking yourself, "What words must I use to be sure that my readers will grasp exactly what I mean?"

In figuring out which words to use, consider a plain, natural style. Don't be tempted to drag out your SAT vocabulary just to snow your readers. After all, AP readers are not world-class intellectuals who scoff at all but the most sophisticated prose. Rather, they're just teachers with plenty of experience evaluating students' writing. They won't be impressed by formal, pompous, or elegant writing. Think of them as everyday folks who appreciate straight, plain, everyday language. You have a natural voice. Use it. Don't try to pass yourself off as someone you are not. Readers can smell pretension a mile away.

In the time you have to write each essay, you'll be doing well if you develop a single idea fully. You won't have time to try to write the definitive essay on your subject. An essay that tries to do too much may end up as a jumble of unsubstantiated opinions. Therefore, concentrate on a single main idea that you develop with supporting ideas and examples.

Poor essays often suffer from lack of development. The writer states ideas and then drops them. You're not apt to do that, however, if you think of your readers as skeptics who doubt your veracity unless you show them that their skepticism is unfounded—that what you have said is the truth. An undeveloped statement, no matter how strongly worded, usually won't suffice.

Putting a reader's skepticism to rest means nothing more than backing up your general ideas with illustrative material that can take any number of forms. Use facts, statistics, common sense, your experience, and—especially in analyzing a poem or passage—quotations taken directly from the work itself. Don't overdo it, however. Don't rely too heavily on quoted material. Don't let the quotes constitute the bulk of your essay. Rather, state ideas in your own words, then support them with direct quotations. Whatever you do, demonstrate that your views are based on something more solid than a feeling or on personal preference. The kind of writing expected on the AP test is rational discourse, not emotional blabber. The left side of your brain, the logical side, is being examined along with the right, the creative, side. The best essays reveal that both sides of your brain are in good working order.

Editing Time

In general, first drafts (and even second drafts) are too wordy. Given two essays on the same topic, one verbose and the other to the point, the tightly written one would come out ahead. In short, economy is a virtue. If a point can be made with thirty words, you should not use sixty, forty, or even thirty-five. Economical writing, with the verbiage squeezed out, is far more interesting to read.

Therefore, as you edit your essays, be alert for needless words, for redundancy, and for nice-sounding but empty ideas and phrases that will put your reader to sleep. As William Strunk wrote in the definitive book on writing, *The Elements of Style,* "Vigorous writing is concise. A sentence should contain no unnecessary words, a paragraph no unnecessary sentences. . . . This requires not that a writer make all his sentences short, or that he avoid all detail and treat his subjects only in outline, but that every word tell." In keeping with that advice, don't gum up your prose with fuzzy, all-inclusive statements that try to encompass the history of mankind or the universe, such as "Since the beginning of time, men have pondered moral questions . . . ." Such overblown and pretentious writing has no place on the AP test. If you feel compelled to say something seemingly profound to get started, do so, by all means, but afterwards, cross it out unless it is essential to the point of your essay.

It goes without saying that some editing time should be spent proofreading your essays for spelling, punctuation, and proper grammar. You won't be penalized for one or two isolated errors, but AP readers will take a dim view of papers that are crowded with mechanical mistakes. Also, check your essay for legibility. Sloppy, hard-to-read handwriting is not supposed to count against you, but think of the readers: they want to get the job done. If they are bogged down in a barely legible paper, they could develop a bias against you. They're not supposed to, but humans, being human, often can't control their feelings. Face it, messy handwriting works against you; a neat hand works in your favor.

Unless you are lightning-quick, you won't have time to copy over the first draft of each essay. In fact, don't even think of trying. Your time will be better spent reorganizing and clarifying your ideas or looking for ill-chosen words and phrases. Feel free to cross out and to move sentences and paragraphs. If you rearrange the sequence of ideas in an essay, however, be sure to lead the reader through it with arrows, numbers, or other markers.

Writing Essays: What You Need to Know About Language and Rhetoric

No essay question on the AP exam is likely to ask you specifically about the grammar in a poem or passage. On occasion, however, it may be desirable, even opportune, to discuss certain aspects of grammar and usage in your essays.

The following paragraph by Washington Irving practically cries out for a comment about its sentence structure—particularly its use of parallelism:

> Her mighty lakes, like oceans of liquid silver; her mountains, with their bright aerial tints; her valleys, teeming with wild fertility; her tremendous cataracts, thundering in their solitudes; her boundless plains, waving with spontaneous verdure; her broad deep rivers, rolling in the solemn silence to the ocean; her trackless forests, where vegetation puts forth all its magnificence; her skies, kindling with the magic of summer clouds and glorious sunshine;—no, never need an American look beyond his own country for the sublime and beautiful of natural scenery.

Notice that the paragraph—except for the clause after the dash—consists of a single sentence composed of a series of nouns and modifiers, most followed by a participle phrase. The effect of this pattern is accumulative. It creates an image of the vastness of America, an idea aided not only by the piling up of visual images but by the repeated use of adjectives such as "tremendous," "boundless," and "broad."

Every AP exam contains essay questions that test your understanding of rhetoric. Most often, you are asked to analyze how such rhetorical concepts as tone, diction, syntax, and imagery help to achieve the purpose of a passage. The discussion below is intended to prepare you to make this kind of analysis.

The Rhetoric of Sentences

Long ago you probably learned that the sentence is the basic unit of communication. Individual words have meanings: nouns are the names of persons, places, and things; verbs express action; adjectives describe; and so forth. But only sentences can convey complex relationships between ideas, and the ability to use clear, forceful, and well-constructed sentences is a measure of one's ability to think. Therefore, the type, structure, and length of sentences provide significant clues to the thought processes of a writer or speaker. On the AP exam you will almost certainly have an opportunity, while answering multiple-choice questions or while writing an essay, to demonstrate your awareness of how sentences reveal an author's intent and convey meaning.

Sentence Length

Sentences can vary in length between one word ("Walk!") and hundreds, even thousands, of words. While styles in sentence length change over time, the average number of words in sentences written for a mass, middle-class audience of today is between twenty and thirty. Usually, the complexity of an idea determines the length of the sentence. That means that an author writing for an educated, literate audience is likely to use longer sentences than a writer of children's books. But not always. Profound ideas can also be expressed in pithy sentences: "I think, therefore, I am."

As you analyze a passage on the AP exam, stay alert for sentences that deviate markedly from the average. Speculate why the author may have chosen to write a protracted sentence. Ask why the author may have put a short sentence in a particular place or written a series of short sentences. In general, long sentences allow writers to convey complex ideas, and by subordination and manipulation of phrases, relative clauses, modifiers, appositives, parenthetical ideas, participles, and so forth, may emphasize certain points more than others. By definition, material in subordinate clauses receives less emphasis than material in an independent clause. On the other hand, when a passage consists of several brief sentences in succession, each sentence is hammered separately and emphatically into the reader's consciousness. The author may have a rhetorical purpose for structuring a passage with short sentences. In the case of some writing, however, a series of five- to ten-word sentences may simply indicate that the writer could not distinguish what was important from what was not.

Short sentences are easier to grasp. A short sentence makes its point quickly and often with considerable force, as in this passage about authors and critics:

> A person who pries into the actions of others, with no other desire but
> to discover their faults and publish them to the world deserves the title
> of slanderer of the reputations of men just as a critic who reads with the
> same malevolence should be deemed a slanderer of the reputations of
> books. Both are odious vermin.

The blunt closing sentence, particularly after a windy fifty-four word sentence, produces a mild jolt. The effect is intentional. Juxtaposing a tight, terse sentence against a long one leaves a mark on the reader's consciousness.

Sentence Structure

The order in which sentence elements are arranged affects a reader's response to the sentence. Of the three main sections of a sentence—the beginning, the middle, and the end—the end is the most desirable spot for placing ideas that a writer wants to emphasize. Why this is so can be explained by the fact that the reader's mind comes to a very brief stop at the end of each sentence—brief, but nevertheless long enough for the last idea to sink in. Ideas placed at the beginning of a sentence leave an impression, too, but not as vivid an impression as those at the end. The middle of a sentence is often reserved for the least important ideas.

This principle underlies the use of so-called *periodic* sentences—sentences that save the most important idea for the very end. Compare the following two sentences:

> A false, unnatural, and destructive economic system develops when the poor worker is allowed to work at half price and the good worker is forced to work for an inadequate wage, hardly sufficient to support a family.

> When the poor worker is allowed to work at half price and the good worker is forced to work for an inadequate wage, hardly sufficient to decently support a family, a false, unnatural, and destructive economic system develops.

There is nothing wrong with either sentence. Both state their point clearly. But if the writer wished to stress the point that certain conditions lead to a dysfunctional economic system, the second sentence does it more emphatically by stating that fact at the end—in that part of the sentence that contains the subject and verb (Subject: *destructive economic system;* verb: *develops*). In the first sentence, the main point is stated first but is then pushed into the background by the account of circumstances that lead to a destructive economic system.

In this example of a periodic sentence, the main idea is completely delayed. A variation of this kind of periodic sentence is one in which the main clause is introduced early in the sentence but its completion is postponed by modifiers and other interrupting material, as in

> The tall shapely trees, their branches withered and their trunks bent inward toward the slope of the mountain, showed the effects of raging winds.

What always distinguishes the periodic sentence from its opposite, the *loose* sentence, is that its thought is not completed until the end. The loose sentence, on the other hand, gives away its "secret" at the start. It follows the most common pattern of English sentences—subject-verb, as in *Kevin called,* or subject-verb-object, as in *He used a cell phone.*

As it happens, most English sentences in speech and writing are loose sentences. But an endless progression of loose sentences is monotonous. Likewise, prose consisting of a string of periodic sentences is difficult to read. A balance is best. In the following passage, for example, the sudden appearance of a periodic sentence at the end creates a dramatic effect:

> He had been away from home for five years. He hadn't heard from his family in all that time. His heart started to quicken when he drove into town. He was five minutes from home. The town hadn't changed much since he left. He pressed the accelerator harder, thinking of how surprised his mother would be to see him standing at the front door. Then, suddenly, as he steered his Honda into the driveway, instead of the familiar white house, he saw an empty, garbage-strewn lot.

Here, the climactic sentence provides a surprise to the reader, a pay off that would have been lost or at least diminished if it had been written: *He suddenly saw an empty, garbage-strewn lot instead of the familiar white house as he steered his Honda into the driveway.*

Savvy writers know how sentence parts should be arranged to convey meaning. The arrangement they choose very often amounts to simply highlighting the important ideas and letting secondary, and even tertiary, ideas slide into the background. This is done by subordination.

As you know, every sentence has a main clause consisting of at least a subject and a verb. That's all a *simple* sentence needs to be complete—a subject and a verb. Even if many modifiers and objects are added, it still remains a *simple* sentence.

For example, both of the following sentences, despite the disparity in their length, are *simple* sentences:

> Berkeley admitted Sarah.

> Situated on the eastern side of San Francisco Bay, Berkeley, the University of California's flagship institution, admitted Sarah as a freshman in the class of 2004, to the delight not only of Sarah herself but to the satisfaction of her family, teachers, and friends.

Leaving aside the wordiness and wisdom of including so much miscellaneous information in the second sentence, you still find a simple declarative sentence—*Berkeley admitted Sarah*—lurking within its jumble of modifiers, participles, prepositional phrases, and appositives.

To turn a *simple* sentence into a *compound* sentence, add a conjunction, a word like *and* or *but,* as in

> Berkeley admitted Sarah and she was delighted.

You can infer from this example that a *compound* sentence is made up of at least two simple sentences joined by a conjunction. What is rhetorically noteworthy about a compound sentence is that the author gives more or less equal emphasis to the information in each of the clauses. Clauses of equal rank and structure are called coordinate clauses and are joined by coordinating conjunctions (*and, but, or, nor, yet, so*) and sometimes by a semicolon with connective words like *however, moreover, nevertheless, otherwise, therefore, consequently,* and others. In this case, whether logical or not, Sarah's acceptance has been given equal importance to her reaction to the news.

If the author's intent, however, is to emphasize Sarah's state of mind, the sentence might best be turned into a *complex* sentence—that is, a sentence that contains both a subordinate and a main clause:

> *Because Berkeley admitted her,* Sarah was delighted. (Subordinate clause
> italicized)

Here, the cause-and-effect relationship between the two ideas is made clearer. The addition of a subordinating conjunction *because* gives prominence to the information in the main, or independent clause. (Other widely used subordinating conjunctions include *although, before, even though, while, unless, if,* and *when.*)

By means of subordination, authors are able to convey not only the interrelationship of ideas but also the relative importance of one idea to another. Important ideas usually go into the independent clause of a complex sentence, while secondary or subordinate ideas are relegated to dependent clauses, or to phrases and individual words.

> *Although Sara was not in the top quarter of her class,* Berkeley admitted
> her as a freshman in the class of 2004. (Dependent clause italicized)

Some sentences have a still more elaborate structure. They can combine the elements of a compound and a complex sentence, hence the label *compound-complex.* For example,

> *Although Sara was not in the top quarter of her class,* Berkeley admitted
> her as a freshman in the class of 2004, anyway, and she was delighted.

The Sound of Sentences

In analyzing prose (or poetry, for that matter), it pays to be sensitive to the rhythm of the words. The rhythm of prose is not obvious, as it is in most music and poetry. It is a more subtle quality, hard to define and difficult to measure, except by the roughest standards, but quite noticeable in its absence—when a sentence or passage sounds awkward and stumbling.

That doesn't mean that rhythmic passages have a beat, but rather that the words possess a graceful combination of sounds, accents, phrases, and pauses, often indicated by punctuation. The most important of these rhythmic components may be the rests that are signaled by commas, semicolons, colons, dashes, and periods that break a sentence into rhythmic units. Each rest gives the reader a chance to pause momentarily and let ideas sink in.

Long sentences with a string of prepositional phrases not only rub against a reader's aesthetic grain but lack the pauses that establish a rhythm. For example:

> The account of the building of the section of the road between Bedford
> and the Connecticut border is wrong in its details on account of the
> illegibility of the words written on the order form on the clipboard of
> the supervisor of the project.

Such sentences, while grammatically flawless, sweep the reader along relentlessly from beginning to end. In sentences as unbroken as this one, there is no phrasing and no rhythm.

In passages on the AP exam, you probably won't encounter such poorly written prose. But you may be asked to write about a passage in which the rhythm of the language helps the author convey meaning. Or you may wish to point out that a passage derives its beauty or power from a combination of rhythm and balance—that is, a consistent matching of parallel phrases or clauses, as in this well-known excerpt from *Ecclesiastes:*

> Everything has its appointed hour, there is a time for all things under
> heaven: a time for birth, a time for death, a time to plant and a time to

uproot, a time to kill, a time to heal, a time to break down and a time to
build, a time to cry, a time to laugh, a time to mourn, a time to dance, a
time to scatter and a time to refrain, a time to seek, and time to lose, a time
to keep, a time to throw away, a time to tear, a time to sew, a time for
silence and a time for speech, a time for love, a time for hate, a time for
war, a time for peace.

A reader can hardly help being struck by the repetition in this passage. (The
word *time* is used 27 times.) Considering the intent of the passage—to convey
both the variety and the everlasting cycle of life—such repetition is not only
appropriate but necessary. Without it, reading the passage would be less memorable. Although the passage lacks the metrical regularity of a poem, it is poetic
and exemplifies a rhythmic eloquence.

On the AP exam you may run into a passage characterized by an absence of
regular rhythm. Such a passage may be from a stream-of-consciousness novel or
other work that attempts to recreate a person's random, fragmented internal
thoughts. In the event that you must write about such a passage by James Joyce,
William Faulkner, or the contemporary novelist Dom DiLillo, show how the
words capture the chaos of human thought or suggest the prevailing atmosphere of a character's mind, or provide a visual montage of modern life—or
whatever other intent you may discern.

Authors intentionally use rhythm to arouse emotions. In fact, rhythm can
have at least as much power as well-chosen words to create an emotional
effect. A passage that is meant to create a sense of peace and calm demands a
slow, even rhythm, as in this sample of prose from the pen of the American
naturalist/writer Edward Abbey. Describing early morning in the desert, he
writes:

The sun is not yet in sight but signs of the advent are plain to
see. Lavender clouds sail like a fleet of ships across the pale green dawn;
each cloud, planed flat on the wind, has a base of fiery gold. Southeast,
twenty miles by line of sight, stand the peaks of the Sierra La Sal, twelve
to thirteen thousand feet above sea level, all covered with snow and rosy
in the morning sunlight. The air is dry and clear as well as cold; the last
fogbanks left over from last night's storm are scudding away like ghosts,
fading into nothing before the wind and the sunrise.

In an entirely different mood, Abbey writes on the topic "Transcendence":

It is this which haunts me night and day. The desire to transcend my own
limits, to exceed myself, to become more than I am. How? I don't know.
To transcend this job, this work, this place, this kind of life—for the sake
of something superlative, supreme, exalting. But where? Again, how? Don't
know. It will come of itself . . . like lightning, like rain, like God's gift of
grace, in its own good time. (If it comes at all.)

In this passage, the inner turmoil Abbey feels about himself manifests itself in
the short, choppy phrases, the combination of questions and fragmentary sentences, the clipped rhythm of his thoughts.

Review of Rhetoric

Rhetoric is a broad term. Having come this far in your education, you are
already acquainted with many of its varieties. Everything you have ever written
or read—from a movie review to a college application—is subject to analysis in
rhetorical terms.

The study of rhetoric can be a lifetime occupation. Thick books have been written on the subject. For a thorough treatment of rhetoric, turn to *A Rhetoric Casebook* by Francis Connolly and *The Language of Argument* by Daniel McDonald. For a readable overview, get *Elements of Style* by William Strunk and E.B. White or *On Writing Well* by William Zinsser. For a brief look at the basic rhetorical principles you should know for the AP exam, read on.

The rhetoric of some works is easier to discern than the rhetoric in others. Rhetoric is most obvious in prose and poetry that distinctly convey an author's personality as well as the author's attitude toward the subject. In an advertisement for Nike shoes or in a prosecutor's opening statement at a murder trial, the point and purpose are likely to be transparent. A diplomatic communiqué, on the other hand, may have subtleties of meaning that evade all but the most seasoned foreign service officials.

Virtually all writing has a rhetorical purpose. If authors aim to describe a place, person, or object, they try to recreate the look, the sound, the smell, the taste, and the feel of things. If their aim is to tell a story, they try to communicate an event or a sequence of events by selecting and arranging particulars, usually in the order they occurred. An argumentative author takes a position and offers reasons to support it. And so on. Whatever the mode, the author's choice of words, the syntax (order of words and phrases), the sound and structure of sentences, the sequence of ideas, the selection of details—all these elements and more are meant to serve the purpose of the whole.

The purpose is often more complex than simply conveying an experience or telling a story. Authors may, for example, want to stimulate certain responses in their readers, who may react to a vivid re-creation of an experience as though they themselves had the experience: they may laugh out loud, become tense or frightened, weep, grow angry. A biographer may want to communicate the facts of his subject's life. A. Scott Berg, for instance, wrote a prize-winning biography of Charles Lindbergh. In doing so, Berg established a tone that revealed his own thoughts about Lindbergh. In laying out the facts about Lindbergh, he also meant to convince the reader that Lindbergh was both an admirable and a reprehensible figure. He wants us to admire and despise the man at the same time, just as he, the biographer, does.

What the author intends his readers to think is often called the intellective purpose; what the author wants readers to feel is termed the emotive purpose. Scientific treatises, process analyses (how to do something), definitions, and pieces written solely to inform or instruct may lack emotive purpose altogether, but it is hard to conceive of a piece—including a pure-bred lyric poem—that lacks all intellectual purpose. Regardless, the two purposes are usually not separate or distinct from each other. Thoughts and feelings blend into our total response to the work.

Of course, a writer's attitude toward the subject is not necessarily identical with the response of the reader. An advertising copywriter for Nike may be totally indifferent to the shoes he crows about, but since his job is to make readers feel a certain way, he purposefully uses words to produce a particular response—namely, to turn readers into consumers of Nike products. In short, language molds the reader's attitude toward the subject discussed. And tone determines precisely what that attitude will be.

When you analyze the rhetoric of passages on the AP exam, these are the kinds of concepts that you must deal with. To be prepared, you should be conversant with the intellectual and emotional impact of a writer's tone and diction (connotation and denotation), metaphorical—that is, figurative—language, and allusions.

Tone

In both the multiple-choice questions and essay questions, you will probably need to deal with tone. One of the most common objective questions asks you to identify the tone of a poem or passage, of a sentence, or even of a single word or phrase. To answer the question you will need a sense of the narrator's or speaker's attitude toward the subject of the passage. This may differ from the author's attitude, of course. An author may portray a scoundrel in a favorable way, but that doesn't necessarily mean the author has a soft spot in his heart for scoundrels. Because an author's tone may be complex or may shift part way through a passage or poem, it can be described in innumerable ways, often by one or more adjectives. For example,

> *Negative:* bitter, condescending, contemptuous, disdainful, disgusted, facetious, flippant, indignant, irreverent, mocking, patronizing, pedantic, petty, sarcastic, satiric, scornful, teasing, threatening,
> *Positive:* benevolent, compassionate, determined, ecstatic, effusive, elegiac, enthusiastic, hopeful, laudatory, learned, supportive, sympathetic,
> *Neutral:* bantering, colloquial, confident, detached, didactic, factual, informal, objective, restrained, scholarly.

In essence, tone is the psychological quality of the words. The words themselves and the manner in which they are expressed work together to establish the tone. Consider the simple question, "Who are you?" Depending on the tone in which the words are expressed, the question may be funny, sassy, inquisitive, challenging. Because the inflection of a voice is not available to writers, they must rely more on diction—the writer's choice of words, including figures of speech—to establish a tone. The differences between "Shut your mouth," "Please keep still," and "Would you be kind enough not to talk now?" are apparent. In a general sense the three locutions mean the same thing. The tone in each sentence, however, could hardly be more different from the tone of the others because the words chosen to convey the meaning evoke very different feelings.

While the form of sentences significantly influences tone, other rhetorical elements also play a major part, especially diction, metaphors, and other figures of speech such as symbols and allusions.

Sentence Forms

One way an author reveals tone is by the form of sentences. An exclamatory sentence, for example, expresses a wish, a desire, a command—and is often, but not always, indicated with an exclamation point:

> Heads up!
> May the force be with you!
> Have a nice day!

Such sentences can express various gradations of begging, beseeching, praying, imploring, apologizing, requesting, advising, commanding, persuading, and so on. "Let the word go forth," intoned John F. Kennedy in his inauguration address, "that the torch has been passed to a new generation . . . ." Kennedy's inspirational tone is initiated by the use of the imperative verb *let*. The high-sounding verb *go forth* and the metaphorical use of *torch* also contribute a sense of mission to the mood of the occasion.

An *interrogative* sentence also offers a writer a variety of tones. Questions are usually asked in order to obtain information: "When is the next train to Mt. Kisco?" But the tone of a question can also be a challenge ("Who are you calling a nerd, Mac?), a denial ("Do you actually think I'm capable of such a thing?"), disbelief (Can you believe the nerve of that driver?"), hesitation ("Do you really think I should step off the edge of the cliff ?), and so on. On the AP exam, the questions you may find within passages are most likely to be rhetorical questions—questions that have only one correct answer, implied in the question itself. Used in argumentation, a rhetorical question calls attention to an obvious proposition or idea. Although phrased as a question, it has the force of a strong assertion. Lincoln used the power of rhetorical questions, for example, in a letter to one of his critics:

> You dislike the Emancipation Proclamation, and perhaps would have it retracted. You say it is unconstitutional. I think differently. I think the Constitution invests its commander-in-chief with the law of war in time of war. The most that can be said—if so much—is that slaves are property. Is there, has there ever been, any question that, the law of war, property, both of enemies and friends, may be taken when needed? And is it not needed whenever taking it helps us or hurts the enemy?

Some passages may also contain questions that function as guides to the discussion. A rhetorical device, technically known as *ratiocinatio* and used to make an argument more dramatic and convincing, is a series of questions and answers, structured somewhat like a dialogue or an author's interview with himself:

> When our ancestors condemned women for one crime, they considered that by this single judgment she was convicted of many transgressions. How so? Judged unchaste, she was also deemed guilty of poisoning. Why? Because, having sold her body to the basest passion, she had to live in fear of many persons. Who are these? Her husband, her parents, and the others . . . .

A *declarative* sentence, the most common form of sentence, makes a factual statement. Unlike the exclamatory and interrogative sentence, the declarative sentence does not blatantly reveal its tone. Much of the time, the tone of a declarative sentence is neutral. It merely states information in a matter-of-fact way:

> In 1897, Columbia University moved from 49th Street and Madison Avenue, where it had stood for forty years, to its present location on Morningside Heights at 116th Street and Broadway.

While this matter-of-fact tone is prevalent in scientific and other informational prose, declarative sentences can also be highly charged with emotion:

> People who knew Thomas Wolfe recall that he habitually roamed down the long aisles of the library stacks, grabbing one book after the other from the shelves and devouring its contents as if he were a starving man suddenly let loose in an immense storehouse of food. He wrote with abandon, turning out incredible quantities of manuscript, filling whole packing cases with the product of his frenzied pen.

On the surface, this may seem like a factual description of Thomas Wolfe. The writer is informing us that Wolfe read many books and wrote prodigiously. But the words create a portrait of an awe-inspiring, larger-than-life figure. The simile, "as if he were a starving man suddenly let loose in an immense storehouse of food," while possibly overstating Wolfe's behavior in the library, does not exaggerate the passion Wolfe must have felt for reading books.

Diction

In large measure, tone is created by diction. In the following passage, from an article titled "Fenimore Cooper's Literary Offenses," Mark Twain comments on the diction of a well-regarded American writer.

> Cooper's word sense was singularly dull. When a person has a poor ear for music, he will flat and sharp right along without knowing it. He keeps near the tune, but it is not the tune. When a person has a poor ear for words, the result is a literary flatting and sharping; you perceive what he is intending to say, but you also perceive that he doesn't say it. This is Cooper. He was not a word musician. His ear was satisfied with the *approximate* word. I will furnish some circumstantial evidence in support of this charge. My instances are gathered from half a dozen pages of the tale called *Deerslayer*. He used "verbal" for "oral"; "precision" for "facility"; "phenomena" for "marvels"; "necessary" for "predetermined"; "unsophisticated" for "primitive"; "preparation" for "expectancy"; "rebuked" for "subdued"; "dependent on" for "resulting from"; "fact" for "condition"; . . . "brevity" for "celerity"; "distrusted" for "suspicious"; "mental imbecility" for "imbecility"; "eyes" for "sight"; "counteracting" for "opposing"; . . . . There have been daring people in the world who claimed that Cooper could write English, but they're all dead now.

Apparently, Cooper's diction left much to be desired. In Twain's view, Cooper was insensitive to the connotation of many, many words. He may well have known the definitions of words, but he had a so-called tin ear when it came to understanding the words in context. He seems deaf to the feelings that words represent, and, therefore, chose his words badly.

Diction is one of the elements of *style* that give each person's writing, for good or ill, a quality that is uniquely his/her own.

Tone, another element of style, involves not only a manner of writing that shows a certain attitude, but also an emotional and intellectual quality, more or less pronounced, that arises from the urge to set down on paper some experiences, some views, some ideas that the writer wants to share with the reader. It arises from a deep commitment of the writer to his/her art.

Two other elements that enter into style are as follows:

1. The variety of the forms of the writer's sentences and paragraphs.
2. The pace and the sequence of the presentation of everything the writer has to say. This attribute of a work arises to a great extent from an instinctive sense. The choice of words, the structure of the sentences, the rhythm created by arranging the words so that accents fall into a pleasing pattern—all play a part in the pace of a work.

These many elements are what you will have to examine and comment on, not only when you look critically at the writing of others, but also when you look critically at your own writing and seek to refine it. Part of your preparation for the exam should include close critical study of the many elements that comprise style.

Below is a list of adjectives culled from Roget's *Thesaurus* from which you can choose apt terms to describe the style of the various passages that you will be studying for the examination.

clarity	obscurity	plainness	embellishment
lucid	obscure	unvarnished	ornate
explicit	vague	severe	flowery
	involuted	commonplace	turgid
		unimaginative	bombastic
		sparse	florid

conciseness	diffuseness	elegance	inelegance
brief	verbose	polished	graceless
terse	prolix	classic	vulgar
laconic	rambling	graceful	labored
succinct	protracted	symmetrical	ponderous
sententious	wordy	felicitous	tasteless
	convoluted		

vigor	feebleness	conformity	unconformity
forcible	prosaic	ordinary	singular
mordant	unvaried	commonplace	amorphous
incisive	sketchy	bromidic	bizarre
graphic	weak	exemplary	extraordinary
impassioned	puerile		
trenchant	inferior		
	ineffective		

Look up these words in the dictionary for precise meanings. What other words can you think of to describe style?

Furthermore, you will need to sharpen two additional skills: (1) the power to judge aspects of the character and personality of the writer that are reflected in the way he/she fuses the many elements of the work; and (2) the power to arrive inferentially and logically at conclusions related to the work and supported by evidence within the work.

If, for example, a writer's tone is objective or ironic or sentimental, it will not only determine the language, metaphors, symbols, and allusions the writer uses but also reflect his/her attitude toward the subject. The reader needs to sharpen the skill to judge the character and personality and the purpose and beliefs of a writer who deals with the tools of his/her trade in a particular fashion. If style makes the man or woman, then the reader must be able to make judgments about the writer from the totality of style and content. The ability to make such judgments, as well as to arrive at logical conclusions suggested but not directly stated, comes from inferential reading.

Refining Writing Skill

Consider the following two paragraphs. Both deal with the same content. The first is a series of simple declarative sentences arranged in logical sequence. The passage has no structural sentence errors. Its intellectual content is ably recorded, and the diction is reasonably good. Yet you will agree that it is dull and lifeless and that you would find it intolerable to read a full chapter written in this way.

Analyze what the writer has done in the second paragraph to communicate the same information more interestingly and more dramatically. What few facts has she added? Judge how she has achieved sentence variety, how she has vitalized the style of her presentation, how the pace and rhythm of the account have added an emotional tone to the intellectual content, and how a greater sense of the personality of the writer is apparent. Finally, determine what inferential conclusions can be drawn from this account about the events recorded.

Paragraph 1

Parliament had hitherto bestowed very little attention on our Eastern possessions. George the Second died. There was a succession of weak administrations. Each administration was flattered and betrayed by the court. The administrations had held the semblance of power. There were intrigues in the palace. There were riots in the capital. There were insurrectionary movements in the American colonies. The advisers of the Crown had little leisure to study Indian politics.

Paragraph 2

Parliament had hitherto bestowed very little attention on our Eastern possessions. Since the death of George the Second, a rapid succession of weak administrations, each of which was in turn flattered and betrayed by the court, had held the semblance of power. Intrigues in the palace, riots in the capital, and insurrectionary movements in the American colonies had left the advisers of the Crown little leisure to study Indian politics. When they did interfere, their interference was feeble and irresolute. Lord Chatham, indeed, during the short period of his ascendancy in the councils of George the Third, had meditated a bold attack on the [East India] Company. But his plans were rendered abortive by the strange malady which about that time began to overcloud his splendid genius.

Connotation and Denotation

Words derive their connotation from two sources: people's common experience and an individual's personal experience. Because we are all creatures of our society, our personal response to a word may be the same as the general response. On the AP exam you would not be expected to recognize the kinds of private connotations of words found in some poems and in books like Joyce's *Finnegan's Wake*. Rather, you can depend on passages containing words with more general connotations.

Words represent not only ideas, events, and objects, but also the feelings we attach to ideas, events, and objects. Thus, the word *rat* represents a certain kind of rodent—among other things. That is its denotative meaning. But a rat also evokes in us feelings of fear and disgust—its connotation. What is true of *rat* is also true of countless other words: *mother, home, candy, money, grease, America, dog,* and so on. Connotations may change over time, and our personal experience often adds connotative value to words that may at first mean nothing beyond their definition. Scientific words that at one time merely named physical phenomena or technical achievements—*cloning, abortion, www.com*—might easily acquire rich connotative meanings as we become familiar with them.

Take note of the connotative power of the words in the following passage, written by one of the first lexicographers, Dr. Samuel Johnson. Johnson surely used richly connotative words to stimulate a specific emotional response in his readers:

> It is the fate of those who toil at the lower employments of life
> to be rather driven by the fear of evil than attracted by the prospect of
> good; to be exposed to censure without hope of praise, to be disgraced
> Line by miscarriage or punished for neglect whose success would have been
> (5)   without applause, and diligence without reward.
>   Among these unhappy mortals is the writer of dictionaries, whom
> mankind have considered, not as the pupil, but the slave of science, the
> pioneer of literature, doomed only to remove rubbish and clear obstructions

from the paths through which Learning and Genius press forward to
(10) conquest and glory, without bestowing a smile on the humble drudge that
facilitates their progress. Every other author may aspire to praise; the
lexicographer can only hope to escape reproach, and even this negative
recompense has been yet granted to very few.

Although Johnson was a man of intellect and wit, you must have noticed the
despair in his words. In spite of the self-pity implied in the passage, Johnson must
have loved writing his dictionary. Otherwise he would not have undertaken such
a mammoth job. His tone, therefore, may be somewhat ironic, for a person of his
stature on the London literary scene of the eighteenth century could hardly be considered a "humble drudge" (line 10). Rather, he is trying to make readers feel
respect for him and appreciate the work that goes into writing a dictionary.

Metaphorical Language

Figures of speech often reveal an author's tone. The most common figures of
speech—no doubt familiar to you—are metaphor, simile, metonymy, synecdoche, personification, and allusion, which, taken as a whole, may be called
metaphorical language. Basically, metaphorical language functions as a means
of making comparisons. When an author can't find the exact words to describe
a feeling or to capture experiences that seem almost inexpressible, a metaphor
may come to the rescue: "She has a voice of gold," says the music critic, using a
metaphor to express not only the beauty of her voice but also its value. Indeed,
in a particular context the metaphor could mean that the singer makes big money
with her voice. In short, figures of speech have the power to make something
clearer or more vivid, or turn a vague impression into something concrete.

Furthermore, figures of speech are economical. They condense a lot of
thought and feeling into a few words. Ernie Pyle, a famous World War II news
correspondent, reported his stories as though they were being told by the average GI lying in a foxhole. He said, "I write from a worm's eye point of view."
The idea gives a fresh slant to an old expression and cogently fixes Pyle's position on the battlefield.

Because metaphorical language evokes mental images, it has a good deal to
do with the emotional content of a piece of writing. If an author relies on trite,
second-hand expressions to convey an idea, using such metaphors as *walking
on air* or *life in the fast lane,* you can fairly well conclude that the author may
have nothing new or surprising to say. On the other hand, a passage full of fresh
metaphorical language may give readers rich new insights and understandings.
An allusion—an implied or direct reference to something in history or culture—is, like a richly connotative word, a means to suggest far more than it
says. An allusion of a single word or phrase can expand the reader's understanding more completely than a long, discursive comparison. You may know
Robert Frost's poem "Out, Out . . . ," a narrative poem that recounts a farmyard
accident that takes the life of a young boy. A theme of the poem, the uncertainty
and unpredictability of life, is alluded to in the title, which you may know
comes from Macbeth's soliloquy upon hearing of his wife's death: "Out, out,
brief candle./Life's but a walking shadow, . . ." Macbeth's speech is a reflection
on both the tragedy of a premature death and the impermanence of life. While
readers unfamiliar with *Macbeth* may read "Out, Out . . . " with insight and
pleasure, the allusion to Shakespeare's play enriches the experience.

Although there is a danger that you may not catch all instances of metaphorical language on the AP exam, be confident that you will grasp enough of them

to comment in your essays about how figures of speech affect the tone of a passage. The breadth and depth of your literary experience will enable you to see that figures of speech tell you about the author's attitude, as well as the attitude the author wishes readers to have toward the subject.

Figurative language sways readers because, like individual words, each figure of speech has a connotation. If an author wishes to establish a friendly tone, metaphors will be drawn from ordinary, everyday experience. Figurative language sways readers because, just like individual words, each figure of speech has a connotation. To say that a marathoner "runs like the wind" evokes an unambiguous image of a swift runner striding effortlessly along the course.

On the other hand, an author hoping to establish an elevated tone will create metaphors that have an elevated quality. "Prose has no stage scenery to hide behind, as poetry has," wrote H.L. Mencken. "It cannot use masks and wigs. It is not spontaneous, but must be fabricated by thought and painstaking effort. Prose is the ultimate flower of the art of words." Although Mencken might be accused of being carried away by metaphorical language, the description conveys the author's cynicism about poetry and his respect for prose. Prose is compared to a play. Unlike poetry, the meaning of which can be obscured—presumably by odd syntax, unusual words, idiosyncratic usage—prose must be clear and carefully crafted. Then he compares prose to the "ultimate flower," a metaphor suggesting one of nature's most beautiful objects. Through his use of metaphorical language, Mencken expresses his admiration for good prose. The words he uses suggest that he would like you, the reader, to admire it, too.

Good writers choose metaphors carefully, for metaphorical language that seems inappropriate to the general tone and purpose of the passage will grate on readers and weaken the overall effect that the author may have in mind. It also suggests that the author lacks a clear sense of purpose or just doesn't know how to achieve a particular purpose. Take, for example, this attempt to describe how memories of childhood fade with the passing of time:

> As you grow older, your memory of childhood is obliterated like
> Hiroshima after the bomb.

Isn't it obvious that the author missed the point? After all, memories fade slowly, not cataclysmically. Whatever tone the author may have intended is lost in the incongruity of the simile. A more appropriate way to capture the idea that memories erode gradually may have been

> As you grow older, memories of childhood vanish like sand dunes
> at the edge of the sea.

Of course, there may be another possibility. Perhaps the author purposely wrote an incongruous metaphor for a particular purpose. Authors often try to surprise their readers to heighten interest. They introduce an inappropriate or contradictory metaphor, for instance, for the sake of contrast. They invent a figure of speech with a connotation that is off kilter in order to create a kind of tension or to make an ironic or amusing comment. During the Spanish Civil War, Ernest Hemingway, writing a dispatch from the front lines, said of the enemy planes, "If their orders are to strafe the road on their way home, you will get it [be wounded or killed]. Otherwise, when they are finished with their jobs on a particular objective, they go off like bank clerks, flying home." The comparison of deadly fighters and bank clerks may seem frivolous, but it does make the point effectively. Both are eager to scurry away from their jobs as quickly as possible. Moreover, by contrasting bank clerks—generally harmless, well-meaning functionaries—with ruthless fighters, Hemingway heightens the viciousness of the enemy aircraft strafing the people on the road.

Another form of comparison is the *analogy,* usually defined in words like these: A comparison of two objects or situations that have several common characteristics. An extended analogy, showing parallels between two unlike things, can simplify a complicated idea and leave a powerful impression on a reader. Consider the tone established in the following excerpt from a speech by President Woodrow Wilson:

> I had a couple of friends who were in the habit of losing their tempers, and when they lost their tempers they were in the habit of using very unparliamentary language. Some of their friends induced them to make a promise that they never would swear inside the town limits. When the impulse next came upon them, they took a street car to go out of town to swear, and by the time they got out of town they did not want to swear . . . . Now, illustrating the great by the small, that is true of the passions of nations.

Wilson used this analogy in support of his position that a country must not jump into a war in the heat of passion. By using colloquial words (e.g., "a couple of friends) and telling a personal anecdote, Wilson established a folksy tone. The analogy, which would be accessible to every listener, draws on everyday experience, and makes good common sense. Wilson, in effect, has taken on the persona of one of the guys. Neither moralistic nor panicky, he creates the image of a fellow whose judgment the country can trust in a crisis.

An author's use of metonymy and synecdoche also contributes to the establishment of tone. Unlike metaphors, which make comparisons, these two figures of speech make substitutions—usually something abstract for something concrete (or vice versa), a container for the thing contained (or vice versa), a part for the whole, a cause for the effect, and so on.

In the statement, "Marv has a good head," the word *head* has been substituted for *brain* (the container for the thing contained). But *head* also means "IQ" or "intelligence"—both abstract concepts that are made more tangible by the use of *head.* In general, metonymy tends to bring a kind of vitality to a phrase or idea. To some degree, it can simplify an idea—unlike a metaphor, which tends to complicate a thought—particularly when a concrete substitution is made for an abstraction, as in "Your hands made you rich," in which *hands* means occupation, or trade, or line of work.

Synecdoche is a variety of metonymy, in which a part is substituted for the whole, or vice versa. Any time you use the word *sail* for ship ("A fleet of a hundred sails"), or call a truck an *eighteen-wheeler,* you are using synecdoche. When Hamlet is about to remove the body of Polonius from Gertrude's bedchamber, he says "I'll lug the guts into the neighbor room." His synecdoche *guts* clearly stands for corpse, but its connotation also suggests the disdain that Hamlet felt for Polonius. Indeed, both metonymy and synecdoche can be rich with implied meaning.

As you consider the metaphorical language in passages on the AP exam, keep in mind the passages' purpose and tone. Ask yourself whether each figure of speech is appropriate, and how it contributes to or detracts from the reader's response.

Categories of Prose Discourse

Exposition

Exposition is a form of discourse in which the writer attempts to explain a subject, any subject. It is an attempt to communicate ideas about people as individuals and as groups, about institutions created by people to order their lives, about the meaning of events occurring in the lives of people and in the history of nations, about the values and dogmas of faith and culture, about the meaning of a work of art or literature, about the relationships within families—in short, just about anything. Elements of other forms of discourse—narration, description, argumentation—may enter into exposition, but the fundamental aim is to explain; and information and views are communicated, not as cold, statistical details, such as a computer printout (which may, however, appear in an expository work as a form of proof), but as a carefully thought-out composition that reveals a human, not a mechanical, touch in its expressions.

The essays you will write in answer to the questions in the Language and Composition examination will be to a great extent expository. You will be writing on a proposed subject. Also, in presenting your thoughts and ideas on this subject, you will be following guides set up by experienced writers and teachers so that what you record will have order, control, and interest and reveal the disciplines acquired by knowledge, practice, and imagination.

You need also to be aware that every subject on which you write requires to some degree a unique approach, though certain fundamental principles apply to all writing. For example, in exposition some essays may focus on definition; others may be developed by examples, by proof, or by comparison, contrast, antithesis; still others, like those dealing with historical, biological, or biographical topics, may concentrate on causal or chronological development interspersed with occasional comment. The subject and theme that are enunciated, as well as the tone and spirit manifested in the writer's conception of the subject, will color the manner of the treatment.

Argumentation

In argumentation, the writer attempts to prove the verity, validity, and efficacy of a point of view, a belief, an interpretation, a condition, a principle, a process. The writer expresses what he/she seeks to prove in a proposition, another term for thesis statement. Whereas exposition is concerned with analysis and explanation, argumentation seeks to win assent, to convince. In order to convince others to accept ideas, the writer needs evidence. Much evidence is to be found in the self-evident truths of civilized society, the universal beliefs and traditions accepted over long periods. Other forms of evidence are the beliefs and opinions of authorities and experts in particular fields.

The mental process involved in argumentation is reasoning, that is, the application of modes of thinking to establish premises and to draw truths from them. The modes of reasoning are as follows:

1. *Deduction.* Deduction is reasoning from a known premise to an unknown one that must in logic be accepted; from a general truth to a particular truth. A familiar example is the following:

All men are mortal.	general truth
Socrates is a man.	general truth
Socrates is mortal.	particular truth

Such a series is called a *syllogism.* Mathematicians frequently begin with premises called axioms and from these draw the particulars of a system.

2. *Induction.* Inductive reasoning involves the gathering of particulars to arrive at a conclusion; the more data, the more cases gathered, the greater is the likelihood that a truth of some validity will emerge. Induction is the scientific approach. In experimentation a conclusion becomes valid when a great number of particulars support the conclusion. The process begins with an intuitive percept, later couched in a hypothesis; then follows the search for the particulars.

Many written arguments that you will encounter in your reading will also be persuasions, not only to present and/or justify a belief or view, but also to move the reader to action of some kind. Lawyers' briefs, for example, are arguments seeking to persuade. Speeches by politicians seek most frequently to win some active response from colleagues or voters. On TV programs on current events, speakers defending opposing views appear nightly. Among them are many urging some vigorous action from listeners. This is true also of editorials and featured writers' columns in newspapers. Most, however, are arguments that provide information.

What is important to remember is the difference between argument and persuasion: in argument one attempts to win assent to a belief or opinion, whereas in persuasion one presents arguments as prods for some proposed action. The style of persuasive discourse is likely to be more vigorous, more dramatic, more emotional. A good example is Antony's speech to the populace at the funeral rites for Julius Caesar in Shakespeare's play of the same name.

Description

Description is a form of exposition. Whatever is being described—a scene in nature, a structure, a public square, an art show, a mechanical process, an event witnessed—the writer must, without necessarily saying so, establish a point of vantage and a logical order that readers can follow so that they can visualize the parts easily as each contributes to the total picture. This does not mean that the writer cannot move about. However, the movements cannot be random. The reader should not be expected to join the writer when he/she makes a sudden and unexpected leap to another vantage point without, in some clear way, preparing the reader.

Another matter requiring consideration is the occasional necessity to record the effect of the object or scene or event being described upon the senses. It is not too difficult, when one is trained to do it, to describe what one sees. But how does one go about describing what is heard or smelled? It becomes important to integrate what one perceives through all the senses into a total portrait.

All of the foregoing is true also when the writer is describing a person. There must be order in the description—from the whole person, his/her appearance and dress, to different parts; from physical appearance to temperament, disposition, and behavior. Sometimes the two aspects can be sequentially combined. What must be avoided is confusing randomness.

Narration

You will have occasion to use narrative passages in your expository writing: the citing of a story or incident to support or illustrate an idea. What the writer of narration seeks to do is draw the reader into the scene by 1) focusing on the action, including details made vivid by language, style, and tone, and frequently by quotation; 2) using apt figures of speech; and 3) establishing an order in which an increasing intensity leads toward the resolution. The kind of narration that occurs in expository or argumentative prose is punctuated by comment or serves as proof for a critical statement, a philosophy, or a view of the experiences of life.

Passages Illustrating the Various Categories of Prose Discourse

Below are paragraphs from various sources. They are printed sentence by sentence, or, in the first instance, clause by clause, so that you may identify the proposition or thesis in the passage even when it is omitted, and see more clearly how it is developed.

Consider 1) the grammatical structures of the sentences to judge their variety, and 2) the order and substance of the ideas, examples, illustrations, and proofs to judge how well the proposition is supported.

Exposition: Definition

[The educated man is one] who has been so trained in youth that his
body is the ready servant of his will and it does with ease and pleasure
all the work that, as a mechanism, it is capable of;
whose intellect is a clear, cold logic engine, with all its parts of equal strength
and in smooth working order; ready, like a steam engine, to be turned to any
kind of work, and spin the gossamers as well as forge the anchors of the mind;
whose mind is stored with the knowledge of the great fundamental truths
of nature and of the laws of her operations;
one who, no stunted ascetic, is full of life and fire, but whose passions are
trained to come to heel by a vigorous will, the servant of a tender conscience;
who has learned to love all beauty, whether of nature or of art, to hate
all vileness and to respect others as himself.

Thomas Henry Huxley
(1825–1895)

This paragraph consists of one sentence listing the characteristics of the educated man. It is organized in parallel structure with a series of expanded relative clauses. Can you separate the figurative language from the description?

Exposition: Opinion

Can science heal that neurotic flaw in us?
If science cannot, then nothing can.
Let us stop pretending.
There is no cure in high moral precepts.
We have preached them too long to men who are forced to live how they can:
that makes the strain which they have not been able to bear.
We need an ethic which is moral and which works.
It is often said that science has destroyed our values and put nothing in their place.
What has really happened of course is that science has shown in harsh relief the division between our values and our world.
We have not begun to let science get into our heads; where then was it supposed to create these values?
We have used it as a machine without will, the conjured spirit to do the chores.
I believe that science can create values: and will create them precisely as literature does, by looking into the human personality; by discovering what divides it and what cements it.
That is how great writers have explored man, and this whether they themselves as men have been driven by the anguish in *Gulliver's Travels* or the sympathy in *Moll Flanders*.

The insight of science is not different from that of the arts.
Science will create values, I believe, and discover virtues, when it looks into man; when it explores what makes him man and not an animal, and what makes his societies human and not animal packs.

Can you construct a reasoned argument in which you either 1) demonstrate with evidence what values science can create to help men and women understand themselves and make better lives for themselves and others, or 2) prove with evidence that science, because of its very nature, is incapable of creating the right values for a world like ours?

Exposition: Idea

There is still another aspect under which the beauty of the world may be viewed, namely, as it becomes an object of the intellect.
Besides the relation of things to virtue, they have a relation to thought.
The intellect searches out the absolute order of things as they stand in the mind of God, and without the colors of affection.
The intellectual and the active powers seem to succeed each other, and the exclusive activity of the one generates the exclusive activity of the other.
There is something unfriendly in each to the other, but they are like the alternate periods of feeding and working in animals; each prepares and will be followed by the other.
Therefore does beauty, which, in relation to actions, as we have seen, comes unsought, and comes because it is unsought, remain for the apprehension and pursuit of the intellect; and then again, in its turn, of the active power.
Nothing divine dies.
All good is eternally reproductive.
The beauty of nature re-forms itself in the mind, and not for barren contemplation, but for new creation.

Ralph Waldo Emerson
(1803–1882)

Can you provide evidence to support or to disprove Emerson's view that the intellect applied to the interpretation of the nature of beauty can produce the virtues that give meaning to life?

Description: Of Persons

1.   Emma Bovary, from *Madame Bovary* by Gustave Flaubert (1821–1880)

Charles noticed that her lips were full, and that she had the habit of biting them in moments of silence.
Her neck rose out of the low fold of a white collar. The two black sweeps of her hair, pulled down from a fine center part that followed the curve of her skull, were so sleek that each seemed to be one piece.
Covering all but the very tips of her ears, it was gathered at the back into a large chignon,* and toward the temples it waved a bit—a detail that the country doctor now observed for the first time in his life.
Her skin was rosy over her cheekbones.
A pair of shell-rimmed eyeglasses, like a man's, was tucked between two buttons of her bodice.

---

*chignon: a knot or coil of hair, usually worn at the back of the neck.

2. Gerald Crich, from *Women in Love* by D. H. Lawrence (1885–1930)

> Her son was of a fair, sun-tanned type, rather above middle height,
> well-made, and almost exaggeratedly well-dressed.
> But about him also was the strange, guarded look, the unconscious glisten, as if
> he did not belong to the same creation as the people about him.
> Gudrun lighted on him at once.
> There was something northern about him that magnetised her.
> In his clear northern flesh and his fair hair was a glisten like sunshine refracted
> through crystals of ice.
> And he looked so new, unbroached, pure as an arctic thing.
> Perhaps he was thirty years old, perhaps more.
> His gleaming beauty, maleness, like a young, goodhumoured, smiling wolf, did
> not blind her to the significant, sinister stillness in his bearing, the lurking
> danger of his unsubdued temper.

In each of the foregoing descriptions from novels by Flaubert and Lawrence, the impressions of the appearance and personality of a character are presented through a particular view of another character. Can you compare and contrast the two descriptions, emphasizing the details and language by which each view is highlighted?

Description:
Of a Place

> The appearance of San Francisco at night, from the water, is unlike
> anything I ever beheld.
> The houses are mostly of canvas, which is made transparent by the lamps
> within, and transforms them, in the darkness, to dwellings of solid light.
> Seated on the slopes of its three hills, the tents pitched among the chapparal* to
> the very summits, it gleams like an amphitheatre on fire.
> Here and there shine out brilliant points, from the decoy-lamps of the gaming-
> houses; and through the indistinct murmur of the streets comes by fits the sound
> of music from their hot and crowded precincts.
> The picture has in it something unreal and fantastic; it impresses one like the
> cities of the magic lantern, which a motion of the band can build or annihilate.
>
> Bayard Taylor
> (1825–1878)

Can you, like Taylor, describe a place, a scene, or a person that is familiar to you? If you describe a person, you may wish to describe him or her at a number of different places or occasions.

Description:
Of Nature

> The inhabitants of cities suppose that the country landscape is pleasant
> only half the year.
> I please myself with the graces of the winter scenery and believe that we are as
> much touched by it as by the genial influences of summer.
> To the attentive eye, each moment of the year has its own beauty, and in the
> same field, it beholds, every hour, a picture which was never seen before, and
> which shall never be seen again.
> The heavens change every moment, and reflect their glory or gloom on the
> plains beneath.
> The state of the crop in the surrounding farms alters the expression of the earth
> from week to week.
> The succession of native plants in the pastures and roadsides, which makes the
> silent clock by which time tells the summer hours, will make even the divisions
> of the day sensible to a keen observer.

---

*chapparal (dictionary spelling, chaparral): a dense thicket of shrubs, thorny bushes, etc.; origi-
nally of evergreen oaks.

The tribes of birds and insects, like the plants punctual to their time, follow each other, and the year has room for all.
By watercourses the variety is greater.
In July, the blue pontederia or pickerel-weed blooms in large beds in the shallow river, and swarms with yellow butterflies in continual motion.
Art cannot rival this pomp of purple and gold.
Indeed the river is a perpetual gala, and boasts each month a new ornament.

Ralph Waldo Emerson
(1803–1882)

Emerson describes scenes in nature, and the changes that occur in the appearance of earth and sky and in the behavior or plants, birds, and insects when summer follows winter. There is no mention in this passage about the changes in the behavior of human beings.

Have you observed that people behave differently according to the season? Do you think that the essential character of people, as opposed to their behavior, remains the same or changes with the seasons?

Argument

The next three selections are arguments in which each famous writer presents a view calling for a policy or an action in which he believes strongly.

As you analyze each selection, determine what policy or action is called for. Examine the order of the arguments presented and discuss their persuasiveness. For each selection, judge also whether it appeals to reason or to emotion.

Argumentation: 1

How can the Union be saved?
There is but one way by which it can with any certainty; and that is, by a full and final settlement on the principle of justice, of all questions at issue between the two sections.
The South asks for justice, simple justice; and less she ought not to take.
She has no compromise to offer but the Constitution; and no concession or surrender to make.
She has already surrendered so much that she has little left to surrender.
Such a settlement would go to the root of the evil, and remove all cause of discontent, by satisfying the South that she could remain honorably and safely in the Union, and thereby restore the harmony and fraternal feelings between the sections, which existed anterior to the Missouri agitation.
Nothing else can, with any certainty, finally and forever settle the question of issue, terminate agitation, and save the Union.

John Coldwell Calhoun
(1782–1850)

Argumentation: 2

Whether there ought to be a federal government intrusted with the care of the common defense is a question in the first instance, open for discussions; but the moment it is decided in the affirmative, it will follow that that government ought to be clothed with all the powers requisite to complete execution of its trust. And unless it can be shown that the circumstances which may affect the public safety are reducible within certain determinate limits; unless the contract of this position can be fairly and rationally disputed, it must be admitted as a necessary consequence, that there can be no limitation of that authority which is to provide for the defense and protection of the community, in any matter essential to the formation, direction, or support of the national forces.

Alexander Hamilton
(1757–1804)

Argumentation: 3

Men of passive tempers look somewhat lightly over the offences of
Britain, and still hoping for the best, are apt to call out, "Come, come, we shall
be friends again for all this."
But examine the passions and feelings of mankind; bring the doctrine
of reconciliation to the touchstone of nature, and then tell me, whether you can
hereafter love, honor, and faithfully serve the power that hath carried fire and
sword into your land?
If you cannot do all these, then are you only deceiving yourselves and by your
delay bringing ruin upon posterity.
Your future connection with Britain, whom you can neither love nor
honor, will be forced and unnatural, and being formed only on the plain of
present convenience, will in a little time, fall into a relapse more wretched than
the first.
But if you say, you can still pass the violations over, then I ask, "Hath
your house been burnt? Hath your property been destroyed before your face?
Are your wife and children destitute of a bed to lie on, or bread to live on?
Have you lost a parent or child by their hands, and yourself the ruined and
wretched survivor?"
If you have not, then are you not a judge of those who have?
But if you have, and still can shake hands with the murderers, then are
you unworthy the name of husband, father, friend, or lover, and whatever may
be your rank or title in life, you have the heart of a coward, and the spirit of a
sycophant.

Thomas Paine
(1737–1809)

Avoiding Fallacies in Argumentation

In writing arguments, you must be careful to avoid ten common fallacies.

Argumentum ad hominem (the argument to the man)

Turning from the issue addressed to the person involved, questioning his
character, knowledge, and/or competence.

Example: You have been a socialist all your life. How can you possibly
understand any justification this corporation has for its policies?

Begging the question

Assuming as a fact the very thing one professes to prove; assuming a conclusion that in reality needs proof.

Example: There is no doubt that our schools are failing to educate our children. That is why our businesses can't get competent help.

[These statements require proof. They are presented as facts.]

Equivocation

Being deliberately ambiguous; being purposely misleading; having two or
more meanings.

Example: John Smith is a true believer in civil rights. Therefore we know
that he supports prayer in the schools.

False analogy

Drawing a wrongful comparison between two dissimilar elements or situations.

Example: Our son Mortimer is an excellent math student. He is likely to
become a successful scientist.

Faulty dilemma

Presenting, as the major premise, a choice that does not exhaust the possibilities.

Example: If we do not introduce bilingual education for the Hispanic children in our schools, we will fail to educate them for successful living in American society.

Hypothesis contrary to fact

Beginning with a premise that is not necessarily true.

Example: Children inherit from parents and ancestors criminal tendencies that rule their lives.

Ignoring the question

Avoiding, consciously or unconsciously, the point under dispute; dodging the issue.

Example: Question: Why is your country preventing the U.N. inspectors from leaving with the information they gathered?

Diplomat: We want you to know that our people are proud of their country, happy to be its citizens, and willing to obey its laws.

[The diplomat ignores the question and makes a comment that is extraneous.]

Overgeneralization

Providing too few instances or inadequate evidence to support a premise or conclusion.

Example: The school system in this city is dreadful. No child can get a decent education in our schools.

Nonsequitur (it does not follow)

Drawing a conclusion or inference that does not follow from the premises or from the preceding arguments.

Example: Lyndon Johnson's Great Society program abandoned many policies of the past. As a result we had a rebirth of true democracy in the land.

Post hoc ergo propter hoc (after this, therefore because of this)

Arguing that a happening that follows another must result from it.

Example: Mr. Smith was brought up in the miserable slums of this city. He tasted the evils of poverty and discrimination and survived. He is therefore the perfect candidate for mayor.

Narration

A short time ago some builders, working on a studio in Connecticut, left a huge square of plate glass standing upright in a field one day.

A goldfinch flying swiftly across the field struck the glass and was knocked cold.

When he came to, he hastened to his club, where an attendant bandaged his head and gave him a stiff drink.

"What the hell happened?" asked a sea gull.

"I was flying across a meadow when all of a sudden the air crystallized on me," said the goldfinch.

The sea gull and a hawk and an eagle all laughed heartily.

A swallow listened gravely.

"For fifteen years, fledgling and bird, I've flown this country," said the eagle, "and I assure you there is no such thing as air crystallizing. Water, yes; air, no."

"You were probably struck by a hailstone," the hawk told the goldfinch.

"Or he may have had a stroke," said the sea gull. "What do you think, swallow?"

"Why, I—I think maybe the air crystallized on him," said the swallow.

The large birds laughed so loudly that the goldfinch became annoyed and bet them each a dozen worms that they couldn't follow the course he had flown across the field without encountering the hardened atmosphere.

They all took his bet; the swallow went along to watch.

The sea gull, the eagle, and the hawk decided to fly together over the route the goldfinch indicated.

"You come, too," they said to the swallow.

"I—I well, no," said the swallow. "I don't think I will."

So the three large birds took off together and they hit the glass together and they were knocked cold.

Moral: He who hesitates is sometimes saved.

"The Glass in the Field" by James Thurber

Although this fable seems more story than essay, it is "essay" because it deals not only with a subtle idea of how knowledge is acquired but also with the belief that inaccurate knowledge acquired from observed experience can also be a "truth" if it brings peace of mind and/or keeps people from harm.

Try writing a paragraph of about 100 words in which you discuss, with reference to the fable, one of the following subjects:

1. The nature of inductive reasoning.
2. The determination of what is truth.
3. Illusion as an antidote to the pains and fears of existence.

The following passage from Thomas Henry Huxley's "The Method of Scientific Reasoning" may help you to write the paragraph based on James Thurber's fable:

There is a well-known incident in one of Molière's plays, where the author makes the hero express unbounded delight on being told that he had been talking prose during the whole of his life. In the same way I trust that you will take comfort, and be delighted with yourself, on the discovery that you have been acting on the principles of inductive and deductive philosophy during the same period. Probably there is not one here who has not in the course of the day had occasion to set in motion a complex train of reasoning, of the very same kind, though differing of course in degree, as that which a scientific man goes through in tracing the causes of natural phenomena.

A very trivial circumstance will serve to exemplify this. Suppose you go to a fruiterer's shop, wanting an apple—you take up one, and on biting it, you find it is sour; you look at it, and see that it is hard and green. You take up another one and that too is hard, green and sour. The shopman offers you a third; but before biting it, you examine it, and find that it is hard and green, and you immediately say that you will not have it, as it must be sour, like those you have already tried.

Nothing can be more simple than that, you think; but if you will take the trouble to analyze and trace out into its logical elements what has been done by your mind, you will be greatly surprised. In the first place you have performed the operation of induction. You found that, in two experiences, hardness and greenness in apples went together with sourness. It was so in the first case, and it was confirmed by the second. True, it is a very small basis, but still it is enough to make an induction from; you generalize the facts, and you expect to find sourness in apples where you get hardness and greenness. You found upon that a general law that all hard and green apples are sour; and that, so far as it goes, is a perfect induction. Well, having got your natural law in this way, when you are offered another apple which you find is hard and green, you say, "All hard and green apples are sour; this apple is hard and green; therefore this apple is sour." That train of reasoning is what logicians call a syllogism, and has all its various parts and terms—its major premise, its minor premise, and its conclusions. And, by the help of further reasoning, which, if drawn out, would have to be exhibited in two or three other syllogisms, you arrive at your final determination, "I will not have that apple." So that, you see, you have, in the first place, established a law by induction, and upon that you have founded a deduction, and reasoned out the special particular case.

PART TWO

CHAPTER 4 Overview of the Test

The Literature and Composition exam emphasizes the analysis of imaginative literature in several genres, primarily novels, plays, short stories, and poems. To prepare for this exam you should have substantial practice in careful reading and critical analysis of texts from roughly the sixteenth century to the present and written originally in English, although selections from high-quality literature in translation (Greek drama, Russian novels) are sometimes included on the exam.

You should also be familiar with the ways that authors use language to convey meaning in their works. In analyzing a work of literature, you may be asked to consider its structure, style of writing, and dominant themes. You should also be able to recognize and discuss such elements as figurative language, imagery, allusion, symbolism, diction, and tone.

To perform well on the test, you should know intimately several works of literary merit by such fiction writers as Jane Austen, Joseph Conrad, F. Scott Fitzgerald, and John Updike—in other words, recognized authors whose works are likely to endure. Dramatists whose works are equally durable include Shakespeare (of course), Chekhov, Ibsen, and Eugene O'Neill. And among the poets—Lord Byron, Robert Browning, Marianne Moore, and William Butler Yeats.

In addition to having a thorough grasp of particular works of literature, you should know how each work reflects and embodies the time and place in which it was written. You won't be asked specific questions about a work's historical context, but such a background often leads to greater understanding and more insightful interpretation of a text.

To demonstrate your grasp of literature, you will be given one hour to complete about fifty multiple-choice questions, and another two hours to write three essays. On the short-answer section of the test, you will be given four or five selections—two or three passages from a work of fiction and two or three short poems. The questions about each selection will cover such matters as the meaning of individual words and sentences; the structure of the piece; and its imagery, style, tone, figures of speech, mood, and implications.

Of the three essay questions, one is on poetry. After reading the given poem, you must write an essay that explains how the poem conveys its meaning. You may be asked to consider its theme, structure, language, or any number of poetic devices used by the poet.

A second essay question asks you to write an essay that analyzes an excerpt from a novel or story, a series of letters, a speech in a play, or some other literary passage.

And the last question asks you for an essay on a book or play of your choice. The question, or "prompt," as it is called, makes a general observation about life or literature. Your job, then, is to discuss the observation as it applies to a work of "literary merit." Several appropriate titles are included with the question, but you may choose any other book or play of "comparable literary merit," a phrase whose meaning is far from clear-cut, but suggests books that teachers and scholars would generally regard as excellent, serious, adult literature.

Answering Multiple-Choice Questions

Answering the multiple-choice questions demonstrates your ability to read and extract meaning from poems and passages of fiction, or, on occasion, from a play. Questions range from the meaning of the entire poem or passage to the implications of a particular word. Indeed, anything that the author or poet has done while creating the passage is grist for the test maker's mill. Therefore, in the ten or dozen questions about each selection, you may be asked to recognize structural components, types of language, tone, rhetorical devices, writing styles, and more. If any one type of question predominates, it is the sort that asks you to comprehend or interpret the meaning of a segment of the poem or passage.

The selections are taken from contemporary literature as well as the literature of previous eras. In most cases, the authors and poets are not identified, although the titles of poems are usually included and sometimes can help you unlock a poem's meaning.

Here are some suggestions for answering the multiple-choice questions:

1. If the poem or passage has a title, consider it carefully. Some titles, unfortunately, yield few or no clues to what follows; if you are not already familiar with the poem, a title like "Ozymandias," "Sonnet 146," or "The Eve of St. Agnes" does not tell you very much. Other titles, however, are completely forthright: "To a Skylark," "Hawk Roosting," "The World is Too Much with Us." A third type of title is suggestive of the content; you are not sure how the theme will be developed, but you have a hint as to what the selection is about. Examples include "Any Human to Another," "The Ebb and Flow," and "Mending Wall."
2. Because the prose passage will have no title, look for a topic sentence that tells you what the passage is about. Usually such a sentence occurs at or near the beginning of the passage, but sometimes it is at the end.
3. Read the selection carefully, sentence by sentence. Don't skip over sentences that seem involved and confusing. In reading lines like these from A.E. Housman:

   > And bound for the same bourn as I,
   > On every road I wandered by,
   > Trod beside me, close and dear,
   > The beautiful and death-struck year.

   keep looking for the subject—in this case, the last word.
4. Take advantage of helpful footnotes on the examination. These define unusual or archaic words and explain obscure references.
5. As you read, underline words or sentences that seem especially important to you.
6. Note the imagery—analogies, metaphors, symbols, allusions. They should help to clarify the content.

7. Don't guess unless you can eliminate at least one answer choice as obviously incorrect. In scoring multiple-choice questions, the examiners apply a correction factor to compensate for random guessing. For this reason you will do better to omit a question if you have no idea of the correct answer. To earn a total grade of 3, you need to answer about 50 to 60 percent of the multiple-choice questions correctly.

Poetry Questions

Printed below are a number of poems. After each poem is a series of multiple-choice questions. Read each poem carefully and answer the questions. Then check your answers with the key on page 87.

SONNET 146
William Shakespeare (1564–1616)

Poor soul, the center of my sinful earth.
Thrall to these rebel powers that thee array.
Why dost thou pine within and suffer dearth,
Line   Painting thy outward walls so costly gay?
(5)   Why so large cost, having so short lease,
Dost thou upon thy fading mansion spend?
Shall worms, inheritors of this excess,
Eat up thy charge? is this thy bod's end?
Then, soul, live thou upon thy servant's loss,
(10)   And let that pine to aggravate thy store;
Buy terms divine in selling hours of dross;
Within be fed, without be rich no more:
So shall thou feed on Death, that feeds on men,
And Death once dead, there's no more dying then.

1. The speaker of this poem
   (A) has lived wisely
   (B) looks forward to death with resignation
   (C) regrets his sins and is repentant
   (D) is not afraid of death
   (E) has lived in abject poverty

2. In this poem the speaker states that death can be defeated by
   (A) being ignored
   (B) acquiring courage through life
   (C) caring for one's physical health
   (D) making a pact with the devil
   (E) attending to the soul

3. The inheritor of the human body, according to the poem, is
   (A) God
   (B) Satan
   (C) the landlord
   (D) the worm
   (E) the state

4. All of the following are metaphors used in the poem EXCEPT
   (A) master and servant
   (B) landlord and tenant
   (C) seller and purchaser
   (D) clothing and feeding
   (E) worms and corpse

5. "Death once dead" is an example of
   (A) hyperbole
   (B) paradox
   (C) simile
   (D) irony
   (E) metonymy

6. An irony of the poem is that
   (A) neglecting the body fosters immortality
   (B) one cannot really defeat death
   (C) the center of the body is the brain, not the soul
   (D) spiritual happiness is an inherent, not a purchased, element
   (E) not even the soul can live without food

7. The "rebel powers" in the poem are the
   (A) material demands of the body
   (B) four horsemen of the Apocalypse
   (C) seven deadly sins
   (D) fears of penury and illness
   (E) specters of death and decay

8. In the poem, clothing is a metaphor for
   (A) nobility
   (B) delusions
   (C) prayer and worship
   (D) indulgence or extravagance
   (E) reality

9. The best interpretation of line 12 is:
   (A) man should seek happiness rather than wealth
   (B) the destiny of man is to be food for worms
   (C) man should consider his soul of greater worth than his body
   (D) spiritual sustenance is inferior to material gain
   (E) man's wealth disappears when he dies

10. The *dominant* metaphor of the poem is related to
    (A) clothing the body
    (B) investment in a house
    (C) a battlefield against death
    (D) the terms of a will
    (E) the cost of food

AFTER GREAT PAIN, A FORMAL FEELING COMES
Emily Dickinson (1830–1886)

After great pain, a formal feeling comes—
The Nerves sit ceremonious, like Tombs—
The stiff Heart questions was it He, that bore,
Line   And Yesterday, or Centuries before?
(5)   The Feet, mechanical, go round—

Of Ground, or Air, or Ought—
A Wooden way
Regardless grown,
A Quartz contentment, like a stone—
(10)   This is the Hour of Lead—

Remembered, if outlived,
As Freezing persons, recollect the Snow—
First—Chill—then Stupor—then the letting go—

11. The poem deals with the
(A) numbing effects of bitter cold
(B) gradual numbing of the body before death
(C) progression of deep grief
(D) suffering of the Crucifixion
(E) nature of contentment

12. The "Hour of Lead" is the
(A) weight of remorse
(B) period of grief
(C) moral decadence of age
(D) coming of death
(E) advent of winter

13. The images in the last line of the poem represent
(A) dying
(B) protest
(C) escape
(D) defeat
(E) acceptance

14. The "He, that bore" in line 3 of the poem is a reference to
(A) the person who died
(B) death
(C) an unknown martyr
(D) Jesus
(E) the speaker

15. The speaker can best be characterized as
(A) incoherent with grief
(B) philosophical
(C) resigned
(D) indifferent
(E) stoical

16. The effectiveness of the poetic statement in the first stanza is heightened by
    (A) personification
    (B) paradox
    (C) understatement
    (D) hyperbole
    (E) synecdoche

17. The first line of the poem
    (A) is an outburst of pain
    (B) introduces the speaker
    (C) states the subject
    (D) is cold and formal
    (E) cites the first illustration of the theme

18. The formal feeling that comes after great pain is a
    (A) return to normal routines
    (B) willingness to profit from experience
    (C) desire to begin again
    (D) quiet acceptance of tragic loss
    (E) refusal to accept the reality of death

19. Which of the following best describes the speaker's approach to her subject?
    (A) She states her theme in the first line, develops it in the first and second stanzas, and resolves it in the third.
    (B) She does not state her theme but expects the reader to infer it.
    (C) She obscures her theme with dramatic metaphors that color her poem with ambiguity.
    (D) She states her theme in the first stanza and expands on it throughout the poem.
    (E) She provides metaphor and illustration in the first two stanzas and states her theme in the third.

20. The mood of the poem is best described as
    (A) solemn
    (B) euphoric
    (C) bitter
    (D) sanguine
    (E) pessimistic

21. Which of the following is NOT true of the statements in the poem?
    (A) The formal feeling of grief suggests no overt demonstration.
    (B) To grieve excessively is necessary for catharsis.
    (C) Grief is a universal experience.
    (D) The pain in the poem is not a physical one.
    (E) If one is religious, he/she will associate pain with the sufferings of Jesus.

22. All of the following are suggested by images in the poem EXCEPT
    (A) lifelessness
    (B) the pain of the Crucifixion
    (C) death by freezing
    (D) mechanical movement
    (E) quiet weeping

MUSÉE DES BEAUX ARTS
W. H. Auden (1907–1973)

About suffering they were never wrong,
The Old Masters: how well they understood
Its human position; how it takes place
While someone else is eating or opening a window

Line   or just walking dully along;
(5) How, when the aged are reverently, passionately waiting
For the miraculous birth, there always must be
Children who did not specially want it to happen, skating
On a pond at the edge of the wood.
They never forget
(10) That even the dreadful martyrdom must run its course
Anyhow in a corner, some untidy spot
Where the dogs go on with their doggy life and the torturer's horse
Scratches its innocent behind on a tree.

In Breughel's *Icarus,* for instance: how everything turns away
(15) Quite leisurely from the disaster; the ploughman may

Have heard the splash, the forsaken cry,
But for him it was not an important failure; the sun shone
As it had to on the white legs disappearing into the green
Water; and the expensive delicate ship that must have seen
(20) Something amazing, a boy falling out of the sky,
Had somewhere to get to and sailed calmly on.

23. The "Old Masters" mentioned in the poem are
    (A) poets
    (B) painters
    (C) martyrs
    (D) saints
    (E) novelists

24. The antecedent of the pronoun "they" in line 9 is
    (A) children
    (B) Old Masters
    (C) the aged
    (D) someone else
    (E) There is no antecedent

25. The allusion in the poem to the "dreadful martyrdom" probably refers to the
    (A) fall of Icarus
    (B) suffering of the ploughman
    (C) pain of childbirth
    (D) Crucifixion of Christ
    (E) massacre of the innocents

26. In the poem, the drowning of Icarus is
    (A) an event that could have been avoided
    (B) an act determined by fate
    (C) a sign of God's displeasure
    (D) an added illustration of martyrdom
    (E) a subject appropriate for art

27. The poem begins with
    (A) a general statement
    (B) a vivid image
    (C) a bemused ironic statement
    (D) a mythological allusion
    (E) an apostrophe to artists

28. The speaker states that Icarus's death was
    (A) the result of failure to obey
    (B) a sign of God's wrath
    (C) a moment of historic importance
    (D) an event that produced no reaction
    (E) the result of a misjudgment of the sun's power

29. The speaker suggests that the "miraculous birth" was
    (A) an event that pleased only the aged
    (B) a great moment in the history of religion
    (C) the beginning of Christianity
    (D) a popular subject of art
    (E) an event that drew the ploughman to the manger

30. The poem expresses
    (A) moral indignation
    (B) religious fervor
    (C) esthetic appreciation
    (D) direct and matter-of-fact comment
    (E) misanthropy

31. The tone of the poem is
    (A) sublime
    (B) sentimental
    (C) ironic
    (D) indignant
    (E) vitriolic

EIGHTH AIR FORCE
Randall Jarrell (1914–1965)

If, in an odd angle of the hutment,
A puppy laps the water from a can
Of flowers, and the drunk sergeant shaving
Line   Whistles *O Paradiso!*—Shall I say that man
(5)   Is not as men have said: a wolf to man?

The other murderers troop in yawning;
Three of them play Pitch, one sleeps, and one
Lies counting missions, lies there sweating
Till even his heart beats: One; One; One.
(10)   *O murderers!* . . . Still this is how it's done:

This is a war. . . . But since these play, before they die,
Like puppies with their puppy; since, a man,
·I did as these have done, but did not die—
I will content the people as I can
(15)   And give up these to them: Behold the man!

I have suffered, in a dream, because of him,
Many things; for this last saviour, man,
I have lied as I lie now. But what is lying?
Men wash their hands in blood, as best they can:
(20)   I find no fault in this just man.

32.   Throughout the poem, the speaker moves back and forth, characterizing the airman alternately as
(A)   wolf and saviour
(B)   child and adult
(C)   hero and coward
(D)   murderer and victim
(E)   loner and mixer

33.   The "murderers" in the poem are
(A)   puppies whose ancestors were wolves
(B)   all humankind
(C)   the airmen at the air base
(D)   the leaders of the warring nations
(E)   the enemy airmen

34.   The poem is
(A)   a satire against war
(B)   a dramatic monologue
(C)   a ballad of despair
(D)   an ode to humanity
(E)   an elegy for the victims of bombardment

35. "This just man" in line 20 refers to
    (A) Judas Iscariot
    (B) Jesus
    (C) the drunk sergeant
    (D) the sleeping airman
    (E) the speaker himself

36. "Men wash their hands" in line 19 is an allusion to
    (A) murdering airmen who feel no guilt
    (B) warmakers
    (C) Peter the Apostle
    (D) war profiteers
    (E) Pontius Pilate

37. All the following questions concern the speaker deeply EXCEPT:
    (A) Is man a heartless animal?
    (B) Is modern man the last saviour?
    (C) How can men live and play together and later kill?
    (D) Does killing ease the evil in man?
    (E) Am I a murderer like the others?

38. The subject of the poem is the
    (A) brutality of war
    (B) callousness of flyers
    (C) domestic activities in a barracks
    (D) danger of flying on air missions
    (E) sense of guilt of an airman

39. The theme of the poem is effectively stated in stanzas
    (A) one and four
    (B) one and two
    (C) three and four
    (D) two and four
    (E) one and three

40. The end-rhyme repetition of the words "man," "one," and "die" is effective because it
    (A) separates the speaker from his comrades
    (B) intensifies the speaker's emotional guilt
    (C) concentrates the reader's attention on personal responsibility
    (D) emphasizes the dullness of barracks existence
    (E) suggests the carnage of war

41. The speaker in the poem concludes that man can be a
    (A) crier for a scapegoat
    (B) hero
    (C) redeemer
    (D) sinner
    (E) penitent

42. The poem is about all of the following EXCEPT
    (A) war in our day
    (B) man's potential for goodness
    (C) man's potential for evil
    (D) the individual's sense of guilt
    (E) the physical suffering of airmen facing death

43. The drunken sergeant's whistling of *O Paradiso* (line 4) is an example of the poet's use of
    (A) apostrophe
    (B) personification
    (C) paradox
    (D) irony
    (E) metaphor

44. The speaker is moved by the fact that, having himself engaged in missions against the enemy,
    (A) he is still alive
    (B) he feels no guilt
    (C) he envies his callous comrades
    (D) he feels superior to his comrades
    (E) he is in no position to make judgments

HOLY SONNET 5
John Donne (1572–1631)

I am a little world made cunningly
Of elements, and an angelic sprite;*
But black sin hath betrayed to endless night
Line My world's both parts, and, O, both parts must die.
(5) You which beyond that heaven which was most high
Have found new spheres, and of new lands can write,
Pour new seas in mine eyes, that so I might
Drown my world with my weeping earnestly,
Or wash it if it be drowned no more:
(10) But, O, it must be burnt! Alas the fire
Of lust and envy have burnt it heretofore,
And made it fouler; let their flames retire,
And burn me, O Lord, with fiery zeal
Of Thee and Thy house, which doth in eating heal.

45. This poem is
    (A) an appeal to an honored friend
    (B) a prayer to God
    (C) an appeal to the king for forgiveness
    (D) a complaint about injustice
    (E) a lament for a dead friend

---

*spirit.

46. The speaker asks that
    (A) he be washed in the blood of the lamb
    (B) his sins be cleansed in water and tears
    (C) his dwelling place be away from court
    (D) his sins be cleansed by fire
    (E) he be permitted to be near his Lord

47. The speaker conceives of himself as being made of
    (A) chemical elements
    (B) sin and virtue
    (C) body and soul
    (D) fire and water
    (E) lust and envy

48. The "You" in line 5 is
    (A) Satan
    (B) the speaker's beloved
    (C) a dead friend
    (D) the speaker's soul
    (E) God

49. The speaker fears that he is doomed to
    (A) be drowned in a flood
    (B) be burned at the stake
    (C) dwell in an empty and newer sphere
    (D) dwell in eternal darkness
    (E) weep forever

50. The last line of the poem ends in a
    (A) metonymy
    (B) simile
    (C) metaphor
    (D) paradox
    (E) personification

51. The speaker uses fire as a symbol of
    (A) hell
    (B) both sin and virtue
    (C) heaven
    (D) a monarch's wrath
    (E) a friend's displeasure

52. In line 7 of the poem, there is an example of
    (A) hyperbole
    (B) pathetic fallacy
    (C) affective fallacy
    (D) metaphor
    (E) synecdoche

53. The word "house" in line 14 refers to
(A) heaven
(B) the king's palace
(C) milord's castle
(D) purgatory
(E) a cathedral

54. The inference to be drawn from the statement in lines 5 and 6 is that
(A) heaven is boundless
(B) astronomical study has revealed to man that there is a greater heaven
(C) victories have brought new lands to the king
(D) friendship has no limits
(E) a poet's imagination has no limits

55. All of the following are elements of the imagery of the poem EXCEPT
(A) night and darkness
(B) chemistry
(C) fire
(D) worship
(E) water

Answer Key for Multiple-Choice Questions on Poetry

1. C	7. A	13. E	19. A	25. D	31. C	36. E	41. C	46. D	51. B
2. E	8. C	14. D	20. A	26. E	32. A	37. D	42. E	47. C	52. A
3. D	9. C	15. B	21. B	27. A	33. C	38. E	43. D	48. E	53. A
4. E	10. B	16. A	22. E	28. D	34. B	39. A	44. A	49. D	54. B
5. B	11. C	17. C	23. B	29. D	35. B	40. B	45. B	50. D	55. D
6. A	12. B	18. D	24. B	30. D					

Prose Questions

Read each of the following passages carefully, and answer the questions that follow. Then check your answers with the key on page 93.

PASSAGE 1

Sometimes—once or twice a week—that lady visited the upper regions in which the child lived. She came like a vivified figure out of the *Magasin des Modes*—blandly smiling in the most beautiful new clothes and little
Line gloves and boots. Wonderful scarfs, laces, and jewels glittered about her.
(5) She had always a new bonnet on: and flowers bloomed perpetually in it: or else magnificent curling ostrich feathers, soft and snowy as camellias. She nodded twice or thrice patronisingly to the little boy, who looked up from his dinner or from the pictures of soldiers he was painting. When she left the room, an odour of rose, or some other magical fragrance, lingered
(10) about the nursery. She was an unearthly being in his eyes, superior to his father—to all the world: to be worshipped and admired at a distance. To drive with that lady in the carriage was an awful rite: he sat up in the back seat, and did not dare to speak: he gazed with all his eyes at the beautifully dressed princess opposite him. Gentlemen on splendid prancing horses
(15) came up, and smiled and talked with her. How her eyes beamed upon of them! Her hand used to quiver and wave gracefully as they passed. When he went out with her he had his new red dress on. His old brown holland was good enough when he stayed at home. Sometimes when she was away, and Dolly his maid was making his bed, he came into his mother's room.

(20) It was as the abode of a fairy to him—a mystic chamber of splendour and delights. There in the wardrobe hung those wonderful robes—pink and blue, and many-tinted. There was the jewel-case, silver-clasped: and the wondrous bronze hand on the dressing-table, glistening all over a hundred rings. There was the cheval-glass, that miracle of art, in which he could just see his own

(25) wondering head, and the reflection of Dolly (queerly distorted, and as if up in the ceiling), plumping and patting the pillows of the bed. Oh, thou poor lonely little benighted boy! Mother is the name of God in the lips and hearts of little children; and here was one who was worshipping a stone!

1. The best title for this passage is
    (A) A Victorian Family
    (B) A Portrait of Mother
    (C) A Little Boy's World
    (D) A Child's Delusions
    (E) Life with Mother

2. The attitude of the narrator toward the mother is
    (A) humorous
    (B) admiring
    (C) bitter
    (D) satiric
    (E) bemused

3. By "upper regions" as the dwelling place of the child, the narrator suggests that the
    (A) child's life was dull
    (B) mother made the dwelling a heaven
    (C) mother's visits were accompanied by physical effort
    (D) child's world was a unique one
    (E) child's room was in the upper story of the building

4. According to the passage, which of the following is true?
    (A) The father paid no attention to the boy.
    (B) The mother took no part in the physical care of the child.
    (C) The boy hated his father.
    (D) The mother's visits to the boy and their drives in the carriage were motivated by love.
    (E) The maid Dolly was unconcerned about the boy.

5. All of the following are true of the mother, as portrayed by the narrator in this passage, EXCEPT:
    (A) She was flirtatious.
    (B) She followed the fashions of her day.
    (C) She was a beautiful woman.
    (D) She was worldly.
    (E) She was deeply in love with her husband.

6. The view of the mother that the reader gets from this passage is that of the
   (A) townspeople
   (B) child
   (C) narrator
   (D) narrator and child
   (E) husband

7. This passage describes in greatest detail
   (A) the world of the mother
   (B) the world of the child
   (C) upper-class Victorian society
   (D) a neglected child
   (E) the tragedy of wealth

8. "Stone" in this passage is associated with
   (A) idolatry
   (B) wealth
   (C) selfishness
   (D) pursuit of pleasure
   (E) vanity

9. "Oh, thou poor lonely little benighted boy!" is an example of
   (A) sentimentality
   (B) epigram
   (C) bathos
   (D) apostrophe
   (E) personification

PASSAGE 2

The objection to conforming to usages that have become dead to you is
that it scatters your force. It loses your time and blurs the impression of
your character. If you maintain a dead church, contribute to a dead Bible-
Line   society, vote with a great party either for the government or against it,
(5)   spread your table like base housekeepers,—under all these screens I have
        difficulty to detect the precise man you are: and of course so much force is
        withdrawn from your proper life. But do your work, and I shall know you.
        Do your work, and you shall reinforce yourself. A man must consider what
        a blind-man's-bluff is this game of conformity. If I know your sect I antic-
(10)   ipate your argument. I hear a preacher announce for his text and topic the
        expediency of one of the institutions of his church. Do I not know before-
        hand that not possibly can he say a new and spontaneous word? Do I not
        know that, with all this ostentation of examining the grounds of the insti-
        tution, he will do no such thing? Do I not know that he is pledged to himself
(15)   not to look but at one side, the permitted side, not as a man, but as a parish
        minister? He is a retained attorney, and these airs of the bench are the
        emptiest affectation. Well, most men have bound their eyes with one or
        another handkerchief, and attached themselves to some one of these com-
        munities of opinion. This conformity makes them not false in a few partic-
(20)   ulars, authors of a few lies, but false in all particulars. Their every truth is
        not quite true. Their two is not the real two, their four not the real four; so
        that every word they say chagrins us, and we know not where to begin to set

them right. Meantime nature is not slow to equip us in the prison-uniform
of the party of which we adhere. We come to wear one cut of face and

(25)   figure, and acquire by degrees the gentlest asinine expression. There is a
mortifying experience in particular, which does not fail to wreak itself also
in the general history; I mean "the foolish face of praise," the forced smile
which we put on in company where we do not feel at ease in answer to
conversation which does not interest us. The muscles, not spontaneously

(30)   moved but moved by a low usurping wilfulness, grow tight about the outline of the face with most disagreeable sensation.

10. This passage deals with all of the following EXCEPT
     (A)   the need to be one's self
     (B)   the virtues of independence
     (C)   the damage done by conformity
     (D)   the pursuit of truth
     (E)   the faults of tradition

11. To the writer of this passage, the views of men usually are formed by all
     of the following EXCEPT
     (A)   their religion
     (B)   their political affiliations
     (C)   their club memberships
     (D)   the opinions of their neighbors
     (E)   the books they read

12. "Spread your table like base housekeepers" (line 5) is an example of
     (A)   simile
     (B)   antithesis
     (C)   climax
     (D)   euphemism
     (E)   hyperbole

13. "Do I not know beforehand that not possibly can he say a new and spon-
     taneous word?" is an example of
     (A)   period structure
     (B)   ironic comment
     (C)   a rhetorical question
     (D)   a double negative equaling a positive statement
     (E)   a simple question

14. This paragraph is developed by
     (A)   argument
     (B)   proof
     (C)   detail
     (D)   illustration
     (E)   exposition

15. To the writer of this passage, conformity
    (A) brings success
    (B) wins friends
    (C) creates an impression of intelligence
    (D) makes possible the survival of social institutions
    (E) creates doubt about a person's integrity

16. All of the following are used metaphorically EXCEPT
    (A) "blind-man's-bluff" (line 9)
    (B) "retained attorney" (line 16)
    (C) "asinine expression" (line 25)
    (D) "cut of face and figure" (lines 24–25)
    (E) "prison-uniform" (line 23)

17. The chief place of conformity cited by the writer of this passage is the
    (A) government
    (B) community
    (C) school
    (D) church
    (E) home

18. By "one cut of face" the writer of this passage means all of the following EXCEPT
    (A) creed
    (B) level of wealth
    (C) opinions
    (D) dress
    (E) relationships

PASSAGE 3

He resumed his walk, and was glad to perceive that the street now
became wider, and the houses more respectable in their appearance. He soon
discerned a figure moving on moderately in advance and hastened his steps to
Line overtake it. As Robin drew nigh, he saw that the passenger was a man in years,
(5)   with a full periwig of gray hair, a wide-skirted coat of dark cloth, and silk
stockings rolled above his knees. He carried a long and polished cane, which he
struck down perpendicularly before him at every step; and at regular intervals he
uttered two successive hems, of a peculiarly solemn and sepulchral intonation.
Having made these observations, Robin laid hold of the skirt of the old man's
(10) coat, just when the light from the open door and windows of a barber's shop fell
upon both their figures.
    "Good evening to you, honored sir," said he, making a low bow and
still retaining his hold of the skirt. "I pray you tell me whereabouts is the
dwelling of my kinsman, Major Molineux."
(15)   The youth's question was uttered very loudly; and one of the barbers,
whose razor was descending on a well-soaped chin, and another who was
dressing a Ramillies wig, left their occupations, and came to the door. The
citizen, in the mean time, turned a long-favored countenance upon Robin, and
answered him in a tone of excessive anger and annoyance. His two sepulchral
(20) hems, however, broke into the very centre of his rebuke, with most singular
effect, like a thought of the cold grave obtruding among wrathful passions.

"Let go my garment, fellow! I tell you, I know not the man you speak
of. What! I have authority, I have—hem, hem—authority; and if this be the
respect you show for your betters, your feet shall be brought acquainted with
(25)   the stocks by daylight, tomorrow morning!"

Robin released the old man's skirt, and hastened away, pursued by an
ill-mannered roar of laughter from the barber's shop. He was at first
considerably surprised by the result of his question, but, being a shrewd youth,
soon thought himself able to account for the mystery.
(30)   "This is some country representative," was his conclusion, "who has
never seen the inside of my kinsman's door, and lacks the breeding to answer a
stranger civilly. . . ."

19. This passage concerns itself with all of the following EXCEPT
    (A)   a search for a kinsman
    (B)   the rudeness of an elderly citizen
    (C)   the rudeness of spectators
    (D)   the rudeness of Robin
    (E)   the dwelling of Major Molineux

20. The word "passenger" in this passage means
    (A)   vagabond
    (B)   foot traveler
    (C)   citizen
    (D)   visitor
    (E)   native

21. The narrator of this passage invites the reader to infer
    (A)   that Robin was a suspicious-looking character
    (B)   that the town was a rough place
    (C)   that there was some mystery concerning the Major
    (D)   that people are generally suspicious of strangers
    (E)   that Robin had arrived home in disgrace

22. The style of this selection is
    (A)   laconic
    (B)   florid
    (C)   simple and direct
    (D)   leisurely
    (E)   verbose

23. Suspense is created by all of the following EXCEPT
    (A)   the old man's rebuff
    (B)   the laughter from the barber shop
    (C)   Robin's holding the skirt of the old man's coat
    (D)   the mention of Major Molineux
    (E)   the retreat of the old man

24. The setting of this story is
    (A) an eighteenth-century town
    (B) the mind of Robin
    (C) a town in Elizabethan England
    (D) a world of fantasy
    (E) the present

25. As far as the reader knows, Robin's comment about the old man could be any of the following EXCEPT
    (A) an intelligent deduction based on available evidence
    (B) an error in judging character
    (C) an inaccurate deduction based on dislike
    (D) the only sensible conclusion
    (E) an irrational response by a stupid youth

Answer Key for Multiple-Choice Questions on Prose

1. B	2. D	3. E	4. B	5. E	6. D	7. A	8. C	9. D	10. D
11. E	12. A	13. C	14. D	15. E	16. C	17. D	18. B	19. D	20. B
21. C	22. D	23. C	24. A	25. E					

For your information, here are the sources of the preceding passages:

1. William Makepeace Thackery, *Vanity Fair*
2. Ralph Waldo Emerson, "Self-Reliance"
3. Nathaniel Hawthorne, "My Kinsman, Major Molineux"

Answering Essay Questions

What follows are synopses of the essay questions given in recent years. Although the types of questions have remained the same, the order of questions 1 and 2 varies. That is, the question on poetry or on a prose passage may come either first or second. Invariably, however, the essay question on a novel or play of your choice is given last.

On the exam, you may write the essays in any order your choose. Because forty minutes is suggested for the writing of each essay, it is crucial that you apportion your time so that you'll finish all three essays. Guard against getting caught up in the first or the second essay so you won't have time to write the third. It is better to write three less-than-perfect essays than to hand in only two essays.

1994

1. Read a passage from "A White Heron," a short story by Sarah Orne Jewett. Then write an essay that shows how Jewett dramatizes the young heroine's adventure. Consider discussing diction, imagery, narrative pace, and point of view, among other literary elements.

2. After reading two short poems about Helen of Troy, write an essay that contrasts the two speakers' views of Helen. Consider elements such as diction, imagery, form, and tone.

3. Write an essay about a novel or play in which a character who appears briefly—or does not appear at all—is still a significant presence. Describe how the character functions in the work and how he or she affects such matters as action, theme, or development of other characters.

1995

1. After reading a poem by John Donne, write an essay that analyzes how the speaker uses imagery to show his attitude toward love.
2. Read "Eleven," a short story by Sandra Cisneros. Then write an essay that shows how the author uses literary techniques to characterize the main character, Rachel.
3. Write an essay about a play or novel that contains a character who is alienated from a culture or society because of gender, race, class, or creed. Show how that character's alienation reveals the values and assumptions of that culture or society.

1996

1. Read an excerpt from *The House of the Seven Gables* by Nathaniel Hawthorne. Then write an essay that analyzes how the narrator reveals the character of Judge Pyncheon. Emphasize any significant literary element, including tone, choice of detail, syntax, or point of view.
2. After reading a poem by Anne Bradstreet, write an essay that shows how the poem's primary metaphor conveys the attitude of the speaker.
3. Write an essay about a novel or play that ends with some kind of "spiritual reassessment or moral reconciliation." Identify the reassessment or reconciliation, and explain its significance to the work as a whole.

1997

1. After reading a poem by Richard Wilbur, write an essay that shows how such formal elements as structure, syntax, diction, and imagery reveal the speaker's reaction to the death of a toad.
2. Read a passage from Joy Kogawa's novel, *Obasan*. Then write an essay analyzing how changes in perspective and style mirror the narrator's attitude toward the past. Include such elements as point of view, structure, choice of detail, and figurative language.
3. Base an essay on a novel or play that includes a wedding, funeral, party, or other social event. Show how the event contributes to the meaning of the work as a whole.

1998

1. After reading "It's a Woman's World," a poem by Eavan Boland, write an essay that analyzes how the speaker reveals her conception of a "woman's world."
2. Read an excerpt from George Eliot's *Middlemarch*. Then write an essay that characterizes the narrator's attitude toward Dorothea Brooke, and explain the literary techniques used to convey this attitude.
3. After reading a brief assessment of literature by Thoreau, write an essay about a novel, play, or epic poem that you may initially have thought to be conventional and tame but that you now value for its "uncivilized free and wild thinking." Explain why you value the work and how "uncivilized free and wild thinking" contributes to its value.

1999

1. After reading "Blackberry-Picking," a poem by Seamus Heaney, write an essay that explains how the intensity of the language conveys both the act of picking blackberries and the deeper meaning of the whole experience. Consider such elements as diction, imagery, metaphor, rhyme, rhythm, and form.
2. After reading about a dramatic experience in Cormac McCarthy's novel *The Crossing,* write an essay that shows how the author's techniques convey the impact of the experience on the main character.
3. Write an essay on a novel or play in which a character faces competing desires, ambitions, obligations, or influences. Identify the conflicting forces and explain how the conflict illuminates the work as a whole.

Before you commit a word to paper, be sure you understand the question. Read the question at least twice. Underline the key words and ideas on which to focus as you plan your essay.

Writing a Thesis Statement and Introductory Paragraph

When you are sure you know what you are asked to do, the next step is to express the subject of your essay in a clear thesis statement that encompasses the theme or themes of the question.

When you have done this, you are ready to write your introductory paragraph, in which you define your thesis and mention the works or aspects of the works you will discuss in your essay. There will undoubtedly be a number of subtheses, which will be the themes of the paragraphs and which together will develop your central thesis. You will need to know the connection between the subtheses and the central subject, and you will need to plan to arrange the themes in the most effective and dramatic order. For example, suppose the question on the examination asks you to discuss the nature of evil in a novel or play. It states that evil is dormant in human beings and does not manifest itself unless some impetus is given by an external force, and that, once evil is let loose in a man or woman, it leads to disaster. As you think about the statement, your thesis takes shape. Human beings are capable of evil. Inner censors—the moral values of society—and external ones—fear of danger and punishment— keep the wickedness in control. Some forces release it, overwhelm the power of the censors, and movement begins on a path to suffering and disaster. You decide to choose *Macbeth* or *Wuthering Heights* and to discuss the careers of Macbeth or Heathcliff. Your elaboration and interpretation of the examination question in the form of a thesis statement and an explanation of its meaning, your choice of *Macbeth* or *Wuthering Heights,* and your reasons for that choice will constitute your first paragraph.

Suppose you believe that the evil in Macbeth and Lady Macbeth was released through their close relationship, their partnership; that if Macbeth had been married to someone like Lady Macduff, or if the Macbeths had had a large family, ambition in Macbeth would have been diminished. That would be a subthesis to be proved.

Suppose you chose *Wuthering Heights.* A subthesis would arise from your interpretation of what particular external forces triggered Heathcliff's cruelty toward innocents like Isabella, Linton, Hareton, and the young Catherine. In the case of Heathcliff there would be a subthesis with explanations demonstrating that, once the evil was let loose, it had to lead to suffering and tragedy.

All the interpretations combined and presented in logical order with appropriate transitions would provide the evidence to support the central thesis expressed in your first paragraph.

Sample Introductory Paragraphs

The ten sample paragraphs below illustrate how a writer might incorporate an essay's main thesis into the opening paragraph of an essay. In each case, the writer also makes clear the gist of the question being addressed.

1. Characters in literature are often thoughtful people troubled by the injustices they see in the world about them. They find themselves incapable of adapting themselves to the realities of poverty and social injustice. Their intellectual concern leads them to question the beliefs of their faith and the institutions of their society. Their torment occasionally generates unique, unexpected responses. One such character is Raskolnikov in *Crime and Punishment* by Fyodor Dostoevsky.

2. The course of a man's life is never determined purely by his own character and decisions. Since man does not live alone in a vacuum, whatever happens to him is the product of his decisions and the influences and direction of the people who surround him and are close to him. Women are important in men's lives, and they will color those lives for good or ill. In literature, we frequently find women who lead men to actions that eventually destroy or defeat them. One such woman is Eustacia Vye in *The Return of the Native* by Thomas Hardy.

3. Satirists are basically angry persons. In contemplating human ugliness and inhumanity, their fury is roused, and they strike out against cruelty and injustice with all the weapons of language and imagery at their command. For this reason, satirists are accused of misanthropy. But this is not true. If one carefully reads *Candide* by Voltaire, he/she will discern a vein of compassion for humanity that pervades the work.

4. The specter of death and decay haunts the lives of many people. Philosophers have advised men and women to live each day as though they were to die tomorrow. However, very few people live daily lives of excitement and novelty, and death in the form of pattern and routine permeates their lives. One such character in literature concerned with death and affected by that concern is Gabriel Conroy in "The Dead" by James Joyce.

5. Equilibrium is the essence of comedy. The fun and the subtlety of comedy lie in the disturbance of the lives of characters who are so unhappy by the turn of events as to seem at the moment to be on a course toward a tragic resolution. However, all is straightened out in the end. The equilibrium is restored, and that makes for comedy. A comedy that perfectly illustrates this view is *The Way of the World* by William Congreve.

6. Dullness is the bane of the lives of men and women. When sameness rules daily existence, when there is not enough to fill a day, people will look for change in activities and relationships that promise excitement but at the same time lead to disappointment and misery. This is a familiar subject in literature and is best illustrated through the career of Emma Bovary in Gustave Flaubert's novel, *Madame Bovary*.

7. Minor characters in different works perform different functions. They can serve as narrators, either of the entire story or of important events that they have been in position to witness. They can serve as foils and highlight, by

contrast, qualities of the main characters. They can help to fill out the milieu of the story. They can present the views of the author or views that are anathema to him. They can by their words and deeds move the main characters to certain behavior or to fresh understandings. In short, they serve in a variety of ways. In *Lord Jim* by Joseph Conrad, Marlow, the narrator of the story and Jim's confidant, lets us see the career of Jim through his "voice."

8. Failure of communication is frequently the cause of failure of a relationship. Individuals in the closest of alliances, like parent and child, husband and wife, employer and employee, teacher and student, find themselves isolated because they cannot explain themselves. The isolation may lead to quarrels, to suffering, to tragedy. Where understanding occurs, and there is some exchange, there is hope for a change for the better. In *Death of a Salesman* by Arthur Miller, Willy Loman's tragedy lies in part in his inability to explain himself to his sons, his employer, or to anyone else except perhaps his wife.

9. Isn't it possible for a character in a play or novel to be a tragic hero even though his personality is a negative one, even though his attitude toward life is one of indifference, even though in terms of contemporary values he is a cipher, even though his carelessness or stupidity causes others pain? His suffering and his heroism lie in his inability, try as he may, to comprehend what is happening to him, in his perplexity as he seeks to determine his position in the universe, in his realization finally that he is a thing and his resigned, almost noble, acceptance of this role, and lastly, in the courage with which he faces the annihilation, the disappearance, of his "self" from the world of human beings. Two such characters are Rosencrantz and Guildenstern in *Rosencrantz and Guildenstern Are Dead* by Tom Stoppard.

10. Commonplace objects appear in many works of literature. Writers devote much space to descriptions of things in nature, religious objects, pieces of furniture, dining room and kitchen utensils, farm implements, factory tools, and the like. Frequently, these descriptions fill out a scene, but occasionally, the objects take on meaning beyond the literal and add a symbolic dimension to the story. The pickle dish accidentally broken by the cat in Edith Wharton's *Ethan Frome* is such an object. The snow in James Joyce's "The Dead" is important symbolically to the story. The handkerchief in William Shakespeare's *Othello* and the hallucinatory dagger in Shakespeare's *Macbeth* are inherent elements of the story line of the plays.

Evaluating Your Answer

How do you go about checking the essay you have written in answer to a question on the Advanced Placement examination to determine whether it is the best answer to the question?

Suppose the question pertained to "Stopping by Woods on a Snowy Evening" by Robert Frost.

The question asserts that in literature readers often encounter experiences that may not occur in their own lives. You are asked to read "Stopping by Woods on a Snowy Evening" and then write a well-organized essay in which you show how the poet uses language, including such elements as diction, syntax, tone, and choice of details, to provide a rich, vicarious experience for the reader.

Essay 1

Now suppose you were examining the following essay written in answer to this question. How would you evaluate it?

A Study of "Stopping by Woods on a Snowy Evening"

Through an isolated and seemingly insignificant incident the reader vicariously experiences, rather than being told, a man's feelings. The author achieves this by his choice of words and by the structure of the poem. He uses only soft sounds and breaks up each four-line stanza with an unrhymed line. The soft sounds help to reinforce the feeling of peace and tranquility, and the unrhymed line slows down the pace of the poem, in keeping with the unhurried pace of both the man and country life.

Robert Frost's main image is, of course, the woods, which he depicts as tranquil and isolated. He contrasts this with the owner's house in the village, which represents warmth and shelter, and thereby emphasizes the isolation of the scene. In the second and third stanzas he continues to strengthen the image of the woods and further the contrast with the village. The lines "My little horse must think it queer/To stop without a farmhouse near" and "He gives his harness bells a shake/To ask if there is some mistake" equate the horse with the lack of variety in his life and the impatience and hurried pace of the village.

By the anonymity of the man and the location, the author has avoided encumbering the poem with unnecessary details. More important, he has given the reader freedom to universalize the experience, and therefore identify to a greater degree with the man.

The repetition of the final line is very significant. Beyond the symbolic possibilities of "And miles to go before I sleep" representing the road of life, with sleep representing the final sleep, death, which the author might repeat for emphasis, there is again the pace of the poem. The repetition slows down the pace of the poem, and transfers to the reader the conflict of the man's desire (to stay in the woods), and his responsibility to continue on with his journey.

OUTLINING THE ESSAY

Try to outline this essay. When you do this, you will find that the outline reads approximately as follows:

I. The reader experiences a man's feelings vicariously through an isolated and seemingly insignificant incident.
  A. The author achieves this by
    1. Choice of words
    2. Structure of the poem
    3. Use of soft sounds
    4. Breaking up each four-line stanza with an unrhymed line
  B. The soft sounds reinforce the feeling of peace.
  C. The last device (number 4 above) slows down the pace of the poem.

II. Frost's main image is the woods, depicted as tranquil and isolated.
  A. The woods are contrasted with the owner's house, which is warm.
  B. This emphasizes the isolation of the woods.
  C. The lines describing the horse's action equate the lack of variety in the man's life with the hurriedness of the village.

III. By anonymity of man and location, the author avoids encumbering the poem with unnecessary detail.
    A. He gives the reader freedom to universalize the experience.
    B. Therefore the reader can identify more with the man.

IV. The repetition of the final line is significant.
    A. Beyond the symbolic meaning of
        1. Road of life
        2. Sleep being equated with death
    B. There is the pace of the poem.
    C. The repetition slows down the pace.
    D. The repetition transfers to the reader the conflict in the man between a desire to stay in the woods and the responsibility to continue the journey.

COMPARING THE ANSWER WITH THE QUESTION

You will notice, as you look at the outline, that the student writing this paper has not answered the question. The subject of the question is vicarious experience and the way in which such experience enriches a reader's life. The writer of this paper states the theme in her first sentence, but she does not develop it. In fact, she drops it until the last sentence in her essay. She does mention that there is a relationship between the poet's technique and the feelings of the man in the poem, but makes no attempt until the last sentence to define these feelings and to show how they can be experienced vicariously by the reader.

There are a number of questions that should arise in your mind as you read the student's paper and the outline of it.

1. Take the first sentence, for example. It is the thesis statement: "Through an isolated and seemingly insignificant incident the reader vicariously experiences, rather than being told, a man's feelings." Your first response is that the sentence is awkward and not clear. To whom does the incident happen—the man or the reader? Why is the phrase "rather than being told" included? The writer then goes on to discuss technique. Shouldn't she at this point have focused her attention on the incident and the feelings and discussed *later* how the technique accented the thesis?

2. In the second paragraph, the student discusses Frost's image of the woods and contrasts it with the house in the village, stating that the contrast emphasizes the isolation of the scene. What happened to the man? He is mentioned as the owner of the house, but the focus has shifted to Frost. Also how *is* the isolation emphasized, not solely by contrast with the house in the village? Does the horse's behavior emphasize the contrast? In what ways do the actions of the horse highlight the lack of variety in the man's life? How does the student know that the man's life lacked variety? Is there evidence in the poem for this conclusion?

3. In paragraph three: *Does* the anonymity give the reader freedom to universalize? Couldn't the reader universalize—as he/she does in poems like "Richard Corey"—even if the man's name or the name of the village was known?

4. Finally, in paragraph four: Why, when the student begins to deal with meanings and conflicts and experience, does she digress to "pace"? Does the repetition, in fact, transfer this conflict to the reader?

You can judge from this analysis that the student writing this paper had a number of thoughtful observations to record. Mainly, she was concerned with technique. But she failed to show what the subject of the poem was and how technique clarified and dramatized the subject. Because of this omission, she did not answer the question. The paper, therefore, would be unacceptable and would probably receive a rating of 1 from the AP examiners.

This analysis is included to help you make accurate evaluations of your own essays, and to encourage you to direct careful attention to the subject or the theme you are discussing, and to caution you against including content that is irrelevant to your subject.

On the examination you will, of course, not have time to check your essays by outlining them. However, in your preparation for the examination, you will find that this approach to the evaluation of your work will refine your skills of thinking and organization and help you to write spontaneously thoughtful and well-organized essays.

Many teachers encourage students to prepare outlines in advance of writing. This is, of course, a time-honored aid to clear thinking and clear planning before writing. But many students complain that stopping to outline before writing hampers the flow of their thoughts and stifles their imagination. For such students, the technique of outlining their writing after it is finished is a helpful one. It focuses their attention on the major faults of their thinking. It reveals any tendencies to stray from the subject and encourages them to discipline their expression.

Essay 2

Let us try an answer to another question.

> Literature frequently deals with the struggle for dominance between opposing forces. Write a well-organized essay defining the struggle in a play or a novel and showing how the struggle is resolved.

Evaluate the following answer to this question.

The Theme of Dominance in *Macbeth*

Struggle for dominance in drama or fiction may take many forms. On one level it is a conflict between two people for power; on a more complex level it is a conflict between two people for power over a third person; on a psychological level it is the conflict in the mind and heart of a person between forces that move him toward evil and forces that move him toward good.

Macbeth is basically the struggle for dominance between good and evil, good being embodied by Macbeth's conscience, and evil by his desires and ambitions. Macbeth is unable to cope with either of these forces; therefore, he alone is the cause of his downfall.

Neither conscience alone nor ambition alone creates such a problem. Rather, it is the dynamic imbalance between the two that does. Macbeth, realizing his susceptibility to attacks from his conscience, says: "Glamis hath murdered sleep, and therefore Cawdor/Shall sleep no more: Macbeth shall sleep no more!" He suggests by thinking of himself as Glamis, Cawdor, and Macbeth that all of him is now subject to sleeplessness.

The witches are the stimuli for each of Macbeth's actions, but the plans were already in his mind. The witches added certainty to Macbeth's speculations. They were the link between fantasy and reality. Assured success moved Macbeth to action.

After the murder, Macbeth is sucked rapidly into the realities of self-preservation. He is forced to commit other murders to maintain his tenuous hold on the throne, and he realizes the futility of his efforts when the witches show him eight descendants of Banquo who were to rule in Scotland. It becomes increasingly harder for good to achieve dominance.

In the end Macbeth realizes he has failed completely. He cannot control his own destiny. His conscience has turned upon him for his moral transgressions. His ambitions are thwarted; Banquo's descendants, not his, will ascend the throne. His wife is sick, obsessed by imaginary blood stains she cannot wash from her hands. Macbeth himself has found only infrequent and fleeting moments of happiness, so even his interlude as king has come to naught. As Macbeth himself acknowledges when the armies of Siward and Macduff approach the castle and news of his wife's suicide reach him, life is a huge nothing.

Outlining the Essay

An outline of this essay would be something like the following.

I. Dominance takes many forms.
   A. Struggle of two people for power.
   B. Struggle of two people for power over a third.
   C. Struggle within a character between two forces.

II. *Macbeth* is a struggle for dominance between good and evil.
   A. Macbeth's inability to cope with the two forces.
   B. Imbalance in Macbeth between conscience and ambition the cause of his downfall.
   C. Conscience the cause of his sleeplessness.

III. Macbeth through self-preservation is forced to commit other murders.
   A. The futility of the murders.
   B. Banquo's descendants to rule in Scotland.

IV. Macbeth fails.
   A. His conscience turns on him.
   B. His ambition is thwarted.
   C. His wife is ill.
   D. He has had only fleeting moments of happiness.
   E. His life has become meaningless.

EVALUTING THE ESSAY
A study of the composition and the outline should reveal the following to you.

If *Macbeth* deals with a struggle between conscience and ambition, where in the play and how is this struggle highlighted? The student has not supplied the detail—the scenes immediately before and after the murder of Duncan as well as those depicting Macbeth's tensions and hallucinations—to support his thesis. The paragraph on Macbeth's murders to preserve his throne is irrelevant. The last paragraph is a satisfactory conclusion, but it needed to be preceded by the illustrations to prove the thesis. The rating of this paper would be 5 on the 0–9 scale used in evaluating AP essays. See pages 43–44 for a description of the scoring scale.

Essay 3

Struggle for dominance in drama may take many forms. On one level it is a conflict between two people for power, one representing the power of government and the other the power of the gods.

Choose a novel or play in which such a struggle occurs. Then, in a well-organized essay, identify the conflicting forces and explain how this conflict illuminates the meaning of the work as a whole. You may choose one of the novels or plays listed below or another work of comparable literary quality.

The Adventures of Huckleberry Finn
Anna Karenina
Antigone
The Awakening
Beloved
Billy Budd
Ceremony
Crime and Punishment
Dr. Faustus
An Enemy of the People
Equus
The Glass Menagerie
Hamlet
Heart of Darkness
Jane Eyre
Jasmine
Light in August
A Lesson Before Dying
Macbeth
The Mayor of Casterbridge
Native Speaker
The Piano Lesson
A Portrait of the Artist as a Young Man
A Raisin in the Sun
The Scarlet Letter
Wuthering Heights

Antigone deals with a struggle between two antagonists for power. Creon, as king of Thebes, seeks to strengthen his political power so that he can rule his land without danger of rebellion. Antigone, too, wants power, not for herself, she says, but for the gods. But she knows that winning power for the gods gives her authority to override the laws of the state. In burying the body of Polyneices, Antigone becomes more powerful than Creon and she becomes the spokeswoman for a new state.

Like her father, Antigone is stubborn and proud. She has not learned much from what happened to him and from what he had to say in the years she cared for him. She is different from her father because she is incapable of acknowledging that someone else is right. Oedipus insisted on learning the truth that destroyed him. Antigone cannot acknowledge the truth that, if she violates Creon's decree, she weakens his power to rule. She considers herself greater than Creon and therefore perhaps more deserving to rule. She can remain unmoved by his arguments and can taunt him into the action that eventually destroys her and him.

Antigone is different from her sister, too. Ismene sees her situation realistically and realizes that Creon cannot bury Polyneices and remain a strong ruler. Antigone, stronger, perhaps remembering that she had been a king's daughter, is ready to challenge Creon. She sees herself as greater than Creon, being closer in blood to Thebes's previous rulers.

Regardless of whose cause was more just, the winner of the battle becomes the ruling power in Thebes. Creon knows this, and so Antigone, whom he loves, must die. Antigone knows this, too, and so she is ready to defy Creon and to die if need be. Had Antigone not been the daughter of Oedipus and the bride of Haemon, Creon would have had no problem. The relationship of Antigone to Creon brings about the doubts that finally destroy Creon's wife and son, as well as Antigone, and leave Creon a broken but nevertheless resolute ruler.

OUTLINING THE ESSAY

If you were to outline this essay, you would get something like the following.

I. *Antigone* is a struggle for power.
    A. Creon seeks to strengthen his temporal power.
    B. Antigone seeks power for the gods.
    C. If Antigone wins, Creon's power is undermined.

II. Antigone, like her father, is stubborn and proud.
    A. She has not learned from her father's plight.
    B. She is inflexible and willing to die for her beliefs.

III. Antigone is different from her sister.
    A. Ismene understands Creon's position.
    B. Antigone sees herself as greater than Creon and is ready to challenge him.

IV. The winner of the battle rules in Thebes.
    A. Antigone must die.
    B. Antigone's relationship to Oedipus and Haemon aggravates the problem.
    C. Creon is the victor but at tragic expense.

EVALUATING THE ESSAY

A study of the composition and the outline should reveal the following to you.

If *Antigone* is a struggle for power between Antigone and Creon (and this is a thesis that can be supported), the emphasis in the supporting evidence should be on Antigone's ambition. Did Antigone hope to rule by marrying Haemon? Was her burial of Polyneices not solely an act of filial piety? Was she moving also to undermine Creon's authority? Did she expect Creon to be weak, to surrender to her wishes? Did she hope that this weakness would also diminish his power in Thebes and make possible a coup that would dethrone him and place her and Haemon on the throne? This is an interesting view, but it needs to be more strongly supported. The paragraphs on Antigone and her father and on Antigone and her sister require a different emphasis. They need to show that Antigone, like Oedipus, sought power and wanted to be a ruler in Thebes.

Nevertheless, this is a thoughtful and well-developed essay. The student reveals a close knowledge of the play. The discussion of Antigone is subtle and detailed, but the thesis is not substantially supported. The rating of this paper would be 5 on the 0–9 scale used to evaluate AP essays. See pages 43–44 for a description of the scoring scale.

Typical Student Essays with Teacher Analyses

Below are two questions similar to the ones you will find on the Advanced Placement examination. For each question, there is a sample student answer, followed by a teacher's comments and a rating on the basis of 1 to 5. Read the questions; study the student answers and the teacher's comments. Make a judgment about the quality of the student essay, and determine to what extent you agree or disagree with the teacher's evaluation.

Question 1. Authors often reveal the themes of their work by the use of metonymy, symbols, and images. In a well-organized essay, show how an author or playwright has used metonymy, symbols, or a recurring series of images in a novel or play to clarify two important themes of the work.

Sample Essay

                 The Status of Symbols in Shakespeare's *Hamlet*
When one reads various works of literature, added insight and increased appreciation of the many levels of meaning may be gained if we are able to grasp the symbolic meaning of common-place objects strategically placed throughout the work. Thus, important themes are revealed to the reader by subtle means. The observant reader will look for hidden meanings everywhere since good authors select objects not only to represent themselves, but to enrich and enlarge a theme. If an author chooses objects well, they will have many symbolic connotations for the reader, even if the author did not intend it that way. Thus, a work of literature can grow in meaning even after it has been completed. That is what separates good literature from literature that is mediocre or poor.

The use of symbolism is not restricted to any particular literary genre or era. Indeed, Shakespeare developed the technique to the epitome of perfection, and his *Hamlet* is rich with many subtle yet powerful symbols. The image of flowers in *Hamlet* is used to develop the central idea of the play in several ways. By their very nature, flowers are beautiful and fragrant, yet they are also extremely fragile and wilt easily. Flowers are continually associated with Ophelia, especially when she goes mad. We come to identify flowers with Ophelia's equally lovely and frail personality. The entire world would be one of beauty and grace if allowed to remain undisturbed, but caught in the midst of the great conflict and turmoil of *Hamlet,* such weak and early-fading charms must perish. In *Hamlet* the entire world does crumble before us, and with it Ophelia and her flowers, and all the fair and beautiful things in life that they stood for. Hamlet, seeing all the degradation about him, contemplating his mother's incest in particular, is made to say of the world that it is an unweeded garden growing to seed. All of the flowers of the world, the flowers of mankind, the flowers of human experience, were growing rank and were being decayed by the evil and ugliness of the world.

Another theme in *Hamlet* is appearance and reality. All through the play, characters have difficulty knowing what is real and what only appears to be real. Hamlet himself puts on an antic disposition in which he pretends to be mad. He acts mad some of the time, but then he acts sane. Yet at one of his most rational moments he contemplates suicide, an act of insanity. Symbolizing the dichotomy between appearance and reality are the players who visit Elsinore. As actors, they play many parts, just as people in life play parts. Hamlet plays the madman, Claudius the rightful king. Gertrude plays the good wife and Polonius the wise counselor and especially Rosenkrantz and Guildenstern pretend to be Hamlet's faithful friends, when they are not faithful at all but have been summoned to Denmark by the new king. The actors, then, are a central symbol, the epitome of how difficult it is to separate appearance and reality, and a theme in *Hamlet* that begins when Hamlet cannot tell whether the ghost is really his father or an agent of the devil and does not end until the scene when Hamlet and Laertes have a duel which on the surface seems fair and honest, but in reality is stacked against Hamlet.

In conclusion, symbols used by authors are very powerful tools to convey themes in works of literature. Without them, it would be more difficult for authors to reveal their ideas to their readers.

EVALUATING THE ESSAY

The writer is obviously familiar with *Hamlet.* He has cited numerous examples of how symbols clarify and expand the meaning of the play. The essay is clearly organized, although not very inspired. The writing is pedestrian. Although the paper contains good ideas, it's not terribly interesting to read.

The opening paragraph rehashes the question and digresses into a related, but not particularly germane, discussion of symbolism in literature. Overall, it does not add much to the reader's understanding of the interrelationship of symbol and theme. It isn't necessary on an AP exam to provide elaborate introductions. A straightforward presentation that quickly focuses on the main point of the essay is sufficient.

In the second paragraph the student begins a discussion of the flower imagery in *Hamlet* as the symbol of corruption. Although the second sentence in the paragraph is unnecessarily effusive, the rest explains articulately and with reasonably good detail how flowers contribute to a theme of the play.

Beginning with an uninspiring transition, the third paragraph contains several good examples to show how the troupe of players adds to the pervasive theme of appearance vs. reality in the play. Although one could argue with the writer's assertion that the players are symbolic, their presence adds substantially to the development of the appearance/reality theme.

The concluding paragraph adds nothing to the discussion and could easily be left out.

Because of the writer's insights and logical treatment of a fairly difficult topic, the rating for the paper is 7 on the 0–9 scale used to evaluate AP essays. See pages 43–44 for a description of the scoring scale.

Question 2. Read the well-known poem "Fern Hill" by Dylan Thomas. Then write a well-organized essay in which you discuss how the poem's language expresses the speaker's complex attitude with the past. Consider such poetic devices as tone, diction, choice of details, and imagery.

Sample Essay

                    Diction in "Fern Hill" by Dylan Thomas
Dylan Thomas's "Fern Hill" deals with feelings about the past, particularly feelings of childhood in a country setting. The language used by Thomas captures the feelings of innocence and the carefree days of youth. Thomas has set up a purposeful synesthesia that continues throughout the poem.

He uses unusual phrases to describe common objects. He writes of a "lilting house," of "singing as the farm was home," of a sabbath that "rang slowly in the pebbles," of "fire green as grass," and of "the horses flashing into the dark." These are not ordinary ways of describing such definite things as horses, fires, or houses. He does this because he is writing from a young child's point of view, and they use imaginative, unconventional language. A child also tells a story by adding up details with simple sentences joined by "and's." Thomas does the same by starting numerous sentences with "and," making each detail equally important, just like a young child who can't separate the important from the trivial facts. Also, like a child, Thomas uses short words. Nearly every word in the poem is either one or two syllables long.

Beginning with the first two verses, he has opened the door of childhood and allowed for the entry of the reader. With tense mixing and euphony, he creates words that are pleasing to the ear and evoke pleasant images. The very first verse has the words "young and easy." "Easy" has the long *e* sound softened by the *s* and made lyrical by the *y*. The second verse contains the words "house and happy," following the musical precedent of the first verse. The word "green" at the end of the second verse has this long *e* sound that was noted in the first verse. The alliterations "house and happy" and "grass and green" also contribute to the tone of the opening verses. In several places in the poem, there are internal rhymes such as "time let me . . . climb," and "time let me play and be," which again are euphonious combinations. It is also interesting that most of the final sounds of the words may be linked with the following word without sudden changes in the position of the lips as "golden in," and "heydays of his eyes." Where this liaison cannot be made, the words seem naturally to flow into one another. The rhythm of each stanza is constant, and within itself "lilting."

The poem deals with paradoxes and human helplessness. It summarizes the persona's response in the last few lines. There is an irony of situation: the difference between what should be and what is, which is often true of life itself, and in this context, the likeness is not a clue to new frontiers of thought.

It is an interesting exercise to write about diction and idea in a poem, but in order to structure my ideas through words most effectively, to bring justice to the poet and his work, I fear I must be a poet myself.

Evaluating the Essay

In the essay, the writer probably tried to cover too much ground. As a result, a good deal of unrelated matter is included, particularly in the last two paragraphs. As for the analysis of the poem, the bulk of the essay focuses on diction. The writer has done a good job in pointing out unusual uses of language and sound. The relationship between diction and content is dealt with cursorily, however. Except for the second paragraph, in which the writer shows that the language has child-like qualities, the content of the poem is ignored. The third paragraph lists several examples of words apparently chosen for their sound but fails to explain how these choices relate to the meaning of the poem.

The essay reveals the writer's potential for excellent and thoughtful insight. Some of the thoughts, however, are extremely vague or unclear. The phrase "tense mixing and euphony" is one puzzling example. What, precisely, does that mean? Likewise, what is the meaning of "opened the door of childhood and allowed for the entry of the reader"? Such an idea may sound good, but its meaning is elusive. Although the writer lists examples of alliteration and internal rhyme, the sequence of illustrations lacks coherent order.

The idea that "Fern Hill" illustrates synesthesia shows the writer's awareness of the concept, but very little of the essay shows just how images fired by colorful, dramatic diction create a multiple-sense response. In other words, it's one thing to recognize synesthesia, it's another to clearly explain and illustrate its function.

In the fourth paragraph the writer refers very generally to the theme of the poem: "paradoxes and human helplessness." Nowhere in the essay, however, is there a clear and cogent indication that the writer understands that the poem is really about the inevitable ravages of time. Thomas recalls a childhood of joy, a time when his imagination overflowed with delight. But the poem is more than a childhood idyll. Rather, it is a reminder that "young and easy" days soon vanish and that time puts an end to innocence. A thorough discussion of diction should probably point out words and phrases that illustrate the speaker's awareness of this darker side of life.

This response to the question has much to commend it. But as a piece of writing, it lacks organization and coherence. Moreover, it falls short of fully dealing with the question. The rating for this paper is 5 on the 0–9 scale used to evaluate AP essays. (See pages 43–44 for a description of the scoring scale.)

5 Poetry on the AP Exam

The most obvious way to distinguish poetry from prose is to search for rhyme and meter. Prose almost never rhymes (unless by accident), and metered prose is a rarity. But this is an inadequate distinction, since a great deal of modern poetry—like prose—lacks both meter and rhyme. Therefore, a more useful way to tell prose and poetry apart is to say that poetry relies more fully on figurative language, although that, too, is an overgeneralization.

Suffice it to say, therefore, that the study of individual poems reveals that metaphorical language, connotation of words, and verbal irony, while not the exclusive domain of the poet, are used frequently in poetry and are crucial in giving readers what may be called the poetic experience.

On the AP Literature exam, you will invariably find both multiple-choice questions and an essay question that will require you to analyze one or more poems. Although it is generally agreed that poetry should be read for pleasure, the poems on the exam are not there for your enjoyment. You might enjoy reading them, of course, but your task is to find out as much as you can about the poem—how it sounds, what it means, how its pieces are arranged, how it conveys its meaning. To describe a poem adequately, you must be familiar with the vocabulary of poetry.

In the multiple-choice questions, you may be asked to name poetic devices contained in a given poem. You may, for example, be required to recognize *assonance, consonance,* or *alliteration.* Or you may be expected to identify a *quatrain* or a *rhyming couplet.*

While writing an essay, you won't have time on the AP exam—nor would it be very desirable—for you to take the trouble of including a lengthy explanation of a rhyme pattern in a poem such as Tennyson's "Blow, Bugle, Blow," for instance. The poem happens to use rhymes, not only at the end of poetic lines, but within lines as well. Thus, "The splendor falls on castle walls" contains two words that rhyme, as does "The long light shakes across the lakes." By knowing the term "internal rhyme," you might dispense with the matter expeditiously and spend your time more profitably discussing other matters. In other words, mastering the poet's lexicon will serve you well as you prepare to take the AP test.

The poetry review that follows contains many of the terms that may help you to answer several questions on the exam.

Types of Poems

1. **Lyric:** subjective, reflective poetry with regular rhyme scheme and meter that reveals the poet's thoughts and feelings to create a single, unique impression.
   Matthew Arnold, "Dover Beach"
   William Blake, "The Lamb," "The Tiger"
   Emily Dickinson, "Because I Could Not Stop for Death"
   Langston Hughes, "Dream Deferred"
   Andrew Marvell, "To His Coy Mistress"
   Walt Whitman, "Out of the Cradle Endlessly Rocking"

2. **Narrative:**   nondramatic, objective verse with regular rhyme scheme and meter that relates a story or narrative.
>   Samuel Taylor Coleridge, "Kubla Khan"
>   T. S. Eliot, "Journey of the Magi"
>   Gerard Manley Hopkins, "The Wreck of the *Deutschland*"
>   Alfred, Lord Tennyson, "Ulysses"

3. **Sonnet:**   a rigid 14-line verse form, with variable structure and rhyme scheme according to type:

   a. Shakespearean (English)—three quatrains and concluding couplet in iambic pentameter, rhyming abab cdcd efef gg or abba cddc effe gg. The Spenserian sonnet is a specialized form with linking rhyme abab bcbc cdcd ee.
   >   Robert Lowell, "Salem"
   >   William Shakespeare, "Shall I Compare Thee?"

   b. Italian (Petrarchan)—an octave and sestet, between which a break in thought occurs. The traditional rhyme scheme is abba abba cde cde (or, in the sestet, any variation of c, d, e).
   >   Elizabeth Barrett Browning, "How Do I Love Thee?"
   >   John Milton, "On His Blindness"
   >   John Donne, "Death Be Not Proud"

4. **Ode:**   elaborate lyric verse that deals seriously with a dignified theme.
>   John Keats, "Ode on a Grecian Urn"
>   Percy Bysshe Shelley, "Ode to the West Wind"
>   William Wordsworth, "Ode: Intimations of Immortality"

5. **Blank Verse:**   unrhymed lines of iambic pentameter.
>   Robert Frost, "Birches"
>   John Milton, "Paradise Lost"
>   Theodore Roethke, "I Knew a Woman"
>   William Shakespeare, *Macbeth*
>   Robert Frost, "Mending Wall"

6. **Free Verse:**   unrhymed lines without regular rhythm.
>   Walt Whitman, "The Last Invocation"
>   William Carlos Williams, "Rain," "The Dance"
>   Richard Wilbur, "Juggler"

7. **Epic:**   a long, dignified narrative poem that gives the account of a hero important to his nation or race.
>   Lord Byron, "Don Juan"
>   John Milton, "Paradise Lost"
>   Homer, "The Illiad," "The Odyssey"

8. **Dramatic Monologue:**   a lyric poem in which the speaker tells an audience about a dramatic moment in his/her life and, in doing so, reveals his/her character.
>   Robert Browning, "My Last Duchess"
>   T. S. Eliot, "The Love Song of J. Alfred Prufrock"

9. **Elegy:**   a poem of lament, meditating on the death of an individual.
>   W. H. Auden, "In Memory of W. B. Yeats"
>   John Milton, "Lycidas"
>   Theodore Roethke, "Elegy for Jane"
>   Alfred, Lord Tennyson, "In Memoriam A. H. H."

10. **Ballad:**   simple, narrative verse that tells a story to be sung or recited; the folk ballad is anonymously handed down, while the literary ballad has a single author.
   John Keats, "La Belle Dame sans Merci"
   Edward Arlington Robinson, "Richard Cory"
   William Butler Yeats, "The Fiddler of Dooney"

11. **Idyll:**   lyric poem describing the life of the shepherd in pastoral, bucolic, idealistic terms.
   Alfred, Lord Tennyson, "Idylls of the King"
   William Wordsworth, "The Solitary Reaper"

12. **Villanelle:**   a French verse form, strictly calculated to appear simple and spontaneous; five tercets and a final quatrain, rhyming <u>aba</u> <u>aba</u> <u>aba</u> <u>aba</u> <u>aba</u> <u>abaa</u>. Lines 1, 6, 12, 18 and 3, 9, 15, 19 are refrain.
   Theodore Roethke, "The Walking"
   Dylan Thomas, "Do Not Go Gentle into That Good Night"

13. **Light Verse:**   a general category of poetry written to entertain, such as lyric poetry, epigrams, and limericks. It can also have a serious side, as in parody or satire.
   Vachel Lindsay, "The Congo"
   Lewis Carroll, "Jabberwocky"

14. **Haiku:**   Japanese verse in three lines of five, seven, and five syllables, often depicting a delicate image.
   Matsuo Basko,   The lightning flashes!
   And slashing through the darkness,
   A night-heron's screech.

15. **Limerick:**   humorous nonsense-verse in five anapestic lines rhyming <u>aabba</u>, <u>a</u>-lines being trimeter and <u>b</u>-lines dimeter.
   Edward Lear,   There was an old man at the Cape
   Who made himself garments of crape
   When asked "Will they tear?"
   He replied, "Here and there,
   But they keep such a beautiful shape!"

Meter

Meter is poetry's *rhythm,* or its pattern of stressed and unstressed syllables. Meter is measured in units of *feet;* the five basic kinds of metric feet are indicated below. Accent marks indicate stressed (´) or unstressed (ˇ) syllables.

Type of Metric Foot	Accent/Stress	Example
Iambic	ˇ ´	bă-loón
Trochaic	´ ˇ	só-dă
Anapestic	ˇ ˇ ´	cŏn-tră-díct
Dactyllic	´ ˇ ˇ	má-nĭ-ăc
Spondaic	´ ´	mán-máde

Metrical units are the building blocks of lines of verse; lines are named according to the number of feet they contain:

Number of Metric Feet	Type of Line
one foot	monometer
two feet	dimeter
three feet	trimeter
four feet	tetrameter
five feet	pentameter
six feet	hexameter
seven feet	heptameter
eight feet	octometer (rare)

Scansion is the analysis of these mechanical elements within a poem to determine meter. Feet are marked off with slashes (/) and accented appropriately (´—stress, ˘—unstress). Emily Dickinson's "Because I Could Not Stop for Death" is scanned here:

> Bĕcaúse / Ĭ coúld / nŏt stóp / fŏr Déath
> Hĕ kínd- / lў stoppéd / fŏr mé
> Thĕ Cár- / riăge héld / bŭt júst / oŭr-selvés
> Ănd Ím- / mŏrtál-/ ĭtý.

The feet in these lines are iambic (˘´). The first and third lines have four feet and can be identified as iambic tetrameter. The second and fourth lines, with three feet each, are iambic trimeter. Therefore, the basic meter is iambic tetrameter.

Metric feet make up lines, which make up *stanzas*. A stanza is to a poem what a paragraph is to a narrative or essay. Stanzas are identified by the number of lines they contain:

Number of Lines	Type of Stanza
2	couplet
3	tercet
4	quatrain
5	cinquain
6	sestet
7	septet
8	octet (octave)
9	x-lined stanza
(or more)	

Other Metric Terms

amphibrach: a foot with unstressed, stressed, unstressed syllables (˘´˘): Chĭcágŏ.

anàcrusis: an extra unaccented syllable at the beginning of a line before the regular meter begins.
"*Mine* / bў thĕ ríght / ŏf thĕ whité / ĕlećtiŏn"
(Emily Dickinson)

amphimacer: a foot with stressed, unstressed, stressed syllables (´˘´): áttĭtúde.

catalexis: an extra unaccented syllable at the ending of a line after the regular meter ends (opposite of anàcrusis).
"I´ll téll / yŏu hów / thĕ sún / róse" (Emily Dickinson)

caesura: a pause in the meter or rhythm of a line.
> Flood-tide below me! ‖ I see you face to face!
> (Walt Whitman: "Crossing Brooklyn Ferry")

enjambement: a run-on line, continuing into the next without a grammatical break.
> Green rustlings, more-than-regal charities
> Drift coolly from that tower of whispered light.
> (Hart Crane: "Royal Palm")

Rhyme

1. **Rime:** old spelling of rhyme, which is the repetition of like sounds at regular intervals, employed in versification, the writing of verse.

2. **End Rhyme:** rhyme occurring at the ends of verse lines; most common rhyme form.

> I was angry with my *friend,*
> I told my wrath, my wrath did *end.*
> (William Blake, "A Poison Tree")

3. **Internal Rhyme:** rhyme contained within a line of verse.

> The splendour *falls* on castle *walls*
> And snowy summits old in story:
> The long light *shakes* across the *lakes*
> And the wild cataract leaps in glory.
> (Alfred, Lord Tennyson, "Blow, Bugle, Blow")

4. **Rhyme Scheme:** pattern of rhymes within a unit of verse; in analysis, each end rhyme-sound is represented by a letter.

> Take, O take those lips away,—a
> That so sweetly were forsworn;—b
> And those eyes, the break of day,—a
> Lights that do mislead the morn:—b
> But my kisses bring again, bring again;—c
> Seals of love, but seal'd in vain, seal'd in vain.—c
> (William Shakespeare, "Take, O Take Those Lips Away")

5. **Masculine Rhyme:** rhyme in which only the last, accented syllable of the rhyming words correspond exactly in sound; most common kind of end rhyme.

> She walks in beauty like the *night*
> Of cloudless climes and starry *skies;*
> And all that's best of dark and *bright*
> Meet in her aspect and her *eyes:*
> Thus mellowed to that tender *light*
> Which heaven to gaudy day *denies.*
> (Lord Byron, "She Walks in Beauty")

6. **Feminine Rhyme:** rhyme in which two consecutive syllables of the rhyming words correspond, the first syllable carrying the accent; double rhyme.

> Trembling, hoping, lingering, *flying.*
> O the pain, the bliss of *dying!*
> (Alexander Pope, "Vital Spark of Heavenly Flame")

7. Half Rhyme (Slant Rhyme): imperfect, approximate rhyme.

> In the mustardseed sun,
> By full tilt river and switchback sea
> Where the cormorants scud,
> In his house on stilts high among beaks
> (Dylan Thomas, "Poem on His Birthday")

8. Assonance: repetition of two or more vowel sounds within a line.

> Burnt the fire of thine eyes
> (William Blake, "The Tiger")

> And I do smile, such cordial light
> (Emily Dickinson, "My Life Had Stood, A Loaded Gun")

9. Consonance: repetition of two or more consonant sounds within a line.

> And all is seared with trade; bleared smeared with toil;
> And wears man's smudge and shares man's smell: the soil
> (Gerard Manley Hopkins, "God's Grandeur")

> Love, all alike, no season knows, nor clime,
> Nor hours, days, months, which are the rags of time.
> (John Donne, "The Sun Rising")

10. Alliteration: the repetition of one or more initial sounds, usually consonants, in words within a line.

> Bright black-eyed creature, brushed with brown.
> (Robert Frost, "To a Moth Seen in Winter")

> He clasps the crag with crooked hands
> (Alfred, Lord Tennyson, "The Eagle")

11. Onomatopoeia: the use of a word whose sound suggests its meaning.

> The buzz saw snarled and rattled in the yard
> (Robert Frost, "Out, Out")
> Veering and wheeling free in the open
> (Carl Sandburg, "The Harbor")

12. Euphony: the use of compatible, harmonious sounds to produce a pleasing, melodious effect.

> I knew a woman, lovely in her bones,
> When small birds sighed, she would sigh back at them.
> (Theodore Roethke, "I Knew a Woman")

> And the smooth stream in smoother numbers flows
> (Alexander Pope, "Sound and Sense")

13. Cacophony: the use of inharmonious sounds in close conjunction for effect; opposite of euphony.

> Or, my scrofulous French novel
> On grey paper with blunt type!
> Simply glance at it, you grovel
> Hand and foot in Belial's gripe;
> (Robert Browning, "Soliloquy of the Spanish Cloister")

> But when loud surges lash the sounding shore
> (Alexander Pope, "Sound and Sense")

Poetic Devices and Figurative Language

1. **Metaphor:** a figure of speech that makes a direct comparison of unlike objects by identification or substitution.

> All the world's a stage
> (William Shakespeare, *As You Like It*)

> Death is the broom
> I take in my hands
> To sweep the world clean.
> (Langston Hughes, "War")

2. **Simile:** a direct comparison of two unlike objects, using like or as.

> The holy time is quiet as a nun
> (William Wordsworth, "On the Beach at Calais")

> And like a thunderbolt he falls
> (Alfred, Lord Tennyson, "The Eagle")

3. **Conceit:** an extended metaphor comparing two unlike objects with powerful effect. (It owes its roots to elaborate analogies in Petrarch and to the Metaphysical poets, particularly Donne.)

> If they be two, they are two so
> As stiff twin compasses are two;
> Thy soul, the fix'd foot, makes no show
> To move, but doth, if th' other do.
> (John Donne, "A Valediction: Forbidding Mourning")

4. **Personification:** a figure of speech in which objects and animals have human qualities.

> When it comes, the landscape listens,
> Shadows hold their breath.
> (Emily Dickinson, "A Certain Slant of Light")

> Into the jaws of Death.
> Into the mouth of Hell.
> (Alfred, Lord Tennyson, "The Charge of the Light Brigade")

5. **Apostrophe:** an address to a person or personified object not present.

> Little Lamb, who made thee?
> (William Blake, "The Lamb")

> O loss of sight, of thee I most complain!
> (John Milton, "Samson Agonistes")

6. **Metonymy:** the substitution of a word that relates to the object or person to be named, in place of the name itself.

> The *serpent* that did sting thy father's life.
> Now wears his crown.
> (William Shakespeare, *Hamlet*)

> A *spotted shaft* is seen (snake).
> (Emily Dickinson, "A Narrow Fellow in the Grass")

7. **Synecdoche:**   a figure of speech in which a part represents the whole object or idea.

> Not a *hair* perished (person).
> (William Shakespeare, *The Tempest*)

> And all mankind that haunted nigh
> Had sought their *household fire* (homes).
> (Thomas Hardy, "The Darkling Thrush")

8. **Hyperbole:**   gross exaggeration for effect: overstatement.

> Love you ten years before the Flood,
> And you should, if you please, refuse
> Till the conversion of the Jews.
> (Andrew Marvell, "To His Coy Mistress")

> Our hands were firmly cemented.
> (John Donne, "The Ecstasy")

9. **Litotes:**   a form of understatement in which the negative of an antonym is used to achieve emphasis and intensity.

> He accused himself, at bottom and *not unveraciously,* of a fantastic,
> a demoralized sympathy with her.
> (Henry James, "The Pupil")

10. **Irony:**   the contrast between actual meaning and the suggestion of another meaning.

> a. *Verbal*—meaning one thing and saying another.
> next to of course god america i love you
> (e.e. cummings)

> b. *Dramatic*—two levels of meaning—what the speaker says and
> what he/she means, and what the speaker says and the author means.
> I stood upon a high place,
> And saw, below, many devils
> Running, leaping,
> And carousing in sin.
> One looked up grinning,
> And said, "Comrade! Brother!"
> (Stephen Crane, "I Stood Upon a High Place")

> c. *Situational*—when the reality of a situation differs from the antici-
> pated or intended effect; when something unexpected occurs.
> What rough beast, its hour come round at last
> Slouches toward Bethlehem to be born?
> (William Butler Yeats, "The Second Coming")
> (The second coming of Christ is intended, but a rough beast will come
> instead.)

11. **Symbolism:**   the use of one subject to suggest another, hidden object or idea.

> In Robert Frost's "The Road Not Taken," the fork in the road represents a major
> decision in life, each road a separate way of life.
> In Alexander Pope's "The Rape of the Lock," "Cupid's flames" symbolizes love.
> In Gerard Manley Hopkins's "The Caged Skylark," "a dare-gale skylark scanted in
> a dull cage" symbolizes the human spirit contained within the domains of society.

12. **Imagery:** the use of words to represent things, actions, or ideas by sensory description.

> Night after Night
> Her purple traffic
> Strews the land with Opal Bales—
> Merchantmen—poise upon Horizons—
> Dip—and vanish like Orioles!
> (Emily Dickinson, "This Is the Land Where Sunset Washes")

> And the May month flaps its glad green leaves like wings
> (Thomas Hardy, "Afterwards")

> He clasps the crag with crooked hands;
> Close to the sun in lonely lands,
> Ringed with the azure world, he stands.
> The wrinkled sea beneath him crawls;
> He watches from his mountain walls,
> And like a thunderbolt he falls.
> (Alfred, Lord Tennyson, "The Eagle")

13. **Paradox:** a statement that appears self-contradictory, but that underlines a basis of truth.

> Elected silence, sing to me.
> (Gerard Manley Hopkins, "The Habit of Perfection")

> Were her first years the Golden Age; that's true,
> But now she's gold oft-tried and ever-new.
> (John Donne, "The Autumnal")

14. **Oxymoron:** contradictory terms brought together to express a paradox for strong effect.

> Beautiful tyrant! fiend angelical!
> Dove-feathered raven! wolvish-ravening lamb!
> (William Shakespeare, *Romeo and Juliet*)

> All things counter, original, spare, strange;
> Whatever is fickle, freckled (who knows how?)
> With swift, slow; sweet, sour; adazzle, dim;
> He fathers-forth whose beauty is past change:
> Praise him.
> (Gerard Manley Hopkins, "Pied Beauty")

15. **Allusion:** a reference to an outside fact, event, or other source.

> World-famous golden-thighed Pythagoras
> Fingered upon a fiddle-stick or strings
> What a star sang and careless Muses heard
> (Pythagoras—Greek mathematician; Muses—mythological goddesses
> of beauty and music)
> (William Butler Yeats, "Among School Children")

> In Breughel's great painting, *The Kermess,*
> the dangers go round, they go round and around
> (William Carlos Williams, "The Dance")

Aspects of Poetry

Tone

Tone is the author's attitude toward his/her audience and subject. In real life, you can easily discern the tone of someone's spoken words. On a sunny, cloudless day, a friend might say, "What a beautiful day," and you easily sense the sincerity of the remark. But if it is rainy, cold, and gray, and your friend exclaims, "What a beautiful day," you can just as easily recognize the sarcasm in the statement.

In poetry, however, the speaker reaches you through his/her own written words. In order to understand the poet's tone and to decide whether it is earnest or facetious, happy or melancholic, serious or ironic, somber or playful, intimate or condescending, you must trace *all* the elements of the poem—form, rhyme, connotation, figurative language, and the like. The task of the good poet is to remove your disadvantage of not hearing the inflection of the speaker's voice by inserting subtle, consistent clues of meaning throughout the poem.

Theme

To determine the author's major idea or meaning you must ask two questions: What is the dominant purpose behind writing the poem? How does the poet achieve this purpose? In arriving at the dominant, core meaning of the poem, again you must scrutinize all elements of the poem. This is possible on many levels, each increasing in generality.

Unfortunately, too many readers of poetry make the fatal error of substituting a tidy, mellifluous group of words that they call the theme for the poem itself. The theme of a poem is not to be abstracted like the moral of a fairy tale, for it is inextricably linked to the elements of the poem itself. The theme of the poem is the abstract idea upon which the poem is built, rendering it concrete through the speaker, events, or images within the poem.

Dramatic Situation

Several important questions must be asked after reading any poem: Who is the speaker? To whom is he speaking? What are the circumstances? Does this situation contribute to the total meaning and impact of the poem?

The dramatic situation of a poem is the interrelationship of the answers to these questions. It depends on the speaker, who develops in a poem much like a character in a play. All that you come to know about him/her is derived only through the poem itself. To understand any poem, we must identify the dramatic situation.

Analysis of Two Sonnets

Consider the following two sonnets.

GOD'S GRANDEUR
Gerard Manley Hopkins (1844–1889)

Line The world is charged with the grandeur of God.
2   It will flame out, like shining from shook foil;
            It gathers to a greatness, like the ooze of oil
4   Crushed. Why do men then now not reck his rod?
            Generations have trod, have trod, have trod;
6   And all is seared with trade; bleared, smeared with toil;
            And wears man's smudge and shares man's smell: the soil
8   Is bare now, nor can foot feel, being shod.

And for all this, nature is never spent;
10   There lives the dearest freshness deep down things;
And though the last lights off the black West went
12   Oh, morning, at the brown brink eastward springs—
Because the Holy Ghost over the bent
14   World broods with warm breast and with ah! bright wings.

THE WORLD IS TOO MUCH WITH US
William Wordsworth (1770–1850)

Line   The world is too much with us; late and soon,
2   Getting and spending, we lay waste our powers;
Little we see in Nature that is ours;
4   We have given our hearts away, a sordid boon!
This Sea that bares her bosom to the moon,
6   The winds that will be howling at all hours,
And are up-gathered now like sleeping flowers,
8   For this, for everything, we are out of tune;
It moves us not.—Great God! I'd rather be
10   A Pagan suckled in a creed outworn;
So might I, standing on this pleasant lea,
12   Have glimpses that would make me less forlorn;
Have sight of Proteus rising from the sea;
14   Or hear old Triton blow his wreathed horn.

The reader of Hopkins's sonnet is met with a dazzling array of sounds. The tone of the poem is developed in union with the sound of the poem. You could divide the poem into four sections:

1. Lines 1–4: a presentation of God's grandeur
2. Lines 5–8: a statement of man's feeble efforts
3. Lines 9–12: a praise of nature's resilient power
4. Lines 13–14: a return to God's benign power

In the first section, Hopkins develops a conceit of God's grandeur flaming out, charging the world, "like shining from shook foil." The image of God that Hopkins presents to us is magnificent. Through alliteration, assonance, consonance, and onomatopoeia, Hopkins chooses words and sounds to match the meaning of his lines (see chart following)—a brilliant arrangement of the consonants r, k, and l.

In the second section, after Hopkins develops the greatness of God, he turns to mankind with the transition phrase, "Why do men then now not reck his rod?" Why do men fail to recognize and respect God's power and why do they fail to have concern about God's punishment? Again the sound of the lines parallels their meaning—dreary, long consonants dominate the lines—r's and d's (see chart following).

In the third section, Hopkins states that, in spite of all this waste and devastation, nature is never exhausted. Again, the sound and the sense are linked.

In the final two lines, Hopkins returns to another image of God, this time not a galvanized, electric one, but a gentle, brooding picture of God as a great bird resting on his nest. And here again the sound is significant.

You should be alert to the incredible varieties of internal rhyming devices Hopkins develops throughout the poem. The following chart lists the major occurrences; note how the pattern changes appropriately for each section of the poem:

Alliteration:

Line 1	world, with; grandeur, God
2	flame, from, foil; shining, shook
3	gathers, greatness; ooze, oil
4	now, not; reck, rod
6	trade, toil
7	smudge, shares, smell, soil
8	now, nor; foot, feel
9	nature, never
10	dearest freshness; deep down
11	last, lights; West, went
12	brown, brink
13	Because, bent
14	World, with, warm, with, wings; broods, breast, bright

Assonance:

Line 2	like, shining
4	men, then, reck
6	seared, bleared, smeared
8	feel, being
10	dearest, deep
13	Holy, Ghost, over

Consonance:

Line 1	world, charged, grandeur; world, charged, God
2	will, flame, like, foil; it, out; flame, from; like, shook
3	gathers, greatness; gathers, ooze
4	crushed, reck, rod; men, then
6	seared, trade, bleared, smeared; all, bleared, toil
7	wears, man's, shares, man's; wears, shares man's, smudge, man's, smell
9	nature, never; this, spent
10	There, dearest, freshness lives, dearest, freshness, things
11	last, lights, West last, lights, West, went
12	morning, brown, brink, eastward, springs eastward, springs at, eastward
13	Ghost, bent
14	world, broods, warm, breast, bright broods, breast, wings

Onomatopoeia:

Line 1	charged
2	shining from shook foil
3	ooze of oil

6	seared, bleared, smeared
7	smudge
10	dearest freshness; deep down
14	broods

The tone of this poem moves from a powerful capitulation of God's omnipotence, to a dreary expression of man's ruining his earth, to a delicate statement of nature's everlasting fecundity, and finally to a gentle image of God protecting His creation. Above all, you should sense the tone of hope that echoes at the conclusion of the poem.

However, in Wordsworth's sonnet, in spite of the similarities of theme, you may detect a sharp difference in tone. Whereas in Hopkins, hope resounds, in Wordsworth, disillusionment prevails.

Wordsworth, too, employs sound vividly to develop the tone of his poem. This sonnet divides into two sections, an octave and a sestet:

1. lines 1 to 8: a lamentation for lost reverence of nature
2. lines 9 to 14: a statement of preference for a pagan creed that at least allows worship of and communion with nature

In the octave, Wordsworth says we are so caught up in "getting and spending" that "little we see in nature." By laying waste our communicative powers, "we have given our hearts away." He calls this a "sordid boon"; by this he means that the act of giving our hearts away is a sordid, or squalid, occurrence because the capacity to feel is gone. Then he chooses some natural images: the sea (personified), the moon, howling winds; in a simile, he states that, like unprotected "sleeping flowers," these things are "up-gathered" or lost. The state of mankind is abysmal: "we are out of tune" with nature. "It moves us not." Like Hopkins, Wordsworth uses internal rhyme to accentuate his meaning (see following chart). Heavy, sonorous sounds underline the sadness and disillusionment of the speaker.

In the sestet, Wordsworth exclaims that he would rather embrace a "pagan" creed than lose contact with nature. His tone is not so much one of praise for the "creed outworn" as one of dissatisfaction with the tendency to "lay waste our powers."

You should be sensitized to the magic of Wordsworth's language. His use of rhyme is extremely effective, as the following chart attests.

Alliteration:

Line 1	world, with
2	we, waste
4	have, hearts
5	bares, bosom
6	winds, will
9	Great, God
12	make, me
14	hear, his, horn

Assonance:

Line 1	too, soon
2	lay, waste

   3   we, see
   6   howling, hours
 11   might, I
 13   sight, rising; Proteus, sea
 14   old, blow

Consonance:
Line 1   us, soon
     2   our, powers; spending, waste, powers
     3   Nature, ours
     4   hearts, sordid
     5   bares, bosom
     6   will, howling, all
     7   are, up-gathered, flowers; like sleeping, flowers
     8   For, for, everything, are; out, tune
     9   It, not; Great, rather
   10   creed, outworn
   11   might, pleasant; pleasant, lea
   12   glimpses, less
   13   sight, Proteus, rising, sea; Proteus, rising from
   14   Or hear, Triton, wreathed, horn; old, blow

Onomatopoeia:
Line 6   howling
   10   suckled
   12   forlorn

By his constant use of heavy sounds, such as the alliteration of w and the consonance of r, we sense the melancholic, disillusioned tone of the speaker as he frets over humanity's great loss in its lack of communion with nature.

Moving through the four clearly marked sections of Hopkins's poem, you may be able to articulate the basic theme: man is so caught up in the daily affairs of his life (his "trade" and "toil," or, as Wallace Stevens says, the "malady of quotidian") that he fails to recognize the beauty and power of God; regardless of this, nature will always remain a source of freshness and inspiration, and God will continue to brood over and to protect His world.

Examine each section carefully to discern how Hopkins develops his ideas. Many interpretations have arisen over his conceit of God's grandeur flaming out, "shining from shook foil." The image of tin foil shaking and reflecting brilliant light is one possibility. Another is an image of a Leyden jar, an electrical condenser shaped like a glass jar and coated on the inside and outside by metal foil, connected internally to a conducting rod. The beautiful world is "charged" with its rich connotative meanings such as electricity, aggressiveness, power, and control. This is coupled with the "ooze of oil/Crushed," another phrase abundant in interpretations. One possibility is olive oil pressed from branches, another is lubricating oil working in large machines (due in part to the rising industrialization at the time the poem was written and to the image of electricity), and a third is the rare oil of perfumery, squeezed into an essential distillate. The overall conceit radiates a ubiquitous, omnipotent, brilliant God.

In vivid contrast to the arresting quality of lines 1 to 4, the next section moves from sharp, crisp sounds and images of God's grandeur to a depiction of man's despoiled, filthy, slimy world. The repetition of the phrase "have trod" marks a cycle of futile waste, and the onomatopoetic words following enhance the notion. The picture of man's ceaseless trodding on his earth is a powerful one. He leaves smudged footprints, and a layer of filth on arid ground that his feet, "being shod," can no longer feel—he is far removed from verdant nature.

In the next section, Hopkins obliterates the smears, smudges, and toils and cracks open the soil to find that, in spite of the sordid cover, there is a "dearest freshness" in "deep down things." The amazing quality of this section is that no divisions exist between it and the previous four lines—the poet uses identical sounds in the words, but he transforms them from ugliness to beauty. Incredibly, the sonnet itself does what the opening lines say divinity can do. By including west and east he captures more than a cycle, as if to say, "Tomorrow is another day," and in spite of the ruination in the world and the ignorance of the grandeur of God, hope "springs" eternal at the "brown brink," below the level of filth. The "dearest freshness" is inside, both in the soil and in man; and although each is covered with a dirty exterior, the natural beauties, here vegetation and perhaps honor or virtue, are just beneath the surface.

In the end, Hopkins returns to his beatific, benevolent God. Enhanced by the gentle exclamation of "oh," the lines recall the medieval icon of the dove. God, the gentle creature, will always protect His brood. The world may be "bent," another very connotative word (rounded: man improperly shown the way to spiritual bliss, the earth devalued by the constant trodding of man), but always God will protect. The poet's final words, "bright wings," recall the opening conceit of brilliance, and unify the poem.

The theme of Wordsworth's sonnet is closely aligned with that of Hopkins. The woes of the world and the attention to daily details of life have hidden from the souls and minds of men the great joys and spiritual blessings found in close communication with nature. By becoming "out of tune" with nature, humanity has lost one of its greatest gifts: the ability to respond to nature and to be moved by its simple beauty and awesome power. "The world is too much with us"; we are too easily ensnared by the chore of earning a living and providing a home.

Nature for Wordsworth represents a "presence" that links human beings to God. In his immortal poem, "Lines Composed a Few Miles Above Tintern Abbey," he expresses this feeling.

> And I have felt
> A presence that disturbs me with the joy
> Of elevated thoughts; a sense sublime
> Of something far more deeply interfused,
> Whose dwelling is the light of setting suns,
> And the round ocean and the living air,
> And the blue sky, and in the mind of man:
> A motion and a spirit, that impels
> All thinking things, all objects of all thought,
> And rolls through all things. Therefore I am still
> A lover of the meadows and the woods,
> And mountains; and of all that we behold
> From this green earth; of all the mighty world

Of eye, and ear—both what they half create,
And what perceive; well pleased to recognize
In nature and the language of the sense
The anchor of my purest thoughts, the nurse,
The guide, the guardian of my heart, and soul
Of all my moral being.

lines 93–111

You should sense that the poet has lost some faith in the present way of life, and to compensate for it he turns to ideas and personages from the past.

His allusions in "The World Is Too Much with Us" to Proteus (the *Odyssey* figure who was a man of the sea capable of assuming many shapes) and to Triton (a sea deity who was portrayed as blowing on a conch) are efforts to "have glimpses that would make me less forlorn." Although he believes that the ancient Greek religion is a "creed outworn," he does find one fact particularly delightful: even though these people were pagans, they could sense the beauty and meaning in nature and searched to find an apocalypse of it. However, unlike the "Pagan," Wordsworth does not begin to believe that gods will present themselves with revelations, but he does sense that a divine spirit, a presence in nature, is all around him.

Dramatic Situation

Here the poems are remarkably similar. In each poem, the speaker is an omniscient observer of mankind, probably the poet himself. He is speaking to all mankind in an effort to bring man to a realization about his life.

Both sense severe errors in their species. For Hopkins, man fails to recognize the grandeur of God and instead is content to tread His earth and to waste His vast resources. For Wordsworth, man fails to escape his daily life of "getting and spending" and in the process is missing the myriad natural beauties of the earth.

Both sonnets appeal to higher sensitivity and to awareness of the bountiful joys offered us by nature.

The Lyric Poem

Characteristics and Types

The lyric is the most widely used type of poem, so diverse in its format that a rigid definition is impossible. However, several qualities are common to all lyrics:

1. They are limited in length.
2. They are intensely subjective.
3. They are personal expressions of personal emotion.
4. Each expresses the thoughts and feelings of a single speaker.
5. They are highly imaginative.
6. Each has a regular rhyme scheme.

Actually, many other types of poems are lyrics, but they occur so frequently that they merit a separate classification. Among them are the following:

1. **Aubade:**   a song written to praise the coming of dawn.
2. **Ballad:**   a simple poem, usually created for singing, dealing with a dramatic episode.
3. **Ballade:**   a French poem of three stanzas and an envoy, a four-line refrain recited to another person.

   4. **Dirge:**　a poem or song of lament, usually a commemoration for the dead.
   5. **Eclogue:**　a bucolic or pastoral poem such as Spenser's *Shepheardes Calender.*
   6. **Elegy:**　see separate entry.
   7. **Epithalamion:**　a poem written in celebration of marriage.
   8. **Hymn:**　a poem of religious emotion usually written for singing.
   9. **Monody:**　a poem similar to a dirge; a Greek poem of mourning sung by one person.
  10. **Ode:**　see separate entry.
  11. **Pastoral:**　many forms of literature fit this category; its setting is a created world marked by constant summer and fecund nature.
  12. **Rondeau:**　a French poem for light topics; it has 15 lines, with short refrains at lines 9 and 15, rhymed aabba, aabc, aabbac.
  13. **Rondel:**　a poem very similar to a rondeau, with 13 or 14 lines.
  14. **Song:**　a poem for musical expression, usually brief, straightforward, and emotional.
  15. **Sonnet:**　see separate entry.
  16. **Threnody:**　a poem similar to a dirge; in Greek poetry it mourns the dead and is sung by a chorus.
  17. **Vers de société:**　light verse, written in a congenial, witty, amorous way.
  18. **Villanelle:**　see separate entry.

Analysis of "Any Human to Another"

ANY HUMAN TO ANOTHER
Countée Cullen (1903–1946)

The ills I sorrow at
Not me alone
Like an arrow,
Line　Pierce to the marrow,
(5)　Through the fat
And past the bone.

Your grief and mine
Must intertwine
Like sea and river,
(10)　Be fused and mingle,
Diverse yet single,
Forever and forever.

Let no man be so proud
And confident,
(15)　To think he is allowed
A little tent
Pitched in a meadow
Of sun and shadow
All his little own.

(20)　Joy may be shy, unique
Friendly to a few,
Sorrow never scorned to speak
To any who
Were false or true.

(25)　Your every grief
Like a blade
Shining and unsheathed

       Must strike me down.
       Of bitter aloes wreathed,
(30)   My sorrow must be laid
       On your head like a crown.

Poets frequently try to universalize their poems, to write of themes and ideas applicable to all humanity. Such a poem is Countée Cullen's, "Any Human to Another." Even from the title you should sense his attempt to write about the brotherhood of man; rather than "a" or "one" human, he chooses "any" human.

The specific images in each stanza build toward the conclusion. Stanza 1 points out that a person does not sorrow alone (1–2) and that sorrow is intense (3–6). By employing the simile "Like an arrow,/Pierce to the marrow" the poet underscores the suffering. Stanza 2 adds to this idea by stating that "Your grief and mine/Must intertwine"; all persons must sympathize with sorrow, regardless of the individuality of the griever. Again a simile adds impact to the notion: like a river running into a sea, "fused and mingle,/Diverse yet single," the sorrows of human beings may be personally different but universally similar. Stanza 3 advances the doctrine that no one can escape from the grief in the world. Here the image of "A little tent/Pitched in a meadow/Of sun and shadow" emphasize his point. The "little tent" represents separateness, or removing oneself from the rest of the world, while "sun and shadow" correspond with happiness and sadness, or, as Cullen states elsewhere, joy and sorrow. Stanza 4 states that, although joy does not come to all because it can be a private emotion unique to one person, sorrow is universal. The poet personifies joy as a "shy, unique" person, and "sorrow" as a person who "never scorned to speak." Stanza 5 emphasizes that "grief" to any one person really is sorrow for all. First, Cullen develops a simile that grief is "Like a blade" that will "strike . . . down" any human being. Second, he alludes to the wreaths of laurel worn by victors in antiquity; "aloes" is a drug often associated with sorrow and bitterness. To paraphrase: "My sorrow must be laid/On your head like a crown" of sadness, rather than the laurel wreath (symbol of victory). Cullen presents the wreath of aloes (symbol of grief), emphasizing the necessity for sharing grief among all persons as well as sharing victory. You might also notice the possible reference to Christ and the crown of thorns, another manifestation of the theme of suffering.

"Any Human to Another" is a fine example of how the poet works with figurative language and poetic devices to develop a theme. Each stanza contains an important example:

Stanza

1	simile	(sorrow hurts like a pierced arrow)
2	simile	(grief is individual yet universal, like a river running into the sea)
3	images	(the tent indicates aloofness)
		(the sun and shadow indicate joy and sorrow)
4	personification	(joy as one who is shy, and sorrow as one who speaks to all)
5	symbol	(aloes as wreath of sorrow)
	simile	(grief pains like a shining blade that strikes someone down)
	allusion	(to laurel wreath ceremony)
		(possibly to Christ and crown of thorns)

That all persons are affected by one another and need to fuse the human spirit is Cullen's statement to the reader.

Analysis of "A Valediction: Forbidding Mourning"

A VALEDICTION: FORBIDDING MOURNING
John Donne (1572–1631)

As virtuous men pass mildly away,
    And whisper to their souls to go,
Line   Whilst some of their sad friends do say
(4)   The breath goes now, and some say, No;

So let us melt, and make no noise,
    No tear-floods, nor sigh-tempests move,
'Twere profanation of our joys
(8)   To tell the laity of love.

Moving of th' earth brings harms and fears,
    Men reckon what it did and meant;
But trepidation of the spheres,
(12)   Though greater far, is innocent.

Dull sublunary lovers' love
    (Whose soul is sense) cannot admit
Absence, because it doth remove
(16)   Those things which elemented it.

But we by a love, so much refined
    That our selves know not what it is,
Inter-assured of the mind,
(20)   Care less, eyes, lips, and hands to miss.

Our two souls therefore, which are one,
    Though I must go, endure not yet
A breach, but an expansion,
(24)   Like gold to airy thinness beat.

If they be two, they are two so
    As stiff twin compasses are two;
Thy soul, the fixt foot, makes no show
(28)   To move, but doth, if th' other do.

And though it in the center sit,
    Yet when the other far doth roam,
It leans and hearkens after it,
(32)   And grows erect, as that comes home.

Such wilt thou be to me, who must
    Like th' other foot, obliquely run;
Thy firmness makes my circle just,
(36)   And makes me end where I begun.

John Donne's "A Valediction: Forbidding Mourning" is rich in figurative language, and therefore is frequently misread. Because of the title and of the death images in the first stanza, readers often go awry in their interpretations of the poem. The dramatic situation in the poem consists of a speaker delivering a valediction (words uttered as people part from each other) to his beloved as he embarks on a journey. He is not dying; in fact at the end of the poem he talks of returning.

Donne develops a contrast between two types of lovers, the "laity" (8), or the people with religious faith separate from the clergy, and the true lovers of deep conviction. The former are "dull sublunary lovers" whose soul or essence is the "sense" or physical sensations of their love. They "cannot admit/Absence," "because it doth remove/Those things which elemented" or made up their love. Simply, they cannot endure separation. But the true lovers, whose "two souls therefore, . . . are one" and with "a love, so much refined," can with their "inter-assured . . . mind" bear separation. Theirs is a love of the souls and not of the senses. Hence even when separated, they will never lose their conviction.

This idea is presented by a series of four devices—a simile (stanzas 1 and 2), a metaphor (stanzas 3, 4, 5), another simile (stanza 6), and perhaps the most famous conceit in English poetry (stanzas 7, 8, 9).

In the first simile the speaker compares the separation of the true lovers to the parting of "virtuous men" from life. You should see that the opening stanza is not the primary subject of the poem, but a scene used for a comparison (marked by "As," the first word in the poem). Here a virtuous man lies on his deathbed passing so quietly or "mildly away" that his "sad friends" are unsure whether or not he is breathing. The speaker states that, as such virtuous men, he and his beloved should "make no noise,/No tearfloods, nor sigh-tempests" at their parting. It would be a "profanation of [their] joys," an irreverent, vulgar act to "tell the laity of love," to reveal to more base lovers that their love cannot stand the test of separation.

In a metaphor the speaker compares the "trepidation of the spheres" (this refers to celestial disturbances that do not affect the earth, as conceived of in Ptolemaic cosmology) with the true lovers. Just as the great movements of the heavenly spheres do not cause as much "harms and fears" in human beings as earthquakes, "Moving of th' earth" (which are inferior to "trepidation of the spheres"), so true lovers can separate without causing major disturbances, whereas the "dull sublunary lovers" who depend on physical love "cannot admit/Absence."

The second simile compares the parting of the true lovers to the expansion of gold when it is beaten into gold leaf. Their separation will not be a real or permanent break "but an expansion,/Like gold to airy thinness beat."

The final device, a conceit, is a hallmark of John Donne and other Metaphysical poets. This is a figure of speech that establishes a striking and extended parallel between two dissimilar things or situations. Here we see the poet compare the relationship of the parting lovers to the coordinated movement of the two feet in a compass. (Elsewhere in his poetry, Donne uses a flea who bit two lovers to deride the lady's coyness, and in "The Canonization" a comparison of two lovers with a series of bizarre things—commercial items, birds, historical monuments—and of physical love with the spiritual love of heavenly saints.) On a compass-drawn circle the moving or "obliquely run" foot "hearkens after" and "comes home" to the "fixt foot"; so the lover will return to his beloved after his journey. The speaker thinks of himself as the moving foot of the compass that leaves from the center (their love) and draws the circle. His beloved, the "fixt foot," keeps his circle constant. Thus he promises "Thy firmness makes my circle just,/And makes me end where I begun": during their parting she will be in his heart and on his mind.

This poem should alert you to the elaborate poetic devices available to poets as they develop their work.

The Narrative Poem

Characteristics

The narrative poem tells a story, sometimes simple, sometimes complicated, sometimes brief, sometimes long (as in the epic). Because of the increasing acceptance of the novel and shorter forms of prose fiction, narrative verse appears less frequently today. Almost the opposite of the lyric, it can be characterized as follows:

1. It is highly objective.
2. It is told by a speaker detached from the action.
3. The thoughts and feelings of the speaker do not enter the poem.
4. The rhyme scheme is regular.

Analysis of "La Belle Dame sans Merci"

LA BELLE DAME SANS MERCI
John Keats (1795–1821)

O what can ail thee, Knight-at-arms,
  Alone and palely loitering?
Line The sedge has withered from the Lake,
(4)   And no birds sing!

O what can ail thee, Knight-at-arms,
  So haggard and so woebegone?
The squirrel's granary is full
(8)   And the harvest's done.

I see a lily on thy brow
  With anguish moist and fever dew,
And on thy cheeks a fading rose
(12)   Fast withereth too.

I met a lady in the Meads,
  Full beautiful, a faery's child,
Her hair was long, her foot was light
(16)   And her eyes were wild.

I made a Garland for her head,
  And bracelets too, and fragrant Zone;
She looked at me as she did love
(20)   And made sweet moan.

I set her on my pacing steed,
  And nothing else saw all day long,
For sidelong would she bend and sing
(24)   A faery's song.

She found me roots of relish sweet,
  And honey wild, and manna dew,
And sure in language strange she said
(28)   "I love thee true."

She took me to her elfin grot
  And there she wept and sighed full sore,
And there I shut her wild wild eyes
(32)   With kisses four.

And there she lulled me asleep,
  And there I dreamed, ah! Woe betide!
The latest dream I ever dreamt
(36)   On the cold hill side.

I saw pale Kings and Princes too,
  Pale warriors, death-pale were they all;
They cried, "La belle dame sans merci
(40)   Hath thee in thrall!"

I saw their starved lips in the gloam
  With horrid warning gaped wide,
And I awoke and found me here
(44)   On the cold hill's side.

And this is why I sojourn here,
  Alone and palely loitering;
Though the sedge is withered from the Lake
(48)   And no birds sing.

John Keats's "La Belle Dame sans Merci" is an interesting narrative type of poem because it possesses elements of narrative, ballad, and lyric poetry. The dramatic situation of the poem consists of a speaker (stanzas 1–3) who discovers a "Knight-at-arms" "palely loitering" by a lake in autumn. The knight then responds (stanzas 4–12) with his sad story of how he met a beautiful lady, fell in love, was led by her "to her elfin grot," slept and experienced a horrible dream, and awakened alone.

Significantly, the poem takes place in autumn, as indicated by many details: "The sedge has withered from the Lake" (3), "no birds sing" (4), "The squirrel's granary is full" (7), "the harvest's done" (8), "the cold hill side" (44), repetition of the withered sedge and the absence of birds (47, 48). Just as the fecund joy of summer fades in autumn and eventually disappears in winter, so the strange lover of the knight has left him, despairing, to face her absence. The use of weather and seasons to reflect the state of characters or theme of the work is quite common in literature.

The knight, bewitched by his lady, is forlorn after her spell of love has been lifted, and is unable to face a normal life. The tone of the poem is deeply melancholic, tragic, and mysterious. Several types of images develop the tone:

1. Those that present the deep sadness of the knight as he relates his tale.
2. Those that develop the magical charm of the lady.
3. Those that tell of the terror of the knight's dream.

The knight explains why he "sojourn(s) here,/ Alone and palely loitering." First, the lady that he fell in love with vanished from his sight. Second, his dream revealed to him that she is "La belle dame sans merci," the beautiful lady without pity, who has already placed "pale Kings and Princes too;/ Pale warriors, death-pale were they all" "in thrall." She has entranced him as well.

The lady is "a faery's child," "Full beautiful" and captivating. She reveals her magical powers by riding with him on his steed, by confessing that she loves him, by luring him to her cave, by letting him kiss her, and by lulling him to sleep after she wept. She symbolizes a woman who with some magical ability can attract men to fall deeply in love with her. This fatal attachment leads them to fall into a swoon and then to waken to wander helplessly about, feeling remorse for their departed love. The knight here suffers from a strange physical affliction; as the speaker says:

> I see a lily on thy brow
>   With anguish moist and fever dew,
> And on thy cheeks a fading rose
>   Fast withereth too.

Keats uses the dramatic situation of this poem to symbolize hopeless love. Another argument for you to consider is how important biographical information might be in understanding the poem. Keats suffered from tuberculosis, and his description of the tragic knight's hopeless suffering in stanza 3 fits a description of the pain of this disease. Also, Keats was immersed in a fruitless love affair with a woman named Fannie Brawne; his unrequited love might have been similar to the knight's.

The Sonnet

Form and Types

The sonnet is a lyric of 14 lines, usually in iambic pentameter, written about one important subject. Although many variations of the form exist, basically two kinds predominate.

The *Italian sonnet,* developed by the medieval poet Petrarch and sometimes called the Petrarchan sonnet, is usually in two sections, an octave and a sestet. The rhyme scheme is abba abba cde cde (or any variation of c, d, e). With its two divisions, usually two ideas are developed, either compared or contrasted. Frequently the octave develops a question, a story, or an idea, and the sestet presents an answer, a comment, or a proposition. Naturally, many variations can occur, but the Italian form should be easily recognizable.

The *English sonnet,* sometimes called the Shakespearean sonnet, tends to be divided into four sections, three quatrains and a couplet. The rhyme scheme is abab cdcd efef gg. Each of the three quatrains develops a different aspect of the subject, and the couplet makes a final comment.

Two slight variations made famous by their greatest practitioners are the Miltonic and the Spenserian sonnet. The former has the same octave scheme as the Italian sonnet (abba abba) but keeps the sestet as an integral part of the meaning of the poem rather than coming to a conclusion. The latter combines the English and Italian forms, using three quatrains and a couplet in an abab bcbc cdcd ee linking scheme.

Many great poets have maintained the sonnet tradition, among them (in addition to those already mentioned) Sidney, Wordsworth, Rossetti, Elizabeth Barrett Browning, Wyatt (who first wrote them in English) and Surrey, along with Americans Longfellow, Robinson, Millay, and cummings.

A very legitimate question to ask is why this form has existed so long, given the incredible limitations and rigors it imposes on the poet. The most obvious answer is that these very restrictions tax the poet's skill to make the poem seem to escape the form. What the sonneteer seeks is to adhere to the form but to make the form totally subservient to the meaning and movement of the poem. The compressed form invites intense expressions of idea, sound, and devices. With little ground to dig into, the poet must be very exacting as he/she plants ideas.

As an adjunct to this notion, many poets have chosen to write a series of sonnets unified by subject. This is called a sonnet sequence. Some of the better known ones include Spenser's *Amoretti,* Sidney's *Astrophel and Stella,* and E. B. Browning's *Sonnets from the Portuguese.*

Frequently, a poet tries to praise the beauty and uniqueness of a loved one by comparing her/him to certain objects. To see the endless variations available in what seems to be a restricted poetic form, consider the following three sonnets, which bear interesting relationships to each other.

Analyses of Three Sonnets

A. LONG WHILE I SOUGHT. . .
Edmund Spenser (1552–1599)

Line Long while I sought to what I might compare
(2) Those powerfull eyes, which lighten my dark spright,
Yet find I nought on earth to which I dare
(4) Resemble th' image of their goodly light.
Not to the sun, for they do shine by night;
(6) Nor to the moon, for they are changed never;
Nor to the stars, for they have purer sight;
(8) Nor to the fire, for they consume not ever;
Nor to the lightning, for they still persever;
(10) Nor to the diamond, for they are more tender;
Nor unto crystal, for nought may them sever;
(12) Nor unto glass, such baseness might offend her;
Then to the Maker self they likest be,
(14) Whose light doth lighten all that here we see.

B. SONNET XVIII
William Shakespeare (1564–1616)

Line Shall I compare thee to a summer's day?
(2) Thou art more lovely and more temperate:
Rough winds do shake the darling buds of May,
(4) And summer's lease hath all too short a date:
Sometime too hot the eye of heaven shines,
(6) And often is his gold complexion dimmed;
And every fair from fair sometimes declines,
(8) By chance or nature's changing course untrimmed;
But thy eternal summer shall not fade
(10) Nor lose possession of that fair thou ow'st;
Nor shall death brag thou wander'st in his shade,
(12) When in eternal lines to time thou grow'st:
So long as men can breathe, or eyes can see,
(14) So long lives this, and this gives life to thee.

C. SONNET CXXX
William Shakespeare (1564–1616)

Line My mistress' eyes are nothing like the sun;
(2) Coral is far more red than her lips' red;
If snow be white, why then her breasts are dun;
(4) If hairs be wires, black wires grow on her head.
I have seen roses damasked, red and white,
(6) But no such roses see I in her cheeks;
And in some perfumes is there more delight
(8) Than in the breath that from my mistress reeks.

I love to hear her speak, yet well I know
(10)   That music hath a far more pleasing sound;
I grant I never saw a goddess go;
(12)   My mistress, when she walks, treads on the ground.
And yet, by heaven, I think my love as rare
(14)   As any she belied with false compare.

   A. In Spenser's "Long While I Sought . . . " you should see the clear division of three sections in the sonnet: a statement of the problem, an exploitation of the problem, and a solution of the problem.

1. Lines 1–4: a statement that the poet can find nothing suitable with which to compare the "powerfull eyes" of his beloved.
2. Lines 5–12: a series of images to which he attempts to compare the eyes, but fails.
3. Lines 13–14: a resolution that only the Lord shows a brilliance worthy of comparison.

   In the opening quatrain the speaker reveals the magnetic attraction he feels for the eyes of his beloved, "which lighten my dark spright [spirit]." In the octave, the speaker attempts to find a suitable object of comparison. In an odd method, the speaker chooses a series of images in a decrescendo effect, beginning with a powerful celestial body, the sun, and ending with a common manufactured object, glass. The conflict of celestial versus worldly and natural versus artificial emphasizes the uniqueness of the eyes, for nothing serves as a worthwhile metaphor. Note the deceleration and the shortcoming of each image:

sun —shines not eternally, only during day
moon —changes shapes and cycles
stars —fade according to sky conditions
fire —consumes itself into destruction
lightning—lasts but a brief time
diamond—displays an extremely hardy quality
crystal —possesses too fragile a composition
glass —tends to be too common

   Seemingly, the repetition of the phrases "Nor to" to defeat the comparison and "for they" to emphasize the advantage of the eyes is intrinsically not an interesting way to go about constructing a poem. Does Spenser relieve the tedium? You should see how he tries to achieve a good effect.

1. Repetition in itself can be an effective rhetorical device. Using a similar speech pattern lends unity to writing, enabling the reader to anticipate what comes next. It is a simple syntactical formula used both to repeat (the pattern) and to vary (the subject).
2. Spenser invites comparison with seemingly dissimilar objects. However, if you notice, each of the eight possesses a quality similar to the eyes—it involves light.
3. Each negative assertion really is a positive predication of the beauty of the woman, since her eyes are superior.

4. Spenser uses metrics very carefully. Notice that each of the celestial objects is developed in a line with a strong, masculine ending.

> Nŏt tŏ the sún, fŏr théy dŏ shíne bў níght
>
> Nŏt tŏ the stárs, fŏr théy haʼve púrĕr síght

Each is a clear iambic pentameter. In an excellent variation, however, the earthly objects are developed in a line with a weak feminine ending.

> Nŏr tŏ the fíre, fŏr théy cŏnsúme nŏt éveŭr
>
> Nŏr úntŏ gláss, sŭch básenĕss míght ŏffénd hĕr

Each adds the additional unstressed syllable to the regular iambic pentameter. The poet underscores the inferiority of the earthly to the celestial by changing the consistency of the meter.

5. Spenser establishes a consistent use of the caesura to break from the object of comparison to the superiority of the eyes.
6. By employing a varying rhythm and pattern of stress, Spenser develops an effective interplay of the regular and expected with the different and unexpected.

By elevating the sonnet in the closing couplet and comparing the eyes to God's infinite light, the poet is able to transform what seems to be a statement of failure into an assertion of the affirmative.

B. As a second variation on sonnet technique, consider Shakespeare's "Shall I Compare Thee to a Summer's Day?" Like Spenser, Shakespeare finds his beloved superior even to natural wonders. She surpasses each for specific reasons:

1. A summer's day—she is more beautiful and more gentle.
2. Summer's lease—time passes and summer ends.
3. The sun—sometimes the "eye of heaven" (a very effective metaphor) is too hot, and the goldness of his light (a personification of his complexion) is sometimes clouded.
4. Fair weather—it changes to poor weather as "nature's changing course" develops.

In the octave, the poet states his observation that his beloved maintains a steadier and brighter beauty than summer.

In the sestet, he establishes a resolution. Rather than merely develop a comparison to a series of objects, he will immortalize his beloved in poetry, ironically the "eternal lines" of this very poem. Unlike summer, whose beauty fades with the season, a poem is constant, so that "So long as men can breathe, or eyes can see" the words and ideas will be permanent. The poet captures an eternal summer. "So long lives this" verse of adoration, it "gives life" to his beloved and recalls memories of his attitude and her beauty. Rather than praise her as heavenly, as Spenser does, he grants her immortality.

C. In a third variation, Shakespeare seemingly makes light of all the absurd quests of poets to compare their beloveds with objects of great beauty or natural wonder. He takes the same idea as Spenser, the uniqueness of his mistress, but he strives to describe her essential humanness.

In the octave, he speaks of how much more pure certain objects are than are aspects of her physical state.

eyes   —the sun is brighter
lips   —coral is redder
breasts—snow is whiter
hair   —like wire it entangles
cheeks—roses are their own beauty
breath —perfume is sweeter

In the sestet he establishes his basic premise. His mistress speaks well, but music sounds better; a goddess must be more nearly perfect; his mistress walks like anyone else. But, he believes, she is rare and incomparable, so much her own person that it is folly to try to say she is like something else.

Analysis of "The Cambridge Ladies Who Live in Furnished Souls"

THE CAMBRIDGE LADIES WHO
LIVE IN FURNISHED SOULS
e. e. cummings (1894–1962)

the Cambridge ladies who live in furnished souls
are unbeautiful and have comfortable minds
(also, with the church's protestant blessings
Line   daughters, unscented shapeless spirited)
(5)   they believe in Christ and Longfellow, both dead,
are invariably interested in so many things—
at the present writing one still finds
delighted fingers knitting for the is it Poles?
perhaps. While permanent faces coyly bandy
(10)   scandal of Mrs. N and Professor D
. . . . the Cambridge ladies do not care, above
Cambridge if sometimes in its box of
sky lavender and cornerless, the
moon rattles like a fragment of angry candy

The poet e. e. cummings manages to escape any form of traditional response within the sonnet form. In "the Cambridge ladies" he describes with clear acrimony the upper class, pseudoliberal, emotionally controlled inhabitants of Cambridge, Massachusetts.

He experiments with a different rhyme scheme from the schemes of the two traditional sonnet forms. The poem, in an octave and a sestet, rhymes abcddcbaeeffee. Perhaps the enclosed nature of the rhyme scheme is created in this way not so much to depart from tradition as to fit the subject matter; that is, the closed-minded Cambridge ladies who "have comfortable minds" and who "do not care" box themselves in through their lifestyle just as the rhyme scheme of the octave and the sestet boxes itself in.

In the octave, cummings launches a frontal assault on many qualities and characteristics of the "ladies":

1. They live in "furnished souls." By playing on the idea of furnished houses and juxtaposing the essential spirit of the soul with the vacuum of a house to be filled, the poet effectively attacks their way of life. Threadbare, worn-out, spoon-

fed precepts dominate their souls just as accessories of unoriginal taste dominate a furnished house. Like a furnished house, the ladies do not choose the contents of their mind, but are fitted out with prescribed thoughts.

2. They are "unbeautiful" and possess "comfortable minds." Because they are so rigid and interchangeable, cummings prefers to call them, not hideous, but just "unbeautiful." Because they accept what has been handed down to them willingly, they own "comfortable minds."

3. They have daughters who, like them, are "unscented shapeless spirited." Everything about them is unostentatious, having just the right amount of decorum and propriety. Their shapelessness, like their "comfortable" lives, is attributed to their lack of initiation into life. Ironically, they are sanctioned "with the church's protestant blessings," because there they can meet in their Sunday best and reaffirm to each other that their lifestyle is perfect.

4. They "believe in Christ and Longfellow, both dead" because both are fashionable (although hardly similar) heroes. Because of their predilection for just the appropriate Christian feelings, they find it right to espouse Christ. And because of Longfellow's stature as a good poet and a native of Cambridge, they find it right to support him. Ironically, they are "both dead" physically, but, more importantly, they are "both dead" in the minds of the ladies, who do no more to live by the teachings of Christ than to challenge their existence.

5. They "are invariably interested in so many things" because it is fashionable in an intellectual community to be well informed, even if superficially, to be interested in hearing about people and ideas, and to be conversant with these for social gatherings. The tone of this line is extremely bitter.

6. With "delighted fingers" they are "knitting" for any charitable cause or minority groups. It is fashionable to support a charity, even though the ladies are more interested in the social approval they receive for their "work" (their knitting may hardly be useful) than in the work itself. By using the phrase "is it Poles?" cummings satirically underscores their uncertainty about whom the knitting is for, and the phrase "delighted fingers" effectively emphasizes the shallowness of their commitment.

7. The staid members of the community, the "permanent faces," constantly search for gossipy tidbits to "coyly bandy" about in a scandal. The anonymity created by Mrs. N (she's married of course) and Professor D (he's an important person of course) heightens the idea that the scandal is more significant than the people.

8. Clearly they "do not care" about human nature; they display an insouciance and a distance toward people other than those in their own tight little circle.

The poet then closes the sonnet with a brilliant metaphor and devastating statement. Throughout, the poem is a sardonic, wry commentary about the superficiality and banality of these ladies' lives. To them, the moon is no more than a piece of candy in a lavender box; their rigid attachments to their own select society hinder them from seeing any natural phenomenon as it actually is and prevent them from translating it from their own perceptions (the moon is not a moon but a piece of candy in a tidy box that they give for a present and that symbolizes their culture). The moon symbolically conjures up many possibilities for the reader—it is such a traditional symbol for so many different values and ideas that you can make it mean whatever you want (love, natural beauty, night, freedom, or change, which the moon does twenty-eight times a month), so long as you see it as distinct from the confining world of the Cambridge ladies.

The key changes in cummings' tone are expressed through the words "rattles" and "angry." The moon "rattles" in the box like a "fragment of angry candy" because it refuses to be trapped, "cornerless" in the void the Cambridge ladies create for it. Here cummings is no longer sardonic, but downright indignant and "angry." He chooses aggressive words and aggressive actions, phenomena alien to the ladies, but perhaps, he might be urging, not alien to the reader. One must seek to shatter illusory, preset "furnished" worlds and become an initiating, challenging person.

The Ode

Characteristics and Types

An ode is an exalted, complex, rapturous lyric poem written about a dignified, lofty subject. The original ancient odes were written in Greece, delivered by a chorus singing and performing an elaborate dance. The Greek poet Pindar developed the first odes consisting of complex stanzaic forms in units of three: the strophe, antistrophe, and epode. Each section had a movement of the chorus in dance rhythm; together they were meant to correspond to ebbs and flows of emotion.

In English there are three approximate types of odes:

1. The *Pindaric* or *regular ode* consists of the same strophe, antistrophe, epode division of its historical antecedent. Metrics and verse lengths vary at times, but a regular rhythmic pattern emerges.
2. The *Horation* or *homostrophic ode* is patterned after the subject, form, and tone of the Roman poet Horace's verse. It consists of one repeated stanza type, although it may vary within its form (e.g., Keats's "Ode to Autumn").
3. The *irregular ode,* growing from the work of the seventeenth century poet Abraham Cowley, imitates the spirit of the Pindaric or regular ode, but disregards the strophe and stanza rules. It is very flexible and offers the poet an opportunity to change stanza line structure, length, meter, and rhyme to suit his/her subject, mood, and tone. Because of the freedom in the irregular ode, it is the most common in English poetry.

Analysis of "Ode: Intimations of Immortality from Recollections of Childhood"

ODE: INTIMATIONS OF IMMORTALITY
FROM RECOLLECTIONS OF EARLY
CHILDHOOD
William Wordsworth (1770–1850)

> The Child is father of the Man;
> And I could wish my days to be
> Bound each to each by natural piety.

1

There was a time when meadow, grove and stream,
The earth, and every common sight,
To me did seem
Apparelled in celestial light,

The glory and the freshness of a dream.
It is not now as it hath been of yore;—
        Turn whereso'er I may,
            By night or day,
The things which I have seen now I can see no more.

Line   2
(10)   The Rainbow comes and goes,
            And lovely is the Rose,
            The Moon doth with delight
Look round her when the heavens are bare,
            Waters on a starry night
            Are beautiful and fair;
        The sunshine is a glorious birth;
        But yet I know, where'er I go,
That there hath passed away a glory from the earth.

                3
Now, while the birds thus sing a joyous song,
(20)   And while the young lambs bound
            As to the tabor's sound,
To me alone there came a thought of grief:
A timely utterance gave that thought relief,
            And I again am strong:
The cataracts blow their trumpets from the steep;
No more shall grief of mine the season wrong;
I hear the Echoes through the mountains throng,
The Winds come to me from the fields of sleep,
            And all the earth is gay;
(30)   Land and sea
Give themselves up to jollity,
            And with the heart of May
Doth every Beast keep holiday;—
        Thou Child of Joy,
Shout round me, let me hear thy shouts, thou happy
            Shepherd-boy!

                4
Ye blessed Creatures, I have heard the call
        Ye to each other make; I see
The heavens laugh with you in your jubilee;
(40)   My heart is at your festival,
            My head hath its coronal,
The fullness of your bliss, I feel—I feel it all.
            Oh, evil day! if I were sullen
            While Earth herself is adorning,
            This sweet May-morning,
        And the Children are culling
            On every side,
            In a thousand valleys far and wide,
            Fresh flowers; while the sun shines warm,
(50)   And the Babe leaps up on his Mother's arm:—
            I hear, I hear, with joy I hear!
            —But there's a Tree, of many, one,
A single Field which I have looked upon,
Both of them speak of something that is gone:

The Pansy at my feet
Doth the same tale repeat:
Whither is fled the visionary gleam?
Where is it now, the glory and the dream?

5

Our birth is but a sleep and a forgetting:
(60)   The Soul that rises with us, our life's Star,
Hath had elsewhere its setting,
And cometh from afar:
Not in entire forgetfulness,
And not in utter nakedness,
But trailing clouds of glory do we come
From God, who is our home:
Heaven lies about us in our infancy!
Shades of the prison-house begin to close
Upon the growing Boy,
(70)   But he beholds the light, and whence it flows,
He sees it in his joy;
The Youth, who daily farther from the east
Must travel, still is Nature's Priest,
And by the vision splendid
Is on his way attended;
At length the Man perceives it die away,
And fade into the light of common day.

6

Earth fills her lap with pleasures of her own;
Yearnings she hath in her own natural kind,
(80)   And, even with something of a Mother's mind,
And no unworthy aim,
The homely Nurse doth all she can
To make her Foster-child, her Inmate Man,
Forget the glories he hath known,
And that imperial palace whence he came.

7

Behold the Child among his new-born blisses,
A six years' Darling of a pygmy size!
See, where 'mid work of his own hand he lies,
Fretted by sallies of his mother's kisses,
(90)   With light upon him from his father's eyes!
See, at his feet, some little plan or chart,
Some fragment from his dream of human life,
Shaped by himself with newly-learned art;
A wedding or a festival,
A mourning or a funeral;
And this hath now his heart,
And unto this he frames his song:
Then will he fit his tongue
To dialogues of business, love, or strife;
(100)   But it will not be long
Ere this be thrown aside,
And with new joy and pride
The little Actor cons another part;

Filling from time to time his "humorous stage"
With all the Persons, down to palsied Age,
That Life brings with her in her equipage;
    As if his whole vocation
    Were endless imitation.

8

Thou, whose exterior semblance doth belie
(110)   Thy Soul's immensity;
Thou best Philosopher, who yet dost keep
Thy heritage, thou Eye among the blind,
That, deaf and silent, read'st the eternal deep,
Haunted, forever by the eternal mind,—
    Mighty Prophet! Seer blest!
    Oh whom those truths do rest,
Which we are toiling all over lives to find,
In darkness lost, the darkness of the grave;
Thou, over whom thy Immortality
(120) Broods like the Day, a Master o'er a Slave,
A Presence which is not to be put by;
Thou little Child, yet glorious in the might
Of heaven-born freedom on thy being's height,
Why with such earnest pains dost thou provoke
The years to bring the inevitable yoke,
Thus blindly with thy blessedness at strife?
Full soon thy Soul shall have her earthly freight,
And custom lie upon thee with a weight,
Heavy as frost, and deep almost as life!

9

(130)   O joy! that in our embers
    Is something that doth live,
    That nature yet remembers
    What was so fugitive!
The thought of our past years in me doth breed
Perpetual benediction: not indeed
For that which is most worthy to be blest;
Delight and liberty, the simple creed
Of Childhood, whether busy or at rest,
With new-fledged hope still fluttering in his breast:—
(140)   Not for these I raise
    The song of thanks and praise;
  But for those obstinate questionings
  Of sense and outward things,
  Fallings from us, vanishings;
  Blank misgivings of a Creature
Moving about in worlds not realised,
High instincts before which our mortal Nature
Did tremble like a guilty Thing surprised:
    But for those first affections,
(150)   Those shadowy recollections,
  Which, be they what they may,
Are yet the fountain light of all our day,
Are yet a master-light of all our seeing;
    Uphold us, cherish, and have power to make

Our noisy years seem moments in the being
Of the eternal Silence: truths that wake,
                 To perish never:
Which neither listlessness, nor mad endeavour,
                 Nor Man nor Boy,
Nor all that is at enmity with joy
(160)   Can utterly abolish or destroy!
                 Hence in a season of calm weather
                 Though inland far we be,
Our souls have sight of that immortal sea
                 Which brought us hither,
             Can in a moment travel thither,
And see the Children sport upon the shore,
And hear the mighty waters rolling evermore.

10

Then sing, ye Birds, sing, sing a joyous song!
(170)   And let the young Lambs bound
                 As to the tabor's sound!
We in thought will join your throng,
                 Ye that pipe and ye that play,
                 Ye that through your hearts today
                 Feel the gladness of the May!
What though the radiance which was once so bright
Be now for ever taken from my sight,
Though nothing can bring back the hour
Of splendour in the grass, of glory in the flower?
(180)   We will grieve not, rather find
                 Strength in what remains behind;
                 In the primal sympathy
                 Which having been must ever be;
                 In the soothing thoughts that spring
                 Out of human suffering;
                 In the faith that looks through death,
In years that bring the philosophic mind.

11

And O, ye Fountains, Meadows, Hills, and Groves,
Forbode not any severing of our loves!
(190)   Yet in my heart of hearts I feel your might;
I only have relinquished one delight
To live beneath your more habitual sway.
I love the Brooks which down their channels fret,
Even more than when I tripped lightly as they;
The innocent brightness of a new-born Day
                 Is lovely yet;
The Clouds that gather round the setting sun
Do take a sober colouring from an eye
That hath kept watch o'er man's mortality;
(200)   Another race hath been, and other palms are won.
Thanks to the human heart by which we live,
Thanks to its tenderness, its joys, and fears,
To me the meanest flower that blows can give
Thoughts that do often lie too deep for tears.

William Wordsworth's "Ode: Intimations of Immortality from Recollections of Early Childhood" represents one of the most complex, yet finest poems in the language. In many ways it is a poem about poetry, about the growth of a poet's mind and imagination. In spite of a modern reader's possible disagreement with the religious statements about the human soul existing in heaven before turning toward earth, the development of the poet's ideas remains especially intricate and subtle, a source of satisfaction to explicate.

As for all great poems, myriad interpretations exist. Basically, you should know several of Wordsworth's fundamental philosophical assumptions before delving into a close reading of the poem. He believed that his transcendent visionary experiences with nature were more real to him than his actual sensory experiences; you may be skeptical about such a viewpoint, but for Wordsworth this was quite true. At time he lived in a world of vision, not just in a world of sight. Also, the experiences in a visionary world were closely associated with his imagination and creative powers. And for Wordsworth, these moments of vision were timeless; they allowed him to see and to understand the eternity of God's creation and the immortality of the soul.

In the Ode, the poet asks for a restoration of the fading imaginative visions of childhood. Only through recollection of these spots of time can the poet recapture the heights of "visionary gleam" that the child reaches with nature. The epigraph (the concluding lines from "My Heart Leaps Up") of the Ode spells out this notion:

> The Child is father of the Man;
> And I could wish my days to be
> Bound each to each by natural piety.

In essence, "the Child is father of the Man" because the events and actions of childhood have a great effect on the events and actions of adulthood. The man is the sum total of all the experiences of his childhood; he learns from his early life and becomes a personality because of it. Wordsworth wishes to join his childhood with his powers as a poet; "I could wish my days to be/Bound each to each." By "natural piety," he means a passionate, almost religious response to the glories of nature, a worshipping of her powers.

You must understand the idea of preexistence, even though you may not agree with it. In fact, it is doubtful whether Wordsworth was wholeheartedly espousing a philosophical idea or merely developing it for poetic reasons. The soul, in heaven before birth, arrives to man and immediately begins a process of forgetting its origins.

You should see the poem dividing into three separate sections:

1. *Stanzas 1–4:* In childhood man sees nature's wonders, but this perception slowly diminishes as he matures.
2. *Stanzas 5–8:* The preexistence of the soul is developed, along with the insight into divinity.
3. *Stanzas 9–11:* The fading of the insight as the man grows is replaced with a belief in immortality and a heightened awareness of fellow beings.

SECTION ONE: STANZAS 1–4:

In Stanza 1, Wordsworth laments the fact that "There was a time when . . . every common sight/To me did seem/ Apparrelled in celestial light," but "these things which I have seen I now can see no more." The beauty and brilliance of nature and of heaven permeated the world for him and swelled his heart; but that occurs no more in adulthood.

Stanza 2 portrays the many natural beauties of the world. But as a man, although the poet still sees the "Rainbow" and the "Rose," their radiance is not as glorious, for "there hath passed away a glory from the earth." What is absent from the world is the "celestial light" (line 4) or the "visionary gleam" (57); these suggest remnants of his previous existence and his visionary experience, a feeling of divinity touching "every common sight."

Wordsworth adds to the mood by the sound and rhythm of his poem. The sounds of the words are beautiful and the rhythm is musical. The following words are excellent examples: "Apparelled," "glory," "freshness," "starry," "glorious," "joyous." The meter flows very smoothly, solidly iambic; for example:

> Apparelled in celestial light
>
> The Rainbow comes and goes
>
> The Moon doth with delight
>
> But yet I know, where'er I go

Another factor is the intricate balance between the long and short lines, creating a musical feeling. Also the rhyme scheme is varied.

In Stanzas 3 and 4 Wordsworth shows that nature rejoices, but that he feels melancholic. Notice the difference in the following lists:

Nature	The Poet
joyous song	a thought of grief
cataracts blow their trumpets	evil day
the earth is gay	sullen
jollity	something that is gone
heart of May	Where is it now?
holiday	
happy shepherd-boy	
jubilee	
festival	
coronal	
fullness of your bliss	
adorning	

A shout from a shepherd boy and the joy of animals and children in springtime make him feel once again "the fullness of [their] bliss." But nature imbues in him a counter-feeling, reminding him of "something that is gone." As he asks, "Whither is fled the visionary gleam?/Where is it now, the glory and the dream?" you should sense the disillusionment and melancholy in his tone.

SECTION TWO: STANZAS 5–8:

In Stanza 5 the poet articulates his dominant idea of the preexistence of the soul. "Our birth is but a sleep and a forgetting" because the soul eventually loses its attachment to heaven. Wordsworth presents this principle as an extended metaphor in which the span of human life from birth to maturity is compared to the first half of a day. The poet answers the questions posed at the end of Stanza 4. He presents a different conception of life, where, rather than daily life remaining most important to us and our other spiritual existence being "a sleep and a forgetting," here our birth into real, daily life is the "sleep and . . . forgetting" and the spiritual existence is most significant. When we come into this life we bring with us a sense of our former existence with its celestial light. "Heaven lies about us in our infancy" because the recently born child keeps a certain contact with heaven. But the child matures and the heavenly ties fade as the "prison-house" of daily life keeps him from remembering his background. "The Youth, who daily farther from the east/Must travel," leaves his birth (symbolized by east, where the "clouds of glory" or sunrise begins), but "still is Nature's priest," retaining a subconscious sense of the heavenly vision and extolling nature as he senses the divine presence. But as an adult, man forfeits his "visionary gleam" in the demanding light of pragmatic reality, "the light of common day." Upon losing this vision, we become more dependent upon the mortal light of this world, no longer the glory of sunrise but the glowing of midday.

In Stanza 6 Wordsworth metaphorically calls the earth a "homely Nurse," emphasizing that the child's real attachment belongs to another world as the earth becomes a surrogate mother, and terms the child a "Foster-child," underlining the loss of his origins in "that imperial palace" and the fact that he appears on earth only for a time. Man's true home is in this palace, in a state of union with God.

In Stanza 7 the child becomes immersed in the everyday affairs of the world ("the getting and spending" of which Wordsworth speaks in "The World Is Too Much with Us"). Eventually, the child is "Shaped by himself with newly-learned art," forced to change himself in the many roles life demands, a "little Actor." Even to the last, "down to palsied Age," life makes demands, "As if his whole vocation/Were endless imitation."

In Stanza 8 the poet states that the child is wiser than the man. Addressed as "thou," the child is depicted as a prophet, a seer, and a philosopher. In spite of his youth, the child has within him a gigantic soul. His wisdom stems from his divine attachments at the time of his birth; then he instinctively was cognizant of the eternal truths that man must search out during his lifetime. Maturing means a certain surrender to the world and a certain evanescence of those truths. The child is the "best Philosopher," an "Eye among the blind," because he still retains his divine heritage and vision: the intimations of immortality that he possesses grant to him an awareness of life's unknowns that as an adult he loses. Compared with man, the child has an instinctive insight that makes him "a Master o'er a Slave." Those life mysteries that men try feebly to comprehend are inherited by the child. Wordsworth questions why the child "with such earnest pains dost . . . provoke/The years to bring the inevitable yoke" of maturing, life's "earthly freight." In the concluding lines you should see another example of Wordsworth's power with images; here the "frost" of mature life clashes with the warmth and happiness of the May Day celebration. The actions, habits, and social demands of everyday life eliminate the blessed state of the child.

In the first two sections Wordsworth shows man as he slowly fades away from his recollections of immortality and questions what solace man can find during his life.

SECTION THREE: STANZAS 9–11:

In the last section Wordsworth answers the questions he has posed. Stanza 9 opens with a rapturous release of feelings. Although mature man misses his glimpses of immortality, his "embers" or remains of his earlier being burned away by daily life retain a dim memory of those years. He praises "the thought of our past years" for the "Perpetual benediction" that it brings; his intimations of immortality, even though dim and "fugitive" (recalling the prison image), are a constant blessing because they assure him of a return to a heavenly status. The past is not only a memory of happiness and freedom, but a source of "High instincts." These "shadowy recollections" produce "the fountain-light of all our day," a "master-light of all our seeing." This is the reservoir of our true understanding of life and our hope for immortality. With this illuminated memory, man can view the "noisy years" of life as only a small part of the grand scheme. No sadness or tragedy can dim the promise of this truth. In a wonderful contrast, Wordsworth states that, "Though inland far we be," apart from our sources of immortality, "Our souls have sight of that immortal sea." This stanza particularly demonstrates the poet's genius at developing ideas. The following list demonstrates the powerful contrasts that ebb and flow through the stanzas, as Wordsworth moves from the tribulations of day-to-day living to the brilliance of immortality.

Earthly Troubles
embers
fugitive
obstinate questionings
outward things
fallings
vanishings
blank misgivings
mortal Nature
listlessness
mad endeavour
abolish and destroy
inland far we be

Heavenly Prospects
Perpetual benediction
new-fledged hope
High instincts
fountain-light of all our day
master-light of all our seeing
eternal silence
truths that wake
a season of calm weather
sight of that immortal sea
Children sport upon the shore
hear the mighty waters rolling evermore

(You should consider making such lists of progressive ideas to help you explicate a poem.)

The poet did not create a "song of thanks and praise" to revel in "the simple creed of Childhood," but to praise an increasing awareness of the world. The "first affections" of the vague memories of preexistence will help to bring about immortality, but a man must also acquire, with maturity, the knowledge and wisdom to understand mankind and to adhere to the value of the human heart.

In Stanza 10, the poet asks "Birds," "Lambs," and other creatures of nature to rejoice in their natural state and to "Feel the gladness of the May!" Although the poet cannot recreate the radiance of his childhood, "Of splendour in the grass, of glory in the flower," he can instead find solace in his recognition of a "primal sympathy" in all of nature, in his acceptance of "human suffering," and "in the faith that looks through death."

The final stanza presents an apostrophe of nature as Wordsworth addresses its various aspects. Man's physical enjoyment of nature is replaced by a sober appreciation:

> Thanks to the human heart by which we live,
> Thanks to its tenderness, its joys, and fears,
> To me the meanest flower that blows can give
> Thoughts that do often lie too deep for tears.

Man clearly can learn from nature. Truly the "Child is father of the Man"; the mature man learns from the experiences of his earlier life; he is what childhood has made of him. Man desires to retain the natural wisdom of childhood.

In many ways, this ode manifests the best in poetry. You should discern the emotional force and imaginative power. The Ode's pantheistic credo enables the sensitive reader to be spiritually refreshed by Wordsworth's sense of the holiness of all natural things.

Blank Verse

Characteristics

Blank verse is unrhymed, but each line is basically iambic pentameter (˘ / ˘ / ˘ / ˘ / ˘/). Generally, we find this type used most often in plays, especially Shakespeare's. The tone of blank verse tends to be serious. Today, critics employ the term to include many unrhymed metric forms, where iambic pentameter occurs but not constantly.

Good blank verse is hard to write. The absence of rhyme seemingly would leave a great deal of latitude for the poet, but he must compensate for this in many other ways. The use of enjambement (run-on lines) and caesuras (pauses within a line) must be meticulously done. In addition, the form must accommodate many different emotions: humor, solemnity, happiness, melancholy, exaltation, condescension, praise, anger, and others.

In "Mending Wall" Robert Frost makes excellent use of blank verse to comment on a traditional way of looking at life. Using the common language of rural people, Frost establishes a dialogue between the speaker and his neighbor as they meet at a stone wall that serves as a boundary between their farms. Each is there, since it is spring, to mend the gaps made in their stone walls by winter's frost.

Analysis of "Mending Wall"

MENDING WALL
Robert Frost (1874–1963)

Something there is that doesn't love a wall,
That sends the frozen-ground-swell under it
And spills the upper boulders in the sun,
And makes gaps even two can pass abreast.
(5)   The work of hunters is another thing:
I have come after them and made repair
Where they have left not one stone on a stone,
But they would have the rabbit out of hiding,
To please the yelping dogs. The gaps I mean,
(10)   No one has seen them made or heard them made,
But at spring mending-time we find them there.
I let my neighbor know beyond the hill;
And on a day we meet to walk the line
And set the wall between us once again.
(15)   We keep the wall between us as we go.
To each the boulders that have fallen to each.
And some are loaves and some so nearly balls
We have to use a spell to make them balance:
"Stay where you are until our backs are turned!"
(20)   We wear our fingers rough with handling them.
Oh, just another kind of outdoor game,
One on a side. It comes to little more:
There where it is we do not need the wall:
He is all pine and I am apple orchard.
(25)   My apple trees will never get across
And eat the cones under his pines, I tell him.
He only says, "Good fences make good neighbors."
Spring is the mischief in me, and I wonder
If I could put a notion in his head:
(30)   "*Why* do they make good neighbors? Isn't it
Where there are cows? But here there are no cows."
Before I built a wall I'd ask to know
What I was walling in or walling out.
And to whom I was like to give offense.
(35)   Something there is that doesn't love a wall,
That wants it down. I could say "Elves" to him,
But it's not elves exactly, and I'd rather
He said it for himself. I see him there,
Bringing a stone grasped firmly by the top
(40)   In each hand, like an old-stone savage armed.
He moves in darkness, as it seems to me,
Not of woods only and the shade of trees.
He will not go behind his father's saying,
And he likes having thought of it so well
He says again, "Good fences make good neighbors."

The speaker contrasts two ways in which gaps are made in the wall. One is clearly stated in lines 5 to 7:

The work of hunters is another thing:
I have come after them and made repair
Where they have left not one stone on a stone

As they trail rabbits, the hunters scatter the stones recklessly. But the other source of gaps is presented as an ambiguity. Frost repeats the same line twice in the poem (1, 35) to emphasize it: "Something there is that doesn't love a wall."

By using the word "something" he creates a feeling of uncertainty that runs throughout the poem as the speaker shows us his view of human existence. You should look at the two implications; that the "something" is a part of nature or a part of man. These gaps appear mysteriously. "No one has seen them made or heard them made." On a literal level, the gaps could result from the winter frost that expands the wall and topples the "upper boulders." On a figurative level, the gaps could serve as an indication of something in human nature that tries to break down barriers, to create gaps in the walls that separate people and inhibit freedom and honesty.

To explore this idea you must look carefully at the character of the speaker. Look at these instances:

> 1.   Oh, just another kind of outdoor game,
>   One on a side. It comes to little more: (21–22)

Here the speaker demonstrates his wry, ironic attitude toward much of human action; it is a "game" with each person playing out a part. In this poem the contestants are the speaker and his neighbor as they argue about the wall.

> 2.   My apple trees will never get across
>   And eat the cones under his pines, I tell him.   (25–26)

The speaker possesses not only a sense of humor but also a subtle method of dealing with his neighbor.

> 3.   Before I built a wall I'd ask to know
>   What I was walling in or walling out,
>   And to whom I was like to give offense.   (32–34)

The speaker questions the value of erecting walls, often artificial, between human beings.

You should discern the attitude of the speaker toward his neighbor and toward his wall. The tone is very significant. Clearly he is critical, although tolerant; friendship and respect exist, although complete trust does not. The key to the relationship is the speaker's reaction to his neighbor's espousal of his father's epigram about boundaries between lands and people. "Good fences make good neighbors." Because his neighbor blindly accepts an existing custom or tradition and fails to modify it to suit new situations or relationships, the speaker deeply questions him:

> He moves in darkness, as it seems to me,
> Not of woods only and the shade of trees.   (41–42)

At one point he even describes his neighbor as an "old-stone savage," conjuring up the image of Stone Age man relying upon crude stone utensils for protection and living. The speaker finds this attachment inscrutable and by saying "He moves in darkness" implies that his neighbor lives in an ignorant, perhaps superstitious, and certainly backward way. When the neighbor refuses to budge from his position of supporting a tradition merely because it was handed down to him, the speaker is wryly amused.

The theme of the poem lies in the relationship between the two men. Neither will change his position. The neighbor, by insisting on maintaining the annual custom of mending the wall, shows his approach toward life to be inflexible, cautious, distrustful, and wary. The speaker, by preferring a humane and practical approach toward the stone wall, shows his approach toward life to be malleable, friendly, accepting, and open. In spite of the speaker's detailed philosophical questioning, the neighbor can only mimic the tradition of his father.

Frost, then, seems to imply many interrelated statements:

1. The wall could symbolize the ignorance of people in dealing with one another.
2. People must question existing customs and traditions to solve new problems and conditions.
3. People must question artificial barriers between themselves and others.
4. Only through questioning obstacles and developing understanding can human beings break down artificial barriers.
5. People must constantly try to illuminate themselves, to fight "darkness" and ignorance.
6. A person must recognize the value of past belief but must also question a blind acceptance of it.

The dramatic situation of the poem lends itself to interpreting the conflict of the two Yankee farmers on a far more universal level. The wall literally separates those two, but many walls figuratively separate all humanity.

Frost's use of blank verse is very effective here. The unrhymed lines and consistent meter lend themselves very well to the colloquial speech of the two farmers. Without being too repetitive, Frost is able to tie the poem together. Note the following:

1. Line 1 and line 35 are identical: "Something there is that doesn't love a wall."
2. Line 10 establishes a rhythm through repetition: "No one has seen them made or heard them made."
3. "The wall between" is repeated in lines 14 and 15, serving to emphasize the basic theme in the poem.
4. The advice of the neighbor's father, "Good fences make good neighbors" occurs twice (27, 45) to underscore the unflinching acceptance of the past tradition.

The poet employed the form perfectly to his purpose and to his advantage.

You could go one step further in discussing this poem. In many ways it is a paradox. Although the speaker seems to argue the removal of barriers, Frost, through the structure of this very poem, leaves the barriers between the two farmers unchanged. What does he imply by this?

Free Verse

Characteristics

Free verse or *vers libre* as it is sometimes called, is free from the limitations of fixed meter and rhyme; but this is not to say that it lacks poetic techniques. In fact its freedom allows the poet to pick and choose among many rhyming, metric, and language devices to develop each line successively. Free verse is very rhythmic, often patterned after the spoken word.

In the mid-1800s Walt Whitman introduced it extensively, and free verse has since grown in usage. Given the extreme mechanization and technology of the twentieth century, many modern poets turn to free verse in an effort to escape formal conventions and to give freedom and life to their poetry.

In free verse, the poet makes frequent use of such devices as image, symbol, internal rhyme, and figurative language. The difficulty of writing free verse lies in achieving unity within the poem, given the endless possibilities for developing the ideas. Deciding lines, grammar, and rhythm are formidable tasks. When the poet succeeds in gathering his/her resources to create a consistently unified poem, a great work develops. This characteristic of unit is what separates excellent from mediocre free verse poems.

Analysis of "Thirteen Ways of Looking at a Blackbird"

THIRTEEN WAYS OF LOOKING AT A BLACKBIRD
Wallace Stevens (1879–1955)

I
Among twenty snowy mountains,
The only moving thing
Was the eye of the blackbird.

II
I was of three minds,
Like a tree
In which there are three blackbirds.

III
The blackbird whirled in the autumn winds.
It was a small part of the pantomime.

IV
A man and a woman
Are one.
A man and a woman and a blackbird
Are one.

V
I do not know which to prefer,
The beauty of inflections
Or the beauty of innuendoes,
The blackbird whistling
Or just after.

VI
Icicles filled the long window
With barbaric glass.
The shadow of the blackbird
Crossed it, to and fro.
The mood
Traced in the shadow
An indecipherable cause.

VII

O thin men of Haddam,
Why do you imagine golden birds?
Do you not see how the blackbird
Walks around the feet
Of the women about you?

VIII

I know noble accents
And lucid, inescapable rhythms;
But I know, too,
That the blackbird is involved
In what I know.

IX

When the blackbird flew out of sight,
It marked the edge
Of one of many circles.

X

At the sight of blackbirds
Flying in a green light,
Even the bawds of euphony
Would cry out sharply.

XI

He rode over Connecticut
In a glass coach.
Once, a fear pierced him,
In that he mistook
The shadow of his equipage
For blackbirds.

XII

The river is moving.
The blackbird must be flying.

XIII

It was evening all afternoon.
It was snowing
And it was going to snow.
The blackbird sat
In the cedar-limbs.

Wallace Stevens's "Thirteen Ways of Looking at a Blackbird" is a problematic poem because of its many possible interpretations. This difficulty can be attributed to Stevens's mastery of images. Succinct and vivid, the images in this poem release the imagination to interpret each stanza separately and to gather the separate meanings into a whole. It is much like variations on a theme in music. The omniscient speaker, probably the poet himself, accomplishes two concurrent themes: he describes a series of scenes involving a blackbird (stanzas I, III, VI, IX, XII, and XIII) and reveals his attitude about some situations involving the blackbird (stanzas II, IV, V, VII, VIII, X, and XI).

As the speaker relates his attitudes in graphic images, the reader learns much about him and the situations and people that evoked his thoughts. He reports the condition of a group of "thin men," as he calls them; these poor souls are men who have no power of mind. The reason this situation exists is that they refuse to perceive the reality of their lives. Because of their imperception and insensitivity, these men will be forced to live a life in which their imaginations stagnate. To represent the reality (realities) that these shallow men fail to perceive, Stevens chooses something simple in nature, something seemingly insignificant in the scheme of the world, a blackbird.

This poem, then, is about thirteen ways of looking at a blackbird, or to translate this, thirteen ways of looking at reality. Stevens seems to imply that any real object in the world does not have a prescribed thirteen ways of looking at it or interpreting it. Rather, the number thirteen is an open-ended one that suggests that what one person sees as reality may not correspond exactly to what another person sees as reality. This difference is superficial so long as people seek out the real world and avoid living in a sheltered, unreal one. The poem, then, seems to be about ways of looking at reality, ways that, if people fail to observe them, can lead to a cold, sterile, meaningless life (as Stevens relates in the poem).

The speaker, the poet himself, is not one of the "thin men." He is not a poet who deals simply with mechanics and sounds that are pleasant rather than having significant meaning (what is called in the poem a "bawd of euphony"), but a poet who understands the necessity to recognize reality and then to order it with his imagination. The resultant frame of mind, the perception of reality tempered by an imaginative interpretation of it, is what Stevens calls in other poems the "Supreme Fiction," a form of poetry, to quote a title from another Stevens poem, wherein "reality is an Activity of the Most August Imagination." Basically, Stevens creates four poetic worlds:

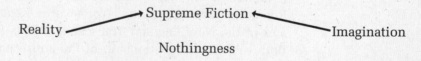

A poet can deal exclusively with reality or with imagination, but for Stevens neither by itself is suitable subject matter for poetry. What the poet needs to do is to select a real phenomenon in the world, interpret it in his own mind and imagination, and order it into poetry. This results in the Supreme Fiction. And the antithesis of the Supreme Fiction, a state of inertia and inactivity, figuratively the absence of either reality or imagination, is the world of Nothingness. Throughout the canon of Stevens's poetry, you can find individual poems that deal with each of the four realms.

To return to "Thirteen Ways," you should attempt to explicate the images in each stanza by itself, building toward an overall interpretation. The remainder of this discussion follows that format.

Stanza I: One method for the mind to encounter reality is to compare and contrast two phenomena in the real world. Here we have the blackbird set against mountains. They differ on several levels: the blackbird's eye moves while the mountains stand impassively; there are twenty mountains and only one blackbird; the mountains are covered with white snow while the bird is black. Rather than merely describe the mountains and the blackbird, Stevens presents a vivid image based on their differences. Stevens's graphic image invites differentiating real phenomena as one way of establishing reality.

The blackbird seems insignificant in this landscape, but an understanding of it and what it represents is integral to an understanding of life. By using this difference Stevens emphasizes the necessity to scrutinize life carefully to find meaning, order, and satisfaction.

Stanza II:　This problematic simile describes the mental state of the speaker. He ties his own openness to different interpretations ("I was of three minds") to the blackbird. For every real event, every blackbird, so to speak, any person can have a separate interpretation. He seems to be underlining the myriad minds in existence or the ways of looking at one real event available to anyone.

Stanza III:　Both the blackbird (symbol for reality) and the "autumn winds" (symbol of the passing of the summer, the movement of seasons, the running of time) are only "a small part of the pantomime" of all of nature. Any event or person is related to the whole pattern by nature. The great word here is "pantomime," a performance in which a whole story is told only through bodily and facial movements. In other words, the blackbird whirling in the autumn winds is really only a small part of the whole show of nature; its seeming insignificance is overcome when it is considered part of the whole.

Similarly, one event or occurrence in a person's life may not seem meaningful. But when it is considered as part of the whole, as a happening that helps to shape the composite person, it has meaning. Stevens seems to be urging the reader to try to discover and to realize the significance of all events, no matter how small, to his/her life. All reality is important.

Stanza IV:　Stanza IV follows Stanza III in establishing the relationship of many aspects of nature. The acceptance of a man and a woman as a unified whole should lead to an inclusion of other aspects of the real world into that unified whole. Hence a man and a woman and a blackbird (or any natural phenomena) are one, also. This idea is reminiscent of the pantheistic creed of the Romantic poets in England (Wordsworth, Keats, Coleridge, Shelley, and others) and of the New England Transcendentalists (Emerson, Thoreau, and others). Both see an interrelationship of the entire natural world; human beings and nature possess a unity or oneness.

On another level Stevens could be suggesting that the unity a man and a woman can achieve will not remain a wholeness or oneness unless they reach out beyond their immediate ties to interpret and to incorporate the real world (the blackbird) around them into their relationship. People should relate to all things.

In another poem Stevens considers life to be a search for an apprehension of order.

> To impose is not
> To discover. To discover an order as of
> A season, to discover summer and know it.
> To discover winter and know it well, to find,
> Not to impose, not to have reasoned at all,
> Out of nothing to have come on major weather,
> It is possible, possible, possible. It must
> Be possible. It must be that in time
> The real will from its crude compoundings come.

The blackbird, "the real," no matter if it is a "small part of the pantomime," is part of an order, and a person must search relentlessly for that order to make the real "from its crude compoundings come."

Stanza V: The indecision of the speaker, in choosing between the blackbird whistling and the period just after, is significant because both events possess "beauty." By "inflections" he means the delightful music of the blackbird whistling, and by "innuendoes" he means the pleasing hints of the whistling as one plays it back in the mind. As an analogy, you could consider a great symphony while it is played. You directly perceive its "inflections," you find beauty and majesty and satisfaction in the music; but when it ends and you think of or play back the music in your own mind, the "innuendoes" are just as beautiful as the real experience. Which do you prefer?

In other words, people should seek out real and vital experiences with reality and think about them while they occur. But a person must also realize the significance and importance of the meditation over the meaning of those experiences for his/her life. Thus the real sounds of the blackbird and the reflection on those sounds are both pleasurable to the speaker, and he does not know which to prefer. Simply speaking, the real world and an imagined world have separate but equal attractions.

Although the world of meditation does not possess the power of immediacy that the world of reality does, it, too, can inspire beauty. Consider this passage from Keats's "Ode on a Grecian Urn":

> Heard melodies are sweet, but those unheard
> Are sweeter; therefore, ye soft pipes, play on;
> Not to the sensual ear, but, more endeared,
> Pipe to the spirit ditties of no tone

For Keats the perception of beauty is transitory. The permanent source of joy comes with the ideal embodiment of that moment in art. In this poem and in "Ode to a Nightingale," Keats searches to achieve a timeless world. And although he believes in the immortality of ideal beauty, he also loves the ecstasy of the actual moment. As he says in "Ode to a Nightingale":

> Still thou wouldst sing, and I have ears in vain—
> To thy high requiem become a sod.

Despite the efforts of his fancy, he still remains in the world of time. Both Keats and Stevens are acutely aware of the dilemma of the beauty of the moment and the beauty of reflection upon it.

Stanza VI: In this stanza reality is obscured as only the shadow of the blackbird and not the blackbird itself can be seen. Whereas in Stanza V the blackbird was the cause of the beauties and the speaker did not know which aspect of the beauty to prefer, here the bird is remote. The tone of the stanza is dissatisfaction and fear as reality is obfuscated by the "icicles" in the "long windows." Stevens affixes the adjective "barbaric" to the icicles, heightening his tone and accentuating their sharpness and danger. In the winter landscape in Stanza I, nature is frozen and impassive, and the reality of the bird is intangible. A cold, thoughtless, transient life is anathema to Stevens. In many of his poems, he symbolizes the state of nothingness with ice and snow.

> For the listener, who listens in the snow,
> And nothing himself, beholds
> Nothing that is not there and the nothing that is.

This excerpt from "The Snow Man" reveals the impoverished world of no feeling and no activity that Stevens detests. This nothingness hinders the apprehension of reality, in this case the blackbird, thus its resignation to an "indecipherable cause."

Stanza VII: The speaker addresses his questions to the "thin men of Haddam." Haddam is a suburban town in Connecticut, not far from Stevens's home in Hartford. He characterized Haddam in another poem, "The River of Rivers in Connecticut":

> The river is fateful,
> Like the last one. But there is no ferry man.
> He could not bend against its propelling force.
> It is not to be seen beneath the appearances
> That tell of it. The steeple at Farmington
> Stands glistening and Haddam shines and sways.

The river, given additional meaning with the allusion to the river Styx in Dante's *Inferno,* in its sad omnipotence seems to nourish Haddam, the home of the "thin men" doomed to a life in which the imagination dies.

The poet wants to know why the "thin men" are so caught up in their pursuit of the ideal (the "golden birds") that they miss the availability of the real (the "blackbird"). The golden birds symbolize an abstract concept of reality, whereas the blackbird represents a concrete notion of reality.

Stevens's use of the word "thin" to describe the inhabitants of Haddam could be a statement of the meager quality of their minds. They miss the obvious—the blackbird "Walks around the feet" of their women. (Significantly, they fail to grasp the attachment of the blackbird to the women, showing the "thin men" are so involved with their own dreams of success that they cannot see the reality of the blackbird or the sensuality of the women. Recall Stanza IV, where "a man and a woman and a blackbird/Are one." Clearly the "thin men" of Haddam have no chance of attaining the unity of being possible to any person who perceives reality.)

It may be more than foolish conjecture to say that Stevens anticipated the growing image of the suburban stereotype with its plastic life and porcelain emotions, so familiar to the 1960s, 1970s, and 1980s, and so often a target of the acerbic pen of contemporary writers. Pursuing inane and material goals, dreaming of unobtainable "golden birds," impervious to the realities around them, these "thin men" lack the perspicacity and foresight to perceive the reality of their shallow lives.

On an artistic plane of interpretation, Stevens may be referring to the necessity to integrate a firm apprehension of reality with a subtle usage of imagination. One must first perceive reality, then order it, shape it, structure it with the imagination before it reaches the heights of art. As mentioned earlier, Stevens calls this infinite expression of an infinite reality the "Supreme Fiction" (fully developed in his poem "Notes Toward a Supreme Fiction"). Poetry, Stevens argues, is an apprehension of order. You should sense the undercurrent of a poem about poetry running through "Thirteen Ways."

Stanza VIII: The speaker recognizes and somewhat applauds certain devices employed by artists, particularly poets with their "noble accents/And lucid, inescapable rhythms." But this alone is not enough to evolve good art. The speaker knows of another factor: "the blackbird is involved/In what I know"; that is, artists must choose their material from the real world before tempering it with their imagination. If they are not involved with reality, they may slip into obscure separation from their contemporaries, rendering their art recondite, esoteric, and unavailable to the world. An artist cannot live entirely within the confines of his/her own imagination.

Stanza IX: Although the mind has the capability to perceive nature, the mind has limits. Because human beings are imperfect, human efforts to understand the complexities of life will never be fully achieved. The enclosed circles could represent this limitation to human knowledge. The blackbird "flew out of sight"; its circle is all that people know about it. But the blackbird's leaving "marked the edge of one of many circles." Different people have different limitations on their knowledge (just as they have different ways of apprehending reality). The fact that there are limits is no excuse for people to be satisfied with minimal knowledge. The more we search in reality, the more we will learn, the bigger the circle will become. Hence, the blackbird represents many things to many people and "marks the edge of one of many circles." If we work at interacting with reality, the potentials will increase.

Stanza X: Stevens characteristically employs colors to symbolize his four poetic realms. Usually blue means Imagination, green means Reality, white means Nothingness, and purple means the Supreme Fiction. In this stanza he emphasizes the blackbird as a symbol of reality by declaring that

> At the sight of blackbirds
> Flying in a green light,
> Even the bawds of euphony
> Would cry out sharply.

A bawd is a panderer or prostitute. Euphony (as opposed to cacophony) is the mixing of sounds to produce a pleasing effect. Perhaps Stevens makes a pun on "bard" (in modern use, another word for poet) to emphasize that the "bawds of euphony" create their own pleasant sounding but meagerly meaningful verse of, as stated in Stanza VIII, "noble accents/And lucid, inescapable rhythms." But if these half-poets were to be shaken by the sight of a blackbird in a green light, figuratively reality squared, or a powerful happening in the real world, they would "cry out sharply" in a moment of realization that all poetry must have as its goal the presentation and interpretation of reality and not merely a pleasing conglomeration of rhyme, meter, and rhythm. The light that tracks the blackbird is mental as well as physical illumination. Perhaps the sight of the blackbird in a "green light" would shock even the "thin men," forcing them out of their world of delusions and "golden" dreams.

Stanza XI: A single man, possibly one of the "thin men of Haddam," rides in a "glass coach," an image of rising technology. (Considering this poem was written in 1917, the image is particularly apt.) The interesting point about this gentleman is that he cannot distinguish between the "shadow of his equipage" and "blackbirds." His mistaken identification further emphasizes his inability and the inability of people like him to perceive reality. In a way reminiscent of the "barbaric glass" in Stanza VI (where the blackbird was obscured from reality and only its shadow visible through the icy glass), Stevens again creates an image of the shallow person who cannot recognize the reality of his/her life. In fact, the man in the poem fears reality, "a fear pierced him," for it would prevent him from leading a life of self-delusion.

What it does leave for the "thin men" and (tying both levels of the poem together) for the half-poets ("bawds of euphony") is a world isolated from reality and imagination. This is the world of Nothingness, an impoverished world where lack of feeling and lack of deep living go on. Throughout his poetry Stevens uses the color white, the symbol glass, the season winter to represent this realm. In this poem you find all three, in stanzas I, VI, XI, and XIII.

Stanza XII: All nature, perhaps symbolized by the river, does not stand still. Time moves on, and man must perceive the realities in his world before they depart. "The blackbird must be flying": reality must move on, for man seems to have failed to grasp the tangible aspects of the natural world. He too easily returns to his insouciant, indifferent life: his chance to experience this particular aspect of reality has come and has gone.

Stanza XIII: The autumn of Stanza III here turns to winter. The snow, static on the mountains in Stanza I, now begins to fall. Because man missed his chance to grasp the reality of the blackbird, the world of Nothingness prevails. The blackbird, flying into man's life, so to speak, giving him the opportunity to apprehend a real moment, now departs and silently sits in the "cedar-limbs" apart from humanity. Stevens emphasizes the dreary results of the world minus reality by two excellent devices. One is the paradox of "It was evening all afternoon." Night, the time of darkness and of sight cut off by the absence of light (physical and mental illumination), predominates in the scene, casting a grim shadow over the light of day because man failed to encounter the blackbird. The other is the repetition of the snowfall: "It was snowing/And it was going to snow." Stevens underlines the permanence of the snow, suggesting that for this period of time man had failed to interact with reality and to escape his limitations. The poet, disturbed at human indifference and illusions, watches reality evanesce into the dark cold of night as the blackbird retreats.

Although this is a grim outlook on the human condition and seems to represent a frequent occurrence, Stevens leaves one note of hope, and perhaps of warning. Even though the blackbird retreated to the "cedar-limbs," rendered invisible by the falling snow, it did not flee the landscape altogether. The poet might be implying that human beings miss much of the reality of their lives, but given the constant nature of reality, it could appear again to give them another chance. The poet pleads with the reader not to miss the opportunity as the "thin men" or the "bawds of euphony" did.

Conclusion: Wallace Stevens very carefully fits his style to the subject. The succinct, vivid images are matched by the tight, brief stanza constructions. Free verse is appropriate for the wide range of images and observations; since each is different, a different construction is necessary. This style provides the poet with the necessary format for the rapidly changing objects of consideration in the poem—the blackbird, the speaker, nature, art (more specifically, poetry), certain men, and all humanity in general. As he combines terse statement with vibrant image, you should react to each of the thirteen stanzas. The word "blackbird" appears in every stanza, reinforcing the idea of thirteen ways of looking at it and at what it symbolizes. The poem possesses an essential unity.

The theme of the poem runs concurrently on two tracks. On the one hand, Stevens urges man to recognize the necessity of apprehending the reality of his life so that he can order it, understand it, and enjoy it. On the other hand, Stevens implies that all poetry or art must attempt to create order, and the poet or artist accomplishes this by coming to grips with the real world and by structuring the perceived reality with his/her imagination. The thirteen stanzas, interdependent but unified, are ramifications and variations of these themes.

Analysis of "Dream Deferred"

DREAM DEFERRED
Langston Hughes (1902–1967)

What happens to a dream deferred?
Does it dry up
Like a raisin in the sun?
Or fester like a sore—
And then run?

Does it stink like rotten meat?
Or crust and sugar over—
Like a syrupy sweet?

Maybe it just sags
Like a heavy load.

Or does it explode?

"Dream Deferred," the famous poem by Langston Hughes, is an excellent example of developing ideas in free verse through metaphor and simile. In the well-known play, *A Raisin in the Sun,* Lorraine Hansberry chose this poem as an epigraph for the play, because the theme of deferred dreams and ideas lost or tarnished by years of desire unsatisfied dominates the play.

Hughes answers the question "What happens to a dream deferred?" in five similes. Each of these powerful images produces a different meaning and impact. "Does it dry up/Like a raisin in the sun?" recalls the once fecund grape, a passionate, voluptuous fruit, now desiccated. Original promises of dreams create happy and jocund feelings, but failure to deliver the promises eventually causes the dreamer to become moribund and listless. The simile "fester like a sore—/And then run" summons up a picture of a flayed, open wound never healed. A dream put off eventually turns to bitterness and despair. "Does it stink like rotten meat?" triggers associations of poverty, garbage, and malodorous trash, phenomena common to ghetto blacks. The idea "crust and sugar over—/Like a syrupy sweet" conjures feelings of staleness, hardness; a once attractive candy no longer appetizes. The promise of dreams unfulfilled leaves the dreamer bitter, with a hard, crass, tough exterior frequently evident in his/her dealings with others. "Maybe it just sags/Like a heavy load" recreates the onus of black slaves pushed too hard, beyond their virile capacities.

But it is the last line, italicized for emphasis, that elevates the poem into a dynamic warning to the oppressor. By continually making false promises and creating dreams and illusions, a society stands in danger of having the impatient dreamers explode into frantic and frenetic action to snatch their dreams. Blacks grow tired of waiting for the promises and hopes of freedom, of equality, of a better life. The dream has been deferred since 1865; how long can an oppressed people wait for salvation?

The poem "Dream Deferred" is not restricted to a particular time or context, although quite clearly Hughes speaks of the ugly and unjust conditions of blacks. This poem should stand the test of time; its message is appropriate for the experience of any culture or civilization. Of course, the idea of a deferred promise exploding in the face of procrastinating societies is a powerful, devastating notion. Hughes creates an image that is a prominent and permanent expression of the black experience and of human experience in general.

The Dramatic Monologue

Characteristics

Another form of the lyric, the dramatic monologue, was brought to great heights by the Victorian poet Robert Browning. As the title suggests, it is a poem told by one speaker about a significant event. Several qualities exist in the form:

1. The speaker reveals in his/her own words some dramatic situation in which he/she is involved.
2. The speaker demonstrates his/her character through the poem.
3. The speaker addresses a listener who does not engage in dialogue but helps to develop the speech.

We enter the psyche of the speaker, and the skillful poet makes much of his/her own nature, attitudes, and circumstances available in words to the reader who discerns the implications of the poem.

The dramatic monologue differs from a soliloquy in a play in that, in drama, time and place are developed before the character ascends the stage alone to make his/her remarks, whereas the dramatic monologue by itself establishes time, place, and character.

Analysis of "Ulysses"

ULYSSES
Alfred, Lord Tennyson (1809–1892)

It little profits that an idle king,
By this still hearth, among these barren crags,
Matched with an aged wife, I mete and dole
Line   Unequal laws unto a savage race,
(5)   That hoard, and sleep, and feed, and know not me.
I cannot rest from travel; I will drink
Life to the lees. All times I have enjoyed
Greatly, have suffered greatly, both with those
That loved me, and alone; on shore, and when
(10)   Through scudding drifts the rainy Hyades
Vexed the dim sea. I am become a name;
For always roaming with a hungry heart
Much have I seen and known—cities of men
And manners, climates, councils, governments,
(15)   Myself not least, but honoured of them all—
And drunk delight of battle with my peers,
Far on the ringing plains of windy Troy.
I am a part of all that I have met;
Yet all experience is an arch wherethrough

(20)   Gleams that untraveled world whose margin fades
        Forever and forever when I move.
        How dull it is to pause, to make an end,
        To rust unburnished, not to shine in use!
        As though to breathe were life! Life piled on life
(25)   Were all too little, and of one to me
        Little remains; but every hour is saved
        From that eternal silence, something more,
        A bringer of new things; and vile it were
        For some three suns to store and hoard myself,
(30)   And this grey spirit yearning in desire
        To follow knowledge like a sinking star,
        Beyond the utmost bound of human thought.

        This is my son, mine own Telemachus,
        To whom I leave the scepter and the isle—
(35)   Well-loved of me, discerning to fulfill
        This labour, by slow prudence to make mild
        A rugged people, and through soft degrees
        Subdue them to the useful and the good.
        Most blameless is he, centered in the sphere
(40)   Of common duties, decent not to fail
        In offices of tenderness, and pay
        Meet adoration to my household gods,
        When I am gone. He works his work, I mine.

        There lies the port; the vessel puffs her sail;
(45)   There gloom the dark, broad seas. My mariners,
        Souls that have toiled, and wrought, and thought with me—
        That ever with a frolic welcome took
        The thunder and the sunshine, and opposed
        Free hearts, free foreheads—you and I are old;
(50)   Old age hath yet his honour and his toil.
        Death closes all; but something ere the end,
        Some work of noble note, may yet be done.
        Not unbecoming men that strove with Gods.
        The lights begin to twinkle from the rocks;
(55)   The long day wanes; the slow moon climbs; the deep
        Moans round with many voices. Come, my friends,
        'Tis not too late to seek a newer world.
        Push off, and sitting well in order smite
        The sounding furrows; for my purpose holds
(60)   To sail beyond the sunset, and the baths
        Of all the western stars, until I die.
        It may be that the gulfs will wash us down;
        It may be we shall touch the Happy Isles,
        And see the great Achilles, whom we knew.
(65)   Though much is taken, much abides; and though
        We are not now that strength which in old days
        Moved earth and heaven, that which we are, we are—
        One equal temper of heroic hearts,
        Made weak by time and fate, but strong in will
(70)   To strive, to seek, to find, and not to yield.

In his dramatic monologue, Tennyson interprets the myth of Ulysses. Dante, Shakespeare, Joyce, and many others have recast the role of the legendary hero. Interpretations have varied, from Dante's condemnation of him to the circles of hell as a symbol of overreaching pride and ambition, to Tennyson's espousal of him as a symbol of the human desires for experience, physical prowess, courage, adventure, and knowledge.

You must establish the dramatic situation. Ulysses is now an elderly king as he addresses the people of Ithaca. He is about to set off again in quest of great adventures and plans to leave the management of the kingdom to his son Telemachus. To establish the character of the speaker, consider the following excerpts.

> I will drink/Life to the lees (6–7)

Ulysses is an active, vibrant human being who wants to experience as much as possible in life. He wants to move out into realms of the unknown in an effort to live life to the fullest and to increase the knowledge of all people.

> It little profits that an idle king
> . . . mete and dole
> Unequal laws unto a savage race. (1–4)

Ulysses plans to leave Ithaca because he feels no challenge in the calm, rustic routine of slowly building a society from a backward nation.

> I am a part of all that I have met (18)

Ulysses is inextricably linked to the past experiences that built his fame: "I am become a name." He needs to reach out into experience, to sail again the seas of the unknown and to grow even more. His past shaped his present character.

> How dull it is to pause, to make an end,
> To rust unburnished, not to shine in use! (22–23)

For him to stand is tantamount to an admission that his abilities have died. He must set out again on a quest.

> . . . Life piled on life
> Were all too little, and of one to me
> Little remains (24–26)

Even one lifetime cannot contain his infinite energies and desires.

> And this grey spirit yearning in desire
> To follow knowledge like a sinking star (30–31)

Even in his old age Ulysses' spirit still yearns to uncover new lands and to explore new vistas of human life.

> 'Tis not too late to seek a newer world (57)

For Ulysses, human beings must never surrender their spirit of exploration and their desire for knowledge.

> Though much is taken, much abides (65)

In spite of the many victories he has won, there are always more awaiting the adventurous person.

> To strive, to seek, to find, and not to yield. (70)

This famous closing line of the poem has become a credo for all that is great in human fortitude and strength.

In direct contrast to Ulysses is his son Telemachus. Tennyson purposely establishes this contrast to represent two separate ways of life. Ulysses, as is quite obvious above, represents the heroic vision of the explorer. But Telemachus, of whom his father says, "He works his work, I mine," represents a different but in many ways equally important role in life. The hero can seek out new experiences, but his constant wanderings leave him little time to contemplate the meaning of his discoveries, to discern what societal benefits they may reap. Telemachus is the thoughtful man of society who places its well being above his own. He can face the daily challenge of dealing with an unenlightened race in an attempt to build a culture and a civilization. Telemachus possesses a "slow prudence to make mild/A rugged people, and through soft degrees/Subdue them to the useful and the good" (36–38). He has "tenderness" coupled with a strength to deal with "common duties."

In this poem Tennyson clearly sides with the individual who seeks personal actualization rather than social involvement. But this is not to condemn the value of either goal. In fact, the biographical fact that Tennyson wrote this poem after the death of his close friend Arthur Hallam in an attempt to emphasize the need to go forward and brave the struggle of life makes his meaning and intention clear.

The many lines that have universal significance (6–7, 11–12, 24–26, 31–32, 70) reflect the poet's desire to have his speaker relate the value of the heroic way of life. His tone of commitment to his ideals and of lofty aspirations serves to enhance the poem.

The Elegy

Characteristics

During the Classical Age in Greece the elegy took on a specific form (couplets in metric unison) to deal with the poet's attitude not only about death, but also about life and love. Now the term refers specifically to poems that mourn the death of an individual, the absence of something deeply loved, or the transcience of mankind.

A form of the lyric, the poem has a solemn, dignified tone as it laments the loss of something dear to the poet or to man.

A particular subset is the Pastoral Elegy, a mourning poem with a joyous ending. The format involves a shepherd set in a pastoral world, a rustic, fertile environment marked by eternal summer and fecund nature. Among the more famous ones are Milton's "Lycidas" and Shelley's "Adonais."

Analysis of "Elegy for Jane"

ELEGY FOR JANE
My Student, Thrown by a Horse
Theodore Roethke (1908–1963)

I remember the neckcurls, limp and damp as tendrils;
And her quick look, a sidelong pickerel smile;
And how, once startled into talk, the light syllables leaped for her,
Line   And she balanced in the delight of her thought,
(5)   A wren, happy, tail into the wind,

Her song trembling the twigs and small branches.
The shade sang with her;
The leaves, their whispers turned to kissing;
And the mold sang in the bleached valleys under the rose.

(10)   Oh, when she was sad, she cast herself down into such a pure depth,
Even a father could not find her;
Scraping her cheek against straw;
Stirring the clearest water.

My sparrow, you are not here,
(15)   Waiting like a fern, making a spiny shadow.
The sides of wet stones cannot console me
Nor the moss, wound with the last light.

If only I could nudge you from this sleep
My maimed darling, my skittery pigeon.
(20)   Over this damp grave I speak the words of my love:
I, with no rights in this matter
Neither father nor lover.

Roethke's elegy is a unique one, both in subject and in form. He accomplishes several statements in the poem: a penetrating look into the speaker's intense feelings and emotions; a sensitive tribute for the fresh personality and endearing character of a dead young woman; and a poignant lament for the loss of this lovely, energetic person.

He indicates the passage of time by moving from a recollection of what his student was like to a presentation of grief over her death. He chooses deeply connotative words to describe the paradox he feels: words of death and gloom to convey the melancholy about her loss, and words of action and youth to convey the ebullience of her life.

Death	Life
limp, damp (1)	neckcurls (1)
shade (7)	tendrils (1)
mold (9)	quick look (2)
bleached valleys (9)	pickerel smile (2)
sad (10)	light syllables (3)
scraping (12)	delight (4)
spiny shadow (15)	happy wren (5)
wet stones (16)	trembling song (6)
moss (17)	leaves . . . kissing (8)
last light (17)	clearest water (13)
sleep (18)	sparrow (14)
damp grave (20)	fern (15)
maimed darling (19)	skittery pigeon (19)

The series of bird metaphors stands as one of the central devices in the poem. The movement from "wren" to "sparrow" to "skittery pigeon" accomplishes many basic thematic purposes. The changes reveal the depth of the speaker's feelings for the girl, and the gentle comparisons help to define these deep feelings. Each metaphor by itself might be inappropriate, but the entire series is provocative.

Roethke employs antithesis on several levels in the poem; sharply contrasted ideas are presented in parallel form. Here we find life and death, action and stasis, melancholy and elation. Certainly he feels that Jane was a special human being, as is indicated by his use of the bird metaphors and nature images (e.g., "shade," "leaves," "mold," "wet stones," and "moss") to suggest the two poles of the series of antitheses.

The thrust of the poem involves the speaker's attitude toward Jane. He expresses this on three levels: his deep feelings for his student; his intense insight into her nature; and his emotional response to her death. The closing of the poem expresses his futility: in spite of his affection for her and his knowledge of her, he has "no rights in this matter," for he is "Neither father nor lover." But he can speak the "words of [his] love" by an elegiac tribute to Jane, his student, thrown by a horse, robbed of life in an accident that underlines her very aliveness.

The Villanelle

Characteristics

Although a highly specialized form, the villanelle is a difficult kind of poem to write without seeming trite or repetitive. A French verse form, the poem has 19 lines divided into 5 tercets and 1 quatrain. Two rhymes or repeated lines predominate. With the rhyme scheme *aba aba aba aba aba abaa*, line 1 is repeated exactly in lines 6, 12, and 18, while line 3 is repeated exactly in lines 9, 15, and 19.

Although originally a light, pastoral verse, the villanelle has been used by modern poets to outstanding effect.

Analysis of "Do Not Go Gentle into That Good Night"

DO NOT GO GENTLE INTO THAT GOOD NIGHT
Dylan Thomas (1914–1953)

Do not go gentle into that good night,
Old age should burn and rave at close of day;
(3) Rage, rage against the dying of the light.

Though wise men at their end know dark is right,
Because their words had forked no lightning they
(6) Do not go gentle into that good night.

Good men, the last wave by, crying how bright
Their frail deeds might have danced in a green bay,
(9) Rage, rage against the dying of the light.

Wild men who caught and sang the sun in flight,
And learn, too late, they grieved it on its way,
(12) Do not go gentle into that good night.

Grave men, near death, who see the blinding sight
Blind eyes could blaze like meteors and be gay,
(15) Rage, rage against the dying of the light.

And you, my father, there on the sad height,
Curse, bless, me now with your fierce tears, I pray.
Do not go gentle into that good night.
(19) Rage, rage against the dying of the light.

Thomas's villanelle "Do Not Go Gentle into That Good Night" is such a flashing amalgam of rhyme, rhythm, and meaning that he completely escapes what could be a crippling adherence to the rigorous demand of the poetic form.

Look at the poem prosodically. The meter is predominantly iambic, although Thomas substitutes trochees for emphasis (lines 1, 5, 10, 13) as well as spondees ("Rage, rage" appears throughout the poem and begins many lines.) The entire poem is developed around the rhymes of -ight and -ăy. He follows perfectly the aba aba aba aba aba abaa scheme. The alternating lines of refrain are "Do not go gentle into that good night" (1, 6, 12, 18) and "Rage, rage against the dying of the light" (3, 9, 15, 19). These refrains serve a specific purpose: not only do they unify and bring the poem together, but they also underline the basic theme that no one should accept death "gently" but rather wage a battle, "burn and rave," against it. Of course, the repetitions of the refrains lend an abundance of internal rhyme to the poem. But even the other lines deal with a variety of sound effects.

Assonance:

Line 2	age, rave, day
4	wise, right
7	by, crying, bright
8	deeds, green
11	late, they, way
13	men, death; blinding, sight
14	Blind, eyes, like; meteors, be; blaze, gay
17	me, fierce, tears

Consonance:

Line 2	old, should, day; burn, rave
4	their, dark, right
5	their, words, forked; Because, words
7	crying, bright
8	Their, frail, green
10	caught, flight
11	learn, grieved; late, it, its
13	Grave, near; death, with
14	Blind, blaze, like; eyes, blaze, meteors
16	father, there
17	Curse, bless, fierce, tears

Alliteration:

Line 1	go, good
5	their, they
7	by, bright
8	deeds, danced
10	sang, sun
11	learn, late
14	Blind, blaze, be
16	there, the

Onomatopoeia:

Line 1   gentle
     2   rave
     3   dying
     5   forked no lightning
     7   bright
    10   flight
    11   grieved
    14   blaze like meteors
    17   fierce tears

For Thomas a victory of sounds! Note how the consonant sounds (the heavy, dolorous *r*'s) seem to capture death, while the assonance sounds (the bright, long vowels, *a, i, e,*) seem to emphasize living. Truly an amazing accomplishment!

In Stanza 1 Thomas urges that in spite of old age man should never give up his life; he should fight ("rage") against the coming of death ("the dying of the light"). Then he addresses different types of men:

Stanza 2—"wise men"	Stanza 5—"Grave men"
Stanza 3—"Good men"	Stanza 6—his own father
Stanza 4—"Wild men"	

The "wise men" know "dark is right"; they sense the inevitability of death. However, because "their words had forked no lightning," because they have not made an impression on their world, they will not stop fighting death and they "Do not go gentle into that good night."

The "good men" are confident about their accomplishments on a personal level. They need not be judged by all of mankind (symbolically the "wave" of humanity) when they can find satisfaction in being judged on a smaller scale (the "green bay"). They will not give up life but "Rage, rage against the dying of the light."

Even the "wild men" who forsake responsibility and spend their time in senseless endeavors (catching and singing "the sun in flight") gain awareness that they must take up the battle against death to preserve their free spirits.

And even the "grave men, near death" realize that they have led too sad and serious a life, and hope for a flicker of joy (wishing their "Blind eyes could blaze like meteors and be gay") before death and therefore are willing to fight it.

With that in mind the poet urges his father, "there on the sad height," not to give up his fight for life. He emphasizes this by having both refrains that urge a maintaining of the life spirit modify his father, whereas the other men have only one refrain. Actually, Thomas wrote his poem at a time in his life when he believed his father was near death.

The villanelle, on a larger level, urges all men to experience life to its fullest before it slips away. The poet accomplishes this theme, as stated before, through rhyme, and also through imagery.

Dark or Night Images (Death)	Light Images (Life)
"good night" (1)	"burn and rave" (2)
"close of day" (2)	"rage" (3)
"dying of the light" (3)	"lightning" (5)
"dark" (4)	"bright" (7)
"good night" (6)	"sun in flight" (10)
"dying of the light" (9)	"rage" (9)
"good night" (12)	"see with blinding sight" (13)
"Grave," "death" (13)	"blaze like meteors" (14)
"Blind eyes" (14)	"rage" (15)
"dying of the light" (15)	"rage" (18)
"sad height" (16)	
"Curse" (17)	
"good night" (18)	
"dying of the light" (19)	

Thomas brings the sounds, rhymes, and images of his poem together in a complete, very effective way.

Poetry in Translation

Traditionally, the poetry read and studied in AP English is British, Irish, and American. It won't surprise you, however, that this so-called "canon" of poetry represents but a fraction of the output of the world's poets. Consequently, you should be aware of some of the outstanding poets from non-English-speaking countries whose poetry has been translated into English.

Translations of poems present numerous problems to serious readers. First of all, you can never be sure that the translator has accurately represented the original work. A good translator tries to duplicate all that a poet has done, but differences between languages often make the task next to impossible. All languages contain extraordinary subtleties of meaning and expression distinctive only to themselves. Many metaphors and similies don't translate well, if at all. An original poem is a unique work of art, and tampering with it in the slightest way—even changing a single word—will necessarily alter it. The limits of the translator's language may force him into choosing less-than-accurate words and expressions. Or when he aims to create a carbon copy of the original, he may find himself resorting to awkward and ill-sounding phrases in English.

Writing a poem in one's own language is a complex task involving innumerable choices of subject matter, style, tone, structure, diction, sound, rhythm and even the appearance of the poem on the page. Translating a poem respecting all these elements can be a daunting challenge. Although respecting the sound is probably the most difficult because of differences between languages, translators often devise ways to bend and manipulate English to their bidding. Where there should be no flexibility, though, is in maintaining the essential meaning of the poem. To alter meaning for the sake of beauty, musicality, accessibility, or any other aim is a disservice to both the poet and the reader.

Ideally, a student of literature should be able to read poetry and prose in the language in which it was written. (Literary history, incidentally, is full of examples of dedicated scholars who actually learned Latin in order to read Virgil in the original, or studied German in order to read Goethe, or Russian to read Dostoevsky.) Barring your taking the time to learn a new language, you must depend on the integrity of translators for meaningful encounters with poetic works from other countries.

ODE TO THE AMERICAS
Pablo Neruda (1904–1973)

To enter the world of this work, you should probably know a few basic facts about Pablo Neruda, the Chilean, Nobel Prize-winning poet. During the 1930s, Neruda spent time in Spain, where his poetical interests, which until then had been predominantly self-reflective and lyrical, enlarged to include political and social issues. In the 1940s, after Neruda became a communist, his poetry took on an overt political flavor, seen particularly in his most famous work, "The Heights of Macchu Picchu," a meditation on the ancient ruins of the Andes. Among his concerns were the material condition of his native Latin America and the people's historically weak resistance to North American imperialism. These matters were in Neruda's mind as he wrote "Ode to the Americas."

ODE TO THE AMERICAS

Oh, pure Americas,
ocean-guarded lands
kept
Line   purple and intact,
(5)   centuries of silent apiaries,
pyramids and earthen vessels,
rivers of bloodstained butterflies,
yellow volcanos
and silent peoples,
(10)   shapers of pitchers,
workers of stone.

Today, Paraguay, water-formed
turquoise, buried rose,
you have become a prison.
(15)   Peru, heart of the world,
eagles'
aerie,
are you alive?
Venezuela, Colombia,
(20)   no one hears
your happy voices.
What has become of
your silvery morning chorus?
Only the birds
(25)   of ancient plumage,
only the waterfalls,
display their diadems.
Prison bars have multiplied.
In the humid kingdom of
(30)   fire and emerald,

between
paternal rivers,
each day
a new despot arises and with his saber

(35)   lops off mortgages and auctions your treasure.
Brother begins
to hunt brother.
Stray shots sound in the ports.
Experts arrive

(40)   from Pennsylvania,
the new conquistadors,
meanwhile,
our blood

(45)   feeds
the putrid
plantations and the buried mines,
the dollars flow,
and

(50)   our silly young girls
slip a disk learning the dance
of the orangutan.
Oh, pure Americas,
sacred lands,

(55)   what sadness!
A Machado dies and a Batista is born.
A Trujillo remains in power.
So much room
for sylvan freedom,

(60)   Americas,
so much
purity, ocean
waters,
solitary pampas, dizzying

(65)   geography, why do
insignificant blood merchants
breed and multiply?
What is happening?
How can the

(70)   silence continue
interrupted
by bloodthirsty parrots
perched in branches
of Pan-American greed?

(75)   Americas, assailed
by broadest expanse of foam,
by felicitous seas
redolent
of the pepper of the archipelagos,

(80)   dark
Americas,
in our orbit
the star of the people
is rising,

(85)   heroes are being born,

                new paths being garlanded
                with victory,
                the ancient nations
                live again,
(90)   autumn passes
                in the most radiant light,
                new flags
                flutter on the wind.
                May your voice and your deeds,
(95)   America,
                rise free from your
                green girdle,
                may there be an end
                to love imprisoned,
(100)   may your native dignity
                be restored,
                may your grain rise toward the sky
                awaiting with other nations
                the inevitable dawn.

Analysis of "Ode to the Americas"

An ode, an ancient form of poetic song, has long been used to declaim on elemental subjects such as nature, basic human emotions, and everyday objects. Odes are rarely intellectual. In fact, they often seem consciously anti-intellectual, glorifying the ordinary features of daily life. The form fits Neruda perfectly, for as a champion of the common folk, he wrote in a manner that common readers would understand and appreciate. That doesn't necessarily mean that Neruda's odes are simplistic. To the contrary, "Ode to the Americas" raises several ponderous issues relating to Latin America's past, present, and future.

The narrator of the poem is not personalized, but speaks with the voice of someone apparently ashamed of his people's behavior. The speaker rebukes the "Americas" for their passivity in the face of centuries of exploitation. His outspokenness stands in sharp contrast to the silence of the masses, a tension that echoes throughout the poem. He addresses the "Americas" in the first line. It remains unclear whether he means the people of the Americas or the geographical entities that make up the continent. Perhaps he means both, hence the plural "Americas." Either way, the tension created by such ambiguity is carried forward throughout the first stanza, which consists of a mixture of human and natural images.

This opening stanza is used to address the now-silent civilizations that existed on the western half of the earth before the European invasion. It acknowledges the existence of an ancient harmonious relationship between man and nature, when people made "earthen" vessels and were "workers of stone." Their lands were protected from foreigners by vast oceans, and their societies were like "apiaries," or beehives, suggesting that they were aswarm with purposeful activity and life. Students of Latin American history may question whether pre-Columbian Indians were as contented and unspoiled as Neruda implies, but for the sake of the poem, the romantic myth of an earthly paradise before the coming of the white man should be accepted.

After portraying an idealized Latin America of the past, the speaker turns to the continent today (line 12). At present, the land is artificially divided into countries—Paraguay, Peru, and so forth—each with its own woeful story of oppression. At one time Peru had eagles, Venezuela and Colombia, "happy voices." Nature's riches, described in terms of "silver," "diadems," "emerald[s]," "a treasure," continue to exist but are now remote from the people. Instead of enjoying nature's benificence, people are imprisoned, both literally, by prison bars and new despots, and figuratively, by their condition in life. The natural wealth of Latin America, which for centuries was its greatest blessing, has turned into a curse by attracting powerful economic and political interests, termed "blood merchants" (line 66). Had not nature been so bounteous, Latin America's people would have been left in peace. What formerly sustained the people has now turned them into slaves. Twentieth-century conquistadores in the form of "experts" from Pennsylvania (read United States or any neocolonial imperialist nation) now force people to spill their blood not on ancestral lands but on "putrid/plantations and buried mines." People and nature have been torn apart by economic exploitation that has also led to moral and cultural degeneracy embodied by young girls learning the dances of apes.

Part way through this recitation of woe, the narrator, no longer able to contain his grief, laments again "Oh, pure Americas," as he did in the poem's first line. His desperate cry recalls once again the differences between the Americas of the past and of the present and also serves as a brief hiatus in the Whitmanesque catalogue of abuses at the core of the poem. One cause of horrendous conditions is the rise of the proverbial Latin dictator. Three dictators are named, not as individuals but as a class of ruthless men: a Machado, a Batista, and a Trujillo. All are "bloodthirsty parrots" (line 72), that is, puppets mindlessly mouthing the words of the exploiters. The tragedy of today's Latin America is reinforced still further by brief glances at nature's now-ignored blessings—ocean waters, solitary pampas, dizzying geography—phrases that remind the reader of differences between then and now.

When the outspoken narrator asks rhetorically (line 69) how the people's silence can continue, the contrast between his own passion and the people's passivity is emphasized. The earlier silence, that of the Indians in harmony with nature, and the present silence, one of guilt and shame, stands in vivid juxtaposition to the narrator's cry for change, which now shifts the poem's focus to the future (line 75). Suddenly, images of nature recur. Somewhat surprisingly, the narrator sees hope, a vision of the rising star of the people, new heroes being born, "new paths being garlanded with victory." He urges America to raise its voice and to free itself from nature's "green girdle," which for centuries has kept the people chained to the land. Through a new relationship with nature, the people will reclaim their former dignity. Henceforth, nature will cooperate with people, but when the inevitable new dawn breaks, people will be in control.

Neruda's poem deals with power, politics, and economics, all rather unpoetic subjects. Yet it follows the customary tripartite form of the ode: strophe, antistrophe, and epode. This structure is a particularly ingenious choice considering the Marxist thrust of the poem. The dialectic of Marx's social philosophy also contains three parts: thesis, antithesis, and synthesis. To a degree the three sections of "Ode to the Americas" correspond to this dialectic structure. The poem's last lines suggest that Neruda has faith in the international communist crusade. As he sees it, the Latin countries, along with other oppressed peoples, will wait for the coming of a new era.

IN PRAISE OF DARKNESS
Jorge Luis Borges (Argentina, 1899–1986)

Old age (this is the name that others give it)
may prove a time of happiness.
The animal is dead or nearly dead;
Line   man and soul go on.
(5)   I live among vague whitish shapes
that are not darkness yet.
Buenos Aires,
which once broke up in a tatter of slums and open lots
out toward the endless plain,
(10)   is now again the graveyard of the Recoleta,
        the Retiro square,
the shabby streets of the old Westside,
and the few vanishing decrepit houses
that we still call the South.
(15)   All through my life things were too many.
To think, Democritus tore out his eyes;
time has been my Democritus.
This growing dark is slow and brings no pain;
it flows along an easy slope
(20)   and is akin to eternity.
My friends are faceless,
women are as they were years back,
one street corner is taken for another,
on the pages of books there are no letters.
(25)   All this should make me uneasy,
but there's a restfulness about it, a going back.
Of the many generations of books on earth
I have read only a few,
the few that in my mind I go on reading still —
(30)   reading and changing.
From south and east and west and north,
roads coming together have led me
to my secret center.
These roads were footsteps and echoes,
(35)   women, men, agonies, rebirths,
days and nights,
falling asleep and dreams,
each single moment of my yesterdays
and of the world's yesterdays,
(40)   the firm sword of the Dane and the moon
        of the Persians,
the deeds of the dead,
shared love, words,
Emerson, and snow, and so many things.
(45)   Now I can forget them. I read my center,
my algebra and my key,
my mirror.
Soon I shall know who I am.

Analysis of "In Praise of Darkness"

This lyrical poem brings to mind an elegy, a poem of loss. Earlier in this book, you read that elegies often mourn an individual who has died or recall fondly some time or deeply loved place. Elegies, considering their subject matter, are typically solemn and dignified. In each of these respects, "In Praise of

Darkness" qualifies as an elegy, but one with an ironic twist. In this poem, the speaker, instead of lamenting a loss, welcomes it. He praises the approach of his blindness and the loss of his youth. The poet, Borges, incidentally, lost his sight gradually over the course of his life. During his last decade he was totally blind. Therefore, it's safe to assume that the speaker in "In Praise of Darkness" is the poet himself.

He says that "Old age . . . may prove a time of happiness," a somewhat puzzling comment when you consider that old age usually implies a withering of one's faculties, sickness, and approaching death. The speaker, however, rejects the label "old age,"—"this is the name that others give it"—with its grim connotations. Although he knows that youth, or "The animal," is dead or near dead, the better parts of him, "the man and soul," will continue to live on, and as his vision diminishes, he will, ironically, be able to "see" more clearly.

How the coming of darkness leads to greater self-awareness or enlightenment is the paradoxical story of the poem. "All through my life things were too many," he says (line 15), as though he'd devoted too much of his life to the relentless pursuit of "things." Blindness, however, puts an end to his quest and allows him, instead, to contemplate and savor all that he has experienced, from books read and friends made to the places he's been and seen. "This growing dark is slow and brings no pain," he declares. Rather, there is a "restfulness" about it, a peaceful return to the past and reliving of all that has made him who he is. His past is captured metaphorically by an image of converging roads "from south and east and west and north" all leading to a "secret center" (line 33). In the end, he discovers that "each single moment of [his] yesterdays" (line 38) is forgettable, and once he casts his clutter of memories aside, he can find the key to what really counts in life. In blindness he sees himself in the mirror and exclaims, "Soon I shall know who I am."

The poet's allusion to Democritus (lines 16–17) is particularly apt. In ancient Greece, Democritus theorized that genuine knowledge comes from the intellect not from the senses. Therefore, he blinded himself, believing that his eyesight kept him from the true knowledge of reality. It remains unclear whether Democritus actually found what he sought, but in this poem Borges discovers a self that remained concealed to him while he still had sight.

POEMS BY ANNA AKHMATOVA
(Russia, 1889–1966)

Anna Akhmatova is one of Russia's most acclaimed twentieth-century poets. Most of her poems are rooted in her personal experiences: She lived in the center of pre-Revolutionary St. Petersburg literary circles, abided an unhappy marriage, and endured political changes during and after the Revolution. She suffered through two World Wars, the Stalinist purges of the 1930s, the exile and execution of loved ones, and many excruciating years of artistic repression. Through much of her career, she was censored and silenced. In order to save her poetry, she had to memorize it. Toward the end of her life, she was rehabilitated by the Soviet authorities, but neither she nor her work ever shed the bitterness and anger felt by artists during the dark years of communist totalitarianism. In spite of the autobiographical basis of her poems, the themes are widely applicable to human experience.

PUSHKIN
Tzarskoye Selo, 1911

A swarthy youth rambled
by the forlorn lakeshore.
A century passes, and we hear
his crackle on the path.

Pine needles, thick, thorny,
bury the stumps of trees . . .
Here lay his tricorn hat,
his dog-eared verses by Parny.

The nineteenth-century poet Alexander Pushkin, considered the father of Russian literature, is a revered national hero. By chance, young Anna Akhmatova grew up in the same town, Tzarskoye Selo, as Pushkin. In this poem, Akhmatova acknowledges the mysterious influence that Pushkin's spirit must have had on her decision to become a poet. The "swarthy youth" is Pushkin, whose black great-grandfather had been an Ethiopian visiting the court of Peter the Great. The poem suggests the power that a place can exert on a person's emotions. Just as English-speaking people are drawn to Stratford-on-Avon to walk where Shakespeare walked, Russians regard Tzarskoye Selo as a hallowed shrine. To occupy Pushkin's space, to see his sights and breathe his air has the power to stir up irresistible feelings.

Akhmatova's life, like the life of many Russians, was disrupted by World War I and by the unrest that preceded the Bolshevik Revolution of October, 1917. "All Has Been Taken Away" (1916) conveys frustration over finding herself blocked from doing what she loved most—writing poetry. Her Muse seems to have taken time off, "doesn't say a word,/and lays her head, in its dark wreath,/exhausted, on my breast." At first, she blames her writer's block on the fact that she has been uprooted from her familiar surroundings (St. Petersburg). Although she is in Sevastopol, a sunny and attractive resort on the Black Sea, she takes no pleasure in it. Daily, she grows increasingly disappointed in her performance and suffers from guilt. Finally, she recognizes that no one will rescue her from her own frustration. Having "run out of tears and excuses," she must take up her pen again. The result of her resolve, of course, is a poem.

"I Am Not One of Those Who Left the Land . . ." (1922) was written during the period of Russia's Civil War, a time of sickness, famine, shootings (Akhmatova's husband was shot by the Bolsheviks in 1921 for allegedly conspiring against the new regime), pitch-dark apartments, damp firewood, and fear. In the first stanza Akhmatova refers to the fact that the Soviet government forcibly seized all land and private property in the name of the people, causing many upper- and middle-class citizens to flee the country with nothing except the clothes they wore. Rather than abandon her homeland, Akhmatova decided to stay, believing that she would endure oppression unflinchingly and that things would get better "after the passing of this cloud." In the meantime, she would continue to write her "songs" (i.e., poems) for herself, not for the approval of the authorities. (In fact, many of her poems were barred from publication in the Soviet Union on the grounds that they were too individualistic, served no social purpose, and did nothing to glorify the people or the state.)

As one who refused to give in to the new regime, Akhmatova pities those who chose exile. Homeless and poor, they are a "half-dead" class of people, infected by "wormwood," a woody herb with an extremely bitter taste. In the last half of the poem, Akhmatova's pity turns scornful. Proudly, she proclaims that "survivors" like herself "do not flinch/from anything." Not only are they brave, but they are "people without tears,/straighter than you . . . more proud . . ." Considering Akhmatova's generally defiant tone, it is hardly surprising that the Soviets banned her work. For years, Akhmotova refused to submit her work for publication. It would have been too risky to herself and her family.

Akhmatova wrote a poem of utter despair, "The Last Toast" (1934), during the apex of the Stalinist terror and at the nadir of her life. In the 1930s Akhmatova was officially ostracized by the Soviet authorities. Moreover, she suffered material hardship and was intermittently ill with tuberculosis. She had lost touch with her family, whose unknown fate increased her distress and isolation.

The poem, as its title says, is a toast, addressed an unnamed person, possibly to Nikolai Punin, an art historian with whom she was living at the time. It might also be addressed to Stalin, whose "lying lips" and "dead-cold, pitiless eyes" had spread fear and anguish throughout the country. The toast might also be for the long-suffering Soviet people who lived in what Akhmatova termed a "ruined house," despoiled by the Revolution and its aftermath. Regardless of the audience, the poem reflects both Akhmatova's recognition that "the world is brutal and coarse" and, in spite of her devotion to the Russian Orthodox Church, her belief that "God in fact has not saved us."

There is a kind of irony in proposing a toast to a litany of woes. Toasts, after all, are usually made in the name of something desirable: good health, happiness, a friend, a new venture. By toasting her despair, Akhmatova may be suggesting just how low she has sunk. On the other hand, that she has the vision to propose a toast at all may be a saving grace, the only sign of hope in this self-portrait of misery.

Early in World War II, Akhmatova, along with thousands of others, was evacuated from Leningrad during the famous Nazi siege. For two and a half years she resided in Tashkent in Central Asia, far from the city she loved, which she once described as "the city of Peter, the city of Lenin, of Pushkin, Dostoyevski, and Blok." A poem, "This Cruel Age Has Deflected Me . . ." (1944), written upon her return to Leningrad, reflects on the consequences of having had her life seriously disrupted.

First, Akhmatova likens herself to a river whose course has been diverted into a "sister channel." In other words, life has taken turns that kept it from following its natural flow. Detours from life's main route have diminished her. She has missed "spectacles," failed to make friends, and has lost opportunities to travel, but her greatest regret is that she has been unable to write all that she had expected—nay, all that she had been destined to write: "And how many verses I have failed to write!" The lost words haunt her and may someday "strangle" her, but it is unclear whether she expects to be overrun by a flood of repressed words or will continue to be overwrought with remorse about words not written.

Having led a fragmented life, Akhmatova claims to know "beginnings" and "endings," as well as things she'd "rather not recall just now," presumably things that are worse even than "life-in-death." Her knowledge of beginnings and endings may allude to a rich lode of ideas for poems stored inside her that have never been written because "this cruel age has deflected" her. In a sense, she lives not as Anna Akhmatova was meant to live. She leads a parallel but different life, recalling the earlier image of a "sister channel." Another woman—not the real Anna Akhmatova—seems be residing in her body. The name is the same, but not the person who should have been Anna Akhmatova. In fact, if the pretender could step outside herself and view objectively what Anna Akhmatova should have been, she "should know at last what envy is."

The concluding thought in the poem is likely to resonate with many readers:

> But if I could step outside myself
> and contemplate the person that I am,
> I should know at last what envy is.

Who, after all, has never imagined himself as a new and improved version of himself—perhaps richer, happier, smarter, fairer, more talented—someone so much better than the original that, were he real, you might actually envy him.

Written toward the end of her career, "Alexander at Thebes" (1961) succinctly summarizes Akhmatova's career. Metaphorically, and somewhat grandly, she invents an episode from the life of Alexander the Great on the verge of proving his awesome power by burning to the ground the ancient city of Thebes. At the last moment, however, Alexander has second thoughts and says, "Only be sure the Poet's House is spared." Why he orders that house to be spared is the puzzle of the poem. Perhaps the decision reveals Alexander's humanistic streak. Another possibility is that Alexander wished to preserve the house of the one person in the city who could record for the ages the story of Alexander the Great's conquests. In that sense, Akhmatova resides in the poet's house. Through much of her life, she was silenced by Soviet censorship. Yet she continued to write secretly, believing that it was her duty to tell the story of Russian life during its darkest days. Her poems, then, bear witness and record for posterity the destruction of her country and the suffering of her people during a major portion of the twentieth century.

Writing an Essay on Poetry

The poetry about which you will write an essay on the AP exam may have been written several centuries ago or just last April. Regardless of its age, however, poetry from one era will have certain characteristics in common with poetry from any other. Poetry expresses insights in language meant to arouse some sort of emotion. In the poetry of every age, you'll find connotation, imagery, symbolism, understatement, hyperbole, paradox, and so on.

When you write your poetry essay on the AP exam, the task you face is to show how these and any other appropriate poetic devices create or contribute to the meaning of the poem.

The next several pages contain numerous poetry exercises that will help you do just that.

One caveat before you begin: Be sure that whatever interpretations you make can be supported by specific evidence in the poems. Don't fall prey to the common temptation of believing that a poem means whatever its reader wants it to mean.

Exercises in the Interpretation of Poetry

A.   SONNET XIV

John Donne (1572–1631)

Batter my heart, three-personed God; for You
As yet but knock, breathe, shine and seek to mend;
That I may rise and stand; o'er throw me, and bend
Line   Your force to break, blow, burn and make me new.
(5)   I, like an usurped town, to another due,
Labor to admit You, but Oh! to no end!
Reason, your viceroy in me, me should defend
But is captivated and proves weak or untrue.
Yet dearly I love You, and would be loved fain,
(10)   But am betrothed unto Your enemy:
Divorce me, untie or break that knot again,
Take me to You, imprison me, for I,
Except you enthrall me, never shall be free
Nor ever chaste, except You ravish me.

1.   Who is the speaker? Whom is the speaker addressing? Is the poem a prayer? What is the mood of the speaker? What is the source of his anguish?
2.   The unifying principle of this poem is a paradox. What is the paradox? How would you explain the paradoxes in line 13 and line 14?
3.   The theme of the poem is expressed by means of three images or metaphors. What are the three comparisons? Are these comparisons apt in terms of the statement of the poem and the emotional state of the speaker?
4.   The poem is addressed to the three-personed God: the Father, the Son, and the Holy Ghost. How is the number three related to the qualities of God used imaginatively and symbolically in the poem?
5.   Write an essay in which you demonstrate how the speaker in this poem uses paradox to express the intensity of his emotion and to strengthen his arguments in his appeal for God's help.

B.   LONDON

William Blake (1757–1827)

I wonder thro' each chartered street
Near where the chartered Thames does flow
And mark in every face I meet
Marks of weakness, marks of woe.
Line
(5)   In every cry of every Man,
In every Infant's cry of fear,
In every voice; in every ban,
The mind-forged manacles I hear.

How the Chimney-sweeper's cry
(10)   Every black'ning Church appalls
And the hapless Soldier's sigh
Runs in blood down Palace walls.

But most thro' midnight streets I hear
How the youthful Harlot's curse
(15)   Blasts the new-born Infant's tear
And blights with plagues the Marriage hearse.

1. What is the organization of this poem? The speaker is a walker in the city of London. He records what he sees and what he hears. How does the speaker see London? What is the order of his presentation? Is the order climactic?

2. Blake uses vivid concrete images to make his indictment. What are these images? How does Blake use "chartered" in its two meanings to suggest the enslavement of London's streets and people? What effect does Blake achieve in using the word "mark" as verb and noun? How does the repetition of the words "chartered" and "mark" in Stanza 1 intensify the criticism and indictment?

3. What effect does the speaker achieve in Stanza 2 by relating cries to the clanking of fetters? In what way are the fetters mind-forged? In the speaker's view who or what is responsible for the enslavement of children and adults?

4. What is the speaker's view of the church? Both the chimney-sweeper and the church are blackened by soot. What effect is achieved by relating the two? What blackens the chimney-sweeper? What blackens the church?

5. The speaker says the soldier's sighs flow like blood. This is an unusual image. What is its effect? What is Blake criticizing?

6. Why is the last stanza climactic? Is it that the source of creation, the union of the sexes, is blighted by the exploitations of the city? What is the effect of matching "youthful" to "harlot" and "marriage" to "hearse" and juxtaposing the harlot's curse against the infant's tear? How is it ironic? What has happened to the holy conceptions of love? What effect is achieved by capitalizing words like "Infant," "Harlot," and "Chimney-sweeper" and words like "Church" and "Palace"? Does it crystallize the confrontation between those who exploit and those who are exploited? Does the capitalizing of "Infant," "Harlot," "Soldier," "Chimney-sweeper" raise them from the particular to the universal and give them the halo of martyr? Is this too strained a reading?

7. Write an essay in which you demonstrate that there is a logical order in the poem, leading to the climactic statement of the last stanza.

C. THE PERSIAN VERSION
Robert Graves (1895–1985)

Truth-loving Persians do not dwell upon
The trivial skirmish fought near Marathon.
As for the Greek theatrical tradition

Line   Which represents that summer's expedition
(5)   Not as a mere reconaissance in force
        By three brigades of foot and one of horse
        (Their left flank covered by some obsolete
        Light craft detached from the main Persian fleet)
        But as a grandiose, ill-starred attempt
(10)   To conquer Greece—they treat it with contempt;
        And only incidentally refute
        Major Greek claims, by stressing what repute
        The Persian monarch and the Persian nation
        Won by this salutary demonstration:
(15)   Despite a strong defence and adverse weather
        All arms combined magnificently together.

A question arises in connection with this poem: Whose version are we getting, the Persian version, the Greek version, or neither? Read the following short essay written by a student; then write an essay of your own expressing agreement or disagreement with the views expressed.

A View of "The Persion Version"

The poem may be read seriously or ironically. If it is read seriously we get the version of the honest historians of Persia. To them the battle at Marathon was a trivial skirmish and a minor defeat magnified into a great victory by the hyperbole of Greek patriotic tradition. What actually happened was that a small force reconnoitering a position, their left flank defended by obsolete vessels, met the Greek force and was defeated. But it was no serious defeat. The maneuvers, they say, were admirably handled; the various forces combining magnificently in an encounter that won repute for the Persian monarch and nation.

The language of the poem crystallizes the view of the speaker. The Persians recording the event are truth-loving. The tone suggests a gentle contempt for the Greek theatrical tradition. "Theatrical" is used ironically. The forces were engaged in a "summer's expedition." The defeat was made possible by a "strong defence and adverse weather." The maneuver was a "salutary" demonstration of military adeptness.

There is another way to read the poem. The reader knows the historical fact as it was recorded in Greek and Persian history. The fact is the Persians suffered a serious defeat. The Persians, therefore, try to restore Persian prestige and they do so by belittling the Greek achievement. This is, of course, customary procedure among historians of defeated nations. The speaker, cognizant of the Greek victory and recognizing the futile efforts of the Persians, clothes his account in a tone of irony. The Persians recording the events are not truth-loving but self-defensive and apologetic; and the facts are not facts but distortions. The speaker presents the Persian view as a lie, and he therefore believes that the true version is the Greek one.

As you prepare to comment on this essay, determine how much is paraphrase and how much is interpretation. Determine also whether the conclusions have been satisfactorily supported by evidence from the poem. Be sure that the views expressed in your essay are a valid interpretation and are supported by evidence.

D.   BASE DETAILS
Siegfried Sassoon (1886–1967)

If I were fierce, and bald, and short of breath,
    I'd live with scarlet Majors at the Base,
And speed glum heroes up the line to death.
Line   You'd see me with puffy petulant face,
(5)   Guzzling and gulping in the best hotel,
    Reading the Roll of Honor. "Poor young chap,"
I'd say—"I used to know his father well;
    Yes, we've lost heavily in this last scrap."
And when the war is done and youth stone dead,
(10) I'd toddle safely home and die—in bed.

1. Who is the speaker in this poem? What is the tone of his comment? What is the relationship between the tone and the speaker's pretending he is an officer?
2. What conflicting attitudes toward the activity of war are there in the poem? Which attitude does the speaker hold?
3. What effect on the poem would the following changes have?
   a. In line 8 to substitute "battle" or "engagement" for "scrap."
   b. In line 5 to substitute "sipping" and "imbibing" for "guzzling" and "gulping."
   c. In line 10 to substitute "totter" or "march" for "toddle."
4. What is the speaker's attitude toward the "glum heroes"? What is the officer's attitude toward the "glum heroes"?
5. Why is the poem called "Base Details"? How do the two meanings of "base" strengthen the comment the speaker is making?
6. Write an essay in which you demonstrate how the technique and language of the poem enforce the poet's attitude toward the activity of war. Is the indictment against war minimized by the concentration of the speaker upon officers?

    E. MUSEUM PIECE
      Richard Wilbur (1921–   )

The good gray guardians of art
Patrol the halls on spongy shoes,
Impartially protective, though
Perhaps suspicious of Toulouse.

Line
(5)   Here dozes one against the wall,
Disposed upon a funeral chair.
A Degas dancer pirouettes
Upon the parting of his hair.

See how she spins! The grace is there,
(10)   But strain as well is plain to see.
Degas loved the two together:
Beauty joined to energy.

Edgar Degas purchased once
A fine El Greco, which he kept
(15)   Against the wall beside his bed
To hang his pants on while he slept.

There are in this poem three attitudes toward art. Write an essay in which you define the three attitudes and support with evidence from the poem the attitude that you believe the speaker held.

To help you, you should know that Toulouse-Lautrec was a French painter who painted scenes in a house of prostitution. Such scenes may have disturbed the museum guards. Edgar Degas painted ballet dancers. El Greco painted mystic religious subjects with elongated spiritual figures. Look for the tone and spirit of each of the stanzas to help you arrive at your conclusions.

Sample Advanced Placement Questions with Student Responses and Teacher Analyses

Question 1. In a brief essay discuss the significance to human action found in the image of the heart.

SUGGESTED TIME: 40 MINUTES

IN THE DESERT

In the desert
I saw a creature, naked, bestial,
Who, squatting, upon the ground,
Held his heart in his hands,
And ate of it.
I said, "Is it good, friend?"
"It is bitter-bitter," he answered;
"But I like it
Because it is bitter,
And because it is my heart."

Sample Student Response

The poem "In the Desert" illustrates one way man attempts to cure his sorrows; that is, to abandon humanity and chastise himself. Because the self-affliction of punishment relieves tension and rids guilt, man will impose suffering upon himself. Representing emotional, animalistic man, the creature in the poem secludes himself in the desert and devours the cause of his sorrow, his "bitter-bitter" heart.

The image of the bestial creature, squatting naked in the desert, is especially appropriate for the poet's purpose. It is man stripped to the basics, devoid of culture and civilization. The thought of eating the heart not only supplies a graphic image, but conjures up powerful symbolic associations: the heart has long been thought of in a variety of meanings—emotion, desire, sensitivity, love, humanness, life-blood, the very essence of man himself.

The key point is that the creature chooses to eat his heart. In that sense the image parallels many human actions; any one in which a man can choose to destroy himself. Among all creatures, only man exercises this activity. Think for instance of war, or drugs, or alcohol; in each case man knows that he will ultimately bring about self-destruction, but engages in it anyway.

The parallel to human action in the image of eating the heart, then, is man's ability to determine his own actions. Here we see man, naked and bestial, destroying his very core, but nonetheless enjoying the prerogative; "I like it . . . because it is my heart," even though it is a "bitter" action.

ANALYSIS OF STUDENT ESSAY

This paper reaches to the basic issue of the poem; the poet employs an image to represent a much larger significant action. The paper moves in a lucid direction.

The poem has overtones of meaning and, like a parable, makes a comment on the ugliness in human nature that causes man to destroy so much that is beautiful and good in himself and his world. The image chosen by the poet is the heart, conceived as the center of human emotions and the yearning for the good things of life. A second image is that of a human being become a bestial creature squatting in a world turned desert, eating his heart and enjoying it. It is this devouring of the heart, representing all that is good, just, and civilized, that, according to the speaker, has returned man to the primitive, animalistic state from which he emerged and has converted his world into an empty desert.

The writer of this essay has chosen to interpret the poem in more personal and individual terms, focusing on the element of free will, of choice. He sees the image of a creature in a desert devouring his heart; this being, through weakness and self-indulgence, has brought misery into his life and, to escape the sorrows and ills of human experience, acquires behaviors and habits that turn him into a beast. The irony is that the awareness of what he is doing does not distress him. He enjoys it.

This paper is well organized, as follows:

Theme: Man, through the opiate of rooting out all emotion and through the paralysis of conscience, tries to rid himself of the pains, sorrows, and regrets that torment his soul.

Proof (Inferences That May Be Drawn):
1. To cure his sorrows, man abandons humanity, turns his world into a desert, and finds pleasure in destroying whatever emotion is left him.
   a. Through self-punishment man relieves tension and rids himself of guilt.
   b. Man, turned bestial creature, hides in a desert and devours his heart.
2. The image of man as a creature is a fitting symbol for this theme.
   a. The image is of a primitive, animal-like, uncivilized creature.
   b. The heart is the symbol of the essences of good in humanity.
3. The eating of the heart symbolizes actions by means of which man destroys himself.
   a. He destroys himself through war, alcohol, and other drugs.
   b. He is free to make choices.
   c. He makes the wrong ones and enjoys the evil they bring upon him.

The central themes of this paper are well stated and well developed.

The rating for this essay is 9 on the scale of 0–9 used to score AP essays. (See pages 43–44 for a description of the scoring scale.) (The poem is by Stephen Crane, 1871–1900.)

Question 2:   Write an essay in which you explain how the experience of the last line relates to the rest of the poem.

SUGGESTED TIME: 40 MINUTES

SUMMUM BONUM

All the breath and the bloom of the year in the bag of one bee;
All the wonder and wealth of the mine in the heart of one gem;
In the core of one pearl all the shade and shine of the sea;
Breath and bloom, shade and shine,—wonder wealth, and—
    how far above them—
    Truth, that's brighter than gem,
    Trust, that's purer than pearl,—
Brightest truth, purest truth in the universe—all were for me
    In the kiss of one girl.

Sample Student Response

In "Summum Bonum" the poet suggests that "highest good" can be found even in the simplest of things. He describes the "kiss of one girl" as an image of one of the purest, most perfect acts of nature and human emotions.

The poet points out that all the freshness of spring can be captured "in the bag of one bee," all splendor of jewels in "one gem," and all the depth of the sea "in the core of one pearl." Each of these images represents some form of natural perfection.

Then he presents two heights of human excellence—"Truth . . . brighter than gem" and "Trust . . . purer than pearl." Each of these is perhaps even greater than the perfections of nature.

He concludes that at least as wonderful as all this was "the kiss." It was rooted in simple emotions, in truth; it was perfect. The poet uses his rhyming devices to underscore his contention. The detailed alliteration, assonance, and onomatopoeia in the three images of nature and the two statements of human values appear ornate compared to the simple monosyllabic line "In the kiss of one girl." To enhance the theme, the sound matches the sense.

Below are two analyses of this student's essay with ratings. Comment on your agreement or disagreement with each of these evaluations and ratings.

ANALYSIS 1 OF STUDENT ESSAY
Consider the poem as a mathematical metaphor.
A = the three images of natural perfection in the first three lines
B = the two statements about human perfection in the lines about "Truth" and "Trust"
C = the kiss of one girl (a metonymy for any moving, simple emotional experience)

The poem reads $A + B < C$.
In other words, this student responds with a clear explication of each section of the poem.

Thesis: The "highest good" (summum bonum) can be found in the simplest of emotional experiences (the "kiss of one girl") just as easily as in natural and human perfection

Proof: 1. Define three images of natural perfection: the coming of spring, the value of a rare gem, the beauty of a pearl
           2. Define two statements of human perfection—"Trust" and "Truth"

Conclusion: The simple experience of the kiss has more value than the others, and the poet uses rhyme and sound to parallel his theme.

Clearly the essay rates the highest score, 9.

ANALYSIS 2 OF STUDENT ESSAY
The paper is well organized, but it tends to be more paraphrase than interpretation. The aspects of nature presented as symbols of perfection are objects that appeal to the eyes, objects of color, design, symmetry. Trust and truth are ethical and philosophical concepts of a different perfection, and these challenge the mind. But to the speaker, moved by the ecstasy of love, the kiss of one girl is of even greater perfection because it involves a closer participation in an expe-

rience, a sharing of deep feeling. It becomes the center of a world of wonder and realization that can be built between two people, and in the mind of the speaker is a symbol of a greater perfection than is encountered in nature and human thought. These are logical inferences that can be drawn from the statements in the poem. Failure to draw inferences often leads to paraphrasing.

The paper also mentions the technical poetic elements that give form, design, and color to the emotional, deep-felt tone of the poem: detailed alliteration, assonance, onomatopoeia, the contrast between ornate and simple diction to highlight the perfection of the kiss. This is good, but the writer needs examples to illustrate her statements. Something should also be said about the variation of meter—anapest, dactyl, iamb—that adds a musical flow to the lines of the poem.

Because of the careful organization of the paper, the clear understanding of its subject and theme, and the awareness of the poetic devices used by the poet, the rating of this paper is 5.

(The poem is by Robert Browning, 1812–1889.)

Question 3. Discuss the relationship of the final two lines to the preceding ones. In your answer consider the poet's attitude (emotional response) toward the central concern of the poem.

SUGGESTED TIME: 40 MINUTES

LINES WRITTEN IN DEJECTION

When have I last looked on
The round green eyes and the long wavering bodies
Of the dark leopards of the moon?
All the wild witches, those most noble ladies,
For all their broom-sticks and their tears,
Their angry tears, are gone.
The holy centaurs of the hills are vanished;
I have nothing left but the embittered sun;
Banished heroic mother moon and vanished,
And now that I have come to fifty years
I must endure the timid sun.

Sample Student Response

In the last two lines, the speaker, who has passed the youthful part of his life, regrets that he can no longer enjoy the imagination of his younger years, but instead must confront reality directly. His tone is dejected and melancholic.

The poet employs two central symbols, the sun and the moon, to represent the qualities of older life and youthful life, respectively. It seems that the sun might symbolize rationality, intellect, objectivity, sensibility, and reality, all inherent to older age; the moon, however, might symbolize imagination, intuition, emotion, subjectivity, sensitivity, and fantasy, all indigenous to youth.

Dejected and dispirited because his "banished heroic mother moon" has vanished, the poet sees that age has caught up with him and he can never experience his youth again. Clearly he favors the "moon" qualities he once possessed. To express his love for this, he employs three beautiful images. The "dark leopards," with their "round green eyes" and "long wavering bodies," depict the fierce, unpredictable, lithe, sensuous aspects of youth. The "wild witches," despite their broomsticks and their tears, still characterize the phenomenal imaginative capacity of youth; hence they are really "noble ladies." The "holy centaurs" portrays an even more ultimate imaginative leap into the mythic, representing the animal-like, instinctive side of early life.

But the poet, left only with bitter reality, must silently "endure the timid sun," the daily reality of life. He has "nothing left but the embittered sun"; his "heroic . . . moon," and all that it represents, are "vanished" now that he has "come to fifty years." The poem is a lament for the passing of youth.

ANALYSIS OF STUDENT ESSAY
Certainly the paper possesses a clear, direct organization.

Thesis: The last two lines show a dejected middle-aged poet lamenting his lost youth.

Proof: 1. Sun and moon symbols are differentiated:

sun	moon
rationality	imagination
intellect	intuition, emotion
objectivity	subjectivity
sensibility	sensitivity
reality	fantasy

2. The poet favors his "moon" qualities, developed in three images:
"dark leopard"—unpredictable, sensuous
"wild witches"—imaginative capacity
"holy centaurs"—mythic, instinctive

Conclusion: The poet employs words such as "endure," "timid," and "embittered" to express his dejection about the passing of youth.

Certainly the paper explicates the poem and is written very well. Notice how the student makes use of two effective writing devices: 1) parallel series, such as the description of sun and moon symbols, and 2) weaving quotes from the text into the actual sentences of the essay, such as the concluding paragraph. It rates a score of 9.
(The poem is by William Butler Yeats, 1865–1950).

Typical Advanced Placement Essay Questions on Poetry

What paradox cited by the poet explains the loss of a beloved one?

SUGGESTED TIME: 30 MINUTES

A SLUMBER DID MY SPIRIT SEAL

A slumber did my spirit seal;
   I had no human fears:
She seemed a thing that could not feel
   The touch of earthly years.
No motion has she now, no force;
   She neither hears nor sees;
Rolled round in earth's diurnal course,
   With rocks, and stones, and trees.

How does the speaker prepare the reader for the statement of the last three lines?

SUGGESTED TIME: 30 MINUTES

WHEN I HAVE FEARS

When I have fears that I may cease to be
    Before my pen has glean'd my teeming brain,
Before high-piled books, in charact'ry,
    Hold like rich garners the full-ripen'd grain;
When I behold, upon the night's starr'd face,
    Huge cloudy symbols of a high romance,
And think that I may never live to trace
    Their shadows, with the magic hand of chance;
And when I feel, fair creature of an hour,
    That I shall never look upon thee more,
Never have relish in the faery power
    Of unreflecting love!—then on the shore
Of the wide world I stand alone, and think
Till Love and Fame to nothingness do sink.

1. What is the relationship of the subject of the poem to the title?

or

2. What outcome to the relationship of the lovers is suggested in the poem?

SUGGESTED TIME: 30 MINUTES

NEUTRAL TONES

We stood by a pond that winter day,
And the sun was white, as though chidden of God,
And a few leaves lay on the starving sod;
    —They had fallen from an ash, and were gray.

Your eyes on me were eyes that rove
Over tedious riddles of years ago;
And some words played between us to and fro
    On which lost the more by our love.

The smile on your mouth was the deadest thing
Alive enough to have strength to die;
And a grin of bitterness swept thereby
    Like an ominous bird a-wing . . . .

Since then, keen lessons that love deceives,
And wrings with wrong, have shaped to me
Your face, and the God-curst sun, and a tree,
    And a pond edged with grayish leaves.

CHAPTER **6** Fiction on the AP Exam

The AP exam asks more questions about fiction than about any other genre. Two of the essay questions and at least half of the multiple-choice questions pertain to passages of fiction. Most passages come from novels and short stories. On occasion, the passage is an entire short story, hardly more than a page or two in length. The multiple-choice questions range from broad to narrow—from the meaning of the passage to the use of a single word or phrase. You may be asked about themes, structure, character, setting, tone, purpose, language. In fact, every aspect of the passage is fair game for the multiple-choice questions.

The fictional passage in the essay section of the exam will also be an excerpt from a longer work or a short story printed in its entirety. After you have read the passage, you are expected to write a well-organized essay that analyzes the story. In most cases, the question will suggest the aspects of the passage on which to focus your essay—usually such elements as tone, imagery, use of language, choice of details, and so on. Your analysis is then supposed to show how such elements are used to contribute to the meaning or effect of the passage.

The open-ended essay question invariably instructs you to choose a novel or a play about which to write an essay. Although novels and plays are drastically different creatures, the question makes no distinction between them. Both are "works of literature," with such common characteristics as plot, structure, conflict, settings, themes, major and minor characters, and some sort of resolution.

The present chapter reviews the elements of fiction. In addition, several works of literature are analyzed in detail in order to familiarize you with the sort of literary analysis expected of you on the AP exam. You probably have studied some of the works in school. In such cases, you will become reacquainted with their form and substance. If a work is new to you, however, perhaps you will be inspired to go out and read it.

The Nature of Fiction

The following story appeared in *The New York Times:*

> A 15-year old student at the Fashion Industries High School was stabbed to death on the subway yesterday by another teen-age girl who wanted to steal her gold earrings, the police said.
>
> The victim, Maribel Feliciano of 188 Lincoln Avenue in the East New York section of Brooklyn, was on her way home from school on a southbound C train at 3:35 P.M. when the stabbing occurred. She was taken to St. Vincent's Hospital, where she died at 4:20.
>
> Stunned family members and friends gathered in front of Ms. Feliciano's home late into the night, recalling a cheerful girl with a generous spirit, who seemed to have a promising future in the fashion industry.

Yesterday evening, Inspector Thomas Naff of the transit police said
the killing appeared to be the result of "a robbery that went sour." It was
the 15th homicide in the subway this year, the police said.

The story recounts a tragic experience, an event that was fated, an ironic one,
since Maribel, the victim, was pursuing the normal activities of her life when
she was accosted. She refused to give up her gold earrings. It was a death that
should not have occurred.

The question that arises is whether this news account is a short story. It has
characters, incident, rising action and suspense, and climax. We must, however,
distinguish between story and short story. Any experience in daily life, usual or
unusual, is a story. A child in a hurry to catch a bus to school falls and breaks
an arm. That is a story. An elevator breaks down, stops running between floors,
and imprisons four people for two hours. That, too, is a story. But these incidents are not *short stories*. A short story is a literary form. It requires some special doing to give it shape. An incident, whether related by word of mouth, or
printed, if it is newsworthy, in a newspaper is raw, basically untreated experience. It becomes a short story when it is treated by a writer. This involves
selecting from the raw experiences those that best fit a conception in the mind
of the writer; it requires emphases on and elaborations and contractions of
experiences; it needs delineation and particularizing of character; and it
demands the creation of a world in which the events occur. In addition, the raw
experiences of life are "fictionalized"; that is, the writer changes events, characters, and world to fit his/her view of life and purpose in telling the story. In
the hands of a skilled writer, however, the changes do not distort life; they give
form and meaning to life. The events, characters, and places acquire a verisimilitude, a truth to life, that arouses a sense of recognition in the reader and an
acknowledgment that what is portrayed is so.

Ernest Hemingway wrote a story about gangsters on a mission to kill a victim. His story, "The Killers," tells of the experience in a diner of two men who
have a contract to kill a worn-out prizefighter. It is the prizefighter's habit, they
have learned, to come into the diner at six o'clock, and so, after tying up the
cook and Nick Adams, a boy whom they find in the diner when they first come
in, they terrorize the counterman as they wait for their victim. The prizefighter
does not show up. They leave the diner. Nick decides to warn the prizefighter,
knowing that he may be putting himself in some danger. But when he talks to
the fighter, he learns that the fighter is resigned to his fate and that, when he
gets up enough courage, he will go out to be shot at. Hemingway has turned the
raw experience of a gangland murder into a short story, and he has done this by
giving personalities to his killers and to their victims and by coloring his
account with two views that governed many of his short stories. First, the prizefighter reveals a resignation and a courage that Hemingway found in many of
the defeated of the world. The brave suffer or die with heroism and acceptance
and without a whimper or cry. Second, those who are human cannot avoid participation in the lives of others regardless of the cost. Involvement is an aspect
of maturity. Nick Adams, growing to manhood, feels impelled to warn Ole
Andreson, the fighter, of the danger to his life.

For Hemingway the cold-blooded killers' stalking of a defeated and resigned
victim becomes an experience for heroism on the part of a sensitive boy. This
is the emphasis in the Hemingway story.

There are the elements of a fine short story in the news account, cited above, of the killing of an innocent victim by a youthful criminal made cruel and vicious by the ugly world in which she grew up. To become a story, however, it needs treatment by a skilled writer.

The Form and Structure of Fiction

The Short Story

It is not always easy to tell the difference between the short story and the novel. One difference has to do with length. A short story can be read swiftly. Another difference deals with the subject. A short story concentrates on one central incident or one central character. However, how does one characterize the long short stories or the short novels? Terms like *novella* and *novelette* are used to describe such works. The best way to judge the difference between short story and novel and at the same time to determine the tone or spirit of the work is by means of the following guides:

Let us use a quadrilateral figure to represent a work of fiction. The story begins at a point in human experience; the reader becomes involved in the experience, motivated by the skill of the writer in creating interest and suspense; the reader is led to the climax or resolution of the problems or conflicts in the story; and the story is brought to a close. Sometimes the story ends at the climax; sometimes a few loose ends are quickly gathered together; sometimes a long explanation is necessary to conclude the story. Sometimes a new experience is introduced related to the events preceding it, showing the results of the climactic event or explaining how the climactic event came to be. Sometimes a new series of events flows from the climax and culminates in a new climax.

These are the shapes stories may take.

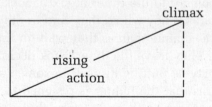

The story ends at the climax.
Example: "Flowering Judas"
by Katherine Anne Porter

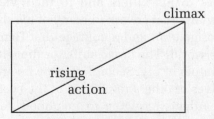

*Some loose ends need to be
gathered after the climax.*
Example: "The Dead"
by James Joyce

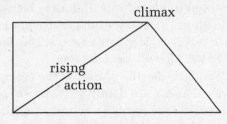

A long explanation follows the climax.
Example: "The Purloined Letter" by Edgar Allan Poe

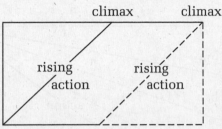

A second series of events follows the climax of the first series and culminates in a concluding climax.
Example: "Noon Wine" by Katherine Anne Porter

The Novel   If a third series of incidents needs to be added to expand further the events leading to the first climax or to recount the effects produced by the events leading to the first climax, we have moved into the realm of the novel. A typical novel is a series of experiences happening to a central character or to a group of central characters, each of which culminates in a climactic event. The final climactic event resolves the conflicts and the dilemmas of the characters and brings the novel to a close. The shape it takes is as follows:

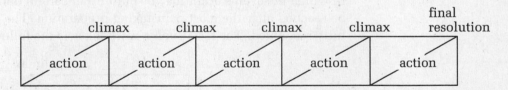

New characters may be introduced in the secondary incidents and characters may suffer and die or leave the scene before the end, but all characters are dealt with in some form before the final resolution or at the final resolution. The final resolution may occur swiftly, or it may be followed by a short or long account of what happens after. In Charles Dickens's *A Tale of Two Cities,* what happens after the climax is presented as a vision of Sydney Carton before he dies. In *The Return of the Native,* Thomas Hardy concludes the novel with a long account of what happens to Clym, Diggory, and Thomasin after the death of Eustacia and Wildeve.

The experiences in a novel need not be sequential or chronological. They may occur at random in the work. But when the final resolution occurs, the reader should be able to visualize the sequence and chronology and to see the story whole. Such a novel is Joseph Conrad's *Lord Jim.*

Frequently, a novelist will concentrate attention on one central character or on a few characters and on a related series of experiences leading to one culminating climax. The novelist will give the reader thorough portraits of his/her character or characters, including detailed psychological analyses, and will build up an elaborate environment in which the characters perform and which affects their lives. In short, he/she will expand what is basically a short story into a novel. Such a novel is Stephen Crane's *The Red Badge of Courage* or Thornton Wilder's *The Bridge of San Luis Rey.*

In *The Bridge of San Luis Rey* the climax is the collapse of the bridge, killing five people. The novel deals in detail with these people and with others involved in their lives. Wilder creates a world of faith and loyalties in which the events occur and which influences all the characters. What we have is a story that moves as follows:

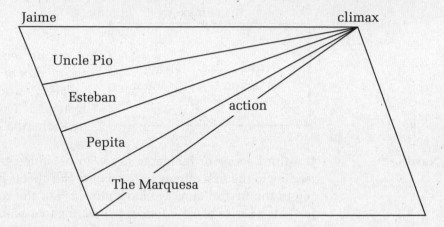

A short story may be expanded into a novel by the inclusion of detail. The central character or characters may be fully described and analyzed, the world in which the events occur may be built up in careful detail, and the climax will be reached after the most painstaking preparation. The aftermath, too, may be fully recounted. The form such a work takes is the following:

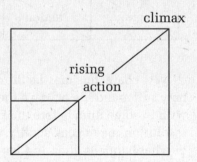

The Modes of Fiction

Quadrilaterals may also be used to clarify certain critical classifications of novels. The experiences in serious novels may be described basically as good or bad. Let us use a quadrilateral this time to represent the experiences of life, and let us divide the experiences into those that depict human goodness and those that depict human malevolence. We will divide the quadrilateral in half, though we recognize that life is never exactly half good and half evil.

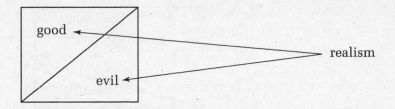

Suppose a writer deals with both the good and bad experiences in the lives of his/her characters, telling it "as it is." We call such a writer a *realistic* writer. There are not many completely realistic writers because, if writers include in their work too many of the everyday experiences of their characters, they are likely to be dull. However, there have been some excellent realistic writers, their work attaining brilliance because of the symbolic significance they were able to give to ordinary things. Leo Tolstoy's *Anna Karenina,* Gustave Flaubert's *Madame Bovary,* and James Joyce's stories in *Dubliners* are realistic.

There are two basic approaches to exposing evil in the world: one is the *satiric* and the second, the factual, or *naturalistic.* The naturalistic writer, aware of evil, describes it in all its ugliness. What we get are scenes of cruel exploitation, dismal poverty, repulsive depravity—all the ills that flesh is heir to, and all the suffering that human beings are capable of inflicting upon their fellows. The writer is moved by misery to expose its causes. Some melodrama, exaggeration of the horror, may enter such a story when the writer is moved to strengthen his/her indictment. Emile Zola's *Germinal,* Theodore Dreiser's *Sister Carrie,* John Steinbeck's *The Grapes of Wrath,* and Stephen Crane's *Maggie, a Girl of the Streets* are naturalistic works.

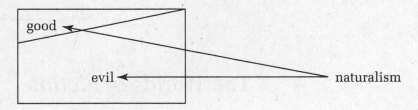

A naturalistic work will, of course, have characters capable of nobility, heroism, and self-sacrifice. Such characters serve to accentuate the ugliness that engulfs them.

If a reader of a particular work finds that the world is good and that human beings are capable of friendship, love, sacrifice, nobility, honor, devotion, patriotism, dedication, heroism, we have a romantic work. Of course, in such a work evil forces will threaten the hero and his friends, but the hero will triumph. If he does not triumph, he will face his doom with courage and without fear, engaging death, as Cyrano did, in a duel.

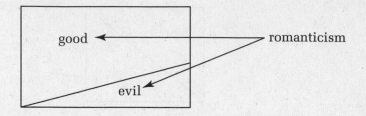

Finally, all three of these forms can occur in an unreal world, a world of *fantasy*. A man, defeated by a dull job and a demanding and parasitic family, can imagine himself as a beetle. A young girl may see death as a dark, handsome, debonair gentleman come to woo her. A boy driven to despair by the demands of home and school may find peace in imaginary snow which fills his house and room and eventually buries him as he lies in bed. A man whose loved one, married to another, dies after bidding him a stormy farewell and after giving birth to a child is haunted by her spirit until his death unites them. The unreal world can be made real, and realism or romanticism can be the spirit of such a work.

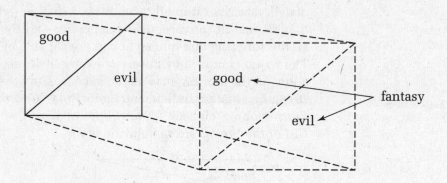

The Worlds of Fiction

You will encounter in your reading of fiction many varied worlds, real and unreal.

The first and most familiar will be the world of everyday experience. The stories you will read will concern themselves with family life, with birth, growth, love, marriage, age, death. They will deal with school, with other places of learning, with work and recreation, with moments of excitement and days of dullness, with heroism and cowardice. A novel such as D. H. Lawrence's *Sons and Lovers* describes the everyday life of a family in a mining town and records the conflicts between husband and wife and the love between mother and son, as well as the love between man and woman. It tells also of a boy's growing to manhood. A short story such as James Joyce's "Araby" records the anguish of a young boy coping with his first love.

Whatever the setting of the story, whether it be a bleak mill town in England, the city of Dublin, or a farm in the Midwest, it is a familiar one because the values and loyalties that move the people in this world are the basic ones that govern our own lives. The problems of those who have great wealth or who live in abject poverty do not enter this world. Its people may not be rich, but they work hard and have enough to eat.

You will notice, however, when you read the best of these works that ordinary objects and ordinary events assume symbolic significance. A reference to a chalice in "Araby" details the religious element in a young boy's love, and the snow in James Joyce's "The Dead" reflects Gabriel Conroy's inner yearning to escape from the stifling milieu of his aunts.

A second world is the world of economic extremes, the kind of world most of us look at from the outside, the world of great power and wealth and the world of soul-starving poverty. From such works we learn how monarchs and millionaires live and what values govern their lives; we learn how the poor and the disinherited of the earth struggle to survive and how their values are eroded. The people that live in these worlds face many of the everyday problems of the everyday world. They, too, are concerned with family loyalties but with a difference. They live with greater tensions, and the climaxes of their lives tend to be more dramatic. In William Faulkner's *As I Lay Dying,* the Bundren family goes through flood and fire to bury the dead mother in Jefferson City, and the enmity among Darl, Jewel, and Dewey Dell ends with Darl's incarceration in an insane asylum.

The values that motivate the rich and powerful and the ones that rule the lives of the poor and exploited are similar to those that operate in the everyday world, but arrogance of the rich and necessity among the poor will lead them more readily to flaunt these values and produce more dramatic outcomes. In addition, among the rich there are the problems of snobbery and boredom and among the poor the devastating problems of hunger, work, misery, and anguish. Often in these worlds the values acquire a nicety, and there is an exaggerated adherence to nobility verging on the sentimental. Peter Brench in Henry James's "The Tree of Knowledge" loves Mrs. Mallow but will not tell her, and he and Mrs. Mallow separately support Mr. Mallow's delusions that he is a great sculptor. Kino, a poor pearl fisher, in John Steinbeck's *The Pearl* learns that finding a pearl sparks an envy that turns almost the entire village against him. In the best of these works, too, familiar objects and events take on symbolic meaning. The pearl, for example, becomes the symbol of Kino's dreams and his assertion of manhood.

A third world is the dramatic one in which the malignant force of nature or the innate evil in human beings turns the universe into a battleground for survival. It is a restless, anxious world, one in which human beings face the slings and arrows of storms, floods, famine, war, revolution, and crime. Caught up in a maelstrom of events they cannot control, people fight for survival, using all the powers of arm and mind granted them by nature. Their values are shaped by two basic drives, to stay alive and to protect those who depend upon them. They will defy God and state and betray values to remain alive and to keep those close to them safe. They will sacrifice much for ideals. The ideals may bear some relation to existing values, or they may break with old values to establish brave new ones. Much self-sacrifice is demanded and offered, and identity and personal needs disappear in the struggle for survival or in the movements to effectuate change. Laura, in Katherine Anne Porter's "Flowering Judas," for example, betrays herself to work for revolution and learns at last that her oblations have been vain.

A fourth world is the "sick" world. The stories deal with people and places gone awry. The atmosphere and the action are ugly, weird, strange, supernatural, shocking. The people are maladjusted, perverted, insane, suicidal, retarded. It is the world of idiots, drug addicts, pimps, prostitutes, sexual perverts, criminals, lunatics. It is a dark world where evil triumphs, preying on human weakness and converting a man or woman into a monstrous being. Sometimes the evil growth-forces in nature produce a pathetic misfit, incapable of governing his life, trying desperately to comprehend his nature and his world and failing because comprehension is beyond him. Such figures, like Benjy in William Faulkner's *The Sound and the Fury,* move through their paces like sad automata, unaware of meaning or purpose in their lives. Other forms of disturbed personalities appear in many stories. In Franz Kafka's "Metamorphosis" a man awakes one morning and discovers himself to be a beetle. In Conrad Aiken's "Silent Snow, Secret Snow," a boy, unable to cope with life, slowly goes mad. In D. H. Lawrence's "The Rocking Horse Winner" a boy kills himself to get for his mother the money he thinks will make her happy. In Katherine Anne Porter's "Noon Wine" a homicidal maniac who has found peace and friendship working for the Thompsons is destroyed by Mr. Hatch, who seeks to bring him to justice. In the worlds of these stories the sacred values are questioned. A murderer may be a decent man. A devoted mother may be a monster. A gentle-appearing schoolmaster may be a sadist.

The fifth world is the world of fantasy. It is an unreal world in which dreams unattainable in the real world are often fulfilled. It is a romantic world in which Heathcliff and Cathy (characters in Emily Brontë's *Wuthering Heights*) are united in death, where the Walter Mittys are daredevil heroes.

It is also often a satiric world created by writers to expose the evils of the real world. It is the world of Swift's *Gulliver's Travels* and Voltaire's *Candide;* of Huxley's *Brave New World* and Orwell's *1984;* of Carroll's *Alice in Wonderland* and Orwell's *Animal Farm;* of Golding's *Lord of the Flies* and France's *Penguin Island.* Everything is possible in a world of fantasy. Animals talk, create institutions, quarrel, and destroy what they have created. Lilliputians find the giant Gulliver asleep on the shore of their land and capture him. Alice attends a mad tea party.

In a world of fantasy, strange and wonderful and terrible things can happen. A boy rides a rocking horse with wild abandon and thereby learns what horse will win a race. A woman is stoned to death by friendly neighbors because she picks the lot with the black spot. Such stories are not always diverting. They hint at the dark elements in the mind and heart of human beings and probe into the darkness of their past. In these stories, too, the values of a particular society are either upheld and strengthened or questioned and ridiculed.

Reading and Responding to Literature

Elements of Literary Interpretation

As an AP English student you are expected to respond to a short story, a play, or a novel with something more substantial than "It's good," or "I didn't like it." Not that a snap judgment about a piece of literature is wrong, but you might render the same verdict about a song by Elton John or a dish of pudding. A piece of literature on which an author toiled, sometimes for years, deserves more than a simple thumbs up or thumbs down. The next several pages explain and illustrate what thoughtful people think about when they read fiction or go to the theater. By studying this material, your repertoire of responses to literature should grow broader and more piquant. As you prepare for the AP English exam, that's a goal worth striving for.

Subjective, or visceral, responses. Typically, an initial response to a work of literature is emotional. It comes from your heart rather than your head. Perhaps the beauty of the language has moved you, the author's passion has stirred your soul, or you've been struck by the force of a new idea. Perhaps you identify with a character, or the story is so compellingly presented that you lose yourself in the work and must exert some effort to jolt yourself back into reality. Do you recall the gripping scene early in Herman Hesse's *Siddhartha,* when the young Siddhartha, hoping to exact his father's permission to leave home to join the wandering Samanas, stands waiting silently all through the night? Siddhartha's vigil proves to his father how desperately his son wishes to leave. Whether you empathize with the young man on the verge of adulthood or feel pity for his hapless father who wants to protect his only son from harm, or even if you don't take sides at all, it's hard to resist being caught up in the timeless and universal conflict between generations that the incident epitomizes.

No doubt you can think of other scenes from literature that for a time drew you away from the world of reality into the world of fiction. During those moments you literally gave yourself up to the world of the book or story. How, you might ask, does a work elicit such a hypnotic response? The answer, of course, lies partly within you. As a reader, you are willing to surrender yourself to the world created by the author. More specifically, your sensibilities are stimulated by esthetic and psychological forces that a skillful author marshals through use of language, style, form, rhythmic patterns, allusions, figurative expression, and much, much more, including the so-called world of the work. Basically, the intensity of an emotional response to a piece of literature is determined by how thoroughly you become immersed in its world. When you give yourself completely, you tend to like, even to love, the work. When you can't "get into" the work, or the work holds you at arm's length, your response will be unfavorable or, at best, indifferent.

Understanding the "world of the work." Like strangers arriving in a town for the first time, readers try to get their bearings when they enter a fictional world. They want to know almost immediately where they are, what kind of place it is, and what sort of people they should expect to meet. Broadly speaking, they need to make sense of the "world of the work" in which they find themselves, and from the first page seek such information as: In what kind of community does the action occur? What are the customs, the beliefs, the values of the community? What is sacred in this society and what is held in scorn? What forms of behavior and response are expected from those who live within its boundaries? What are the patterns of daily life, what patterns of faith are typical, and what patterns are considered atypical and therefore suspect? What institutions exist in this society, and how effectively are they functioning? What causes tension among the different members of this society? Are there conflicts and disagreements? What forms do they take? Are they open or secret?

With a profusion of details, some of which may at first strike you as trivial and unnecessary, authors often present a full-blown portrait of a society to their readers. In *War and Peace,* Tolstoy, never one to skimp on words, piles facts on facts and details on details to help readers understand what it meant to be a Russian noble at the time of Napoleon's ill-fated attempt to conquer Russia in the early 1800s. Likewise, Thomas Mann in *Buddenbrooks* draws a well-rounded picture of middle-class life—the births, christenings, marriages, divorces, deaths, the commercial successes and failures—all the commonplace happenings in the lives of four generations of a wealthy burgher family in Germany during the nineteenth century. And William Faulkner, in his fourteen Yoknapatawpha novels and many stories, creates a fictional county in northern Mississippi with a long social history, a culture, and a population of 6,298 whites and 9,313 blacks. Some readers are impatient with long passages of background material. They skim over matters that describe the setting, the social and cultural milieu, and the history of a place in order to get to the meat and potatoes of the story. Try to avoid doing that. Be assured that an author has portrayed the world of the work, not to make the book longer or more tedious, but to orient you to the world of the work. Moreover, because surroundings profoundly influence the thoughts, emotions, and actions of the characters, a place can be as significant to a story as any of the people in it. If you accustom yourself to carefully reading the descriptions of setting and other background matters, your experience with the book will be that much richer, and you will soon grow aware of the reasons for the selection of details.

As you read a work of literature and become involved in its world, you can hardly avoid making judgments about it, first in terms of your own values and then in terms of the esthetic, philosophical, and moral values that prevail in your own culture and society. When you enter the world of Franz Kafka's *The Castle,* for example, you are suddenly transported to a weirdly illogical place where the individual struggles against ubiquitous, elusive, and anonymous powers. As someone accustomed to a degree of freedom and autonomy, you are likely to be repelled by the world Kafka has created. Yet, you read on because the story of "K," the novel's protagonist, resonates with you and perhaps causes you to reflect on the pathos of a place where human isolation is the norm and an individual's quest for freedom and responsibility never succeeds. Certainly you wouldn't choose to live in a world such as Kafka's. In fact, you couldn't even if you wanted to. His world doesn't exist except in the pages of his novel, but in spite of knowing that fact, readers suspend their disbelief, even their rationality at times, and go along with the illusion. Thus, the worlds of Oedipus's Thebes, Hamlet's Elsinore, Ethan Frome's Starkfield, and Madame Bovary's Rouen seem as real to readers as their own home towns—more real, perhaps, while the folks next door, not to mention members of your own family, can be forever strangers.

The conclusions that readers draw about the world of the work usually are the most enduring. Readers may soon forget the names of characters, subplots, elements of form and structure, twists and turns of the story, and stylistic conceits. What remains embedded in the mind is that which gives a piece of literature its general identity. Thus, the world of Hemingway's *The Sun Also Rises* is the American expatriate subculture drifting through Europe after World War I. The world of Dickens's *A Tale of Two Cities* is London and Paris during the time of the French Revolution and the Reign of Terror. Flaubert's *Madame Bovary* depicts the plight of a middle-class woman in nineteenth-century France.

Responding to characters. While the "world of the work" helps to identify a piece of literature, what attracts most readers to a story, novel, or play is usually its cast of characters. After all, literature is about people, and in literature you meet such interesting and unusual types, from monsters to heroes, from losers to people you'd die to know in real life. Unless you are a self-centered, antisocial, reclusive egomaniac, you probably have an abiding curiosity about other people—how they live, what they think, and most of all, what they are like. That may explain why so much of one's daily conversation and thinking are about other people, and also why character analysis is often the most agreeable aspect of literary criticism.

In books, characters' innermost lives are often revealed as they rarely are in life. You are privy to others' desires and dreams and to secrets that would be virtually impossible to know if the character actually existed. In *Moby Dick,* for instance, you learn in the very first paragraph that Ishmael is subject to bouts of depression, that he follows funerals, pauses in front of coffin warehouses and has a hard time resisting the urge to knock people's hats off. You learn too that "whenever it is a damp, drizzly November" in Ishmael's soul, he casts off his anger and spleen by going to the ocean and boarding a ship to see "the watery part of the world." Were Ishmael a fellow you just met on a bus, how long would it take to learn so many intimate facts about him?

At the start of *Crime and Punishment,* you learn that the protagonist, Raskolnikov, is a "crushingly poor" student, that he is frightened by his landlady, to whom he owes money, and that he's got murder on his mind. In fact, when you meet him, he's going out to rehearse the murder he soon expects to commit. Because would-be killers usually don't advertise their intentions, you know something about Raskolnikov that would never be revealed to you in real life.

On the other hand, in a work of literature not everything about a character is presented. You see only that portion of a person the author chooses to show, sometimes a more circumscribed and limited view than you might see in reality. This is necessary because people are multidimensional, and there are countless elements of a character's behavior, speech, emotional life, and personality that are extraneous to the author's purpose. To include what Romeo liked to eat for breakfast or how often Richard III took a bath might thrill a gossip-hound but would only befuddle Shakespeare's aims. Even though you see only part of a character's whole being, however, an author's skill can transmute the selected elements we are given into a revelation of the entire person. Functioning like a metonymy, the parts you see provide a pretty accurate picture of the whole character. Thus you can easily speculate that, given the choice of staying home and reading a book on Friday night or going bowling with the gang, Elizabeth Bennet in *Pride and Prejudice* would sit in the parlor and read, and McMurphy in *One Flew Over the Cuckoo's Nest* would end up at Bowl-o-Rama.

Like people in real life, characters in literature reflect the world in which they live. Because they have been shaped by the customs, beliefs, and values of their time and place, their thoughts and actions shed light on the world of the work and may reveal aspects of their society that might otherwise remain hidden. For example, Macbeth first resists murdering the king because Duncan is his overnight guest at Inverness. Macbeth's thoughts reveal the sanctity of the relationship between a monarch and his subjects as well as his particular responsibility to keep his guests safe from harm. Knowing that by murdering Duncan, Macbeth violates a "double trust," you can more fully understand why guilt drives him to ruin later in the play. In *A Tale of Two Cities,* the actions of memorable Madame Defarge embody the anger and resentment of the French lower classes against the aristocracy at the time of the Revolution. In Richard Wright's novel, *Native Son,* Bigger Thomas, for all practical purposes, represents the victimization of blacks in America during the 1950s. Such characters, while having distinctive and discrete personalities, function also as docents to their unique worlds. In a sense, they reveal the lay of the land and show you around.

In any work of literature, you are likely to meet an assortment of minor characters who show up once or twice in a play or novel, help to move the story along or add local color to the world of the work. They are not throwaway characters. Pay attention to them, especially when they touch the lives of the main, more fully developed people in the story. In Steinbeck's *The Grapes of Wrath*, the Joad family, en route to California, meets scores of minor characters, among them a one-eyed junk dealer, portrayed as a pathetic and defeated loser whose chief joy in life is to feel sorry for himself. Why give the man more than a glance? On the surface, he is just another hapless victim of the Depression and Dust Bowl of the 1930s. His presence in the book, however, serves another function: to contrast vividly with Tom Joad, whose troubles are no less burdensome than the junk dealer's. Yet Tom won't be defeated. He endures, and when you consider how easy it was succumb to self-pity, Tom's fortitude is all the more impressive.

Fully comprehending fictional characters takes time and vision. Examine not only their individual personalities but their relationships with one another, their actions and thoughts in response to the demands of these relationships, and their behavior in response to the demands of the community. Like a detective, seek motives for their actions, especially in terms of what the characters presently are and what they hope to be or to achieve. Ask how they see themselves and how they are seen by others, and try to determine how the narrator or author wishes you to see them.

In general, look for information about characters in three main places.

1. *What the author or narrator tells you.* What you learn about a character is determined, of course, by what the author wishes to tell you. Thus, the author wields great power in influencing your attitude toward a character. In *Crime and Punishment*, Dostoevsky describes the old pawnbroker this way: "She was a tiny dried-up scrap of a creature, about sixty years old, with sharp, malicious little eyes and a small sharp nose. . . Her fair hair, just beginning to go grey, was thick with grease. A strip of flannel was twisted round her long thin neck, which was wrinkled and yellow like a hen's legs . . . ." Perhaps you'll agree that Dostoevsky was trying to stack the cards against the old lady. He seems to want the reader to feel repulsed by her appearance, just as Raskolnikov is, and to feel, as Raskolnikov and others do, that her death will be no great loss to society. Descriptions such as that of the pawnbroker not only help to define characters but sometimes provide clues to the author's overall purpose. In part, *Crime and Punishment* attacks the nihilists of mid-nineteenth-century Russia, who rejected all traditional moral values. To Dostoevsky, a nihilist had no right to take another's life, even if the victim were a wretched old hag.

2. *What other characters say.* When information comes from other characters, you must be more circumspect. Don't accept the information at face value, not at the outset, at least. Like people in real life, characters in literature have hidden motives, vested interests, propensities to distort the truth or to exaggerate—all qualities that keep them from describing others with complete accuracy and objectivity. After you're familiar with an informant's background and personality, you'll then be in a somewhat better position to judge the validity of the information given to

you. Better still, try to define the relationship between the speaker and the character about whom he or she is talking, as well as the dynamics between speaker and listener. Each of these relationships may subtly alter what the speaker says. When, for instance, Mr. Collins in *Pride and Prejudice* first describes his patroness, Lady Catherine de Bourgh, in a letter to the Bennets, you might well believe that the honorable lady has a kind, benevolent soul. After meeting Mr. Collins in person, however, and hearing from Jane Austen that he is "not a sensible man," but rather a "mixture of pride and obsequiousness, self-importance and humility," your preconceptions of Lady Catherine's bounty must be cast aside. Why does Mr. Collins present Lady Catherine as an exalted figure when, in fact, she is a rancorous shrew? In the answer lies a clue to Mr. Collins's personality and values. Consider also the works of Joseph Conrad. Does Marlow's view of Jim in *Lord Jim* and of Kurtz in *Heart of Darkness* coincide with the actual characters? Or is Marlow's vision slightly blurry? If Marlow is not seeing Jim and Kurtz clearly, why not?

Before drawing your conclusions about characters, it pays to identify the sources of your information and weigh the validity of the evidence. Are the sources reliable? Is there any reason to believe that the sources themselves have been misled or that shading or distorting the truth is in their own best interest?

3. *What characters say and how they act.* The words and actions of characters are probably the surest indicators of who they truly are. Nevertheless, proceed cautiously in making definitive character analyses because fictional people, like those in real life, often lie, put on airs, wear masks, and disguise their true nature in countless other ways. Stories told in first person are particularly resistant to easy analysis because narrators will often be very selective in choosing what to reveal about themselves. At the beginning, any judgments you make should be extremely tentative. Through much of *Huckleberry Finn,* Huck, the narrator, calls himself "ornery" and "low down." In other words, he doesn't think much of himself because no one has ever thought much of him. By the end of the book, though, you realize that Huck has many admirable qualities—basic kindness, loyalty, love of life, and a well-tuned sense of right and wrong. In short, don't be swayed by everything that characters say about themselves. Only after reading the last page should you feel reasonably sure that you fully grasp what makes a character tick.

Whether the old observation that "actions speak louder than words" applies to analysis of characters in literature is a question worth pondering. Do actions or do words provide more helpful clues? Hamlet has customarily been seen as confused and contemplative. In soliloquies and speeches, he grieves at his own inability to act decisively. Yet, as the play goes on, Hamlet adopts an "antic disposition," writes some lines for the traveling players, kills Polonius, plots against Rosenkrantz and Guildenstern, fights Laertes, and more. He may be more of a man of action than he claims to be.

When analyzing a character it is equally important to take into account who is telling the story. The narrator or speaker will deeply affect your perceptions. In the short story by Willa Cather, "Paul's Case," Paul, a troublesome teenager, is someone people loved to hate. Had the tale of his adventures been told from his own viewpoint, however, he might have explained and justified his delinquent behavior, causing you to judge him less harshly. But had his bitterly disappointed father told the story, Paul would probably lack a single redeeming trait. Since Cather assumes the role of omniscient narrator, you get all the facts about Paul but no cues as to the way you should feel about the facts. Therefore, your attitude toward Paul is likely to fall somewhere between scorn and pity.

Of all the characters in a play, novel or story, those that require the most careful scrutiny are the protagonist and the antagonist. The protagonist particularly deserves your attention because that person very often bears messages from the author. Consider such characters as King Lear, Elizabeth Bennet (*Pride and Prejudice*), and Lieutenant Frederic Henry (*A Farewell to Arms*). Lear's division of his kingdom unleases the forces that lead ultimately to the catastrophic ending of the play. Shakespeare uses Lear to show the consequences of upsetting the natural order that Elizabethans held dear. Through Elizabeth Bennet, Jane Austen comments on issues of marriage and the burdens borne by single women in the polite society of her time, and Lieutenant Henry's life and experience vividly illustrate the loss of innocence and the disillusionment that Hemingway means to convey in his story of love and death in World War I.

Usually it is quite clear who the protagonist is in a work of fiction. Occasionally, however, especially when the conflict pits two equally "good" forces against each other, or when two appealing personalities clash, it is not so easy. Generally a case can be made for either character. Is it Phaedra or Hippolytus who is the protagonist of Euripides' *Hippolytus*? Is it Antigone or Creon who is the protagonist of Sophocles' *Antigone*? Who is the protagonist of Conrad's *Heart of Darkness*? Is it Marlow, the narrator, who receives from Kurtz's experience a revelation of the potential for evil in man? Or is it Kurtz, who is destroyed by the baleful consequences of living in the tropics and acquiring supreme power over the natives of the region?

Identifying the true protagonist is not necessarily a critical issue, of course, but it often forces you to think deeply about the characters, events, and themes in a work of literature. In that sense, it is a valuable exercise in literary analysis. Similarly, the identity of the antagonist, the force that opposes the protagonist, is worth pondering. Antagonists range from individual adversaries, who for various reasons seek to thwart the protagonist, to inner psychological demons that threaten or even destroy him. Consider Akaky Akakievich, the protagonist of Gogol's "The Overcoat." He falls prey to his associates at work, to the Russian bureacracy, to the frigid St. Petersburg winter, and to the muggers who steal the coat. All seem to conspire to defeat Akaky, but he is really brought down by an internal nemesis, his inability to cope with the slings and arrows of workaday life. The protagonist of Eugene O'Neill's play *The Emperor Jones* is pursued through the jungle by rebel tribesmen who seek to dethrone him, but it remains unclear whether he is finally subdued by the hunters or by the accumulated horrors of his life that appear in his mind's eye as he tries to avoid capture. Hamlet must overcome the thinking that "puzzles the will" before he can move to avenge the murder of his father. Othello falls prey to jealousy, the "green-eyed monster." In both *Hamlet* and *Othello,* the protagonists face physical adversaries (Claudius, among others, and Iago), but the main sources of their tragedies lie within themselves.

In many works, protagonists encounter forces that are other than human. Nature and God can also deal a cruel hand. The central conflicts in Ole Rolvaag's *Giants in the Earth,* Willa Cather's *My Antonia,* and Pearl Buck's *The Good Earth* find humans struggling against nature. Per Hansa, the Shimerda family, and Wang Lung face unrelenting hardships while scraping a living from the land or trying to survive in the face of nature's freakish, seemingly antagonistic, behavior. Opposition from the gods often comes in the form of fate that, for good or ill, determines human destiny. In the works of Thomas Hardy, fate invariably shapes the lives of the characters. No matter how hard she tries to pick herself up from despair, Tess, the protagonist of *Tess of the d'Urbervilles,* experiences one setback after another. Her destiny is to suffer and die. Fate plays a crucial role in classical Greek drama. Oedipus, Antigone, Agamemnon, Clytemnestra, and Orestes cannot avert the disasters that the oracles decree for them. Like Hamlet, Othello, and King Lear, they also suffer from a personal flaw that to a large extent contributes to their fate.

Economic, social, and political forces also serve as the grist of literature. How people cope with poverty and hunger, oppression and greed, is the theme of works like John Steinbeck's *The Grapes of Wrath,* Emile Zola's *Germinal,* and Upton Sinclair's *The Jungle.* How people of color respond to prejudice and alienation is dealt with in novels like Ralph Ellison's *Invisible Man,* Toni Morrison's *Beloved,* and David Guterson's *Snow Falling on Cedars.* The laws and institutions that a society establishes to maintain order sometimes produce injustice that overwhelms innocent members of the society. Such situations occur in John Galsworthy's *Justice,* Victor Hugo's *Les Miserables,* and Theodore Dreiser's *An American Tragedy.* Frequently also, idealists—those who see flaws in society and try to fix them—run headlong into the opposition of vested interests who want to preserve the status quo. Such confrontations are the stuff of Hendrick Ibsen's *An Enemy of the People,* George Bernard Shaw's *Saint Joan,* and Ernest Hemingway's *For Whom the Bell Tolls.*

In the end, the crux of a work of literature, and the very reason you are apt to keep reading, is the struggle between the protagonist and the antagonist. A story ends in either victory or defeat, but it could just as well end in a stalemate. Victory leads most often to a happy ending, defeat to a tragic one, although many works end ambiguously by balancing a bit of both. With the human condition being so subtle and the human personality so complex, it is not surprising that what sometimes appears as disaster may be a triumph, particularly when an assertion of moral force accompanies the fall or when the protagonist's collapse is accompanied by the promise of a resurrection of good. As *Wuthering Heights* draws to a close, for instance, Heathcliff's fury is spent. Heathcliff joins his beloved Catherine in death, and the tempests subside. Young Catherine and Hareton now can find tranquility in a world cleansed of the passionate extremes of love and hate. Oedipus blinds himself after he discovers the truth about the murder of Laius. The act, however, restores clarity to his vision of himself. Yes, he was wronged by the casual and wanton actions of the gods, but he sees clearly that his quest for power and his arrogance have caused his downfall. He paid the price of thinking that he was an equal of the gods. In disaster he finds the peace that had eluded him throughout his life.

Hearing the voice of the author. Every piece of literature has a narrator or speaker. Sometimes, as in essay and biography, it is the author's voice you hear. In fiction and poetry, on the other hand, the identity of the narrator may not be so apparent. In order to fully appreciate the piece, however, you should try to figure out who is speaking. It is not always easy to do so. It takes practice to examine the language and imagery, the characters and conflicts, the themes and plots—virtually every aspect of a literary work—to discover whether the narrator or speaker is the author, a surrogate assigned to speak for the author, or an invented voice whose beliefs and values differ from the author's. Because an author's views are often signaled in the tone of a work, you must be alert for clues to the narrator's attitude. By scrutinizing language you will detect satire, irony, humor, sentimentality, detachment, foreboding, melancholy, anger, and countless other states of the narrator's mind and feelings.

Gustave Flaubert uses *Madame Bovary,* in part, to express disapproval of the treatment of women in France in the 1850s. Moreover, the novel's focus on Emma's inner life—her memories, dreams, and fantasies—might very well reflect Flaubert's own obsessions with love, sexuality, and art. Because straight-laced Germans of the early 1900s spurned romantic writers, Herman Hesse wrote the novel *Steppenwolf* to tell the reading public of his displeasure about how artists and intellectuals felt ostracized. Some critics consider *The Grapes of Wrath* a piece of literary propaganda that Steinbeck wrote to espouse his socialist views. *Women in Love* by D. H. Lawrence has a pervasive note of gloom that undoubtedly reflects the author's response to World War I. Novels like *Johnny Got His Gun* by Dalton Trumbo and *All Quiet on the Western Front* by Erich Maria Remarque are statements that passionately convey their authors' antiwar positions.

When a story is told in first person, the narrator may or may not represent the author's views. The narrator in "Family Happiness," a story by Tolstoy, is Masha, an innocent young woman from the country who falls in love with and marries an older man. Masha is swept up by the social whirl when her new husband introduces her to big city life. In every way, she's a world apart from Tolstoy himself, who was well over fifty and firmly entrenched in his country estate when he wrote the story. In *Wuthering Heights,* several narrators, including Lockwood, Catherine, Ellen Dean, Heathcliff, and Isabella, tell the story. None of them speaks for Emily Brontë, the author. Nick Carraway narrates *The Great Gatsby,* but he is not F. Scott Fitzgerald, although they both came from Minnesota and attended Ivy League colleges. (If anything, Jay Gatsby is more like Fitzgerald.) Similarly, David Copperfield is not Charles Dickens, nor is Ishmael Herman Melville in *Moby Dick,* although some parallels exist between the lives of the characters and the lives of the authors. Poetry offers the same kinds of ambiguities as prose fiction. Shakespeare's sonnets are assumed to express the poet's love for the so-called dark lady, but you can't be sure. The poems of the romantics (Wordsworth, Keats, Shelley, and Coleridge) seem also to have been written straight from the heart, but there are exceptions. One certainty, however, is that in dramatic monologues, such as "My Last Duchess" by Robert Browning, the speaker is always someone other than the poet. In drama, except when a playwright deliberately uses a narrator, as in *Our Town* and *A Man for All Seasons,* there seems to be no omniscient narrator, although one or more characters in a play may very well represent and express the author's views.

Third-person narrators are often trickier to pin down, for authors are wont to invent voices completely different from their own. The narrator may be the author, but often is not, and there is a danger of misinterpretation in ascribing to the author the views and attitudes of the narrator. Would it be fair to say that the author of *Studs Lonigan,* James T. Farrell, is anti-Catholic or anti-Irish because he presents a critical portrait of Irish-Catholic life in Chicago? Is Philip Roth of *Goodbye, Columbus* fame antisemitic because so many of the Jewish characters in his novels behave badly? Are James Joyce's views of Catholicism in *Portrait of the Artist as a Young Man* the same as those of his protagonist Stephen Dedalus? Contrary to what many readers think, Jonathan Swift, the author of *Gulliver's*

Travels, did not accept entirely the beliefs by which the Houyhnhnms governed their lives. Nor did Voltaire, who wrote *Candide,* find perfection and the answer to the ills of mankind in the values of El Dorado.

Omniscient narrators complicate the task of identifying the author's views because they move in and out of characters' minds, know everything about everybody and may even pause occasionally to editorialize on the story they are telling you. In order to thoughtfully judge the psychological and social connection between authors and narrators, study carefully the manner in which narrators tell the story and the range and completeness of their knowledge of characters and events. Do they know all about the characters' lives and background? Who is their source? Do they know what characters are thinking and dreaming? Are they privy to confidential information? Is the narrator a character in the story or just an observer? Answers to such questions help to unravel the tone of a story. Edith Wharton's *Ethan Frome* is narrated by a young man who hears the story from Ethan himself twenty-four years after the events occurred. Since memory is highly selective, readers should not unquestioningly accept everything in the account of Ethan's love affair with Mattie Silver as the absolute truth. Similarly, because *First Love* by Ivan Turgenev is a story of sixteen-year-old Vladimir's first brush with love told by Vladimir in middle age, distortions and semitruths are bound to occur.

In brief, readers should be aware of the distance between the narrator and the events in the story. They should also try to ascertain the distance between the narrator and the author. In calculating this distance, it may be tempting to read a life story of the author in search of traces of autobiography in the fiction. Perceptive readers ordinarily eschew such aid because they are able to find sufficient evidence in the text itself to draw reasonable conclusions about the purpose and meaning of the work—conclusions, that is, about what the author thinks.

But no simple formula or prescription will provide a technique for determining the author's point of view. Works of literature are often too complex and subtly written to yield easy answers. As you know, a work of literature frequently may be read or interpreted in various ways. One reader may draw from the content, form, and language a valid meaning amply supported by evidence in the text, while another reader may find an equally valid alternate meaning. The threat of being dead wrong is real, but feeling strongly about an interpretation and wishing that it were valid won't make it so. Whenever you have doubts, go back to the text to look for supporting evidence. A careful rereading may either strengthen your position or expose its weaknesses.

On pages 291–297 you'll find a number of different interpretations of Shakespeare's *Hamlet.* Each can be supported by the text of the play. Which is the most accurate? And which the most compelling?

Responding to the art of literature. Although it is often said that literature imitates life, it doesn't. A literal imitation or realistic recreation of life suits filmmakers (thus the popularity of *cinema verité*) more than writers of fiction. Authors select experiences from the vast context of life and redesign them to suit their purposes. By doing so, authors abstract life and give it a form and a semblance of order rarely found in the chaotic universe in which we lead our lives. The result is often a unified and coherent literary work. All its parts—the world of the work, the action, the characters, the theme, the language, the imagery—combine to produce a pleasing artistic structure.

Structure, in fact, applies to all the arts. A medieval cathedral, for example, has a specific floor plan, usually in the shape of a cross. It has a central nave, side aisles, transepts, an apse, and three entrances, symbolizing the Holy Trinity. Huge pillars, surrounded by smaller satellite pillars, hold up the heavy slate roof using a system of rib vaults. Flying buttresses transfer structural forces to strong outer walls. Stained glass windows and a large centrally located rose window permit a wash of iridescent light throughout the dim interior. Tall towers reach toward the heavens. In its composition, the cathedral is a harmonious work of art, its pieces, when taken as a whole, reflecting a coherent faith in God.

This kind of organic unity is a characteristic of good literature, too. As a student of literature, you should be aware that individual elements work together to create a sense of unity in a novel, story, play, or poem. If you focus on only one element (the characters, for example), you'd find yourself in the position of the blind men and the elephant, using only a small piece of evidence to generalize about the whole thing. Determining how individual parts blend with each other to achieve organic unity is not always easy to pin down or to articulate. Yet you know organic unity when you see it and miss it when it's not there. Of course, no one says, "Okay, I'm going to read this book for its organic unity." Rather, a reader's intuition or sense of harmony and balance will serve as a guide. You know that neon lights don't belong in a cathedral, nor a rumble seat on a sleek new Porsche. Likewise, an incongruous turn of events, trite ideas, senseless sequences, a character's inconsistent or impossible behavior, figurative language that seems forced, dialogue that is stylized and artificial, as well as many other writing sins tend to tear organic unity apart.

Unity is achieved partly through the structure of a work. For instance, the Italian sonnet, discussed earlier in this book (pages 130–136), consists of two parts. The first part, the octave, develops a question, a story, or an idea. The second section, the sestet, offers an answer, a comment, or a proposition. If either part were missing or out of synch with the other, the coherence and unity of the piece would be lost. Similarly, plays, discussed in detail in a previous chapter, are often constructed like a pyramid, the moment of their greatest tension at the apex. A play with a too early climax would flop. Because novels are often long and far-ranging, discovering their structure takes time and practice.

One simply structured work is Conrad's "The Secret Sharer." Like its style of writing, the tale is straightforward, with no shifts in time and space. The story's structure consists simply of a character's movement from ignorance to knowledge. By the end of the story the young captain knows himself more thoroughly. As a consequence, he is a better leader than he was at the start. You'll find a more complex structure in *The Great Gatsby*. Fitzgerald begins the story in the present, using the first three chapters to describe the novel's four main locales: Daisy's house, the valley of ashes, New York City, and Gatsby's house. The plot of the novel is developed in the next several chapters. Only toward the middle of the book, when he is pretty sure that the reader will be curious about the enigmatic Gatsby, does Fitzgerald begin to tell the story of Gatsby's past. In the climactic last chapter, the past and the present come together. This design seems to suit the novel perfectly because Fitzgerald reveals information as Nick Carraway gets it, in bits and pieces over a period of time. As the story approaches its climax, the reader learns more and more about Gatsby so that by the end, Gatsby's motivation and behavior are thoroughly understandable. The technique that Fitzgerald employs—first-person narrative combined with gradual revelation of the past—works well and endows the novel with unity and coherence.

The unifying structure of Joyce's *Portrait of the Artist as a Young Man* invites several interpretations, the simplest being that each of the book's five chapters represents a stage in Stephen Dedalus's growth from childhood to maturity. The book has also been thought to have a three-part structure that reflects the three phases of Stephen's increasing self-awareness. An alternate view is that the book is structured as a series of rhythmic waves. Each chapter moves from a trough of Stephen's self-doubt to a peak of triumph. Since the action rises slowly, only to fall at the start of the next chapter, the pattern has also been likened to the myth of Daedalus, Stephen's mythic namesake. Each chapter recounts Stephen's attempt to break away, and at each chapter's end, he breaks another link in the chain that binds him to his roots. Finally, at the book's climax, Stephen leaves for good. Whether he will succeed in the world like Daedulus or fall like Icarus remains unclear.

In general, unity achieved through the structure of a work plays subtly on a reader's response. Far more direct is storytelling technique. Readers are perpetually aware of *how* the story is told. Because there are innumerable ways to tell a tale, no one method is superior to another. What counts is whether the manner of storytelling fits the point and purpose of the story being told. The most elementary way, of course, is chronological. What happens first is told first, what happens next is told next, and so on. Children's stories are usually told chronologically, as are picaresque novels like Cervantess *Don Quixote* and Henry Fielding's *Tom Jones,* in which a central character undergoes numerous adventures, one after another. Most chronological works, however, refer to things past, often to give readers background for comprehending what comes next. For example, Homer's *The Odyssey* begins with Telemachus's decision to journey forth to seek news of his absentee father. Why the young man undertakes the search is not made clear until Homer goes back in time to tell the story of Odysseus's adventures after the Trojan War. In almost all of Shakespeare's plays, as well as in dramas by Ibsen and others, early dialogue informs the audience of the events that occurred before the curtain rose.

A backward look can also provide a window into a character. When Billy Budd, the title character of Melville's story, is impressed into His Majesty's navy, the captain of Billy's ship explains to the British lieutenant (and to the reader) that Billy is no ordinary sailor. He's "the best man . . . the jewel of 'em," the crewmember whose presence turned the ship from a "rat-pit of quarrels" to a place of peace and good will. This description accounts for Billy's subsequent actions and makes his tragic fate all the more poignant. Then, too, Jay Gatsby is a more intriguing character because we are told that long ago he may have been not only a crook, a bootlegger, and a companion of criminals, but also a German spy and a killer. Similarly, in *Candide,* characters frequently stop to relate tales of their past misfortunes. Still other stories, such as Melville's "Bartleby the Scrivener" and Turgenev's "First Love," begin with a narrator in the present recalling events of long ago, another popular storytelling device.

Conrad's *Lord Jim,* Faulkner's *As I Lay Dying,* and Toni Morrison's *Beloved* use another narrative technique for relating the story. Each of these novels depends for its effectiveness on the compatibility between the content and form. In other words, their form follows their function. Events are recounted by multiple voices that move forward and backward in time. Because the voices change repeatedly, we are told of the same events again and again, but each time from a different perspective. In *Beloved,* for example, we hear of Paul D's arrival in Cincinnati related first from Denver's point of view, then later by Sethe and then by Paul D. Some readers react negatively to this kind of storytelling, claiming that it's too repetitious and confusing, or that the author's virtuosity as an artist seems to overshadow the point of the book itself. To a point, such responses may be valid. (Certainly they're valid for those readers.) On the other hand, life is often like a Gordion knot: disorderly, chaotic, and too complex to unravel easily, and in order to be faithful to reality, stories should not oversimplify human experience.

Clearly, a piece of literature need not be realistic to reflect real life. Even the most improbable stories can mirror reality. Think of the fantastical occurrences in works by authors from Hawthorne to Hesse, the absurdist plays of Ionesco, Albee, and Becket, and the remarkable story by Nikolai Gogol, "The Nose," in which a man discovers one morning that his nose has vanished from his face, only to have it show up in the breakfast muffin of his barber, who lives across town. Literature is filled with unnatural events and supernatural beings. The story of Hamlet is launched by the appearance of a ghost, the setting of *Beloved* is haunted by the spirit of a dead child, and Gulliver for a time is taken prisoner by a horde of people no taller than his thumb. Does this mean that Shakespeare, Morrison, and Swift and their fellow authors have a distorted sense of reality? No, it means that they give expression to reality rather than recreate it. Having apprehended reality, authors transmute it and give it a shape and a clarity by focusing on meticulously selected elements that depict their vision sharply and truthfully. Artistic license permits authors to shuffle sequences, omit or enlarge happenings, change and combine characters, spin the world in any way they like, but there are limits to their freedom. On the whole, unless there is an artistic reason for doing so, they should not introduce implausible psychological distortions in human response or behavior. If an incident could not happen in any world, real or imagined, or if a character with a certain personality acts inconsistently, or if historical anomalies creep into the work (e.g., the use of jet planes in World War II) the author may well have betrayed the truth, misrepresented reality, and written a flawed work—but not always.

Before you can respond somewhat intelligently to a work of literature, therefore, it helps to be a little dry behind the ears, that is, to have tasted a little bit of life, either in person or vicariously. If you didn't know anything about individual freedom, for example, reading Kafka's *The Castle* would be a totally meaningless exercise, or if you had no understanding of religion, it would be pointless to read, say, *Portrait of the Artist as a Young Man.* In other words, responses to books involve assessing how effectively authors have remolded the raw material of life into works of art. It takes a passion for real life to react passionately to the life in books. You can't be out to lunch and also appreciate good literature.

Perhaps the feature of a work of literature that you're apt to notice first is writing style. After a few paragraphs you'll know whether the language is poetic or plain, flowery or simple, lofty or down-to-earth, figurative or literal. Almost from the outset you can tell whether the narrator is humorous or serious, bitter or cheerful, proud or humble, hard-boiled or romantic. Sentence length and structure, word choice, figures of speech, allusions, use of dialogue—with all of these the author establishes a mood and tone. More important than simply recognizing the components of a writer's style, however, is determining whether the language is appropriate for the purpose of the work and assessing whether the language contributes to the work's impact on the reader, decisions that you can't make until you've read most of the work. Hemingway's distinctive style of writing is a case in point. You probably know that Hemingway wrote simple, spare, journalistic prose, full of sensory detail. In a way, his style resembles his characters—tough, terse, and not given to wearing emotions on their sleeves. Frederic Henry, the protagonist in *A Farewell to Arms,* distrusts abstract concepts like *patriotism* and *honor.* His wound in battle has nothing to do with bravery or glory. His leg hurts; that's all that matters. Hemingway's writing has a hard edge to it. Using short, concrete, tangible words and phrases (a glass of wine, hot bath, soft bed) rather than multisyllabic, abstract words, he captures the more-or-less macho personalities of men and women caught up in the conflicts of war, the bull ring, the sea, and the big game hunt.

James Joyce's style is a world away from Hemingway's. Using all the resources of the English language, Joyce sets a mood, creates a tone, and captures the essence of the characters. In *Portrait of the Artist as a Young Man,* he portrays Stephen Dedalus and his world by taking liberties with language that might give an English teacher fits. He coins words, expands meanings, plays with rhythms and sounds, spells whimsically, ignores punctuation when it suits him, and pours his thoughts into streams of consciousness, apparently not giving a hoot whether the reader will understand or not. Much of the language is meant to suggest the confused state of young Stephen's emotions, the boy's inner turmoil. The style changes with Stephen's age, starting with the short, choppy sentences of a tot, developing complexity as Stephen grows to manhood. In his inimitable way, Joyce integrates language with the meaning and purpose of his novel.

At some point you'll probably run into authors who employ a style that seems antithetical to the content of the work. For example, murder and suicide are pretty grim topics. Yet they can be given a light touch or written about in poetic language of great beauty. Likewise, violent and painful death can be described with the detachment of a scientist taking lab notes, and an everyday occurrence like spreading cream cheese on a bagel can be related in ornate, bombastic, grandiloquent words. Such oppositions between language and content or between style or form and content are called *tensions,* created for a humorous, satirical, or in some cases, a bitterly ironic effect. When Jonathan Swift, in "A Modest Proposal," advances the idea of eating babies to put an end to lower-class starvation, he uses a no-nonsense, objective style of writing. The contrast between the horror of his culinary idea and its cool, impersonal presentation makes the piece one of the most enduring satirical essays ever written. In his many stories and novels, Franz Kafka records bizarre and frightening experiences—waking up to discover yourself turned into a cockroach, for one—in simple, direct, deceptively innocent language. Alexander Pope's poem "The Rape of the Lock" focuses on an attractive young woman about to have a lock of hair snipped from her head. Written in the style of a grand epic worthy of Homer or Virgil, the piece is known aptly as a "mock" epic. By using inflated language, Pope has trivialized (i.e., mocked) the event.

Figurative language also adds dimension to a piece of literature. Broadly defined, figurative language is a way of saying something in other than the ordinary way. Authors get mileage (a metaphor) by using allusions, similes, personifications, tropes, or any other of 250 separate figures that have been identified.

(See Poetry on the AP Exam [Chapter 5] for definitions and examples.) In poetry as well as prose, nothing enriches and broadens meaning like a fresh and original figure of speech.

Two figures, perhaps, deserve your particular attention: the metaphor and the metonymy. Both extend objects, people, and experiences into innumerable imaginative and symbolic forms. Simply stated, a metaphor compares two essentially unlike things. A metaphor such as "All the world's a stage" evokes, among other things, the thought that our lives are fleeting dramas, that life from birth to death is a performance that succeeds or fails according to our skill as actors. The parallels can be extended much farther. By thinking of what it takes to mount a play from its birth to final curtain, and thinking then of what it takes to make a life, the power of Shakespeare's metaphor is bound to become obvious. Metonymy, the use of a closely related idea for the idea itself, is also a comparison. In the phrase "The pen is mightier than the sword," *pen* stands for the writer, *sword* for the warrior. The sentiment (that a writer wields more power with words than a warrior with arms) is conveyed vividly and is actually a living example of its meaning.

Metaphor and metonymy provide access to a deeper meaning in many works of literature. A modern work rooted in a biblical tale or in ancient Greek myth or drama can be viewed as a metaphor for its source. *East of Eden* by John Steinbeck, for one, is a modern adaptation of the story of Cain and his brother Abel. *The Grapes of Wrath* has numerous parallels to the Old Testament's account of the Israelites' search for the promised land. In reading modern literature, you can hardly go far without running into Christ-like figures, people who sacrifice themselves to save others from death or indignity, like Sonia in *Crime and Punishment,* McMurphy in *One Flew Over the Cuckoo's Nest,* and the hero of *The Informer* by Liam O'Flaherty. No doubt you can think of stories and novels in which a parent, acceding to a higher moral duty, gives up a child. Chances are those works are metaphors for the story of Abraham's obedience to God's command to sacrifice his son Isaac. If you have read tales of children defying their parents, it's likely that they are metaphorical adaptations of the parable of the prodigal son.

Greek myth and drama have also served as the source of modern works. A story in which a child slays a parent alludes metaphorically to Oedipus. Antigone's compulsion to bury her brother in defiance of the law serves as the basis for works in which family loyalty takes precedence over loyalty to the state. Much of Clytemnestra is to be found in such modern characters as Ibsen's Hedda Gabler. James Joyce's mammoth novel *Ulysses* is a latter-day transmutation of *The Odyssey,* in which the hero, instead of wandering around the waters and isles of the ancient Mediterranean, roams the streets and sites of modern Dublin.

Finally, consider the metonymic significance of certain literary characters; Arthur Miller's Willy Loman (*Death of a Salesman*) as the modern worker lost in changing economic times; Kafka's Joseph K. (*The Trial*) as the modern citizen lost in the bureaucratic maze; Beckett's Didi and Gogo (*Waiting for Godot*) as modern man lost in a meaningless existence.

Analysis of "Give It Up"

Let us begin a series of literary analyses with the following selection from the work of Franz Kafka (1883–1924). It is a short parable called "Give It Up," which was found among Kafka's papers after his death.

It was very early in the morning, the streets clean and deserted; I was on my way to the station. As I compared the clock tower with my watch, I realized it was much later than I thought and that I had to hurry. The shock of this discovery made me feel uncertain of the way. I wasn't very well acquainted with the town as yet. Fortunately, there was a policeman at hand. I ran to him breathlessly, asked him the way. He smiled and said:

"You asking me the way?" "Yes," I said, "since I can't find it myself." "Give it up! Give it up!" said he, and turned with a sudden jerk, like someone who wants to be alone with his laughter.

What is the world of this short story? We are in a town quite early in the morning. No mention is made of inhabitants. There is a clock tower, a station, a policeman. But the impression is one of emptiness, loneliness, of clean, almost desolate, space. The speaker, lost in this barrenness, looks for direction and guidance. He needs to get to the station. The individual whose function it is to help him not only refuses assistance but also considers the appeal a huge joke. The world of this story, then, is a frightening one in which lost beings can expect no aid from a fellow being. People are not around. They are away, asleep or hiding; authority scorns and is, in fact, irritated by appeals for help. This may not be quite the world as we know it. But it has characteristics we have often encountered, especially in our dealing with government and bureaucracy, a refusal on the part of those in authority to offer direction to individual members of society.

One wonders what the author intended. The speaker is beginning a journey. He appears in the clean, deserted streets of the town quite early. Is this the beginning of a life, and is there urgency, since time is moving, to get on with the business of living? The beginning movements are tentative and fearful ones, and direction is needed. Where should it come from? Certainly, one expects the authority figures—father, minister, king, God—to help; but no help is forthcoming, only ridicule and an urging to "Give it up." The world of the story, as conceived by Kafka, is an empty and frightening one in which a human being can get easily lost—lost physically and lost spiritually. The author has apparently created *this* world because he sees *his* world, *our* world, in this way, a world of betrayal where duty and responsibility have lost their meaning.

An important image is the clock tower. It obviously is a symbol of time, and the clock tower reminds the narrator that he has promises to keep and that he must get to the station. But the likelihood of his getting anywhere is slim. Lost in a deserted town, he cannot reach the station and cannot proceed on his journey without help. But help is not forthcoming, nor will it be later when the town streets fill up with people. (This is an inference that the narrator invites us to accept from his account.) Alone, therefore, he floats in the town aimlessly, and what is a joke for the policeman is a tragedy for him. Is this the tragedy of modern humanity as Kafka conceives it?

There are two characters in the story: the narrator and the policeman. They are apparently not intended to be real people. They are symbolic figures, the narrator being man and the policeman, authority—God, king, father. Over the centuries, man has created institutions and figures whose purpose was to give order to his existence, to enable him to believe that his stay on earth had some meaning, some purpose. Is this story saying that man has failed, that his institutions are unworkable, particularly his religious and/or political institutions? If one equates policeman with father, then Kafka intimates that even the basic institution of the family, created for survival in primitive times, is failing, possibly because the fathers, too, are turning away with grimly humorous disdain from their children's appeal for guidance.

The story is a parable. It is a fictitious narrative from which a spiritual truth is to be drawn. It is told in bare, simple terms. Its place, events, characters are unreal, vague. Nothing has any clear form or shape. One doesn't know, for example, what the narrator looks like or what kind of clock tower is in the town, or what town it is. But the story does express a spiritual truth about the human condition, as Kafka conceived it and as man encounters it so often, and has sensed it, the indifference of God, or state, or father to human need.

The analysis of this brief parable simulates a process that you might follow in your explication of the meaning of a short story.

Read Hemingway's "In Another Country." It's about an American soldier who was wounded fighting in the Italian army in World War I. He is in a hospital near Milan for treatment, and he makes friends with an Italian major who is also being treated for a wound. In analyzing the story, look for answers to the following questions.

1. Who is the narrator of the story? How does the narrator see himself? How does he see the world in which he is now living—the city of Milan and the hospital where he receives treatment? How does he view his fellow patients? What sights, sounds, and smells of wartime Milan register upon the narrator?

2. Whose story is this? Is this the story of the narrator, or is it the story of the Italian major? What facts about the background and life of the Italian major does the narrator learn? Why is the major viewed by the narrator as a defeated man? How does the major react to his defeats? In what ways is the major heroic?

3. What are the narrator's chief concerns? Why does he feel a sense of isolation? What interest does the major hold for him? What final picture of the major does the narrator give us?

4. How has Hemingway treated the raw experience of an American soldier in an Italian hospital to make it into a short story? What views of life color the telling of this story? Is the story more effective because it is told by a narrator? Does the narrator present the author's views, or is it necessary for the reader to infer the author's views from the manner of the telling? Is there any distance between narrator and author?

The Short Story

General Questions to Consider in Analyzing a Short Story

1. Who is telling the story? How much does he/she know? To what extent is this knowledge or vision limited? Is the storyteller the author or a narrator created by the author? How much *distance* is there between the author and the narrator?

2. What are the raw facts of this story? How has the author embellished the raw facts?

3. What objects or people appear in the story to represent more than their basic elements or reality? What, in your view, do they represent?

4. What purpose does the author have in telling the story? What are his/her intentions? How do you determine these intentions? Are the intentions clear or must they be inferred from the details and the emphases of the story?

5. What is the author's view of the characters? How do you know this? How do the characters view one another? How do you know this?

6. What is the author's view of life? What evidence in the story supports your conclusions about the author's philosophy?

7. What is the world of the story? Is it a real or an unreal one? What are the basic values that govern this world? How do these values affect the actions, beliefs, decisions of the characters? What is the author's view of this world?

Analysis of "A Clean, Well-Lighted Place"

A CLEAN, WELL-LIGHTED PLACE
Ernest Hemingway (1899–1961)

THE BEGINNING

It was late and every one had left the cafe except an old man who sat in the shadow the leaves of the tree made against the electric light. In the day time the street was dusty, but at night the dew settled the dust and the old man liked to sit late because he was deaf and now at night it was quiet and he felt the difference. The two waiters inside the cafe knew that the old man was a little drunk, and while he was a good client they knew that if he became too drunk he would leave without paying, so they kept watch on him.

"Last week he tried to commit suicide," one waiter said.

"Why?"

"He was in despair."

"What about?"

"Nothing."

"How do you know it was nothing?"

"He has plenty of money."

This is how the story begins. Is there anything in the first paragraph that prepares the reader for the remark of one of the waiters that the old man had attempted suicide? What is the tone of the first paragraph? How is the old man described? Why is he at the cafe? Why is he drinking? What can you infer about the old man before the waiter makes his remark? If the narrator has introduced the old man well, the waiter's remark should not come as a surprise.

In this first dialogue, the narrator does not distinguish between the waiters. Why? We learn later that one is young and one is middle-aged. Which one of the waiters do you think made the first remark? How do you know? Which of the waiters is the more sympathetic? Apparently, one of the waiters had gone to the trouble of finding out something about his customer. What attitude toward life does this waiter have? Is there anything in the first paragraph to suggest the despair of the old man? Read it carefully. How much life is there in the old man?

POSSIBLE INTERPRETATIONS

Read the entire story. See whether you can find evidence in the story to support the following interpretations.

1. "A Clean, Well-Lighted Place" presents three views of the human condition: that of a young man; that of a middle-aged man; and that of an old man. How does each of the three men react to his life?

2. The narrator of the story wishes the reader to accept the view that "a clean, well-lighted place" is a metaphor for all the institutions and relationships that give meaning to people's lives. In an absurd world, there needs to be some place, some belief, some relationship that makes existence tolerable, a light in the night.

3. The narrator of the story presents a totally nihilistic view of life. Before the top of the universe blows off and after it blows off, there is nothing.

4. In this realistic story there are many romantic elements created by the contrasting images of light and darkness.

5. Since "youth implies age, love is an apple that must fall from its tree, the dew will dry, the light will go out," the title "A Clean, Well-Lighted Place" is ironic. Is the narrator suggesting that the middle-aged waiter's belief in the necessity in the world of clean, well-lighted places is a vain delusion?

Analysis of "Noon Wine"

NOON WINE
Katherine Anne Porter (1890–1980)

POSSIBLE INTERPRETATIONS

Read this story carefully. Which of the interpretations summarized below do you accept? Can you support these with evidence from the text?

1. This is a story of a simple, proud man to whom status, integrity, and dignity are of paramount importance. When the values that give meaning to his life are destroyed, when his wife and children see him as a murderer, he has no recourse but to commit suicide.

2. This is a story of a close, human relationship between an ordinary family and a disturbed, lonely man. In some curious way, they learn to live together. Mr. Helton's skill as a farmer and dairyman gives Mr. Thompson what he wants most—position and dignity. Mr. Helton has helped to raise the Thompsons from failure to security. In return, they respect his privacy and leave him alone. They are not disturbed or annoyed by his ways. An affection, born of mutual assistance, springs up between them and becomes cemented over the years. There is peace on the Thompson farm until Mr. Hatch appears. Mr. Thompson's violence seems born of heat, discomfort, and irritation, which turns to fury at Mr. Hatch's obnoxious ways. But in reality the blow he strikes is struck in defense of a friend and in defense of the peaceful world Mr. Helton had helped to create.

3. This is a paradoxical story of a conflict between good and evil. The force that represents evil also represents law and order. Whatever his motive, Mr. Hatch is at Mr. Thompson's farm to return a homicidal maniac to custody. In defending Mr. Helton, Mr. Thompson is protecting a criminal from the punishment which is his due. Another paradox is that Mr. Thompson, who is a decent, law-abiding man, commits a crime to defend a criminal, and Mr. Helton, the criminal, rushes to defend his friend instead of running away to escape Mr. Hatch.

4. This is a story of an Eden-like existence that is destroyed by the intrusion of Satan. The relationships in the Thompson family are good ones. It is a satisfying existence of mutual respect and concern and of accommodations. With Mr. Helton as a guardian angel taking care of the economics, peace reigns in the Thompson world. The appearance of Mr. Hatch brings violence to this Eden-world and destroys it.

5. This is the story of a lonely, disturbed man who wants peace and privacy. With the Thompsons he finds what he seeks, a place where he can work and where he will be left alone to play on his harmonicas. He is a good man despite his insanity and potential for violence. The narrator tells us very little about his crime; only that he had killed his brother because his brother had taken one of his harmonicas and lost it. There is no mention of any torments and ridicule to which Mr. Helton might have been subjected, other than that he had been committed to an asylum and had escaped. Mr. Helton takes on the quality of a recluse, idiot, sensitive fool, who can be roused to violence when one of his harmonicas is touched and who wants no part of the human world.

STRUCTURE

The story is divided into eight sections, each one being a short unit in itself and related to what has preceded.

Section 1: This section deals with the character of Mr. Thompson and his world and his hiring of Mr. Helton.

Section 2: Mrs. Thompson meets Mr. Helton and is aware that he does his work well.

> Mrs. Thompson was perfectly accustomed to all kinds of men full of all kinds of cranky ways. The point was to find out just how Mr. Helton's crankiness differed from any other man's and then get used to it, and let him feel at home.

Section 3: This section describes the Thompson family, their relationships to one another, and their responses to the presence of Mr. Helton. Their view of Mr. Helton is defined.

Section 4: This section describes Mr. Thompson's character and values juxtaposed against the character and ways of Mr. Helton. An ominous note is introduced with the matter of Mr. Thompson's boys' fooling with Mr. Helton's harmonicas and Mr. Helton's violent response. Mr. Thompson warns his sons. Peace is restored; the world of Mr. Thompson settles down. We reach the end of the first half of the story.

Section 5: Nine years have passed. The section describes the pleasant, peaceful existence at the Thompson farm.

Section 6: Mr. Hatch appears. There is a conversation between him and Mr. Thompson, ending in violence. Mr. Hatch is dead, and Mr. Helton has run off.

Section 7: This section deals with the aftermath of the slaying of Mr. Hatch and the killing of Mr. Helton by the sheriff's men. Mrs. Thompson blames her husband.

> Mr. Thompson can't argue with a man and get him off the place peaceably; no she thought . . . he has to kill somebody, he has to be a murderer and ruin his boys' lives and cause Mr. Helton to be killed like a mad dog.

Section 8: This last section deals with the defeat of Mr. Thompson, his loss of pride and self-esteem and the destruction of his values. He is driven to do penance, to tell his story to his neighbors over and over, hoping they will believe him. He forces Mrs. Thompson to lie. He creates fear in her and his sons. Life has lost its meaning, and he commits suicide. Mr. Thompson has been driven out of Eden. There is a failure of redemption. Ironically, Mr. Helton found redemption after a murder. Mr. Thompson does not.

The story recounts the growth and the cementing of a relationship over a period of nine years, the sudden violent destruction of that relationship, and the aftermath following the violence. (The sane and the insane are capable of sudden bursts of homicidal violence, given a certain atmosphere and sufficient provocation.) The highlights of the story are presented in elaborate detail. A few touches are added to round out a character or relationship. The unimportant is sketched quickly. The technique gives a three-dimensional vitality to the characters and makes the violent and bizarre action real and believable.

TONE
The tone of the first half of the story, as well as the pace, builds us the world of Mr. Thompson and establishes the relationship between the Thompsons and Mr. Helton. An ominous note enters in Mr. Helton's violent punishment of the boys for touching his harmonicas. In the peaceful world of the Thompsons, Mr. Helton's violence potential is controlled. With the appearance of Mr. Hatch, the tone and the pace change. The style of Mr. Hatch's speech and the substance of what he says builds up resentment in the reader, as it does in Mr. Thompson.

IS MR. THOMPSON A TRAGIC FIGURE?
1. Is there nobility, humanity, in the character of Mr. Thompson? If there is, how is it shown in the story?
2. Is there a tragic flaw in his nature? If there is, what is the flaw? Is it pride? What is the nature of Mr. Thompson's pride? Why is Mr. Thompson so anxious to convince everybody that his killing of Mr. Hatch was justifiable? He was exonerated in court.
3. What is the nature of Mr. Thompson's suffering? Does it add substance and depth to his character? Does his pain enlarge or diminish him as a man? Is his suicide inevitable? How does he kill himself? What is his mood at the moment of self-destruction?
4. After the killing of Mr. Hatch and the death of Mr. Helton what does Mr. Thompson protest against? Who is responsible for the destruction of Mr. Thompson's paradise? Whom does he really blame? Is it Mr. Hatch? Is it society with its rigid laws, its inhumanity in dealing with those different from the norm?
5. What about the human condition is revealed in the tragedy that befalls Mr. Thompson? Is Mr. Thompson a hero or a fool?

Analysis of "The Dead"

THE DEAD
James Joyce (1882–1941)

SEQUENCE OF EVENTS
The reader attends the annual Christmas party of the Misses Morkan and finds himself/herself in the midst of a provincial, middle-class, cultivated society at the turn of the century. Is this the world of "the dead" suggested by the title of the story? Why does the narrator see this world as dead?

Lily, the servant, is literally run off her feet receiving the guests. The reader learns about Kate and Julia Morkan and about their niece, Mary Jane, who supported the household by playing the organ and giving music lessons.

Gabriel and Gretta arrive late. Gabriel stops to scrape the snow from his galoshes. Gretta goes upstairs. They are separated most of the evening. The snow becomes symbolic of Gabriel's inner unrest, an unrest that will be resolved to some degree at the conclusion of the story. The physical separation of husband and wife at the party symbolizes the lack of communication between the two, created, as we later discover, by Gabriel's excessive great absorption in self and his intellectual arrogance.

Lily is disturbed, answers bitterly, when Gabriel gaily comments about the possibility of her being married. Her bitter retort reinforces the narrator's view of this world as being dead. Gabriel gives Lily a coin, a Christmas present, and embarrasses her even more. This is Gabriel's first rebuff at the party.

Gabriel, as has become the custom at his aunts' annual party, will deliver a speech. He is worried about what he plans to say despite his awareness of his intellectual superiority to the guests. Gabriel seems to be a complacent, self-satisfied intellectual.

The Conroys have decided this year not to go home from the party but to spend the night at the Gresham Hotel. Gabriel seems concerned about Gretta's well-being, saying that she'd walk home in the snow if she were let. To the aunts, Gabriel's solicitude about Gretta was a standing joke. In view of what happens later, this solicitude of Gabriel's is ironic. Why?

Freddy Malins appears. As usual, he has been drinking and Gabriel takes care of him. Refreshments are served. Mr. Browne escorts three young ladies. He offends them by making a vulgar remark in a low Dublin accent. The company dances a quadrille. Freddy tells Mr. Browne a story he has just told Gabriel and keeps laughing before he can finish it. What is the significance of all these details?

Mary Jane entertains the company by playing the piano. Gabriel is not happy about the piece she is playing, especially since no one is paying any attention to her. The level of culture of the people at the party is delineated. Gabriel's eyes wander to pictures on the wall, the balcony scene in *Romeo and Juliet* and the two murdered princes in the tower. Gabriel is reminded of his mother. (There is a picture of her before the pierglass.) He recalls her sullen opposition to his marriage to Gretta who, she had said, was country cute. The theme of love is here suggested. The balcony separation of lovers, a parent's objections, and the present separation at the party. How much does Gabriel love his wife? Have his mother's objections strengthened or weakened this love? Mary Jane's playing ends. The narrator has taken the reader into the mind of Gabriel and given us an additional insight into his character. What more has the reader learned?

The guests dance the lancers. Gabriel's partner is Miss Ivors. She has "a crow to pluck with him." She calls him a West Briton and says he should be ashamed to write a book review for the *Daily Express,* an English newspaper. Gabriel had reviewed the poems of Browning. A discussion about Gabriel's feelings about Ireland is precipitated by an invitation from Miss Ivors that Gabriel and Gretta join her during the summer in an excursion to the Aran Islands. Gabriel plans to go to Europe and in pique says, "To tell you the truth, I'm sick of my own country." This is a second rebuff Gabriel experiences. His complacency is again jolted. But the reader recognizes that Gabriel is torn between the attractiveness of the culture of Europe and the emotional demands of his homeland. This dualism is made clearer when Gretta joins Gabriel for a moment, comments on his row with Miss Ivors, and, when she learns of the invitation, says she would like a holiday to the west of Ireland. Gabriel coldly says, "You can go if you like." Some of the reason for the subconscious distance between Gabriel and Gretta becomes apparent in this exchange.

Gabriel thinks again of his speech. He longs to be out in the snow. The snow becomes again a cleansing force, and the reader begins to notice that a change is being initiated in the spirit of Gabriel. It is still a small voice and barely heard. His complacency returns, and he considers including in his speech a critical comment on Miss Ivors and her love of Ireland. He plans to praise the old ways represented in the lives and values of his aunts. "What did he care that his aunts were only two ignorant old women?" He sees his aunts and their world clearly. He doesn't yet see himself clearly.

Aunt Julia sings—it's an old song, "Arrayed for the Bridal." Freddy praises Julia's singing. There is talk about Aunt Julia's wasting her talents singing in a choir. Mary Jane comments, "Isn't it for the honor of God?" Aunt Kate is critical of the Pope for turning women out of choirs and substituting boys. Miss Ivors leaves and refuses Gabriel's offer to see her home. The reader sees more of the deadness of ways grown stale with time. The view is emphasized by the departure of Miss Ivors and by her refusal of Gabriel's assistance.

The table is set for dinner. It is a sumptuous repast, and the narrator describes it in detail. Gabriel carves the goose—perhaps a symbol of the Ireland whose indigenous vitality has been stifled by the second-hand culture of the "West Britons." During the meal there is talk of the opera company at the Theatre Royal and of singers past and present, some more of the decaying, borrowed culture. Then the pudding is served, and there is more talk, this time about Mount Melleray, where the air is bracing, where the monks are hospitable, never speak, get up at two in the morning, and sleep in their coffins.

Gabriel is ready to deliver his speech. He sees himself again out in the snow. He talks about Irish hospitality. He praises his aunts. He criticizes the new generation. "We are living in a sceptical and if I may use the phrase, a thought-tormented age—educated or hyper-educated as it is." The guests sing "For they are jolly gay fellows." The door is opened. "The piercing morning air came into the hall." Again, the cleansing power of the outdoors touches the stagnant indoors of the Morkan sisters.

The guests begin to leave. Julia recalls the horse Johnny, and Gabriel again tells the story of Patrick Morkan and his horse, Johnny, who, attracted by a statue of King Billy on a horse, insisted upon going round and round the statue oblivious to the cries of his master. The Malins leave with Mr. Browne amid talk of where Mr. Brown is to be dropped and amid a chorus of laughter and adieus. The detail enforces the realism of the account and the dullness of the lives of the people.

Looking up, Gabriel sees that his wife is standing near the top of the first flight. He sees the panels of her skirt. She appears to him a figure of grace and mystery. He thinks he would like to paint her if he could and call the painting *Distant Music*. Gretta is listening to Bartell D'Arcy sing "The Lass of Aughrim." D'Arcy stops suddenly, claiming that he is as hoarse as a crow, and gets ready to leave. Mary Jane comments about the snowstorm. "We haven't had snow like it for over thirty years. The snow is general all over Ireland." "Poor Mr. D'Arcy doesn't like the snow," says Aunt Kate. Mr. D'Arcy belongs, with Miss Ivors, to the generation of lovers of Ireland and the culture of Ireland. The snow seems to represent the cleansing force of the new movement. Why would Mr. D'Arcy not like the snow? Is it Aunt Kate's obtuseness that is exposed here? The snow attracts Gabriel. Shouldn't it be D'Arcy's natural element? All the guests leave.

Gretta walks ahead with Mr. D'Arcy. Gabriel, contemplating her, is moved by a deep passion for her. He recalls memories of their past life together. They hail a cab and are driven to their hotel, where they bid D'Arcy farewell. A riot of passionate memories has swelled Gabriel's brain during the walk and in the cab, and the excitement in Gabriel mounts as they climb the stairs to the hotel room. After some trivial conversation Gabriel approaches Gretta. He thinks for a moment because Gretta kisses him lightly that she feels a similar intense longing for him. But she turns from him, bursts into tears, tells him she is thinking of the song D'Arcy sang, breaks loose from him, runs to the bed, and hides her face in her arms. As Gabriel follows her, he sees a reflection of himself full length in a mirror.

When Gabriel questions Gretta, he learns that the song had awakened in her memories of a boy, Michael Furey, who used to sing "The Lass of Aughrim." The boy had loved Gretta. He was a delicate lad who died at the age of seventeen. Gretta believed that Michael had died because on a cold wintry night he had come to say good-bye to her before she left to go to the convent. Michael had thrown gravel at her window, and she had come out into the cold to bid him good-bye.

And so Gabriel sees for the first time the distance between himself and Gretta. She was in truth upstairs away from him. This is his third rebuff. His love for her was a selfish thing concerned only with his gratification. Michael Furey, a lost boy, had known what love was. He sees himself "as a ludicrous figure, acting as a penny boy for his aunts, a nervous, well-meaning sentimentalist, orating to vulgarians and idealising his clownish lusts, the pitiable fatuous fellow he had caught a glimpse of in the mirror." This is Gabriel's epiphany, his revelation, his realization of his true self.

Before Gabriel falls asleep, he watches the snow falling from the window of their room. And he believes that the time has come for him to set out on his journey westward. The snow falling on all of Ireland is cleansing the land, and it is cleansing him, slowly tearing him away from the world of the dead and drawing him westward to the land of Gretta and Michael.

Questions for Discussion

Do you accept the interpretation given above of the closing paragraphs of "The Dead"? If you do not, how do you interpret the closing paragraphs? Defend your view with evidence from the text.

Defend with evidence from the text the view expressed in each of the following critical statements:

1. Joyce lifts the objective details of his material to the symbolic level. He manipulates what at first sight seems to be mere physical detail into dramatic symbolism.
2. Joyce's method is that of the Central Intelligence Agency. The author suppresses himself, but he does not allow Gabriel to tell his own story.
3. From the beginning to the end of the story we are never *told* anything; we are *shown* everything.
4. There is in "The Dead" a movement toward reversal, resurrection, the beginning of a new life, and it is initiated by Lily.

Make a study of the element of distance in "The Dead." What is the distance between the narrator and Gabriel? Is there any moment in the story where the views of the narrator and of Gabriel coalesce? Discuss the distance between Gabriel and Gretta, Gabriel and his aunts, Gabriel and Mrs. Ivors, Gabriel and Ireland.

Analysis of "A Country Doctor"

A COUNTRY DOCTOR
Franz Kafka (1883–1924)

Kafka's story ends with the following passage:

> . . . Naked, exposed to the frost of this most unhappy of ages, with an earthly vehicle, unearthly horses, old man that I am, I wander astray. My fur coat is hanging from the back of the gig, but I cannot reach it, and none of my limber pack of patients lifts a finger. Betrayed! Betrayed! A false alarm on the night bell once answered—it cannot be made good, not ever.

One is reminded of Rosencrantz and Guildenstern in Tom Stoppard's play. The moment the two friends of Hamlet answer the summons from King Claudius, all goes awry. The laws of nature are suspended, and they become souls lost in space. A similar fate befalls the country doctor. He answers a false alarm on the night bell, and the world envelops him. His experiences become irrational, illogical, unreal. And at the end he is lost in space, naked, on a vehicle drawn by unearthly horses. The unreal becomes his reality.

It is obvious that the speaker is a disturbed man. What elements in what he says reveal that he is disturbed? What information concerning the speaker is revealed in this passage? Why does he feel betrayed? What does he expect? What are his regrets? Does he evoke any sympathy from you, the reader? What is your response to his outburst? What symbolic significance can you attach to the following: that the doctor is naked, that he is alone, that he is frozen, and that he seeks to escape?

Read the entire story. You learn that the speaker is *a* country doctor, not *the* country doctor. Does the *a* make the doctor a universal and symbolic figure? The story is told in *one* paragraph. What does this signify? Are we to conclude that this is the outpouring of an insane man? It is apparent that the story is a confession of a troubled man. He is a doctor. He has done something very shocking, seemingly out of an excessive sense of duty, and he is so appalled by his misdeed that it has unhinged his mind. The need to confess is overwhelming, and so he pours out his story in an endless flow. He cannot accept the reality of being the one who betrayed another, and so he conceives himself as having been betrayed. It is a punishment due him to be betrayed.

The story makes sense only if you recognize that the speaker is hiding his fault behind a symbolic façade. He tells his story as if it were a dream, with the symbols and distortions of a dream. The listener may be a psychiatrist, a friend, the world, or the reader who represents the world. What kind of man does the speaker reveal himself to be? Prove with evidence from the text that he seeks to justify his overweening sense of duty and that he seeks also to explain his failures and his betrayals. In his account, whom has he betrayed? What were his failures? Where in the story is there evidence of betrayal in response to a sense of duty? Look for the narrator's failure to protect Rose, his superficial first diagnosis of the boy's illness, his desertion of the boy to escape the villagers' wrath.

The doctor is moved by self-pity. He exaggerates his generosity and helpfulness. Why does he feel a need to do this? Here is his defense when he learns the boy is wounded and decides to do nothing about it.

> I am no world reformer and so I let him lie. I was the village doctor and did my duty to the uttermost, to the point where it became almost too much. I was badly paid and yet generous and helpful to the poor. I had still to see that Rose was all right, and then the boy might have his way and I wanted to die too. What was I doing there in that endless winter! My horse was dead, and not a single person in the village would lend me another.

This is more than self-pity. It is a rationalization, a justification, for some gnawing betrayals or failures. One involves Rose, who haunts him all through his nightmarish account. The others apparently involve criticism of him by his patients. What is the doctor's attitude toward his patients as stated in this passage? Is he sincere about this? What is the real reason for his criticism of the people in the village?

The doctor's confession reveals that he is the product of a Christian world. As you read the story look for Christian concepts and symbols. How are these symbols used? What is their significance? There are references to the conflict between good and evil: the doctor is helped by a groom who attacks Rose, the doctor's servant girl; the wound in the boy's right side—the wound of Jesus on the cross—is filled with worms. How is death conceived by the narrator-doctor? Whom does the woodsman represent?

To what extent is the doctor's devotion to science revealed in his account? Is his scientific objectivity and detachment affected by his faith? Does he feel that his concern with science has been a betrayal of spirit? From the text can you prove that the speaker has been a good doctor? Has he also been a good man? If not, what were his failings? How do you know? Why does the doctor exaggerate the demands of his patients, the people of the village? Why does he feel that they will kill him if he does not cure the boy?

Not everything in the story is clear. The reader gets only snatches of insights. Is there any intention in the confusing ambiguities of the story? What in your estimation was Kafka's purpose in making the doctor's story ambiguous? Edgar Allan Poe often wrote stories in which the narrators or speakers were madmen. Poe's madmen were lucid, almost objective and logical in their explanations of their actions. Is Kafka's technique better? What is your view?

The Novel

Analysis of *Wuthering Heights*

WUTHERING HEIGHTS
Emily Brontë (1818–1848)

STRUCTURE
It will be helpful in your study of *Wuthering Heights* to know the vital statistics of the characters. Emily Brontë gives us this information throughout a work that deals with the lives of people in three generations. It is summarized by Mark Schorer in his Introduction to the Rinehart edition of *Wuthering Heights* (1950).

The story at Wuthering Heights begins with Mr. and Mrs. Earnshaw. They have two children, Hindley and Catherine. Mr. Earnshaw adopts a waif, Heathcliff, whom he picked up on a visit to Liverpool. Mrs. Earnshaw dies in the spring of 1773 and Mr. Earnshaw dies in October 1777, leaving Heathcliff to the tender mercies of Hindley, who hates him and mistreats him. At this time Hindley, who was born in the summer of 1757, is twenty years old. Heathcliff is thirteen, and Catherine, with whom Heathcliff is inseparable, is twelve. In 1777 Hindley marries Frances, and a year later they have a son, Hareton. Frances dies the following year.

Catherine, believing she is in love with Edgar Linton of Thrushcross Grange and thinking through this marriage to be able to help Heathcliff, marries Edgar in April, 1783. Heathcliff had left, and she did not know whether he would return. At this time Edgar is twenty-one and Catherine is eighteen.

Heathcliff, who left Wuthering Heights when he overheard Catherine tell Nelly Dean that she was planning to marry Edgar, returns three years later to find Catherine ill. In January of 1784 Heathcliff, bent on revenge, marries Isabella Linton, who is nineteen. Unable to bear Heathcliff's cruelty, Isabella leaves him soon after their marriage and goes off to London, where, in September, her son Linton is born. Meanwhile, in March 1784, Catherine has died after giving birth to a girl, also named Catherine.

Hindley, weakened by drink, dies in September 1784, six months after the death of his sister Catherine and the same month in which his nephew, Linton Heathcliff, is born. Hindley's son, Hareton, is now in the care of Heathcliff, who treats him as a servant. Isabella dies in June 1797 at the age of thirty-two, at which time her son is thirteen.

To further his revenge, Heathcliff plans to own Thrushcross Grange by arranging a marriage between his son Linton, a sickly boy, and his niece Catherine. He manages this by forcing Linton to come home to Wuthering Heights, by arranging meetings between Catherine and her cousin, and finally by locking up Catherine, away from her ailing father. The two young people are married in August 1801. Both are seventeen years old. In September of that year Edgar dies at the age of 39, and the following month young Linton dies. Heathcliff is now the owner of Wuthering Heights and Thrushcross Grange. Young Cathy is forced to live with him.

Life at Wuthering Heights is a dismal existence. Cathy and Hareton quarrel, but a feeling of concern for one another begins to grow in them. Heathcliff's fury is spent. He realizes that in death he can rejoin his beloved Catherine. He neglects his health and dies in May 1802, at the age of thirty-eight. Love between Cathy and Hareton grows, and they are married in January 1803. Hareton is twenty-five and Catherine is nineteen. Calm is restored to Wuthering Heights.

This summary is useful for two reasons. First, it shows that *Wuthering Heights* is a carefully planned novel, not a wild, amorphous work. Second, it helps you to visualize the characters and to see the story more clearly. This is a story about young people who live tortured and violent lives and who, except for young Catherine and Hareton, and except for Nelly Dean and Lockwood, who tell the story, die at a young age. The ones who die are subject either to the cruelties of the climate, the raging passions that burn within them and destroy them, or the fierce cruelty of the satanic Heathcliff.

The story has two settings—Thrushcross Grange and Wuthering Heights. Thrushcross Grange reflects the character of Edgar Linton. It is a quiet, civilized place where the amenities are observed and where the passions of its inhabitants have been disciplined to make possible a genteel existence. Wuthering Heights, on the other hand, reflects the characters of Hindley and Heathcliff. It is a wild, desolate place surrounded by howling nature that constantly threatens the people that dwell there and imbues them with some of its fierceness. Within Wuthering Heights there is an undisciplined energy and a stark malignity that infects its inhabitants and leads to violent and destructive actions. In a drunken stupor, Hindley Earnshaw drops his son Hareton over the bannister, and had Heathcliff not caught the child, Hareton would have been killed. It is a place of twilight and night and of a brooding and submerged anger that frequently bursts into fury.

When Catherine moves into Thrushcross Grange, she brings much of the unrest of Wuthering Heights into its peaceful interiors. When Isabella, as Heathcliff's wife, moves to Wuthering Heights, she is unnerved by the cruelty and ferocity of its atmosphere and must escape.

The novel and its centers reflect metaphorically the world of nature as Emily Brontë experienced it on the moors. There seems in nature a constant struggle between the forces of turbulence and the forces of serenity, the forces of destructiveness and the forces of regeneration. One does not react in revulsion against storm and tempest. One is fascinated by it. At the same time one yearns for the calmness and peace of nature's quiet moments. *Wuthering Heights* metaphorically transfers into its characters and places the conflict between the satanic forces of violence and the beneficent forces of temperateness which one finds in nature. With a deranged Hindley and a demonic Heathcliff in control of Wuthering Heights, the world there is frenzied and insecure. When the people of this world invade Thrushcross Grange, the gentle, civilized life of the Lintons is upset. There is a wild and passionate loyalty in the love of Heathcliff and Catherine, a subsurface turbulence in the marriage of Catherine and Edgar, a volcano of demonic tension when Heathcliff returns and upbraids the sick Catherine for betraying him, and fury, passion, and savage grief when Catherine dies.

There follow quiet years while the younger Catherine and young Linton grow up. Again the fury begins when Heathcliff schemes to take over Thrushcross Grange, and Cathy and Linton, like Hareton, are trapped by his malevolence. But Heathcliff's fury is spent. He at last joins his Catherine in death, and calm is finally restored in the marriage of Cathy and Hareton.

The reader finds fascinating the intense love between Catherine and Heathcliff and feels deep sympathy for the mistreated Heathcliff, especially when he feels rejected by his beloved. The reader is repelled by Heathcliff's cruelties but is again won over by a Heathcliff exhausted by his furies of revenge and aching for the death that will enable him to rejoin Catherine. If Heathcliff and Catherine represent the demonic forces of nature, and Edgar, Isabella, and young Cathy the beneficent forces, then we can understand the skill of Emily Brontë in being able to involve the reader in the anguish of the lovers. The reader is frightened and fascinated by the power of their passion, as he/she would be frightened and fascinated by the power and passion of tempestuous nature. The resolution is a peace that follows the tension of conflict.

HEATHCLIFF AS A TRAGIC HERO

Is the story of *Wuthering Heights* the tragedy of Heathcliff? Apply the criteria of the following questions to his character and experiences as they are portrayed in the work. Cite evidence from the text to support your conclusions.

1. How does Heathcliff see his world? Is there order in his universe? Does he feel that his suffering is part of the scheme of the gods? Or does he recognize that the source of his failures and losses lies within him? Heathcliff overhears Catherine tell Nelly Dean that she is thinking of marrying Edgar Linton, and he leaves in anger and pain. Had he waited a while longer, he would have heard Catherine confess to Nelly that she could have no life without him. Catherine would never have married Edgar while Heathcliff was near. Didn't Heathcliff know this? Where lies the fault of this misunderstanding that caused the tragedy of their lives? What part did Hindley play in this tragedy?

2. Is Heathcliff a man of freedom and courage? Does he have the power to face the results of his choices? Does he display qualities that make him heroic? Is he more a man wronged than a man who wrongs others?

3. *Wuthering Heights* is in part a story of revenge. Is Heathcliff justified in the actions he takes to avenge the insults he has been subjected to and the pain he suffered? Do you excuse or justify his harsh treatment of Isabella, his son Linton, and young Cathy? Is he a man of great pride? Does his pride give him power and dignity?

4. How do you react to Heathcliff's suffering? Do you think he is foolish for suffering so intensely his loss of Catherine? Do you accept, admire, and feel pity for a man who loves not wisely but so well? Has Heathcliff the power to endure the pains of his existence? How does he meet his death? Is his end heroic? Does the romantic or melodramatic quality of his death prevent your feeling sympathy for him?

5. How could Heathcliff have stopped the course of events that destroyed him psychologically before they destroyed him physically? Is there an inevitability to the course of the tragic events that destroyed both Catherine and Heathcliff? Were Catherine and Heathcliff playthings of an indifferent nature or the tragic products of their own perverse, tempestuous personalities? At what point does Heathcliff realize that the struggle avails him naught?

6. Does Heathcliff protest against the situation he is in? Whom does he blame? What form do his protests take? Does he show strength or weakness in his final surrender? Are his final actions signs of weakness or strength? Does Heathcliff at any time blame the gods, or nature, or himself for his suffering? Isabella blames him for Catherine's death, and he flings a knife at her. Does he acknowledge to himself that he was responsible for Catherine's death?

7. Is Heathcliff at any time humanized by his suffering? Does he learn anything about the human condition from his agony? Does his attitude toward Hareton or toward young Cathy change at any time? Is there the suggestion of any remorse in his behavior during the final days of his life? Is he ennobled by his suffering, and does he see some meaning to his existence before he dies?

8. What conceptions about the human condition did the experiences of Heathcliff give you, as a reader? Did Hareton and Cathy learn anything from the tragedy of Heathcliff? Despite everything, Hareton seems to have had some affection and respect for Heathcliff. Did he also learn anything from Heathcliff's suffering? Did Lockwood and Nelly Dean, outsiders involved in the affairs of Thrushcross Grange and Wuthering Heights, come to any conclusions about Heathcliff?

The answers to many of these questions should enable you to determine whether *Wuthering Heights* is a tragic novel and whether Heathcliff is a tragic hero. You should be able to support your conclusions with evidence from the work.

**The Narrators
of *Wuthering Heights***

Emily Brontë creates two narrators to tell the story of *Wuthering Heights:* Mr. Lockwood, a visitor from the city, comes to the moors to forget that his cold manner had frightened away a girl he had loved and hoped to marry; and Miss Nelly Dean, a serving girl in the Earnshaw household. Nelly is more than a servant. Because her mother, too, was a servant of the Earnshaws, she was brought up with the Earnshaw children, was probably their playmate, though she knew her place, and has, therefore, become a confidante, too. Catherine confides many things to her, as does Heathcliff. She takes care of young Cathy, born just before the death of her mother. As a servant so close to the family, she cannot help but interfere in their lives. She tries to encourage the child Heathcliff to run away from Wuthering Heights; she incites Catherine to violence in the presence of Edgar; she arranges for Heathcliff to visit the sick Catherine when Edgar goes to church; she gives little Cathy provisions for a ride to Wuthering Heights. She participates in many other ways in the lives of Thrushcross Grange and Wuthering Heights. She is in part the catalyst of some of the tragic events of the novel.

But Nelly serves a more important purpose. She is a vigorous, healthy young woman, untroubled by any emotional or psychological drives beyond her control. She is governed by strong moral principles, but her morality is not a harsh, rigid piety. Hers is a wholesome personality. She can join with pleasure the entertainment and dances of the village. She becomes the exemplar of morality, of equilibrium. The intense, troubled, passion-ridden behavior of Catherine and Heathcliff, of Hindley and Isabella, of young Cathy and Hareton is measured against her normality. The reader is at first inclined to accept her views, but as the story progresses, he/she begins to recognize that Nelly is a poor judge of people whose lives are fashioned by adversity and who are moved to fervent and morbid actions by overwrought minds and uncontrollable emotions. Nelly makes critical judgments that the reader will not accept; the reader's judgments go beyond Nelly's, and, in objection to her comments, the reader moves more closely into the heart, the center, of the story.

Nelly is, in short, an important character in the story. She was created by the author to guide the reader to the point from which he/she is forced, because of the need to challenge Nelly's views, to share more deeply the pain of the dwellers of Thrushcross Grange and Wuthering Heights, and by sharing their pain to understand them better, to be moved by their plights, and not to be shocked by their excesses. The catharsis of the reader is impelled by Nelly.

Lockwood performs a different function, and yet an important one. He provides the reader with the view of an outsider, the city dweller, unfamiliar with the mores of the people of the moors. He seeks solitude, he says, but it is a pose. Solitude is not what he wants. Even though he is poorly treated on his first visit to Wuthering Heights, he must return for a second visit; and he is not deterred by threatening weather. He is sentimental about relationships, though afraid to make a gesture that will involve his life with another's. He is sufficiently sensitive to suggestion to dream that the ghost of Catherine knocks on the window of his bedroom, when he spends the night at Wuthering Heights, and tries to enter. Later he thinks that he may be able to charm and to win as bride the winsome young Cathy.

He is, of course, fascinated by the story that Nelly tells him and which he records for the reader in Nelly's words. He is inclined to accept Nelly's judgments because he, too, represents a normal view, a little different from Nelly's, and because his is the view of an outsider, a male, and a romantic. He is perhaps more sympathetic to the supranormal passions of the dwellers at Wuthering Heights, but his sympathies are those of a sentimental spectator rather than, as in Nelly's case, those of an active participant.

The story, therefore, filters through two different normal minds, one healthy, one troubled, and takes on added appeal as the reader responds part in agreement, part in protest, to their views.

There is in the novel a myriad of views. There are the views of the characters themselves, for example, Heathcliff's account of how Catherine, bitten by the Linton dogs, came to stay at Thrushcross Grange; Catherine's passionate avowal to Nelly of what Heathcliff means to her. In addition, there are Nelly's views and Lockwood's views. Finally, there are the reader's views, complex and varied, fashioned by the author through this intricate approach.

Do you agree or disagree with the above analyses concerning the functions of Nelly Dean and Mr. Lockwood in *Wuthering Heights*? Support *your* view with evidence from the text. You may see Nelly Dean's function and Mr. Lockwood's function differently. State your interpretation and defend it.

Another View of the Novel

Wuthering Heights is a romantic novel. It deals basically with two love stories in two generations, one tragic and one felicitous. Both are presented as existing on an ideal level. The love between Catherine and Heathcliff, fostered in childhood and nurtured on the wild moors, transcends the normal passions of reality. Despite its tragic consequences, it is a love that exists in a world of dreams. It is a love also that is so demanding that it devours its participants. It is a love that men and women yearn for and find unattainable. It is because of this that the ungovernable and tortured Catherine and the Byronic and suffering Heathcliff are appealing.

The love between young Cathy and Hareton is of another kind, and it, too, exists on an ideal level. It is a love that begins with disgust on Cathy's part and hatred on Hareton's part. But below the surface of the antagonism of the two lurks a physical attraction fostered by health and vigor. Alone together, and not troubled by Heathcliff's aggressions and Nelly's moralizings, the two become aware of one another as individual beings, and they begin to try to please one another. It is a more normal love, and it works out well because it is idealized in terms of a resolution of the inherited passions of the two lovers. Cathy, with her mother's stubborn, passionate nature, and Hareton, with the potential of his father's self-indulgent and violent nature, subdue the unrest and submit to the beauty of mutual respect and mutual help. They are on the way, the story suggests, to a good life on the wild and rough moor, ready to match their strengths as free spirits and as partners against anything the moor can offer. This is the ideal and romantic ending of *Wuthering Heights* and forms a companion fade-out to the phantom appearances on the moor of the ghosts of Catherine and Heathcliff.

Do you agree or disagree with this analysis? Can you support this view with additional evidence from the text? What other romantic elements do you find in the story? Is the world of Wuthering Heights a romantic one? How would you define the love between Catherine Earnshaw and Edgar Linton? How would you define the love between young Cathy Linton and her cousin, Linton Heathcliff? Do you feel any romantic pity for the suffering of young Linton?

Analysis of *Lord Jim*

LORD JIM
Joseph Conrad (1857–1924)

STRUCTURE
Lord Jim can be divided into five sections as follows:
1. Chapters 1–4   Beginnings
2. Chapters 5–17   The *Patna* disaster
3. Chapters 18–20   Jim in flight
4. Chapters 21–35   Jim's success at Patusan
5. Chapters 36–45   The Patusan tragedy

The story of *Lord Jim* is told by two narrators: the first, an omniscient story-teller, introduces Jim, tells the reader about Jim's background, explains how he came to be chief mate on the *Patna,* and describes the court inquiry; the second, Marlow, tells most of the story from the moment when Jim's demeanor at the trial catches his attention to the end. Marlow is not omniscient. He gets his information from various sources, and he intersperses in his account histories of other characters, descriptions of scenes, and philosophical comments. In addition, Marlow presents facts and incidents at random and he ignores chronology. The omniscient storyteller reappears for short sections. Marlow tells the story in two ways: Jim's experience from the *Patna* trial to success at Patusan in talk to after-dinner companions on the veranda of his home, and Jim's last days by means of a long letter to a friend in England.

Marlow's account is diffuse. In his pursuit of truth, Marlow recounts to his listeners different versions of the *Patna* disaster. His sources for the *Patna* incident are the court inquiry, Jim's own version, the stories of the first engineer on the *Patna* and of the French lieutenant who aided in towing the *Patna* to safety, and the testimony of the Malays who were at the ship's wheel.

Marlow tells also about the actions of other people. He stops to describe the different people who enter his and Jim's story, even those who appear in incidental and minor roles. The most important stories concern the suicide of Brierly, the conscious heroism of Stanton, the casual heroism of the French lieutenant, and the histories of Stein, Cornelius, and Gentleman Brown.

From Jim's letters, from letters written to him by friends, and from information given to him by friends whom he meets in his travels, Marlow learns of Jim's middle period, his various jobs and his running away from one employer to another to escape the stigma attached to him because of the *Patna* incident.

Marlow finally asks his friend Stein to help Jim escape from himself, and Stein "immerses Jim in the destructive element" by giving him the job at Patusan.

Marlow visits Jim at Patusan two years later, and he again lets Jim tell his story. Happy that Jim seems to have found himself at Patusan and wishing to ease Jewel's fears that Jim will leave her, Marlow says farewell to Jim, saying he will never return.

The rest of Jim's story Marlow learns from Gentleman Brown, dying from asthma in a squalid Bangkok hovel, from Jewel, from Tamb' Itam, and from a trader who has been at Patusan. Marlow tells of Brown's arrival at Patusan, of his aborted attack on the village, of the treachery of Kassim and Cornelius, of the killing of Dain Waris, and of Jim's surrender to Doramin's vengeance.

The story of Jim, as Marlow relates it, contains many flashbacks. For example, Jim recounts to Marlow his experiences when he first came to Patusan. Marlow stops to tell Stein's past history.

**Problems in
Analyzing *Lord Jim***

1. *Narrative Technique:* The first problem for you to work out in the study of *Lord Jim* is the effectiveness of Conrad's use of an omniscient narrator outside the story, and an involved and limited narrator, Marlow, who becomes Jim's friend, who tries to help him, who gets his information about Jim from various sources, and who tries to tell Jim's story in a way that will make his view of Jim clear.

What is the omniscient narrator's view of Jim? Does he sympathize with Jim? Is he objective? Does he represent Conrad's view?

What is Marlow's view of Jim? Is Marlow's view the same as Conrad's? Is it the same as the narrator's? How does it change during the story? What is Marlow's difficulty in dealing with the character and history of Jim? How is this difficulty revealed in the story? Does Marlow reveal any personal limitations or biases in telling Jim's story? Does Marlow's affection for Jim color his account in any way? Does he make Jim more attractive and more heroic than he was in reality? Is Marlow fair to the villains of the story?

2. *The Relevance of the Seemingly Extraneous Materials:* A second problem to consider is the relevance or irrelevance of the many additional stories the narrator and Marlow introduce into the account. What relationship to the basic story, if any, do the following stories have?

   a. Jim's failure to get into a cutter that set out to rescue two ships in trouble after a collision in a storm.
   b. The different versions of Jim's cowardice on the *Patna*.
   c. The heroism of the French lieutenant.
   d. Brierly's suicide.
   e. Stanton's heroism.
   f. The past histories of characters like Stein, Gentleman Brown, Cornelius, Jewel.

Would it be natural for a verbose talker like Marlow to color his story of Jim with many asides, or do these seemingly extraneous tales reveal the questions and doubts Marlow had about Jim?

3. *Imagery in Lord Jim:* As you read *Lord Jim,* you should also try to record the kinds of images Conrad uses in the work. How many times and in which particular scenes are there references to shadow, darkness, clouds, mist, fog? How often and in which situations are there references to light, sun, whiteness, color? What relationship is there between the imagery and the characters of the story and between the imagery and the incidents of the story?

Stein is a collector of butterflies and beetles. Do these insects symbolize the benign and malevolent characters of the story? If so, who are the beetles? Why is Stein given the role of collector and caretaker of butterflies and beetles? What significance, if any, is there in the story of Stein's finding and catching a rare and beautiful butterfly after killing his enemies?

As you read the novel, do you discern any religious (Christian) allusions or imagery? Is Jim's death a sacrifice? Who is saved by this sacrifice? Is Jim's death an act of redemption? Is Jim a sinful creature? Is he portrayed as a saintly figure? Are any of his enemies satanic creatures? Are any of his enemies Judas-like creatures? Is there any significance to the friendship, loyalty, and love of Dain Waris, Tamb' Itam, and Jewel?

How does Conrad see the world of his story? Does Marlow represent the values of this world? Does Jim represent the values? How do you see Tamb' Itam and Jewel? How do you see Stein? What do these three characters represent? How do you see the villains: the Rajah, Kassim, Sherif Ali, Cornelius, Gentleman Brown? Do they represent the satanic forces of the universe? Is the story a struggle between the benign and the evil forces of life for the soul of Jim? Who wins?

4. *Lord Jim—a Romantic Novel?* Can you prove that *Lord Jim* is a romantic novel? Analyze the following to support the view that the novel is romantic:
   a. The world of the novel—the sea, the Far East, the hidden, tropical village of Patusan. In what ways does Conrad make this world unique, strange, exotic, phantasmal?
   b. The characters in the novel. Are they bigger than life either in nobility or in villainy?
   c. The incidents in the novel. Are some incidents in the realm of ideal action and behavior; for example, the friendship between Jim and Marlow and between Jim and Dain Waris, the suicide of Bierly, the heroism of Stanton and the French lieutenant, the love between Jim and Jewel, the friendship between Marlow and Stein, the loyalty of Tamb' Itam? Are some incidents in the realm of romantic villainy; for example the cowardice of the officers on the *Patna,* the suspected cannibalism of Captain Robinson, the treachery of Cornelius and Gentleman Brown? Are some incidents in the realm of melodrama; for example, the defeat of Sherif Ali, Tamb' Itam's revenge upon Cornelius, Gentleman Brown's ugly last hours?
   d. The love story in the novel. Is the love between Jewel and Jim an ideal relationship? Is Jim's renunciation of Jewel a gesture of greatness of spirit? Is Jewel the perfect wife for the man in the tropics?

5. *Jim as a Tragic Hero:* Is Jim a tragic hero? Or is Jim not a tragic hero but a saintly hero, like Oedipus in Sophocles' *Oedipus at Colonus,* who finds redemption and fulfillment in death? You should be able to cite evidence to support either view. Here are some questions to ask about Jim.
   a. Does he have a belief in his own freedom? Does he make choices when faced with dilemmas, and has he the faith and courage to accept the outcomes of his choices?
   b. Is he a man of pride? What is the source of his pride? What doubts distress him? Does he conceive of himself as superior to those about him? Does he have a superior uniqueness? Does he have courage, dignity, and strength? Is there in his character dimensions of nobility?
   c. Is he strong in the way he bears his suffering? What is the source of his anguish? Is his guilt understandable or does he seem a fool? Is his code an admirable one? Does he question the forces within and without him that cause his suffering?
   d. Is there an inevitability, granted the nobility of his character and his values, that must lead to his tragic end? Are the values that lead to his sacrifice the result of nobility of character or profound weaknesses?
   e. What is his tragic flaw? Is it his sense of guilt? Is this exaggerated sense of guilt believable? Do you admire him for it? Is it the flaw that leads to the events that make Jim's dying inevitable?
   f. Is there protest on Jim's part against forces beyond his control that bring out the weaknesses that in the beginning and finally at the end defeat him? Whom or what, if anyone or anything, does he blame? Does he believe that life was unkind, that many forces over which he had not control defeated him?

g. *Was* he defeated? Did he learn from his agony? Was he ennobled by his suffering? Did his death leave a memory of glory? Or was it a futile gesture as Tamb' Itam and Jewel believed? Did he at his death see more clearly his place and function in his world? Was his death an act of courage, or was it a meaningless gesture?

h. What kind of impact does his experience have upon the reader? Does the reader identify with him? Does the reader see him as a good and noble man who has redeemed himself for an act of cowardice and who has finally found the greatness he dreamed of when, as a young man, he began his career as a seaman?

6. *The Psychology of the Characters:* Read carefully the actions and the behavior of the various characters in the story, especially those of Jim, Marlow, Jewel, Cornelius, and Gentleman Brown; study the motivations for their behavior and actions, and determine whether they were psychologically sound. For example, Jim describes the long sequence of events that culminated in his jumping from the stricken *Patna* into the lifeboat. He describes also the thoughts that were going on in his mind. Is what goes on in his mind psychologically sound? Is the story of Brierly's suicide psychologically acceptable? What explanation can you offer for Brierly's desperate action? Is Cornelius's hatred of Jim despite Jim's kindness to him believable psychologically?

7. *Major Themes in Lord Jim:* There are two themes of the work that require analysis. The first deals with its morality and the second with its conception of truth. As a romantic work, *Lord Jim* is concerned with the conflict of good and evil and with the triumph of good. What conceptions of good and evil do you find in the work? Is there any ambiguity about the nature of good and the nature of evil? The death of Dain Waris, for example, was due to the treachery of Cornelius and to the indifferent sadism of Gentleman Brown. Why should Jim have had to suffer for it? Is the novel saying that sacrifice for a vain ideal is foolish? Was Jim's final act another act of cowardice, or was it an act of supreme courage and morally necessary?

The second theme concerns truth. What relationship is there between the structure of the story and the concept of truth that shaped it? What relationship is there between the imagery of the story and Conrad's notion of the ambiguity of truth? For example, the court of inquiry into the matter of the *Patna* sought *facts*. Were the facts of the case the truth? What, if anything, was missing? Was Jim's account the truth? What, if anything, was missing from his story? What is the whole truth about Jim? Is it possible to define it, to give it form and expression? What is the whole truth about any of the characters? Is Conrad saying that truth is elusive? Is this notion of truth an area in which there is no distance between author and narrator?

Thesis Statements

Select a number of the following thesis statements, and see whether you can find evidence in the text to support or refute them.

1. The stories of Brierly, Stanton, and Stein serve to highlight Jim's character and his psychological and moral problems.
2. When we first meet Jim and learn a little of his early background, we find hints of personality that foreshadow the events of the novel.
3. Marlow is in part responsible for Jim's tragic defeat.
4. Jim's jump into the lifeboat is a symbolic act. Jim's action becomes a metaphor for the moral weakness of human beings and is an action that, in Conrad's

view, disturbs the order of the universe. (As Conrad sees it, the order of the universe reflects ideal moral behavior.)

5. Jim's dying restores the moral order of the world of *Lord Jim*.

6. The world of *Lord Jim* is shadowy and foggy, and there are only occasional moments of clarity.

7. Marlow's presentation of facts and actions at random, his ignoring of the natural continuity of time, and his adding to the action comments and descriptions of scene—all reflect his unsureness about what is truth.

8. Stein's butterflies are symbols of idealism and his beetles are symbols of decadence. In the heroic actions of the ideal characters and in the vile and treacherous actions of the villains, we see the conflict in life between good and evil.

9. Jim does not come through to the reader as a clear, finally understood personality, because neither the author nor Marlow could see him clearly.

10. There are two father-son relationships in *Lord Jim*. Marlow looks upon Jim as his son. Marlow looks upon Stein as his father. The novel begins with the son and ends with the father.

11. The real hero of *Lord Jim* is Marlow.

12. *Lord Jim* deals with the failure of the idealist in a world of fact. Lost in dreams of perfection, the idealist misjudges the motives of mean and vicious characters and comes to grief.

Analysis of
Madame Bovary

MADAME BOVARY
Gustave Flaubert (1821–1890)

STRUCTURE

The story begins with a narrator who is a classmate of Charles Bovary and who records Charles's first day in a new school. Charles is an ungainly boy of fifteen placed in a class with pupils younger than he. Then, imperceptibly, another narrator takes over, an omniscient observer, who, knowing all, penetrates the minds of his characters, records their experiences and thoughts, and stops frequently to comment, generally in a quiet, ironic tone, on character and events. The narrator transfers his major attention from Charles to Emma and at the end turns back to Charles. But the narrator is also concerned with the bourgeois society in which the Bovarys live. It is not so much Emma's dreams and illusions that lead her into the adulteries that destroy her as the petty, malicious, hypocritical world of Homais, Lheureux, Father Bournisien, Rodolphe, Boulanger, and the others.

As a story of the ecstasies and despairs of Emma Bovary, it falls into three sections. Each section concerns a different place in which the romantic dreams of Emma are fostered and in which she is made ready for a romantic encounter with a "hero" who turns out in time to be made of dust. The first place is the convent where Emma is educated and where her reading of romantic and sentimental literature makes her ready for Charles Bovary. She idealizes Charles, as she later idealizes Rodolphe and Leon. She marries Charles, not at all aware of his dull, stodgy personality.

Emma's romantic ardor is reawakened when she and Charles are invited by the Marquis d'Anderevilliers to a ball at La Vaubyessard. Emma is too excited and too blinded by the richness of the surroundings to see the moral decay and the empty pursuits of a nobility made stale by time and indulgence. The ball makes her ready for the seductive appeals of Rodolphe.

The third attachment, this time to Leon, is sparked by Emma's visit to the opera at Rouen, where she is moved by the love laments of *Lucia di Lammermoor* and the gallant appearance of opera star Edgar Lagardy. Here, once more, she loses herself in romantic fantasies, and when she again meets Leon, she is ready for a liaison with him.

THE OMNISCIENT NARRATOR

The omniscient narrator has complete control of his story. He tells you what he thinks of people. For example, his treatment of his characters is objective. He does not see Emma or Charles as tragic. He records what happens to them with dispassionate honesty. (By contrast, for example, Arthur Miller's treatment of Willy Loman in *Death of a Salesman* is subjective and therefore a tone of compassion pervades the work.) There is no compassion for Emma except possibly in the scene where she seeks solace from the priest Bournisien. The tone of *Madame Bovary* is ironic, as though the narrator were saying, "What fools these mortals be." There are a few people whom the narrator admires—Dr. Lariviere, for example—and he tells us so. But his attitude toward most of his people is critical because he feels they destroy life by petty living.

Let us examine a few passages from the book.

To hide her affair with Leon, Emma lies to her husband. The narrator makes the following comment:

> Lying became a need, a mania, a positive joy—to such a point that if she
> said that she had walked down the right-hand side of the street the day
> before, it meant that she had gone down the left.

This comment of the narrator appears objective and to a degree it is, but it is tinged with an irony that indicates that the narrator sees Emma as a foolish woman and that he has little sympathy for her position as an unfaithful wife hiding a liaison.

The narrator comments on Leon's response to Emma's allurements:

> He [Leon] marveled at the sublimity of her soul and at the lace of her pet-
> ticoat. Besides—wasn't she a "lady," and married besides? Everything, in
> short, that a mistress should be?

Here the narrator, in juxtaposing soul and petticoat, makes an ironic comment on the selfishness and foolishness of Leon's ardor. In addition, the narrator moves into Leon's mind to record his thoughts.

Look for similar ironic passages. They run all through the work; analyze the comments the narrator makes.

Look also for passages in which the narrator records the thoughts of characters and frequently includes a comment of his own. For example:

> And all this time she [Emma] was torn by wild desires, by rage, by
> hatred. The trim folds of her dress hid a heart in turmoil, and her reti-
> cent lips told nothing of the storm. [This is the narrator's description of
> Emma's state. Now he moves into her thoughts.] She was in love with
> Leon, and she sought the solitude that allowed her to revel undisturbed
> in his image. . . .

There is here a combination of two voices. The voice of the narrator, because of the romantic exaggeration, suggests his ironic view of Emma's transports. The voice of Emma is more subdued and records her passion as she herself experiences it.

There are three additional elements of technique that you should look for when you read the text.

The first is the use of poetic descriptive passages that provide an aura of lyricism to the mundane and petty world of the book. It is as though the narrator were painting a front portrait of real and ugly and deluded humanity against a colorful backdrop of nature's beauty. You will notice, though, that many of Flaubert's nature scenes convey a humidity and ripeness that anticipates decay. Here is an example:

> . . . The summer weather had reduced its [the river's] flow and left uncovered the river walls and water steps of the gardens along the bank. It ran silently, swift and cold-looking; long fine grasses bent with the current, like masses of loose green hair streaming in its limpid depths. Here and there on the tip of a reed or on a water-lily pad a spidery-legged insect was poised or crawling. Sunbeams pierced the little blue air bubbles that kept forming and breaking on the ripples; branchless old willows mirrored their gray bark in the water; in the distance the meadows seemed empty all around them. . . .

Here is another example:

> The moon, a deep red disc, was rising straight out of the earth beyond the meadows. They could see it climb swiftly between the poplar branches that partially screened it like a torn black curtain; and finally, dazzlingly white, it shone high above them in the empty sky illumined by its light. Now, moving more slowly, it poured onto a stretch of the river a great brightness that flashed like a million stars; and this silvery gleam seemed to be writhing in its depths like a headless serpent covered with luminous scales. It looked, too, like a monstrous, many-branched candlestick dripping with molten diamonds. . . .

A second element of the narrator's technique is his use of dramatic imagery. Watch for the various images as you read the text. Determine the relationships of the images to the themes of the story. Images of water and boats run through the work. For example, the narrator tells us that the bed in the hotel room where Emma and Leon met was in the form of a boat. Love is frequently expressed in images of water. There are images of ripening fruit, melting snow, moonlight on river. There are references to "drops" of water "keeping time and creating a palpitation" or "giving a semblance to feelings numbed by the monotony of desire." There are images of cathedral and hospital related to the delusions of holiness with which Emma clothes her desires, to Charles's defeat in his treatment of Hippolyte, and to Emma's suicide.

The circle becomes a significant metaphor in the book, reflecting Emma's way of reasoning and the repetitive nature of her adulteries, the circular movement of love, passion, satiety, termination: "All the feelings in her [Emma's] soul converged in this love as the spokes of a wheel around the axle which supports them." Finally, there is the metaphoric use of two minor characters whose influence upon Emma is profound: the viscount at La Vaubyessard, who symbolizes her illusions about a romantic life, and the blind beggar, who haunts her last days and who symbolizes the reality of despair and death.

The third element and the one that shapes the work most completely is the cold, objective realism in the recording of scenes in the life of Emma, Charles, and their world, especially Emma's last days and her dying. The narrator spares us few details in describing the dullness of Emma's life with Charles, the pointless arguments between Homais and Bournisien, the failure of Charles's attempt to cure Hippolyte's club foot, and finally Emma's death and Charles's utter disintegration.

Here is a typical example:

> He [Charles] came home from his rounds late—ten o'clock, sometimes midnight. He was hungry at that hour, and since the servant had gone to bed it was Emma who served him. He would take off his coat to be more comfortable at table, tell her every person he had seen, every village he had been to, every prescription he had written; and he would complacently eat what was left of the stew, pare his cheese, munch an apple, pour himself the last drop of wine. Then he would go to bed, fall asleep the minute he was stretched on his back, and begin to snore.

As you read the text, select realistic passages to support the conclusion that *Madame Bovary,* despite its poetic descriptions, its imaginative imagery, its ironic tone, its profound criticism of the bourgeois values of small-town French life, its emphasis on the hypocrisies of people like Homais and Bournisien, is fundamentally a realistic work.

PLOT MOVEMENTS

The main plot of the novel concerns Emma Bovary. Though readers follow her external actions, they are asked by the narrator, through his treatment of Emma's life and through the emphases in his account, to be concerned more with her inner life. The story of Emma is in part a psychological analysis of the way her mind works and the effects of her experiences upon her psyche. Emma is herself not too aware of the extent to which the world of Yonville affects her, but it does in subtle and destructive ways. There is in the novel, therefore, an outer movement that coincides with the inner movement in Emma's mind and heart and that thrusts at her in many ways, eventually to destroy her. Her enemies are Lheureux, who involves her in debt until she has nowhere to turn; Homais, who persuades her to encourage Charles to attempt the fateful operation on Hippolyte; and Bournisien, to whom she turns in a time of deep misery for spiritual consolation and who is too obtuse to perceive her plight. Emma moves in her inevitable course to destruction. Yonville and its petty inhabitants move in their repetitive routine from day to day, touching Emma's life in ways she does not comprehend and finally assisting most efficiently in destroying her. An ironic scene climaxes the effect of Yonville on Emma when Homais and Bournisien, sitting with the dead Emma, totally oblivious to the panic that drove her to suicide and to the part they played in her defeat and totally unmoved by her sad end and Charles's misery, engage in their usual clerical argument.

A visual representation of the inner and outer movements of the novel would take the following form:

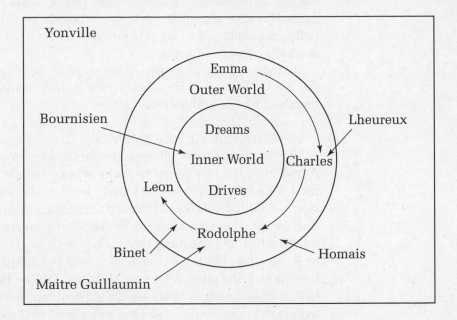

Discussion Questions   How would you answer the following questions?

1. Whose views of the various events in the story do we get?
2. What distance is there between Flaubert and the narrator of the story?
3. Why doesn't Flaubert have Emma tell part of her own story?
4. Why does Flaubert start and end his story with Charles?
5. What is the narrator's view of Emma?
6. What is the narrator's view of Charles?
7. What is the narrator's view of Homais?
8. Why does the end of the story include a comment about Homais?

Analysis of *As I Lay Dying*

AS I LAY DYING
William Faulkner (1897–1962)

STRUCTURE

As I Lay Dying is a unique novel. The story is told in fifty-nine monologues, spoken by fifteen characters. It concerns a journey of some twenty miles from the small farm of the Bundrens in Yoknapatawpha County to Jefferson, the main city of the county. The journey is undertaken by Anse Bundren and his children to bury Addie Bundren, wife and mother, near her family. Addie Bundren made Anse promise to bury her in Jefferson City, and he aims to keep his word. A heavy storm arises, the river the family needs to cross turns into a flood and destroys the bridges, and the Bundrens encounter all kinds of obstacles getting the body of Addie to Jefferson City. Friends and neighbors try to help the Bundrens in their trouble. Dewey Dell, the daughter, who is pregnant and who tries to get some medicine to abort her child, is given kindly advice by one pharmacist in Mattson and is taken advantage of by another in Jefferson. No one but Darl knows of Dewey Dell's plight, but Darl cannot help her because he is more concerned about the indignities suffered by the corpse of his mother and by the physical suffering of his brother Cash, whose leg is broken when their wagon is overturned crossing a ford in the river. Addie is finally laid to rest nine days after she died, and Darl, who has been considered queer by everybody, is committed to an asylum because he fired Gillespie's barn to free his mother's corpse in flames.

By means of the monologues the story of Addie and her family unfolds, and the reader learns the complex psychological relationships existing among the members of Addie Bundren's family.

PSYCHOLOGICAL MOVEMENTS

The center of the psychological relationships in the novel is Addie Bundren. Addie becomes indifferent to Anse, whose "words" of love she comes to distrust. She loves her first child Cash, born of early passion, and before disillusion set in, but she is cold toward Darl, her second child, born in the days of distrust. She has an affair with Whitfield, the preacher. Jewel is the child of that relationship, and she loves Jewel above both her other children. She turns back to Anse when the fire of her feelings for Whitfield flickers out, and to "negative" Jewel, she gives Anse two children, Dewey Dell and Vardaman. She is a matter-of-fact mother to all her children except Jewel. From this coldness Darl suffers the most, and it spurs his anger toward Jewel.

As you read the story, work out the movements of love and hate among the members of the Bundren family and prove your conclusions with evidence from the text. Here are some questions to consider:

1. What qualities made Addie Bundren the dominating figure in her family?
2. In what ways did her influence on her children affect their feelings toward one another?
3. Why didn't Cash feel the same ambivalent antagonisms that Darl felt?
4. Why did Dewey Dell move toward Jewel and away from Darl?
5. Whom among his brothers did Vardaman love the most?

PROBLEMS IN INTERPRETING AS I LAY DYING

1. One of the problems in analyzing *As I Lay Dying* is determining whose story it is. Who is the central protagonist? Is it Addie Bundren? Is it Darl? Is it the Bundren family? Nineteen of the fifty-nine monologues are in Darl's voice. Vardaman's voice is heard ten times; Cash's, five; Dewey Dell's, four. Addie speaks but once and so does Jewel. Who dominates the story? Who moves you the most?

Write an essay proving with evidence from the text that the central protagonist of *As I Lay Dying* is Addie Bundren or Darl.

2. Another problem in analyzing *As I Lay Dying* is determining what the themes are and which of the themes is the dominant one. Below are some of the themes of the story. See whether you can find evidence in the text to prove that each is a theme of the novel. Select one and prove that it is the dominant one.

a. *As I Lay Dying* is an exploration of the psychological relationships within a family.

b. The Bundrens in *As I Lay Dying* are an archetypal family. The structure and relationships have a Biblical tone and are a metaphor for all families since human beings created the family as an institution for survival.

c. *As I Lay Dying* is concerned most with faith and sin and with the rituals and conflicts associated with the journey from life into death.

d. In *As I Lay Dying* the accumulated insults heaped upon the body of Addie Bundren symbolize the fear, horror, and humiliation of death.

e. The fire and flood in *As I Lay Dying* symbolize the rituals in primitive times associated with the journey from life into death. The passage is celebrated with the frenetic forward and backward movements of the sons and is accompanied by the sacrifice of one of the sons.

f. The chief concern of *As I Lay Dying* is the nature and meaning of death, its physical elements, its pathetic and its grotesque elements.

g. *As I Lay Dying* belongs in the category of dark humor. The macabre events that accompany the journey of the body of Addie Bundren to Jefferson City are grotesquely comic. (In preparing to write a discussion of this aspect of the novel, select the scenes that are exaggerated and those in which shocking and unexpected incidents occur.)

h. *As I Lay Dying* deals preeminently with the conflict between word and deed, between what people say and what they do.

Writing a Critical Paper

Read the essay printed below and write a short critical commentary indicating your agreement or disagreement with the view expressed in it.

Vardaman's Role in As I Lay Dying

What we see of Vardaman in the barn-burning sequence is an extension of what the author has invited us to see about him in the earlier passages of the story. Basically, this reveals how a child reacts to the death of his mother and to the various actions of the adults around him, centered in the final illness, death, and burial of Addie Bundren.

In addition to our view of a child groping blindly and pathetically to understand the phenomenon of death and the "weird" behavior of the adults around him, we see the other figures in the story through his vision. Our estimate of them is sharpened by his childish insights and responses. One view becomes more crystallized than others, and that is the relationship between Vardaman and Darl. As the story proceeds, we become more clearly aware of the nature of this relationship and its function in the novel.

It is Vardaman, troubled by the buzzards and wondering where they stay at night, who discovers Darl setting fire to Gillespie's barn. He tells Dewey Dell, probably because he seeks an explanation, but she tells him not to tell anybody about it. After the fire, he finds Darl lying on the coffin, "there so the cat won't come back," he believes. Darl is crying, and Vardaman tries to console him by saying, "You needn't cry, Darl. Jewel got her out." The remark is profoundly ironic in view of what Darl was seeking to do. A few sentences later, Vardaman repeats to himself what has troubled him, "I saw something that Dewey Dell says I mustn't never tell nobody."

Vardaman could not understand why Darl set fire to the barn, but he could understand why Darl was crying. To him, at that moment, Darl was feeling the anguish he felt. The spectacle of Darl's firing the barn disturbed him. It runs like a refrain through his tortured musings. We can infer from this and from all the novel tells us that Vardaman idolized Darl and that the barn-burning created doubts in his mind which were dissipated when he found Darl crying on Addie's coffin.

The novel depicts the deep love of a child for an older brother. After Darl is taken to Jackson, Faulkner shows us Vardaman with Dewey Dell. All through this monologue, Vardaman shows a perplexed agony similar to that which he experienced at the death of his mother. He keeps repeating, "Darl is my brother. My brother Darl." It runs through his soliloquy like a tragic lament. What heightens the effect of Vardaman's suffering throughout the story is that he does not know what is happening. For example, it is Vardaman who describes what he believes are Darl's futile efforts to get the coffin out of the river. And when Darl comes empty out of the water, Vardaman's cry is, "You never got her, Darl, Darl, Darl." All Vardaman's love for Addie and Darl is in that cry of disappointment. But Darl's actions are beyond his comprehension.

From all of this, the reader can reach a number of conclusions concerning Vardaman's role in the novel. By the end of the novel, the reader has some understanding of both Vardaman and Darl, though the portraits are not clearly outlined. The reader sees Darl as a sensitive, poetic personality with so deep a knowledge of the people about him, their beliefs, habits, and ways, that he can reconstruct scenes that he has not witnessed. We believe that Darl's description of Addie's death and of the reactions of those present is true because we know that his omniscience is like that of the artist describing places and people that have penetrated his/her deepest understanding. Despite his awareness of his world or perhaps because of it, Darl is pursued by demons that pull him in many directions. He loves his mother and he hates her. He is tormented by what his intelligence considers to be an insult to the dignity of his mother, prolonging her burial. When Cash, Jewel, and he cross the ford and the log causes the wagon to turn over, he tries to let the flood carry the coffin away. His burning of the barn is an attempt to put an end to his father's vain pilgrimage. Its failure brings him to tears. Despite his belief that Addie must be quickly buried, he objects to delaying attention to Cash's leg. He believes that care for the living comes before care for the dead. We are aware of his concern for Cash. He is not troubled by Dewey Dell's plight because hers is due to natural causes and does not endanger her physically. He is aware, however, of Vardaman's love and Vardaman's pain, but he is himself too lost in the indignity and insult to which his mother's corpse is being subjected to help his little brother. Throughout the story, he is moved to actions of participation and actions of withdrawal. His attitude toward all his family is ambivalent.

Vardaman, like Darl, is a sensitive, poetic personality, but Vardaman responds to the tragic experiences of his life in a confused and frightened way. He is moved by instinct and by his limited awareness of reality. In a curious way, he associates his mother with a fish. The vivid image of the fish "cut up into pieces of not-fish now, not-blood on my hands and overalls" is associated in his mind with his dead mother, "not-mother." He thinks Dr. Peabody killed her, and he takes revenge by driving Peabody's team of horses loose. After his mother dies, he keeps opening the window so that she can get air. Upset by the realization that the coffin is airtight and recalling how suffocated he was when he got "shut up in the crib," he bores holes in the top of the coffin with an auger that bores into his mother's face. He insults her as much in his innocence as other members of the family do in sophistication. He has a fantasy that his mother got out through the holes he bored and got into the water and became a fish. But it is a fantasy the reality denies.

Here, therefore, is a naïve, imaginative child, horrified, and tormented by events, responding in bizarre, touching ways to a tragedy with which he cannot cope. Despite the exaggerated and even grotesquely humorous nature of his responses, perhaps because of them, the reader is deeply moved by his plight.

In a similar fashion, Darl, responding on an adult level to the same tragedy, is defeated, suffers, in fact, a more tragic end because, like Vardaman, he cannot cope with reality and because in him, too, there are movements which he does not understand and which he cannot control. This interplay between Vardaman and Darl, between the innocent and the sophisticated view of tragic human experience, is one of the main themes of this novel.

Write an essay in which you define in similar fashion the relationship between Darl and Jewel or between Cash and Darl.

Write an essay in which you prove with evidence from the text that Addie's influence on the lives of her children was a destructive one.

Analysis of *Invisible Man*

INVISIBLE MAN
Ralph Ellison (1914–1994)

Invisible Man by Ralph Ellison is an account of incidents in a life as recorded by a sensitive writer. Like many such works, it presented a series of experiences by means of which the protagonist learns many things about himself and about the world in which he lives.

Whether the author creates a narrator who recounts significant episodes in his life in chronological or logical order, or one who in maturity recalls the past and records the revelations of the particular experiences that brought him to his present state, the impact upon the reader is more or less similar. In both cases, the author informs the reader how the insights either produced the values that in maturity governed the narrator's life and molded his beliefs, or gave him the knowledge of how good or evil came to dominate him and the domain of his limited world. Usually, the smaller world that is the center of the action becomes a metaphor for the wider world of humankind.

TWO TYPES OF SYMBOLISM

Writers also distinguish between symbolism of events and symbolism of objects. In *Invisible Man,* symbolism of both events and objects is prominent. For example, the Battle Royal, which is the first event recounted, becomes a symbol of much of the exploitation and agonies of the innocent; and the blindfold covering the eyes of the young black students who are forced to engage in battle for the amusement of the white gentry becomes the symbol of the successive periods of misunderstandings and blunders that haunt the career of the *Invisible Man* as he searches for meaning and a true and acceptable identify in his life. The realization on the part of the narrator in *Invisible Man* that all who play serious and humane roles on the stage of life are blindfolded much of the time and that seeing comes in dramatic spurts of traumatic experiences, when the blindfold is consciously or accidentally removed, is a central theme of the novel. The replacement or the removal of the blindfold with each shaking experience occurs in the progress of a life, and with each instance comes knowledge that redeems or destroys.

ELLISON'S VIEW OF INVISIBILITY

According to Ellison, everybody during his or her lifetime is largely invisible. The physical person may be seen, but *who* the person is in reality, and *what* that person is, is seldom perceived. Visibility comes in moments of realization, learning, sharing, recognition, achievement, wonder. As the result of such moments, in time one begins to accept the knowledge of who he or she is, and it is at such a time that one attains some self-esteem, some identity to be proud of, and an acceptable visibility to the world outside the self. Ellison seems to conclude that visibility is a healthy state when it occurs in a pause during the vicissitudes of life, when the individual has come to know him- or herself and attains a proud identity, when he or she is ready to form or reform his or her life in more humane and positive ways, and take a place in the moral and social milieu of the time.

But this does not always happen. Often the knowledge, the revelation, destroys, as was the case with Tod Clifton in *Invisible Man,* when the realization is that humanity is fundamentally evil, that no philosophy, no system, no measure, no dream can stop humankind in its march through cruelty and destructiveness to disenchantment, exploitation, defeat, and pain, that particular individuals and groups are destined to suffer, and that any vision, any faith, any institution for human betterment is doomed to failure. When this happens to a sensitive individual, he or she is moved to seek some escape, the most desperate being death. The majority, however, eschew suicide. They take a break, run off to an isolation to meditate, to review their place in what appears to be a hopeless chaos, and to make some effort to find a meaning and an identity that make possible and tolerable some participation, some contribution, some relationships and friendships in this struggle called existence.

By having the Invisible Man serve as the narrator and having him recount his experiences and his thoughts and views in stream-of-consciousness passages at each stage in his development, Ralph Ellison is able to present a subtle and penetrating overview of the world and problems of the black population of America. Through the rationality and the passion of the narrator's response in all the encounters that shape his life and his values, through the melodramatic and occasional surrealistic descriptions of individual and mass behavior in confrontations and explosions of violence, and through satiric exaggerations of the ways some of the people in the book act, Ellison presents with clarity and honesty a series of portraits of the blacks of his day, their community in a Southern town and in New York's Harlem, and the problems they face. In Ellison's view the black person in a white society seems permanently to be invisible, not known, not understood. In addition, the atmosphere of the white culture so affects the view of the ambitious black held by his fellows that he or she often becomes invisible to them, too. This is the paradox, the irony, that affects the black's expectations.

The fundamental goal of the Invisible Man is identity: an identity that includes knowledge, special talents, and uniqueness. He is aware that he possesses these qualities even though only a few recognize them. What Ellison states is that, as long as the world retains a stereotypical view of the black's character and personality and as long as African-Americans, facing the competitiveness of a world dominated by whites, tend to belittle their own qualities and the potential areas of achievement open to them, they will remain invisible men and women, and their progress toward dignity, acceptance, and success will be hampered. What can save them, Ellison suggests, is to know themselves and to determine the extent to which their invisibility will aid them in attaining the best outcomes for whatever values they hold sacred, especially values that concern the common good. This is not easy because determining what is best for the common good and for fulfilling one's own economic and social needs without demeaning one's self requires a unique intelligence and sensitivity.

One need not be an intellectual or a saint, however, to attain one's goals. In *Invisible Man,* Ellison has created a protagonist who has nobility and civic concern and who values his freedom as an individual. Sharpened by experience, he is ready to engage in a mission of worth, as well as to fulfill his needs as a thinking person. Paradoxically, what the narrator attains is a perfected invisibility that makes him visible to those who sense in him the nobility and strength of his character and the selflessness of his efforts and his message. The narrator states that he did not come to be truly alive until he discovered the force and flexibility of his invisibility.

The Invisible Man's Story

The nameless Invisible Man makes a kind of pilgrim's progress in the novel. He begins as a young Southern black who has undertaken a program of education to make something worthwhile of himself and his future. His dream is to become a successful, respectable gentleman. He believes that what is required is that he get a good education, acquire the social manners of the white society that befriends him, dress properly, and, above all, know his place in the controlled world of white supremacy. His role model at first is Dr. Bledsoe, the head of the college for black students to which he has been admitted on the basis of his abilities and his accomplishments in the lower schools.

The following is a summary of the key experiences recorded in a first-person narrative by the Invisible Man, who is hiding in an underground haven where he is safe from enemies and where he can relive the past and see more clearly what he has learned from the events of his life thus far. He must also decide where he is to go in terms of career and mission from this time on.

EARLY EXPERIENCES

His first experience occurs when he is invited to give the speech he had delivered at his graduation from high school to a gathering of the town's leading white citizens. When he gets there, he is pushed into an entertainment called the Battle Royal, to be fought in a ring by nine of his schoolmates. The contestants, clad in shorts for the fighting match, are first subjected to the sight of a stark-naked blonde woman who dances sensuously. They are then blindfolded and ordered to attack one another, urged on by the sadistic white onlookers, who have cast off all civilized restraints. When this second phase of the evening's program is over, the boys are supposedly rewarded. They are ordered to gather, on signal, coins and bills from an electrified rug. The agony of being subjected to shock after shock keeps them from gathering anything, and one by one they rush out of the ring. A few, including the Invisible Man, manage to gather some "coins" only to discover later that they are brass tokens. The boys are paid five dollars each for their performance; the last one to rush off gets ten dollars.

The Invisible Man finally gets his chance to deliver his speech to the raucous audience, who interrupt him frequently. When he finishes, however, they praise him and give him his rewards, a gleaming calfskin briefcase and a scholarship to the State College for Negroes, for which he is grateful. He accepts his place in this unbalanced society where he must tolerate being insulted, demeaned, and cruelly treated as long as he is rewarded for his accomplishments and is given a beautiful briefcase and the opportunity to get a good education.

THE COLLEGE YEARS

A second stage in the life of the Invisible Man occurs when he is a junior at the college. Dr. Bledsoe, the college president, asks him to drive Mr. Norton, a wealthy businessman who is a generous contributor to the college, about the campus and its precincts. The Invisible Man learns from Mr. Norton that his generosity in supporting the college arises from a belief that in some mystic way the contributions to American society of the graduates of this school will keep alive the memory of his daughter. He claims that the future of the young narrator and that of each of the school's students is part of his own destiny, a belief that is totally beyond the comprehension of the young student.

Driving away from the college grounds, Dr. Norton and the Invisible Man come upon the home of Jim Trueblood, a poverty-stricken sharecropper, who has brought disgrace upon himself and upon the black community by committing incest with his daughter. Both wife and daughter are pregnant. Mr. Norton is at first appalled. But when he meets Trueblood, he lets the farmer tell his story—an account that is a masterpiece, fascinating, and shocking in its simple, lurid realities and showing the influence of writers like Kafka and Faulkner.

The incest, as Trueblood tells it, arose out of the closeness in their living quarters that compelled them to sleep together when the weather got very cold and out of a strange, erotic dream. Trueblood is a decent, hardworking man caught up by the forces of a hard life. His wife and daughter are furious with him, but resigned. Although the black community wants the family out of town, his story interests the whites, and they keep the blacks from driving him out. Trueblood's confession reminds Mr. Norton of his own feelings toward his daughter. Visibly moved, he gives Trueblood a one-hundred-dollar bill, and he and his student guide leave.

Mr. Norton says he needs a drink. The only place where the Invisible Man can take him is the Golden Day, a house of prostitution. It proves to be a mistake because on this day a group of insane men from the local asylum are visiting the brothel. What follows is another descent into hell. A violent riot occurs. During all the tumult Mr. Norton, an elderly man in poor health, faints several times. He is restored by one of the insane, a doctor who calls himself Vet. All that the narrator tells the reader about the tragedy of Vet's life is that "ten men in masks drove him out from the city at midnight and beat him with whips for saving a human life." Whose life he saved and what the circumstances were are not told, but it probably had to be the life of someone whom the worst of the whites in the city wanted destroyed.

The Golden Day events, like those of the Battle Royal, deal with the most cruel and the most insane behavior of human beings, even those who are considered pillars of society. Nevertheless, this behavior is punctuated with a few scattered gestures of concern and assistance, such as the actions of Vet and a few of the prostitutes. The riot becomes a shocking metaphor for those times in community existence when a segment of its population goes mad. Sometimes, on such occasions the instigators, the participants, if they are caught, may be punished, but the tragedy is that many innocents also suffer.

Another series of events occur when the Invisible Man returns with Mr. Norton to the college. These events initiate the process of enlightenment that will go on for some time before the young protagonist achieves a raison d'etre for his life and an identity he respects.

1. This phase begins with self-reproach for having taken Mr. Norton to the back of the slave-quarter section.
2. He is upbraided by Dr. Bledsoe for being so insensitive as to take Mr. Norton to so depraved an area of black existence.
3. He attends chapel, where he listens to an emotional retelling by a Reverend Barbee from Chicago of the life and death of the founder of the school and of the founder's trust in Dr. Bledsoe to continue his work.
4. He returns to see Dr. Bledsoe. This time Bledsoe tears into him, calling him a "nigger" and blaming him for causing damage to the school by taking Mr. Norton into a black slum. Bledsoe talks to him of the virtues of lying and hypocrisy in dealing with white benefactors and sympathizers. The narrator fights back and asserts his innocence. He reminds Bledsoe that Norton was not offended and had forgiven him. The college president realizes that the boy is a fighter, not a docile creature to be molded in any way he wishes, and that he must get him out of the way. He changes his tune. He tells the young man that, if he will go to New York, he will be provided with letters of recommendation to businessmen who are friends of the school, one of whom will surely give him a job. Feeling some sense of guilt, the narrator accepts.

THE REST OF THE STORY

The rest of the novel continues in a similar vein. The narrative takes various forms: realistic accounts of dramatic experiences; surrealistic descriptions of places and events, especially of mob actions, of violent confrontations, and of the bizarre behavior of particular personalities; detailed portraits of a variety of persons, including one of a white leader of a radical group dedicated to establishing a communal society where the citizens sacrifice freedom for the good of the programs envisaged by the leaders; the use of metaphors and symbols dealing with sight and blindness, truth and falsehood, honesty and hypocrisy, freedom and servitude, victory and defeat, idealism and cynicism, ignorance and knowledge. The work is a rich, vivid, original, and singular presentation of the character and problems of the blacks in America as Ralph Ellison saw them at the time he wrote the novel. In innumerable ways, it reflects the struggles and the values of American blacks in rural and urban America.

The following is a sequence of scenes in the career of the Invisible Man in New York, especially in Harlem, that leads to his self-knowledge as a black and to a realization of the needs of his people. The attempts, presented in detail in this novel, to improve the lot of blacks in American society are not all positive. Most, in fact, appear to end in disappointment. Nevertheless, the novel depicts people and problems as the author views them and in some ways suggests what can be done.

1. In New York the Invisible Man feels a greater sense of alienation, as well as a feeling of being under surveillance. From a Mr. Emerson, Jr., the rebel son of the last of the businessmen to whom he applies for work, he learns that Dr. Bledsoe's letters of recommendation were actually letters of betrayal. Mr. Emerson, Jr., helps him get a job in a paint factory.

2. In the factory his job is to add drops of a black liquid into buckets of brown paint that when stirred, turns white. The added black makes the paint even whiter. This is a symbolic comment on the tendency of blacks to emulate whites.

3. Accused of carelessness, he is given the job of assisting a black engineer, called Brockway, who runs the power source of the factory. Thinking at one point that the narrator is a union man, Brockway attacks him. During the fight an explosion occurs. The Invisible Man is hurt and is taken to a hospital, where the cold, sterile indifference gives him a sense of imprisonment.

4. He finds a home in a rooming house owned by Mary Rambó, who symbolizes the warm mother figure so prominent in black life and literature.

5. Coming upon the eviction of an elderly couple from their home because they cannot pay their rent, he addresses the many people whose anger is rising as they watch. There is a riot, and the police are called. The narrator escapes arrest by going to the roof of the building, jumping from one to the next, and leaving by way of the last building on the street.

6. This escapade brings him to the attention of Brother Jack, the white leader of an active black Brotherhood, with a program of setting up a solidarity to improve conditions for the blacks, and of establishing an egalitarian society where blacks and whites can work together for the common good. Brother Jack needs the Invisible Man's eloquence and his passion to articulate the grievances of people. He is to be well paid. He is also expected to be educated in the ideology of the Brotherhood by Brother Hambro and trained to sell its message to the masses.

7. What bothers him about the organization is that he is expected to take orders from the Brotherhood without question, to give up his freedom to have personal views.

8. His first speech to an audience is on dispossession and on humanitarian values. Although the response from his listeners is good, the Brotherhood doesn't like the speech. It tends to advocate an individualism contrary to the substance of their ideals.

9. He is made leader of the Harlem district and meets other members of the Brotherhood. He gets to know two members well. Brother Tarp, who represents the heroic black, who asserts his rights, and who is ready to suffer for his actions, becomes a father figure to the young man; the other, Tod Clifton, is a young but extremely sensitive idealist who, when the Brotherhood fails him, reverts to a past stereotype. One brother, Wrestrum, doubts the Invisible Man's dedication and his sincerity. He also meets Ras the Exhorter, a fiery, rabble-rousing activist leader, furiously antiwhite and devoted solely to rousing the masses to violence.

10. The Invisible Man is relieved by the Brotherhood of his duties in Harlem. The members find that he is incapable of following to the letter the rigid doctrines and the disciplines of the Brotherhood ideology. Brother Jack's weakness and his obsessions are symbolized by his loss of an eye in one of his encounters for his cause. His vision of a better life for mankind, in the view of the Invisible Man, was thereby marred.

11. Like the Invisible Man, Tod Clifton, too, is disenchanted, but, unlike him, Tod gives up. The Invisible Man finds him selling mechanical Sambo dolls and is present when Tod is shot during a quarrel with the police.

12. Without consulting the Brotherhood, he arranges for a public funeral for Clifton. Before a tremendous crowd, he delivers a raging and impassioned

oration, which is followed by mob unrest. Admonished by Brother Jack and other members of the Brotherhood, he is sent back to Brother Hambro for further indoctrination.

13. After a violent quarrel with Ras, he finds himself the object of the anger of Ras's men, who seek to kill him. He assumes a disguise that creates a resemblance between him and Rinehart, a Harlem character of many faces and many activities, one ready to take advantage of the masses, to sacrifice them supposedly for their own best interest, to promise them the good life, and at the same time to draw every possible benefit for himself. Having seen the splendid home of Brother Jack, the Invisible Man realizes that this is the way not only of the Brotherhood but also of the rabid, antiwhite activism of Ras.

The novel ends with an account of a violent riot, with the Invisible Man hiding in a cellar, reviewing his past and aware that he has been invisible, because he is black, in all his contacts and experiences, never really known, and never, until this moment, never really knowing himself. The blindfold has fallen from his eyes. And yet, he believes, there is some mystery to his inner being that has yet to be revealed.

The Novel's Timelessness

Ralph Ellison has written a novel about many aspects, elements, and concerns of African-Americans in the United States. What he wrote in the 1950s has cogent relevance in our day as well. He does not offer solutions. The revelations of his work provide the materials and the direction for the leaders. When leaders go astray, writers are there to remind them of their betrayals and to reproach them for their failures. But one must remember that writers also are fallible. They, too, are invisible men and women who are mysteries to others and mysteries to themselves.

Writing an Essay Based on *Invisible Man*

1. Each of the major characters in *Invisible Man* represents a personality that Ellison finds in the African-Americans in his time. Choose two of these characters who espouse opposing philosophies, and write an essay supporting the view that they are clearly defined and recognizable individuals or that they are merely stereotypes to support Ellison's view of his world.

2. Ellison is critical of many of the African-Americans of his day and of the values that ruled their lives. He also comments on the baleful effect of the white culture upon the lives of the blacks. Write an essay in which you argue either that many changes have occurred since the fifties and that the lot of the African-American is much improved, or that Ellison's criticisms and comments are as true today as they were in his time.

3. Write an essay in which you discuss the moral problems faced by the Invisible Man and the manner in which he coped with them. Comment, with reasons, on whether you agree or disagree with his judgments and his actions.

Analysis of *Gulliver's Travels*

GULLIVER'S TRAVELS
Jonathan Swift (1667–1745)

Gulliver's Travels is considered one of the greatest satirical works. You will need to study it carefully to determine what it satirizes and how Swift goes about satirizing the objects of his scorn. In general terms, what Swift does is to create worlds of fantasy which mirror in exaggerated forms the patterns that exist in his real world. Into these fantastic worlds, he places his protagonist, an educated, but at the same time naïve and gullible Englishman, who responds to his experiences in simple, uncritical ways. His final response is to turn away from human beings because he can no longer tolerate the stench that they create and that exudes from them. Gulliver is engaged in his four voyages in a process of education. His study is humanity and its institutions. What he learns is that humanity is ugly and is best avoided.

In reading the text, you need to concern yourself with particulars, with the specific techniques used by Swift and the specific evils he exposes. Your first problem is to determine the distance between Swift and Gulliver. Throughout the work, Gulliver expresses many views about the nature of humanity, about human activities, customs, habits, behavior. He has, for example, much to say about the behavior of the Yahoos, the debased man-creatures he encounters in the land of the Houyhnhnms. In addition, he comments much on human institutions and relationships, on the endeavors of human beings to deal sensibly and scientifically with their environment. The problem for you to consider is this: How much of Gulliver's philosophy is Swift's? Where do author and character agree? Where do they disagree? For example, Gulliver sees the world of the Houyhnhnms as utopian. The educated horses in his view have solved the problems of relationships and social structure that human beings have been unable to resolve for centuries. Does Swift, also, see the Houyhnhnms as ideal? Does Swift agree with Gulliver that human beings are to be spurned and avoided because their Yahoo-nature is fixed, impervious to any attempt to change it for the better? Watch for this agreement or disagreement between Swift and Gulliver as you read the book.

Second, Swift directed his ire at specific evils and specific people in his day. But he also exposed evils that were universal, that exist in all time. You need not trouble yourself trying to determine the specific persons represented, for example, by the different Lilliputians. If you are interested there are notes in the Norton Critical Edition of *Gulliver's Travels* that will give you that information. You should concern yourself with the more universal customs, practices, values of Swift's England that led him to write this comic and bitter satire. You should seek also to determine the justice of Swift's criticism.

Third, in your study of *Gulliver's Travels,* you should seek to place Swift in a chain of being that runs from purely animal behavior and thinking to purely intellectual and spiritual behavior and thinking. Does Swift, for example, excuse or justify the sensual elements in human nature? Does he see the answer to the ugliness of life in some ideal realm where mind and spirit direct human energies to sublime ends? Is he a pragmatist who conceives that the answer lies in benevolent but authoritative men and women and institutions that will justly rule humanity?

Fourth, *Gulliver's Travels* indicts human institutions and ways. It would be an interesting and challenging project to make a study of the criticism directed by Swift and Gulliver against a particular group or a particular activity. For example, what are Gulliver's and Swift's views of women, of leaders in government, of scientific research, of religious conflicts, of law and government, of child-parent relationships, of patriotism, of war?

Fifth, *Gulliver's Travels* is a satire on the four aspects of human beings—the physical, the political, the intellectual, and the moral. What human physical attributes are satirized? What political aspects? What intellectual aspects? What moral aspects? Be specific. Find passages that comment critically on the way people prostitute mind and body for egotistic and often self-destructive ends.

Sixth, Gulliver begins in Lilliput as an innocent but ends back home in England, after his sojourn among the Houyhnhnms, sophisticated and alienated. Having had an education in human nature among the Lilliputians, the Brobdingnagians, the Laputans, and the Houyhnhnms, he has come to see men and women as ugly creatures whose contact he must avoid. What conclusions do you arrive at concerning Swift's intention? Does Gulliver represent the alienation that Swift himself feels? Does Swift believe that Gulliver's knowledge of humanity has driven him insane? Is Gulliver conceived as a tragic protagonist whose experiences have so exalted his sense of superiority that, acting as a prideful being, he separates himself from humanity and becomes tragically lost and insane among his horses in the stable?

Satire

The *Oxford English Dictionary* defines satire as "the employment in speaking or writing of sarcasm, irony, ridicule, etc., in exposing, denouncing, deriding, or ridiculing vice, folly, indecorum, abuses, or evils of any kind." Another definition in the OED defines a *satire* as "a poem, or in modern use sometimes a prose composition, in which prevailing vices or follies are held up to ridicule. Sometimes, less correctly, satire is applied to a composition in verse or prose intended to ridicule a particular person or class of persons."

Satire we may say, then, is a literary form of criticism. A society may over the years have come to accept a custom, a tradition, a belief, or an institution as embodying truth. The satirist sees in the world of reality that the particular custom, tradition, belief, or institution, instead of making human existence secure and rich, is, on the contrary, causing serious damage. The satirist sees this world no longer as one embodying truth but rather as one embracing a lie, as one founded on evil. To correct the harm, to expose the fault, he/she attacks. But the approach is not to reveal the ugliness totally in realistic terms, to show the cancer as it is. The satirist prefers to achieve his/her aims through ridicule, and uses the weapons of exaggeration, understatement, incongruity, sarcasm, irony, humor, wit, burlesque, invective, parody, and any other instrument of destruction in the literary arsenal, including cold, realistic detail.

Two Approaches to Satire

Basically, there are two approaches a satirist may take, depending on the nature of the vice or evil under attack and on the satirist's response to that vice or evil.

THE BEMUSED SATIRIST

The satirist may be a detached, bemused critic with no deep desire to effectuate change. In such a case, the purpose may be to hold a mirror up to the readers or spectators and let them see themselves and their world honestly. To such a satirist, the vices and follies commented upon are not destructive. They are a reflection of the obtuseness and stupidity of people, of the superficiality and meaninglessness of their lives, and of the barrenness and lack of substance in their values. In such a world, form is everything and substance nothing. The satirist applies wit and irony in commenting on the emptiness of such an existence and on the aridity of such a world. There is much fun and some hurt in the dissection, but no one is too seriously affected. This is the satire one finds in the novels of Jane Austen and in the plays of William Congreve, Richard Brinsley Sheridan, George Bernard Shaw, and Noel Coward.

THE ANGRY SATIRIST

The satirist, on the other hand, may be angry. The vices and follies perceived in the world and in the people that inhabit it are intolerable and enraging. The satirist, appalled by the suffering he/she sees, lashes out with bitterness and fury. The basic weapons are sarcasm and irony, and the tirades abound with vitriolic invective and venomous denunciation. In any tongue-in-cheek comments the poison of the satirist's hatred is readily apparent. Many satirists are often people inwardly beside themselves, frequently controlling their anger with cleverness, but more often letting loose with bitter vituperation. This is the kind of satire one finds in Jonathan Swift's *Gulliver's Travels*.

Take this characterization of man expressed in Swift's *Gulliver's Travels* by the king of Brobdingnag:

> . . . by what I have gathered from your [Gulliver's] own relation, and the answers I have with much pains wringed and extorted from you, I cannot but conclude the bulk of your natives to be the most pernicious race of little odious vermin that nature ever suffered to crawl upon the surface of the earth.

This is vigorous, angry denunciation, and it is directed against all humanity. Its power comes from the fact that it is a conclusion arrived at by a supposedly honest and impartial listener in response to Gulliver's descriptions of the customs and ways of civilized Europeans. Gulliver is aghast at the conclusion of the king of Brobdingnag because, at this time in his career, he does not see human beings in so ugly a light. The contrast between the king's sophisticated view and Gulliver's innocent view heightens the impact of the denunciation. The view of the king of Brobdingnag is obviously an exaggeration, but in light of Gulliver's accounts of human institutions and history and his descriptions of the behavior of human beings, as well as the reader's awareness of the depths to which they can descend, there is enough truth in the characterization to make the satirical comment powerful and effective.

The Satirist and the Audience

The clever satirist must consider his/her audience. The satirist needs to choose the tone and the technique that are most consonant with the temper of the readers. The majority of the audience may be hostile or indifferent or they may agree with the writer. For each class of readers the tone must be right if the work is to make any impact. What are the tones satirists have used? A satirist may adopt a tone of complete scientific detachment. What is being told, he/she will insist, is the truth, recorded with dispassion and moderation. But if the truth arouses horror, that is due not to the writer but rather to the matter being reported. For example, consider this passage from "A Voyage to Brobdingnag" in Swift's *Gulliver's Travels*.

> . . . One day the governess ordered our coachmen to stop at several shops, where the beggars, watching their opportunity, crowded to the sides of the coach, and gave me the most horrible spectacles that ever an

English eye beheld. There was a woman with a cancer in her breast, swelled to a monstrous size, full of holes, in two or three of which I could have easily crept, and covered my whole body. There was a fellow with a wen in his neck, larger than five woolpacks, and another with a couple of wooden legs, each about twenty foot high. But the most hateful sight of all was the lice crawling on their clothes. I could see distinctly the limbs of these vermin with my naked eye, much better than those of an European louse through a microscope, and their snouts with which they rooted like swine. . . .

How does Swift see human beings in this passage? They are creatures subject to the ravages of illness and made disgusting by disease. Poverty, too, makes them disgusting because they become dirty, evil-smelling, and infested with vermin. In this passage, Swift is not faulting society entirely, nor is he faulting humanity entirely. It is nature with its cruel conditions that turns men and women into revolting objects. But society and human beings bear some responsibility. This is an inference we must draw from the statement. In Brobdingnag, which Swift considers to be an enlightened country, there are poverty and disease, and nothing is done to remedy the horror. The satire is directed, therefore, first against nature and God and then against society and humanity for failure to deal with the ravages produced in men and women by neglect, time, and disease. The account is objective, scientific. The reader's reaction is one of horror.

Satirical Comment— Lilliput

What was Swift satirizing in the following?
1. The description of the king of Lilliput. His treatment of Gulliver. His view of himself.
2. The account of party conflicts: the high heels versus the low heels.
3. The account of religious conflicts: the Big-Endians versus the Little-Endians.

    It is computed that eleven thousand persons have, at several times, suffered death rather than submit to break their eggs at the smaller end.

4. The conflict between Lilliput and Blefescu.

    Blefescu constantly fomented these civil commotions and supported the cause of the Big-Endians.
    The emperor of Lilliput wished to reduce Blefescu to a province and thereby become the sole monarch of the world.

5. The conspiracy against Gulliver organized by a number of ministers. The king's attitude.

    Of so little weight are the greatest services to princes when put into the balance with a refusal to gratify their passions.

6. Ways of obtaining and maintaining position at court.
7. Laws and customs: laws against informers, laws against those guilty of fraud, rewards for those who observe the law, burial customs, education of children, parent-child relationships, treatment of the old and the sick.
8. Attitude toward intellectuals.

    . . . the want of moral virtue was so far from being supplied by superior endowments of the mind, that employments could never be put into such dangerous hands as those of persons so qualified. . . .

Satirical Comment— Brobdingnag

1. Gulliver at Brobdingnag, a tiny man among giants, is subjected to many dangers and harassments:*

    a. A child gets Gulliver's head in his mouth and then drops him. (p. 104)
    b. He is attacked by rats. (p. 106)
    c. A schoolboy aims a hazel nut at his head. (p. 111)
    d. A dwarf drops him into a bowl of cream. (p. 122)
    e. He is bothered by flies and wasps. (p. 124)
    f. A dwarf shakes an apple tree when Gulliver walks under it. (p. 130)
    g. He is pelted by hail.
    h. He is carried off by a spaniel and almost carried off by a kite. (p. 131)
    i. He is treated as a toy by the maids of honor. (p. 132)
    j. He is carried off by a monkey. (p. 136)

Why did Swift include these adventures in his account of Gulliver's experiences in Brobdingnag? Are these incidents comic or satiric? If you think they are comic, what creates the humor? If you think they are satiric, what faults of Brobdingnag is Swift exposing?

2. Gulliver describes religion, laws, government, learning, and manners of Europe to the king. (p. 121) The king's comment is: "How contemptible a thing was human grandeur which could be mimicked by such diminutive creatures such as Gulliver." Gulliver reacts by saying to the reader, "My color came and went several times with indignation to hear our noble country so contemptuously treated." How is irony used in this exchange as a weapon of satire? Read the entire passage. What is Swift satirizing?

Gulliver describes the English system. (p. 141) "How often have I wished for the tongue of Demosthenes or Cicero that might have enabled me to praise my own dear native land in a style equal to its merits and felicity." Swift's satiric technique is to exaggerate virtues beyond truth and to describe faults as if they are virtues. The king propounds some questions. (p. 143) The questions expose the corruption and hypocrisy in the system. The king also expresses his wonder and amazement at various institutions described to him by Gulliver. (p. 146) The king presents his view of European history (p. 147) and his reactions to Gulliver's panegyric upon England. His final comment is: "The bulk of your natives are the most pernicious race of little odious vermin that nature ever suffered to crawl upon the surface of the earth." Gulliver's naïve comment is: "I was forced to rest with patience while my noble and beloved country was so injuriously treated." How is irony used in this passage to carry out Swift's satiric intention? How effective is it? Is Swift's criticism justified?

Gulliver describes to the king the destructive power of gunpowder and offers to show the king how to manufacture and how to use it to extend his power. The king is horrified at the suggestion. (pp. 149, 150) Gulliver's comment is: "A strange effect of narrow principles and short views!" Gulliver is a good man. Why does he propose the use of gunpowder to the king? Why does he not see the virtue in the king's view? What is Swift saying about the effect of custom and general usage of weapons of war upon the typical populace?

3. Gulliver is taken to the town. He sees ugly sights among people in the streets. (p. 127) This is apparently a description of sights in London streets, highly enlarged. What kind of satirical comment appears in this scene?

---

*All page references are to *Gulliver's Travels* published by New American Library.

Satire 249

4. Gulliver describes the Brobdingnagian system as being limited and defective; yet it has elements of practicality and common sense. Can you tell from this account what elements of government and law Swift approves of? Is there a satirical tone in any of the descriptions of the Brobdingnagian system?

Satirical Comment—Laputa, Balnibarbi, and Other Places

In Laputa and its surrounding lands, Gulliver enters a world in which human beings seek to solve the problems of existence. There is in this world a concern with the speculative and the intellectual, but instead of solving problems, the inhabitants compound them; and they convert truth into superstitions, freedom into rigidity, love into caprice, power into tyranny, and good into evil.

1. The people of Laputa are taken up with intense speculation. Their heads are inclined either to the left or right. They can be brought back to reality by being tapped with flappers. "Although they are dexterous enough upon a piece of paper in the management of the rule, the pencil, and the divider, yet in the common actions and behavior of life, I have not seen a more clumsy, awkward, and unhandy people, nor so slow and perplexed in their conceptions upon all other subjects, except those of mathematics and music." (p. 180)

What classes of people and what activities is Swift satirizing here? Do you accept his criticism?

Gulliver tells us also that the people of Laputa live under continual disquietudes. (p. 180) They believe their world is in danger of annihilation from changes in the celestial bodies. What in the field of science is Swift satirizing here? Do you agree with his criticism?

Gulliver visits the academy of projectors, where scientists are engaged in various projects and schemes. There are elements both of comedy and of satire in his descriptions of the various enterprises in which the scientists are engaged. See whether you can define the comic elements as well as the satiric elements in these descriptions. Swift apparently finds a curious paradox in the researches of the scientists. In seeking solutions to problems, they attempt to create a world of facts that will function well and make the daily operations of humanity effective and satisfying. Instead, they destroy the old world of facts, the bases for a tolerable existence, and create a world of illusion, superstition, fear, and ugliness. The builders of a better life create an uglier life. Was this criticism of scientific research valid in Swift's day? Is it valid in our own day? Even if you do not agree with Swift's indictment, how would you evaluate his method and technique, his use of the devices of comedy and satire?

2. Gulliver comments on the women of Laputa. "The women have an abundance of vivacity; they condemn their husbands and are exceedingly fond of strangers." (p. 181) "The caprices of women are not limited by any climate or nation." (p. 182) Can we infer from these statements and from others that appear in the text, especially Gulliver's descriptions of the behavior of female Yahoos, that Swift was a misogynist? What satirical devices does Swift use in satirizing the personalities and behavior of women?

3. Gulliver admires Lord Munodi, whom he meets in Balnibarbi. Lord Munodi's countrymen despise him. Why? What in Balnibarbi does Swift criticize? Against what evil in his own society is Swift inveighing? Is Lord Munodi a model of virtuous behavior? What qualities in him does Swift admire? What form of satiric comment do we have when Swift juxtaposes Lord Munodi's values alongside of Balnibarbian values and reports the contemptuous attitude of the Balnibarbians toward Lord Munodi?

4. How would you characterize the satirical substance of a passage such as the following, concerned with an enterprise of one of the political projectors?

> He likewise directed that every senator in the great council of a nation, after he had delivered his opinion and argued in the defense of it, should be obliged to give his vote directly contrary; because if that were done, the result would infallibly terminate in the good of the public.

5. In Luggnag, Gulliver, with grandiose illusions concerning how he would spend his existence if he were immortal (p. 226), encounters the immortal Struldbrugs. (p. 228) How are his views on immortality changed by this encounter? (p. 231) Is this experience with immortality satirical? Is Swift ridiculing the conceptions of physical immortality offered to human beings by most of the religions they have created and accepted? Is there enough content in the text to support this view? Is this view a logical inference that one may draw from the content?

Satirical Comment—The Country of the Houyhnhnms

1. Gulliver spends a little over three years among the Houyhnhnms. When he comes home, he is a changed man, unable to tolerate proximity to human beings and spending almost all of his time in the stable with his beloved horses. Can we agree that at the close of the story the distance between Gulliver and Swift is great? Swift may see humanity as ugly, but not in the way Gulliver does. When you read the text, list the human beings who show Gulliver sympathy and kindness, especially Don Pedro de Mendez, who treats the queer Gulliver with such humanity and civility, and Gulliver's wife and children, who remained faithful and devoted to a husband and father who was seldom at home.

2. We learn much of the ways of the Houyhnhnms from the text. We learn about:
    a. Their homes and the food they ate. (p. 250)
    b. Their notion of truth and falsehood. (pp. 259, 260)
    c. Their manners and customs: marriage, education of women, education of the young. (pp. 288–290)
    d. The assembly of the Houyhnhnms. How they dealt with political and social problems. (pp. 291, 292)
    e. Their arts and crafts. (pp. 294, 295)
    f. Their treatment of death and their manner of burial. (p. 296)
    g. Their behavior in company. The nature and conduct of conversation and discussion.

In contrast to this, Gulliver describes the dirty and degenerate behavior of the Yahoos.
    a. Their eating habits: Their quarrelsomeness at food. (p. 280)
    b. The behavior of the ruling Yahoo and the manner by which he could be deposed. (p. 283)
    c. The flirtatious behavior of female Yahoos. (p. 284)
    d. The capacities of Yahoos for learning. (p. 287)

The description of the country of the Houyhnhnms smacks of Utopia. Read this part carefully. Gulliver may think this land Utopia, but does Swift? What is missing and what is wrong in Houyhnhnm-land? Look for criticisms. You will need to do inferential reading to find the faults in this world.

The descriptions of Yahoo behavior are angry, savage, and acrimonious. Human beings are depicted in their ugliest, most degenerate aspect. What satiric techniques does Swift use in this portrait of animal man? Is the satire effective? If you think the satire is powerful, what makes it so?

3. Among the Houyhnhnms, as among the Brobdingnagians, Gulliver has occasion to describe the institutions and customs of his native land. Gulliver tells his Houyhnhnm master how he views England and its people. He talks about wars among nations and the causes of war; about religious differences and the quarrels resulting from these differences; about the way law is practiced and the way judges are chosen; about the importance of money and the depths to which the English will sink to get it; about the habit of drinking, which destroys character and humanity; about the physical illnesses that afflict people, especially the horror of venereal afflictions, and the methods employed by physicians to cure the sick; about the way to rise to become prime minister; and finally about the qualities of the nobility. Gulliver gave a similar account to the king of the Brobdingnagians but with a difference. To the king, Gulliver described Europe, its peoples, institutions, and customs, as noble. The king looked below the surface and saw the ugliness that was there. To the Houyhnhnm master, Gulliver describes the foul reality. He now sees his world precisely as the Brobdingnagian king sees it. What effect does this vision of his world have upon Gulliver? What has happened to him? Which of his views is truer? Does Swift agree with him? As satire, which approach is more effective? Is there irony in Gulliver's account to the Houyhnhnm master?

Analysis of *Candide*

CANDIDE
Voltaire (1694–1778)

Cease then, nor ORDER imperfection name:
Our proper bliss depends on what we blame.
Know they own point: this kind, this due degree
Of blindness, weakness, Heav'n bestows on thee.
Submit—In this, or any other sphere,
Secure to be as blest as thou canst bear:
Safe in the hand of one disposing Power,
Or in the natal or the mortal hour.
All Nature is but art, unknown to thee;
All chance, direction, which thou canst not see;
All discord, harmony, not understood;
All partial evil, universal good;
And, spite of pride, in erring's reason's spite,
One truth is clear, whatever IS, is RIGHT.

This passage from the first epistle of Alexander Pope's *Essay on Man* expresses a philosophy that was popular in the eighteenth century. It is this view of life, of human beings' relationships to God and nature that, among other things, is satirized in *Candide*.

Let us first paraphrase the passage from Pope to see clearly what this optimistic philosophy of life was. The poem is addressed to humanity, and the speaker is one, perhaps the poet, who believes strongly in this view. He tells human beings to stop protesting, not to call the order in the universe imperfect. Order by definition contains perfection. Our happiness is related to what we find fault with. If we blame fate or God or ourselves for our pain, how can we be happy? Know yourself. Your form, your blindness, your weakness is

God-given. Resign yourself to what you are. In this world or in any other world, try to be as happy as you can. Feel secure in that you are, at birth or at death or through life, in the hand of a benevolent power. Nature is a creation whose comprehension is beyond human power. What appears to be an accident is part of a plan that you cannot understand. What is discordant is harmony; what seems evil is good. Your pride may prevent acceptance of this truth; your reason may lead you to err. One truth, however, is clear: the world, as it is, is right and good.

It is this view that Voltaire holds up to ridicule through the character of Pangloss, who throughout the work reiterates that everything happens for the best and that this is the best of all possible worlds. Opposed to Pangloss's view is the one held by Martin. Martin believes that evil is real and that it is an inherent element in nature and in human beings. He insists that the universe is torn between the supernatural forces of good and evil, and that evil rather than good has been the triumphant power since the beginning of time.

The work deals in part with the education and disillusionment of Candide, who seems at the close of the book to arrive at the conclusion that the problem of the existence of brutality and savagery, of pain, sorrow, and suffering, in a world supposedly created by a beneficent God is insoluble, that speculation on the subject is useless, and that human beings might be better employed in other pursuits.

Questions for Analysis

In studying *Candide,* you should deal with the following questions:

1. What kind of characters do we find in the work? How real are Voltaire's people? How much depth do they reveal? If you believe that the characters—Candide, Pangloss, Cunegund, Martin, Cacambo, Jacques, the Old Woman, Pacquette, Pococurante, and the many others—are all surface creations, is this due to a limitation in the author or to the nature and purpose of the work? Support your view with evidence from the text.

2. What are the unifying elements of the book? The following three have been mentioned by critics: the process of disillusionment in the mind and heart of Candide; the search for Cunegund, who represents the ideal that human beings strive toward; the testing of Pangloss's theories by juxtaposing them against reality. Do you accept any or all of these as unifying elements? Can you support any or all of them as unifying elements with evidence from the text?

3. What are the objects of Voltaire's satirical thrusts? Is Voltaire's satire directed against the following: organized religion in general and the Catholic Church in particular; monasticism as an institution harmful to the individual and injurious to society; the horrors and stupidity of war; the city of Paris with its follies and vices; the fatuous pride of noble families; the unreal Utopias envisioned by naïve and impractical idealists; the optimistic philosophy of German thinkers like Leibnitz and Wolff? See whether you can find evidence in *Candide* to support Voltaire's criticism of these institutions, behaviors, places, beliefs, attitudes. See also whether you can define Voltaire's satirical method.

4. *Candide* is a work filled with scenes of carnage, torture, and savagery. How does Voltaire undercut the horror of these scenes? Study the characters. How easily can you identify with them? If they were real, three-dimensional people, would you be able to tolerate the sequence of atrocities heaped upon them? Study the tone. What qualities of the tone neutralize the dread and terror of the

frightful events? Study the pace and movement of the scenes. How much detail does Voltaire provide? How is Voltaire's purpose aided by the quick, short scenes without elaboration? What makes many of the experiences of his characters unreal? Is there any element of fantasy to the work that leavens the shock? Study also Voltaire's use of comedy in the book. Select a number of scenes you consider comic and show how these, too, make bearable the abominations depicted in the work. What characters in the work do you consider comic? In what ways are they comic? Be specific.

5. What is the form of the work? It is a story of adventures of the hero and his friends. Find out what a picaresque novel is. Determine in what ways *Candide* is picaresque. What variations, if any, of the picaresque novel has Voltaire introduced? Voltaire introduces a number of interruptions in the sequence of his narrative. The narrative pauses while characters recount their adventures. The old woman tells her history before she joined Candide and his friends. So do Cunegund, Pangloss, and the Baron when they reappear after having been given up for lost. What is the effect of these interruptions? The narrative pauses frequently also for philosophical discussions about the nature of the universe and the concern of God in human welfare. What is the effect of the philosophical interruptions? Do they detract from the interest of the story, or do they add interest to the story? Why are they necessary?

6. How do you characterize the style of the work? Voltaire's sentences are short. The pace is fast. There is a pungent brevity to his scenes. His tone is light, comic, sardonic, bemused. Disgust is generated by the irony that runs through the entire work. What is the effect of having the voice of optimism and brightness comment on the ugly and evil reality? What is the effect of matching heroic demeanor, gay uniforms, cheerful music against cruelty, destruction, torture, and misery? How would you characterize the following statements from the work?
   a. Private misfortunes are public benefits; therefore the more misfortunes there are, the greater the general good.
   b. He came to a village which had been burned to the ground by Bulgarians in accordance with international law.
   c. They obliged him to make a choice and he determined by virtue of that divine gift called free will to run the gauntlet six and thirty times.
   d. By dint of purging and bleeding, Candide's disorder became very serious.
   e. In this country it is found requisite to put one admiral to death to spirit up the others.

7. What attitude toward his world does Voltaire reveal in *Candide*? Some readers have called Voltaire—and Swift, too—a misanthrope. Is this true? Can it be supported with evidence from the text? Can you support the following statement with evidence from the text: Underlying everything is Voltaire's horror of suffering and injustice and his compassion for the victims of oppression and cruelty?

8. Below is Voltaire's picture of El Dorado, a Utopia visited by Candide and Cacambo. Is there any satire in this account? If you find satire in this description, what is being satirized? What satirical techniques does Voltaire use?
   a. The useful and the agreeable are equally blended. The country is cultivated equally to provide delight for the eye and to produce the necessaries. The roads are adorned with carriages formed of glittering materials.
   b. The men and women are of a surprising beauty. Children wear tattered garments of the richest gold brocade and play at quoits with precious gems.

   c. Houses are built after the manner of European palaces. Delightful music is played in all parts of each house. Agreeable smells come from the kitchen. A typical dinner menu consists of four dishes of different soups, two young parakeets, a boiled condor, two roasted monkeys, three hundred hummingbirds in one dish, excellent stews, delicious tarts served in dishes of rock crystal, several sorts of liquor extracted from sugar cane.

   d. Inns are maintained by the government. Lodging and food are free.

   e. Everybody is of one opinion. There is no need for disputes, for government, for intrigue, for burning people who do not agree with you.

   f. The king's palace is a magnificent structure. To greet the king, one walks between two files of musicians, each file consisting of a thousand. The king is greeted by an embrace and a kiss on both cheeks. Twenty beautiful young virgins-in-waiting conduct Candide and Cacambo to the bath and dress them in robes woven of the down of hummingbirds.

   g. The city has magnificent public structures. The market place is decorated with thousands of columns. Fountains spurt spring water, rose water, and liquors. The squares are paved with precious stones emitting odors of cloves and cinnamon.

   h. There is a Palace of Sciences with a gallery two thousand feet long with various apparatus of mathematics and natural science.

9. When Candide and Martin are in Venice, they meet Signor Pococurante, a wealthy Venetian, whom Candide thinks to be a prodigious genius since nothing can please him. Pocourante regales Candide and Martin with his literary and esthetic views. Below are some of his opinions.

(Is Pococurante a satiric figure? What characteristics of the esthete nobleman is Voltaire satirizing? What are your reactions to Pococurante's dogmas?)

   a. Painting is esthetically satisfying only when it reproduces nature herself.

   b. Music, to be esthetically pleasing, must be easy to perform.

   c. Tragedies set to music are wretched contrivances. The songs of operas are ridiculous.

   d. Homer is a dull poet. His work abounds with descriptions of battles endlessly repeated. His gods are unbelievable creatures. His events are prolonged beyond the interest of the reader. Helen, the important character in his work, hardly appears.

   e. The characters in Virgil's *Aeneid* are flat and disagreeable.

   f. Since Cicero doubts everything, one should never read him. All one can learn from him is ignorance.

   g. The volumes of scientists are filled with chemical systems, none of which are the least bit useful.

   h. John Milton is a slovenly imitator of the Greeks. He disfigures creation. He represents in an absurd fashion devils and angels cannonading each other in heaven. His work abounds with melancholy reveries. In his work Lucifer rehashes the same thing over again a hundred times and eternally argues theology. The work is obscene, whimsical, and disagreeable.

Which of these views do you find comic? Why? Which of these views do you find satiric? Why? Which of these views express a serious, acceptable judgment? Did Voltaire intent Pococurante to be occasionally intelligent? How do you explain the Pococurante views that you find intelligent?

**Summary
Questions
on *Candide***

1. What beliefs is Voltaire satirizing in *Candide*?
2. What kind of characters do we meet in *Candide*?
3. Why isn't the reader appalled by the horrible scenes of violence in *Candide*?
4. Why do characters who have been killed come back to life?
5. What in your estimation are the fundamental conditions of life? Does Voltaire satirize these conditions?
6. What in your estimation were the social conditions in Voltaire's time? Does Voltaire satirize these conditions?
7. Prove or disprove: Voltaire believes in the existence of God, but he conceives of God as an evil force.
8. Prove of disprove: In Voltaire's view, one's garden hardly seems worth cultivating.
9. Do you agree or disagree with Candide's first conclusion about Pococurante, that he was the happiest of human beings?
10. What in your estimation is wanting in Voltaire's vision of Utopia as described in the chapters on El Dorado?

**Summary of
Satirical Content
of *Gulliver's Travels*
and *Candide***

What is Swift satirizing?

1. Rationalism: the emphasis on intellectual ideas and concepts; the rejection of the wisdom of the past.
2. Experimental and theoretical science: science deluded humanity with promises of a better future; it secularized society; it was antireligious.
3. New conceptions of humanity: the notion of the essential goodness of human nature seemed to Swift to be sentimental, optimistic, and unrealistic.
4. The new moneyed class: this new class in British society seemed to Swift to be corrupting social and political institutions.
5. Increasing power of the centralized government: power lay in a small group, the crown, a few ministers, the court.

What is Voltaire satirizing?

1. Organized religion in general and the Catholic Church in particular: Voltaire believed that the Church stifled intellectual pursuits.
2. Monasticism: to Voltaire this kind of separation from society was harmful both to society and to the individual.
3. The horrors and folly of war: Voltaire was especially incensed at the profession of soldiery, where men served as murderers for a price.
4. The city of Paris with its follies and vices: its pseudo-culture, its vicious critics, its pleasure, and its entertainments.
5. The fatuous pride of noble families: birth and ancestry counted for more than inherent nobility and ability.
6. The optimistic follies of German thinkers like Leibnitz and Wolff: they seemed to believe suffering to be part of the basic plan of the universe.

Analysis of *Catch-22*

CATCH-22
Joseph Heller (1923–1999)

Given *Catch-22*'s intricate narrative structure, detailed and numerous characters, complex time sequence, and varied moods and tones, you need to create a lucid, consistent framework for analysis of this extraordinary novel. On the one hand, the novel is humorous, savagely against the follies of war, insightful, and well-characterized; but, on the other hand, it is disturbing, vulgar, gruesome, and alien. Therefore, to enter the universe of this work is not an easy task. The richest, most complete reading of the novel becomes a value-generating critical endeavor only when you successfully enter that universe.

One method of accomplishing this involves searching for what can be called structuring principles. These are controlled overviews which not only produce understanding and appreciation, but also create order and organization. To obtain a structuring principle you need to ask specific questions. What ideas does the author develop thoroughly throughout the text? Which reappear at critical junctures? What is at stake in the action? What are the value centers of the work? You must consider how the novelist employs such elements as action, characters, dialogue, imagery, symbolism, irony, tone, and mood.

Developing structuring principles is practical, not theoretical, criticism. However, you must remember that a structuring principle is not the meaning of a work. It proves useful when you can bring it to the work, and it illuminates itself and the text, enabling you to comprehend the universe of the work emotionally and intellectually. By their very nature, structuring principles are inadequate and incomplete, for they cannot possibly include all elements of the novel.

From the following list of structuring principles about *Catch-22,* you can peruse the text, cataloguing references and page numbers, and then attempting to enunciate a summary statement of the breadth, scope, and effectiveness of the principle in question. Below the list are samples of how to cite textual evidence to support a structuring principle. In your analysis of the novel, you can choose to explicate the remaining structuring principles or to generate even more.

STRUCTURING PRINCIPLES

1. *Constant increase in the number of missions:* As if to underscore the folly of war, Colonel Cathcart constantly raises the number of missions his squadron flies. The fact that this is done to win the war is obfuscated by Cathcart's desire to become the most famous bomber squadron commander. The missions vary from 25 to 80 throughout the book, raised capriciously with no concern for the men.

2. *The inverted chain of command:* In a devastating irony, Heller reverses the power structure of the Army. Possibly the two most driveling idiots in the book are General Dreedle and General Peckem, a modern-day Tweedle-Dee and Tweedle-Dum. Possibly the most powerful person in the book is ex-PFC Wintergreen, the communications expert across whose desk flows every order and letter in the whole theater, waiting for his whimsical changes and censors. The higher the rank, the more incompetent the person; the lower the rank, the more influential the person.

3. *Milo's economy:* Backed by frequent doubletalk and inscrutable logic, Milo Minderbinder begins with buying eggs and ends by owning practically all of Europe. In a savage indictment of the free enterprise system carried to its illogical extreme, Heller allows one man to control his friends and his enemies.

4. *Catch-22:* The catch phrase of irrefutable logic, Catch-22 sweeps up everyone in its devastating path. As the book descends into a nightmarish tale of the macabre, the rampant destructions of war become obvious. Catch-22 grows cancer-like in its scope and power, enmeshing everyone in an endless net of agony and pain.

5. *Censorship:* To prevent the leak of crucial information, each officer in the hospital is given the task of censoring all incoming and outgoing mail.

Given this incredible power to wipe out any phrases, words, or addresses, the officers assume pseudonyms and launch a powerful campaign. Another expression of this phenomenon involves ex-PFC Wintergreen, who reads and censors all mail and memos coming into headquarters.

6. *Paranoia:*   Many of the characters in the work, particularly the protagonist, suffer from a deep-rooted fear that someone or something is out to get them. This fear governs many of their actions, and in turn creates many of the absurd regulations that bring terror and anxiety to their lives.

7. *Circular logic:*   In many of the dialogues and army rules in the book, Heller carries logic to an absurd extreme. The very logic of *Catch-22* is a prime example. In order to stop flying missions, a man must prove he is insane. But only a sane man would recognize that flying more missions and creating more opportunities to die is an insane proposition. Therefore, any man who requests to stop flying more missions must be sane. In many other cases, the characters in the book use this form of logic to their advantage.

8. *Double-talk:*   Closely allied to circular logic is the repetitious and nonsensical dialogue. During Clevinger's trial, the prosecuting colonel asks the recording secretary to read him back his last line. The response: "Read me back my last line." The following exchange is another example from the same trial. Clevinger: "I never said you couldn't punish me." Colonel: "Now you're telling us when you did say it. I'm asking you to tell us when you didn't say it." Clevinger: "I always didn't say you couldn't punish me, sir." This type of double-talk echoes throughout the novel.

9. *Constant attempts to escape:*   Because of the absurdity and dangers of the war, many of the characters attempt to escape. Interestingly, however, only the junior officers and enlisted men try, because the superior officers are so wound up in the follies of war as to remain inextricable.

10. *The folly of hospital treatments:*   One way to escape the war is to enter the hospital. However, the supposed cures for the sick and nonsick are just as ridiculous as those in the world outside. Yossarian's liver condition, painting one's gums purple as a remedy for any sickness, and the sad basket cases all underline the folly of the hospitals.

11. *The fact that everyone is dying in one form or another:*   In addition to the multitude of characters in the book who are physically killed, many others live a type of death in life or are victimized by the vicious system. By tracing what happens to the major characters, one can see the cruel fates the war offered.

12. *The soldier in white:*   As a living (or shall we say dying?) manifestation of death in life, the cast- and gauze-covered soldier in white, whose life fluids seep placidly from a jar through his body, emerging into another jar, symbolizes the cruelty and absurdity of war. Others' reactions to him show us much about their characters as well.

13. *The dead man in Yossarian's tent:*   Like the soldier in white, Mudd, the dead man in Yossarian's tent, who some swear is there and others swear was never there, demonstrates the weird ways of war. How others react to him shows us much about them.

14. *The man who saw everything twice:*   As a further example of symbolic absurdity, the hospital patient who saw everything twice deeply affects Yossarian and others. His particular malady is an especially effective expression of the ludicrous war.

15. *Competition within a rank:*   As if the desire to gain a higher rank were not enough, the way in which colonels plot against colonels, generals against

generals, majors against majors, and so on, underlines the foolishness of the officers. They openly deceive one another to look better to their peers, their troops, and their superior officers. Of course, in the end, their clandestine conniving only underscores their ridiculousness.

16. *Déjà vu:*   The feeling of having been somewhere before or seen something before serves to attack the horrors of war. After one has flown many, many missions and experienced many, many atrocities, the horrors all seem to blur together in one unending, unfocused vision of the world.

17. *The whores:*   The many prostitutes that men seek out in Rome and in other places demonstrate the futility and frustration of their lives (and of course speak of what happens to women and marriages during war). In many cases, the libidinal energies of the men redirect the entire action.

18. *Snowden:*   Poor Snowden, the man wounded by the flak, presents a haunting and ineradicable nightmare for Yossarian. Bleeding to death and freezing in the plane, Snowden mindlessly whimpers, "I'm cold" as Yossarian tries to bandage his wounds. But then Snowden spills his secret, along with his insides, and leads Yossarian to a final judgment about the war. Interestingly, Mike Nichols, in his direction of the film "Catch-22," chose the Snowden incident as his recurring theme and source of continuity with his many references to the grisly scene.

19. *Significance of characters' names:*   Partly to refer to an illusion, partly to choose a name to fit the character, partly to generalize about all nationalities, Heller chose a battery of names for his characters that astounds and challenges the readers, ranging from the obvious Scheisskopf to the ridiculous Major Major Major to the subtle Major-de Coverly.

Structuring principle 1—constant increase in number of missions:*

page
   22—raised to 50 from 44
   54—originally 25
   60—raised by Cathcart to 55
   66—Cathcart keeps 5
106—explains rise from 40 to 55
111—was 35 at one point
169—set at 40
219—Cathcart contemplates 70, 80, 100, 200, 300, 6000
222—raised to 60
376—raised to 70
397, 410, 414—set at 80

The pure folly with which Cathcart raises the missions becomes clear. Furthermore, the time sequence of the novel proves to be quite complex as Heller shifts from event to event.

Structuring principle 4—Catch-22:

page
   8—Each censored letter bears the censor's name.
47—Doc Daneeka and Yossarian discuss the number of missions the men must fly when they are sane.

---

*All page references are to Joseph Heller's *Catch-22* published by Dell Publishing Co., Inc.

60—Yossarian discusses whether he can go home after flying a number of missions, is told he must fly more.

108—If ex-PFC Wintergreen goes over the hill once more, he will be sent to the stockade.

118—Captain Black enforces his Loyalty Oath crusade through starvation and Catch-22.

179—Doc Daneeka won't ground Yossarian.

416—The MPs can do anything one can't stop them from doing—even the old woman understands the implications.

416—The MPs stomp around mumbling Catch-22 and don't have to show it to the people they chase out because the law (Catch-22) says they don't have to.

430—Before Yossarian is sent home by Cathcart and Korn, he must obey one final Catch-22 and declare they are his friends. Obviously Catch-22 is the law [sic] which enables the Army to do anything it damn well pleases. It brings about the total subjugation of men to a principle. The book is a vicious cycle of traps for the men.

Structuring principle 8—double talk:*

Double-talk is a language that mixes sense and nonsense, and exemplifies the stupidity and incompetence that exist in the Army.

page 13—Yossarian talking to the Chaplain: He says he didn't know there were any other Captain Yossarians. As far as he knows, he is the only Captain Yossarian he knows, but that is only as far as he knows.

page 17—Yossarian talking to Clevinger about those who want to kill him: Clevinger responds he doesn't know who is trying to kill Yossarian, so Yossarian responds by asking how Clevinger knows they aren't trying to kill him.

page 29—Colonel Cargill talking to the officers about the accordion player: How can Appleby see to tell whether he has flies in his eyes when he has flies in his eyes?

page 59, 91—Colonel Cathcart tells Major Major that he is the new squadron commander, but relays that he shouldn't think it means anything, because it doesn't. All it does mean is that he's the new squadron commander.

page 62—Yossarian, in talking to Milo about his liver condition, reveals that no one really understands the ailment.

pages 77–83—Clevinger's trial is a fascinating exercise in futile double-talk.

page 98—Major Major and the C.I.D. man discuss the absurd Washington Irving pseudonym on official documents.

Structuring principle 11—the fact that everyone is dying in one form or another:

We will use the following key to indicate the different types of death the men face:

1. physical death
2. the men are "disappeared" by the Army
3. missing in action
4. death in life—a spiritual nonentity
5. Catch-22 gets them

The only alternative is total escape, which we will label no. 6. One other factor in their deaths is the extent to which the men were aware of what was happening to them.

(*) stands for they knew all along.
(**) stands for a certain level of deadness in which they existed.

1, 2 Mudd	1 Snowden
1 Soldier in white (*)	2 Dunbar (*) (**)
1 Chief White Halfoat (*)	4, 5 Doc Daneeka (*)
1 Kraft	3 Clevinger (*)
1 Hungry Joe	4 Major Major (**)
1 Kid Sampson	2 Milo Minderbinder
1 McWatt	2 Gen. Peckem
1 Soldier who saw everything twice	2 Gen. Dreedle
2 Scheisskopf	4 Aarfy (*)
2 Wintergreen	6 Chaplain Tappman
5 Whores and the Old Man	6 Yossarian

The realization that maybe everyone is dying is powerful enough to drive the characters in *Catch-22* to the paranoia and escapism that form the substance of the book. There are dead and dying people throughout the book; and beginning with the deaths of Kid Sampson and McWatt (348–350) and Yossarian's counting the roll call of all the dead people he knew (355), the novel plunges into the steady extermination of many of the characters (the worst and most profound being Snowden, 445–450).

Characters and Chapter Sequences

Two other key considerations for a study of *Catch-22* involve an understanding of the many characters and of the sequence of the chapters. Reprinted below is a list of the major and minor characters. As you read the novel, try to keep clear the interrelationships of these characters and the intricate organization of the chapters, both chronologically and thematically.

Major Characters

1. Yossarian	6. Major Major Major
2. Milo Minderbinder	7. Lieutenant Scheisskopf
3. Chaplain Tappman	8. ex-PFC Wintergreen
4. Colonel Cathcart	9. Doc Daneeka
5. Colonel Korn	10. Nately's whore

Minor Characters

1. Hungry Joe	11. McWatt
2. Appleby	12. Kid Sampson
3. Snowden	13. Nately's old man
4. Major-de Coverly	14. Old lady in Rome
5. Havermeyer	15. Nately's whore's kid sister
6. Clevinger	16. Captain Flume
7. Nately	17. Aarfy
8. Colonel Moodus	18. Orr
9. Captain Black	19. Chief White Halfoat
10. Dunbar	20. The Texan

21. Dobbs	33. Kraft
22. Corporal Whitcomb	34. Danby
23. Sergeant Towser	35. Colonel Cargill
24. Piltchard and Wren	36. Colonel of Communications
25. Nurse Duckett	37. Mrs. Daneeka
26. Nurse Cramer	38. Dr. Ferredge
27. Dori Duz	39. Gus and Wes
28. Scheisskopf's wife	40. Luciana
29. C.I.D. man	41. Major Sanderson
30. Mudd	42. General Dreedle
31. Soldier in white	43. General Peckem
32. Soldier who saw everything twice	44. Old man in Rome

Satirical Nature of *Catch-22*

Yossarian is a bombardier. He is in an army hospital, having suffered from a pain in his liver. The pain is gone but he is kept in the hospital because he runs a fever. In the morning, because he is an officer, he is given the task of censoring letters. In the hospital among the many patients are a Lieutenant Dunbar, a warrant officer, an artillery captain, a fighter captain, a soldier in white who is badly wounded and wrapped in plaster and gauze, and a middle-aged colonel who is dying of a mysterious ailment not fully diagnosed. They are joined by a Texan whom in three days no one can tolerate. The soldier in white dies. In a short time, to escape from the Texan, many of the patients stop complaining of illness, say they are well, and return to duty. Before this, a chaplain comes to the hospital to visit the sick; Yossarian and the chaplain "hit it off."

This is an account of the raw events that occur in the first chapter of *Catch-22*. The narrator of this account could have handled these events differently. He could, for example, have described them realistically, depicting for the reader a typical scene in an army hospital in which his protagonist spent a few days to recover from a liver ailment. He might also have described the events melodramatically, highlighting the dramatic efforts which the doctors and nurses made to save the life of a soldier in white and that of the dying colonel, and expanding on the exemplary devotion of the chaplain, who made every effort to bring comfort to the sick patients and to offer last rites to the dying.

But the narrator had another purpose in mind, and that was to present a satirical view exposing the maladministration and incompetence of upper echelon army personnel and the blundering and stupidly impersonal handling of the fighting men that characterized army life during World War II. In addition, he wanted to comment, in a wry and bitterly humorous way, on the effects of combat on the thinking and actions of the soldiers. For these reasons, the account abounds in 1) descriptions that exaggerate and distort the shapes of objects and places and the speech, demeanor, and conduct of the characters; 2) behavior that is either unmotivated and pointless or motivated by the worst possible considerations; and 3) conversations among the characters that are replete with *non sequiturs* and do not communicate with any clarity.

Read the following passages carefully.

Passage 1.   Mrs. Daneeka, Doc Daneeka's wife, was not glad that Doc Daneeka was gone and split the peaceful Staten Island night with woeful shrieks of lamentations when she learned by War Department telegram that her husband had been killed in action. Women came to comfort her, and their husbands paid condolence calls and hoped inwardly that she would soon move to another neighborhood and spare them the obligation of continuous sympathy. . . . Just as she was growing resigned to her loss, the postman rang with a bolt from the blue—a letter from overseas that was signed with her husband's signature and urged her frantically to disregard any bad news concerning him. . . . Mrs. Daneeka was overjoyed. . . . She dashed a grateful note off to her husband pressing him for details and sent a wire informing the War Department of its error. The War Department replied touchily that there had been no error. . . . The letter to her husband was returned unopened, stamped KILLED IN ACTION.

Passage 2.   The chaplain's summer-tan shirt was soaking with perspiration by the time he arrived there and rushed breathlessly back inside the orderly room tent, where he was halted peremptorily by the same treacherous, soft-spoken, staff sergeant with round eyeglasses and gaunt cheeks, who requested him to remain outside because Major Major was inside and told him that he would not be allowed inside until Major Major went out. . . .

"I'm sorry, sir," he said regretfully in a low, courteous, melancholy voice. "But those are Major Major's orders. He never wants to see anyone."

"He wants to see me," the chaplain pleaded. "He came to my tent to see me while I was here before."

"Major Major did that?" the sergeant asked.

"Yes, he did. Please go in and ask him."

"I'm afraid I can't go in, sir. He never wants to see me either. Perhaps if you left a note."

"I don't want to leave a note. Doesn't he ever make an exception?"

"Only in extreme circumstances. The last time he left his tent was to attend the funeral of one of the enlisted men. . . ."

Passage 3.   There were usually not nearly as many sick people inside the hospital as Yossarian saw outside the hospital, and there were generally fewer people inside the hospital who were seriously sick. There was a much lower death rate inside the hospital than outside the hospital, and a much healthier death rate. Few people died unnecessarily. People knew a lot more about dying inside the hospital and made a much neater, more orderly job of it. They couldn't dominate Death inside the hospital, but they certainly made her behave. They had taught her manners. They couldn't keep Death out, but while she was in she had to act like a lady. People gave up the ghost with delicacy and taste inside the hospital. There was none of the crude, ugly ostentation about dying that was so common outside the hospital. They did not blow up in mid-air like Kraft or the dead man in Yossarian's tent or freeze to death in the blazing summertime the way Snowden had frozen to death after spilling his secret to Yossarian in the back of the plane. . . .

They didn't take it on the lam weirdly inside a cloud the way Clevinger had done. They didn't explode into blood and clotted matter. They didn't drown or get struck by lightning, mangled by machinery, or crushed in landslides. They didn't get shot to death in hold-ups, strangled to death in rapes, stabbed to death in saloons, bludgeoned to death by parents or children, or die summarily by some other act of God. Nobody choked to death. People bled to death like gentlemen in an operating room or expired without comment in an oxygen tent. There was none of that tricky now-you-see-me-now-you-don't business so much in vogue outside the hospital. . . . There were no famines or floods. Children didn't suffocate in cradles or iceboxes or fall under trucks. No one was beaten to death. People didn't stick their heads into ovens with the gas on, jump in front of subway trains, or come plummeting like dead weights out of hotel windows with a *"whoosh!"*

Reread these passages, and then write short analyses of them that define and describe their satirical nature. Be sure to mention the evils or faults that are being exposed, the satirical intent, and the techniques and devices used by the author to achieve his goals.

Magic Realism

"Magic realism" is a genre that fuses fantasy and reality so seamlessly that it seems almost natural for a whole town to be infected with a plague of insomnia and a ghost of a child to return to the living as an adult. By blending the supernatural with the normal, magic realism raises questions about the nature of reality and truth. The following two selections, *One Hundred Years of Solitude* and *Beloved,* typify this genre.

ONE HUNDRED YEARS OF SOLITUDE
Gabriel García Márquez (1927–   )

Background   *One Hundred Years of Solitude* is many things to many people. Casual readers, literary scholars, specialists in myth, students of literary archetypes—critics of all types and persuasions feast in this novel's richness and diversity. It isn't a novel that goes down easily, however. On the contrary, it requires intense reading and rereading, always with a willing suspension of disbelief. Nor is it a book that can be fully understood without a bit of help. The purpose of this section is to give you some insight into what the author, Gabriel García Márquez, had in mind. When you are finished reading this material and the novel itself, perhaps you will share the pleasures that readers all over the planet have found in the book. Perhaps you will discover that Macondo, an otherworldly locale, seems strangely like a real place.

Basically, *One Hundred Years of Solitude* is the story of six generations of the renowned Buendía family. It is also the history of a community that never was and never will be. It's not that Macondo is a mythical place; rather, it operates outside the usual boundaries of time. It's a place where the passage of time is more or less irrelevant. Some people seem to live forever. Others die and return. Macondo is simultaneously primitive and technologically advanced. Its residents, dominated by the Buendías, embrace the bizarre, see fantasy in reality and reality in fantasy, and are embarked on a century-long quest to establish a functioning society.

As you read the book, you see a small city or state (one can never be sure) in the process of discovering itself and developing features common to civilized society. Macondo forms a government, develops commerce, law, religion, and technology. Its people learn to think, speak, read, and write. It engages in war, art, scientific research, politics, and in all the other activities emblematic of a modern civilization. In its rise and fall, Macondo invites comparison to both ancient and contemporary societies.

In telling you the story, the author invents a unique reality. A character flies off on a carpet, two children come into the world adorned with a pig's tail, a trail of human blood snakes its way around town looking for the mother of the bleeding man. Everything and everyone in Macondo is unusual in some way, perhaps larger than life, perhaps endowed with inhuman qualities, such as a mammoth sex organ or the desire to eat only dirt. Macondo is a weird place, populated by eccentric people. *One Hundred Years of Solitude* is part image, part dream, partly a metaphor for the growth and dissolution of a civilization.

Critics have categorized *One Hundred Years of Solitude* as a novel of "magic realism." Is there any rational way, for example, to account for José Arcadio's amazement over Melquíades' ice? How do you explain Melquíades' two deaths or the beautiful Remedios' rise into the air one calm afternoon?

Although magic runs amok throughout the novel, García Márquez claims that the book is grounded in reality, an assertion that at first glance may seem ludicrous. But if you think of the book as a metaphor, García Márquez can be given the benefit of the doubt. Remedios the Beauty, after all, is so gorgeous that men literally die for her. She is a virtual goddess, in a class by herself and, therefore, not bound by the rules that apply to the rest of us. Why not, then, launch into the sky and let her fly?

By taking the long view, you will see that this epic book represents, among other things, a kind of metaphorical history of Colombia (García Márquez's native land), of Latin America, and perhaps of the human race, from genesis to apocalypse.

Structure

One Hundred Years of Solitude consists of twenty unnumbered episodes, or chapters, that, in a basically linear fashion but with frequent dips into the past and the future, tell the story of the Buendía family and of Macondo. The first sentence in the book sets the pattern: "Many years later, as he faced the firing squad, Colonel Aureliano Buendía was to remember that distant afternoon when his father took him to discover ice." At once, three dimensions of time are invoked: the future, "many years later as he faced the firing squad"; the past, "that distant afternoon"; and the present, the time in which the narrator is speaking. Although the action is basically chronological, it is also cyclical. You can hardly help noticing that many events recur and that one generation of the Buendía family is not very much different from the others. For example, early Buendías begat a son with a pig's tail. Generations later, another Buendía son is born with an identical appendage.

Because of the narrator's numerous digressions into the past, the present is portrayed as a continuation of the past, not as a separate unit of time. Actually, it may help to think of the narrative as a spiral in time, a möbius strip, which keeps revolving into itself. Ice, for instance, is a central element in the organization of the first chapter. From ice, the narrator moves to Melquíades' other discoveries, but the chapter closes with José Arcadio Buendía's introduction to ice. This kind of circularity is repeated in chapter after chapter and in the novel's overall structure. At the end of the book you see Aureliano decoding the meaning of Melquíades' enigmatic parchments, which contain the Buendía family history, past, present, and future. As he reads, Aureliano finds himself in the peculiar position of reading the story of himself reading the parchments, as though he is looking into a "speaking mirror." In the parchments he also discovers that he is fictional and that Macondo never really existed. In fact, Aureliano never existed, yet he is reading about his own nonexistence.

Plot

One Hundred Years of Solitude is a history of a place and its people. It consists of a progression of events and episodes tied together by the adventures of several generations of the Buendía family. Some chapters introduce characters who set in motion a series of events that you don't see resolved until much later in the book. Some of the episodes resemble what might happen in reality, others seem like pure fantasy.

The first chapter focuses on the family background of the Buendías, especially on the patriarch José Arcadio Buendía and his efforts to make use of scientific inventions and technology. In particular, he is amazed by a magnet that the gypsy Melquíades has introduced to Macondo and declares that magnets are to be used for extracting gold from the earth. José Arcadio Buendía spends his days trying to figure out uses for a telescope, a magnifying glass and other wonders of the modern world recently brought to Macondo. Practical-minded Úrsula, his wife, shows little patience with José's scientific speculations, and one day, after José declares that the earth is round like an orange, loses patience and tells him that if he's going to go crazy, he will have to do it alone. It's an idle threat, however; she stays with him except for a short-lived sojourn to the world outside Macondo.

Of the Buendía family's children, the first son, José Arcadio, is quiet and physically well endowed. The younger, Aureliano, the first person born in Macondo, seems to have been blessed with supernatural powers. For example, he predicts that a pot will fall from a table seconds before it plunges to the floor. At the end of the chapter, Melquíades introduces José Arcadio Buendía to ice, which the patriarch declares is the greatest invention of their time.

Early in the book, you also become acquainted with Macondo, an isolated tropical paradise with roughly three hundred inhabitants, none over thirty years old. No one has ever died in Macondo, and it has been immune from the changes occurring in the outside world except for some inventions brought by the gypsies.

The second chapter steps into the past and describes how Macondo owes its origins to Úrsula and José Arcadio Buendía. Many years before, an uncle of José Arcadio Buendía had married an aunt of Úrsula, resulting in the birth of a child with a pig's tail. Believing that a union of other members of the two families might result in a similar birth defect, Úrsula stays clear of the marriage bed for a year. As a result, a townsman, Prudencio Aguilar, calls into question the masculinity of José Arcadio Buendía. Spurred by ridicule, José Arcadio kills Prudencio and drags Úrsula to bed. Prudencio's death weighs so heavily on José Arcadio and Úrsula, however, that they leave town, cross the mountains, and found a seacost community they name Macondo.

Some time later, Úrsula disappears, but returns in five months bringing people with her to help modernize the backward peninsula of Macondo. Rebeca, an orphan of distant relations, is made welcome by the family and later marries José Arcadio, the son of José Arcadio Buendía and Úrsula. Rebeca has an odd quirk: she prefers to eat dirt. Melquíades, who had died some time ago, returns to Macondo, bored with the solitude of death and ready to devote his life to the operation of a daguerreotype laboratory. After a time the national government assigns Don Apolinar Moscote to be the magistrate of Macondo. Moscote's authoritarian, bureaucratic ways are unwelcome. After Moscote orders all of Macondo's houses to be painted blue in honor of the conservative government, José Arcadio Buendía threatens him to within an inch of his life. Moscote, convinced that he should change his ways, sends away the retinue of soldiers who have served him and permits residents to paint their homes in any political color they choose. Moscote has seven daughters, one of whom, Remedios, is a notable beauty, although only nine years old. Despite her age, José Arcadio Buendía's son, Aureliano, who is old enough to be the girl's father, falls headlong in love with her. Later, after Remedios reaches child-bearing age, she marries Aureliano, in spite of her immaturity and childish ways.

One day, a case of mass insomnia overcomes the citizens of Macondo. With the inability to sleep comes the loss of memory. Suddenly, no one can remember what's what or why's why. José Arcadio Buendía helps to solve the problem by placing little signs on everyday objects: *table, chair, clock, door, wall, cow, goat, pig, caladium,* and so forth. For a time, though, he worries that people will remember the names of things but not what they are used for. He even places a sign saying MACONDO on the outskirts of the town and works on the invention of a "memory machine" that every morning will review for the people what they knew the night before. Melquíades finally invents a magic potion that restores memory to everyone.

Soon after, political rivalries between the Conservatives and Liberals bring on a long series of civil wars. Aureliano, made a colonel, fights in thirty-two battles, losing all of them. When peace temporarily breaks out, Colonel Aureliano retires to devote his days to fabricating little gold fish. His brother, Arcadio, in the meantime is executed by a firing squad of the conservative faction.

Perpetual conflict between opposing political parties, each vying for power, leads to an endless cycle of wars and rebellions. One thing both sides agree to, however, is to open Macondo to prosperity and modernization by welcoming American investment. A company moves in, builds banana plantations and dominates the economy of Macondo, but the owners treat the workers so poorly that José Arcadio Segundo instigates a workers' strike. Soldiers massacre thousands of strikers, but take no responsibility for their actions. In fact, the regime offers "proof" that the workers never existed and therefore, no massacre could have occurred. Gradually, the event is erased from the collective memory of Macondo.

Then come the rains. For almost four and a half years, it rains constantly. Unable to continue its business, the fruit company withdraws, leaving Macondo poor, corrupt, and in ruins. Macondo is ripe for rebirth as a fresh new town. But it is too late for the innocent past to be recreated. Finally, a child with a pig's tail is born to the family. The birth brings the story back to where it began, and the book ends with the last Aureliano reading the parchments that tell the story of Macondo and its people.

Narrative Voice

On the surface, *One Hundred Years of Solitude* is a traditional novel with a not-quite-omniscient narrator. Sometimes, the narrator reveals what the characters think, as in the novel's first sentence, but most of the time the narration comes to you via a detached, impartial observer. Complete neutrality is an impossible ideal in any case, but the narrator of *One Hundred Years of Solitude* comes relatively close. For the most part, you are permitted to draw your own conclusions and make your own judgments about the characters and events in the story.

Except for background material, what you see and hear is limited to what characters can see and hear. When you are told, for instance that Aureliano Segundo was "a slob, a sponge, a good-for-nothing" it may seem as though the narrator is speaking. In actuality, these are the opinions of Fernanda, Aureliano

Segundo's wife, who seems to have had enough with her ne'er-do-well husband. At the end of the book you discover that Melquíades, the wise gypsy, has written the history of the Buendías and Macondo in Sanskrit and left his parchments behind for Aureliano to decipher and translate. What you read are the words of a magician who has created the illusion of the narrator being outside the story when in fact he was very much a part of the story the whole time.

The narrator casts a satirical eye at the people of Macondo. He tells of stupefying events in the most matter-of-fact, ho-hum language, as though such miracles as Remedios' launch into the sky and Melquíades' two returns from the dead occur every day of the week. José Arcadio Buendía threatens Prudencio Aguilar: "You go home and get a weapon, because I'm going to kill you." Ten minutes later he throws a spear into Prudencio's throat, with no more effort or concern than if he were breaking an egg. Nor is there anything noteworthy about Úrsula encountering Prudencio in her kitchen a few nights later searching for water to wash his wound. Deadpan depiction of the extraordinary happenings is meant to be humorous. It portrays the foolishness of the people in Macondo, especially when contrasted to the exaggerated, highly charged language used to describe the most mundane events. In the first chapter, touching ice fills José Arcadio Buendía's heart with fear and jubilation. Later, the ignition of a pile of dry hay with a magnifying glass is called a "startling demonstration."

Themes

THE FLEXIBILITY OF TIME

By manipulation, *One Hundred Years of Solitude* obliterates the usual linear conception and measurement of time. From the very first sentence, in which the narrator at once anticipates the future and recalls a distant past, time is compressed. Throughout the novel, time present, past, and future can be recounted at any moment by a narrator who is equidistant from them all and creates the illusion that a century of daily episodes coexists in one instant. As a consequence, the book upsets our thinking regarding sequence. Pilar Ternera's function during the insomnia plague, for example, is to read the past rather than the future in her cards. Fernanda is described as a widow whose husband has not yet died yet. Remedios is a fourteen-year-old great-grandmother, Úrsula a newborn old lady. Melquíades the magician has transcended time altogether. His parchments are the history of the Buendía family and also its prophecy because they predate the actions they describe. Yet, in the course of the book you see Melquíades working on them and often giving members of the Buendía family clues to their interpretation.

This disregard for time's usual progression calls into question the very time of the book itself. The narrator uses conventional expressions to indicate the passage of time: "several months later," "after several weeks," "when the mourning had gone on so long that the needlepoint sessions began again." But such vague markers of time evoke a sense of imprecise, legendary time in stark contrast to the startling figure that the rain lasted four years, eleven months, and two days. Time, according to Einstein, is relative. Perhaps the famous theory of relativity is implied by José Arcadio Segundo's notion that "time also stumbled and had accidents and could therefore splinter and leave an eternalized fragment in a room."

REPETITION, CYCLES

The action in *One Hundred Years of Solitude* is circular. The book begins and ends with the birth of Buendía boys, each adorned with the tail of a pig. Individual chapters often focus on a topic, digress, and then return to the original topic. You can't avoid being struck by the repetition of characters' names. Aureliano has seventeen illegitimate sons all named Aureliano. Pilar Ternera returns again and again to serve the amorous needs of generations of Buendía men. Melquíades dies twice and returns. To a great extent, the circularity in the story resembles the countless cycles of time, life, and nature that occur during any span of a hundred years.

Although there are different types of Buendías, there is precious little to distinguish between two of the same name, even if separated by half a century. The Arcadio branch of the family tree, like José Arcadio Segundo, likes to tinker, invent crazy schemes, and decipher manuscripts. The Aurelianos are more interested in politics, although they often shut themselves up in the laboratory, too. The twins are exceptions to the rule, but they may have swapped identities during their early childhood. The longest-living member of the family, the matriarch Úrsula, sagely observes that the family is trapped in a cyclical labyrinth, that time did not pass but just turned in a circle. Frustrated over José Arcadio Segundo's plan to make a port of Macondo by digging a channel from the sea, she is reminded of José Arcadio's earlier hare-brained scheme and says plaintively, "I know all of this by heart. It's as if time had turned around and we were back at the beginning."

Circularity is apparent in the family's habit of making things in order to unmake them later: The little gold fishes are sold for coins to be made into other fishes. Amaranta, recalling Penelope, weaves a shroud only to unravel it and weave it again. And Úrsula is seen to be busy doing a thousand things poorly so that she can do them over the next day.

José Arcadio Buendía, struck by time's unwillingness to move on instead of circling back again and again, seeks to prove that time is linear. He spends hours examining people and things, trying to find changes in appearance from the previous day. But he concludes that Tuesday is no different from Monday. Nor is Wednesday different from Tuesday. Since he detects no changes, he cannot prove that time passes, a failure that drives him insane.

The notion of repetition in the book is strengthened by frequent references to twins, mirror images, reflections, and oppositions. The identical twins José Arcadio Segundo and Aureliano Segundo are a case in point. They are so similar that their mother dresses them in color-coded clothes and makes them wear name bracelets, but they deliberately sabotage her efforts to tell them apart. Neither follows in the footsteps of his namesake. Rather, they eventually become exact opposites, at one point performing a mirror-image ritual, one doing with the left hand what the other does with his right. As older boys, José Arcadio Segundo begs to watch an execution, while Aureliano Segundo is loathe to be witness. All the while, Úrsula believes that the boys have actually swapped identities, and when they die, each is buried in the other's grave. The idea of reflections culminates in the book's final episode when Aureliano reads about himself looking at the parchments "as if he were looking into a speaking mirror."

INCESTUOUS LOVE

The theme of incest winds its way into the story of the Buendía family. In spite of the social taboo against incest, Macondo, being a rather claustrophobic place, is fertile ground for incestuous relationships. José Arcadio weds his cousin Rebeca and is ostracized by the family. The first Amaranta loves her nephew,

José Arcadio, and although they don't marry, every time she bathes him she experiences sexual desire for her little great-great-nephew. The Colonel, on the verge of execution by firing squad, finds that he cannot keep thoughts of his wife separate from thoughts of his mother and daughter. Only near the end of the book, however, does an incestuous coupling lead to a child, the final Aureliano, who is born with the tail of a pig.

Incest often breeds where people spurn outsiders or shun social relationships. Those who don't communicate outside their immediate families turn inward and often become lonely and eccentric. Several of the book's characters, by choice or circumstance, live at least part of their lives as victims of appalling solitude. One is locked for years in a room, another is tied to a tree, and another is long forgotten in an empty house. Amaranta's incestuous leanings are both caused by and lead to bitter fruitlessness and loneliness. José Arcadio commits suicide. His widow prefers to live the rest of her life as an isolate. Neither she nor Amaranta would consider breaking out of their xenophobia by marrying the eligible Italian, Pietro Crespi. Finally, at the end of the story, the incestuous pairing of Aureliano and Amaranta Úrsula contributes to the social breakdown of Macondo. Having no interest in anything but each other, they permit the environment to overrun them.

THE SEARCH FOR KNOWLEDGE AND REALITY

Macondo is fresh, innocent, even primitive, its people unsullied by the outside world. But José Arcadio Buendía, Macondo's most conspicuous citizen, wants to change that. He wants to modernize Macondo, and he devotes his days to the pursuit and creation of the knowledge that will help him do it. He invents a memory machine as an antidote to mass amnesia. For a time, he isolates himself to think of ways to use a magnifying glass as a weapon of war. He studies alchemy and clairvoyance as intently as he examines Pietro Crespi's mechanical toys. By the end of José Arcadio Buendía's life, Macondo has inched forward. By no means a modern place, it nevertheless has acquired contemporary problems: political fighting, civil war, labor unrest. Like many other Third World places, Macondo has adopted the worst of the modern world instead of the best. Macondo has come of age, but not very happily.

By creating a backwater Macondo beset with modern problems, García Márquez, a keen political and social observer, has probably used his own country as a model. Colombia is a land of contrasts with a long, chaotic history of conquest, civil war, political violence, social upheaval, guerrilla warfare, drug dealing, and economic dependence on a single crop: coffee. In that sense, Macondo exists in the real world, but since literally anything can happen there, *One Hundred Years of Solitude* is far from a conventionally realistic novel.

As a critical reader, you can dismiss Macondo's odd and unnatural history as a product of García Márquez's overactive fantasy life. Or you can try to go beyond the appearance of things by expanding your concept of reality and viewing the strange goings-on in Macondo as metaphors for real-life occurrences. Macondo's mass memory loss, for instance, has numerous parallels, not only in the history of Colombia but worldwide. Think of instances when a populace has deliberately purged from its collective conscience some terrible atrocities committed by its fellow countrymen. Nazi Germany, Cambodia, and Argentina come to mind. The events are neither talked about nor acknowledged, and after a generation or two nobody remembers them. Actually, this kind of conspiracy of silence was very much on García Márquez's mind when he tells the story of the fruit company massacre. A large-scale killing of workers occurred in Colombia early in this century. The facts were suppressed, and in *One Hundred Years of Solitude* García Márquez attempts to let the truth be known.

You might also notice that fantasies in the novel often spring from characters' distorted or declining faculties of perception. Drunkenness, blindness, madness, guilt, and senility all play a part in the creation of fantasy. Thus, Úrsula, agonizing over Prudencio's death, encounters the dead man walking around in her kitchen two days after he has been killed. Objectively, Úrsula was hallucinating, but to her, Prudencio's present was as palpable—as real—as her own. Is the apparition of Prudencio real or is it unreal? Trying to answer such a question condemns you to wallow in ambiguity, for the line that separates reality from unreality is too blurry, and furthermore, keeps changing according to context.

That's why, in a very practical sense, the seemingly "unreal" events in Macondo may be hardly more outrageous than events you see on TV or read about in the newspaper, and not only in *The National Enquirer.* How often have you heard someone say, "Unreal!" in reaction to an outlandish situation? Such a response is brimful of meaning, for it suggests that something real can also seem unreal. By extension, then, something "unreal" can also be real. To put it another way, the rampant fantasy of *One Hundred Years of Solitude* may not be as fantastic as you might suppose.

The Novel as History

The novel's numerous allusions to actual events and people suggest that *One Hundred Years of Solitude* is a dreamlike rendition of Colombian history from the pre-Columbian times until today. Because Macondo completes the universal cycle of birth, development, prosperity, decadence, and death, some critics see *One Hundred Years of Solitude* as the history not only of Colombia, but all of Latin America and of the world's civilizations.

Colombia's past parallels that of Macondo. For untold centuries, indigenous people, like the original Macondans, lived in a primitive, prehistoric state. Then Columbus, like Úrsula discovering the route between Macondo and the outside world, opened the door to exploration and settlement. The church arrived. Merchants arrived. Eventually, a government was formed. Conservatives supporting the church and a powerful central government tussled with liberals, who advocated the separation of church and state, and stood for freedom of religion, a free press, and a federalist government. Decades of intermittent civil war broke out. Meanwhile, railroads and utilities were developed, giving the country a more modern face. Near the end of the nineteenth century the United Fruit Company started doing business in Colombia and permanently changed the economy and society of the country. Conflict between the owners and the workers tore the country apart.

The fictional version of the strike and subsequent massacre of workers in *One Hundred Years of Solitude* may be closer to the truth than is generally acknowledged in the history books. The facts are that the fruit company hired the cheapest labor it could find and often made a case for the nonexistence of the workers, in order to avoid complying with regulations governing pay and working conditions. In the novel, of course, the slaying of the workers is erased, like chalk on a blackboard, from the minds of the public. The soldiers responsible for the mass killings tell the people they must be dreaming: "Nothing has ever happened, and nothing will ever happen. This is a happy town." Records and references to the banana company are gradually eliminated. History has been revised.

If you believe that those who forget history are doomed to repeat it, then you will understand why Macondo was in for a bad time. The city's amnesia plague wiped out the memory of its past. As a result, the gypsies returning to Macondo find a population in such a forgetful state that they reintroduce magnets, magnifying glasses, and false teeth. This crisis of memory is also indicative of how much actual history has been lost, forgotten, or concealed, an issue of vital concern to García Márquez, who has tried to preserve the legacy of Latin America in his novels and stories.

Questions for Writing and Discussion

Defend or refute with evidence from the text of *One Hundred Years of Solitude* the views expressed in each of the following statements.

1. The exuberant use of hyperbole in the language of the novel is a reaction to officialdom. The novel is full of precise yet inflated dates and numbers, of meticulous yet incredible descriptions. The resultant atmosphere is one of a parody.
2. The main reason for the success of *One Hundred Years of Solitude* is that it can be read on many levels.
3. Solitude is a hereditary infirmity of the Buendías. Alienation prevents them from communicating and frustrates them in all their undertakings. They are unable to adapt to a world they don't understand and to a society in which everything seems possible, except happiness.
4. Although *One Hundred Years of Solitude* can make readers laugh, there is something rather serious going on within its pages.
5. All the characters feel the pressures of time from two directions: past and future. Memories and premonitions burden their present lives and keep them separate from one another. Unlike many other fictional characters who leave the past behind in order to remake themselves according to their own design, García Márquez's characters are inextricably bound to the past.

BELOVED
Toni Morrison (1931–   )

Background

The subject of *Beloved* is slavery. The time is 1873, eight years after the Emancipation. The mood is horror, misery, anguish, and a sense of unspeakable woe. Most of the characters are ex-slaves who cannot rid themselves of the physical and emotional scars of having been victims of cruel and inhumane treatment by a social and economic system that viewed them as pieces of merchandise to be bought, sold, and traded. The novel is naturalistic but also contains a strong element of "magic," first in the form of a baby ghost that haunts the house where most of the action occurs, and then in the flesh-and-blood resurrection of the dead baby, now grown to a twenty-year-old woman. The language of the book is rooted in spirituals, gospel music, and biblical cadences and alludes frequently to jazz, blues, and the slave experience. Although the narrator tells the story of a small group of blacks, once slaves but now free or dead, Toni Morrison's vision is broader than that. The author tries to distill from the experience of a few survivors the essense of the entire black experience. The characters are real people yet also symbolic of the long-term damage wrought by slavery in America. They can't wash away their horrific memories and over-whelming grief. Some say that Morrison has attempted the impossible: to put into words that which cannot be put into words, the unutterable monstrousness of slavery. As the book shows, to purge a dreadful past is excruciatingly difficult and far more painful that it has any right to be.

Structure

Perhaps the pivotal moment in *Beloved* is the slaying of Sethe's two-year-old child, an event that took place at the time of the Sweet Home slaves' dash for freedom. Much of what occurs in the book is tied to the child's death—what leads up to it and what occurs as a result of it. The murder, if not justifiable, is made understandable by the conditions and practices of slavery, not only at Sweet Home but all over the South.

No single section of the book fully portrays slavery. Rather, it is revealed in pieces, implied by the thoughts and actions of the characters. You, as reader, must put the fragments together. Plenty of help is provided by Sethe and Paul D, whose recollections paint a vivid picture of the systematic dehumanization and psychological control endured by slaves. By controlling every aspect of the slaves' lives, masters convinced slaves of the hopelessness of their condition and taught slaves to be totally dependent on them.

Because slaves were considered property, they could be bought, sold, and traded. This feature of slavery is what led Sethe to perform the unnatural act of slitting her baby's throat. Being sold "down the river" meant permanent and irrevocable separation from one's family—from spouse, parents, children—a prospect so dire that to a slave it was more fearful than physical punishment or even death.

The specter of separation is made more real at Sweet Home after the death of the somewhat kindly master, Mr. Garner. His successor, known as Schoolteacher, is a sadistic tyrant. In fact, one of the Sweet Home regulars, Paul F, has recently disappeared, sold who-knows-where in order to raise some cash for paying bills. Conditions for the Sweet Home slaves have become so precarious that risking a mass escape is preferable to waiting helplessly for misfortune to strike. During the escape, Sethe is brutally assaulted by two white boys and then is whipped without mercy for reporting the attack.

Considering this background, it may be less puzzling that Sethe chooses to murder the child. She regards it a mercy killing, an act of love, to save her daughter from a life of pain and suffering. One can argue, of course, that no one has the right to commit such a heinous crime. Besides, most slave mothers did not kill *their* babies. Why should Sethe be put in a class by herself? But those are rational arguments that may not apply to slavery, one of the most emotionally charged, irrational institutions ever created.

What happens thereafter in the novel turns on that terrible moment. Sethe, devastated by what she has done, is overcome with self-loathing. But for Howard and Buglar, her two young sons, she might even do away with herself.

The first phase of Sethe's punishment lasts for eighteen years. Heavily burdened with guilt and by memories of frightful days as a slave, she is ostracized by her community and lives a lonely life with her daughter Denver. Feeling that she deserves punishment for her grisly deed, she tolerates the presence of the baby's ghost in her house. Some might say the ghost is only in Sethe's mind, a manifestation of her guilt. To some extent that could be true, but then some other explanation than the presence of a ghost in the house must be found for

Howard and Buglar's decision to leave home, for we are told that they "had run away by the time they were thirteen years old—as soon as merely looking in a mirror shattered it (that was the signal for Buglar); as soon as two tiny hand prints appeared in the cake (that was it for Howard)."

With the arrival of Paul D, Sethe's life changes. Paul D comes hoping for a measure of peace and love denied him during many years of wandering. He chases the ghost from the house and provides Sethe with companionship and emotional support. Although Sethe doesn't know it, Paul D's presence begins to prepare her, finally, for redemption for her sinful act.

The second phase of Sethe's punishment begins when Beloved appears. Beloved, the embodiment of Sethe's guilt, has come for vengeance. Underneath her veneer of innocence lurks a fearsome figure, bent on setting things right between her and Sethe. Malevolently, she seduces Paul D, deprives the others of good food, sets a snare to catch her anguished mother's heart. Her aim is to incarcerate Sethe in a prison of guilt forever. In a sense, she re-enslaves her mother. In Beloved, Sweet Home lives on.

Over time, however, Beloved learns the story of the child's murder. She remembers vaguely how her mother once loved her. She begins to understand that Sethe killed out of compassion and that ever since that day Sethe has known no peace. Meanwhile, Paul D and Denver stand by Sethe, helping her to strengthen mind and soul. Eventually, with help, they drive Beloved away, reemancipating Sethe. For her sinful act, Sethe has suffered, and by suffering has earned release and forgiveness. At the end of the book, she has been purged of her sin.

Narrative Technique

If you find *Beloved* a difficult book to read, blame it on the narrative technique. It's complicated and diffuse.

The omniscient narrator of the book records a shocking, frightful, and deeply moving story of blacks during and after slavery. In telling of the events that occur over a period of about twenty years, the narrator assumes the voice and point of view of several characters, each with a unique story to tell. The central story belongs to Sethe, but you also hear the voices of her friend and eventual lover Paul D, Sethe's mother-in-law Baby Suggs, her remaining child Denver, and later on, the voice of Beloved herself. Each of their stories amplifies or modifies Sethe's narrative. The stories also speak to and comment on one another.

The overall story is presented in fragments that must be pieced together like a jigsaw puzzle. The characters drop hints and allusions to people and events that you don't know much about until well into the story. Many questions are raised quickly, many tragic incidents foreshadowed. In the end, of course, the bits and pieces coalesce and the full story can be told. (See The Story, which follows.) When the pieces are together, you have the story of a woman's crime, punishment, and redemption. More specifically, you have Sethe, a slave, killing her baby daughter in order to save the child from life as a slave.

Since the narrator tells the story from the vantage point of 1873, several years after many of the events occurred, you hear much of the story filtered through the memory of the characters. Memory is the key. As ex-slaves, Sethe and Paul D remember more than they want to. In fact, Sethe tries to block out such experiences as being beaten by white men, deciding to kill her own child, and paying for an engraving on the child's gravestone with ten minutes of sex. Paul D has his own demons that he can't purge from his memory: seeing the physical and psychological destruction of his fellow Sweet Home men, being forced to wear a bit in his mouth, the atrocities of the chain gang, and so on. These and other painful memories are often triggered by the sights, sounds, and smells of everyday life. Conversations, a word, a look, a smile—anything can open the window of memory. Sethe and Paul D cannot keep the past at bay. Once, after Sethe comes late to work, a brief scolding from her employer brings back a flood of images:

> She had taken pains to keep them out, but knew full well that at any moment they could rock her, rip her from her moorings, send the birds twittering back into her hair. Drain her mother's milk, they had already done. Driven her fat-bellied into the woods—they had done that. All news of them was rot. They buttered Halle's face; gave Paul D iron to eat; crisped Sixo; hanged her own mother." (*Beloved*, Penguin Books, p. 188).

Paul D's arrival in Sethe's home awakens numerous memories of Sweet Home and the bitter years of slavery. Beloved's return forces into the open not only how but why the original child Beloved was killed. By no means, however, are any memories restricted to one segment of the book. Some events, such as Sethe's assault at the hands of two white boys, are recalled fleetingly at many different times, suggesting that the past is never far away.

Throughout the novel, the narrator's language tries to evoke the unspeakable agony of human suffering. But the effort is a far cry from the suffering itself, which cannot be rendered in words. The narrator can do no better than to speak a speakable version of unspeakable woe. To narrate the nightmare, the narrator stands back, observes, and tries to find words that come close to the experience. *Come close* is the key phrase, for no author, however gifted, can actually recreate the horror. The narration in *Beloved* suggests the staying power of the nightmare in the minds of those who lived it. Again and again, it returns to certain images and incidents: the bit in Paul D's mouth, the butter-smeared face of Halle, dead slaves hanging from the sycamore trees, and many others. The repetition, like lashes from a cowhide whip on Sethe's back, soon begin to leave indelible scars in the reader's mind.

The Story

The particulars of the story occur in a building established as a home for free slaves by a Quaker family at 124 Bluestone Road near Cincinnati, Ohio. By the present, 1873, all but two residents have died or gone elsewhere to live. Now Sethe, a woman in her mid-thirties, lives there with her eighteen-year-old daughter Denver, named after a white trash runaway who served as midwife at the girl's birth.

Unexpectedly, a visitor appears. It is Paul D, a former slave who, with Sethe and many others, had run away eighteen years ago from the slave-holding Kentucky plantation called "Sweet Home" (an ironic name, of course, the place being neither "sweet" nor "home"). Paul D's arrival opens memory's door, and the story of the Sweet Home slaves begins to emerge incident by incident, piece by agonizing piece throughout the novel.

Dominant in the group of slaves was an old semi-invalid woman named Baby Suggs, her son Halle, and Paul A, Paul F, Paul D, Sixo, and Sethe. At a time when Baby and Halle had been bought to work under the kindly master of Sweet Home, Halle was permitted to work for others and to receive pay. He earned enough to buy freedom for his mother, who then left Sweet Home and settled at 124, where she became caretaker and host to runaway slaves. Suggs apparently transcended hatred and misery with a faith and spirituality that had made her an eloquent servant and spokesman for the Lord. In a nearby clearing in the woods, she often preached messages of love and kindness.

Meanwhile, back at Sweet Home, the relatively humane master, Mr. Garner, dies, leaving his youthful slaves unprepared to deal with the cruelty and brutality that was typical of slavery. The new foreman, called Schoolteacher, the widower husband of Mrs. Garner's sister, is a brutal and cold businessman who regards slaves as animals. He shows the Sweet Home slaves who is boss by beating them, by measuring them with rulers as though they are livestock, and by selling and trading them without a second thought. Unaccustomed to such treatment, the slaves realize they have to escape. Sethe, married to Halle and pregnant for the fourth time, is the most determined to run because of her three babies whom she fears will be taken from her and sold. Sixo, the most aware of the external world, has learned of the Underground Railroad and persuades others to run off to Baby Suggs' place in Ohio.

During the escape, Paul A is caught and hanged from a tree. Sixo gets caught, too, and is burned alive. Paul D gets no farther; he is quickly apprehended and sent to a chain gang with a bit in his mouth. Halle disappears during the escape and is never heard from again. Sethe manages to get her children on the "train" to freedom, but she is stopped by two white boys, Schoolteacher's nephews. One holds her down while the other laps milk from her breast. As punishment for reporting the assault to Mrs. Garner, Schoolteacher whips Sethe's bare back, leaving permanent scars that Sethe refers to as a "chokecherry tree." Later Sethe continues her flight but stops on the banks of the Ohio River to give birth to another daughter with the help of a young white girl named Amy Denver. The new baby's life is saved by Stamp Paid, a rescuer of runaway slaves, who snatches the newborn from Sethe as she threatened to bash the baby's head in. On the final leg of her journey to Baby Suggs, Sethe is aided by Stamp Paid and his family.

Later we learn that, to prevent herself and her family from being dragged back to Sweet Home, Sethe attempts to kill her own children, but succeeds with only her two-year-old daughter. The murder is the pivotal event of the novel. Almost everything that happens to Sethe from then on is colored by the fact that she killed her own child in what she regarded as merciful act. Eventually, the child's grave is marked with a stone bearing one word, *Beloved*. Sethe had hoped for an ampler inscription, but the engraver gave her only seven letters in exchange for ten minutes of sex.

Now, in 1873, it is eighteen years since the murder. Slavery has been officially abolished. Baby Suggs died eight years ago after a career as a saintly matriarch and spiritual leader of a lively Negro community in and around 124 Bluestone Road. Some time ago, Sethe's two sons, Howard and Buglar, abandoned their mother and sister who now live alone except for the ghost of the slain infant. Everyone else left, too, frightened off by the furniture-rattling, mirror-shattering spirit of a two-year-old whose throat had been cut by her mother. Isolated from others, they have had no visitors. Sethe and Denver accept their lonely life, hoping to find ease from pain and suffering in their love for one another.

Suddenly, Paul D enters their cheerless home after eighteen years of wandering. Sethe is pleased to see one of her old crowd again. The two soon become lovers, but more important, his presence initiates the exchange of stories about Sweet Home, about the escape, and about their lives since then. In telling her story, Sethe does not tell Paul D about killing her daughter, but Paul D reveals, to Sethe's horror, that her husband Halle, while concealed in a barn, had witnessed the assault on her by the two white boys. Paul explains that Halle thought it was pointless to interfere because he would be killed, leaving Sethe with no one to turn to afterward. Driven insane by his inaction, Halle has disappeared in shame and self-hatred.

Unwilling to put up with a ghost in the house, Paul D drives it away, and is himself driven away for a time by Sethe's obsession with Denver. Upon Paul D's return Denver grows resentful of his intrusion, regarding him as a rival for her mother's affections. Although Paul D has rid the house of the ghost, it won't be kept out for long. It returns in the form of an elegantly-dressed, well-scrubbed, strange young woman who talks like a child, can't recall where she came from, and calls herself "Beloved." Sethe willingly takes her in. Denver gradually accepts Beloved as a sister, although she remains suspicious of her motives. Why she has come soon becomes plain: she hopes to exact some kind of revenge on her mother, to whom she clings tenaciously. Everything she does is designed to claim Sethe for herself. She seduces Paul D in order to drag him into the wrong and have him expelled from the house. She gorges herself on the choicest of food, leaving scraps for the others. Denver soon realizes that guilt has made Sethe easy prey for Beloved and watches helplessly as Sethe deteriorates physically and emotionally.

Eventually, Paul D learns that Sethe killed the baby. He is horrified, even as Sethe protests that she acted mercifully. He leaves her for a time, telling her that she has two legs, not four. In her pain, Sethe wishes that Baby Suggs were alive to comfort her. She misses Suggs' strength, faith and love. In a reverie, she reflects on how her life has swung back and forth between Eden and the inferno. She feels fingers on her throat and imagines that they are Baby Suggs' gentle caresses. In reality, though, they are Beloved's deadly grasp, choking the life out of Sethe. Denver observes what is going on and stops Beloved. Sethe is stirred back into consciousness. Denver accuses Beloved of trying to kill Sethe. Beloved protests, of course, but Sethe realizes that Beloved is, in fact, her dead baby come back from death to seek vengeance. Once Sethe knows Beloved's identity, she gives herself over completely to the past and to Beloved's demand for comfort and curing. So complete are Sethe's attempts to make things right with Beloved that she is almost consumed by her. Denver thinks her mother is on the verge of doom and determines to rescue her by banishing Beloved. With the help of Paul D and thirty friends in the community who have noted Beloved's harmful influence on Sethe, she drives Beloved from the house.

Understanding the depth and breadth of Sethe's remorse, Beloved vanishes, apparently satisfied that, through suffering, Sethe has redeemed herself. Beloved forgives her mother and returns to the world of the dead, leaving Paul D and Sethe to begin a new life together.

Slavery as Theme

Writing about the opening of *Beloved,* Toni Morrison said, "The reader is snatched, yanked, thrown into an environment completely foreign, and I want it as the first stroke of the shared experience that might be possible between the reader and the novel's population. Snatched just as the slaves were from one place to another, from any place to another, without preparation, and without defense."[1] In other words, the author wants to yank you into the text, just as the slaves were yanked around by their masters.

---

[1]"Unspeakable Things Unspoken: The Afro-American Presence in American Literature," *Michigan Quarterly Review* 28 [Winter 1989]: 32.

Even though the story is set in 1873, a decade after slavery was declared illegal in the United States, the novel is awash with themes of slavery. The characters have been so profoundly affected by their experience as slaves that time cannot separate them from its horrors or undo its effects. Sethe, in fact, wears a permanent emblem of slavery on her back, and she is perpetually deluged with emotions and thoughts of Sweet Home.

Those who defended slavery in the nineteenth century, and even fought and died to preserve it, considered slavery an institution essential to the well-being of the economy. Indeed, since slaves were regarded as a commodity not different from livestock and cotton, their owners felt justified in treating them like merchandise to be bought and sold. This feature of slavery serves as the catalyst for most of the major events of *Beloved,* for the slaves' determination to run away was a response to the threat that members of their family could be sold, just as Paul F was, at any time. To his dismay, Paul D also realizes that his life could be unalterably changed at the whim of his master, and there was nothing he could do about it. Perhaps Baby Suggs' experience is the most heart-wrenching; she watched as seven of her eight children were taken from her and sold, victims of the most vicious antifamily institution ever devised. Not by accident or stealth, but as a matter of everyday legal policy, young children, parents, mates, brothers and sisters—kin of every stripe—vanished forever.

In the course of doing this kind of business, masters subjected slaves to odious and repulsive treatment. With the fate of slaves in their hands, their behavior illustrates what atrocities men with absolute power are capable of. Slave owners soon started to believe in their own superiority and then justify it by their actions. Even Mrs. Garner, a more-or-less kindly slaveowner, presumes the authority to permit Sethe to marry Halle. If she says it's all right, then it's all right. She, like all the other white folks who adhered to the customs and culture of slavery, had trouble seeing their slaves as people.

Themes and Motifs

MONEY

Ownership is characteristic of slavery. It is a measure of wealth. Because slavery was essentially an economic institution, in which human beings were bought and sold, *Beloved* contains numerous images and references to money, value, debt, exchange, and many other terms related to the marketplace. Baby Suggs' son Halle, in an exceptional arrangement for the time, was able to purchase freedom for his mother by doing extra work. Stamp Paid earned his freedom not with money per se, but with a form of barter. He stood by while the son of his master repeatedly had sex with Vashti, Stamp Paid's wife. "With that gift," says the narrator of *Beloved,* "he didn't owe anybody anything." Whatever his obligations as a slave were, he had paid them off. Stamp Paid (his name is not accidental) now ferries beaten and molested runaway slaves to freedom. He thinks that his customers have paid their debts, and now life owes them.

Indeed, all the characters in the novel who have either escaped or been freed have given more than their weight in gold to the system of slavery. Sethe has paid in full with a scarred back, a lost husband, and a dead daughter. Baby Suggs has given her children, and Paul D has fulfilled his obligation with the sale of one brother, the death of another, a bit in his mouth, and a term on the chain gang.

Images of monetary units (coins, bills, gold, change, and so forth) abound in the novel.[2] Schoolteacher instructs Paul on the "dollar value" of his body. Denver's eyes are as big and round as nickels. When she worries that Beloved may leave if she is pressed too hard with questions about her past, Denver thinks "she might lose the penny that the held-out palm wanted." The book's narrator refers to the "coin of life" when Paul is trying to forge a future with Sethe. A Black Sambo statue in front of the Bodwin house holds coins in its wide-open mouth to pay for deliveries. After revealing to Paul D that Sethe killed her baby, Stamp Paid feels the memory of Baby Suggs "scorching his soul like a silver dollar in a fool's pocket."

Perhaps you will find it odd that money imagery persists throughout the novel because once the slaves are free, economic matters no longer control their lives. Indeed, you might expect the former slaves to shun references to the system that persecuted them. On the other hand, that such images hold on may suggest that the residue of the slave experience cannot be easily shed.

BELOVED

The book's title character functions on both a literal and symbolic level. Basically, Beloved is Sethe's third child, whose death as an infant and return first as a ghost and then as a young woman lie at the core of the novel. As a symbol, though, she plays a far more ambiguous and far-ranging role. The possibilities multiply the more you think about her.

Structurally, the novel needs Beloved to function as a conduit between the past and present. Beloved unlocks her mother's memory, allowing the generally reticent Sethe to tell stories about her past. Via Beloved, then, the dreadful horror of Sweet Home lives on.

Beloved is also the means by which Sethe successfully escapes from slavery. Schoolteacher gives up his claim on Sethe after he sees that she slew her own child. As far as he is concerned, Sethe is damaged goods, no longer usable, so he turns and walks away from her.

As a darker force, Beloved is a manifestation of Sethe's guilt. When she comes walking out of the water as a full-blown young woman, her intentions are strictly malevolent. She aims to capture her anguished mother's heart and to keep the poor woman imprisoned by guilt.

From another point of view, Beloved is a projection of Sethe's longings. Sethe has never gotten over her desperate act of murder. For eighteen years she has continued to love the baby. She suffers constantly and often wishes that she could undo her dreadful deed. Beloved's reappearance is the embodiment of that yearning. She is what lies heavy in her mother's heart, the burden she bears through life. Beloved's resurrection fuels Sethe's psychological escape from the past. Once Beloved understands that Sethe has paid for her sin with an eighteen-year period of atonement, Beloved relinquishes her claim on her mother and returns to the spirit world.

THE LEGACY OF VIOLENCE

Because absolute authority cannot be administered benevolently, slave-owning and violence go hand in hand. Masters controlled their slaves by threatening and inflicting bodily harm on any of them who broke the rules.

---

[2]For example, acknowledgment to Trudier Harris, "Escaping Slavery but Not Its Images," in *Toni Morrison: Critical Perspectives Past and Present*, eds. Henry Louis Gates, Jr. and K. A. Appiah (Amistad Press, NY: 1993), pp. 330–341.

Punishment was swift and brutal. Not surprisingly, then, *Beloved* is crammed with images of black bodies hurt, maimed, scarred, and destroyed. Sethe thinks often of the circular scar under her mother's breast. Paul D is haunted by the memory of wearing a bit in his mouth and irons on his legs. His body trembles with humiliation at the thought of a barnyard rooster who was freer than he. Sethe has her milk stolen. Sixo is roasted alive. Vashti is raped repeatedly by her master's son. Black bodies are whipped and strung up on sycamore trees. But the violence done to black bodies goes deeper than the skin. It also leaves psychic scars. Paul D's heart, for example, is described as a "tobacco tin rusted in his chest," unable to be opened.

Sethe's flowering back bears scars that represent slavery's legacy of violence. The symbolic power of the chokeberry tree in bloom is evident in the number of times that Sethe and other characters refer to it. To Baby Suggs, the imprint of Sethe's back on the bedsheets looks like "roses of blood." Paul D marvels at Sethe's back as though it were a piece of sculpture. He feels it with his fingers and mouth. The scar tissue on Sethe's back has been dead for years, but its symbolism is very much alive.

MEMORY

Much of the story of *Beloved* spills from the characters' memories. As former slaves, Sethe and Paul D might like to repress their painful past, but they can't. The slightest sensation—a smell, a taste, a look—unleashes a flood of flashbacks. Here is Sethe, simply washing her leg:

> The plash of water, the sight of her shoes and stockings awry on the path where she had flung them; or Here Boy lapping in the puddle near her feet, and suddenly there was Sweet Home rolling, rolling, rolling out before her eyes, and although there was not a leaf on that farm that did not want her to scream, it rolled itself out before her in shameless beauty.

Characters in the novel have an adversarial relationship with the past, and much of the narrative explores what it means for them to confront the history of their suffering. By the end, it seems that Sethe and Paul D, finally rid of Beloved, can move beyond their past even though they can't forget it.

The power of memory is clearest in most poetic passages of book, sections 2–5 of Part II, made up of four interior monologues that become a dialogue among the three central female characters. Sethe speaks first of killing her baby, of being beaten, and of being abandoned by her mother. The words, addressed to Beloved, convey recollections so odious that Sethe believes such words should not be uttered by one human being to another. Denver speaks next and expresses fear of her mother and her yearning to be rescued by her father, anxieties that have been left unrevealed until then. Beloved's monologue is the most obscure. Written without punctuation and randomly spaced, it may suggest the disconnectedness between Beloved and the world. Like her life, her words are fragmented but suggest Beloved's yearning to be reunited with her mother. At the same time, the language and style of Beloved's passage connotes the seamlessness of the past and present, an idea borne by the style, content, and structure of the entire novel.

Questions for Writing and Discussion

1. Here are four statements about Beloved with which you may agree or disagree. Choose one to develop into an essay. Use ample specific evidence from the novel to support your ideas.
   a. *Beloved* tells the story of characters bearing the weight of responsibility for their own life and actions.
   b. Although slavery is a system of ownership and possession, *Beloved* illustrates that while slaves might be owned, they were not possessed.
   c. Slavery is a fascinating subject because it provides the ground on which to investigate compelling issues of contemporary culture.
   d. Toni Morrison is careful not to make all the blacks wonderful and all the whites awful. She presents a balanced view of human behavior.
2. About her writing, Toni Morrison has said, "I stand with the reader, hold his hand, and tell him a very simple story about complicated people." Could she have been talking about *Beloved*?
3. Some critics have claimed that the supernatural element in *Beloved* takes away from the power of the book. Do you agree?

CHAPTER **7** Drama on the AP Exam

When you write the third essay on the AP Literature exam, you are offered the option of choosing either a novel or a play as your subject.

Although drama is different from fiction, for purposes of the exam, it is merely another form of imaginative literature. The special techniques that set drama apart from all other literary forms make no difference on the exam. Therefore, many of the comments in the previous chapter that pertain to fiction, for all intents and purposes, apply to drama as well.

Just as there is something called the "world of the work" in prose fiction, there is the "world of the play" in drama.

The World of the Play

To understand successfully the meaning of a play we must effectively enter its world. We must define the particular qualities of its time, place, and society. For instance, Shakespeare's *King Lear* is a play about filial ingratitude. The readers must be able to describe the noble morality of Cordelia, the evil plottings of Goneril and Regan, and the foolish choices made by Lear. But they must see also the graphic scenes of eyes being gouged out, half-naked men raging about in a tempest on a heath, and the genuine remorse growing from a gross misconception of family love. Or consider Shakespeare's *A Midsummer Night's Dream,* where supernatural dream worlds replete with fairies and elves in a mystical forest comprise much of the action.

We must enter that world, and often this demands what Samuel Taylor Coleridge called a "willing suspension of disbelief." Ten years may go by between two scenes, but we must take a leap of the imagination and accept this. Two characters may stand behind others to talk clandestinely; even though the entire theater can overhear the talk, including the characters being discussed, we must accept this. Above all we must absorb a set on stage as a representation of a whole world.

Theme and Meaning in Drama

The theme is the basic idea around which a play develops. You need to draw suggestions of the meaning of a play as soon as possible. After defining the setting, the physical world of the drama, the time, and the atmosphere, you should attempt a statement of what the play is about.

Clearly this is no simple proposition. The ultimate test of the effectiveness of your statement of a theme lies in its consistency and its applicability. When you can define and illuminate a play by one particular statement of its theme, your speculation will be more sophisticated and intelligent.

Greek Tragedy: Analyses of Two Plays

In many literary eras, particular works stand out above the others because they reveal the human condition so profoundly and because they lend themselves to many interpretations that enable spectators or readers better to understand themselves and the world in which they live. In Periclean Athens such works were Aeschylus's *Oresteia* and Sophocles' *Oedipus the King* and *Antigone.*

OEDIPUS THE KING: INTERPRETATIONS

OEDIPUS THE KING
Sophocles (496?–406 B.C.)

Summarized below are a number of scholarly interpretations of *Oedipus the King*. Read each one carefully and see whether you can find in the play evidence to support the view expressed. If you do not accept a view, prove with evidence from the play that such an interpretation, held by some critics, is unsound.

1. *Oedipus deals with the human struggle for knowledge*—first, for knowledge of the evil that besets the state, but ultimately for self-knowledge. Despite the advice of others, Oedipus refuses to remain with illusion; he must find the truth even if it will destroy him.

2. *Oedipus deals with the whimsical and capricious ways in which the gods deal with human beings.* Oedipus's story is fated, and his suffering and anguish serve to amuse the gods. Oedipus has no will, no identity, no force. The divine forces order a crime so as to play havoc with a man. It is an anti-religious play.

3. *Oedipus reflects in human experience the laws by which nature functions.* There is order in nature, but the laws by which this order is maintained exist without special concern for human beings. This creates a remorseless inevitability for the fate of man. He cannot escape tragedy and death. The capriciousness of scientific law is equivalent to the capriciousness of the gods.

4. *In Oedipus Sophocles is supporting the traditional religion against contemporary attacks.* Consciously or unconsciously, Oedipus and Jocasta have sinned against the moral law and must be punished. The gods are justified in the fate they mete out to Oedipus and Jocasta.

5. *The real issue in Oedipus is the conflict between father and son.* In every confrontation with a person old enough to be his father, Oedipus is incapable of the power to reason or to question sensibly. He becomes angry or petty. There are four father figures in Oedipus's life—Laius, Polybus, Teiresias, and Creon. (To help you understand the relationship between Oedipus and Polybus, seek the answer to the question, "Why in Corinth, when Oedipus learned from the drunken reveler at the banquet that he was not the true son of Polybus and later when he learned from the oracle that he was fated to slay his father, did he leave Corinth hastily without checking the truth of the reveler's story with his supposed father, Polybus?" Hint: Is it possible that he sensed some hostility toward Polybus? What might be the source of such hostility?)

6. *Oedipus is a tragic hero according to Aristotle's conception as enunciated in his Poetics.* He is not the victim of fate expressed in the oracles. His tragedy results from within his character. He is a man who sees but one side of a matter, and straightaway, driven by his uncontrolled emotions, acts in accordance with that imperfect vision.

7. *Oedipus's world is an existential one.* It is a nihilistic world in which there is no concern for human beings. In the deepest sense, Oedipus is innocent. He is wronged by the gods. His tragic heroism arises from his refusal to resign himself to the meaningless and purposeless cruelty of his world. If there is any meaning for Oedipus, it is that he can assert the dignity of self in a vacuum of injustice and absurdity.

8.   *The basic conflict in Oedipus is not between man and fate but more profoundly between man and the gods.* If man is cast in the image of the gods, then he possesses godlike qualities. When he acquires power and authority and the right of life or death over a people, he is like a god. At this point the superior greatness of the gods can be demonstrated only by his defeat. Such is the genesis of Oedipus's tragic fate.

9.   *Oedipus is a play about sight and blindness, about truth and falsehood, about reason and want of intellect.* The paradoxes of the play are that profound knowledge and perception exist in the blind Teiresias, that Oedipus's act of blinding himself is a symbol of self-knowledge and an assertion that man can free himself from the careless and capricious decrees of the gods, and that wisdom exists in the simple people of the day, Jocasta and the shepherds, who, though they bring the direst of news, lead to the triumph of truth and the redemption of Oedipus.

10.   *Oedipus, like Orestes, had been placed on trial by the gods.* Oedipus' horrifying crimes—killing his father and marrying his mother—were committed unknowingly. The first, in large measure, was committed either as an act of self-defense or as an assertion of Oedipus's dignity as a man; the second was committed because it was expected of him as the newly selected king of Thebes and, probably, also because Oedipus found Jocasta attractive. Let us suppose further that Jocasta did not kill herself and that Oedipus did not blind himself. The nature of the crimes, the moral values of the society in which the crimes were committed, and the outlook for the future of Oedipus, Jocasta, and their children determine what kind of judgment, if any, the gods could render that would be just and would provide Oedipus and Jocasta with the penance and redemption they would need.

STRUCTURE—SEQUENCE OF EPISODES

Oedipus is composed of six dialogues, each of which has an ode or speech by the chorus. The chorus reacts to the events in various ways. Sometimes it participates in a dialogue.

The first dialogue is a Prologue depicting Oedipus counseling the Theban elders, followed by the first choral ode. Then there are four episodes; in each, one or two confrontations occur, ending with a choral ode. The play concludes with an Exodus, in which the doom of Oedipus is sealed and the chorus turns away from him.

Prologue: Dialogue between Oedipus and a priest of Zeus representing the people of Thebes. The priest calls upon the king to help the plague-stricken city.

Dialogue between Oedipus and Creon. Oedipus sent Creon to the oracle to learn how Thebes might be delivered. Creon delivers the message of the oracle. The murderer of Laius must be found and punished. The choral ode is a prayer to the gods. The chorus recounts the sorrows caused by the plague.

Episode 1:   Dialogue between Oedipus and the leader of the chorus. Oedipus, in a proclamation, calls upon the slayer to confess.

Dialogue between Oedipus and Teiresias. Teiresias at first refuses to give Oedipus the information he seeks. Oedipus accuses Teiresias of being part of a conspiracy that led to the murder of Laius. Teiresias, angered, tells Oedipus he is the defiler of Thebes. The chorus discloses the sense of foreboding that the populace of Thebes feels at the turn of events, and expresses its loyalty toward Oedipus, their king.

Episode 2:   Dialogues in which Oedipus, Creon, Jocasta, and the chorus engage. Oedipus accuses Creon of treason, and of slaying Laius. Creon defends himself, saying he has no desire to be king. Jocasta appears, defends Creon, and seeks to reconcile the two. The chorus urges Oedipus not to dishonor Creon on unproved rumor. Oedipus yields to the urging of the chorus. Then Jocasta wishes to know how the quarrel began. Oedipus tells Jocasta that Teiresias and Creon accused him of murdering Laius. Seeking to allay his doubts and suspicions, Jocasta tells him of the exposure of their child and the manner of Laius's death. Oedipus tells Jocasta the story of his past. He realizes that he *may* be the slayer of Laius, and decides he must speak to the servant who witnessed the murder of Laius.

The chorus praises reverent purity and honor to the gods and is critical of the isolence and *hubris* of rulers who do not fear their justice. It expresses the fear that, if the oracles prove false, reverence for the gods will be undermined.

Episode 3:   Dialogues in which Oedipus, Jocasta, and a messenger from Corinth engage. Jocasta appears as a supplicant calling upon the gods to rid Thebes and her home of the uncleanness. A messenger appears, learns from the chorus where the home of Oedipus is, and informs Jocasta of the death of Polybus. Jocasta calls Oedipus to hear the messenger's news. Oedipus derides the oracles. He explains why he ran away from Corinth. The messenger tells Oedipus that Polybus was not his father and explains how Oedipus came to be cared for by Polybus. Jocasta, now frightened at what the truth might reveal, seeks to dissuade Oedipus from seeking further knowledge about his birth. Oedipus misjudges the reason why Jocasta wishes him to halt the inquiry. He believes the reason is that he was baseborn. Jocasta, now really fearful of what Oedipus's search for the truth will reveal, rushes into the palace in terror.

The chorus in its ode concluding this episode expresses its feeling concerning the parentage of Oedipus. Who were his mother and father?

Episode 4:   Dialogue between Oedipus and the Herdsman. The Herdsman is loath to reveal what he did with the baby Oedipus. When Oedipus threatens him, the Herdsman is forced to tell his story. Oedipus knows at last that he has killed his father and married his mother. Like Jocasta, Oedipus rushes into the palace in shock and terror.

The chorus comments on the shadowiness of life, praises Oedipus again, bemoans the sins of Oedipus, and states that Time in its inexorable movement finally reveals all things.

The Exodus or *Dénouement:*   Dialogues in which Oedipus, Creon, the second messenger, the leader of the chorus, and the chorus engage. The second messenger appears and reports that Jocasta has committed suicide and that Oedipus has blinded himself. Oedipus and the chorus chant responsively in the choral ode of this scene. In this poetic exchange, Oedipus bemoans his fate, blames Apollo, wishes he had been left to die on Mt. Cithaeron. Though moved by his grief, the chorus turns away from him, agreeing that he would be better dead than living and blind. Oedipus asks Creon, who now will assume power, to exile him from Thebes and to care for his daughters, Antigone and Ismene. The chorus concludes the play by commenting on Oedipus's fall from greatness and grace and on the fact that there is no true happiness for one who is mortal.

AN INVESTIGATION INTO A MURDER

Oedipus the King is an investigation into the murder of Laius, king of Thebes. The irony of this investigation is that the prosecutor conducting the inquiry is himself the murderer. He questions a variety of witnesses, and the testimony of each adds to the accumulation of evidence that finally exposes him as the guilty party.

Here are the key questions that he asks of particular witnesses and the answers each gives him:

1. Why has the plague fallen upon the city of Thebes? The answer comes from Creon, who had been sent to consult the oracle. "The oracle says that the plague is being visited upon Thebes because the murderer of Laius has not been found and punished. Justice has not been done."

2. Why was there no attempt to investigate the murder of Laius at the time the crime was committed? Again the answer comes from Creon. "Thebes was in terror of the Sphinx. There was too much unrest in the city. When you, Oedipus, destroyed the power of the Sphinx and saved the city, you were proffered the throne. No one in the city wanted to create any more unrest by investigating Laius's murder. If you want more information, ask Teiresias, the seer."

3. Who murdered Laius? The question is directed at Teiresias, who as a seer and prophet knows the truth. Teiresias at first refuses to answer, but when Oedipus accuses him of conspiring with Creon to overthrow him (Oedipus) and seize the throne, Teiresias says, "You are the one who murdered Laius." At this point Oedipus cannot believe him and suspects him of conspiracy. But there is a doubt.

4. Is there any truth in Teiresias's accusation that I murdered Laius? The answer comes from Jocasta. "The oracle prophesied that Lauis would be slain by his son. The child that was born was therefore exposed and left to die on Mt. Cithaeron."

5. How did Laius die? Again, Jocasta ironically provides the answer. "Laius was killed at a crossroads leading to three cities. He was accompanied by a herald and four armed followers. He and four of his men were killed by foreign robbers. This happened before you came to our city."

6. How much truth did the oracles reveal? "It is true that I, not foreign robbers, killed Laius and four of his followers, but I am not the son of Laius. My father is Polybus, king of Corinth. I am guilty of murder, but not of parricide or of incest."

The answer comes from the first of the messengers. He is a servant in the household of Polybus of Corinth. "Merope and Polybus are not your true parents. You were to be exposed on Mt. Cithaeron. Another shepherd gave you to me. He belonged to the household of King Laius. I gave you to Merope and Polybus, who were childless. They brought you up as their own son."

7. Who were my parents? Am I the child of slaves in Laius's household? The answer comes from the Herdsman, who had been a servant of Jocasta and

Laius. "You were not the child of slaves. Your father was Laius and your mother, Jocasta. They ordered me to expose you, but I through pity saved you."

TRAGIC HEROES

It is possible to support the thesis that both Oedipus and Jocasta are tragic heroes as defined by Aristotle in his *Poetics.* Indicate whether you agree or disagree with the analysis outlined below, which seeks to establish the tragic stature of both Oedipus and Jocasta in Sophocles' play.

Oedipus	*Jocasta*

Pride

He is quick to anger.	She believes it is possible to
He conceives of himself as a father	circumvent the oracles.
to his people and superior to them.	She wishes to remain queen.
He doubts Teiresias.	
He seeks to circumvent the oracles.	
He seeks the truth regardless of the	
consequences.	

Capacity for Suffering

Oedipus's suffering is intense.	Jocasta's suffering is also intense.
It is physical, spiritual, and	It, too, is physical, spiritual,
psychological anguish.	and psychological.
He shows no self-pity though his	She cannot cry out in pain because
crimes were committed in	she cannot add the moment of
innocence.	revelation to her husband's anguish.

Commitment

Oedipus seeks knowledge regardless	Jocasta is committed to her husband
of where it will lead him.	and her children. She, as much as
	Oedipus, must fight the fate decreed
	her by the gods.

Protest

Oedipus cries his protest against the	Jocasta does not cry out, but her quiet
gods that planned so horrible a fate	stoicism in the face of the horrible
for him, against the values and rituals	truth and her suicide express her
that made his actions immoral.	protest against her fate.

Perception

Oedipus is softened, made more	Jocasta has been gentle and human
human by tragedy. He loses	throughout. She seeks to ease
much of his arrogance. He	her husband's suspicions, to draw
acknowledges his errors. He	him away from the investigation.
acquires an even greater dignity	The truth destroys her, but not
in his sorrow.	before she has a revelation of the
	human condition in a world ruled
	capriciously by the gods.

Social and Psychological Effects

The leader and the chorus, the messengers and the Herdsman, the people of Thebes are moved by the fate of Oedipus and Jocasta. All are made aware of suffering as an element of the human condition. They recognize the true nobility of their king and queen. They realize that human beings, despite weakness and sin, can rise to moments of greatness.

DISCUSSION QUESTIONS

Frequently, a person who reads or, as a spectator, sees a play will discover what seem to be illogicalities in the depiction of characters and in the description of their responses to the experiences of the play, or errors in the dramatic narration. The questions that follow seem to indicate flaws in *Oedipus the King.* Consider each of these questions carefully. Do they reveal flaws in the play? Even Homer nodded. Or do you find a satisfactory answer, in human nature or psychology, to each question? Are the elements described Sophocles' mistakes or examples of his unique insight into character?

1. At a banquet, a drunken man tells Oedipus that he is not the true son of his father. Oedipus asks Merope and Polybus whether the drunkard spoke the truth. They say he lied. Why haven't they told Oedipus that he was an adopted child?

2. Oedipus still has doubts. He consults the oracle at Delphi, where he learns that he is destined to slay his father and marry his mother. Why doesn't he go back to Merope and Polybus and again check the drunken man's story? Why does he run off without a word to them?

3. The Greeks in Oedipus's day profoundly believed the prophecies of the oracle. Why, having learned the dire prophecies at Delphi, doesn't Oedipus establish for himself two elementary rules: never get into a quarrel with a man old enough to be your father; never enter into marriage with a woman old enough to be your mother?

4. Why, after killing a man old enough to be his father, and then marrying a woman old enough to be his mother, does he not reflect upon the possible meaning of these actions?

5. Why, upon entering Thebes and finding the throne vacant and the queen a widow, does he never once ask about the fate of the previous king who had been her husband?

6. Why in all the years of their marriage does Oedipus never tell Jocasta the story of his life in Corinth as the son of Merope and Polybus, and the reasons why he left Corinth?

7. Oedipus knew his Corinthian parentage was doubtful. He also knew that an oracle had predicted that he would slay his father and marry his mother. Angered when Oedipus accuses Teiresias, the blind seer, of having had a hand in Laius's murder, Teiresias gives him this dire information. Why doesn't Teiresias's accusation raise any doubts in Oedipus's mind?

Antigone: Structure—
Sequence of Episodes

ANTIGONE

Sophocles (496?–406 B.C.)

There are seven episodes in the play, the first of which, as in *Oedipus the King,* may be considered the prologue. Each episode except the last ends with a poetic statement by the chorus. In each episode, there are not more than three characters and the chorus, a convention that Sophocles and other Greek playwrights observed. The plays could then be performed by three actors, who assumed different roles, plus the chorus.

Episode 1:   Antigone and Ismene talk about the death of their brothers and Creon's decree. The penalty for burying the traitor Polyneices is being stoned to death. Antigone plans to defy the decree, in her belief that the laws of the gods transcend the laws of the state. Ismene is afraid to join Antigone and tries to dissuade her from the act of rebellion. When Antigone remains adamant, Ismene promises to keep Antigone's actions secret. The chorus reviews the war of the seven against Thebes, praises the god that brought them victory, and sings a hymn of joy.

Episode 2:   The chorus of old men, summoned by Creon, hear his statement of the joyous victory of Thebes against its attackers. He affirms his authority as ruler and announces his decree concerning Polyneices, whose body is to be left in the fields unburied. The chorus accepts the decree. A sentry appears to inform the king that someone has strewn dust on the slimy corpse of Polyneices. The sentries guarding the corpse knew of the danger of bringing such news to Creon and so they had thrown dice to determine who was to be the messenger. The leader of the chorus suggests that this may have been an action of the gods. Creon in a rage thinks the guards were bribed and orders them to find the guilty man on pain of death. The chorus concludes this episode by praising man, extolling his powers, his ability to defend himself against any danger except death. They end by praising the force of law in maintaining the security of the city.

Episode 3:   The sentry leads Antigone in, and when Creon appears, the sentry tells of catching Antigone again trying to perform the last rites for her dead brother. It is with some regret that the sentry charges Antigone, but it is his life or hers. The sentry leaves. Antigone defends her action, claiming that the law of the gods has precedence over the law of Creon. Creon, fearing rebellion against his authority and also suspecting Ismene, orders her arrest. Creon and Antigone argue their positions. When Ismene appears, she wishes to confess a share in Antigone's crime, but Antigone will not let her. Ismene reminds Creon that, if he sentences Antigone to death, he will be killing his son's bride, but Creon is unyielding. The chorus ends this episode by commenting on the damnation that has befallen the family of Oedipus, by describing the character of Zeus, whose wrath transcends mortal arrogance, and by reminding the audience that human pleasures are the springs of sorrow.

Episode 4:   Haemon seeks to dissuade his father from punishing Antigone. He begins by acknowledging his father's authority. Creon defends his action, asking Haemon to honor him as father and to forget Antigone. He explains why he has condemned Antigone and tells his son that he fears anarchy. Haemon, in response, tells his father that authority inspires fear in people, that the people are in sympathy with Antigone. He pleads for wisdom, compassion, and flexibility. The quarrel between father and son becomes angry and bitter. Haemon leaves in a fury. Creon shows he has some flexibility by exonerating Ismene. He changes Antigone's punishment from being stoned to being locked in a vault of stone. The chorus concludes this episode with a poem on the power of love.

Episode 5:   Antigone bids farewell to life. She compares herself to Niobe, whose tears are never done and whose death is lonely. She blames her father's (Oedipus's) crime for the tragedy that has befallen her. "Your marriage strikes from the grave to murder mine." The chorus reminds Antigone that her death is the result of a conscious action on her part. Creon, who is present, orders her to be taken and placed in the tomb. Antigone goes "half in love" with a death where she will meet father, mother, brothers. She reminds the Thebans that she dies because she would not transgress the laws of heaven. The chorus ends the episode by recounting punishments meted out by the gods to a number of mortals. (This ode seems irrelevant since Antigone, in defending the laws of the gods, does not deserve the punishment. The chorus members reveal themselves to be simple men. They make simple and unrelated analogies.)

Episode 6:   Teiresias, the blind seer, appears to warn Creon of the disaster that will befall him if Polyneices remains unburied and Antigone dies. Creon responds to Teiresias as Oedipus did, with anger. He accuses Teiresias of taking bribes. Teiresias leaves, prophesying doom on the house of Creon. The leader of the chorus urges Creon to relent. Creon, moved, changes his mind and orders his servants to join him in freeing Antigone. The chorus ends this episode with a hymn to Dionysus (Iacchos), asking the god to restore peace to Thebes.

Episode 7:   A messenger brings news that Haemon has committed suicide "driven mad by the murder his father had done." Eurydice, the wife of Creon, appears. The messenger tells Eurydice that Creon, on his way to free Antigone, had stopped to bury Polyneices. He had, therefore, come too late to the tomb. Antigone had hanged herself, and Haemon was insane with grief. Creon sought forgiveness of his son, but Haemon spat at his father and, drawing his sword, lunged at him. Failing to wound his father, he turned the sword on himself. The news affects Eurydice deeply. She goes off. The grief-stricken Creon appears, the attendants bearing the body of his son. Creon is brought low by the further news that Eurydice, too, has taken her life, cursing him for the death of both her sons. (Megareus, the other son, had been killed in battle between the Argives and Thebans.) Creon blames himself for the disaster and ends by saying, "Fate has brought all my pride to a thought of dust." The leader of the chorus concludes the play with the comment that there is no wisdom but in submission to the gods.

DISCUSSION QUESTIONS
1. The clash between Antigone and Creon is not only a clash of persons. It is also a clash of principles. What principles does each figure espouse?
2. There appear to be a number of discrepancies in the play:
   a. The rites over the body of Polyneices are performed twice. The second time the guards catch Antigone. Why does Antigone go back a second time?
   b. When Creon has exonerated Ismene and reaffirmed his sentence on Antigone, the chorus asks what form of punishment he will inflict. Creon tells them that Antigone is to be locked in a cave with a small amount of food. She will die of starvation. But the decree proclaims that the punishment is death by stoning. Why did Creon change the punishment?
   c. When Creon is beaten down by Teiresias and asks the chorus what he is to do, they reply: "Go and release Antigone." This is what we expect him to do. But he goes first to bury the body of Polyneices and therefore arrives at the tomb too late. Why does Creon stop first to bury Polyneices?
   d. After the tragedy in the cave, Creon brings back on stage the body of Haemon, but not the body of Antigone. The play's central character is supposed to be Antigone. Why is she forgotten?

The discrepancies can be explained as errors on the part of Sophocles or as conscious and pertinent elements of his play. Can you determine any dramatic reasons why Sophocles handled these elements as he did? For example, if Creon stopped to bury Polyneices before freeing Antigone, was he not showing reverence to the gods? Was his worship too late? Were the gods punishing him for his tardy recognition of their authority? What was Sophocles' intention?

3. Sophocles begins his play with the two girls—Antigone and Ismene—two lonely figures, one of whom proposes to defy the king, while the other counsels obedience to the will of the state. Why is this an effective way to begin the play?

4. What expressions in the dialogue highlight the difference in character and view of the two sisters? What is the spectator's emotional reaction to each of the two sisters?

5. What function does the chorus perform when it first appears? What other functions does the chorus perform throughout the remainder of the play? What is the chorus's view of the various events of the play? What impression of the chorus does Sophocles wish the reader or spectator to get?

6. When we first see Creon, he is majestic and powerful. What do we learn of his character from his first speech? What is the dominant force in his personality?

7. Two maxims were well ingrained in the mind of the Periclean Greek: "Remember what you are" and "Nothing in excess." In what way does Creon reveal that he has forgotten these maxims?

8. What function in the play does the guard or sentry serve? What information does he give the audience concerning Creon's relationship with the people he rules? What does Creon fear? What do the guards fear? The guard mentions a curious fact: animals did not get at the body of Polyneices. What inferences does Sophocles wish you to draw from this fact?

9. The chorus recites an ode that extols the virtues of man. What are the limits to man's achievements? Under what conditions can he prosper? In what way is the ode a comment on the flaw in Creon's character and a foreshadowing of the tragedy that is to come?

10. Why is Ismene brought back into the play? Why does Sophocles have Ismene remind Creon that Antigone is Haemon's betrothed? Why is there no scene in the play between Antigone and Haemon?

11. Sophocles wishes us to know that Creon is morally insensitive, that he has a complete lack of ordinary human sympathy and understanding. How are these qualities revealed in his attitude toward Antigone, toward Ismene, toward Haemon, toward Teiresias? How does Creon change after his argument with Teiresias? Is the change believable? Before Eurydice dies, she curses Creon. Is she justified in this hatred of her husband before her death? What, if anything, was wrong in the relationship between husband and wife?

12. The ode of the chorus after Antigone and Ismene are removed is ironic. Why? (Creon is present to hear it. It is recited as a comment on Antigone. It explains why disaster befell her. Actually, it is Creon whom the words fit. How?)

13. What information do we get from Haemon in the angry dialogue with his father? (We learn of the intensity of his love for Antigone. We learn what

the ordinary citizen thinks of Antigone.) How does Sophocles wish us to view the love between Antigone and Haemon? Is there evidence in the play to prove that Antigone loved Haemon? Why is Haemon unable to move his father?

14. The episodes in which the chorus sings of the power of love; in which the chorus admires Antigone, yet considers her a rash, headstrong girl; and in which Creon sends a sorrowful and friendless Antigone to her death highlight the clash of the power and love themes in the play. What references to power and to love do you find in these episodes? Are there similar references in other episodes? What makes Antigone's farewell moving? Why is her farewell ironic?

15. What function, if any, does the ode of the chorus recounting the tragedies of Danae, Lycurgus, and the two sons of Phineus and Cleopatra have in the play? In other words, is this ode pertinent or irrelevant?

16. What is the ironic purpose in Teiresias's prophecy? What relationship is there between Teiresias's prophecy and Creon's subsequent actions? What is ironic in Creon's actions?

17. Why does Sophocles introduce Eurydice so late in the play? What tragic events does she learn from the messenger? How does she react? How are Eurydice's actions related to the power-love theme?

THESIS STATEMENTS

Try writing a critical essay, proving with evidence from Antigone the validity of any one of the following statements:

1. *Antigone* is essentially a political play dealing with the conflict between the laws of state and the conscience of an individual citizen of the state.

2. *Antigone* is conceived in the heroic tradition and is a study of an ideal heroine, rare in the world of reality.

3. *Antigone* is an Aristotelian tragedy of character. Antigone is the perfect tragic protagonist.

4. It is not Antigone who is the tragic protagonist of *Antigone* but Creon, the ruler of Thebes.

5. *Antigone* is a story of conflict and suffering set within a political and religious framework, and thereby universalized.

6. *Antigone* deals with conflicts arising from three demands made upon the human psyche: the demands of religion (Zeus); the demands of the state (Thebes); and the demands of human instincts (Aphrodite).

7. Creon is defeated because he does not realize that there are certain ultimates in human life that must be respected because they are divine.

8. People like Antigone who are desperate enough or noble enough to follow their own instincts or ideals will recoil against short-sighted statecraft, and the defeat of a tyrant will *seem* like the carrying out of a divine law.

Elizabethan Tragedy: Analyses of Two Plays

HAMLET
William Shakespeare (1564–1616)

The following conceptions of Hamlet's world are suggested by two essays: "The World of Hamlet" by Maynard Mack and "Interrogation, Doubt, Irony; Thesis, Antithesis, Synthesis" by Harry Levin. See whether you can support these views with evidence from the play.

1. Hamlet's world is characterized by mysteriousness. The unknown intrudes upon the known and disturbs the logical functioning of the known world. From the depths of Purgatory or Hell, a ghost appears to set in motion a sequence of actions that have an illogical and confused order and result in violence and death. The mind of man, supposedly the seat of reason, is unhinged by events, becomes troubled by doubts, and directs mad and angry actions. How do you explain the cruelty of Hamlet toward Ophelia, Hamlet's heartless and callous treatment of Polonius and of his friends, and the role of Rosencrantz and Guildenstern except as manifestations of inexplicable and mysterious movements of a keen mind gone awry? How do you explain Ophelia's madness and Laertes' perfidy, or the evil that directed Claudius's murder of his brother except as a mystery of life that makes possible the warping of minds?

2. Hamlet's world is also one of riddles, the riddles of the human condition, of human nature. There is the riddle of character. How can a physical, psychological, or spiritual blemish in a man or woman turn him or her into a cruel person capable even of murder? How can Gertrude turn to Claudius? What is the meaning of Ophelia's behavior? How can she be persuaded to betray Hamlet? The greatest riddle of all is the true nature of Hamlet. Is he a noble prince or a devil? When is he most nearly his true self?

3. Hamlet's world is one of uncertainty, perplexity, and doubt. What is real and what is false? So much of the language of the play suggests appearance, pretense, seeming, not being. So much of the action of the play is acting, not living. How real is reality and what is the relation of reality to appearance? The real things are violent and passionate deeds: the murder of the elder Hamlet, the too-hasty marriage of the queen, the suicide of Ophelia, the final slaughter at the play's end. The unreal arises in the acting of parts by the characters: Hamlet's madness, Ophelia at prayer, the king at prayer, Rosencrantz and Guildenstern performing as friends of the prince, the ghost claiming to be the father of Hamlet.

4. Hamlet's world is also one of unanswerable questions, questions related to universals: human nature, the place of human beings in the universe, the nature of life and death, the nature of heaven and hell; and questions related to particulars: the relationships among the characters, the feelings they have for one another, the subsurface motivations that direct their speech and actions, the honest and the equivocal emotions they display in their contacts with one another.

As you read the play, look for the questions. Determine whether they are concerned with the universals or the particulars as outlined above. Determine also whether they are answerable or unanswerable and what they reveal about the mystery of man and his universe. There are questions, for example, about the ghost: Is he an honest ghost? There are questions about love: How deeply does Ophelia love Hamlet? How deeply does Hamlet love Ophelia? Does the queen truly love her son? There are questions about man and God and prayer: Why does Claudius pray to God for forgiveness, knowing that he will not give up what he has gained by crime? There are questions about life and death: Is the paragon of animals only a quintessence of dust? Did Alexander look of this fashion in the earth? Is death a voyage to a place of punishment and reward, or a movement into the unknown?

5. There are ironies and counterfeits in this world of Hamlet. As you read the play, look first for the counterfeits. For example, Hamlet counterfeits madness;

Ophelia counterfeits devoutness at prayer; the king counterfeits the loving father; Polonius—and this is more subtle—counterfeits the concerned parent; Rosencrantz and Guildenstern counterfeit loving friends; the king counterfeits the pious monarch; Laertes counterfeits the forgiving enemy.

There are also many ironies that you will find in the play. There are, for example, the many ironies associated with Hamlet. In seeking to achieve a noble end, the revenge for the death of a father, he destroys many innocent people. His love for Ophelia is not great enough to encompass understanding and compassion. At the moment he makes peace with himself and his world, he drops his guard and is defeated. There are ironies associated with Ophelia. The love she bears her father undoes her. Her essential nature is unable to cope with the demands her world makes upon her. There are ironies associated with the queen. She loves her son, yet is unable to understand or help him. Her passion for Claudius blinds her to the danger her son is in. There are ironies about the ghost, about the king, ironies about cheaters—the king, Polonius, Laertes, Rosencrantz and Guildenstern—being themselves cheated, thinking they are controlling action and being hoisted with their own petard. Look for these and more to prove that Hamlet's world, like our own or any other human world, is filled with counterfeits and ironies. As you study the play, you begin to see how its world becomes a metaphor for all the human worlds created in the history of civilization.

HAMLET'S TRAGIC FLAW

Many critics, accepting the dictum of Aristotle that a tragic hero must have some flaw in character or judgment that will lead them to actions ending in disaster, have sought to discover Hamlet's tragic flaw. They have come up with many views; these are summarized below. Choose two or three of these conclusions and see whether you can find evidence in the play to support them.

1. *Hamlet is indecisive.* He tends to think too carefully, analyze too thoroughly, and intellectualize. The result is that he procrastinates. Because of the delays, he permits the king too many opportunities to escape his (Hamlet's) judgment and prepares the way for his own defeat.

2. *Hamlet suffers from severe melancholia.* This sensation of depression makes participation in daily affairs, like spending time with Ophelia or with his mother or with his friends, or any action, like accusing or attacking the king, appear meaningless.

3. *Hamlet is consumed by an arrogant egotism.* He conceives of himself as being superior to all other persons, especially the ordinary mortals that clutter the earth. This makes him move toward his revenge alone and unaided. Without advice or help, his views distorted by conceit, he must fail.

4. *Hamlet possesses an excessive moral sensibility.* He is so shocked by the evil and corruption of the world that he becomes immobilized. He sees the correction of the world's ills as an impossible task.

5. *Hamlet possesses a high idealism.* He looks for nobility and loyalty in others, especially those he loves. He expects human beings to be ruled by reason and not by the hope of personal gain or the desire for position or power. His disappointments slow him down.

6. *Hamlet is afflicted with an inhuman cynicism.* He recognizes the existence of evil and weakness in man, his institutions, his beliefs, and his professed

ideals. The bitterness generated by the cynicism leads to the excesses that cause the disasters of the play.

7. *Hamlet is troubled by an abhorrence of sex.* His mother's passionate response to the blandishments of Claudius disgusts him. If sex can so move a matron his mother's age, it must be evil and wicked. Obsessed by his disappointment in his mother, troubled by his own feelings toward Ophelia, his mind becomes clouded and he is incapable of the rational action required to revenge his father's murder and place himself on the throne.

8. *Hamlet is excessively concerned with death.* Many things, physical and mental, have died, and their deaths have affected him. His father has died, was possibly murdered. His trust and belief in his mother, Ophelia, and Rosencrantz and Guildenstern are dead. His hopes to be king, married to Ophelia, supported by his mother, are dead. He becomes absorbed with death, speaks to his father's ghost, thinks of suicide, discusses the ravages of death with the gravedigger, comments on the base uses of death to the skull of Yorick, and inflicts death upon Polonius, whose body he drags about the palace. Fascinated by death, he is hampered in his movements to establish a viable situation for himself in a living world.

INTERPRETATIONS OF HAMLET

1. *Something is rotten in the state of Denmark.* It is ruled by evil. Claudius has made himself king by secretly killing his brother and winning the support of the nobles. He has won his brother's wife and by marrying her has strengthened his position on the throne. He is a shrewd politician and rules by clever manipulation of authority, ready to use any means, open and devious, to win his ends. His nephew, Hamlet, is safe so long as he is no threat to his power.

The queen is ruled by passion. She apparently had little feeling for her former husband, and has readily responded to Claudius's overtures of love.

Polonius is a poor father. He does not trust his son in Paris and sends a servant to spy on Laertes and to learn about his habits in the most devious of ways. Seemingly concerned about his daughter, he warns her to stay away from Hamlet; yet he uses her as a decoy to betray Hamlet and shows no awareness of her suffering in the encounter. He will hide behind curtains, betray any confidence, in order to be in the good graces of the king.

His son Laertes seems an honorable young man; yet, angry over his father's death, he will, instead of openly accusing Hamlet and challenging him for an explanation and a reparation, agree to the king's plan to kill Hamlet in an underhanded way.

Rosencrantz and Guildenstern, sufficiently intelligent as courtiers to guess Claudius's intentions toward their close friend, Hamlet, are willing to play the king's game and to betray their friend. In short, this world of Denmark is an evil and corrupt place.

Into this world comes a gentle, idealistic young prince who is a scholar and a courtier, everything that Ophelia says he is when his mad behavior upsets her. He learns his father has been murdered. He makes it his mission to avenge the murder. The evil, corrupt world he has entered contaminates him. It poisons his very soul, and leads him to actions that are as extreme as those engaged in by his enemies. When he dies, having sought to slough off the disease that infected him, it is too late. The damage has been done. A number of people, not deserving of death, have died.

2. *Denmark is not rotten.* It is a typical, normal community with its good and evil. Claudius is a wise ruler. He has committed an evil act in killing his brother to be king, but he is a better king than his brother, and the country benefits. Under the elder Hamlet, Denmark seems to have been a nation at war. Claudius prefers diplomacy to battle and sends ambassadors to resolve the quarrel with Norway. The courtiers respect him and acknowledge his authority. His love for the queen is deep and honest. He will not harm her son, though Hamlet is a danger to him, because Hamlet's death will naturally distress her. He wants peace between himself and his nephew.

The queen cannot be labeled lustful or corrupt because she loves Claudius. Apparently, her life with the elder Hamlet was not fulfilling. With Claudius she is happy. That her son does not approve is something she cannot help though she is unhappy about his disapproval.

A case can be made for Polonius as a concerned father. He has brought his children up himself, watched over them perhaps too carefully, but they all live in a sophisticated court, and there is some danger that an innocent and unwary maiden like Ophelia may be hurt. Within his limitations, he is a good father. His greatest loyalty is to his king. His job is the foundation of his life, and he can be forgiven if he thoughtlessly uses his daughter (because he is unaware of her feelings) to learn more about Hamlet's intentions toward his king. In short, the world of the court at Elsinore, except for the horrid deed that gave Claudius the power, is a normal world. You can develop this interpretation further regarding the qualities of Laertes and Hamlet's two friends, Rosencrantz and Guildenstern.

Suppose Hamlet had not entered this world; what would have happened? The characters would have lived out their lives in peaceful dullness. Only the king would have suffered—we can guess this from what Shakespeare tells us. He would for the rest of his life have suffered the pangs of a poignant conscience and might perhaps have sought to do penance for his dire deed. And in terms of statecraft, the murder of the elder Hamlet can perhaps be defended as necessary for the stability of the land.

But Hamlet *does* enter this world. What is the effect? Things begin to stir, and when the stir is over, eight people including Hamlet are dead, and at least four of them are undeserving of the fate that befell them. They are innocents destroyed in a conflict of powerful opposites. Hamlet has been the contaminating force that converted a normal world, not an Eden it is true, into a hell. He has done shockingly cruel, even corrupt, things. He has driven an innocent girl who loved him into a suicidal insanity. He has killed her father and insulted his corpse by dragging the body about the palace. He has cruelly insulted his mother. And callously, he has sent to their deaths two friends, whose crime was, at the king's behest, to seek the cause of Hamlet's madness. Surely, the criminal in the play is this antihero, this seemingly gentle scholar who in reality possesses a force of evil that consumes all who come in contact with him. Only Horatio survives. But he survives because his is too bland and too simple a nature to be worthy of Hamlet's corrupt talents.

How do you react to these contradictory interpretations of *Hamlet*?

3. *The essential evil of human beings arises in time of crisis.* In Shakespeare's play, before the first scene there are in Denmark two peaceful homes where life is serene and pleasant: the home of the elder Hamlet and that of Polonius, one of the courtiers. There seems to be a good relationship between parents and children in both homes. Hamlet respects his father and loves his mother. Both

parents are fond of their son, and Hamlet is trained for the kingship. He has all the virtues of a noble prince.

In the Polonius household, the father watches carefully over the children, allows them some freedom, prepares Laertes for the life of a courtier and Ophelia for the life of a noble's wife. Both children love their father though they are often amused by his garrulity.

Outside the homes of the two families, there are worlds that are quite different. There is the world of the sophisticated and corrupt court with its drinking and carousing. There is the world of the battlefield with its bloody destruction and disregard for human life. Finally, there is the world of dark nature, the world of the supernatural with its evil spirits that haunt the night. In the play, the three external worlds of corruption, battle, and darkness move in on the peaceful domestic environment of the Hamlet home. The court corruption that sharpens Claudius's ambition leads Claudius to kill the elder Hamlet. The value of human life has been diminished by the slaughter of battle. The sexual corruption of the court has infected Gertrude. Her *carpe diem* view of life leads her to join Claudius. The dark evil surrounding Elsinore has lodged in the two, and they make a well-matched couple—an evil and corrupt king and a lustful consort.

When Hamlet returns to Elsinore, the nobility of his nature comes again under the influence of court and battlefield values, especially since he sees their influence upon his mother. When the voice of his father calls to him out of the darkness of hell, his nature suffers a change, and he is ready for the corrupt and destructive actions that his revenge requires.

Polonius and his family become corrupted when Claudius becomes king. Polonius's closeness to Claudius requires of him hypocritical demeanor and devious action. The corruptness of Polonius was subdued when Claudius was just a courtier. Now the court takes over his life and invades his home. In addition, Hamlet, the dark avenger, made callous by the spectacle of his uncle's crime, his mother's betrayal, his father's ghost's command, moves into the Polonius household. The coalescence of court, battlefield, and hell and the movement of these combined elements into the two peaceful households destroy all the inhabitants in both homes. This is what the play is about, and it becomes a metaphor for all homes destroyed by the corruption, cruelty, and evil of institutions in the external world—corruption in law and government, cruelty and war, and the essential human evil that comes to the fore in time of crisis.

How do you react to this interpretation of Hamlet? See if you can pick up flaws in this view of the play. Defend your disagreement with evidence from the play.

THE IMAGERY IN THE PLAY

It should be interesting as you read the play to record the great variety of images used by Hamlet in his exchanges with other characters, in his musings on life, and in the demands made upon him by fate and by his world. Hamlet reveals himself as a man of education and imagination. His analogies, his references, are drawn from a wide variety of sources and experiences. He knows classical antiquity. He is well versed in law and business. He is at home at the court, on the battlefield, and in school and sports. He is a man of infinite wisdom and infinite variety. He is capable of profound thoughts and at the same time of vulgar and sarcastic comment.

As you read the play, you will notice also the imagery that appears in the speeches of other characters. Images are drawn from disease and from death, decay, and corruption; they are drawn from flowers and gardens; much of the imagery concerned with fortune is related to the unpredictability and the seductive treachery of fortune. Select the images and see how they make vivid a speech or statement, how they are related to the theme of the speech or statement, and how they are related to the themes and characters of the play.

DISCUSSION QUESTIONS

There are a number of questions raised in the play that require careful reading to answer. Perhaps there are no answers to some of these questions. Determine whether Shakespeare had some clear intention in introducing these problems.

1. Why in the beginning of the play does the relieving sentinel speak first?
2. Why should Francisco be sick at heart? He has had a quiet guard.
3. Marcellus does not know whom he is relieving. Why?
4. How did Horatio, who had been at Wittenberg, get all the information about the elder Hamlet's combat with the elder Fortinbras?
5. If Horatio was at the funeral of the elder Hamlet, why didn't young Hamlet see him?
6. How skeptical a man was Horatio?
7. Why, when Claudius addresses his ambassadors, does he say "good" Cornelius and *not* "good" Voltimand?
8. Why didn't Rosencrantz and Guildenstern attend the funeral of the elder Hamlet?
9. Why does Hamlet ask Horatio and the soldiers to swear *three* times to keep secret his meeting with the ghost?
10. Why, when he is asking his friends to swear to keep his secret, does he address the ghost in familiar, almost insulting terms (true-penny, old mole, this fellow in the cellerage, a worthy pioneer)?
11. The ghost repeats "swear." Why?
12. What actually happened at the performance of *The Murder of Gonzago* before the king and court? Why didn't the dumb-show betray Hamlet's scheme?
13. How did it happen that Hamlet, so aware of the king's hate and his scheming nature, could fall into a trap and accept Laertes's challenge?
14. What actually occurred in the duel between Hamlet and Laertes?

Dr. Faustus:
Juxtaposition of
Serious and
Comic Scenes

THE TRAGICAL HISTORY
OF THE LIFE AND DEATH OF DOCTOR FAUSTUS
Christopher Marlowe (1564–1593)

Christopher Marlowe's *Dr. Faustus,* in one of the versions that is generally accepted, is composed of a beginning in which Dr. Faustus makes his pact with Mephistopheles; a middle in which his actions are parodied in scenes of low comedy and in which he uses the powers granted him in puerile displays of necromancy; and an ending in which, having rejected all pleas of a good angel and an old man to repent and to seek God's mercy and forgiveness, he is dragged to hell in fulfillment of his contract with the devil.

The play presents a juxtaposition of serious scenes and comic scenes in the following order:

Scene I: Faustus announces his intellectual supremacy and his decision to venture "beyond the bounds of human thought" through the power of necromancy.
Scene II: Wagner, Faustus's servant, apes his master's display of learning by "chopping logic" with two scholars.

Scene III: Faustus agrees to sell his soul to the devil for twenty-four years of power and voluptuousness.

Scene IV: The clown considers bartering his soul for a shoulder of mutton and a taste of wenching.

Scene V: Faustus makes his compact with Lucifer.

Scene VI: Faustus discusses astronomy with Mephistopheles. He is concerned with who made the world. Lucifer entertains Faustus with a performance by the Seven Deadly Sins.

Scene VII: Faustus is launched in his career as a magician and conjuror. In Rome, invisible, he snatches away the Pope's food and drink and frightens the Pope's retainers.

Scene VIII: Ralph and Robin, low comic characters, burlesque Faustus's conjurations.

Scene IX: Ralph and Robin, with the help of Mephistopheles, try to steal a goblet from a vintner.

Scene X: Faustus continues with his magic. He entertains the emperor, Charles V, by conjuring up Alexander the Great and his paramour. He puts horns upon the head of an irritating and skeptical knight out of pique and a desire to demonstrate his skills.

Scene XI: He cheats a horse dealer.

Scene XII: He delights the pregnant Duchess of Vanholt by having Mephistopheles fetch for her a cluster of grapes, which at this time of the year were out of season and unobtainable.

We see then that at first Wagner and then the clown, Ralph, and Robin, all simple comic characters, parody the aspirations of Faustus and the powers he attained by selling his soul to the devil. Faustus, also, parodies his own profound yearnings and ambitions, and he demeans and desecrates the greatness of soul that made him willing to sell his heaven for supernatural knowledge and power. At first, Faustus is a grand figure, a Promethean rebel, seeking to encompass all knowledge. As he uses his powers to attain trivial ends, the grandeur drops from him, and he becomes one with the fools who parody his speech and his actions.

Scene XIII: Faustus causes the famed Helen of Troy to appear to delight the scholars visiting him. An old man seeks to win Faustus back to God. Faustus almost repents but is stayed by Mephistopheles, who, at Faustus's request, recalls Helen of Troy to be Faustus's paramour. The old man reappears but he is driven off by demons.

Scene XIV: Faustus bids farewell to the scholars. He is frantic with regret, yearns for forgiveness, wishes as punishment that his soul, like the souls of beasts, be absorbed into the elements. But he cannot escape his contract. He is dragged away, protesting, to hell.

STRUCTURE

There is a question about the organization of this play and about the relationship of the middle scenes of the play to the first and final sections, which deal with the contract with Lucifer and with the fulfillment of the contract. The tone and style of the first and last scenes are grand, befitting the story of a great man daring God and willing to sacrifice what he holds sacred for a glimpse into the unknown. Those who challenge God must die, and Faustus accepts his death in passionate and intense protest.

The middle scenes of the play are colloquial and pedestrian. The comedy is noisy and crude. This has led some critics to conclude that these scenes were written by a collaborator, perhaps Samuel Rowley. Yet a careful reading of the play can support the view that the middle scenes are organically part of the whole. What happens when man seeks to assume the mantle of the gods, when desiring supreme power, by some miraculous happenstance, he attains it? How does man then use his power? He clothes himself in excessive regalia. He dwells in magnificent structures built by slaves and surrounds himself with a coterie of obsequious sycophants and creates a world of artificial splendor. He regiments his world and turns man into a puppet, often a cruel and destructive puppet. He uses his power for self-aggrandizement and self-deification, for base and trivial ends. And he forsakes God. He may conceive of himself as divine and exalted. But he is in the last analysis a strutting and deluded clown, and ends either forgotten or remembered with revulsion.

It does not matter whether this paragon seeks temporal power, spiritual power, or intellectual power. Power breeds arrogance. It corrupts and turns man from a godlike and dignified creature into a clown and a fool. It is only in a moment of revelation or at the time when he must pay the debt for the gift of power that man sees himself as he is and becomes aware of what he has done. It is then that he may be restored to some semblance of manhood. And if his malefactions have been forgivable, if his repentance is genuine and his suffering deep, if his soul is merely soiled and not besmirched, he can become a tragic figure, as Dr. Faustus does in Marlowe's play.

The structure of the play also demonstrates its organic wholeness. Central to the action is Faustus's contract with Lucifer and the payment of the debt after twenty-four years of power and indulgence. The other scenes do not follow in any conscious chronological or sequential fashion. They are separate and seemingly unrelated scenes, each demonstrating Faustus's use of supernatural power for trivial or selfish ends, or parodying his use of power through clownish imitations by common folk, or reporting on the spiritual conflict in his mind as he wrestles between the urges of good and the urges of evil. As the scenes round out the movement of Faustus's venture into the unknown world of supernatural authority and display his human weaknesses and frailties, his delusions and failures, Marlowe's comment on the dichotomy between human aspirations and human achievements becomes clear. The scenes, august and trivial, accentuate the dual nature of human beings: their yearning for greatness and knowledge, on the one hand, and the weakness and baseness that make them turn their intellectual prowess to simple, low, or ugly ends, on the other.

THESIS STATEMENTS

See whether you can support the following thesis statements with evidence from the text.

1. Dr. Faustus makes use of the powers granted him by Mephistopheles to satisfy his burning curiosity and to make humble a bumbling humanity.

2. The baseness of some of Dr. Faustus's acts is justified, for they are directed at people whose stupidity, disbelief, arrogance, and misuse of power make them fit subjects for a well-deserved comeuppance.

3. The evil of Dr. Faustus is not the abhorrent evil that might shock modern readers. It is rather the evil of the traditional theology of the sixteenth century. The punishment for this evil, too, is the traditional one and quite undeserved.

4. The tragedy of Dr. Faustus lies not in his seeking to penetrate the realm of deity but rather in his use of questionable moral means to reach his intellectual goals.

5. It is the admirable nature of Dr. Faustus's quest and the vehemance and eloquence of his protest against his fate that give him the exalted character of the tragic hero.

6. *Dr. Faustus* is a pessimistic statement about the futility of human aspiration.

7. Using the following definition, show that *Dr. Faustus* is a tragedy: "Tragedy arises when a man of noble character, knowing the good, chooses evil and is then moved inexorably to disaster. Having chosen evil, the man is powerless to change his decision, though there appear opportunities for him to do so."

8. Marlowe's *Dr. Faustus* is a flawed tragedy because the worthy doctor has finally repented and his descent into hell is an illogical conclusion to the events of the play.

9. None of Dr. Faustus's actions is so monstrously evil in terms of the values of the play as to make his punishment logically deserved.

10. Mephistopheles in *Dr. Faustus* is more than a symbolic messenger of Lucifer. He reveals a depth and a humanity that make him kin to Faustus. Faustus is a noble scholar tainted by evil movements within his soul. Mephistopheles is a wicked emissary from hell, ennobled by memories of divine goodness and moved by fleeting feelings of compassion.

11. The tragedy of Dr. Faustus is that of a man who would be God but who discovers that the trammels of being human cannot be shaken off and that man was born to die. What makes man great, therefore, is how he lives his life and how he dies.

Greek Comedy: Analysis of *The Frogs*

THE FROGS
Aristophanes (257?–180? B.C.)

STRUCTURE—SEQUENCE OF SCENES

1. The play begins with a slapstick exchange between Dionysus and his slave Xanthias about the weight Xanthias carries on his shoulders.

2. Dionysus meets Heracles. Dionysus plans to go down to Hades to bring Aeschylus back to Athens to restore a sense of purpose to the city. He seeks advice from Heracles, since Heracles has been to Hades, concerning how to get there most easily without harm to himself.

3. Heracles recommends three ways—hanging, poisoning, throwing oneself from a cliff—none of which is acceptable to Dionysus. The fourth way—crossing the river Styx—he finds satisfactory. Dionysus and Xanthias seek to hire a corpse to carry their traps down to Hades. The corpse turns them down because they are unwilling to pay the price the corpse demands for the service.

4. They meet Charon. Charon will ferry Dionysus across the Styx, but not Xanthias. Slaves are denied the privilege. Xanthias must go the circuitous way around the river.

5. On the boat trip across the Styx, Dionysus encounters the chorus of frogs. Dionysus joins the frogs in singing their raucous, ribald song. He complains that the trip is wearisome and is hard on his backside.

6. When Dionysus rejoins Xanthias, Xanthias asks him whether he saw any parricides or perjured folk on his journey across the Styx. Dionysus says no, but he points to the audience and says that he sees them all out there.

7. Dionysus and Xanthias are frightened by Empusa, a frightful hobgoblin, who has the power to change herself into many shapes and does so.

8. Dionysus and Xanthias now meet a chorus of mystics marching in a ritual that is part of the Eleusinian mysteries. The marchers sing hymns to Persephone, Demeter, and Iacchus (Dionysus). They warn off those who are evil from taking part in their worship.

9. Dionysus and Xanthias meet Aeacus, the doorkeeper to the hall of Hades. Because Dionysus wears the lion's skin of Heracles, Aeacus mistakes him for Heracles and reviles him for Heracles' malefactions in Hades when he was last there. Dionysus changes places with Xanthias to avoid punishment for Heracles's misdeeds. However, when a maidservant of Persephone offers the *new* Heracles the pleasures of Persephone's home, Dionysus assumes his original guise.

10. The hostess of a cook shop in Hades and her steward, Plathane, rail against the pseudo-Heracles for Heracles's gluttony and thievery on his previous visit to Hades, and again Dionysus wishes to change clothes with Xanthias.

11. Aeacus appears to thrash the make-believe Heracles. Dionysus insists he is a god and can feel no pain. To determine which of the two—Dionysus or Xanthias—is the god, Aeacus thrashes both. As they are beaten, neither cries out, both controlling their response to the pain and insisting they feel nothing.

12. At this point the chorus appears to recite the *parabasis*—a convention in Attic comedy involving a direct address to the audience, criticizing the ills of the state and the incompetence and corruptness of leaders and officials. The chorus addresses the audience and criticizes mainly the offering of the privileges of free men to a new class of the military.

13. Aeacus and Xanthias appear at this point to discuss the advantages of being slaves. Aeacus informs Xanthias that there will be a contest in Hades between the playwrights, Aeschylus and Euripides, to determine which of the two is the better tragic poet and therefore deserves a seat by the side of Hades in the assembly hall. The winner will also be brought back to Athens to restore the city to its earlier glory. Dionysus, who now drops his clownish demeanor and becomes more godlike, will be the judge.

14. The comedy now presents the *agon* or disputation between Aeschylus and Euripides. The two poets criticize one another's plays—subjects, themes, style, and so on. There are amusing parodies in this exchange.

AESCHYLUS'S ARGUMENTS

1. Aeschylus accuses Euripides of presenting scenes of incest on the stage.

2. He says Euripides as a writer is a chatterer.

3. He states that Euripides' influence upon people has been baleful. He found noble-hearted and virtuous men and women in the myths and altered them.

4. Aeschylus claims to have created noble heroes, not idle loafers, low buffoons, and rascally scamps.

5. Aeschylus says he wrote *The Persians,* which stirred the patriotism of his audience.

6. Aeschylus points out that a function of poets is to raise the quality of human beings.

7. He accuses Euripides of introducing harlotry into his plays. Euripides introduced love-sick women and dealt with adultery.

8. He claims that Euripides' plays led many a noble dame to suicide.

9. Aeschylus insists that certain human behavior should remain hidden from public view.

10. He claims that Euripides encourages young people to question the authority of masters and elders.

EURIPIDES' ARGUMENTS

1. Euripides states that Aeschylus brought figures on the stage who said not a word, but posed tragically. A chorus appeared, recited odes; the tragic figures never moved. This made the audience wonder when the characters would speak. When the tragic people finally spoke, they uttered words no one could understand. The images and symbols were obscure.

2. Euripides claims to have taught all the town to talk with freedom.

3. Euripides claims to have simplified the language of tragedies.

4. All characters in his plays, says Euripides, talked. This was an aspect of his democratic views.

5. Euripides claims that his pupils are finer writers than those of Aeschylus.

6. Euripides claims that he influenced his audience to look into the hearts of people and events.

7. To Euripides the purposes of the poet are to amuse with wit; to counsel wisely; to make better townspeople and worthier citizens.

8. Euripides asks whether his story of Phaedra was untrue, whether it is a distortion of reality for a woman to love her stepson.

9. He insists that Aeschylus is obscure even in the presentation of his events and facts.

10. Euripides states that he put on the stage experiences that came from daily life and from the relationships and conflicts of daily existence.

With which of the views of Aeschylus and Euripides do you agree? Support your views with evidence from plays you have read.

DISCUSSION QUESTIONS

1. According to Euripides, the playwright's purpose is threefold: (a) to amuse with wit (entertainment); (b) to counsel wisely (teaching); (c) to make better townspeople and worthier men and women (improvement of morals). Do you agree?

2. Dionysus and Xanthias are thrashed by Aeacus, doorkeeper for Hades. Since they claim to be gods, they pretend to feel no pain. Do you find this amusing? Why or why not?

3. Dionysus is one of the gods in the Greek pantheon. Is he treated with disrespect? If he is, why? Can you infer from this play that Aristophanes was an atheist?

4. In the *parabasis*, the chorus urges the Athenians to give their brethren back their franchise. Aristophanes thinks it a shame that slaves should be lords. He berates the neglect of native Athenians and the respect shown to strangers. What is Aristophanes complaining about? Are the criticisms voiced by the chorus satiric?

5. Aeschylus insists that certain human behavior or actions should be hidden from public view. Do you agree? What behavior or actions would you keep from public view? What is your view of censorship?

6. Euripides insists that scenes and experiences from everyday life belong on the stage. Do you agree? Why or why not? What aspects of everyday life would you omit? What aspects would you present? Isn't Euripides defending soap opera?

7. Aeschylus states that man, when presented on the stage, should appear heroic. What do you think he means by heroic? Can you mention any public figures whose actions you would characterize as heroic: for example, a soldier who confesses shooting civilians; a formerly powerful politician who defends himself against a charge of bribery; a woman who tries to "make a life" after the death of her famous husband? What characters in plays you have read do you consider heroic? Why?

8. Aeschylus says that idle loafers, low buffoons, and rascally scamps do not belong on a stage. Do you agree? Why or why not? Are Dionysus and Xanthias low buffoons? What do you think?

9. Euripides says that the writing of Aeschylus was bloated and swollen with turgid, gasconading words, haphazardly chosen. Is this a satirical statement? If you think it satirical, what makes it so?

10. Is the portrait of Dionysus in *The Frogs* satirical? If it is, what makes it so?

11. Is the portrait of Euripides in *The Frogs* satircal? If it is, what is being satirized?

12. Are the institutions and values of Athenian democracy being satirized? If they are, what techniques does Aristophanes use?

13. How would you describe the world of *The Frogs*—its beliefs, its values, its entertainments, its customs, its people?

14. Is *The Frogs* a comedy? Support your view with evidence from the play.

Restoration Comedy: Analysis of *The Way of the World*

THE WAY OF THE WORLD
William Congreve (1670–1729)

The Way of the World is an example of high comedy or the comedy of manners. Very little of consequence occurs in such a comedy. The entertainment comes from the humor and wit that pervade the work and from the satirical comment that the author makes about the foibles and foolishness of characters whose lives are empty and who fill this emptiness with social trivia.

A comedy of manners, like any play, follows the forms set for successful playwrighting, so that William Congreve needed to write a first act that established the tone of his play, that acquainted his audience with the antecedent action, that introduced his main characters, that gave the audience an inkling of the world of his play and its values, and, finally, that created the expectations (curiosity, dramatic interest, suspense) to coax the audience to continue viewing his play.

Read Act I of *The Way of the World*. The summary of Act I printed below will help you comprehend more clearly what happens in this act.

SUMMARY OF ACT I

Mirabell and Fainall have been playing cards. Fainall has been winning because Mirabell is distracted and is not paying attention to the game. They stop playing. Fainall guesses that Mirabell has quarrelled with Millament, whom he loves. Mirabell tells Fainall that his visit to Millament was interrupted by the appearance of Witwoud and Petulant and later by the appearance of Lady Wishfort, Mrs. Marwood, and three or four others. It was apparent that everyone wished Mirabell to leave, but he refused for awhile, sat quietly with the others, no one speaking, until direct hints from Lady Wishfort and Millament caused him to withdraw. (We learn that Millament's fortune depends upon her marrying with Lady Wishfort's approbation.) Fainall tells Mirabell that he had apparently barged in on one of the ladies' cabal nights when they gather to discuss the week's murdered reputations. All the male sex, with the exception of Witwoud and Petulant, is excluded. We learn also that Lady Wishfort is fifty-five, that Mirabell pretended to court her to conceal his love for her niece Millament, and that she had become quite angry with him upon discovering his deception. Mirabell describes all he did to flatter Lady Wishfort, but all his efforts came to naught when Mrs. Marwood, who apparently was his enemy, betrayed him. Fainall suggests that Mrs. Marwood's animosity was the result of Mirabell's indifference to her advances. Mirabell suggests that Mrs. Marwood has turned to Fainall for consolation. Fainall leaves to join Petulant and Witwoud in the next room. Betty, the waiting maid, who has stood by through this scene, tells Mirabell the time, and goes off to fetch him some hot chocolate. Mirabell's servant enters to announce that he was made sure Waitwell, Mirabell's servant, has married Foible, Lady Wishfort's maid. Fainall reappears with Betty. Fainall notices that Mirabell's good spirits have returned. Mirabell wonders why Fainall permits his wife to be a member of the women's cabal. Fainall says he is not jealous, certainly not of the male members, who are coxcombs. Mirabell is critical of Millament, and Fainall wonders how he could love her. Mirabell, in an amusing speech, describes how he studied Millament's faults, tried to hate her because of them, but instead came to love her all the more. Fainall says that Mirabell should marry Millament. (p. 393)[*]

A messenger arrives with a letter for Witwoud from his half-brother, Sir Wilfull. Mirabell learns from Fainall that Sir Wilfull Witwoud is expected in town that day. (We learn that Sir Wilfull's mother was Lady Wishfort's sister and that Mrs. Fainall is Lady Wishfort's daughter.) Sir Wilfull, who is over forty, plans to travel. Fainall and Mirabell dissect the character of Sir Wilfull, commenting on the impression he will make as an English traveler, on the mixture of bashfulness and obstinacy in his character, on one's being able to tolerate him now that he's begun to decay, and on his pretending to an understanding of raillery so that no insult angers him. Witwoud enters. He is irritated that his half-brother is coming to town. We learn he does not like Sir Wilfull and thinks him a fool. Mirabell and Fainall have fun with him, and there is an exchange of witty conversation about Witwoud's friend, Petulant, whom Witwoud considers to be something of a fool. Witwoud is not aware that Mirabell and Fainall are laughing at him, but many of the things he says *are* witty, and he defends Petulant against their criticisms of him. (p. 395)

A coachman calls for Petulant. We learn that in the coach are two strumpets and a bawd. They send for two cups of hot chocolate and a glass of cinnamon water. Witwoud comments on Petulant's penchant for a public to watch his actions. Petulant appears and complains about being called at all hours like a midwife. He refers to the ladies calling on him as empresses and later as two cousins and an old aunt. Betty announces that the ladies have left in anger. Petulant is not disturbed. Anger, he says, helps complexion, saves paint. Fainall believes that Petulant has refrained from joining the ladies to brag to Millament that he has abandoned the whole sex for her sake. Mirabell shows irritation at Petulant's waiting upon Millament. Petulant, in response, tells Mirabell that Mirabell's uncle is lately come to town. He has learned that Mirabell and his uncle are not friends and that, if the uncle marries and has a child, Mirabell may be disinherited. Mirabell wants to know what was said about his uncle at the women's cabal, and Petulant takes him aside to tell him. Fainall and

[*]All page references are to *Understanding Drama: Twelve Plays*, edited by Brooks and Heilman.

Witwoud talk about Witwoud's interest in Millament. Witwoud admires her because it is the fashion, but he will not break his heart for her. Witwoud says also that Mirabell's suit is in danger since Lady Wishfort is his enemy. Petulant has not had much to tell Mirabell. He compares himself with Witwoud, calling Witwoud a fine gentleman, but silly; he thinks of himself as witty, though malicious. They all plan to "take a turn before dinner." Mirabell asks Petulant to walk by himself because Petulant puts the ladies out of countenance with his senseless ribaldry. Petulant defends his vulgarity by suggesting that the ladies show their innocence by not understanding what they hear or else show their discretion by not hearing what they would not be thought to understand. Thus ends Act I.

Determine what expectations are aroused in you. You learn the following:

1. Except for Betty, who is a waiting maid and a minor character, none of the women appear in the first act. They are, however, talked about. Is your curiousity about the ladies aroused? Do you want to meet them? Which of the ladies are you most curious to meet? Why?

2. You learn that Mirabell loves Millament and that there are many obstacles in their way. Do you want to know what the obstacles are? Are you interested in learning whether or not they will marry by the play's end? Has the playwright aroused your interest sufficiently in Mirabell and Millament for you to want to learn what happens in their romance?

3. You learn that Fainall is married but that he and his wife have quarreled and are separated and that apparently he is involved in a liaison with a Mrs. Marwood, who hates Mirabell. Has the playwright piqued your curiosity about the difficulty between Fainall and his wife and about the reasons for Mrs. Marwood's negative feelings toward Mirabell? This is beginning to be a play of social and personal intrigues. Are you interested in the secret affairs of members of an upper-social leisure class? What qualities in such a play will arouse and keep your interest? Has the playwright introduced such qualities?

4. You learn that Waitwell has married Foible. The news brings joy to Mirabell. The playwright hopes that you will be interested in knowing why this marriage is good news for Mirabell.

5. A number of additional items of expectation are introduced in the first act. Has your curiosity been aroused by the following?

     a. Sir Wilfull is coming to town. You learn he is over forty and a man of rude manners. You wonder what part he will play in the intrigues.

     b. Two strumpets and a bawd call for Petulant. He sends them away. You meet Petulant, but you may want to know more about him. You wonder what kind of man he is. You would like to know why Petulant and Witwoud court Millament when it is obvious they do not love her.

     c. Finally, the playwright wants you to wonder what really happened between Lady Wishfort and Mirabell to make her Mirabell's enemy.

THE WORLD OF THE PLAY

In this first act, you are introduced to the world of this play. You learn that:

1. It is an artificial world, sophisticated and devious.
2. It is a society of intrigue, schemings, and complex relationships.
3. In this world people make an effort to be witty, shrewd, and cynical. They spice their conversation with epigrams and neat retorts.

4. It is a fashionable world in which the major activities of its members are dressing, gaming, gossiping, parading, and pursuing amours.
5. It is an upper-class world of fine ladies and idle gallants.
6. It is a world of coffeehouses and periwigs and elaborately formal dress.

As you read the rest of the play, see whether you can determine what the themes are. Make sure that you can support your conclusions with evidence from the play. One of the themes of the play is love. The play deals in part with variations on the theme of love.

1. The Fainalls had married without love: he, for money, she, to cover up an amour.
2. Lady Wishfort's chief concern is sex.
3. Fainall and Mrs. Marwood are engaged in an illicit relationship.
4. Mrs. Marwood's passion for Mirabell is unrequited.
5. Mrs. Fainall is aware that her former lover, Mirabell, is wooing Millament. She feels no jealousy, treats his action with equanimity.
6. To the bachelors in the play love is a fashion or a convenience. Emotion or involvement mars love.
7. Mirabell and Millament must seek a relationship that this society opposes. Though they are members of this society and play its games, they have enough character to seek depth and loyalty in a love relationship. The reader, as in *Pride and Prejudice*, measures the members of their world against the virtues of these two people.

You need to examine two more aspects of *The Way of the World.* Read the play to determine its comic elements and its satiric elements. Apply the standards enunciated in the sections on comedy and satire in your evaluation.

Analysis of
Rosencrantz and
Guildenstern
Are Dead

ROSENCRANTZ AND GUILDENSTERN ARE DEAD
  Tom Stoppard (1938–)

Below is a summary of *Rosencrantz and Guildenstern Are Dead* by Tom Stoppard. It is an excellent example of tragicomedy or dark comedy. Read the play and the summary. Do you agree with the views expressed in the discussion that follows the summary? How would you answer the questions included in the discussion?

SUMMARY OF THE PLAY
  Act I: Rosencrantz and Guildenstern are tossing coins. With every toss the coin comes up heads. Rosencrantz's money bag is getting full. The two men are disturbed by his phenomenon—the suspension of the law of probability. It is becoming a bore. Suspense no longer exists.

They discuss reasons why all coins come up heads. Guildenstern is willing it. Time has stopped dead. There is divine intervention. There is a vindication of the principle that each individual coin spins individually. "The scientific approach to the examination of phenomena is a defence against the pure emotion of fear."

Rosencrantz and Guildenstern, searching for an explanation to the phenomenon of coins coming up heads, suddenly realize that all this began at the moment when *they were sent for.*

Another phenomenon troubles them: "For the last three minutes on the wind of a windless day I have heard the sound of drums and flute." They talk of morbid trivia, possibly to keep from recognizing the truth. But the facts must be accepted. A messenger came. They were sent for. They have to hurry, fearful lest they come too late. They are troubled. They have been left in space, abandoned. They don't quite know where to go. They hear drums in the distance. Guildenstern talks about the mystical experience of seeing a unicorn.

Six tragedians appear. They are happy to have found an audience. Introducing themselves, Rosencrantz confuses himself with Guildenstern and introduces himself as Guildenstern. One player offers to perform anything, any kind of performance of any kind of play. (He thinks of the gentlemen as patrons.) He says, "It costs little to watch, and little more if you get caught up in the action." The player king offers to entertain Guildenstern and Rosencrantz with any kind of performance, including a pornographic one. Guildenstern becomes enraged and strikes the player. (Previously they had talked also about the element of chance in the players' lives and chance in their meeting with Rosencrantz and Guildenstern.)

Guildenstern suggests that he has influence at court and may arrange for the players to perform there. The player king describes what the tragedians do. "We do on stage the things that are supposed to happen off. Which is a kind of integrity, if you look on every exit being an entrance somewhere else."

Guildenstern and the player king toss coins. The coin falls heads at all times, and when the player king loses a toss, he is upset. Guildenstern invites the player king to bet that the year of his (Guildenstern's or the player's) birth doubled is even. The player king offers Alfred, one of the tragedians, to Guildenstern. Alfred hesitates to perform. Guildenstern calls upon the players to do a Greek play. The player king offers to do one of the blood, love, and rhetoric school. Guildenstern rejects Alfred's offer, an offer urged by the player king, of a performance with him. As the tragedians get ready to depart, the player king strikes a pose and does not move. He is always in character and always on. When he turns and goes, Rosencrantz finds Guildenstern's coin under his foot. It is tails.

At this point Ophelia and Hamlet appear on stage and do in mime the scene where Hamlet appears, apparently insane, in Ophelia's room. When Hamlet and Ophelia go off, Claudius and Gertrude appear to reenact with Rosencrantz and Guildenstern the scene where Claudius asks them to join the too much changed Hamlet and help to bring him back to sanity. When the court leaves, Rosencrantz tells Guildenstern he wants to go home. He feels out of step. What is happening is over his depth. Guildenstern reassures him: "There were always questions. To exchange one set for another is no great matter." Guildenstern talks about what truth is—"a permanent blur in the corner of your eye and something nudges it into outline. It is like being ambushed by a grotesque." A man called them and they came. Guildenstern says they are presented with alternatives but no chance. Rosencrantz cries, "Consistency is all I ask." He feels he has lost all sense of direction and wants to go home. Guildenstern realizes *they've been caught up.* "The smallest action sets off another somewhere else, as is set off by it." They must wear their daily mask.

Guildenstern and Rosencrantz try to establish what they are expected to do—draw Hamlet on to pleasures, glean what afflicts him. Then Rosencrantz asks, "What are you playing at?" Guildenstern answers, "Words, words. They're all we have to go on." They experience a sense of alienation, not knowing what to do. Guildenstern says, "What a fine persecution—to be kept intrigued without being enlightened."

They play a game of questions. (Life is a game of questions in which words like *love* and *God* play prominent rhetorical parts. The rules are unknown.) Hamlet appears reading a book and goes off. Guildenstern suggests that he (Guildenstern) play Hamlet and that Rosencrantz ask the questions to glean what afflicts the prince. After some confusion, Rosencrantz understands what is expected of him. They review the facts of the elder Hamlet's death, Claudius's usurpation of the throne, and the queen's too-hasty marriage. This is general knowledge. What is there to glean from Hamlet? Hamlet appears with Polonius, and a scene from Shakespeare's play is about to be enacted. Hamlet turns, sees his friends, and greets them as he does in the play.

Act II: The act begins with a continuation of the scene from *Hamlet.* Guildenstern presents the players to Hamlet. When Rosencrantz and Guildenstern are alone, they discuss the conversation with Hamlet. He asked twenty-seven questions. They asked three; answered nineteen. As Rosencrantz says, he (Hamlet) murdered them. They review the information they got from him. Hamlet's comment on "space direction" leads them to a long discussion of where north, south, east, west are. They realize that they have lost all sense of direction and they really do not know where they are. Guildenstern says: "Wheels have been set in motion, and they have their own pace to which we are . . . condemned. Each move is dictated by the previous one—that is the meaning of order. If we start being arbitrary, it'll just be a shambles."

Rosencrantz yells "fire" at the audience to demonstrate the use of free speech. Guildenstern says that they crossed their bridges and burnt them behind them, with nothing to show for their progress except a memory of the smell of smoke, and a presumption that "once our eyes watered." Rosencrantz and Guildenstern play again with coins. They are interrupted by Polonius and Hamlet, who appear with the players. Hamlet is planning the performance of *The Murder of Gonzago.* All leave except Rosencrantz, Guildenstern, and the player king. Rosencrantz and Guildenstern threaten the player. He berates them for not appearing at a performance he had prepared to show them on the way. He says, "You don't understand the humiliation of it—to be tricked out of the single assumption that makes our existence viable—that somebody is watching." (Does man expect God to be watching?)

The player states that anything—anything—Rosencrantz and Guildenstern think or do, *he saw them do it.* (Now the player is God.) Rosencrantz tells the player he lies. The player continues describing in detail the agony of performing before nobody. Guildenstern tells the player they have made up for their neglect. They have brought the players to the court. Rosencrantz tells the player that he and Guildenstern expect that the performances will take Hamlet "out of himself." He warns the player to give Hamlet a good, clean, family show. (Rosencrantz and Guildenstern seem to abhor pornography.)

The player tells Rosencrantz and Guildenstern he has performed for Hamlet before, that Hamlet likes classical plays, but that this time he will perform *The Murder of Gonzago.* Rosencrantz and Guildenstern are afraid to let the player leave. He warns them to "concentrate on not losing their heads." Guildenstern tells him that they have been left too much to their own devices and that they don't know how to act. The player answers that no one really knows anything, that "truth is only that which is taken to be true. It's the currency of living. . . . One acts on assumptions." They discuss whether Hamlet is mad and, if he is, what the cause is. (The dialogue is confused as they probe for answers.)

The player finally leaves. They can't force him to stay. They are again alone—and lost. They talk about the unusual behavior of the coin. Rosencrantz talks about death and the horror of being in a box. "Life in a box is better than no life at all." He believes no one cares. He and Guildenstern count for nothing. He continues talking wildly, recording a few anecdotes, but the point of his frenzied remarks is that they are being taken for granted. No one notices them. (He has talked about the moment in childhood when one realizes he is mortal.) Guildenstern says, "Death followed by eternity—the worst of both worlds. It is a terrible thought."

The king, the queen, Polonius, and Ophelia enter. Rosencrantz and Guildenstern are queried about Hamlet's behavior and inform the king about the play. They are again left alone. They see Hamlet approaching. Hamlet is lost in thought (on suicide). Rosencrantz contemplates approaching the prince to ask him what it's all about. But Ophelia enters and Hamlet approaches her. Hamlet and Ophelia go off. Again, for a moment, Rosencrantz and Guildenstern are alone. A female figure enters, ostensibly the queen. Rosencrantz put his hands over her eyes and says desperately, "Guess who?" It turns out to be Alfred. When the player, who has also appeared, puts a foot down, Rosencrantz places his hand under it and blames the player for stepping on his hand. (This is a desperate effort to be *recognized*.) Soon they are surrounded by players getting ready for a dress rehearsal.

The players perform the dumb-show. The player king explains why the dumb-show comes first. In the midst of the rehearsal—at the end of the mime—Hamlet and Ophelia appear, Hamlet insulting Ophelia and telling her to go to a nunnery. Claudius and Polonius come in after Hamlet has run off. They speak to Ophelia, and they, too, go off. Rosencrantz had made a gesture to console Ophelia, but she had slipped away. Guildenstern warns Rosencrantz to keep back; they are spectators.

The players make ready to continue rehearsal. The play has not yet ended, says the player king, since everyone is still on his feet. The player king comments on tragedy and on the fact that all that happens "has been written." No choice is involved. (Since life ends in death, life is a tragedy.)

As the tragedians perform, the player king provides a commentary for Rosencrantz and Guildenstern. Rosencrantz objects to a scene of passion between the murderer and the queen. They witness a stylized performance of the closet scene and of the murder of Polonius, and they see enacted, also in mime, their participation in the king's treachery against Hamlet and their execution in England. There is talk about death in real life and death performed on the stage. Guildenstern insists that death cannot be acted. To him "death is not gasps and blood and falling about. It's just a man failing to reappear."

The player spies are dead; the orders in their message to the king of England, changed by Hamlet, are carried out. The player king throws their cloaks over their bodies. It is in this way that Rosencrantz and Guildenstern learn what is to become of them.

We find ourselves for a moment in *Hamlet*. Claudius stops the performance. The spies are now Rosencrantz and Guildenstern, who rise. They are alone. Rosencrantz stares out into the audience. The questions are where is east and what the audience is expecting them to do. Claudius appears, tells them that Hamlet has murdered Polonius, and urges them to find Hamlet, who has dragged the body off. They cannot decide which way to go. But one thing is clear; they must not separate. Finally, they decide to stay where they are and bar Hamlet's way. They tie their belts together to serve as a barrier. Hamlet enters, dragging

Polonius's body, makes an arc, and leaves the way he came. (Rosencrantz and Guildenstern have talked about the indifference to Polonius's death.) Hamlet appears again, this time to insult Rosencrantz for being the king's sponge. Rosencrantz and Guildenstern don't know what he's talking about. Hamlet walks off. The king appears. They tell him they can't get from Hamlet where the body is bestowed. The king orders Rosencrantz to bring Hamlet before him. Rosencrantz turns to Guildenstern in helplessness. They are saved embarrassment when Hamlet appears, escorted by soldiers. All the characters go off, leaving Rosencrantz and Guildenstern alone again. They don't understand what is going on, but one thing is clear: they're taking Hamlet to England.

They see Hamlet talking to a soldier. Soon the two appear, Hamlet asking the soldier whose army it is landing on Denmark's shores and where they're going. Rosencrantz and Guildenstern talk about the coldness of the coming autumn. They hear the faint sound of the tragedians' band. Hamlet is lost in thought. Knowing that they're going somewhere, a place from which they may never return, they feel a sense of trepidation. The one comfort is that where they go there will be the same sky.

Act III: Rosencrantz and Guildenstern talk in pitch darkness. They realize that, since they can talk and think and feel, therefore they must be alive. Sailors' shouts tell them they're on a ship. Soon the deck is lit up by a lantern and possibly the moon. There are three casks and a large umbrella on the deck. Guildenstern says, "I've lost all capacity for disbelief." There is too much night on the boat. They talk about the feeling of freedom on a boat. Rosencrantz gets sick and turns to the other side of the boat. Guildenstern realizes that they are the bearers of a letter from one king to another and are taking Hamlet to England. Rosencrantz has discovered Hamlet asleep.

They've had trouble sleeping. They're still worried over what it's all about. They play a game where Guildenstern tries to guess in which hand Rosencrantz holds a coin. Guildenstern wins all the time because Rosencrantz has coins in both hands, his way of trying to make Guildenstern happy.

The king has given them both money, each the same amount. They quarrel, Rosencrantz almost bursts into tears, and Guildenstern is sorry. (Rosencrantz has come to depend on Guildenstern, the dominating personality.) They wonder what will happen in England and remember they have a letter. For a moment they think it is lost, but Guildenstern finds it in his pocket. Rosencrantz cannot picture in his mind what will happen when they arrive in England. The thoughts trouble him:

> We drift down time clutching at straws.
> We might as well be dead. Do you think death could possibly be a boat?
> No, no, no. . . . Death is the ultimate negative. Not-being. You can't not-be on a boat.

They realize that they can't question, can't doubt. They perform. And Rosencrantz insists that he wants put on record that he has no confidence in England. Rosencrantz plays the king of England. They imagine the conversation that might occur when they arrive. In the excitement of the play acting, they open the letter and discover they are taking Hamlet to England to be beheaded. Rosencrantz says in wonder, "We're his friends." Guildenstern rationalizes about the virtues of death—"a release from the burden of life and for the godly, a haven and a reward." He says that it would be presumptuous of them to interfere with the designs of fate or even of kings. It is best to leave well enough alone. He suggests tying up the letter neatly. The broken seal will not be noticed. Rosencrantz insists, "He's done nothing to us," and Guildenstern, relieved, says, "It could have been worse."

Hamlet awakens, appears behind them, and goes to the lantern. Rosencrantz reviews their story from the moment they were sent for to the present. Hamlet blows out the lantern. The stage is black. It is then lit by moonlight. Rosencrantz and Guildenstern are asleep. Hamlet takes the letter from them, disappears behind the umbrella for a while, emerges, replaces the letter, and goes off.

Morning comes. Rosencrantz is up. Hamlet is sitting behind him in a deck chair reading. The morning brightens to high noon. Rosencrantz is perturbed. He reviews how they got the letter, looking for meaning to what has happened. They hear the sound of a recorder. "A thing like that, it could change the course of events." They investigate and discover the sound comes from one of the casks. They soon discover that all the tragedians are in the three casks, even Alfred, who comes out last. They are all garbed in the costumes of *The Murder of Gonzago,* the play they never finished enacting. The player king informs them that the tragedians are running away because their play had offended the king. The player king asks Guildenstern what he makes of all that has happened thus far. Guildenstern asserts that *they are free,* that they have *blundered* into a release.

Hamlet walks down to the footlights, spits out at the audience. It is the wrong side of the boat, and so he gets saliva back in his eye. He goes back upstage. Rosencrantz and Guildenstern summarize the symptoms of Hamlet's antic behavior. They also review how the tragedians got on the boat: "Incidents! All we get is incidents! Dear God, is it too much to expect a little sustained action?"

Pirates attack. All draw swords, including the player king. There is the sound of battle. Hamlet, Rosencrantz, Guildenstern, and the player king jump into the three barrels. When it is quiet, Rosencrantz and Guildenstern and the player king come out of the barrels. One barrel is missing—as is Hamlet. Rosencrantz and Guildenstern are upset. They need Hamlet for their release. Nothing can be resolved without him. "We've traveled too far and our momentum has taken over. We move idly toward eternity without possibility of reprieve or hope or explanation."

England is now a dead end. Again, they reenact what will happen when they face the king of England and again they produce the letter. This time they discover that the king is asked to put *them* to sudden death. The player king gets to his feet, walks over to his barrel, kicks it, and announces "They've gone! It's all over!" The players emerge and form a menacing circle around Rosencrantz and Guildenstern, who are appalled and mesmerized. They talk about where they went wrong. "Who'd have thought that we were so important?" Why were they told so little?

The player king tells them most things end in death. This arouses Guildenstern's scorn. He snatches the dagger from the player's belt, deriding the actor's playing of death. "No one gets up after death. There is only silence and some second hand clothes." And he pushes the blade into the player king's throat. The tragedians watch the player king die. When he finally lies still, they applaud, and the player rises to accept the adulation. It is the only death the audience believes in, a death capped by a resurrection. As the player king declaims on the variety of deaths the stage can offer, the players reenact the deaths in Shakespeare's *Hamlet,* including those of Rosencrantz and Guildenstern. Guildenstern says no. This is not the death for them. Dying is not romantic. It is not a game. "It is the endless time of never coming back."

Rosencrantz and Guildenstern are left alone. "What was it all about?" they wonder. *"There must have been a time where we could have said no. But somehow we missed it."* They disappear. The stage lights up on the last scene of *Hamlet.* Everyone is dead except Horatio, who holds the dead Hamlet in his arms; Fortinbras, who will be the new king; and two ambassadors from England, who have come to report to Claudius that his commandment for the execution of Rosencrantz and Guildenstern has been carried out. Horatio, thinking the report was intended for Hamlet rather than for Claudius, insists that the prince "never gave commandments for their deaths." He promises to explain how all the carnage came about.

The World of *Rosencrantz and Guildenstern Are Dead*

The world is a normal place for Rosencrantz and Guildenstern until the summons from King Claudius calls them to the palace at Elsinore. Then things begin to happen because they are pushed into the roles of spectators. The laws of probability are suspended. They are lost in space, abandoned, waiting. They have no sense of direction. The world becomes for them a *place* of questions for which there are no answers. Living becomes a *game* of questions in which words like *love* and *God* play prominent roles. But words have no reality. There are no truths, only assumptions.

Wheels are set in motion at a particular pace to which Rosencrantz and Guildenstern are condemned. They lose identity. They lose contact with others and see themselves reflected in a group of players who have no reality and therefore no existence since they reenact in repetition what appear to be, but in truth are not, the incidents of life.

The players, too, function in vast space. They seek an audience, but in reality they never find one. Their permanent agony is to perform before nobody. Like the three embittered souls in Sartre's *No Exit,* their punishment for entering the stage of life (or death) is to reenact the same scenes over and over. Their living is a repetition of dull routine; their humanity is a veneer with no substance; their dying is followed by a resurrection that means that they must make ready to die again. Since they are not truly alive but only appear to be, their dying is meaningless, their return to life, meaningless. Nobody sees or knows they exist. Nobody cares.

The plight of Rosencrantz and Guildenstern is reflected by the players except that, being more than actors, their dying is a disappearance into the nothingness from which they appeared. Resurrection is not for them. Their exit on one stage is not for them an entrance upon another.

Rosencrantz and Guildenstern struggle to find identity, to be noticed. Rosencrantz places his hand under the player king's foot. He places his hands over the player queen's eyes. He moves toward the weeping Ophelia in a gesture to console her. But all move away from him. He is not noticed.

Both Rosencrantz and Guildenstern attempt to question Hamlet. They are desperate to discover meaning in their lives, but they are verbally annihilated by him. Not knowing the nature of their mission, they are confused and upset by his insulting remarks. They are troubled by a moral problem. They carry a message to England ordering their friend's death. But not knowing what is going on, they can do nothing about it. Having been thrust into the roles of spectators, they are incapable—it is not in their lifelines—of tearing up the letter. When they learn later that the message they carry orders *their* death, they are puzzled, shocked; but here, too, they can do nothing about it. They accept the event as an incident among the other incidents that shape their formless lives. And they disappear, leaving the tableau that completes Shakespeare's *Hamlet* on the stage, with Horatio promising to explain, as if it were possible, how their deaths came to be.

Rosencrantz and Guildenstern ponder about death and talk about it. They say death is not gasps and blood but just a man failing to reappear. It is not-being, the ultimate negative. It is a disappearance that troubles them. In fact, one of them says that life in a box is better than no life at all. But their destiny is to disappear, to leave not the slightest trace of their ever having had being.

During the play, they wonder about their place in the universe and the opportunities that were available to them to change the sequence of their lives. Was there a time when they could have said *no*? Where and when do you say *no* when your life has no order, no sequence, no meaning?

DISCUSSION QUESTIONS

The play is subtle and ambiguous. The summary should help you understand it better. Here are some problems for you to work on in connection with interpreting the play.

1. To what extent is the play a comedy? Select scenes and dialogue that you consider comic. What elements of the comic do these passages contain?

2. To what extent is the play a tragedy? If it is a tragedy, it is not a tragedy of noble men or common men, but a tragedy of all men who are nonentities, spectators in the play of life. Do Rosencrantz and Guildenstern have any of the characteristics of tragic heroes? Can people who suffer and die because they are caught up by events beyond their comprehension and control be considered tragic? Rosencrantz and Guildenstern are not pathetic creatures. They do not ask for pity. By probing to comprehend who they are and what they are and by trying to determine their place in the cosmic scheme, they win the affection of the audience. Yet their deaths do not move the audience deeply. Is it that the play is too intellectual? Is it that Stoppard succeeds in making them puppets, like the players? Is it that their calm acceptance of their fate cancels the pain of their disappearance? Is it that disappearance is less traumatic for an audience to view than violent or painful death?

3. Can you find evidence to support the conclusion that the play is a tragicomedy or a dark comedy or an existential tragedy? Can you compose, on the basis of the introduction to the play and the discussion that follows the summary, a definition of existential tragedy? Can you show how this play is such a tragedy?

4. What function, in your view, do the players perform in the play? Do they do more than reflect and clarify the situation of Rosencrantz and Guildenstern? What significance can you draw from the various scenes in which they appear?

5. What is your interpretation of the play? Read the sample composition below comparing *Oedipus Rex* and *Rosencrantz and Guildenstern Are Dead*. Do you agree with the interpretation? Is the play concerned with what is truth? How? Does it deal with the condition of the contemporary human being? What view of the relationship of man and God does it present?

From Sophocles to Stoppard

Over two thousand years separate Sophocles' *Oedipus Rex* and Tom Stoppard's *Rosencrantz and Guildenstern Are Dead,* yet these two works both shed brilliant light on the theme of man's search for truth about himself. A careful examination of both dramatists and their respective works will convince even the staunchest conservative that writers of the past do not necessarily excel the best writers of the present. It is more likely, however, that most literary critics will agree that literature of one era cannot justly be placed on the same scale of values as literature of another era without adequate adjustments in frames of reference.

In *Oedipus Rex* the underlying theme is of course man's search for truth, and it is brilliantly accented by the metaphor of light and dark, sight and blindness, truth and deception. From the very beginning of the play, we witness Oedipus' fierce and almost fanatic search for truth. *Oedipus Rex* is in fact simply a stream of interrogations held together by the cement of strophe and antistrophe. Oedipus is the prosecuting attorney at, what he fails to realize, is his own trial. He systematically questions Creon, Teiresias, Jocasta, the messenger, and the shepherd. By the middle of the play he senses some ominous revelations about to descend upon him, but he relentlessly forges onward. Several times he comes close to finding the answer he wants but just as quickly his moral blindness temporarily returns. Finally, when the awful truth is at hand, Jocasta begs Oedipus not to continue but he insists that the truth must be found. At the end of the play the oracles are proven correct, and Teiresias's prediction that the truth will ruin Oedipus has been shown to be valid. Man's search for truth in *Oedipus Rex,* then, leads to physical blindness, but also to a great moral illumination that serves as compensation.

In *Rosencrantz and Guildenstern Are Dead,* Tom Stoppard examines the problem of man's search for truth about himself in a more subtle way. While Oedipus realizes, in an abstract way, what he is looking for, Rosencrantz and Guildenstern never do. Yet questions and quests remain strong themes in Stoppard's play. Both protagonists feel that they are "entitled to some direction." They sense they have a mission and that there must be some reason why they were awakened by a messenger and called to Elsinore. Similarly, their search for truth encompasses the quest for their own identity since they themselves, as much as others at court, confuse their names "Rosencrantz" and "Guildenstern." Just as the interrogations play a major role in Oedipus's search, Rosencrantz and Guildenstern play "question games," too. The questions are answered with more questions, and the search for truth becomes more tragic as it becomes increasingly less fruitful. Of course, one of the most obvious truths that Rosencrantz and Guildenstern are looking for is the source of Hamlet's antic disposition. Unfortunately, the far-from-mad Hamlet learns more from them than they do from him. Ultimately, the search for truth on the part of Stoppard's antiheroes leads to their own disappearances (as opposed to deaths). The audience faces a dark stage, and the Stoppardian message is that there is not truth in this existential world.

After this brief examination of both plays and their respective treatments of the same theme, it becomes even more difficult to compare the two as far as literary value is concerned.

Oedipus Rex is a classic, and two thousand years of worldwide performances testify to this fact. The problems of Oedipus are universal and independent of time, and the artistic, literary, and psychological value of this Greek tragedy is infinite.

Oddly enough, however, modern audiences may react to Stoppard's *Rosencrantz and Guildenstern Are Dead* in an even more enthusiastic manner. True, *Oedipus Rex* is a classic; yet precisely because of this, audience identification will be stronger toward Rosencrantz and Guildenstern than toward Oedipus. This is perhaps so because Stoppard has brought tragedy to the Willy Loman type of "common" man while Sophocles confines himself to kings. Furthermore, *Rosencrantz and Guildenstern Are Dead* is a play for our industrialized, automatized, itemized mass-producing world. The identity crisis of Stoppard's heroes is peculiarly modern. Because of all these factors, *Rosencrantz and Guildenstern Are Dead* is, by modern standards, as excellent as *Oedipus Rex*.

Traditionalists may argue that *Oedipus Rex* is a classic and *Rosencrantz and Guildenstern Are Dead* may hardly survive this decade. The answer to this is, of course, that longevity is more a measure of excellence than old age is a measure of wisdom. Putting this debate aside, however, one must conclude that great writers of one century are not competing in some sort of literary Kentucky Derby with great writers of another century. Literature transcends scaler measurements of excellence. Works of literature must be judged according to different criteria, and each should be examined individually for its own unique message. Asking for more than this is like asking whether prose "excels" poetry, or sciences "excel" humanities. Great writers, fortunately, can be found in all centuries.

Analysis of *Waiting for Godot*	WAITING FOR GODOT *Samuel Beckett* (1906–1989)

THE WORLD OF *WAITING FOR GODOT*

The barren, denuded universe in *Waiting for Godot* may be a particularly difficult one for you to enter. To grasp the basic timelessness and placelessness of the play, consider the concept of cultural erasure. Think of a pen and ink drawing, and imagine a simple black outline of a city skyline in back of a beautiful tree-laden park. If an artist were to color in the blue of the sky, the green of the grass, and so on, this could be an analogy to a play with its own culture, location, and environment. Try to recollect the specific worlds of some other plays that you have read. If, however, the artist took an eraser and removed all the color in the sketch, you would see the mere black outline. This sketch is akin to the dramatic universe in *Waiting for Godot*. In the analogy, the world in Beckett's drama, unlike the worlds of most other plays, is static and barren, devoid of culture or background.

Waiting for Godot is about two men with a pointless existence who do nothing in their lives except wait. But the subject matter itself produces the nonaction in the play. We see Vladimir and Estragon alive, feeling human emotions and functions, but their world is not alive. It consists only of a bare stage with a lone tree and a remote ditch. In fact, this is almost a nonworld, an ontological void, an echo of Vladimir's repeated line "Nothing to be done." At one point in the play, Lucky, the semihuman servant of Pozzo, indulges in a cryptic, garbled speech about mankind. He draws a distinction between the Latin words *essy* and *possy*. These two help to explain one of the central conflicts in the play. Vladimir and Estragon live in *essy* (to be, or merely to exist), so to speak, rather than in *possy* (to be able to, or to effect action). All they do in the play is wait. Like the "hollow men" in T. S. Eliot's famous poem, they are inactive, inert, and bored. The most powerful notion of the drama centers on the fact that, in spite of Vladimir and Estragon's deadly passivity, they *want* to continue living in their wretched, barren world. As one critic states, "It is *not despite* the pointlessness of their life that Vladimir and Estragon want to go on living, but, on the contrary, *just because* their life has become so pointless—by which I mean that, ruined by their habit of inaction or of acting without their own initiative, they have lost their will power to decide not to go on, their freedom to end it all. Or, ultimately, they go on living merely because they happen to exist, and because existence doesn't know of any other alternative but to exist."[*]

The action of the play is quite simple. In Act I Vladimir and Estragon discuss their lives while waiting for Godot; Pozzo and Lucky appear onstage and interact with Vladimir and Estragon; Pozzo and Lucky leave; a messenger from Godot appears and leaves; and then Vladimir and Estragon resolve to continue to wait. In Act II, the exact same series of events unfolds. Thus, you must understand not only the barren universe of the play, but also the barren actions of the play. In fact, the only action is that of waiting, which is not action at all. The fact that Vladimir and Estragon wait for Godot is not nearly as important as that they merely wait. To interpret who or what Godot represents becomes an unfruitful task because he never arrives. Beckett himself stated that he is more concerned with "waiting" than he is with "Godot." Vladimir and Estragon open the play in utter hopelessness and futility, and they end the play on the same note.

> End of Act I:
> *Estragon:* Well, shall we go?
> *Vladimir:* Yes, let's go.
> *They do not move.*   Curtain
>
> End of Act II:
> *Vladimir:* Well, shall we go?
> *Estragon:* Yes, let's go.
> *They do not move.*   Curtain

(The fact that Beckett interchanges between the players the question and the unfulfilled response only serves to underscore the futility of the play.)

Ironically, Godot's nonarrival keeps the two waiting for him, and keeps their faith in him alive.

> *Estragon:* Let's go.
> *Vladimir:* We can't.
> *Estragon:* Why not?
> *Vladimir:* We're waiting for Godot.
> *Estragon:* Ah.
>
> (p. 31b-Act I, repeated on
> p. 45b-Act II)[**]

Vladimir's and Estragon's inaction is so overpowering that Estragon cannot ever remember that they are waiting.

---

[*]Gunther Anders, "Being Without Time: On Beckett's Play *Waiting for Godot*," *Samuel Beckett: A Collection of Critical Essays,* ed. M. Esslin (Englewood Cliffs: Prentice-Hall, Inc., 1965), p. 143.
[**]Alaine Robbe-Grillet, "Samuel Beckett or Presence in the Theater," *Samuel Beckett: A Collection of Critical Essays,* ed. M. Esslin (Englewood Cliffs: Prentice-Hall, Inc., 1965), p. 109.

The incredible impact of the play is evident in its ability to capture an audience for nearly three hours. The plot, such as it is, can be summed up in the following passage from a critical appraisal of the play by Alaine Robbe-Grillet.*

Act I: The set conveys nothing, or practically nothing. A road? Just "out of doors," rather. The only specific object is a tree, and not much of a tree at that— a skeleton tree, stunted and without a single leaf.

Two men are on the stage. They are without age, profession, or family background. They have no home to go to, are tramps, in short. Physically, they seem to be relatively unscathed. One takes off his boots; the other talks of the Gospels. They eat a carrot. They have nothing to say to each other. They address each other by two diminutives, Gogo and Didi, which do not suggest any identifiable names.

They look first to the left, then to the right. They pretend to go, to leave each other, but they always come back to each other in the middle of the stage. They can't go away; they are waiting for someone called Godot, about whom we know nothing except that he will not come. That at least is clear to everyone from the beginning.

So no one is surprised when a boy arrives (Didi thinks he is the one who came yesterday) with a message: "Mr. Godot told me to tell you he won't come this evening but surely tomorrow." Then the light suddenly fails. It is night. The two tramps decide to go away and come back again the next day. But they do not move. The curtain falls.

Earlier, two characters have appeared to create a diversion: Pozzo, of flourishing aspect, and Lucky, his decrepit servant, whom he drives along in front of him by means of a rope tied around his neck. Pozzo sits down on a camp stool, eats a leg of cold chicken, and smokes a pipe. Then he delivers a highly colored description of the twilight. Lucky, on the word of command, executes a few shambles by way of a "dance" and gabbles an incomprehensible speech made up of stammerings and stutterings and disconnected fragments.

Act II: The next day. But is it really the next day? Or after? Or before? At any rate the décor is the same, except for one detail: the tree now has four or five leaves. Didi sings a song about a dog that comes into the kitchen and steals a crust of bread. The dog is killed and buried, and on his tomb is written:

> A dog came in the kitchen
> And stole a crust of bread.
> Then cook up with a ladle
> And beat him till he was dead.

Gogo puts on his boots, eats a radish, and so on. He doesn't remember having been there before.

Pozzo and Lucky return. Lucky is dumb, Pozzo blind and remembering nothing. The same little boy comes back with the same message: "Mr. Godot won't come this evening but he'll come tomorrow." No, the boy doesn't know the two tramps; he has never seen them before.

Once more it is night. Gogo and Didi would like to try to hang themselves— the branches of the tree ought to be strong enough. Unfortunately, they haven't a suitable bit of rope. They decide to go away and come back again the next day. But they do not move. The curtain falls.

---

*All page references are to Samuel Beckett, *Waiting for Godot,* published by Grove Press. A number alone means a left-hand page, a number with a "b" means a right-hand page.

The play is called *Waiting for Godot,* and it lasts nearly three hours. This in itself is astonishing. The play "holds" for the whole three hours without a hiatus although it is made up out of nothingness, holds without faltering although it might seem to have no reason either for going on or for coming to an end. The audience is caught from the beginning to the end. They may be disconcerted sometimes, but they remain riveted to these two beings who do nothing, say practically nothing, have no property but that of being there.

You might try to compare the empty, hollow futility evident in Beckett's play with other works of literature you have read that deal with apathy, boredom, and hopelessness. By keeping these in mind, you may be prepared to enter the static world of nonaction in *Godot* without being tempted to pass it off as totally boring.

AFFECTIVE DATA
1. Sense of an external world (p. 7 ff.)
2. A unit of past time (7b, 12b, ff.)
3. Allusion to *Proverbs* 13:12 (8)
4. The tree plot (8, 10, 40, ff.)
5. The hat plot and the shoe plot (7, 8, 10, ff.)
6. Discussion of two thieves (9)
7. Repetition of the phrase "Waiting for Godot"
8. Religious allusions (11, ff.)
9. Vladimir and Estragon discuss hanging themselves (12, 50–60)—introduction and conclusion
10. The carrot-turnip plot (14)
11. The rope plot
12. Constant changes and falls from vertical stature
13. Pozzo's discourse on twilight (25, 26)
14. The Lucky speech (28b, ff.)
15. The goat-sheep issue (32)
16. Action of the messenger (32, 33)
17. The moon and boots episode (34)
18. The boots and Christ episode (34b)
19. Vladimir gives his coat to Estragon (45b)
20. The Cackon-Macon episode (40)
21. The Pozzo vision (57b)
22. The Vladimir vision (58b)
23. Concluding hanging episode (59–60)
24. Is Godot anthropomorphic?
25. Significance of the names

This list of affective data is by no means exhaustive. But each of the above serves to affect the audience or the reader in some way, whether it is speech, action, symbol, character trait—whatever. If you can come to understand the meaning of each item on this list, you will grasp the profound meaning of Beckett's play.

You can set out to discover the many subtleties of the play on your own after reading some sample explications of certain of the listed data. First, you should peruse the play thoroughly and catalogue in writing every reference to the particular item. Second, after gathering the textual data, try to summarize why the playwright employs particular devices.

For a highly intricate network of references such as the tree, the hat, and shoes, or the sense of an external world, all of which appear many times throughout the text, you should sense just how subtle and consistent Beckett's play really is. From the list you compile, you can probably begin to grapple with the meaning of the pattern of references and begin to generalize about Beckett's purpose in developing them. Consider the following example about *Affective Data 1:* Sense of an external world.

The play's universe consists of the stage, a tree, and two people, Vladimir and Estragon. But, there is evidence of an external world.

Page 7: Enter Vladimir

Vladimir: May one inquire where His Highness spent the night?

Estragon: In a ditch.

Vladimir: A ditch! Where?

Estragon: (without gesture) Over there.

Vladimir: And they didn't beat you?

Estragon: Beat me? Certainly they beat me.

Vladimir: The same lot as usual?

Estragon: The same? I don't know.

Page 7b:

Vladimir: Hand in hand from the top of the Eiffel Tower, among the first. We were respectable in those days. Now it's too late. They wouldn't even let us up.

Page 8:

Vladimir: Hope deferred maketh the something sick, who said that?

Page 8b:

Estragon: I remember the maps of the Holy Land. Coloured they were. Very pretty. The Dead Sea was pale blue. The very look of it made me thirsty. That's where we'll go, I used to say, that's where we'll go for our honeymoon. We'll swim. We'll be happy.

Page 9:

Vladimir: You should have been a poet.

Estragon: I was.

Pages 9 and 9b:

Vladimir tells the story of the two thieves.

Page 11b:

Estragon: Calm . . . calm . . . The English say cawm. (He tells Vladimir the story of the Englishman in the brothel.)

Page 15:

Enter Pozzo and Lucky

Page 16b:

Pozzo: Yes, the road seems long when one journeys all alone. For . . . yes, six hours, that's right, six hours on end, and never a soul in sight.

Page 21:

Pozzo: But instead of driving him away as I might have done, I mean instead of simply kicking him out on his arse, in the goodness of my heart I am bringing him to the Fair, where I hope to get a good price for him.

Page 22:

Pozzo: Let us not then speak ill of our generation, it is not any unhappier than its predecessors. Let us not speak well of it either. Let us not speak of it at all. It is true the population has increased.

Pages 23 and 23b:

Vladimir: Charming evening we're having.
Estragon: Unforgettable.
Vladimir: It's only beginning.
Estragon: It's awful.
Vladimir: Worse than the pantomime.
Estragon: The circus.
Vladimir: The music-hall.

Page 26:

Estragon: Even ten francs would be a help.

Page 27:

Pozzo: He used to dance the farandole, the fling, the brawl, the jig, the fandango and even the hornpipe.

Pages 28b–29b:
Lucky's speech

Page 31:

Pozzo: I must have left it at the manor.

Page 31b:
Exit Lucky and Pozzo

Pages 32–34:
Conversation with messenger

Page 34b:

Vladimir: But you can't go barefoot!
Estragon: Christ did.
Vladimir: Christ! What has Christ got to do with it? You're not going to compare yourself to Christ!
Estragon: All my life I've compared myself to him.
Vladimir: But where he lived it was warm, it was dry!
Estragon: Yes. And they crucified quick.

Page 35:

Estragon: Do you remember the day I threw myself into the Rhone?
Vladimir: We were grape harvesting.
Estragon: You fished me out.
Vladimir: That's all dead and buried.

Pages 37 and 37b:
Enter Estragon and Vladimir

Page 38b:

Vladimir: I wouldn't have let them beat you.
Estragon: You couldn't have stopped them.
Vladimir: Why not?
Estragon: There was ten of them.

Vladimir:	No, I mean before they beat you. I would have stopped you from doing whatever it was you were doing.
Estragon:	I wasn't doing anything.
Vladimir:	Then why did they beat you?
Estragon:	I don't know.

Page 39b:

Vladimir:	All the same, you can't tell me that this (gesture) bears any resemblance to . . . (he hesitates) . . . to the Macon country for example. You can't deny there's a big difference.
Estragon:	The Macon country! Who's talking to you about the Macon country?
Vladimir:	But you were there yourself, in the Macon country.
Estragon:	No I was never in the Macon country! I've puked my puke of a life away here, I tell you! Here! In the Cackon country!
Vladimir:	But we were together, I could swear to it! Picking grapes for a man called . . . can't think of the name of the place, do you remember?
Estragon:	It's possible. I didn't notice anything.
Vladimir:	But down there everything is red.

Page 49b:
Enter Pozzo and Lucky

Page 50b:

Estragon:	I tell you there was ten of them.

Page 52b:

Estragon:	We'll go to the Pyrenees.
Vladimir:	Wherever you like.
Estragon:	I've always wanted to wander in the Pyrenees.

Page 54b:

Pozzo:	You are not highwaymen?

Page 55b:

Pozzo:	It isn't by chance the place known as the Board?
Vladimir:	Never heard of it.

Pages 58b–59:
Conversation with messenger

From their many references to an external world, Beckett seems to be showing the loneliness, futility, and barrenness of Vladimir and Estragon's world. They have some feeling of a past place (which seems to be France, judging from references to the Eiffel Tower, Macon country, the Rhone River, and the Pyrenees), a past culture (the Bible, France), and even past work (grape harvesting, Estragon the poet). But what we have in this play is only a fragmented memory of the world the reader or play watcher knows, only dreams and faint memories. In this bare world, Vladimir and Estragon have no sense of place (only a tree and a ditch), no culture (except Lucky's mixed-up utterings), and no work (except waiting).

Another type of assignment from the list of affective data involves explicating one particular detail. As a sample, consider *Affective Data 25*—Significance of the names.

Vladimir—Russian
Estragon—French
Pozzo—probably Italian
Lucky—American or English, a nickname
Vladimir—also called Didi and Albert
Estragon—also called Gogo and Adam

Perhaps the use of pseudonyms for Vladimir and Estragon indicates the fear and loneliness that they possess; they must search for comfort. You should consider the Biblical, Everyman-type implications of Adam. The fact that Beckett employs names from many nationalities adds to the universal quality of the play. Perhaps he is trying not to say anything about these particular countries, but rather to comment about humanity in general. Beckett must have chosen the names carefully—certainly they are effective.

Another task involves tracing the myriad references to boots and hats (*Affective Data 5*).

Page reference
 7   Estrogen tries to take off boot.
 7b Foot hurts him.
 8   Blaming boot for feet's fault
 8b Massaging feet
10   Vladimir looks in Estragon's boot.
34b Estragon picks up boots, leaves them, goes barefoot.
37   Estragon's boots on stage. Vladimir examines them.
37b Estragon barefoot. Vladimir still examining.
43   Vladimir asks Estragon about boots.
43b Estragon denies boots are his. Vladimir says someone traded them (mix-up of colors—brown, black, gray, green—further enhances meaningless).
44b Boots fit Estragon.
45   They don't hurt him.
58   Estragon sits down, tries to take off boots.
59b Takes them off, places them front and center—play ends with separation and fragmentation.

Conclusion: Estragon fools with his boots when no other action takes place. When Pozzo, Lucky, or the messenger is present, Estragon forgets the boots. They appear on stage at the beginning and ending of each day. This represents an absurd way for Estragon to pass time. Since he has nothing else to do while he waits for Godot, he plays with his boots. It is an immature act, drawing attention while filling time (of which there seems a considerable amount). While Gogo and Didi wait for something to happen to them, they have no recourse but to revert to trivial, meaningless acts. Estragon, concerned with the boots, seems to dwell on basic physical functions (his bladder and his feet), while Vladimir seems to dote on the hat or on more basic intellectual functions (the head). By cataloguing the hat references, you would see that Vladimir constantly becomes concerned about it. Together, Vladimir and Estragon seem to represent the two halves of a whole human being (the physical and the intellectual). The point is, however, that in this play these two, like everything else (such as Lucky's speech), are fragmented.

Again, affective data are not restricted to images or ideas appearing throughout the play. Another example would involve the simple act of Vladimir's giving his coat to Estragon.

On page 45b Estragon, who feels cold, sleeps soundly. Vladimir arises softly, takes off his coat, and lays it across Estragon's shoulders, then starts pacing to and fro, swinging his arms to keep himself warm.

In the bare, valueless setting of this play, a simple, kind response such as this takes on more meaning than in an ordinary play. There are no magnificent actions, no swordfights, no romances, no murders, no tricks in the plot. Thus, the simplest emotional response engenders more poignance and significance.

You would sense this as especially touching if you saw it on the stage, an act of love and friendship that serves to point out the real human quality of Vladimir. It seems tragic for him to be trapped in such a hellish place, for in many ways he possesses great potential.

By engaging in the kind of rigorous analysis that preparing or explicating affective data entails, you can become a discerning and meticulous reader of drama. The whole process of gathering textual evidence to support a contention represents the core of writing about literature.

Waiting for Godot is a rich play, a tragicomedy that makes us laugh at the absurd nonsense that occurs and also makes us feel regret at the deplorable plight of the two men waiting. Clearly Beckett urges us to become doers and participators, not merely listeners and spectators.

PART THREE

PRACTICE TESTS

Answer Sheet for Practice Test A
Language and Composition

Multiple-Choice
Questions
Time—1 hour

1. Ⓐ Ⓑ Ⓒ Ⓓ Ⓔ
2. Ⓐ Ⓑ Ⓒ Ⓓ Ⓔ
3. Ⓐ Ⓑ Ⓒ Ⓓ Ⓔ
4. Ⓐ Ⓑ Ⓒ Ⓓ Ⓔ
5. Ⓐ Ⓑ Ⓒ Ⓓ Ⓔ
6. Ⓐ Ⓑ Ⓒ Ⓓ Ⓔ
7. Ⓐ Ⓑ Ⓒ Ⓓ Ⓔ
8. Ⓐ Ⓑ Ⓒ Ⓓ Ⓔ
9. Ⓐ Ⓑ Ⓒ Ⓓ Ⓔ
10. Ⓐ Ⓑ Ⓒ Ⓓ Ⓔ
11. Ⓐ Ⓑ Ⓒ Ⓓ Ⓔ
12. Ⓐ Ⓑ Ⓒ Ⓓ Ⓔ
13. Ⓐ Ⓑ Ⓒ Ⓓ Ⓔ
14. Ⓐ Ⓑ Ⓒ Ⓓ Ⓔ
15. Ⓐ Ⓑ Ⓒ Ⓓ Ⓔ
16. Ⓐ Ⓑ Ⓒ Ⓓ Ⓔ
17. Ⓐ Ⓑ Ⓒ Ⓓ Ⓔ
18. Ⓐ Ⓑ Ⓒ Ⓓ Ⓔ
19. Ⓐ Ⓑ Ⓒ Ⓓ Ⓔ
20. Ⓐ Ⓑ Ⓒ Ⓓ Ⓔ

21. Ⓐ Ⓑ Ⓒ Ⓓ Ⓔ
22. Ⓐ Ⓑ Ⓒ Ⓓ Ⓔ
23. Ⓐ Ⓑ Ⓒ Ⓓ Ⓔ
24. Ⓐ Ⓑ Ⓒ Ⓓ Ⓔ
25. Ⓐ Ⓑ Ⓒ Ⓓ Ⓔ
26. Ⓐ Ⓑ Ⓒ Ⓓ Ⓔ
27. Ⓐ Ⓑ Ⓒ Ⓓ Ⓔ
28. Ⓐ Ⓑ Ⓒ Ⓓ Ⓔ
29. Ⓐ Ⓑ Ⓒ Ⓓ Ⓔ
30. Ⓐ Ⓑ Ⓒ Ⓓ Ⓔ
31. Ⓐ Ⓑ Ⓒ Ⓓ Ⓔ
32. Ⓐ Ⓑ Ⓒ Ⓓ Ⓔ
33. Ⓐ Ⓑ Ⓒ Ⓓ Ⓔ
34. Ⓐ Ⓑ Ⓒ Ⓓ Ⓔ
35. Ⓐ Ⓑ Ⓒ Ⓓ Ⓔ
36. Ⓐ Ⓑ Ⓒ Ⓓ Ⓔ
37. Ⓐ Ⓑ Ⓒ Ⓓ Ⓔ
38. Ⓐ Ⓑ Ⓒ Ⓓ Ⓔ
39. Ⓐ Ⓑ Ⓒ Ⓓ Ⓔ
40. Ⓐ Ⓑ Ⓒ Ⓓ Ⓔ

41. Ⓐ Ⓑ Ⓒ Ⓓ Ⓔ
42. Ⓐ Ⓑ Ⓒ Ⓓ Ⓔ
43. Ⓐ Ⓑ Ⓒ Ⓓ Ⓔ
44. Ⓐ Ⓑ Ⓒ Ⓓ Ⓔ
45. Ⓐ Ⓑ Ⓒ Ⓓ Ⓔ
46. Ⓐ Ⓑ Ⓒ Ⓓ Ⓔ
47. Ⓐ Ⓑ Ⓒ Ⓓ Ⓔ
48. Ⓐ Ⓑ Ⓒ Ⓓ Ⓔ
49. Ⓐ Ⓑ Ⓒ Ⓓ Ⓔ
50. Ⓐ Ⓑ Ⓒ Ⓓ Ⓔ
51. Ⓐ Ⓑ Ⓒ Ⓓ Ⓔ
52. Ⓐ Ⓑ Ⓒ Ⓓ Ⓔ
53. Ⓐ Ⓑ Ⓒ Ⓓ Ⓔ

Three Essay
Questions
Time—2 hours

Write your essays on standard 8¹/₂ by 11-inch composition paper. At the exam you will be given a bound booklet containing 12 lined pages.

A Language and Composition

SECTION I
Total time—1 hour

Carefully read the following passages and answer the accompanying questions.

Questions 1–13 are based on the following passage.

Questions as to "values—that is to say, as to what is good or
bad on its own account, independently of its effects—lie outside the
domain of science, as the defenders of religion emphatically assert. I
Line   think that in this they are right, but I draw the further conclusion,
(5)   which they do not draw, that questions as to "values" lie wholly
outside the domain of knowledge. That is to say, when we assert that
this or that has "value," we are giving expressions to our own
emotions, not to a fact which would still be true if our personal
feelings were different. To make this clear, we must try to analyze the
(10)   conception of the Good.

It is obvious, to begin with, that the whole idea of good and
bad has some connection with desire. *Prima facie,* anything that we
all desire is "good," and anything that we all dread is "bad." If we all
agreed in our desires, the matter could be left there, but unfortunately
(15)   our desires conflict. If I say "what I want is good," my neighbor will
say "No, what I want." Ethics is an attempt—though not, I think a
successful one—to escape from this subjectivity. I shall naturally try to
show, in my dispute with my neighbor, that my desires have some
quality which makes them more worthy of respect than his. If I want
(20)   to preserve a right of way, I shall appeal to the landless inhabitants of
the district; but he, on his side, will appeal to the landowners. I shall
say: "What use is the beauty of the countryside if no one sees it?" He
will retort: "What beauty will be left if trippers are allowed to spread
devastation?" Each tries to enlist allies by showing that his own
(25)   desires harmonize with those of other people. When this is obviously
impossible, as in the case of a burglar, the man is condemned by
public opinion, and his ethical status is that of a sinner.

Ethics is thus closely related to politics: it is an attempt to
bring the collective desires of a group to bear upon individuals; or,
(30)   conversely, it is an attempt by an individual to cause his desires to
become those of his group. This latter is, of course, only possible if
his desires are not obviously opposed to the general interest: the
burglar will hardly attempt to persuade people that he is doing them
good, though plutocrats make similar attempts, and often succeed.
(35)   When our desires are for things which all can enjoy in common, it
seems not unreasonable to hope that others may concur; thus the
philosopher who values Truth, Goodness and Beauty seems, to
himself, to be not merely expressing his own desires, but pointing the

(40) way to the welfare of all mankind. Unlike the burglar, he is able to
believe that his desires are for something that has value in an
impersonal sense.

Ethics is an attempt to give universal, and not merely personal,
importance to certain of our desires. I say "certain" of our desires,
because in regard to some of them this is obviously impossible, as we
(45) saw in the case of the burglar. The man who makes money on the
Stock Exchange by means of some secret knowledge does not wish
others to be equally well informed: Truth (in so far as he values it) is
for him a private possession, not the general human good that it is for
the philosopher. The philosopher may, it is true, sink to the level of
(50) the stock-jobber, as when he claims priority for a discovery. But this
is a lapse: in purely philosophic capacity, he wants only to enjoy the
contemplation of Truth in doing which he in no way interferes with
others who wish to do likewise . . . .

. . . Every attempt to persuade people that something is good
(55) (or bad) in itself, and not merely in its effects, depends upon the art of
rousing feelings, not upon an appeal to evidence. In every case the
preacher's skill consists in creating in others emotions similar to his
own—or dissimilar, if he is a hypocrite. I am not saying this as a
criticism of the preacher, but as an analysis of the essential character
(60) of his activity.

When a man says "this is good in itself," he seems to be
making a statement, just as much as if he said "this is square" or "this
is sweet." I believe this to be a mistake. I think that what the man
really means is: "I wish everybody to desire this," or rather "Would
(65) that everybody desired this." If what he says is interpreted as a
statement, it is merely an affirmation of his own personal wish; if, on
the other hand, it is interpreted in a general way, it states nothing, but
merely desires something. The wish, as an occurrence, is personal, but
what it desires is universal. It is, I think, this curious interlocking of
(70) the particular and the universal which has caused so much confusion
in ethics.

(1935)

1. The phrase "that is to say" (line 6) is the equivalent of the author saying
   (A) "for example."
   (B) "on the other hand."
   (C) "to be more precise."
   (D) "to put it another way."
   (E) "consider the alternative."

2. The word "this" in the last sentence of the first paragraph refers to
   (A) the author's personal feelings.
   (B) expressions of emotion.
   (C) the fact that values are subject to verification by others.
   (D) the idea that "values" lie wholly outside the domain of knowledge.
   (E) the notion that emotions and facts are different.

3. Which of the following best describes the function of the first paragraph?
    (A)   It states a hypothesis that the author intends to prove in the remainder
          of the passage.
    (B)   It sets up a conflict that the author resolves in the remainder of the
          passage.
    (C)   It defines terms that will be used thoughout the passage.
    (D)   It lays the historical groundwork of an intellectual conflict between
          religion and science.
    (E)   It asserts an opinion that will be supported later in the passage.

4. The author suggests all EXCEPT which of the following about the nature
    of "good"?
    (A)   Goodness and badness are innate qualities.
    (B)   Scientific reasoning is unrelated to questions of values.
    (C)   An assertion of values is a manifestation of personal desire.
    (D)   Good values acquire their "goodness" from their beneficial side effects.
    (E)   Science is ineffectual in ascertaining what is good and what is bad.

5. Which of the following best describes the author's purpose in using hypo-
    thetical quotations in the second paragraph (lines 15–16)?
    (A)   To show that reasonable people can disagree on ethical issues
    (B)   To point out a basic dilemma of ethics
    (C)   To illustrate the problem of identifying what is "good" and what is
          "bad"
    (D)   To ridicule the defenders of religion mentioned earlier (line 3)
    (E)   To define the term "values" used in the first paragraph (line 7)

6. Which of the following most accurately tells what the author feels about
    "plutocrats" (line 34)?
    (A)   Strong antipathy
    (B)   Devoted loyalty
    (C)   Secret admiration
    (D)   Gentle scornfulness
    (E)   Bitter envy

7. The author alludes to a burglar as an example of a person who
    (A)   cannot tell "good" from "bad."
    (B)   has desires at odds with the desires of others.
    (C)   is not worthy of respect.
    (D)   cannot get along with other people.
    (E)   is ethically challenged.

8. According to the passage, which of the following best describes the rela-
    tionship between ethics and personal desire?
    (A)   Secret desires are by their nature unethical.
    (B)   Personal desires made public are likely to be ethical.
    (C)   A desire to improve general human well-being is likely to be ethical.
    (D)   Any plan to improve the condition of mankind is likely to be ethical.
    (E)   The desire to ascertain Truth is an ethical desire.

9. In the passage, the plutocrat, the philosopher, and the preacher share which of the following traits?
    (A) An alleged interest in the general welfare of others
    (B) An unwavering belief in ethical behavior
    (C) An earnest desire to define "good"
    (D) A need to analyze and judge the behavior of others
    (E) A strong commitment to individualism

10. The author's allusion to the stock-jobber (line 50) serves largely to
    (A) cite an example of selfish behavior.
    (B) imply that the work of stock-jobbers is unethical.
    (C) assert the universality of gathering wealth.
    (D) heighten the contrast between adherents of ethical standards and those without ethical standards.
    (E) emphasize the unsavory nature of trading in stocks.

11. The author's tone in the passage might best be characterized as
    (A) arrogant.
    (B) defensive.
    (C) caustic.
    (D) moralistic.
    (E) instructive.

12. According to the passage, determining what is ethical is made difficult by
    (A) the language used to express ethical opinions.
    (B) the relationship between ethics and religion.
    (C) differences of perception between people.
    (D) universal hypocrisy.
    (E) the private nature of ethical views.

13. The passage indicates that the author's position on ethics is that
    (A) ethical values are the equivalent of religious values.
    (B) ethicists have not yet succeeded in accurately defining what is good and what is bad.
    (C) ethics need to be based on feelings rather than intellect.
    (D) ethics should be used for the improvement of the world.
    (E) each person has his or her own set of ethical principles to guide his or her action.

Questions 14–23 are based on the following passage.

You can live a lifetime and, at the end of it, know more about
other people than you know about yourself. You learn to watch other
people, but you never watch yourself because you strive against
Line   loneliness. If you read a book, or shuffle a deck of cards, or care for
(5)   a dog, you are avoiding yourself. The abhorrence of loneliness is as
natural as wanting to live at all. If it were otherwise, men would never
have bothered to make an alphabet, nor to have fashioned words out
of what were only animal sounds, nor to have crossed continents—
each man to see what the other looked like.
(10)   Being alone in an aeroplane even for so short a time as a night and
a day, irrevocably alone, with nothing to observe but your

instruments and your own hands in semi-darkness, nothing to
contemplate but the size of your small courage, nothing to wonder
about but the beliefs, the faces, and the hopes rooted in your
(15)   mind—such an experience can be as startling as the first awareness of
a stranger walking by your side at night. You are a stranger.

It is dark already and I am over the south of Ireland. There are the
lights of Cork and the lights are wet; they are drenched with Irish rain,
and I am above them and dry. I am above them and the plane roars in
(20)   a sobbing world, but it imparts no sadness to me. I feel the security of
solitude, the exhilaration of escape. So long as I can see the lights and
imagine the people walking undernearth them, I feel selfishly
triumphant, as if I have eluded care and left even the small sorrow of
rain in other hands.

(25)   It is a little over an hour now since I left Abingdon, England.
Wales and the Irish Sea are behind me like so much time used up.
On a long flight distance and time are the same. But there had been a
moment when Time stopped—and Distance too. It was the moment I
lifted the blue-and-silver Gull from the aerodrome, the moment the
(30)   photographers aimed their cameras, the moment I felt the craft refuse
its burden and strain toward the earth in sullen rebellion, only to listen
at last to the persuasion of stick and elevators, the dogmatic argument
of blueprints that said she *had* to fly because the figures proved it.

So she had flown, and once airborne, once she had yielded to the
(35)   sophistry of a draughtsman's board, she had said, "There I have lifted
the weight. Now, where are we bound?"—and the question had
frightened me.

We are bound for a place thirty-six hundred miles from here—two
thousand miles of it unbroken ocean. Most of the way it will be night.
(40)   We are flying west with the night.

So there behind me is Cork; and ahead of me is Berehaven
Lighthouse. It is the last light, standing on the last land. I watch it,
counting the frequency of its flashes—so many to the minute. Then I
pass it and fly out to sea.

(45)   The fear is gone now—not overcome nor reasoned away. It is
gone because something else has taken its place; the confidence and
the trust, the inherent belief in the security of land underfoot—now
this faith is transferred to my plane, because land has vanished and
there is no other tangible thing to fix faith upon. Flight is but
(50)   momentary escape from the eternal custody of earth. . . .

At ten-thirty I am still flying on the large cabin tank of petrol,
hoping to use it up and put an end to the liquid swirl that has rocked
the plane since my take-off. The tank has no gauge, but written on its
side is the assurance: "This tank is good for four hours."

(55)   There is nothing ambiguous about such a guaranty. I believe it, but
at twenty-five minutes to eleven, my motor coughs and dies, and the
Gull is powerless above the sea.

I realize that the heavy drone of the plane has been, until this
moment, complete and comforting silence. It is the actual silence
(60)   following the last splutter of the engine that stuns me. I can't feel any
fear; I can't feel anything. I can only observe with a kind of stupid
disinterest that my hands are violently active and know that, while
they move, I am being hypnotized by the needle of my altimeter.

I suppose that the denial of natural impulse is what is meant by
(65)   "keeping calm," but impulse has reason in it. If it is night and you are

sitting in an aeroplane with a stalled motor, and there are two
thousand feet between you and sea, nothing can be more reasonable
than the impulse to pull back your stick in the hope of adding to that
two thousand, if only by a little. The thought, the knowledge, the law
(70)   that tells you that your hope lies not in this, but in a contrary act—the
act of directing your impotent craft toward the water—seems a
terrifying abandonment, not only of reason, but of sanity. Your mind
and your heart reject it. It is your hands—your stranger's hands—that
follow with unfeeling precision the letter of the law.

(75)   I sit there and watch my hands push forward on the stick and feel
the Gull respond and begin its dive to the sea. Of course it is a simple
thing; surely the cabin tank has run dry too soon. I need only to turn
another petcock . . .

(1942)

14. The narration switches from second person to first person in line 17 pri-
marily to
(A)   explain the meaning of "You are a stranger" (line 16).
(B)   indicate that the author has not been talking about herself in para-
graphs 1 and 2.
(C)   give an example of the "abhorrence of loneliness" (line 5).
(D)   show that the narrator speaks from first-hand experience about
issues raised in paragraphs 1 and 2.
(E)   inform the reader that the narrator is an accomplished pilot.

15. In line 10, the phrase "Being alone" is structurally parallel to the phrase
(A)   "your instruments" (lines 11–12).
(B)   "your own hands" (line 12).
(C)   "nothing to wonder about" (lines 13–14).
(D)   "such an experience" (line 15).
(E)   "the first awareness of a stranger" (lines 15–16).

16. With respect to the entire passage, the statement in the first sentence is
(A)   an assertion against which the entire passage argues.
(B)   a piece of common wisdom that the passage will illustrate.
(C)   a paradox that the passage will analyze and explain.
(D)   the moral of the story that the author is about to tell.
(E)   an example that supports the main idea of the passage.

17. The function of the phrase "sobbing world" (line 20) is primarily to
(A)   describe the rain outside the airplane.
(B)   suggest the pulsating sounds of the airplane engine.
(C)   explain the sadness of lonely people everywhere.
(D)   explain the author's sympathy for the Irish people far below.
(E)   indicate that flying serves as a release from everyday cares.

18. The passage makes the point that men, to avoid being alone, have under-
taken all of the following EXCEPT
(A)   creating a written alphabet.
(B)   developing spoken language.
(C)   traveling from place to place.
(D)   learning to fly planes.
(E)   observing the behavior of other people.

19. The sentence in line 27 ("On a long . . . same") has all of the following functions EXCEPT
    (A) presenting information about the way pilots think.
    (B) introducing the anecdote that follows in lines 28–33.
    (C) illustrating how pilots on long flights sometimes become disoriented.
    (D) helping to contrast the tedium of flying with the thrill of the take-off.
    (E) explaining the phrase "like so much time used up" (line 26).

20. The writing style of the passage as a whole can best be described as
    (A) reflective and nostalgic.
    (B) objective and informational.
    (C) academic and pedantic.
    (D) effusive and tumultuous.
    (E) terse and impersonal.

21. In the description of the take-off (lines 28–34) the author employs all of the following EXCEPT
    (A) paradox.
    (B) rising action.
    (C) personification.
    (D) repetition for emphasis.
    (E) shift of pronouns.

22. The main contrast employed by the narrator in the passage is between
    (A) being a daredevil and playing it safe.
    (B) the silence of the heavens and the roar of the airplane.
    (C) human impulses and faith in the laws of physics.
    (D) sensitivity and indifference toward others.
    (E) tranquillity and contentiousness.

23. Which of the following best identifies the function of the two phrases, "the act of directing your impotent craft toward the water" (lines 70–71) and "your stranger's hands" (line 73)?
    (A) Subordinate clauses
    (B) Parenthetical asides
    (C) Double negatives
    (D) Colloquialisms
    (E) Appositives

Questions 24–33 are based on the following passage.

Exile is strangely compelling to think about but terrible to
experience. It is the unhealable rift forced between a human being
and a native place, between the self and its true home: its essential
Line   sadness can never be surmounted. And while it is true that literature
(5)   and history contain heroic, romantic, glorious, even triumphant
episodes in an exile's life, these are no more than efforts meant to
overcome the crippling sorrow of estrangement. The achievements of
exile are permanently undermined by the loss of something left behind
for ever.

(10)   Exiles look at non-exiles with resentment. *They* belong in their surroundings, you feel, whereas an exile is always out of place. What is it like to be born in a place, to stay and live there, to know that you are of it, more or less for ever?

                                        * * *

       Although it is true that anyone prevented from returning home is
(15) an exile, some distinctions can be made between exiles, refugees, expatriates, and émigrés. Exile originated in the age-old practice of banishment. Once banished, the exile lives an anomalous and miserable life, with the stigma of being an outsider. Refugees, on the other hand, are a creation of the twentieth-century state. The word
(20) "refugee" has become a political one, suggesting large herds of innocent and bewildered people requiring urgent international assistance, whereas "exile" carries with it, I think, a touch of solitude and spirituality.
       Expatriates voluntarily live in an alien country, usually for personal
(25) or social reasons. Hemingway and Fitzgerald were not forced to live in France. Expatriates may share in the solitude and estrangement of exile, but they do not suffer under its rigid proscriptions. Émigrés enjoy an ambiguous status. Technically, an émigré is anyone who emigrates to a new country. Choice in the matter is certainly a
(30) possibility. Colonial officials, missionaries, technical experts, mercenaries and military advisers on loan may in a sense live in exile, but they have not been banished. White settlers in Africa, parts of Asia and Australia may once have been exiles, but as pioneers and nation-builders the label "exile" dropped away from them.
(35)   Much of the exile's life is taken up with compensating for disorienting loss by creating a new world to rule. It is not surprising that so many exiles seem to be novelists, chess players, political activists, and intellectuals. Each of these occupations requires a minimal investment in objects and places a great premium on mobility
(40) and skill. The exile's new world, logically enough, is unnatural and its unreality resembles fiction. George Lukács, in *Theory of the Novel*, argued with compelling force that the novel, a literary form created out of the unreality of ambition and fantasy, is *the* form of "transcendental homelessness." Classical epics, Lukács wrote, emanate
(45) from settled cultures in which values are clear, identities stable, life unchanging. The European novel is grounded in precisely the opposite experience, that of a changing society in which an itinerant and disinherited middle-class hero or heroine seeks to construct a new world that somewhat resembles an old one left behind for ever. In the
(50) epic there is no *other* world, only the finality of *this* one. Odysseus returns to Ithaca after years of wandering; Achilles will die because he cannot escape his fate. The novel, however, exists because other worlds *may* exist, alternatives for bourgeois speculators, wanderers, exiles.
(55)   No matter how well they may do, exiles are always eccentrics who *feel* their difference (even as they frequently exploit it) as a kind of orphanhood. Anyone who is really homeless regards the habit of seeing estrangement in everything modern as an affectation, a display of modish attitudes. Clutching difference like a weapon to be used
(60) with stiffened will, the exile jealously insists on his or her right to refuse to belong.
       This usually translates into an intransigence that is not easily

ignored. Wilfulness, exaggeration, overstatement: these are
characteristic styles of being an exile, methods for compelling the
(65)   world to accept your vision—which you make more
unacceptable because you are in fact unwilling to have it
accepted. It is yours, after all. Composure and serenity are the last
things associated with the work of exiles. Artists in exile are decidedly
unpleasant, and their stubbornness insinuates itself into even their
(70)   exalted works. Dante's vision in *The Divine Comedy* is tremendously
powerful in its universality and detail, but even the beatific peace
achieved in the *Paradiso* bears traces of the vindictiveness and
severity of judgement embodied in the *Inferno.* Who but an exile like
Dante, banished from Florence, would use eternity as a place for
(75)   settling old scores?

(1984)

24. The passage as a whole can best be characterized as
(A)   a tribute to exiles.
(B)   an analysis of the problems faced by exiles.
(C)   an objective report on exiles.
(D)   a literary appreciation of exiles.
(E)   a sociological study of exiles.

25. The second sentence of the passage, "It is the unhealable . . ." (lines 2–4)
functions in all of the following ways EXCEPT
(A)   defining the word "exile."
(B)   introducing the author's attitude toward exile.
(C)   highlighting the horrors of exile.
(D)   limiting the subject matter of the passage.
(E)   developing the emotional tone of the passage.

26. The attitude of the author toward exiles is primarily one of
(A)   sympathy.
(B)   superiority.
(C)   pity.
(D)   scorn.
(E)   indifference.

27. Which of the following does the author use as an illustration of an exile
who suffers "resentment" (line 10)?
(A)   Hemingway (line 25)
(B)   A missionary sent to a far-off land (lines 30–31)
(C)   A hero of a European novel
(D)   Achilles
(E)   Dante

28. The primary rhetorical function of the last sentence in paragraph 2 ("What
is it like . . . more or less forever?") is to
(A)   provide evidence to support an idea proposed earlier in the paragraph.
(B)   raise the question that the author intends to answer in the next paragraph.
(C)   provide support for ideas presented in paragraph 1.
(D)   define and clarify ideas presented in paragraphs 1 and 2.
(E)   present a rhetorical question that cannot be answered.

29. The author mentions settlers in Africa, Asia, and Australia (lines 32–33) chiefly as examples of
    (A) voluntary exiles.
    (B) colonists.
    (C) pioneers.
    (D) refugees.
    (E) military adventurers.

30. The sentence structure of the last sentence of paragraph 4 (lines 32–34) is most similar to the sentence structure of
    (A) the second sentence of paragraph 1 (lines 2–4).
    (B) the first sentence of paragraph 3 (lines 14–16).
    (C) the last sentence of paragraph 3 (lines 19–23).
    (D) the seventh sentence of paragraph 4 (lines 30–32).
    (E) the last sentence of paragraph 6 (lines 59–61).

31. Which of the following best describes the initial sentence of paragraph 6 (lines 55–57)?
    (A) An analysis of the classical heroes discussed in paragraph 5
    (B) A conclusion drawn from ideas stated in paragraphs 3, 4, and 5
    (C) A turning point that sends the passage in a new direction
    (D) A restatement of ideas in paragraphs 1 and 2
    (E) An idea that further develops the author's portrait of exiles

32. The author's reference to classical epics (lines 44–54) serves primarily to
    (A) show that the phenomenon of exile has existed for a long time.
    (B) review the history of exile.
    (C) contrast epic tales with European novels.
    (D) describe a major theme of classical literature.
    (E) emphasize the courage of classical heroes.

33. Toward the end of the passage (lines 55–75), the author emphasizes which quality of exiles?
    (A) Patience
    (B) Tranquility
    (C) Obstinacy
    (D) Dedication
    (E) Self-indulgence

Questions 34–43 are based on the following passage.

In a recent bulletin of the Superintendent of the Census for 1890 appear these significant words: "Up to and including 1880 the country had a frontier of settlement, but at present the unsettled area has been so broken into by isolated bodies of settlement that there can
Line (5) hardly be said to be a frontier line. In the discussion of its extent, its westward movement, etc., it cannot, therefore, any longer have a place in the census reports." This brief official statement marks the

closing of a great historic movement. Up to our own day American history has been in a large degree the history of the colonization of the

(10)   Great West. The existence of an area of free land, its continuous recession, and the advance of American settlement westward, explain American development.

Behind institutions, behind constitutional forms and modifications, lie the vital forces that call these organs into life and

(15)   shape them to meet changing conditions. The peculiarity of American institutions is the fact that they have been compelled to adapt themselves to the changes of an expanding people—to the changes involved in crossing a continent, in winning a wilderness, and in developing at each area of this progress out of the primitive economic

(20)   and political conditions of the frontier into the complexity of city life. Said Calhoun in 1817, "We are great, and rapidly—I was about to say fearfully—growing!" So saying, he touched the distinguishing feature of American life. All peoples show development; the germ theory of politics has been sufficiently emphasized. In the case of most nations,

(25)   however, the development has occurred in a limited area; and if the nation has expanded, it has met other growing peoples whom it has conquered. But in the case of the United States we have a different phenomenon. Limiting our attention to the Atlantic coast, we have the familiar phenomenon of the evolution of institutions in a limited area,

(30)   such as the rise of representative government in complex organs; the progress from primitive industrial society, without division of labor, up to manufacturing civilization. But we have in addition to this a recurrence of the process of evolution in each western area reached in the process of expansion. Thus American development has exhibited

(35)   not merely advance along a single line, but a return to primitive conditions on a continually advancing frontier line, and a new development for that area. American social development has been continually beginning over again on the frontier. This perennial rebirth, this fluidity of American life, this expansion westward with its

(40)   new opportunities, its continuous touch with the simplicity of primitive society, furnish the forces dominating the American character. The true point of view in the history of this nation is not the Atlantic coast, it is the Great West. Even the slavery struggle, which is made so exclusive an object of attention by writers like Professor

(45)   von Holst, occupies its important place in American history because of its relation to westward expansion.

In this advance, the frontier is the outer edge of the wave—the meeting point between savagery and civilization. Much has been written about the frontier from the point of view of border warfare

(50)   and the chase, but as a field for the serious study of the economist and the historian it has been neglected.

The American frontier is sharply distinguished from the European frontier—a fortified boundary line running through dense populations. The most significant thing about the American frontier is,

(55)   that it lies at the hither edge of free land. In the census reports it is treated as the margin of that settlement which has a density of two or more to the square mile. The term is an elastic one, and for our purposes does not need sharp definition.

(1920)

34. In the context of the passage as a whole, the quotation from the Super-
    intendent of the Census (lines 1–7) presents
    (A) an analogy that illustrates the theme of the passage.
    (B) an anecdote that introduces the main subject of the passage.
    (C) a problem for which the author of the passage will offer a solution.
    (D) a statement on which the passage will build.
    (E) an opinion that emphasizes the gravity of the issue discussed in the
        rest of the passage.

35. In its context, the phrase "vital forces" (line 14) refers to
    (A) the Census Bureau.
    (B) the U.S. Constitution.
    (C) new laws and regulations passed to deal with changing social and
        economic conditions.
    (D) the natural obstacles faced by settlers in the West.
    (E) the people's urge to go west and to settle there.

36. It can be inferred from the passage that a distinguishing feature of an
    industrial society is
    (A) a division of labor.
    (B) the absence of free land.
    (C) an expanding population.
    (D) a democratic form of government.
    (E) a continually changing economy.

37. Which of the following phrases illustrates "the germ theory of politics"
    (lines 23–24)?
    (A) "and rapidly—I was about to say fearfully—growing" (lines 21–22)
    (B) "development . . . in a limited area" (line 25)
    (C) "rise of representative government" (line 30)
    (D) "process of evolution" (line 33)
    (E) "return to primitive conditions" (lines 35–36)

38. The "different phenomenon" mentioned in lines 27–28 refers to all of the
    following EXCEPT
    (A) a return to a primitive style of life.
    (B) new development in unsettled areas.
    (C) a recurrence of historical events.
    (D) growth within a limited geographical area.
    (E) the potential for further expansion.

39. In context, the word "chase" (line 50) is best interpreted to mean
    (A) the hunt for food.
    (B) survival in primitive conditions.
    (C) the question of slavery in the new territories.
    (D) the expulsion of the indigenous population.
    (E) settlers' competition for free land.

40. In the passage the author employs which of the following rhetorical strategies?
   (A) Extended analogy
   (B) Appeal to patriotism
   (C) Testimony from authority
   (D) Inspiring language
   (E) Statistical support

41. The function of the sentence in line 52 ("The American frontier . . . . pop-ulation) is to
   (A) draw a contrast between American and European frontiers.
   (B) show the superiority of the American frontier.
   (C) reveal the uniqueness of the American frontier.
   (D) help summarize the passage.
   (E) present arguments in opposition to those in the previous paragraph.

42. The attitude of the author toward the closing of the frontier is primarily one of
   (A) regret.
   (B) historical interest.
   (C) disapproval.
   (D) hopefulness about the future.
   (E) satisfaction.

43. Which of the following best captures the main theme of the passage?
   (A) An industrial society has superseded a primitive society on the frontier.
   (B) America's frontier differs sharply from frontiers elsewhere.
   (C) Expansion to the West has helped to define America's character.
   (D) Criteria for taking the U.S. census must remain flexible.
   (E) America's frontier has been characterized by violence.

Questions 44–53 are based on the following passage.

PARRIS ISLAND, S.C.—He is seething, he is rabid, he is
wound up tight as a golf ball, with more adrenalin surging through his
hypothalamus than a cornered slum rat, he is everything these Marine
Line recruits with their heads shaved to dirty nubs have ever feared or even
(5) hoped a drill instructor might be.
   He is Staff Sgt. Douglas Berry and he is rushing down the squad
bay of Receiving Barracks to leap onto a table and brace at parade
rest in which none of the recruits, daring glances from the position of
attention, can see any more of him under the rake of his campaign hat
(10) than his lipless mouth chopping at them like a disaster teletype:
WHEN I GIVE YOU THE WORD YOU WILL WALK YOU WILL
NOT RUN DOWN THESE STEPS WHERE YOU WILL RUN
YOU WILL NOT WALK TO THE YELLOW FOOTMARKS. . . .
   Outside, Berry's two junior drill instructors, in raincoats over dress
(15) greens, sweat in a muggy February drizzle which shrinks the view
down to this wooden World War II barracks, to the galvanized Butler
hut across the company street, the overground steam pipes, a couple
of palmetto trees, the raindrops beading on spitshined black shoes.
Sgt. Hudson mans the steps, Sgt. Burley the footmarks. They
(20) pace with a mannered strut, like men wearing white tie and tails, their

hands folded behind their backs, their jaw muscles flexing. One senses
there's none of the wisecracking "See Here, Private Hargrove," or
"Sgt. Bilko" Army routine here, no hotshot recruits outsmarting dumb
sarge for passes to town.

(25)   In fact, during his 63 days of training at Parris Island, unless a
member of the immediate family dies, a recruit will get no liberty at
all. He will also get no talking, no phone calls, no books or
magazines, no television, radio or record players, no candy or gum,
one movie, one newspaper a week, and three cigarettes a day. Unless
(30) he fouls up, gets sent to the brig or to motivation platoon, and loses
the cigarettes.
           WHEN I GIVE YOU THE WORD TO MOVE OUT YOU
       WILL MOVE OUT DO YOU UNDERSTAND ME?
           Hudson meets the first one at the steps like a rotary mower ripping
(35) into a toad, so psyched he's actually dancing on tiptoe, with
       his face a choleric three-quarters of an inch from the private FASTER
       PRIVATE FASTER JUST TAKE YOUR DUMB TIME
       SWEETHEART MOVE! MOVE! as this hog, as recruits are
       colloquially known, piles out of the barracks in a stumble of new
(40) boots, poncho, laundry bag and the worst trouble his young ass has
       ever been in, no doubt about it when Burley meets him just like
       Hudson, in an astonishment of rage that roars him all the way down to
       the right front set of yellow footprints YOU LOCK YOUR BODY
       AT ATTENTION YOU LOCK YOUR BODY. . . .
(45)   Or maybe Burley writhes up around this private to hiss in his ear—
       and Burley is very good at this—*you hate me, don't you, you hate me,*
       private, you'd better hate me because I hate you, or any of the other
       litanies drill instructors have been barking and hissing at their charges
       ever since the first of more than one million Parris Island graduates
(50) arrived on the flea-ridden sand barren in 1911.
           Until there are 60 of them out there in the drizzle with the drill
       instructors shouting themselves hoarse, 60 volunteers who had heard
       from countless older brothers and street corner buddies and
       roommates that it would be exactly like this but they volunteered
(55) anyhow, to be Marines.
           Right now, with lips trembling, eyes shuttling YOU BETTER
       STOP THAT EYE-BALLING, PRIVATE! fat and forlorn, they look
       like 60 sex perverts trapped by a lynch mob. They are scared. They
       are scared as fraternity pledges during a cleverly staged hell week,
(60) shaking like boys about to abandon their virginity.
           It's a primal dread that drill instructors invoke and exploit in eight
       weeks (soon to revert to the pre-Vietnam 11 weeks) of folk theater, a
       spectacle staged on the scale of the Passion Play at Oberammergau,
       an initiation that may be the only true rite of passage to manhood that
(65) America hasn't yet scoured away as an anthropological anachronism.

                                                                          (1972)

44. Several sections of the passage appear in capital letters and with almost no
       punctuation. This can be explained by all of the following reasons EXCEPT
       (A)   to suggest the volume at which the words are uttered.
       (B)   to indicate a staccato-like manner of speech.
       (C)   to convey the intensity with which the words are spoken.
       (D)   to separate spoken words from narration and description.
       (E)   to heighten dramatic effect.

45. In line 8, "daring" modifies
   (A) "Berry" (line 6).
   (B) "squad bay" (lines 6–7).
   (C) "table" (line 7).
   (D) "none" (line 8).
   (E) "recruits" (line 8).

46. In paragraph 3 (lines 14–18), which of the following rhetorical devices is most in evidence?
   (A) Expressionism
   (B) Metonymy
   (C) Figures of speech
   (D) Impressionistic descriptive prose
   (E) Visual imagery

47. The principal contrast employed by the author in the passage is between
   (A) Sgt. Berry and Sgt. Burley.
   (B) the drill instructors and the recruits.
   (C) the reality of boot camp and sitcom versions of military life.
   (D) modern military training and World War II training.
   (E) basic training and fraternity hazing.

48. The main rhetorical function of the description of Hudson and Burley (lines 19–21) is to
   (A) set the stage for material in the next paragraph.
   (B) reinforce a description given earlier in the passage.
   (C) prepare for the contrast made in the following sentence.
   (D) provide support for a thesis proposed in the first paragraph.
   (E) introduce humor into the passage.

49. The point of view expressed in "In fact . . . day" (lines 25–29) is that of
   (A) the author.
   (B) the recruits.
   (C) the Marine Corps.
   (D) Sgt. Hudson.
   (E) Sgt Berry.

50. To create the greatest effect, all of the following rhetorical techniques are used in lines 45–50 EXCEPT
   (A) repetition.
   (B) use of highly connotative verbs.
   (C) evocation of historical tradition.
   (D) vivid adjectives.
   (E) subordinate clause set off by dashes.

51. In the last paragraph, (lines 61–65), which of the following words is paral-
    lel in function to "dread" (line 61)?
    (A) "theater" (line 62)
    (B) "weeks" (line 62)
    (C) "initiation" (line 64)
    (D) "manhood" (line 64)
    (E) "anachronism" (line 65)

52. The passage as a whole might best be described as
    (A) a parable of modern life.
    (B) a melodramatic evocation.
    (C) a parody.
    (D) a dramatic monologue.
    (E) an exposé.

53. Which of the following best captures the author's attitude toward the
    events and people described in the passage?
    (A) "Outside . . . barracks" (lines 14–16)
    (B) "One senses . . . town" (lines 21–24)
    (C) "Hudson meets . . . tiptoe" (lines 34–35)
    (D) "They are scared" (line 58)
    (E) "an initiation . . . anachronism" (lines 63–65)

SECTION II
Total time—2 hours

Question 1

(Suggested time—40 minutes. This question counts as one third of the total
score for Section II.)

Eric Severeid, an American journalist and news commentator, wrote the following editorial in 1958, at a time when the idea of sending a man to the moon
was first becoming technically feasible. After reading the passage carefully,
write an essay analyzing the rhetorical techniques that Severeid uses to express
his views about the future of the moon.

The Dark of the Moon

	This, thank goodness, is the first warm and balmy night
	of the year in these parts; the first frogs are singing. Altogether
	this is hardly the night for whispering sweet sentiments about the
Line	reciprocal trade act, the extension thereof. But since we are
(5)	confined by tradition to the contemplation of public themes and
	issues, let us contemplate the moon. The lively and luminous moon
	has become a public issue. For quite a few thousand years it was a
	private issue; it figured in purely bilateral negotiations between
	lovers, in the incantations of jungle witch doctors and Indian corn
(10)	planters. Poets from attic windows issued statements about
	the moon, and they made better reading than the mimeographed
	handouts now being issued by assistant secretaries of defense.

The moon was always measured in terms of hope and
reassurance and the heart pangs of youth on such a night as this;
(15)   it is now measured in terms of mileage and foot-pounds of rocket
thrust. Children sent sharp, sweet wishes to the moon; now they
dream of blunt-nosed missiles.

There must come a time, in every generation, when those
who are older secretly get off the train of progress, willing to
(20)   walk back to where they came from, if they can find the way.
We're afraid we're getting off now. Cheer, if you wish, the first
general or Ph.D. who splatters something on the kindly face of
the moon. We shall grieve for him, for ourself, for the young
lovers and poets and dreamers to come, because the ancient
(25)   moon will never be the same again. Therefore, we suspect, the
heart of man will never be the same.

We find ourself quite undisturbed about the front-page
talk of "controlling the earth from the moon," because we do
not believe it. If neither men nor gadgets nor both combined
(30)   can control the earth from the earth, we fail to see how they
will do so from the moon.

It is exciting talk, indeed, the talk of man's advance
toward space. But one little step in man's advance toward man
—that, we think, would be truly exciting. Let those who wish
(35)   to try discover the composition of a lunar crater; we would settle
for discovering the true mind of a Russian commissar or the inner
heart of a delinquent child.

There is, after all, another side—a dark side—to the
human spirit, too. Men have hardly begun to explore these
(40)   regions; and it is going to be a very great pity if we advance
upon the bright side of the moon with the dark side of ourselves,
if the cargo in the first rockets to reach there consists of fear
and chauvinism and suspicion. Surely we ought to have our
credentials in order, our hands very clean, and perhaps a prayer
(45)   of forgiveness on our lips as we prepare to open the ancient
vault of the shining moon.

Question 2

(Suggested time—40 minutes. This question counts as one third of the total
score for Section II.)

Here are two passages from the essays of the renowned physicist Albert
Einstein. After reading them carefully, write an essay that analyzes Einstein's
use of language and rhetoric in each. Consider such stylistic elements as diction, sentence structure, tone, and voice.

Passage A

Physics deals with "events" in space and time. To each
event belongs, besides its place coordinates x, y, z, a time value t.
The latter was considered measurable by a clock (ideal periodic
Line   process) of negligible spatial extent. This clock C is to be
(5)   considered at rest at one point of the coordinate system, e.g., at
the coordinate origin ($x = y = z = 0$). The time of an event taking
place at a point P (x,y,z) is then defined as the time shown on the
clock C simultaneously with the event. Here the concept

(10)   "simultaneous" was assumed as physically meaningful without
       special definition. This is a lack of exactness which seems harm-
       less only since with the help of light (whose velocity is practically
       infinite from the point of view of daily experience) the
       simultaneity of spatially distant events can apparently be decided
       immediately.

Passage B   (15)   I am convinced there is only one way to eliminate these
       grave ills, namely through the establishment of a socialist economy,
       accompanied by an educational system which would be oriented
       toward social goals. In such an economy, the means of production
       are owned by society itself and are utilized in a planned fashion.
(20)   A planned economy, which adjusts production to the needs of
       the community, would distribute work to be done among all those
       able to work and would guarantee a livelihood to every man, woman
       and child. The education of the individual, in addition to promoting
       his own innate abilities, would attempt to develop in him a sense
(25)   of responsibility for his fellow men in place of the glorification of
       power and success in our present society.
           Nevertheless, it is necessary to remember that a planned
       economy is not yet socialism. A planned economy as such may be
       accompanied by the complete enslavement of the individual.
(30)   The achievement of socialism requires the solution of some
       extremely difficult socio-political problems: is it possible, in view
       of the far-reaching centralization of political and economic power,
       to prevent bureaucracy from becoming all-powerful and over-
       weening? How can the rights of the individual be protected
(35)   and therewith a democratic counterweight to the power of the
       bureaucracy be assured?

Question 3

(Suggested time—40 minutes. This question counts as one-third of the total
score for Section II.)

Written toward the end of the nineteenth century, the following passage, by the
author Robert Louis Stevenson, reflects on the nature of life. Read the passage carefully and then write an essay that supports, challenges, or qualifies Stevenson's
ideas about man's preoccupation with conserving life rather than living it. Use specific evidence from your observation, experience, or reading to develop your views.

       We confound ourselves with metaphysical phrases,
       which we import into daily talk with noble inappropriateness. We
       have no idea of what death is, apart from its circumstances and
Line   some of its consequences to others; and although we have
(5)   some experience of living, there is not a man on earth who has
       flown so high into abstraction as to have any practical guess at
       the meaning of the word *life*. All literature from Job to Omar
       Khayyam to Thomas Carlyle or Walt Whitman is but an attempt
       to look upon the human state with such largeness of view as shall
(10)   enable us to rise from the consideration of living to the Definition
       of Life. And our sages give us about the best satisfaction in their
       power when they say it is a vapor, or a show, or made out of the
       same stuff with dreams. Philosophy, in its more rigid sense, has

(15) been at the same work for ages; and after myriad bald heads have
wagged over the problem, and piles of words have been heaped one
upon another into dry and cloudy volumes without end, philosophy
has the honor of laying before us, with modest pride, its contribution
towards the subject: that life is a Permanent Possibility of Sensation.
Truly a fine result! A man may very well love beef, or hunting, or
(20) a woman; but surely, not a Permanent Possibility of Sensation! He
may be afraid of a precipice, or a dentist, or a large enemy with a
club, or even an undertaker's man; but not certainly of abstract death.
We may trick with the word life in its dozen senses until we are
weary of tricking; we may argue in terms of all the philosophies of
(25) earth; but one fact remains true thoughout—that we do not love life,
in the sense that we are greatly preoccupied about its conservation;
that we do not, properly speaking, love life at all, but living. Into the
views of the least careful there will enter some degree of providence;
no man's eyes are fixed entirely on the passing hour; but although we
(30) have some anticipation of good health, good weather, wine, active
employment, love and self-approval, the sum of these anticipations
does not amount to anything like a general view of life's possibilities
and issues; nor are those who cherish them most vividly, at all the
most scrupulous of their personal safety. To be deeply interested in
(35) the accidents of our existence, to enjoy keenly the mixed texture of
human experience, rather leads a man to disregard the precautions,
and risk his neck against a straw. For surely the love of living is
stronger in an Alpine climber roping over a peril, or a hunter riding
merrily at a stiff fence, than in a creature who lives upon a diet and
(40) walks a measured distance in the interest of his constitution.

Answer Key for Practice Exam A
Answers to Multiple-Choice Questions

1. C	12. C	23. E	34. D	45. E
2. E	13. B	24. B	35. C	46. E
3. E	14. D	25. D	36. A	47. B
4. D	15. D	26. A	37. A	48. C
5. C	16. B	27. E	38. D	49. C
6. D	17. E	28. A	39. D	50. E
7. B	18. D	29. A	40. C	51. C
8. C	19. C	30. D	41. D	52. B
9. A	20. A	31. E	42. B	53. E
10. A	21. A	32. C	43. C	
11. E	22. C	33. C	44. D	

Answer Explanations

1. **C** Prior to the phrase, the author generalized about the relationship between values and knowledge. Knowing that a reader may not grasp the meaning of his idea, the author clarifies his thought by using more specific language.

2. **E** The word "this" refers to the contents of the previous sentence, in which the author distinguishes between emotions and facts.

3. **E** Much of the passage is devoted to demonstrating the validity of the author's opinion regarding the nature of what we deem to be good or bad—that is to say, the nature of our values.

4. **D** In lines 1–12, the author asserts the truth of each of these positions except (D).

5. **C** These are hypothetical examples meant to show the difficulty of defining "good" and "bad."

6. **D** By placing plutocrats (people whose power comes from their wealth rather than from their merit) in the same category as burglars, the author shows his scorn of plutocrats.

7. **B** The third paragraph of the passage attempts to show that ethical values reflect the general interest of the group that holds them. The author points out that values held by burglars are not in accord with the general interest.

8. **C** The third paragraph makes the point that individual desires are ethical when they are "not obviously opposed to the general interest."

9. **A** All three are cited as people who profess to have the welfare of others in mind: the preacher (line 57), the plutocrat (line 34), the philosopher (line 37).

10. **A** Citing an example of questionable ethical behavior, the author refers to a man who underhandedly earns money on the Stock Exchange: "Truth . . . is for him a private possession." When a philosopher sinks to the level of a stock-jobber, he, too, has only his self-interest at heart.

11. **E** The author's main purpose is to clarify and explain the concepts of "good" and "bad." To do so, the author discusses values as they relate to emotions. His approach is analytical and rational.

12. **C** The author repeatedly alludes to ethical disagreements brought about by differences in points of view. In the second paragraph, the speaker and his neighbor fall into conflict over their perception of desirable land use.

13. **B** The author's intent is to show the confusion that exists over the nature of ethics. In the end, the author acknowledges that confusion has resulted from the "interlocking of the particular and the universal" (lines 69–70). Until that problem is solved, ethics will remain ill-defined and elusive.

14. D The first paragraph consists of generalizations about man's abhorrence of loneliness. The second paragraph cites an example of extreme loneliness. In the third paragraph the narrator feels obliged to explain that her thoughts about loneliness are based on her own experience. Thus, she relates a personal anecdote about a solo flight she once made.

15. D "Being alone" is a verbal phrase that starts out as the grammatical subject of the sentence. But the verb of the sentence—"can be"—does not appear until line 15, after several intervening prepositional phrases and infinitives. By that time, the writer has chosen to recast the sentence with a new grammatical subject—"such an experience." Consequently, the two phrases together serve as the subject of the sentence.

16. B The author alludes directly and indirectly to the sentiment expressed in the aphoristic opening sentence. She is surprised to meet the "stranger" (herself) in the cockpit of her plane (line 16). Later in the narrative, when her craft has apparently run out of gas, she abandons reason and allows her "stranger's hands" (line 73) to keep her plane from falling into the sea.

17. E Piloting a plane provides the "security of solitude, the exhilaration of escape" (lines 20–21). These feelings contrast with those of the cares of the world below and "the small sorrow of rain," which may call to mind the literary convention of associating rain with death.

18. D The first paragraph of the passage contains a list of several activities that help people avoid loneliness. Only piloting an airplane is not mentioned. In the second paragraph, the author notes that in the cockpit of a plane, in fact, one feels "irrevocably alone" (line 11).

19. C The sentence explains why distance is compared to "so much time used up." But it also serves all the other functions except to show that equating time and distance is an indication of pilot disorientation.

20. A During the first half of the passage the author reflects on loneliness. Then she proudly recalls a solo trans-oceanic flight during which she handled an emergency situation calmly and confidently.

21. A A paradox is a statement that seems to fly in the face of common sense. No such contradiction appears in the given lines from the passage.

22. C Twice in the passage—during the take-off (lines 27–37) and when the motor stalls over the ocean (lines 56–74)—the narrator relies on the immutability of physical laws. Reason says that a large piece of machinery won't fly; it's also reasonable to think that, when an airplane's nose tilts down it ought to be pointed up again, but the laws of flight say otherwise.

23. E Both phrases amplify, or modify, preceding nouns—"act" and "hands." As such, they function like appositives, repeating in more specific words the expressions they modify.

24. B The author stresses the emotional tolls of exile. While objective in parts, the passage consists primarily of one man's thoughts about the phenomenon.

25. D The sentence in question, while defining the word "exile," also conveys the author's attitude toward his subject. It does not limit the subject matter of the passage, however.

26. A In describing exiles, the author seems to understand their plight. Although the author says that artists in exile are "decidedly unpleasant" (lines 68–69), overall, he recognizes that exile is an altogether painful experience.

27. E Dante is described as one who used his writing to settle old scores. His exile embittered him toward those who banished him from Florence.

28. A The sentence (phrased as a question) is meant to support the idea that an exile "is always out of place" (line 11).

29. A The settlers participated in the adventure of nation-building and pioneering in far-off lands. In the passage, the author uses them as examples of people who chose to exile themselves.

30. D The sentence in question is a complex sentence that includes a dependent clause beginning with the subordinating conjunction *but.* The other sentence with similar characteristics is that which immediately precedes it.

31. E Early in the passage (paragraphs 1 and 2) the author describes the "terrible" experience of exile. Here, the author continues to show why a life of exile is a life full of suffering.

32. C The passage says that European novels are "grounded in precisely the opposite experience" (lines 46–47) from that of classical epics. The point is to show that exiled heroes in European novels differ from the heroes of ancient epics.

33. C Several words and phrases ("stiffened will"–line 60; "intransigence"–line 62; "stubbornness"–line 69) suggest that exiles tend to have strong wills.

34. D The quotation announces a change in the manner in which census reports are made. In the remainder of the passage, the author details this change and explains its historic implications.

35. C According to the author, "vital forces" generate institutional changes.

36. A In lines 30–32, the author contrasts primitive industrial society with a manufacturing civilization. The difference between them, he says, is that the former lacks a "division of labor."

37. A The author alludes to the "germ theory" in the context of a discussion about growth and development, described vividly by Calhoun's words. The quotation suggests that in 1817 the nation was expanding uncontrollably—not an altogether sanguine situation in Calhoun's words, but rather, the author believes, like a plague of "germs."

38. D Growth in a limited geographical area is characteristic of Europe and of the original American settlement along the Atlantic coast. All the other features pertain to the frontier in the American West.

39. D According to the paragraph in question, the frontier has been the "meeting point between savagery and civilization," and has been marked by "border warfare." Both phrases imply the existence of a clash between the settlers and those who interfered with their progress—namely the native inhabitants of the land. Indeed, much has been written about the conflict between settlers and the Indians.

40. C Twice in the passage, the author quotes authority figures—the Superintendent of the Census (line 1) and Calhoun (line 21)—and then refers to Professor von Holst (lines 44–45). In all instances, the words serve as a springboard to further discussion.

41. D While the sentence points out that the European and American frontiers differ from each other, the purpose of the entire last paragraph of the passage is to summarize what came before. Thus, the sentence introduces and contributes to a summary of the passage.

42. B The author analyzes the historical meaning of the end of the frontier in America. He expresses no strong feelings about it. Rather, he presents his interpretation.

43. C Throughout the passage, the author refers to the frontier's influence on American life. In the first paragraph he states that American development can be explained by the westward expansion. In the next paragraph, he states that America's institutions have adapted to the needs of expansion. In lines 37–43, the author states outright that the frontier has furnished "the forces dominating the American character."

44. D The capitalized words convey the effect of the drill instructor's speech pattern and loudness.

45. E The phrase "daring glances" is a participial modifying the noun "recruits."

46. E The paragraph is filled with visual images, climaxed by the vivid reference to "raindrops beading on spitshined black shoes."

47. B Most of the passage is devoted to describing the behavior of the omnipotent drill instructors. Their power contrasts starkly with the haplessness of the recruits.

48. C Hudson and Burley, proud, tough Marines, stand in stark contrast to the goofy, wisecracking Hargrove and Bilko of television fame.

49. C While not an exact quote from Marine Corps regulations, the material in these lines is a paraphrase of the rules governing recruits during their basic training.

50. E The paragraph contains all of the techniques except a subordinate clause set off by dashes. The material between the dashes (lines 45–46) is an independent clause embedded in another independent clause.

51. C Because the word "dread" names the subject of the sentence ("It"), it is a predicate nominative. Other words in the sentence that serve the same function are "spectacle" and "initiation."

52. B Each of the choices has possibilities, but the purpose of the passage is best described as the author's attempt to recreate life at Parris Island. The extreme emotions and often inflammatory choice of words contain ample evidence of melodrama.

53. E All the choices are descriptive except the last one, in which the author implies his approval of the methods used by the Marine Corps to train its recruits.

Answers to Essay Questions

For an overview of how essays are graded, turn to "How AP Essays Are Scored," on page 43.

Although answers to the essay questions will vary greatly, the following descriptions suggest a possible approach to each question and contain ideas that could be used in a response to the question. Perhaps your essay contains many of the same ideas. If not, don't be alarmed. Your ideas may be at least as valid as—or even better than—those presented below.

Question 1

Severeid's topic is mankind's relationship with the moon, which, in 1958, was about to undergo a drastic change. For eons the moon had been associated with love; now it has become the focus of government scientists and a destination for future astronauts. At first Severeid regards the impending change with amusement. In the first paragraph, he intertwines the bureaucratic jargon of government and politics with the language of love: "whispering sweet sentiments about the reciprocal trade act, the extension thereof," "bilateral negotiations between lovers."

By the end of the third paragraph, however, Severeid's discussion has turned serious. In two sentences made strong by repetition and parallelism, he expresses apprehension over the changes about to occur: " . . . the ancient moon will never be the same again. Therefore, we suspect, the heart of man will never be the same."

In the remainder of the passage, Severeid develops the notion that we have a great deal to learn about ourselves before we travel into space to learn about the moon. To emphasize his concern, he uses a number of balanced phrases, employing parallel words and repetition to juxtapose contrasting ideas: " . . .discover the composition of a lunar crater" is juxtaposed against "discovering the true mind of a Russian commissar." Similarly, "advance upon the bright side of the moon with the dark side of ourselves" is not only a cleverly phrased, memorable locution, but contains the gist of Severeid's vision of a troubled future.

Question 2

Although the two passages were written by the same person, they are dramatically different from each other. In the first, Einstein explains a phenomenon in physics, a world in which he is very much at home. Much of the passage is factual, precise, and impersonal. He writes, for example, "The latter was considered measurable . . .," using a passive construction in order to avoid using the first person. The technical nature of the passage is evident in several symbols and formulas and in the specialized language of physics, e.g., "negligible spatial extent" and "the simultaneity of spatially distant events."

Unlike the first passage, the second is written speculatively. Gone is the voice of authority and the technical language and formulas—replaced herein by vague generalizations couched in the language of economics and sociology. Consider such phrases as "an educational system . . . oriented toward social goals," and "the education of the individual . . . would attempt to develop . . . a sense of responsibility." This sort of language may sound good, but it lacks substance. It's jargon, plain and simple. We are hearing the views of someone who may be a thoughtful human being, but the words resemble empty platitudes. Instead of stating his case forcefully, Einstein resorts to the repeated use of *would,* a word that suggests tentativeness. Had he been more confident and well-informed on the topic, his language would have reflected greater certainty. He would have used *will,* a far more decisive word.

Question 3

In this passage, Robert Louis Stevenson laments the fact that men fail to appreciate the possibilities that life has to offer. Men are more interested, he thinks, in arranging and preserving their lives than in truly living them. To live fully one must be open to the "accidents of existence." Thus, adventurers, such as Alpine climbers, love life more deeply than "the creature who lives upon a diet and walks a measured distance in the interest of his constitution." Were you to agree with Stevenson, your essay would support the notion, articulated so memorably by Thoreau, that most men lead lives of "quiet desperation." No doubt you can think of people in literature (J. Alfred Prufrock, for one) and in life (a friend, a family member) who are so busy pampering themselves and taking care of the mundane chores of existence that they have shut the door to the surprises and opportunities that life can offer.

On the other hand, it is possible to defend the person who thrives on carefully managing and controlling all aspects of life. You might argue that no one has the right to tell another how to lead his life, and the ordinary citizen who quietly follows daily routines may feel that he is truly sucking the marrow out of life as well as anybody else. Thus, you might take the position that it is wrong for Stevenson to condemn the plain Joe or Jane who claims that life is just something you live "one day at a time."

Answer Sheet for Practice Test B
Language and Composition

Multiple-Choice
Questions
Time—1 hour

1. Ⓐ Ⓑ Ⓒ Ⓓ Ⓔ
2. Ⓐ Ⓑ Ⓒ Ⓓ Ⓔ
3. Ⓐ Ⓑ Ⓒ Ⓓ Ⓔ
4. Ⓐ Ⓑ Ⓒ Ⓓ Ⓔ
5. Ⓐ Ⓑ Ⓒ Ⓓ Ⓔ
6. Ⓐ Ⓑ Ⓒ Ⓓ Ⓔ
7. Ⓐ Ⓑ Ⓒ Ⓓ Ⓔ
8. Ⓐ Ⓑ Ⓒ Ⓓ Ⓔ
9. Ⓐ Ⓑ Ⓒ Ⓓ Ⓔ
10. Ⓐ Ⓑ Ⓒ Ⓓ Ⓔ
11. Ⓐ Ⓑ Ⓒ Ⓓ Ⓔ
12. Ⓐ Ⓑ Ⓒ Ⓓ Ⓔ
13. Ⓐ Ⓑ Ⓒ Ⓓ Ⓔ
14. Ⓐ Ⓑ Ⓒ Ⓓ Ⓔ
15. Ⓐ Ⓑ Ⓒ Ⓓ Ⓔ
16. Ⓐ Ⓑ Ⓒ Ⓓ Ⓔ
17. Ⓐ Ⓑ Ⓒ Ⓓ Ⓔ
18. Ⓐ Ⓑ Ⓒ Ⓓ Ⓔ
19. Ⓐ Ⓑ Ⓒ Ⓓ Ⓔ
20. Ⓐ Ⓑ Ⓒ Ⓓ Ⓔ

21. Ⓐ Ⓑ Ⓒ Ⓓ Ⓔ
22. Ⓐ Ⓑ Ⓒ Ⓓ Ⓔ
23. Ⓐ Ⓑ Ⓒ Ⓓ Ⓔ
24. Ⓐ Ⓑ Ⓒ Ⓓ Ⓔ
25. Ⓐ Ⓑ Ⓒ Ⓓ Ⓔ
26. Ⓐ Ⓑ Ⓒ Ⓓ Ⓔ
27. Ⓐ Ⓑ Ⓒ Ⓓ Ⓔ
28. Ⓐ Ⓑ Ⓒ Ⓓ Ⓔ
29. Ⓐ Ⓑ Ⓒ Ⓓ Ⓔ
30. Ⓐ Ⓑ Ⓒ Ⓓ Ⓔ
31. Ⓐ Ⓑ Ⓒ Ⓓ Ⓔ
32. Ⓐ Ⓑ Ⓒ Ⓓ Ⓔ
33. Ⓐ Ⓑ Ⓒ Ⓓ Ⓔ
34. Ⓐ Ⓑ Ⓒ Ⓓ Ⓔ
35. Ⓐ Ⓑ Ⓒ Ⓓ Ⓔ
36. Ⓐ Ⓑ Ⓒ Ⓓ Ⓔ
37. Ⓐ Ⓑ Ⓒ Ⓓ Ⓔ
38. Ⓐ Ⓑ Ⓒ Ⓓ Ⓔ
39. Ⓐ Ⓑ Ⓒ Ⓓ Ⓔ
40. Ⓐ Ⓑ Ⓒ Ⓓ Ⓔ

41. Ⓐ Ⓑ Ⓒ Ⓓ Ⓔ
42. Ⓐ Ⓑ Ⓒ Ⓓ Ⓔ
43. Ⓐ Ⓑ Ⓒ Ⓓ Ⓔ
44. Ⓐ Ⓑ Ⓒ Ⓓ Ⓔ
45. Ⓐ Ⓑ Ⓒ Ⓓ Ⓔ
46. Ⓐ Ⓑ Ⓒ Ⓓ Ⓔ
47. Ⓐ Ⓑ Ⓒ Ⓓ Ⓔ
48. Ⓐ Ⓑ Ⓒ Ⓓ Ⓔ
49. Ⓐ Ⓑ Ⓒ Ⓓ Ⓔ
50. Ⓐ Ⓑ Ⓒ Ⓓ Ⓔ
51. Ⓐ Ⓑ Ⓒ Ⓓ Ⓔ
52. Ⓐ Ⓑ Ⓒ Ⓓ Ⓔ
53. Ⓐ Ⓑ Ⓒ Ⓓ Ⓔ

Three Essay
Questions
Time—2 hours

Write your essays on standard 8½ by 11-inch composition paper. At the exam you will be given a bound booklet containing 12 lined pages.

B Language and Composition

SECTION I
Total time—1 hour

Carefully read the following passage and answer the accompanying questions.

Questions 1–10 are based on the following passage.

I am not excessively fond of salads or fruit, with the exception
of melons. My father hated every kind of sauce; I like them all. Eating
too much makes me uncomfortable; but in respect of its properties I

Line am not yet very certain that any kind of food disagrees with me. Nor
(5) have I noticed that I am affected by full or new moons, by autumn or
spring.

    We are subject to fickle and inexplicable changes. For
example, radishes, which I first found to agree with me, afterwards
disagreed, and now they agree again. In several things I have found
(10) my stomach and palate to vary in the same way: I have changed more
than once from white wine to claret, and back again from claret to
white wine.

    I have a dainty tooth for fish, and the meatless days are my
meat-days; my fasts are my feasts. Besides, I believe that it is, as some
(15) people say, more easily digested than meat. As it goes against my
conscience to eat meat on fish-days, so my taste rebels against mixing
meat and fish; the difference seems to me too wide.

    From my youth up I have occasionally skipped a meal; either
to sharpen my appetite for the next day (for, as Epicurus used to fast
(20) and make lean meals in order to accustom his greed to dispense with
plenty, I do so, on the contrary, in order to train my greed to take
better advantage of plenty and to enjoy it more cheerfully); or I used
to fast to keep my strength for the performance of some mental or
bodily action; for both my body and mind are made cruelly sluggish by
(25) repletion. (And especially do I hate the foolish idea of coupling so
healthy and active a goddess with that little pot-bellied, belching god,
all swelled up with the fumes of his liquor.) Or again, to cure my
ailing digestion; or for want of congenial company; for with that same
Epicurus I say that we should not so much look to what we eat as to
(30) whom we eat with. And I applaud Chilo, who would not promise to
accept Periander's invitation to a feast until he was informed who
were the other guests.

    To me no dressing is so acceptable, and no sauce so
appetizing, as that derived from good company.

(35)   I think it is more wholesome to eat more at leisure, and less,
and to eat oftener. But I would give hunger and appetite their due; I
should take no pleasure in dragging through three or four wretched

repasts a day, restricted by doctors' orders. Who will assure me that I
can recover at supper-time the good appetite I had this morning? Let

(40)   us old men especially take the first opportunity that comes our way.
Let us leave the making of dietaries to doctors and almanac-makers.

The best fruit of my health is sensual pleasure; let us seize the
first that is present and known. I avoid consistency in these laws of
fasting. He who wishes to benefit by a habit, let him avoid continuing

(45)   it. We become hardened, our powers are dulled by it; six months after
your stomach will be so inured to it, that all the advantage you have
gained will be to have lost the freedom of doing otherwise except to
your prejudice.

I do not cover my legs and thighs more in winter than in

(50)   summer: simple silk hose. For the relief of my colds I gave way to the
habit of keeping my head warmer, and my belly on account of the
colic. But in a few days my ailments became accustomed to them and
scorned my ordinary precautions: from a cap I advanced to a kerchief,
and from a bonnet to a lined hat. The wadding of my doublet is now

(55)   only ornamental. All that would be of no avail unless I added a hare's
skin or a vulture's plumage, with a skull-cap for the head. Continue
this gradual progress and you will go a long way. I shall take care not
to do so, and would gladly go back to where I began, if I dared.

"Have you developed a new ailment? Is the remedy no longer

(60)   of any avail? You have grown accustomed to it? Then try another." In
this way they ruin their health who allow themseves to be fettered by
enforced rules, and superstitiously adhere to them; they need more
and more, and after that more again. There is no end.

(1588)

1. It can be inferred that the sentence in lines 4–6 ("Nor have I . . . spring)
    refers to
    (A) widely held superstitions.
    (B) a discredited astrological prediction.
    (C) a physician's advice to a patient.
    (D) an old saying about overeating.
    (E) a folk remedy for indigestion.

2. The author's references to radishes and to claret (second paragraph) func-
    tion in all of the following ways EXCEPT to
    (A) prove the validity of the second paragraph's topic sentence.
    (B) identify changes that the author has experienced.
    (C) define the word "fickle" (line 7).
    (D) add to the litany of the author's personal quirks.
    (E) hint that the author has switched from a serious to an ironic tone.

3. The author claims to have a "dainty tooth for fish" (line 13) primarily
    because
    (A) he observes meatless days.
    (B) fish is less filling than meat.
    (C) he likes fish better than meat.
    (D) fish is easier to digest than meat.
    (E) fish is more healthful than meat.

4. Lines 13–17 contain all of the following EXCEPT
   (A) alliteration.
   (B) parallel syntax.
   (C) synecdoche.
   (D) a paradox.
   (E) onomatopoeia.

5. The speaker justifies his occasional fasting with which of the following reasons?
   I. To increase his appetite
   II. To overeat without feeling guilty
   III. To give his digestive system a rest
   IV. To derive greater enjoyment from his meals
   (A) I, II, and III
   (B) I, II, and IV
   (C) II, III, and IV
   (D) I, III, and IV
   (E) I, II, III, and IV

6. The passage as a whole can best be described as
   (A) a prescription for a better diet.
   (B) an anecdote about old-fashioned eating customs.
   (C) an account of one man's tastes.
   (D) a comparison of the author and his father.
   (E) ruminations about a man's unhealthful eating habits.

7. Which of the following best describes the rhetorical function of lines 33–34 in the passage?
   (A) They serve as a transition between the paragraphs that come before and after.
   (B) They support the author's assertion that he likes all sauces (line 2).
   (C) They provide evidence contrary to material in a previous paragraph.
   (D) They reiterate an idea presented in the previous paragraph.
   (E) They state a logical conclusion based on statements in the previous paragraph.

8. The speaker's allusion to going back to "where I began" (line 58) refers to
   (A) looking for relief from a head cold.
   (B) an earlier unspecified time of life.
   (C) wearing a skull cap.
   (D) putting on a cap to keep his head warm.
   (E) covering his legs with silk hose.

9. Which of the following phrases is probably exaggerated for effect?
   (A) "from white wine to claret, and back again" (line 11)
   (B) "the little pot-bellied belching god" (26)
   (C) "three or four wretched repasts a day" (lines 37–38)
   (D) "from a bonnet to a lined hat" (line 54)
   (E) "a hare's skin or a vulture's plumage" (lines 55–56)

10. The principal contrast drawn by the author of the passage is between
(A) theory and fact.
(B) conventions and individual preferences.
(C) old wives' tales and modern practices.
(D) idealism and realism.
(E) restraint and freedom.

Questions 11–20 are based on the following passage.

Does history repeat itself? In our Western world in the eighteenth and nineteenth centuries, this question used to be debated as an academic exercise. The spell of well-being which our civilization
Line was enjoying at the time had dazzled our grandfathers into the quaint
(5) pharisaical[1] notion that they were "not as other men are"; they had come to believe that our Western society was exempt from the possibility of falling into those mistakes and mishaps that have been the ruin of certain other civilizations whose history, from the beginning to end, is an open book. To us, in our generation, the old
(10) question has rather suddenly taken on a new and very practical significance. We have awakened to the truth (how, one wonders, could we ever have been blind to it?) that Western man and his works are no more invulnerable than the now extinct civilizations of the Aztecs and the Incas, the Sumerians and the Hittities. So today, with
(15) some anxiety, we are searching the scriptures of the past to find out whether they contain a lesson that we can decipher. Does history give us any information about our own prospects? And, if it does, what is the burden of it? Does it spell out for us an inexorable doom, which we can merely await with folded hands—resigning ourselves, as best
(20) we may, to a fate that we cannot avert or even modify by our own efforts? Or does it inform us, not of certainties, but of probabilities, or bare possibilities, in our own future? The practical difference is vast, for, on this second alternative, so far from being stunned into passivity, we should be aroused to action. On this second alternative,
(25) the lesson of history would not be like an astrologer's horoscope; it would be like a navigator's chart, which affords the seafarer who has the intelligence to use it a much greater hope of avoiding shipwreck than when he was sailing blind, because it gives him the means, if he has the skill and courage to use them, of steering a course between
(30) charted rocks and reefs.
It will be seen that our question needs defining before we plunge into an attempt to answer it. When we ask ourselves "Does history repeat itself?" do we mean no more than "Does history turn out to have repeated itself, on occasions, in the past?" Or are we
(35) asking whether history is governed by inviolable laws which have not only taken effect in every past case to which they have applied but are also bound to take effect in every similar situation that may arise in the future? On this second interpretation, the word "does" would mean "must"; on the other interpretation it would mean "may." On
(40) this issue, the writer of the present article may as well put his cards on the table at once. He is not a determinist in his reading of the riddle of human life. He believes that where there is life there is hope, and that, with God's help, man is master of his own destiny, at least to some extent in some respects.

---

[1]hypocritical

(45)   But as soon as we have taken our stand on this issue between
freedom and necessity that is raised by the ambiguous word "does,"
we find ourselves called upon to define what we mean by the word
"history." If we have to limit the field of history to events that are
wholly within the control of human wills, then, to be sure, for a
(50)   non-determinist no difficulty would arise. But do such events ever
actually occur in real life? In our personal experience, when we are
making a decision, do we not always find ourselves only partly free
and partly bound by past events and present facts in our own life and
in our social and physical environment? Is not history itself, in the last
(55)   analysis, a vision of the whole universe on the move in the
four-dimensional framework of spacetime? And, in this all-embracing
panorama, are there not many events that the most staunch believer in
the freedom of the human will would admit, as readily as the most
thoroughgoing determinist, to be inexorably recurrent and precisely
(60)   predictable?

(1948)

11. In line 9, the phrase "an open book" refers to
    (A) the Western world of the 18th and 19th centuries.
    (B) our grandfathers' notion of history.
    (C) the lessons taught by ancient civilizations.
    (D) the debates of academicians.
    (E) the mistakes of civilizations now fallen into ruin.

12. Which of the following best describes the rhetorical function of the sen-
    tence "To us, in our generation . . . ." (lines 9–11)?
    (A) It reiterates the main idea of the passage.
    (B) It introduces an idea that will be discussed during the rest of the pas-
         sage.
    (C) It introduces a contrast between the past and the present.
    (D) It offers a point of view with which the author disagrees.
    (E) It prepares the reader for the discussion of extinct civilizations.

13. In line 15 the word "scriptures" is best interpreted to mean
    (A) religious beliefs.
    (B) the laws.
    (C) ruins.
    (D) the written record.
    (E) artifacts.

14. The end of the first paragraph (lines 22–30) contains all of the following
    rhetorical features EXCEPT
    (A) an antithesis.
    (B) an extended simile.
    (C) a metaphor.
    (D) alliteration.
    (E) hyperbole.

15. The phrase "this second alternative" (line 23) refers to which of the following?
    (A) History's ability to suggest the future
    (B) The fate we cannot avert or modify
    (C) Predictable events
    (D) Our unknown future
    (E) A navigation chart

16. By comparing an "astrologer's horoscope" (line 25) and a "navigator's chart" (line 26), the author intends to convey the idea that
    (A) unlike our ancestors we have the wherewithal to avoid mistakes of the past.
    (B) our ancestors were more superstitious than we are.
    (C) unlike past civilizations we have the ability to determine our future.
    (D) science is superior to superstition.
    (E) astrology is a dying art.

17. In its context, the word "intelligence" (line 27) can best be defined as
    (A) an understanding of history.
    (B) probabilities.
    (C) information.
    (D) insightfulness.
    (E) techniques used to solve problems.

18. For which of the following reasons does the writer use the expression, "put his cards on the table" (lines 40–41)?
    I. To win the reader's confidence
    II. To indicate that he hasn't yet made up his mind on the question
    III. To admit a personal bias
    (A) II only
    (B) I and II
    (C) II and III
    (D) I and III
    (E) I, II, and III

19. The questions asked by the author in the final paragraph of the passage (lines 50–60) can best be described as
    (A) issues that contradict the point of the passage.
    (B) statements put in the form of questions.
    (C) matters that the author intends to ponder further.
    (D) analogies meant to illustrate the author's point of view.
    (E) a series of conflicting opinions regarding the main question of the passage: "Does history repeat itself?"

20. Which of the following most accurately describes the author's intent throughout the passage?
    (A) To solve a logical problem faced by historians
    (B) To refute theories espoused by other historians
    (C) To speculate on the validity of a historical principle
    (D) To prove an important historical theory
    (E) To define several terms used by historians

Questions 21–30 are based on the following passage.

Line
(5)

(10)

(15)

(20)

(25)

(30)

(35)

(40)

What are the practical results of the modern cult of beauty? The exercises and the massages, the health motors and the skin foods—to what have they led? Are women more beautiful than they were? Do they get something for the enormous expenditure of energy, time and money demanded of them by the beauty-cult? These are questions which it is difficult to answer. For the facts seem to contradict themselves. The campaign for more physical beauty seems to be both a tremendous success and a lamentable failure. It depends how you look at the results.

It is a success in so far as more women retain their youthful appearance to a greater age than in the past. "Old ladies" are already becoming rare. In a few years, we may well believe, they will be extinct. White hair and wrinkles, a bent back and hollow cheeks will come to be regarded as medievally old-fashioned. The crone of the future will be golden, curly and cherry-lipped, neat-ankled and slender. The Portrait of the Artist's Mother will come to be almost indistinguishable, at future picture shows, from the Portrait of the Artist's Daughter. This desirable consummation will be due in part to skin foods and injections of paraffin-wax, facial surgery, mud baths, and paint, in part to improved health, due in its turn to a more rational mode of life. Ugliness is one of the symptoms of disease; beauty, of health. In so far as the campaign for more beauty is also a campaign for more health, it is admirable and, up to a point, genuinely successful. Beauty that is merely the artificial shadow of these symptoms of health is intrinsically of poorer quality than the genuine article. Still, it is a sufficiently good imitation to be sometimes mistakable for the real thing. The apparatus for mimicking the symptoms of health is now within the reach of every moderately prosperous person; the knowledge of the way in which real health can be achieved is growing, and will in time, no doubt, be universally acted upon. When that happy moment comes, will every woman be beautiful—as beautiful, at any rate, as the natural shape of her features, with or without surgical and chemical aid, permits?

The answer is emphatically: No. For real beauty is as much an affair of the inner as of the outer self. The beauty of a porcelain jar is a matter of shape, of color, of surface texture. The jar may be empty or tenanted by spiders, full of honey or stinking slime—it makes no difference to its beauty or ugliness. But a woman is alive, and her beauty is therefore not skin deep. The surface of the human vessel is affected by the nature of its spiritual contents. I have seen women who, by the standards of a connoisseur of porcelain, were ravishingly lovely. Their shape, their color, their surface texture were perfect. And yet they were not beautiful. For the lovely vase was either empty or filled with some corruption. Spiritual emptiness or ugliness shows through. And conversely, there is an interior light that can transfigure forms that the pure aesthetician would regard as imperfect or downright ugly.

21. The word "cult" (line 1) as used in the passage means primarily
(A) a group with a particular obsession.
(B) a subculture dedicated to a pagan rite.
(C) a movement sponsored by patrons of beauty salons.
(D) the devotees of a unique ideology.
(E) the followers of a charismatic leader.

22. The first paragraph raises expectations that the remainder of the passage will be
    (A) a biting indictment.
    (B) an objective description.
    (C) a "pro" and "con" kind of discussion.
    (D) praise for the perpetuation of youthfulness.
    (E) advice on maintaining good health.

23. "'Old ladies' are already becoming rare" (line 10) is an idea that the author develops primarily by means of
    (A) metaphors.
    (B) rhetorical questions.
    (C) examples.
    (D) parallel sentences.
    (E) allusions.

24. The author of the passage can be described in all of the following ways EXCEPT
    (A) probing.
    (B) intellectually curious.
    (C) somewhat condescending.
    (D) scientifically objective.
    (E) perceptive.

25. The author's use of the expression "crone of the future" (line 13) reveals an undercurrent of
    (A) anger.
    (B) bitterness.
    (C) sympathy.
    (D) ridicule.
    (E) irony.

26. "The surface of the human vessel is affected by the nature of its spiritual contents" (lines 38–39) is a statement best decribed as
    (A) an epigram.
    (B) a simile.
    (C) a platitude.
    (D) a witticism.
    (E) a symbol.

27. The point in the passage at which the writer turns to his principal theme is
    (A) at the beginning of paragraph 2.
    (B) when he refers to the Portrait of the Artist's Mother (line 14).
    (C) the last sentence of paragraph 1.
    (D) the beginning of paragraph 3.
    (E) the last two sentences of paragraph 3.

28. The passage contains all of the following EXCEPT
   (A) a description of the success of the cult of beauty.
   (B) a discussion of the link between beauty and health.
   (C) a comparison of inner and outer beauty.
   (D) a sympathetic presentation of the yearning for eternal youth.
   (E) the personal feelings of the author toward the phenomena described.

29. The main intention of the author of the passage is to
   (A) highlight the successful aspects of the beauty cult.
   (B) comment on a phase of female psychology.
   (C) describe a change of values in contemporary society.
   (D) expose the shortcomings and omissions of the beauty cult.
   (E) extol the virtues of aging.

30. The best title for this passage is
   (A) Crones and Fair Ladies.
   (B) Health as a Source of Beauty.
   (C) Staying Young Longer.
   (D) Inner versus Outer Beauty.
   (E) Changing Standards of Beauty.

Questions 31–40 are based on the following passage.

	The faculty of learning is ours that we may find in its exercise
	that delight which arises from the unimpeded activity of any energy in
	the groove nature meant it to run in. Let a man acquire knowledge
Line	not for this or that external and incidental good which may chance to
(5)	result from it, but for itself; not because it is useful or ornamental, but

The faculty of learning is ours that we may find in its exercise
that delight which arises from the unimpeded activity of any energy in
the groove nature meant it to run in. Let a man acquire knowledge
Line   not for this or that external and incidental good which may chance to
(5)   result from it, but for itself; not because it is useful or ornamental, but
because it is knowledge, and therefore good for man to acquire.
"Brothers," says Ulysses in Dante, when with his old and tardy
companions he had left Seville on the right hand and Ceuta on the
other, and was come to that narrow pass where Hercules assigned his
(10)   landmarks to hinder man from venturing farther:[1] "Brothers, who
through a hundred thousand dangers have reached the West, deny
not, to this brief vigil of your senses that remains, experience of the
unpeopled world behind the sunset. Consider of what seed ye are
sprung: ye were not formed to live like brutes, but to follow virtue
(15)   and knowledge." For knowledge resembles virtue in this, and differs
in this from other possessions, that it is not merely a means of
procuring good, but is good in itself simply: it is not a coin which we
pay down to purchase happiness, but has happiness indissolubly
bound up with it. Fortitude and continence and honesty are not
(20)   commended to us on the ground that they conduce, as on the whole
they do conduce, to material success, not yet on the ground that they
will be rewarded hereafter: those whose office it is to exhort mankind
to virtue are ashamed to degrade the cause they plead by proffering
such lures as these. And let us too disdain to take lower ground in
(25)   commending knowledge: let us insist that the pursuit of knowledge,
like the pursuit of righteousness, is part of man's duty to himself, and
remember the Scripture where it is written: "He that refuseth
instruction despiseth his own soul."
       I will not say, as Prof. Tyndall has somewhere said, that all
(30)   happiness belongs to him who can say from his heart "I covet truth."

---

[1]The Straits of Gibraltar are sometimes called the Pillars of Hercules

Entire happiness is not attainable either by this or by any other method. Nay it may be urged on the contrary that the pursuit of truth in some directions is even injurious to happiness, because it compels us to take leave of delusions which were pleasant while they lasted. It
(35) may be urged that the light shed on the origin and destiny of man by the pursuit of truth in some directions is not altogether a cheerful light. It may be urged that man stands to-day in the position of one who has been reared from his cradle as the child of a noble race and the heir to great possessions, and who finds at his coming of age that
(40) he has been deceived alike as to his origin and his expectations, that he neither springs of the high lineage he fancied, nor will inherit the vast estate he looked for, but must put off his towering pride, and contract his boundless hopes, and begin the world anew from a lower level: and this, it may be urged, comes of pursuing knowledge. But
(45) even conceding this, I suppose the answer to be that knowledge, and especially disagreeable knowledge, cannot by any art be totally excluded even from those who do not seek it. Wisdom, said Aeschylus long ago, comes to men whether they will or no. The house of delusions is cheap to build, but draughty to live in, and ready at any
(50) instant to fall; and it is surely truer prudence to move our furniture betimes into the open air than to stay indoors until our tenement tumbles about our ears. It is and it must in the long run be better for a man to see things as they are than to be ignorant of them; just as there is less fear of stumbling or of striking against corners in the daylight
(55) than in the dark.

31. What is the primary rhetorical function of the quotation: "Brothers . . . fol-
low virtue and knowledge" (lines 10–15)?
(A) To add a new dimension to the thesis stated in lines 3–6
(B) To provide an idea that will be questioned later in the passage
(C) To introduce testimony from an authority on the subject of the passage
(D) To appeal to the reader's sense of history
(E) To demonstrate the universality of the impulse to acquire knowledge

32. To make his point in lines 15–19 the author uses which of the following?
(A) An extended metaphor
(B) Emphasis through antithetical statements
(C) Hyperbole
(D) Clichés
(E) Repetition

33. The point made by the analogy in lines 19–28 is that
(A) it is morally wrong to reject learning.
(B) virtue often leads to material success.
(C) knowledge and goodness are always rewarded in the end.
(D) virtue and knowledge are important to survival.
(E) learning and moral behavior are intrinsically worthwhile.

34. In line 24 "lower ground" refers to
    (A) living like brutes.
    (B) material success.
    (C) the promise of rewards.
    (D) immoral behavior.
    (E) lack of faith in Scripture.

35. Which of the following phrases does the author use to illustrate the concept of knowledge?
    (A) "unimpeded activity" (line 2)
    (B) "a brief vigil of your senses" (line 12)
    (C) "a coin which we pay down to purchase happiness" (lines 17–18)
    (D) "Entire happiness" (line 31)
    (E) "the daylight" (line 54)

36. According to the passage, the most important reason for men to acquire knowledge is
    (A) to fulfill their destinies as humans.
    (B) that knowledge is inherently good.
    (C) that men with knowledge need not live like brutes.
    (D) that knowledge leads to happiness.
    (E) that knowledge is useful.

37. In lines 47–53, the author employs a metaphor that compares
    (A) inexperience and disease.
    (B) wisdom and the out-of-doors.
    (C) ignorance and a run-down dwelling.
    (D) self-delusion and prudence.
    (E) enlightenment and good health.

38. Which of the following best describes the relationship between knowledge and happiness discussed in the last paragraph of the passage?
    (A) A wise man is usually happier than an ignorant man.
    (B) Both knowledge and happiness are elusive goals.
    (C) Knowledge may lead to unhappiness.
    (D) Ignorance in bliss.
    (E) One must work for knowledge; happiness comes naturally.

39. Throughout the passage the author's tone might best be characterized as
    (A) provocative and inflammatory.
    (B) inspiring and hortatory.
    (C) self-conscious and placid.
    (D) pompous and impulsive.
    (E) eccentric and uninhibited.

40. The best title for the passage is
    (A) The Dangers of Ignorance.
    (B) The Threat of Anti-Intellectualism.
    (C) The Gifts of Intelligence.
    (D) A Theory of Knowledge.
    (E) The Need for Learning.

Questions 41–53 are based on the following passage.

In 1960 the weekly *l'Express* of Paris published a series of extracts
from texts by American and Russian scientists concerning society in
the year 2000. As long as such visions were purely a literary concern
Line   of science fiction writers and sensation journalists, it was possible to
(5)   smile at them. Now we have like works from Nobel Prize winners,
members of the Academy of Science in Moscow, and other scientific
notables. The visions of these men put science fiction in the shade.

By 2000, voyages to the moon will be commonplace; so will
inhabited, artificial satellites. All food will be completely synthetic.
(10)   The world's population will have increased fourfold but will have been
stabilized. Sea water and ordinary rocks will yield all the necessary
metals. Disease, as well as famine, will have been eliminated; and
there will be universal hygienic inspection and control. The problems
of energy production will have been completely resolved. Serious
(15)   scientists, it must be repeated, are the source of these predictions,
which hitherto were found only in Utopia.

The most remarkable predictions concern the transformation of
educational methods and the problem of human reproduction.
Knowledge will be accumulated in "electronic banks" and be
(20)   transmitted directly to the human nervous systems by means of coded
electronic messages. There will no longer be any need of reading or
learning mountains of useless information; everything will be received
and registered according to the needs of the moment. There will be no
need of attention or effort. What is needed will pass directly from the
(25)   machine to the brain without going through consciousness.

In the domain of genetics, natural reproduction will be forbidden.
A stable population will be necessary, and it will consist of the highest
human types. Artificial insemination will be employed. This, according
to Nobelist H.J. Muller, will "permit the introduction into a carrier
(30)   uterus of an ovum fertilized *in vitro,* ovum and sperm . . . having been
taken from persons representing the masculine ideal and the feminine
ideal, respectively. . . . Such cells will be taken from cell banks and
will represent the most precious genetic heritage of humanity. . . . The
method will have to be applied universally. If the people of a single
(35)   country were to apply it intelligently and intensively . . . they would
quickly attain a practically invincible level of superiority. . . ." Here is
a future Huxley never dreamed of.

Perhaps instead of marveling or being shocked, we ought to
reflect a little. . . . In Muller's distant Utopia, how shall we get
(40)   humanity to refrain from begetting children naturally? How shall we
force them to submit to constant and rigorous hygienic
controls? How shall man be persuaded to accept a radical
transformation of his traditional modes of nutrition? How and where
shall we relocate a billion and a half persons who today make their
(45)   livings from agriculture and who, in the promised ultrarapid
conversion of the next forty years, will become completely useless as
cultivators of the soil? How shall we distribute such numbers of
people equably over the surface of the earth, particularly if the
promised fourfold increase in population materializes? . . .There are
(50)   many other "hows," but they are left conveniently unformulated.

When we reflect on the serious although relatively minor
problems that were provoked by the industrial exploitation of coal and
electricity, when we reflect that after a hundred and fifty years these

(55) problems are still not satisfactorily resolved, we are entitled to ask whether there are any solutions to the infinitely more complex "hows" of the next forty years. In fact, there is one and only one means to their solution, a world-wide totalitarian dictatorship which will allow technique its full scope and at the same time resolve its concomitant difficulties. It is not difficult to understand why the scientists and

(60) worshipers of technology prefer not to dwell on their solution, but rather to leap numbly across the dull and uninteresting intermediary period and land squarely in the golden age. We might indeed ask ourselves if we will succeed in getting through the transition period at all, or if the blood and suffering required are not perhaps too high a

(65) price to pay for this golden age. . . .

When our savants characterize their golden age in any but scientific terms, they emit a quantity of down-at-the-heels platitudes that would gladden the heart of the pettiest politician. Let's take a few samples. "To render human nature nobler, more beautiful, and more

(70) harmonious." What on earth can this mean? What criteria, what content, do they propose? Not many, I fear, would be able to reply. "To assure the triumph of peace, liberty, and reason." Fine words with no substance behind them. "To eliminate cultural lag." What culture? And would the culture they have in mind be able to subsist in this

(75) harsh social organization? "To conquer outer space." For what purpose? The conquest of space seems an end in itself, which dispenses the need for reflection.

We are forced to conclude that our scientists are incapable of any but the emptiest of platitudes when they stray from their

(80) specialties . . . .Their pomposities, in fact, do not rise to the level of the average. They are vague generalities inherited from the nineteenth century, and the fact that they represent the furthest limits of thought of our scientific worthies must be symptomatic of arrested development or of mental block.

(85) Particularly disquieting is the gap between the enormous power they wield and their critical ability, which must be estimated as null. To wield power well entails a certain faculty of criticism, judgment, and option. It is impossible to have confidence in men who apparently lack these faculties. Yet it is apparently our fate to be facing a "golden

(90) age" in the power of sorcerers who are totally blind to the meaning of the human adventure.

(1964)

41. In discussing the "ideal" world of the future (lines 8–36), the author's tone is
(A) appreciative.
(B) captious.
(C) humorous.
(D) satirical.
(E) objective.

42. The author's attitude toward visionary scientists can best be described as
(A) cynical.
(B) confident.
(C) hopeful.
(D) admiring.
(E) fearful.

43. The locution "masculine ideal and feminine ideal, respectively" (lines 31–32) may best be described as
(A) legalistic jargon.
(B) a scientific term.
(C) a common idiom.
(D) a figure of speech.
(E) a pun.

44. The author of the passage can best be described as a person who
(A) is committed to preserving the status quo.
(B) sees the need for international cooperation to carry out scientific research.
(C) is impressed with the contributions of Nobel Prize winners.
(D) is willing to stretch the truth to make a point.
(E) has high hopes for the future.

45. The rhetorical functions of the sentence in lines 38–39 ("Perhaps . . . a little") include all of the following EXCEPT
(A) providing a transition that contributes to the coherence of the passage.
(B) beginning a discussion of the ideas expressed in the previous paragraphs.
(C) alerting the reader to a shift in the focus of the passage.
(D) anticipating the reader's reaction to the foregoing paragraphs.
(E) anticipating objections raised by ideas presented in the previous paragraph.

46. It may be inferred that the purpose of the passage is to
(A) expose the failure of creativity in American society.
(B) present science as a creative force in American life.
(C) warn readers about the dangers that lie ahead.
(D) expose the dangers of scientific domination.
(E) pay tribute to the work of visionary scientists.

47. In arguing against some of the potential effects of the technological revolution (lines 51–56), the author uses
(A) an antithesis.
(B) negative reasoning.
(C) induction.
(D) analogy.
(E) simile.

48. In its context, the word "savants" in line 66 is used
(A) pedantically.
(B) metaphorically.
(C) ironically.
(D) symbolically.
(E) literally.

49. In the paragraph that begins with line 66, which of the following stylistic devices is most evident?
    (A) Rhetorical questions
    (B) A list of facts
    (C) Impressionistic images
    (D) The use of synecdoche
    (E) Abstract generalizations

50. Lines 81–84 contain which of the following grammatical structures?
    (A) A compound sentence
    (B) A periodic sentence
    (C) A restrictive clause
    (D) Subordinate clauses
    (E) A compound predicate

51. The word "null" in line 86 derives force from which of the following?
       I. Its connotation
      II. Its sound
     III. Its location in the sentence
    (A) II only
    (B) I and II only
    (C) I and III only
    (D) II and III only
    (E) I, II, and III

52. The style of the passage can best be described as
    (A) graceful and poetic.
    (B) graphic and lucid.
    (C) formal and abstract.
    (D) erudite and scholarly.
    (E) scientific and technical.

53. The best title for this passage is
    (A) Hopes for Mankind.
    (B) The Blessings of Science.
    (C) Visions of the Future.
    (D) The Failures of the Evolutionary Process.
    (E) Revising Human Values and Goals.

SECTION II
Total time—2 hours

Question 1

(Suggested time—40 minutes. This question counts as one third of the total score for Section II.)

Read the following passage from John Donne's, "Meditation XVII" (Devotions upon Emergent Occasions, 1624), in which the author reflects on death—his own and that of others. Then write an essay in which you analyze the language that Donne uses to convey his thoughts. Consider such rhetorical and stylistic techniques as figures of speech, structure, syntax, and tone.

Nunc lento sonitu dicunt, morieris[1]

Perchance he for whom this bell tolls may be so ill as that he
knows not it tolls for him; and perchance I may think of myself so
much better than I am as that they who are about me and see my state
Line   may have caused it to toll for me, and I know not that. The church is
(5)   catholic, universal, so are all her actions; all that she does belongs to
all. When she baptizes a child, that action concerns me; for that child
is thereby connected to that body which is my head too and ingrafted
into that body whereof I am a member. And when she buries a man,
that action concerns me. All mankind is of one author, and is one
(10)   volume; when one man dies, one chapter is not torn out of the book,
but translated into a better language; and every chapter must be so
translated. God employs several translators; some pieces are
translated by age, some by sickness, some by war, some by justice;
but God's hand is in every translation, and his hand shall bind up all
(15)   our scattered leaves again for that library where every book shall lie
open to one another. As therefore the bell that rings to sermon calls
not upon the preacher only but upon the congregation to come, so
this bell calls us all; but how much more me who am brought so near
the door by this sickness! There was a contention as far as a suit—in
(20)   which piety and dignity, religion and estimation, were mingled—which
of the religious orders should ring to prayers first in the morning; and
it was determined that they should ring first that rose earliest. If we
understand aright the dignity of this bell that tolls for our evening
prayer, we would be glad to make it ours by rising early, in that
(25)   application, that it might be ours as well as his, whose indeed it is.
The bell doth toll for him that thinks it doth; and though it intermit
again, yet from that minute that the occasion wrought upon him he is
united to God. Who casts not up his eye to the sun when it rises? but
who takes his eye for a comet when that breaks out? Who bends not
(30)   his ear to any bell which upon any occasion rings? but who can
remove it from that bell which is passing a piece of himself out of this
world? No man is an island entire of itself; every man is a piece of the
continent, a part of the main. If a clod be washed away by the sea,
Europe is the less, as well as if a promontory were, as well as if a
(35)   manor or thy friend's or of thine own were. Any man's death
diminishes me, because I am involved in mankind, and therefore never
send to know for whom the bell tolls; it tolls for thee. Neither can we
call this a begging of misery or a borrowing of misery, as though we
were not miserable enough of ourselves but must fetch in more from

---

[1]Now this bell tolling softly says, you must die.

(40)   the next house, in taking upon us the misery of our neighbors. Truly it ·
         were an excusable covetousness if we did, for affliction is a treasure,
         and scarce any man hath enough of it. No man hath affliction enough
         that is not matured and riped by it and made fit for God by that
         affliction. If a man carry treasure in bullion or in a wedge of gold and
(45)   have none coined into current money, his treasure will not defray him
         as he travels. Tribulation is treasure in the nature of it, but it is not
         current money in the use of it, except we get nearer and nearer our
         home, heaven, by it. Another man may be sick too, and sick to death,
         and this affliction may lie in his bowels as gold in a mine and be of no
(50)   use to him; but his bell that tells me of his affliction digs out and
         applies that gold to me, if by this consideration of another's danger I
         take mine own into contemplation and so secure myself by making my
         recourse to my God, who is our only security.

Question 2

(Suggested time—40 minutes. This question counts as one third of the total
score for Section II.)

After you have read the following passages—the first by Maxwell Anderson, a
playwright and novelist, the other by Susanne Langer, a philosopher and
teacher—write an essay that compares the ways in which the two authors convey
their views about art. You might consider such rhetorical and stylistic devices as
diction, figurative language, point of view, repetition, and sentence structure.

Passage A

         To the young people of this country I wish to say: if
         you practice an art, be proud of it and make it proud of you;
         if you now hesitate on the threshold of your maturity,
Line   wondering what rewards you should seek, wondering perhaps
(5)   whether there are any rewards beyond the opportunity to
         feed and sleep and breed, turn to the art which has moved you
         most readily, take what part in it you can, as participator,
         spectator, secret practitioner, or hanger-on and waiter at the
         door. Make your living any way you can, but neglect no sacrifice
(10)   at your chosen altar. It may break your heart, it may drive you
         half mad, it may betray you into unrealizable ambitions or blind
         you to mercantile opportunities with its wandering fires. But it
         will fill your heart before it breaks it; it will make you a person
         in your own right; it will open the temple doors to you and en-
(15)   able you to walk with those who have come nearest among men
         to what men may sometime be. If the time arrives when our
         young men and women lose their extravagant faith in the dollar
         and turn to the arts we may then become a great nation, nurturing
         great artists of our own, proud of our own culture and unified by
(20)   that culture into a civilization worthy of our unique place on this
         rich and lucky continent between its protecting seas.

                                                                    (1947)

Passage B

         Art is, indeed, the spearhead of human development,
         social and individual. The vulgarization of art is the surest
         symptom of ethnic decline. The growth of a new art or even

(25)   a great and radically new style always bespeaks a young and
             vigorous mind, whether collective or single.
                What sort of thing is art, that it should play such a
             leading role in human development? It is not an intellectual
             pursuit, but is necessary to intellectual life; it is not religion,
(30)   but grows up with religion, serves it and in large measure
             determines it (as Herodotus said, "Homer made the gods,"
             and surely the Egyptian deities grew under the chisels of
             sculptors in strangely solemn forms).
                We cannot enter here on a long discussion of what
(35)   has been claimed as the essence of art, the true nature of art,
             or its defining function; in a single lecture dealing with one
             aspect of art, namely its cultural significance, I can only give
             you by way of preamble my own definition of art, with
             categorical brevity. That does not mean that I set up this
(40)   definition in a categorical spirit, but only that we have no
             time to debate it, so you are asked to accept it as an
             assumption underlying these reflections.
                Art, in the sense intended—that is, the generic term
             subsuming painting, sculpture, architecture, music, dance,
(45)   literature and drama—may be defined as the practice of
             creating perceptible forms expressive of human feeling. I
             say "perceptible" rather than "sensuous" forms because some
             works of art are given to imagination rather than to the outward
             senses. A novel, for instance, usually is read silently with the
(50)   eye, but is not made for vision, as a painting is; and though
             sound plays a vital part in poetry, words even in poetry are not
             essentially sonorous structures like music. Dance requires to
             be seen, but its appeal is to deeper centers of sensation. The
             difference between dance and mobile sculpture makes this
(55)   immediately apparent. But all works of art are purely
             perceptible forms that seem to embody some sort of feeling.

(1957)

Question 3

(Suggested time—40 minutes. This question counts as one third of the total score for Section II.)

The German poet Goethe once wrote, "Treat people as if they were what they ought to be and you help them to become what they are capable of being." Goethe's statement might be applied to schools, government, social services, business, even to families—anyplace, really, where people interact with each other. Is Goethe just expressing pretty-sounding, idealistic nonsense, or does his ideal have real-life applicability? In a well-organized essay, comment on the validity of Goethe's statement as a realistic guide to human relationships. To support your point of view, you may draw evidence from your reading, personal experience, and observation.

Answer Key for Practice Exam B
Answers to Multiple-Choice Questions

1. A	12. C	23. D	34. E	45. E
2. E	13. C	24. D	35. E	46. D
3. C	14. E	25. E	36. A	47. D
4. E	15. A	26. A	37. C	48. C
5. D	16. A	27. D	38. C	49. A
6. C	17. D	28. D	39. B	50. A
7. D	18. D	29. D	40. E	51. C
8. D	19. B	30. D	41. D	52. B
9. E	20. C	31. A	42. A	53. E
10. B	21. A	32. B	43. A	
11. E	22. C	33. A	44. D	

Answer Explanations

1. **A** The author is alluding to common beliefs held at the time he was writing. Readers at the time would no doubt recognize the references. We can only speculate that the author rejects some widely held superstitions about the relationship between diet and natural phenomena.

2. **E** The first sentence of the paragraph is the topic sentence. The remainder of the paragraph supports the topic sentence and adds to the self-portrait of the author. There is no evidence of a change in the author's tone.

3. **C** In an aside (lines 14–15) the author observes that some people say fish is easier to digest than meat. He prefers fish, however, simply because he likes it more: ". . . meatless days are my meat-days" he says—that is, he regards fish-days as special days.

4. **E** Line 14 contains an alliteration ("my fasts are my feasts"). Two clauses in the last sentence of the paragraph are parallel in structure ("As it goes against . . ." and ". . . my taste rebels against . . ."). The phrase "dainty tooth" is a synecdoche—a figure of speech in which a part stands for the whole. "My fasts are my feasts" is a paradox. Only onomatopoeia is missing.

5. **D** The author enjoys eating and never regrets consuming too much—except wine.

6. **C** The discussion of eating habits appears in the context of a description of how the author manages to lead a pleasurable life—by acceding to his whims and fancies.

7. **D** According to the previous paragraph, one's dining companions at a pleasurable meal are at least as important as the quality of the food. Lines 33–34 reiterate that sentiment.

8. **D** To stay warm, the speaker keeps donning additional layers of clothing. His body, however, shortly craves more layers. Having grown weary of

putting on more and more, the speaker would like to return to the time before he first put a cap on to keep his head warm.

9. E   In the next to last paragraph, the author describes the methods he uses to keep warm. He knows that it would be ridiculous to resort to "a hare's skin or a vulture's plumage." Yet he uses the terms to emphasize the lengths to which he is forced to go in order to remain comfortably warm.

10. B   The passage is devoted to descriptions of the author's preferences, particularly in food and health care. Although his preferences often fly in the face of convention, he makes no apology.

11. E   Because the "open book" records mistakes of past civilizations, readers can infer the lessons that history teaches. The "open book" itself, however, refers to the history of past civilizations, in particular the mistakes and mishaps that led to their downfall.

12. C   Early in the passage the author discusses our grandfathers' view of the question of whether history repeats itself. With this sentence, the author begins to present a more up-to-date perspective.

13. C   As we study past civilizations, we have little to go on except the ruins that have been left behind. From the ruins, we infer lessons that have the force of scripture.

14. E   Lines 21–22 contain an example of an antithesis. The discussion of a navigator's chart (line 26) appears in the context of an extended simile. The phrase "charted rocks and reefs" comprises a metaphor. Combinations of words such as "probabilities/possibilities" and "rocks/reefs" contain alliteration.

15. A   The second alternative is a concept of history that enables us to infer what lies in store.

16. A   The horoscope tells what fate has in store for us. The navigation chart, in contrast, enables us to steer "a course between charted rocks and reefs." In other words, we can learn from the mistakes of past civilizations. Because we know the perils, we can take steps to avoid them.

17. D   A seafarer with "intelligence" uses the data on the navigator's chart to avoid rocks and reefs. In other words, he realizes the usefulness of the information he has before him.

18. D   The colloquial expression tends to create the impression that the writer is going to confide his true feelings to the reader; in short, he's going to be frank and forthright. At the same time, the writer implies that he has definite views on the subject.

19. B   The syntax of each question (for example, " do we not," "are there not") indicates that these are not questions at all, but rather assertions of the author's point of view. Written in question form, the statements pull the reader into the discussion and inevitably lead the reader to concur with the author.

20. C   Throughout the passage the author ruminates on the notion of history repeating itself. He contrasts current thinking about the issue with the

debates of earlier times. While he does not prove the theory that history repeats itself, he draws a tentative conclusion that it does. At least, he suggests that there is enough repetition in history to help us avoid the mistakes of the past.

21. A   The second sentence of the passage suggests what the author means. Those who make up a "cult" have an extreme devotion—an obsession, really—to a particular belief or set of activities, in this case, the desire to create, preserve, or restore physical beauty.

22. C   The unanswered questions and the uncertainties expressed in the first paragraph ("difficult to answer"; "It depends") prepare the reader for a discussion that weighs both sides of the issue.

23. D   Several of the sentences that follow the idea in question are similarly structured. Each begins with the grammatical subject of the sentence and uses the verb "will be."

24. D   The style and content of the passage reveal that the author possesses all the traits listed except scientific objectivity.

25. E   The dubious title "crone of the future" is meant ironically—comparable, in a way, to an accolade like "serial killer of the year" or "airhead of the month."

26. A   In its context, the statement is a concise, thoughtful, and memorable idea. Thus, it can be labeled an *epigram*.

27. D   The author uses the first two paragraphs to provide a context for his main concern, which is the difference between inner and outer beauty. Therefore, paragraph 3 contains the heart of the passage.

28. D   The first paragraph describes the cult of beauty, the second, the beauty/health connection. Inner and outer beauty are compared in the final paragraph. Throughout the passage, the author assumes a somewhat condescending attitude. What is missing from the passage, then, is a sympathetic discussion of the yearning for eternal youth.

29. D   By emphasizing the differences between inner and outer beauty, the author makes clear his disapproval of the commercial cult of beauty, which concerns itself only with the superficial, surface appearance of its clientele.

30. D   The first paragraph questions the efficacy of the "modern cult of beauty." The second paragraph discusses women's techniques for making themselves beautiful. These two paragraphs merely serve as a prelude to the final paragraph, in which the author raises his main concern—the difference between inner and outer beauty.

31. A   Ulysses exhorts his men to take advantage of their capacity to seek knowledge. Why? Because they are human and, as the author states early in the passage, knowledge is "good for man to acquire."

32. B   The author makes his point by setting up a series of juxtapositions between what knowledge *is not* and what knowledge *is*—for example, "it is not merely a means of procuring good, but is good in itself." These are antitheses.

33. **A**   As a minister commends righteousness to his flock, the author of the passage commends knowledge to his listeners. The analogy is made to reveal the rectitude of both. In the author's view, to shun learning is the equivalent of acting immorally.

34. **E**   The promise of material reward motivates people to learn, but the author rejects that approach. Rather, the pursuit of knowledge offers a different kind of reward—the reward of knowing that you have carried out a duty to yourself. Someone who refuses that obligation denies the wisdom of the Scriptures.

35. **E**   According to the last sentence in the passage, for a man to know truth, he needs "daylight." The only other reasonable choice is (C), but notice that the author makes the point that knowledge is not the "coin which we pay down . . . ."

36. **A**   All five reasons are mentioned in the passage. The most all-inclusive is reason, that knowledge enables man to fulfill his destiny, is supported by examples and by quotations from Dante and Scripture.

37. **C**   The "house of delusions" (lines 48–49) is the equivalent of the house of ignorance—a simple, easy-to-build place, but as the author notes, such places are not only unhealthy but also unsafe; they could collapse "about our ears" at any time. If you chose (B), think again; the author never says that the out-of-doors is equivalent to wisdom. It's merely preferable to the "house of delusions."

38. **C**   In spite of the unhappiness that sometimes issues from knowing the truth, it is still "better for a man to see things as they are than to be ignorant of them" (lines 52–53). Yet, there is no denying that knowledge can be painful, or as the passage says, "injurious to happiness" (line 33). Thus (C) most accurately summarizes the point of the paragraph.

39. **B**   The author attempts not only to inform his audience of the delights of knowledge, he tries to convince them that they should embrace knowledge. The early part of the passage contains numerous imperatives: "Let a man acquire knowledge," he says in line 3. Later he adds, ". . . let us insist that the pursuit of knowledge . . . is a part of man's duty to himself " (lines 25–26).

40. **E**   Throughout the passage, the author advocates the virtues of learning. For one thing, learning "has happiness indissolubly bound up with it" (lines 18–19). Near the end of the passage, the author states, "It is and it must in the long run be better for a man to see things as they are than to be ignorant of them" (lines 52–53).

41. **D**   The author, in describing the world to come, aims to ridicule or make fun of many scientists' overblown visions of the future. He even says, "The visions of these men put science fiction in the shade" (line 7).

42. **A**   The author pokes fun at what he considers are outrageous predictions made by scientists concerning the society in the year 2000. Among other things, he regards such scientists misguided, shortsighted, and pompous.

43. A The word "respectively" endows the phrase with the ring of a legal contract or edict. Indeed, the paragraph in which the phrase appears consists of a list of reproductive rules that people of the future must follow.

44. D In 1964, when the passage was written, many of the accomplishments described in the passage may have been considered outrageous descriptions of scientific thinking. Although some of these fantastic notions (*in vitro* fertilization, for example) have come to pass, there's no getting around the fact that the author exaggerates to make his point.

45. E In this transitional sentence, the author, expecting readers to have been amazed or shocked by scientists' vision of the world of 2000, proposes an alternative—to reflect on the consequences of the anticipated changes. At that point, the passage shifts its focus. The sentence in question, then, serves all the functions listed except (E).

46. D The author seems to think that scientific progress is out of control. Because advancements have been proposed that ignore human values, the author describes the dangers inherent in a society dominated by scientists.

47. D The author briefly discusses the past—in particular, the industrial revolution—in order to point out some of the problems of the future.

48. C A savant is someone with exceptional knowledge of a specialized field. The author calls scientists "savants" while he is lampooning them. Thus, he used the term ironically.

49. A The paragraph contains a series of rhetorical questions, asked not to get information but for rhetorical effect—in this case, to mock the empty phrases mouthed by scientists.

50. A The sentence in question consists of two independent clauses joined by the conjunction *and.*

51. C Aside from its literal meaning *zero,* the adjective *null* describes something having no value or significance. It strongly suggests a state of complete vacuousness and emptiness. Locating the word at the end on the sentence—the most emphatic location—gives it a memorable impact.

52. B The passage is full of striking, powerfully-expressed ideas, presented in a clear and lively style. For example: "There will no longer be any need of reading or learning mountains of information . . . . What is needed will pass directly from the machine to the brain without going through consciousness" (lines 21–25).

53. E Throughout the passage the author makes a pitch for reexamining scientists' predictions for the year 2000 because innovations which may be technologically possible are not always humanistically desirable. Therefore, our values and goals ought to be reconsidered.

Answers to Essay Questions

For an overview of how essays are graded, turn to "How AP Essays Are Scored," on page 43.

Although answers to the essay questions will vary greatly, the following descriptions suggest a possible approach to each question and contain ideas that could be used in a response to the question. Perhaps your essay contains many of the same ideas, If not, don't be alarmed. Your ideas may be at least as valid as—if not better than—those presented below.

Question 1

Donne's passage consists of pious thoughts provoked by the pealing of the church bell. Such words and phrases as "perchance" and "I know not" indicate that the speaker is unsure of the meaning of the bell. Yet, as he reflects further, his thoughts become more confident. He asserts, for example, that the "bell doth toll for him that thinks it doth." The passage contains numerous additional assertions about life and death.

Although much of the passage is about abstract subjects like death and God and religion, the speaker uses homely metaphors and allusions that bring his thoughts down to a common, everyday level. He refers to God as an "author," calls a human life a "chapter" and the death of a person a "translation" to a better language. Also, he regards mankind as a "continent," and a person as a "part of the main." To make his example still more concrete, he specifically names the continent—Europe—and equates a piece of land ("a promontory") being washed away with the death of an individual. Using such ordinary language to describe such a metaphysical experience both heightens the contrast between spiritual and mundane matters and also suggests the universality and ordinariness of death. Carrying the point still further, in the middle of his reflections on the significance of the bell (lines 15–19), the author alludes to a trivial argument among the clerics about which group "should ring to prayers first in the morning."

Toward the end of the passage, there appears an extended metaphor that uses the terminology of banking: "gold," "treasure," "money," "bullion," etc.—the very antithesis of the author's spiritual concerns. The contrast is stark. In fact, throughout the passage, the author has used antitheses to heighten contrasts for rhetorical effect: "the bell . . . calls not upon the preacher . . . but upon the congregation;" "no man is an island . . . every man is a piece of the continent"; "never send to know for whom the bell tolls; it tolls for thee."

Question 2

Both passages promote art as a desirable, even a necessary, dimension of life. The first author, Maxwell Anderson, speaks directly to young people. Using imperative verbs, he tells the audience what to do: "be proud," "make it proud," "take what part in it you can," and so on. But not to appear too overbearing, he tempers his comments by repeatedly using "may": "It may break your heart . . . may drive you half mad, may betray you." He also uses several conditional sentences that say, in effect "If you do X, then Y will happen," adopting the tone of a well-meaning advisor.

To suggest his reverence for art, and to encourage his listeners to become active in artistic endeavors, Anderson, like an evangelist, employs the language of religion "neglect no sacrifice at your chosen altar," "it will open the temple doors," "lose . . . extravagant faith in the dollar."

Langer's more scholarly, although equally fervent, support of art, which she terms "the spearhead of human development," also asserts a relationship between art and religion: "It is not religion," she declares, "but grows up with religion."

All told, Langer's approach is more academic than Anderson's. She is concerned about defining art and explaining its various categories. Whereas Anderson clumps all forms of expression into a broad category he calls "art," Langer names the arts she has in mind: painting, sculpture, etc.

Both authors refer to themselves in the first person and address their audiences as "you." But Langer is more aloof, more business-like: ". . . we have no time to debate [a definition of art]. . ., so you are asked to accept it." Notice that she does not say "I ask you to accept it," a locution that sounds more conciliatory. Rather, she sets herself a task—to explain the importance of art—and won't be forsworn.

Question 3

The task in this question is to support, challenge, or qualify Goethe's statement. If you agree with Goethe, your essay should contain examples—possibly in anecdotal form—of people living up to expectations because they were treated with respect and dignity. You may remember a time, for example, when you were treated like an adult, and so you behaved like one, or in contrast, because you were treated like child, you acted silly or immature.

If you cannot subscribe to Goethe's point of view, you should cite examples of people being treated well but acting badly. A striking example occurred not long ago when a high school student in New York murdered his English teacher after the teacher had gone out of his way to help the student deal with both academic and personal problems. One could argue, of course, that this case was an aberration, and cannot reasonably support a generalization about human behavior. In fact, beware of drawing any broad conclusions based on a single event or example—both in your essay writing and in life.

Answer Sheet for Practice Test C
Literature and Composition

Multiple-Choice Questions
Time—1 hour

1. Ⓐ Ⓑ Ⓒ Ⓓ Ⓔ
2. Ⓐ Ⓑ Ⓒ Ⓓ Ⓔ
3. Ⓐ Ⓑ Ⓒ Ⓓ Ⓔ
4. Ⓐ Ⓑ Ⓒ Ⓓ Ⓔ
5. Ⓐ Ⓑ Ⓒ Ⓓ Ⓔ
6. Ⓐ Ⓑ Ⓒ Ⓓ Ⓔ
7. Ⓐ Ⓑ Ⓒ Ⓓ Ⓔ
8. Ⓐ Ⓑ Ⓒ Ⓓ Ⓔ
9. Ⓐ Ⓑ Ⓒ Ⓓ Ⓔ
10. Ⓐ Ⓑ Ⓒ Ⓓ Ⓔ
11. Ⓐ Ⓑ Ⓒ Ⓓ Ⓔ
12. Ⓐ Ⓑ Ⓒ Ⓓ Ⓔ
13. Ⓐ Ⓑ Ⓒ Ⓓ Ⓔ
14. Ⓐ Ⓑ Ⓒ Ⓓ Ⓔ
15. Ⓐ Ⓑ Ⓒ Ⓓ Ⓔ
16. Ⓐ Ⓑ Ⓒ Ⓓ Ⓔ
17. Ⓐ Ⓑ Ⓒ Ⓓ Ⓔ
18. Ⓐ Ⓑ Ⓒ Ⓓ Ⓔ
19. Ⓐ Ⓑ Ⓒ Ⓓ Ⓔ
20. Ⓐ Ⓑ Ⓒ Ⓓ Ⓔ

21. Ⓐ Ⓑ Ⓒ Ⓓ Ⓔ
22. Ⓐ Ⓑ Ⓒ Ⓓ Ⓔ
23. Ⓐ Ⓑ Ⓒ Ⓓ Ⓔ
24. Ⓐ Ⓑ Ⓒ Ⓓ Ⓔ
25. Ⓐ Ⓑ Ⓒ Ⓓ Ⓔ
26. Ⓐ Ⓑ Ⓒ Ⓓ Ⓔ
27. Ⓐ Ⓑ Ⓒ Ⓓ Ⓔ
28. Ⓐ Ⓑ Ⓒ Ⓓ Ⓔ
29. Ⓐ Ⓑ Ⓒ Ⓓ Ⓔ
30. Ⓐ Ⓑ Ⓒ Ⓓ Ⓔ
31. Ⓐ Ⓑ Ⓒ Ⓓ Ⓔ
32. Ⓐ Ⓑ Ⓒ Ⓓ Ⓔ
33. Ⓐ Ⓑ Ⓒ Ⓓ Ⓔ
34. Ⓐ Ⓑ Ⓒ Ⓓ Ⓔ
35. Ⓐ Ⓑ Ⓒ Ⓓ Ⓔ
36. Ⓐ Ⓑ Ⓒ Ⓓ Ⓔ
37. Ⓐ Ⓑ Ⓒ Ⓓ Ⓔ
38. Ⓐ Ⓑ Ⓒ Ⓓ Ⓔ
39. Ⓐ Ⓑ Ⓒ Ⓓ Ⓔ
40. Ⓐ Ⓑ Ⓒ Ⓓ Ⓔ

41. Ⓐ Ⓑ Ⓒ Ⓓ Ⓔ
42. Ⓐ Ⓑ Ⓒ Ⓓ Ⓔ
43. Ⓐ Ⓑ Ⓒ Ⓓ Ⓔ
44. Ⓐ Ⓑ Ⓒ Ⓓ Ⓔ
45. Ⓐ Ⓑ Ⓒ Ⓓ Ⓔ
46. Ⓐ Ⓑ Ⓒ Ⓓ Ⓔ
47. Ⓐ Ⓑ Ⓒ Ⓓ Ⓔ
48. Ⓐ Ⓑ Ⓒ Ⓓ Ⓔ
49. Ⓐ Ⓑ Ⓒ Ⓓ Ⓔ
50. Ⓐ Ⓑ Ⓒ Ⓓ Ⓔ
51. Ⓐ Ⓑ Ⓒ Ⓓ Ⓔ
52. Ⓐ Ⓑ Ⓒ Ⓓ Ⓔ
53. Ⓐ Ⓑ Ⓒ Ⓓ Ⓔ
54. Ⓐ Ⓑ Ⓒ Ⓓ Ⓔ
55. Ⓐ Ⓑ Ⓒ Ⓓ Ⓔ
56. Ⓐ Ⓑ Ⓒ Ⓓ Ⓔ

Three Essay Questions
Time—2 hours

Write your essays on standard 8½ by 11-inch composition paper. At the exam you will be given a bound booklet containing 12 lined pages.

C Literature and Composition

SECTION I
Total time—1 hour

Read each poem or prose passage carefully, and answer the accompanying questions.

Questions 1–11 refer to the following poem.

EIGHT O'CLOCK
A. E. Housman (1859–1936)

He stood, and heard the steeple
    Sprinkle the quarters on the morning town.
One, two, three, four, to market-place and people
    It tossed them down.

Strapped, noosed, nighing his hour,
    He stood and counted them and cursed his luck;
And then the clock collected in the tower
    Its strength, and struck.

1. This poem is about all of the following EXCEPT
    (A) time.
    (B) a hanging.
    (C) mortality.
    (D) injustice.
    (E) fate.

2. "He" in the poem is
    (A) a symbol for Jesus.
    (B) humanity in general.
    (C) a convict.
    (D) a traitor.
    (E) a victim of religious persecution.

3. He "cursed his luck" because he
    (A) was guiltless.
    (B) knew his fate was inescapable.
    (C) believed no one cared.
    (D) was offered no opportunity to confess.
    (E) feared he was doomed to hell.

4. The clock in the tower rang
   (A) every three hours.
   (B) every fifteen minutes.
   (C) every hour.
   (D) every half hour.
   (E) only in the victim's imagination.

5. The words "sprinkle" and "tossed" suggest the
   (A) inevitability of the passage of time.
   (B) misty atmosphere of the morning.
   (C) gentleness of time.
   (D) inevitability of death.
   (E) innocent destructiveness of time.

6. The central figure of speech of the poem is
   (A) personification.
   (B) metonymy.
   (C) simile.
   (D) hyperbole.
   (E) irony.

7. The variation of rhythm in the poem highlights the
   (A) fluency of time.
   (B) change of the seasons.
   (C) tragedy of being human.
   (D) blight of reality.
   (E) urgency of the execution.

8. The crime committed by the subject of the poem is
   (A) desertion.
   (B) murder.
   (C) treason.
   (D) being born.
   (E) apostasy.

9. The effect of the last line in each stanza is to emphasize that
   (A) time is powerful, destructive, and quick.
   (B) criminals cannot escape punishment.
   (C) justice is triumphant.
   (D) hope never dies.
   (E) protest is pointless.

10. In this poem the speaker is saying that
    (A) there is no escape from the law.
    (B) people are unconcerned about the welfare of their neighbors.
    (C) nature is man's chief enemy.
    (D) man was born to struggle.
    (E) death is the prelude to immortality.

11. The town in the poem is
    (A) in England.
    (B) a metaphor for a church.
    (C) a metaphor for a court of law.
    (D) the world.
    (E) heaven on judgment day.

Questions 12–23 refer to the following poem.

VIRTUE
George Herbert (1593–1633)

Sweet day, so cool, so calm, so bright,
    The bridal of the earth and sky:
The dew shall weep thy fall tonight;
    For thou must die.

Line
(5) Sweet rose, whose hue, angry and brave,
    Bids the rash gazer wipe his eye:
Thy root is ever in its grave,
    And thou must die.

Sweet spring, full of sweet days and roses,
(10)   A box where sweets compacted lie;
My music shows ye have your closes,
    And all must die.

Only a sweet and virtuous soul,
    Like seasoned timber, never gives;
(15) But though the whole world turn to coal,
    Then chiefly lives.

12. All of the following are metaphoric images in the poem EXCEPT
    (A) coal (line 15).
    (B) timber (line 14).
    (C) box (line 10).
    (D) gazer (line 6).
    (E) dew (line 3).

13. The subject of the poem is
    (A) mortality.
    (B) immortality.
    (C) the beauty of nature.
    (D) the impact of evil.
    (E) the essence of goodness.

14. According to the poem, the dew represents tears that weep for
    (A) brides.
    (B) the erosion of the earth.
    (C) the clouding of the sun.
    (D) the coming of darkness.
    (E) the death of each day.

15. According to the poem, a gazer is brought to wipe his eyes by a rose's
    (A) brief life.
    (B) rareness.
    (C) mortality.
    (D) deep color.
    (E) fragrance.

16. The "box where sweets compacted lie" is a metaphor for
    (A) any day of the year.
    (B) a piece of music.
    (C) the spring of the year.
    (D) a glowing rose.
    (E) a moon-flooded night.

17. The speaker conceives of the world as
    (A) ending in ashes.
    (B) repeating the cycle of birth and death.
    (C) having the strength of "seasoned timber."
    (D) eternal.
    (E) being the secure dwelling of humanity.

18. The last stanza in the poem
    (A) repeats the theme of the first three stanzas.
    (B) summarizes the ideas in the first three stanzas.
    (C) expresses the theme of the poem.
    (D) introduces a new thought.
    (E) contrasts life with death.

19. Which of the following thoughts are NOT expressed in the poem?
    (A) The virtuous soul never yields and is immortal.
    (B) The things of nature are mortal.
    (C) Music, like the human soul, is immortal.
    (D) The rose contains within its structure elements of its own destruction.
    (E) Spring is like a box of compacted candies.

20. The effect of the terse line at the end of each stanza is to
    (A) emphasize the speaker's pessimism.
    (B) dramatize the fate of the subject of each stanza.
    (C) laud the power of death.
    (D) stress the force of virtue.
    (E) lead to a final positive assertion.

21. The tone of the poem is
    (A) melancholy.
    (B) cynical.
    (C) sanguine.
    (D) pessimistic.
    (E) exultant.

22. Two dramatic figures of speech used in the poem are
    (A) apostrophe and metaphor.
    (B) personification and synecdoche.
    (C) metonymy and simile.
    (D) hyperbole and simile.
    (E) apostrophe and hyperbole.

23. The word "bridal" in line 2 means
    (A) offspring.
    (B) ceremony.
    (C) separation.
    (D) marriage.
    (E) space.

Questions 24–31 refer to the following poem.

A DEEP-SWORN VOW
William Butler Yeats (1865–1939)

Others because you did not keep
That deep-sworn vow have been friends of mine;
Yet always when I look death in the face,
Line   When I clamber to the heights of sleep,
(5)   Or when I grow excited with wine,
Suddenly I meet your face.

24. The theme of this poem is that
    (A) the loss of a friend will always haunt one.
    (B) betrayals are remembered with regret.
    (C) unfulfillment generates self-pity.
    (D) memories of a lost love remain forever in the unconscious.
    (E) memories ease the fear of death.

25. This poem states that the loved one has been forgotten
    (A) because other friendships have been made.
    (B) because the speaker has grown old.
    (C) only on the conscious level of the mind.
    (D) with the help of wine and sleep.
    (E) with the passage of time and the approach of death.

26. The theme of this poem is accentuated by the
    (A) simplicity of the statement.
    (B) casualness of the comment.
    (C) contrast in tone between the opening and closing lines.
    (D) repetition of the word "face."
    (E) rhyme scheme.

27. The "face" of the lost love appears in a vision
    (A) only when the speaker is in a serious mood.
    (B) only in convivial instances.
    (C) in moments of danger.
    (D) when the mind is at rest.
    (E) when the concerns of everyday existence do not occupy the speaker.

28. Which of the following are NOT true of "A Deep-Sworn Vow"?
    (A) There are three instances when the face of the lost love appears to the speaker.
    (B) The three instances the speaker mentions reinforce the same idea.
    (C) The lover falsifies the experience by saying it occurs only when he thinks or fears he is dying.
    (D) The image of the loved one is imprinted on the subconscious.
    (E) The loved one was unfaithful to the speaker.

29. The expression "I clamber to the heights of sleep" is an image that suggests
    (A) simply the restlessness of the speaker's personality.
    (B) that the memory of the lost love is all-pervasive.
    (C) that sleep, like death, frightens the speaker.
    (D) that the vision of the lost love does not appear casually.
    (E) that the lost love haunts the speaker's sleep.

30. Which of the following is a fair and accurate comment about the poem?
    (A) It is a sentimental affirmation of a remembered love experience.
    (B) It is an ironic statement about lovers who focus for a lifetime on a past romance.
    (C) It is a candid and dramatic expression of a universal experience.
    (D) It is a recording of a bitter memory that hampers sleep and spurs unrest.
    (E) It is an exaggerated and romantic outburst of an old man's yearning for a lost love.

31. The speaker in the poem is
    (A) one who has reached old age and finds life empty.
    (B) a self-centered egotist.
    (C) a serious-minded and thoughtful individual.
    (D) a sensitive but romantic dreamer.
    (E) one who spends much time alone.

Questions 32–44 refer to the following passage.

From THE BLIND MAN
D. H. Lawrence (1885–1930)

Isabel Pervin was listening for two sounds—for the sound of wheels on
the drive outside and for the noise of her husband's footsteps in the hall.
Her dearest and oldest friend, a man who seemed almost indispensable to
Line   her living, would drive up in the rainy dusk of the closing November day.
(5)   The trap had gone to fetch him from the station. And her husband, who had
been blinded in Flanders, and who had a disfiguring mark on his brow,
would be coming in from the outhouses.

He had been home for a year now. He was totally blind. Yet they had
been very happy. The Grange was Maurice's own place. The back was a
(10)   farmstead, and the Wernhams, who occupied the rear premises, acted as
farmers. Isabel lived with her husband in the handsome rooms in front. She
and he had been almost entirely alone together in a wonderful and unspeakable
intimacy. Then she reviewed books for a Scottish newspaper, carrying on
(15)   her old interest, and he occupied himself a good deal with the farm. Sight-
less, he could still discuss everything with Wernham, and he could also do
a good deal of work about the place—menial work, it is true, but it gave him
satisfaction. He milked the cows, carried in the pails, turned the separator,
attended to the pigs and horses. Life was still very full and strangely serene
(20)   for the blind man, peaceful with the almost incomprehensible peace of
immediate contact in darkness. With his wife he had a whole world, rich
and real and invisible.

They were newly and remotely happy. He did not even regret the loss of
his sight in these times of dark, palpable joy. A certain exultance swelled
(25)   his soul.

But as time wore on, sometimes the rich glamour would leave them.
Sometimes, after months of this intensity a sense of burden overcame Isabel, a weariness, a terrible ennui, in that silent house approached between a
colonnade of tall-shafted pines. Then she felt she would go mad, for she
(30)   could not bear it. And sometimes he had devastating fits of depression,
which seemed to lay waste his whole being. It was worse than depression—
a black misery, when his own life was a torture to him, and when his
presence was unbearable to his wife. The dread went down to the roots of
her soul as these black days recurred. In a kind of panic, she tried to wrap
(35)   herself up still further in her husband. She forced the old spontaneous
cheerfulness and joy to continue. But the effort it cost her was almost too
much. She knew she could not keep it up. She felt she would scream with
the strain, and would give anything, anything, to escape. She longed to
possess her husband utterly; it gave her inordinate joy to have him entirely
(40)   to herself. And yet, when again he was gone in a black and massive misery,
she could not bear him, she could not bear herself; she wished she could be
snatched away off the earth altogether, anything rather than live at this
cost.

Dazed, she schemed for a way out. She invited friends, she tried to give
(45)   him some further connection with the outer world. But it was no good.
After all their joy and suffering, after their dark, great year of blindness and
solitude and unspeakable nearness, other people seemed to them both,
shallow, prattling, rather impertinent. Shallow prattle seemed presumptuous. He became impatient and irritated, she was wearied. And so they
(50)   lapsed into their solitude again. For they preferred it.

32.   The two sounds Isabel Pervin was listening for reflected
  (A)   antagonism toward her husband.
  (B)   anxiety related to her pregnancy.
  (C)   a hopeful answer to her unhappiness.
  (D)   panic about the future.
  (E)   worry over her husband's blindness.

33. The Pervins lived entirely alone because
     (A) Isabel hadn't learned to cope with her husband's handicap.
     (B) their farmstead was in an isolated area.
     (C) they were uniquely compatible.
     (D) time and aloneness appeared necessary for adjustment to Maurice's blindness.
     (E) Maurice was sensitive about his blindness.

34. Maurice's life was very full and strangely serene in that first year because of all the following EXCEPT which statement?
     (A) He could discuss everything with Wernham.
     (B) Blindness did not keep him from work on the farm.
     (C) He had a rich and satisfying relationship with his wife.
     (D) Contact with his world through touch brought him peace.
     (E) He developed a belief that God provided compensations for loss of any of the senses.

35. This passage is primarily concerned with Isabel Pervin's
     (A) looking forward to a visit from her friend.
     (B) realization that she no longer loved Maurice.
     (C) anticipation of childbirth.
     (D) observations concerning her world.
     (E) irritations with life.

36. The statement of the narrator, "Yet they had been very happy" (lines 8–9), is
     (A) objective and factual.
     (B) ironical and derisive.
     (C) critical and caustic.
     (D) subjective and interprative.
     (E) precise and exact.

37. The word "seemed" in the clause "a man who seemed almost indispensable to her living" (line 3) indicates that
     (A) Isabel was not sure of her husband's love.
     (B) Isabel knew all would go well.
     (C) delusion is a product of unhappiness.
     (D) in desperation, people clutch at straws.
     (E) no happiness is permanent.

38. Which of the following did NOT make Isabel, on occasion, feel she would go mad?
     (A) She could not have Maurice to herself.
     (B) Maurice's fits of depression appalled her.
     (C) She feared the oncoming childbirth.
     (D) The silent house haunted her.
     (E) Their friends, when invited by the Pervins, wearied Maurice and her.

39. The prevailing "voice" in this passage is that of
    (A) a prejudiced narrator.
    (B) Isabel Pervin.
    (C) an objective narrator.
    (D) an omniscient narrator.
    (E) Maurice Pervin.

40. The word "unspeakable" (line 13), describing the nearness of Isabel and Maurice during the first year after he had lost his sight, suggests a relationship that
    (A) was unique and fulfilling.
    (B) was harmful in many subtle ways.
    (C) led to Isabel's panic.
    (D) was the source of Maurice's misery.
    (E) interfered with their social life.

41. Which of the following does the narrator NOT suggest may have been the source of Maurice's depression?
    (A) Existence in darkness became at times oppressive.
    (B) He was fearful he would lose Isabel.
    (C) His contact with the world was limited.
    (D) There was not enough for him to do to fill the time.
    (E) He hated the menial farm work he had to do.

42. The tone of this passage best suggests that the narrator is treating the situation of his characters with
    (A) total sympathy.
    (B) humor.
    (C) honest appraisal.
    (D) horrid fascination.
    (E) irony.

43. The narrator tells the reader that "other people seemed to them" (Isabel and Maurice) to be "shallow, prattling, rather impertinent" (lines 47–48). Which of the following is NOT true of this statement?
    (A) The narrator is presenting a subjective opinion.
    (B) The reader is expected to accept the narrator's opinion.
    (C) The narrator indicates that this is the view of Isabel and Maurice.
    (D) The narrator had a low opinion of Isabel and Maurice's friends.
    (E) The reader needs to see Isabel and Maurice in a situation where company fails to help them.

44. As the narrator presents it, Isabel's love for Maurice is best characterized as
    (A) total and physical.
    (B) selfish and consuming.
    (C) a mixture of joy and fear.
    (D) a frequent yearning to escape.
    (E) a form of revenge for earlier neglect.

Questions 45–56 refer to the following passage.

From PREFACE TO THE NIGGER OF THE NARCISSUS
Joseph Conrad (1857–1924)

A work that aspires, however humbly, to the condition of art should carry its
justification in every line. And art itself may be defined as a single-minded
attempt to render the highest kind of justice to the visible universe, by bringing to

Line light the truth, manifold and one, underlying its every aspect. It is an attempt to
(5)   find in its forms, in its colors, in its light, in its shadows, in the aspect of matter
and in the facts of life what of each is fundamental, what is enduring and essential—their one illuminating and convincing quality—the very truth of their existence. The artist, then, like the thinker or the scientist, seeks the truth and makes
his appeal. Impressed by the aspect of the world the thinker plunges into ideas,
(10) the scientist into facts—whence, presently, emerging, they make their appeal to
those qualities of our being that fit us best for the hazardous enterprise of living.
They speak authoritatively to our common-sense, to our intelligence, to our
desire of peace or to our desire of unrest; not seldom to our prejudices, sometimes
to our fears, often to our egoism—but always to our credulity. And their words
(15) are heard with reverence, for their concern is with weighty matters: with the
cultivation of our minds and the proper care of our bodies, with the attainment of
our ambitions, with the perfection of the means and the glorification of our precious aims. . . .

It is only some such train of thought, or rather a feeling, that can in a measure
(20) explain the aim of the attempt, made in the tale which follows, to present an
unrestful episode in the obscure lives of a few individuals out of all the disre-
garded multitude of the bewildered, the simple and the voiceless. For, if any part
of the truth dwells in the belief confessed above, it becomes evident that there is
not a place of splendour or a dark corner of the earth that does not preserve, if
(25) only a passing glance of wonder and pity. The motive then, may be held to justify
the matter of the work; but this preface, which is simply an avowal of endeavour,
cannot end here—for the avowal is not yet complete. . . .

The sincere endeavour to accomplish that creative task, to go as far on that road
as his strength will carry him, to go undeterred by faltering, weariness or
(30) reproach, is the only valid justification for the worker in prose. And if his conscience is clear, his answer to those who in the fullness of a wisdom which looks
for immediate profit, demands specifically to be edified, consoled, amused; who
demand to be promptly improved, or encouraged, or frightened, or shocked, or
charmed, must run thus:—My task which I am trying to achieve is, by the power
(35) of the written word to make you hear, to make you feel—it is, before all, to make
you *see*. That—and no more, and it is everything. If I succeed, you shall find there
according to your deserts: encouragement, consolation, fear, charm—all you
demand—and, perhaps, also that glimpse of truth for which you have forgotten to
ask.

45. What this passage most expresses is
(A) a criticism.
(B) a retort.
(C) an assumption.
(D) an apologia.
(E) a credo.

46. In Conrad's view a major purpose of art is to
    (A) deal with surface reality.
    (B) create beautiful things.
    (C) present moral concepts in an attractive light.
    (D) attain the right by presenting life in its fundamental essence.
    (E) bring beauty to an appreciative public.

47. According to Conrad, a problem such as whether exploration into space will be of benefit to future generations should be of greatest interest to the
    (A) scientist.
    (B) philosopher.
    (C) politician.
    (D) artist.
    (E) clergy.

48. In Conrad's view the question of whether there is order in the universe should be of greatest interest to the
    (A) thinker.
    (B) scientist.
    (C) clergy.
    (D) artist.
    (E) politician.

49. Conrad believes that scientists speak to all of the following needs in the groups that are their audiences EXCEPT the
    (A) desire for security.
    (B) curiosity.
    (C) concern about their well-being.
    (D) sense of the mythology of life.
    (E) love of life.

50. In which of the following groups would Conrad probably place the literary critic?
    (A) Artists
    (B) Teachers
    (C) Journalists
    (D) Scientists
    (E) Thinkers

51. To which of the following ideas would Conrad be most likely to subscribe?
    (A) Writers who go beneath the surface of their characters' lives do so at their peril.
    (B) A writer is a creator of beautiful things.
    (C) Literature is bound to be antiscientific.
    (D) The problems of the human heart in conflict with itself are the best subjects of great writing.
    (E) Literature cannot establish values as facts.

52. According to Conrad, fiction above all must seek to achieve a structure in which
    (A) there is a union of content and form.
    (B) the author stands apart from the world he/she creates.
    (C) vice as well as virtue is treated with sympathy.
    (D) characters reflect the author's view of life.
    (E) nothing that is not true to life is included.

53. According to this passage, the artists in our society seek to appeal to all of the following qualities in people EXCEPT their
    (A) aspirations.
    (B) dreams and illusions.
    (C) faith in the divine.
    (D) egoism and self-esteem.
    (E) yearnings for a better life.

54. According to the passage, fiction fundamentally
    (A) appeals to the human mind.
    (B) gives the reader a greater knowledge of the world.
    (C) sharpens the reader's intellect.
    (D) helps the reader to evaluate society's attainments.
    (E) appeals to the reader's senses and arouses him/her emotionally.

55. According to Conrad, fiction must above all
    (A) expose human degradation.
    (B) avoid the spectral and visionary.
    (C) recreate a world with universal appeal.
    (D) present a diversity of view and scene.
    (E) penetrate the mind of the reader.

56. In Conrad's view, the major function of literature is to
    (A) amuse and entertain.
    (B) sharpen human sensitivity to people and places.
    (C) educate readers to understand their environment.
    (D) teach readers to accept their world.
    (E) provide a healthy moral code of values.

SECTION II
Total time—2 hours

Question 1

Suggested time—40 minutes

The following passage is a comment about the current state of Man. Read the passage carefully. Then, in a well-organized essay, analyze how the author supports his view that it is no longer possible for "society to find the whole man" (line 7). In your analysis, consider such literary elements as tone, point of view, structure, selection of details, and figurative language.

It is one of those fables which out of an unknown antiquity convey an unlooked-for wisdom, that the gods, in the beginning, divided Man, that he might be more helpful to himself; just as the hand was divided into fingers, the better to
Line   answer its end.
(5)   The old fable covers a doctrine ever new and sublime; that there is One Man—present to all particular men only partially, or through one faculty; and that you must take the whole society to find the whole man. Man is not a farmer, or a professor, or an engineer, but he is all. Man is priest, and scholar, and statesman, and producer, and soldier. In the *divided* or social state these functions are par-
(10)   celed out to individuals, each of whom aims to do his stint of the joint work, whilst each other performs his. The fable implies that the individual, to possess himself, must sometimes return from his own labor to embrace all the other laborers. But unfortunately, this original unit, this fountain of power, has been so distributed to multitudes, has been so minutely subdivided and peddled out, that
(15)   it is spilled into drops, and cannot be gathered. The state of society is one in which the members have suffered amputation from the trunk, and strut about so many working monsters,—a good finger, a neck, a stomach, an elbow, but never a man.
       Man is thus metamorphosed into a thing, into many things. The planter, who is
(20)   Man sent out into the field to gather food, is seldom cheered by any idea of the true dignity of his ministry. He sees his bushel and his cart, and nothing beyond, and sinks into the farmer, instead of Man on the farm. The tradesman is scarcely ever given an ideal worth to his work, but is ridden by the routine of his craft, and the soul is subject to dollars. The priest becomes a form; the attorney a statute-
(25)   book; the mechanic a machine; the sailor a rope of the ship.
       In this distribution of functions the scholar is the delegated intellect. In the right state he is *Man Thinking*. In the degenerate state, when the victim of society, he tends to become a mere thinker, or still worse, the parrot of other men's thinking.

Question 2

Suggested time—40 minutes

When we come to the end of a novel or play, a consistent mood should have been created and our consciousness of certain aspects of life should have been intensified or even altered.

Discuss the mood (tone) of a novel or play you have read and point out the ways in which the story intensified your consciousness of certain aspects of life (made you more keenly aware of realities) or altered your views of certain aspects of life.

You may choose works from the list of authors provided below, or select another appropriate novel or play of comparable literary excellence.

Edward Albee	Nadine Gordimer	Toni Morrison
Jane Austen	Joseph Heller	V. S. Naipaul
Saul Bellow	Henrik Ibsen	G. B. Shaw
Charles Dickens	Henry James	Tom Stoppard
Henry Fielding	Ben Jonson	William M. Thackeray
F. Scott Fitzgerald	Christopher Marlowe	Tennessee Williams
E. M. Forster	Arthur Miller	Richard Wright

Question 3

Suggested time—40 minutes

Read the following poem carefully. You will note that a number of questions are raised in the first stanza and that the speaker's answers to these questions complete the poem. Write an essay in which you discuss the view of life expressed through the questions and answers in the poem. Support your ideas with evidence from the poem, indicating also the poetic devices used by the poet.

WHAT ARE YEARS?
Marianne Moore (1887–1972)

```
            What is our innocence,
        what is our guilt? All are
            naked, none is safe. And whence
Line    is courage: the unanswered question,
(5)     the resolute doubt—
        dumbly calling, deafly listening—that
        in misfortune, even death
            encourages others
            and in its defeat, stirs

(10)        the soul to be strong? He
        sees deep and is glad, who
            accedes to mortality
        and in his imprisonment, rises
        upon himself as
(15)    the sea in a chasm, struggling to be,
            in its surrendering
            finds its continuing.

            So he who strongly feels,
        behaves. The very bird,
(20)        grown taller as he sings, steels
        his form straight up. Though he is captive
        his mighty singing
        says, satisfaction is a lowly
        thing, how pure a thing is joy,
(25)        This is mortality,
            This is eternity.
```

Answer Key for Practice Exam C
Answers to Multiple-Choice Questions

1.	D	13.	E	25.	C	37.	A	49.	D
2.	B	14.	E	26.	C	38.	C	50.	E
3.	B	15.	D	27.	E	39.	D	51.	D
4.	B	16.	C	28.	C	40.	A	52.	A
5.	E	17.	A	29.	D	41.	E	53.	D
6.	B	18.	C	30.	C	42.	C	54.	E
7.	C	19.	C	31.	C	43.	D	55.	C
8.	D	20.	B	32.	C	44.	C	56.	B
9.	A	21.	E	33.	D	45.	E		
10.	D	22.	A	34.	E	46.	D		
11.	D	23.	D	35.	D	47.	B		
12.	D	24.	D	36.	D	48.	A		

Answer Explanations

1. **D** All the themes except "injustice" are stated in or implied by the poem. The passing of time dominates the poem. A "hanging" is suggested by the noose. "Mortality" is indicated by the phrase "nighing his hour"—that is nearing the hour of death. "Fate" is implied by the phrase "cursed his luck."

2. **B** Although it is tempting to say that the poem describes the experience of one man, its themes are broad enough to encompass all mankind.

3. **B** Just as he had no way to stop time from passing, he had no way to alter his fate.

4. **B** "Sprinkle the quarters" refers to quarter-hours, or fifteen minutes.

5. **E** Both verbs describe action that is carefree and random. Thus, time innocently causes destruction.

6. **B** A metonymy is a figure of speech in which an attribute of a person or thing is used to represent the whole person or thing. In the poem, the clock reperesents the passing of time—hence the passing of life. If you chose (A), consider that personifcation is not the poem's *central* figure of speech.

7. **C** The changes in rhythm suggest a kind of disorder and agitation, and by extension, tragedy.

8. **D** Having been born, the subject inevitably suffers and dies.

9. **A** Each last line alludes to a violent act.

10. **D** The poem is all about the struggles of life.

11. **D** Because the poem has universal implications, the "town" must be large, like the world.

12. **D** The "gazer" must be taken literally—the one who gazes at a rose.

13. **E** The first three stanzas lead up to the point of the poem—that a sweet and virtuous soul is sturdy like timber and "chiefly lives."

14. E The day will "fall," or end, tonight, and dew will mark its death.

15. D The rose's hue (line 5), or color, brings tears to the gazer's eyes.

16. C Grammatically, the "box" is an appositive, or an alternate name, for "spring."

17. A Line 15 says the world turns to *coal,* meaning ashes.

18. C The first three stanzas are about beauty that fades and dies, last one about virtue that is immortal.

19. C Although music is mentioned in the poem, it is not mentioned in context of immortality.

20. B The repetition and ominous tone of the ultimate lines in stanzas 1–3 emphasize the power of fate. The last line of stanza 4 stands out in contrast to the others.

21. E The last stanza turns what might be regarded as a morbid poem into a hopeful one.

22. A The poet uses *apostrophe* when he talks to the day, the rose, and the spring. He uses metaphors in the second line of each of the first three stanzas.

23. D The image the poet wishes to convey is the union of the earth and sky on a beautiful spring day. The two—earth and sky—seem meant for each other.

24. D Only a lover is likely to give a "deep-sworn vow." Although the vow was not kept, the speaker cannot forget the person who made it.

25. C Only at special times, when the speaker is troubled or not thinking clearly, does the image of the lost love swim into his (or, possibly, *her*) mind.

26. C At the beginning the tone is sad and regretful. The last line, however, is strikingly upbeat and full of anticipation.

27. E The brink of sleep, the effect of too much wine, and encounters with death all qualify as moments when everyday concerns are put aside.

28. C The speaker "meets" the face of his lost love under *three* different conditions, not *one*.

29. D The verb "clamber" suggests a considerable degree of effort.

30. C It is safe to say that the meanings of good poems transcend their contexts. Therefore, seek out universal implications in this and other poems.

31. C *Serious* and *thoughtful* are adjectives that accurately describe a person who insightfully reflects on what the loss of a lover and a broken vow have meant to him.

32. C Isabel anticipated the sounds of her husband's arrival, always hopeful that her misery would change. Maurice was, after all, her "dearest and oldest friend."

33. D After the war, Maurice and Isabel needed time to adjust to his blindness.

34. E The passage does not discuss Maurice's spirituality.

35. D The author analyzes Isabel's relationship with Maurice and her feelings about that relationship.

36. D The narrator infers that Isabel and Maurice were very happy for a time. He expresses his opinion based on his observations of their lives.

37. A The word "seems" opens the door to speculation that Isabel was uncertain about her need for Maurice's love.

38. C The passage does not allude to Isabel's pregnancy.

39. D The narrator knows all there is to know about Maurice and Isabel. Therefore, he is "omnicient."

40. A By calling the intimacy "wonderful and unspeakable," the narrator is saying that it was beyond description. Such a relationship, in turn, must be unique and fulfilling.

41. E Menial work "gave him satisfaction" (lines 17–18).

42. C Although the circumstances of the characters' life together may seem odd, the narrator of the passage tries to tell the story as he sees it.

43. D The narrator does not pass judgment on Isabel and Maurice's friends. Rather, he describes how Isabel and Maurice felt about their friends.

44. C The passage represents Isabel's love for Maurice as part ecstasy and part agony.

45. E A credo is a statement of beliefs or a guide to action. In this preface Conrad states what he hopes to achieve as a writer.

46. D The core of Conrad's view is found his statement that art is "a single-minded attempt to render the highest kind of justice to the visible universe, by bringing to light the truth" (lines 2–4).

47. B According to the first paragraph (lines 8–18) scientists must also be philosphers because they must be concerned with "weighty matters."

48. A Scientists deal with facts, says Conrad, but also with "the cultivation of our minds . . .etc" (lines 16–18).

49. D The passage alludes to all the needs except the need to sense the mythology of life.

50. E Because the metiér of literary critics is the world of ideas, they must be counted among the thinkers (line 9).

51. D In the second paragraph of the passage, Conrad states that his job is to seek out the truth in every "dark corner of the earth" (line 24), including the depths of the human heart.

52. A The artist's task, according to lines 5–8, is to use forms that will express "what is fundamental, what is enduring and essential—their one illuminating and convincing quality—the very truth of their existence."

53. D Conrad has no desire to foster "egoism and self-esteem" in his readers.

54. E Conrad defines his task as a novelist at the end of the third paragraph: "to make you hear, to make you feel."

55. C In his fiction, Conrad seeks to recreate truth, a universal absolute. Therefore, the world of fiction must have a universal appeal.

56. B Conrad believes that his task as a writer is to make the reader hear, feel, and above all, see—in all ways sharpen his readers' sensitivity to the world.

Answers to Essay Questions

Answers for essay questions will vary widely, but the following answers identify ideas that could reasonably be included an a essay.

Question 1

The author laments the current state of Man because Man has been divided into categories, and it is no longer possible to "find the whole man." Each man is just a piece of the whole and therefore, lacks the perspective to "possess himself" (lines 11–12). That is, a man cannot understand who he is and why he exists.

This state of affairs was brought about, according to fables of "unknown antiquity," when the gods divided Man, expecting that such an arrangement would aid Man in achieving his purpose.

The author confidently articulates his point of view with never a doubt or hint of uncertainty that his assessment of Man is anything but the truth. First, he describes the details of the fable, then discusses its implications. That people are sorted into the functions they perform is emphasized in the third paragraph, where the author uses metaphors to describe the essence of each person: "The priest becomes a form . . ." etc. The categories chosen by the author—farmer, priest, scholar, statesman, and so on—represent a broad cross section of society.

Question 2

Basically, this question asks you to discuss how the tone or mood of a novel or play changed you. The possibilities are endless. Had you read *Beloved* by Toni Morrison, for example, you could describe its dark, violent, somber tone. It seems unlikely that any sensitive reader would walk away from *Beloved* without being shocked by the inhumanity of slavery. Or, if you had studied *Death of a Salesman* by Arthur Miller, you might have been struck by the emptiness of the American Dream. In a sense, Willie Loman—like Sethe, Paul D, and the others—was also a slave. He was trapped in a style of life and emotionally bound to a set of values that destroyed his life.

Question 3

The speaker in the poem seems to be making a statement about how one lives life to the fullest, or more specifically, how one gathers the courage to face the vicissitudes of life nobly and joyfully. The answer is found in the latter half of the poem: accept your mortality, says the speaker in lines 10–16. Then fight like "the sea in a chasm"—a simile that suggests a ceaseless struggle to be free in spite of whatever limits may try to contain you. By doing so, you will gather strength, like the bird who sings his heart out. "The very bird, grown taller as he sings" (lines 19–20) is a metaphor conveying the idea that mere "satisfaction" (line 23) is not a sufficient goal in life. Rather, a life should be full of joy: "how pure a thing is joy" (line 24), says the poet. Then, in spite of your mortality, you will have had a brush with the eternal.

Answer Sheet for Practice Test D
Literature and Composition

Multiple-Choice Questions
Time—1 hour

1. Ⓐ Ⓑ Ⓒ Ⓓ Ⓔ
2. Ⓐ Ⓑ Ⓒ Ⓓ Ⓔ
3. Ⓐ Ⓑ Ⓒ Ⓓ Ⓔ
4. Ⓐ Ⓑ Ⓒ Ⓓ Ⓔ
5. Ⓐ Ⓑ Ⓒ Ⓓ Ⓔ
6. Ⓐ Ⓑ Ⓒ Ⓓ Ⓔ
7. Ⓐ Ⓑ Ⓒ Ⓓ Ⓔ
8. Ⓐ Ⓑ Ⓒ Ⓓ Ⓔ
9. Ⓐ Ⓑ Ⓒ Ⓓ Ⓔ
10. Ⓐ Ⓑ Ⓒ Ⓓ Ⓔ
11. Ⓐ Ⓑ Ⓒ Ⓓ Ⓔ
12. Ⓐ Ⓑ Ⓒ Ⓓ Ⓔ
13. Ⓐ Ⓑ Ⓒ Ⓓ Ⓔ
14. Ⓐ Ⓑ Ⓒ Ⓓ Ⓔ
15. Ⓐ Ⓑ Ⓒ Ⓓ Ⓔ
16. Ⓐ Ⓑ Ⓒ Ⓓ Ⓔ
17. Ⓐ Ⓑ Ⓒ Ⓓ Ⓔ
18. Ⓐ Ⓑ Ⓒ Ⓓ Ⓔ
19. Ⓐ Ⓑ Ⓒ Ⓓ Ⓔ
20. Ⓐ Ⓑ Ⓒ Ⓓ Ⓔ

21. Ⓐ Ⓑ Ⓒ Ⓓ Ⓔ
22. Ⓐ Ⓑ Ⓒ Ⓓ Ⓔ
23. Ⓐ Ⓑ Ⓒ Ⓓ Ⓔ
24. Ⓐ Ⓑ Ⓒ Ⓓ Ⓔ
25. Ⓐ Ⓑ Ⓒ Ⓓ Ⓔ
26. Ⓐ Ⓑ Ⓒ Ⓓ Ⓔ
27. Ⓐ Ⓑ Ⓒ Ⓓ Ⓔ
28. Ⓐ Ⓑ Ⓒ Ⓓ Ⓔ
29. Ⓐ Ⓑ Ⓒ Ⓓ Ⓔ
30. Ⓐ Ⓑ Ⓒ Ⓓ Ⓔ
31. Ⓐ Ⓑ Ⓒ Ⓓ Ⓔ
32. Ⓐ Ⓑ Ⓒ Ⓓ Ⓔ
33. Ⓐ Ⓑ Ⓒ Ⓓ Ⓔ
34. Ⓐ Ⓑ Ⓒ Ⓓ Ⓔ
35. Ⓐ Ⓑ Ⓒ Ⓓ Ⓔ
36. Ⓐ Ⓑ Ⓒ Ⓓ Ⓔ
37. Ⓐ Ⓑ Ⓒ Ⓓ Ⓔ
38. Ⓐ Ⓑ Ⓒ Ⓓ Ⓔ
39. Ⓐ Ⓑ Ⓒ Ⓓ Ⓔ
40. Ⓐ Ⓑ Ⓒ Ⓓ Ⓔ

41. Ⓐ Ⓑ Ⓒ Ⓓ Ⓔ
42. Ⓐ Ⓑ Ⓒ Ⓓ Ⓔ
43. Ⓐ Ⓑ Ⓒ Ⓓ Ⓔ
44. Ⓐ Ⓑ Ⓒ Ⓓ Ⓔ
45. Ⓐ Ⓑ Ⓒ Ⓓ Ⓔ
46. Ⓐ Ⓑ Ⓒ Ⓓ Ⓔ
47. Ⓐ Ⓑ Ⓒ Ⓓ Ⓔ
48. Ⓐ Ⓑ Ⓒ Ⓓ Ⓔ
49. Ⓐ Ⓑ Ⓒ Ⓓ Ⓔ
50. Ⓐ Ⓑ Ⓒ Ⓓ Ⓔ
51. Ⓐ Ⓑ Ⓒ Ⓓ Ⓔ
52. Ⓐ Ⓑ Ⓒ Ⓓ Ⓔ
53. Ⓐ Ⓑ Ⓒ Ⓓ Ⓔ
54. Ⓐ Ⓑ Ⓒ Ⓓ Ⓔ
55. Ⓐ Ⓑ Ⓒ Ⓓ Ⓔ
56. Ⓐ Ⓑ Ⓒ Ⓓ Ⓔ

Three Essay Questions
Time—2 hours

Write your essays on standard 8½ by 11-inch composition paper. At the exam you will be given a bound booklet containing 12 lined pages.

D Literature and Composition

SECTION I

Total time—1 hour

Read each poem or prose passage carefully, and answer the accompanying questions.

Questions 1–10 refer to the following poem.

A LETTER
Anthony Hecht (1923–   )

> I have been wondering
> What you are thinking about, and by now suppose
> It is certainly not me.
> Line   But the crocus is up, and the lark, and the blundering
> (5)   Blood knows what it knows.
> It talks to itself all night, like a sliding, moonlit sea.
>
> Of course, it is talking of you.
> At dawn, where the ocean has netted its catch of lights,
> The sun plants one lithe foot
> (10)   On that spill of mirrors, but the blood goes worming through
> Its warm Arabian nights,
> Naming your pounding name again in the dark heartroot.
>
> Who shall, of course, be nameless.
> Anyway, I should want you to know I have done my best,
> (15)   As I'm sure you have, too.
> Others are bound to us, the gentle and blameless
> Whose names are not confessed
> In the ceaseless palaver. My dearest, the clear and bottomless blue
> Of those depths is all but blinding.
> (20)   You may remember that once you brought my boys
> Two little wooly birds.
> Yesterday the older one asked for you upon finding
> Your thrush among his toys.
> And the tides welled about me, and I could find no words.
>
> (25)   There is not much else to tell.
> One tries one's best to continue as before,
> Doing some little good.
> But I would have you know that all is not well
> With a man dead set to ignore
> (30)   The endless repetitions of his own murmurous blood.

1. The speaker in "A Letter"
   (A) regrets the hurt to his children
   (B) suffers from a heart ailment
   (C) is embarrassed by gossip
   (D) has never married because of a lost love
   (E) although married, is in love with another woman

2. The time of "A Letter" is
   (A) summer
   (B) autumn
   (C) spring
   (D) winter
   (E) eternity

3. In "A Letter," the "sliding, moonlit sea" (line 6) is an image used by the speaker to express the
   (A) time of the year
   (B) yearning for his loved one
   (C) beauty of his dwelling
   (D) memories of past romances
   (E) view from his balcony

4. By "ceaseless palaver" (line 18) the speaker in "A Letter" means
   (A) recurrent memories
   (B) beating of his heart
   (C) secret meetings
   (D) small talk
   (E) endless round of dull activities

5. The children of the speaker in "A Letter"
   (A) approve of their father's love affair
   (B) do not trust him
   (C) have met the woman their father loves
   (D) have come to hate their father
   (E) are innocent victims of a hostile marriage

6. All of the following are romantic images in "A Letter" EXCEPT
   (A) "sliding, moonlit sea" (line 6)
   (B) "spill of mirrors" (line 10)
   (C) "warm Arabian nights" (line 11)
   (D) "two little wooly birds" (line 21)
   (E) "clear and bottomless blue" (line 18)

7. "Blood" in "A Letter" is the symbol of
   (A) passion
   (B) suffering
   (C) contrition
   (D) sacrifice
   (E) heartache

8. In "A Letter," "the tides welled about me" (line 24) refers to
   (A) tears
   (B) fears
   (C) recollections
   (D) remorse
   (E) yearnings

9. In "A Letter," the poet invites the reader to view the speaker as
   (A) a hypocrite
   (B) a philanderer
   (C) a person of superficial feelings
   (D) a decent man
   (E) a base husband and father

10. "Blundering blood" and "bottomless blue" are examples of
    (A) pathetic fallacy
    (B) alliteration
    (C) incremental repetition
    (D) assonance
    (E) consonance

Questions 11–20 refer to the following poem.

WATER
Robert Lowell (1917–1978)

It was a Maine lobster town—
each morning boatloads of hands
pushed off for granite
quarries on the islands,

Line
(5)   and left dozens of bleak
        white frame houses stuck
        like oyster shells
        on a hill of rock,

        and below us, the sea lapped
(10)   the raw little match-stick
        mazes of a weir,
        where the fish for bait were trapped.

        Remember? We sat on a slab of rock.
        From this distance in time
(15)   it seems the color
        of iris, rotting and turning purpler,

        but it was only
        the usual gray rock
        turning the usual green
(20)   when drenched by the sea.

        The sea drenched the rock
        at our feet all day,
        and kept tearing away
        flake after flake.

(25)   One night you dreamed
    you were a mermaid clinging to a wharf-pile,
    and trying to pull
    off the barnacles with your hands.

    We wished our two souls
(30)   might return like gulls
    to the rock. In the end,
    the water was too cold for us.

11. The speaker of "Water" recalls a
    (A) love that is gone
    (B) love that has been reawakened by memories
    (C) fishing holiday
    (D) sweetheart who betrayed him
    (E) lost weekend

12. The speaker of "Water" describes
    (A) memories of his adolescence
    (B) the town in which he was born
    (C) the dreams of his youth
    (D) the ravages of time
    (E) the deterioration of a love

13. The mood of "Water" is one of
    (A) anguish
    (B) resignation
    (C) despair
    (D) regret
    (E) hope

14. In "Water" the sea symbolizes
    (A) beauty of nature ignored
    (B) an eroding force
    (C) burned-out passion
    (D) the hard life of lobster fisherman
    (E) fantasies of eternal love

15. The mermaid and wharf-pile image in "Water" (line 26) is used to describe the
    (A) bleakness of the surroundings
    (B) fairy-tale atmosphere
    (C) realization that love is ephemeral
    (D) attempt to save a waning passion
    (E) hopelessness of a dead love

16. In "Water" the color of iris on the rock (lines 15–16) symbolizes that the love was one of
(A) passion
(B) illusion
(C) apathy
(D) pathos
(E) selfish gratification

17. The rock in "Water" is an image of
(A) fervor
(B) transcience
(C) insensitivity
(D) permanence
(E) callousness

18. The theme of "Water" is:
(A) There is nothing permanent in life.
(B) Passion can never be reawakened.
(C) It is wiser to forget the past.
(D) Time erodes love.
(E) Only nature remains unchanging.

19. All of the following are true of "Water" EXCEPT:
(A) Even a rock can be worn away by the sea.
(B) Love is a transient emotion.
(C) Gulls are more loyal to each other than human beings.
(D) When love dies, it cannot be reawakened.
(E) Love gives beauty to one's surroundings.

20. "We wished our two souls/might return like gulls/to the rock" (lines 29–30) is an example of
(A) metaphor
(B) objective correlative
(C) antithesis
(D) synecdoche
(E) simile

Questions 21–33 refer to the following passage.

From CAT IN THE RAIN
Ernest Hemingway (1899–1961)

She laid the mirror down on the dresser and went over to the window and looked out. It was getting dark.

"I want to pull my hair back tight and smooth and make a big knot at the back
Line   that I can feel," she said. "I want to have a kitty to sit on my lap and purr when I
(5)   stroke her."

"Yeah?" George said from the bed.

"And I want to eat at a table with my own silver and I want candles. And I want it to be spring and I want to brush my hair out in front of a mirror and I want a kitty and I want some new clothes."

(10)   "Oh, shut up and get something to read," George said. He was reading
again.

His wife was looking out of the window. It was quite dark now and still raining
in the palm trees.

"Anyway, I want a cat," she said, "I want a cat. I want a cat now. If I can't have
(15) long hair or any fun, I can have a cat."

George was not listening. He was reading his book. His wife looked out of the
window where the light had come on in the square.

Someone knocked at the door.

"Avanti," George said. He looked up from his book.

(20)   In the doorway stood the maid. She held a big tortoise-shell cat pressed tight
against her and swung down against her body.

"Excuse me," she said, "the padrone asked me to bring this for the
Signora."

21. This passage attempts to evoke a mood of
     (A)   emptiness and sterility
     (B)   conjugal affection
     (C)   hostility between husband and wife
     (D)   homesickness
     (E)   serenity and contentment

22. The story is concerned with a husband and wife who
     (A)   are returning home
     (B)   have lost a child
     (C)   stop at an Italian hotel
     (D)   have lost their way
     (E)   are middle-aged and fearful of growing old

23. The place where the couple is staying faces
     (A)   a city in the tropics
     (B)   an empty town square
     (C)   the house of the padrone
     (D)   a field of palm trees
     (E)   an ocean beach

24. The light images in the story shift to
     (A)   create a sense of impending doom
     (B)   highlight the husband's insensitivity
     (C)   accentuate the setting of the story
     (D)   correspond with the darkening moods of the wife
     (E)   establish a contrast with the unchanging hotel room

25. What the wife most yearns for is probably
     (A)   someone or something to love
     (B)   fun
     (C)   the return of her youth
     (D)   affection from her husband
     (E)   a few beautiful possessions

26. The gift of the padrone is
    (A) a joke he plays on the wife
    (B) an ironic gesture
    (C) an artificial fulfillment of the wife's yearnings
    (D) a present to his guests
    (E) an object to decorate the hotel room

27. In the wife's view, her marriage is
    (A) in jeopardy
    (B) dull but tolerable
    (C) unfulfilling
    (D) a relationship of convenience
    (E) a hateful imprisonment

28. The reader knows from the passage that all of the following statements are true EXCEPT:
    (A) There is an analogy between the setting and the relationship of husband and wife.
    (B) The wife lacks material things that might have enriched her life.
    (C) The gesture of the padrone was motivated by kindness.
    (D) The couple is incapable of having children.
    (E) The narrator feels sympathy for people deprived of meaning in their lives.

29. One can infer from reading the passage that the husband was
    (A) well educated
    (B) a successful business man
    (C) a popular fellow among his friends
    (D) a selfish, self-centered boor
    (E) a recluse

30. All of the following reveal that the wife was dominated by the husband EXCEPT:
    (A) He takes her to exotic places.
    (B) Her hair is short.
    (C) He tells her to keep quiet.
    (D) She feels deprived of fun.
    (E) She will not get a kitten or cat from him.

31. The narrator of this story
    (A) is objective
    (B) is omniscient
    (C) shows sympathy for a husband with a complaining wife
    (D) considers the wife a foolish, vain creature
    (E) presents his account as though it were a clinical case history

412 Practice Test D

32. The reader is told the husband's name but not the wife's because
    (A) the husband is the central character
    (B) the narrator wishes to show his irritation with the wife's personality
    (C) the name is commonplace, as is the husband
    (D) the author wishes to highlight the insignificance of the wife in the relationship
    (E) the author wishes to establish a contrast between the reality of the husband and the dream character of the wife

33. All of the following are true of the story EXCEPT:
    (A) The request for a kitten becomes a request for a cat because the progression in the story is moving toward the wife's humiliation.
    (B) The wife lacks clothing that might make her more attractive to herself.
    (C) The padrone, like the husband, is thoughtless and insensitive.
    (D) The hotel room is a symbol of all that the wife has had out of life.
    (E) The wife is hungry for attention and affection.

Questions 34–43 refer to the following passage.

From MEASURE FOR MEASURE
William Shakespeare (1564–1616)

Ay, but to die, and go we know not where
To lie in cold obstruction and to rot,
This sensible warm motion to become
Line   A kneaded clod; and the delighted spirit
(5)   To bathe in fiery floods, or to reside
In thrilling region of thick-ribbed ice,
To be imprisoned in the viewless winds
And blown with restless violence round about
The pendent world; or to be worse than worst
(10)   Of those that lawless and incertain thought
Imagine howling, 'tis too horrible.
The weariest and most loathed worldly life
That age, ache, penury and imprisonment
Can lay on nature is a paradise
(15)   To what we fear of death.

34. The subject of this selection is
    (A) resurrection
    (B) the good life
    (C) the fear of pain
    (D) death
    (E) the devil's world

35. The best definition of "obstruction" as used in line 2 is
    (A) obscurity
    (B) imprisonment
    (C) death
    (D) stagnation
    (E) oblivion

36. In line 3 "motion" is used
  (A) as a metaphor
  (B) for emotional effect
  (C) as a euphemism
  (D) as a symbol for life
  (E) to highlight the speaker's pessimism

37. The vision of the afterlife recorded in this selection is a reflection of the speaker's
  (A) vivid and poetic imagination
  (B) naïve delusions
  (C) limited education
  (D) desire to shock
  (E) culture and faith

38. In line 4 "kneaded clod" is a metaphor that suggests the
  (A) the act of creation
  (B) loss of sustenance in death
  (C) original substance of man
  (D) change of shape in death
  (E) meaninglessness of life

39. In line 4 "delighted" is used to mean
  (A) incapable of delight
  (B) still spiritually conscious
  (C) deprived of light
  (D) still maintaining a spark of physical existence
  (E) joyful to be freed of physical bonds

40. In this selection death is described as a condition in which the soul may encounter all of the following EXCEPT
  (A) torment in fire
  (B) freezing in ice
  (C) being driven wildly about in space
  (D) separation from the confines of the body
  (E) inexorable, stern judgment

41. The tone of this selection can best be described as
  (A) intense and agitated
  (B) restrained and objective
  (C) fearful and incredible
  (D) resigned and pessimistic
  (E) persuasive and hortatory

42. Which of the following statements is NOT true of this passage?
  (A) No matter what ills one encounters in life, living is preferable to dying.
  (B) The conception of the afterlife is one of dire punishment.
  (C) The speaker is clearly confident that his vision of the afterlife is a true one.
  (D) The conception of death is that of a body immobile and a spirit in torment.
  (E) The speaker apparently has some purpose in depicting death in frightening terms.

43. In the context of this passage "thrilling" (line 6) means
  (A) wearisome and monotonous
  (B) quivering and crushing
  (C) distressingly painful
  (D) piercingly cold
  (E) unbearably beautiful

Questions 44–56 refer to the following passage.

From MONTEREY
Robert Louis Stevenson (1850–1894)

The bay of Monterey has been compared by no less a person than General Sherman to a bent fishhook; and the comparison, if less important than the march through Georgia, still shows the eye of a soldier for topography. Santa
Line Cruz sits exposed at the shank; the mouth of the Salinas River is at the middle of
(5) the bend; and Monterey itself is cozily ensconced beside the barb. Thus the ancient capital of California faces across the bay, while the Pacific Ocean, though hidden by low hills and forests, bombards her left flank and rear with never dying surf. In front of the town, the long line of sea beach trends north and northwest, and then westward to enclose the bay. The waves which lap so qui-
(10) etly about the jetties of Monterey grow louder and larger in the distance; you can see the breakers leaping high and white by day; at night, the outline of the shore is traced in transparent silver by the moonlight and the flying foam; and from all round, even in quiet weather, the low, distant, thrilling roar of the Pacific hangs over the coast and the adjacent country like smoke above a battle.
(15)   These long beaches are enticing to the idle man. It would be hard to find a walk more solitary and at the same time more exciting to the mind. Crowds of ducks and sea gulls hover over the sea. Sandpipers trot in and out by troops after the retiring waves, trilling together in a chorus of infinitesimal song. Strange sea tangles, new to the European eye, the bones of whales, or sometimes a whole
(20) whale's carcass, white with carrion gulls and poisoning the wind, lie scattered here and there along the sand. The waves come in slowly, vast and green, curve their translucent necks, and burst with a surprising uproar, that runs, waxing and waning, up and down the long keyboard of the beach. The foam of these great ruins mounts in an instant to the ridge of the sand glacis, swiftly fleets back
(25) again and is met and buried by the next breaker. The interest is perpetually fresh. On no other coast that I know shall you enjoy, in calm, sunny weather, such a spectacle of Ocean's greatness, such beauty of changing color, or such degrees of thunder in the sound. The very air is more usually salt by this Homeric deep.
      In shore, a tract of sand hills borders on the beach. Here and there a lagoon,
(30) more or less brackish, attracts the birds and hunters. A rough, spotty under-

growth partially conceals the sand. The crouching, hardy live oaks flourish sin-
gly or in thickets—the kind of wood for murderers to crawl among—and here
and there the skirts of the forest extend downward from the hills with a floor of
turf and long aisles of pine trees hung with Spaniard's beard. Through this
(35)   quaint desert the railway cars drew near to Monterey from the junction of Salinas City—though that and so many other things are now forever altered—and it
was from here that you had the first view of the old township lying in the sand,
its white windmills bickering in the chill, perpetual wind, and the first fogs of
the evening drawing drearily around it from the sea.
(40)   The one common note of all this country is the haunting presence of the
ocean. A great faint sound of breakers follows you high up into the inland canyons; the roar of water dwells in the clean, empty rooms of Monterey as in a shell
upon the chimney; go where you will, you have but to pause and listen to hear
the voice of the Pacific. You pass out of the town to the southwest, and mount
(45)   the hill among pine woods. Glade, thicket, and grove surround you. You follow
winding sandy tracks that lead nowhither. You see a deer; a multitude of quail
arises. But the sound of the sea follows you as you advance, like that of wind
among the trees, only harsher and stranger to the ear; and when at length you
gain the summit, out breaks on every hand and with freshened vigor, that same
(50)   unending, distant whispering rumble of the ocean; for now you are on the top of
Monterey peninsula, and the noise no longer only mounts to you from behind
along the beach towards Santa Cruz, but from your right also, round by China-
town and Pinos Lighthouse, and from down before you to the mouth of the
Carmelo River. The whole woodland is begirt with thundering surges. The
(55)   silence that immediately surrounds you where you stand is not so much broken
as it is haunted by this distant, circling rumor. It sets your senses upon edge; you
strain your attention; you are clearly and unusually conscious of small sounds
near at hand; you walk listening like an Indian hunter; and that voice of the
Pacific is a sort of disquieting company to you in your walk.

44. The dominant impression in this passage is the
    (A) shape of the bay of Monterey
    (B) glow of the long stretches of beach
    (C) chorus of ducks, sea gulls, and sandpipers
    (D) continuing impact of the sea
    (E) bickering of the white windmills

45. The point of view of the narrator is that of
    (A) a geologist
    (B) an observer moving from place to place
    (C) a traveler from another land
    (D) a sailor on leave from his ship
    (E) a fixed observer standing on a hilltop

46. All of the following places are described in this selection EXCEPT
    (A) the Monterey peninsula
    (B) the inshore countryside
    (C) California's coastal mountain range
    (D) the beaches of Monterey
    (E) the panorama of the Monterey bay area

47. Which of the following statements best describes the first paragraph?
    (A) It focuses mainly on the ocean.
    (B) It ignores completely the observer's feelings.
    (C) It presents the historical background of the area.
    (D) It presents solely the location of Monterey.
    (E) It is an objectively accurate description of the area.

48. The narrator's use of language like "ensconced beside the barb" (line 5), "bombards her left flank" (line 7), "traced in transparent silver by the moonlight" (line 12) adds all of the following to the description EXCEPT:
    (A) It impedes the visual accuracy of the scene.
    (B) It challenges the reader's imagination.
    (C) It encourages the reader to view the scene as a painting.
    (D) It provides an emotional ingredient to the scene.
    (E) It converts what might have been a pedestrian account to literature.

49. The comparison of the bay of Monterey to a "bent fishhook" (line 2) is an example of
    (A) apostrophe
    (B) epigram
    (C) paradox
    (D) metaphor
    (E) symbol

50. Expressions like "flying foam," "trilling together," "first fogs," are examples of
    (A) euphemism
    (B) alliteration
    (C) simile
    (D) assonance
    (E) scanning

51. As the narrator describes the scene, there is most clearly
    (A) a movement from the trivial to the profound
    (B) a growing sense of religious wonder
    (C) a suggestion that the traveler is home
    (D) an intensification of feeling
    (E) a change in weather

52. The response of the narrator to Monterey reaches a climax in
    (A) the last two sentences of paragraph 2
    (B) the last sentence of paragraph 1
    (C) all of the last three paragraphs
    (D) the last four sentences of the passage
    (E) the first sentence of paragraph 2

53. "The waves come in slowly, vast and green, curve their translucent necks" (line 22) is an example of
    (A) symmetry
    (B) antithesis
    (C) apostrophe
    (D) hyperbole
    (E) personification

54. The phrase "same unending, distant whispering rumble" (lines 49–50) is an example of
    (A) onomatopoeia
    (B) poetic license
    (C) a trope
    (D) naturalism
    (E) metonymy

55. All of the following can be said to be true of the passage EXCEPT:
    (A) It is an objectively accurate description
    (B) It loses its effectiveness because there is no fixed point of observation.
    (C) It achieves a consistent point of view.
    (D) It adds emotional response to fact.
    (E) The comparison with a bent fishhook shapes the scene.

56. The unifying element in this passage is the
    (A) woodland
    (B) birds
    (C) narrator
    (D) bay and river
    (E) ocean

SECTION II
Total time—2 hours

Question 1

Suggested time—40 minutes

Read the following passage carefully. Then write an essay in which you analyze how the writer develops his concept of an ideal government. Consider the point of view, tone, use of figurative language, the structure of the passage, or any other appropriate elements of writing.

The authority of government, even such as I am willing to submit to—for I will cheerfully obey those who know and can do better than I, and in many things even those who neither know nor can do so well—is still an impure one: to be strictly
Line   just, it must have the sanction and consent of the governed. It can have no pure right
(5)   over my person and property but what I conceded to it. The progress from an absolute to a limited monarchy, from a limited monarchy to a democracy, is a progress toward a true respect for the individual. Even the Chinese philosopher was wise enough to regard the individual as the basis of the empire. Is a democracy, such as

(10)   we know it, the last improvement possible in government? Is it not possible to take a
step further towards recognizing and organizing the rights of man? There will never
be a really free and enlightened State until the State comes to recognize the individual as a higher and independent power, from which all its own power and
authority are derived, and treats him accordingly. I please myself with imagining a
State at last which can afford to be just to all men, and to treat the individual with
(15)   respect as a neighbor; which even would not think it inconsistent with its own
repose if a few were to live aloof from it, not meddling with it, nor embraced by it,
who fulfilled all the duties of neighbors and fellow men. A State which bore this
kind of fruit, and suffered it to drop off as fast as it ripened, would prepare the way
for a still more perfect and glorious State, which also I have imagined, but not yet
(20)   anywhere seen.

Question 2

Suggested time—40 minutes

When we read and study a novel or a play, we want to be offered something
new—not absolutely new, perhaps because human nature doesn't change very
much, but at least a new combination of human traits, a new illustration of how
human beings behave, of just how much they are capable of—in any one of
innumerable directions.

Discuss a novel or a play that you have read and studied. In your essay, point
out the new views or new experiences this work offered and the ways in which
these views or experiences helped (or did not help) to make the work appealing to you.

The works below are listed as examples. You may wish to choose from
among them or to provide your own appropriate example.

Jude the Obscure	*The Wild Duck*
Wuthering Heights	*Murder in the Cathedral*
As I Lay Dying	*Rosencrantz and Guildenstern Are Dead*
Pride and Prejudice	*Oedipus Rex*
Gulliver's Travels	*The Crucible*
Lord Jim	*Dr. Faustus*
Sons and Lovers	*The Glass Menagerie*
Catch-22	*Amadeus*
The Handmaid's Tale	*Beloved*

Question 3

Suggested time—40 minutes

Read the following poem carefully. Then write an essay in which to discuss how poetic techniques highlight its intellectual and emotional content.

HAMPSTEAD REVISITED
Alfred Levinson (1925–1990)

D.H. Lawrence Lived Here in 1915
Poet and Novelist

Tagore in 1912

Line   A barechested man pats his dog
(5)   in the sun a woman on the doorstep
    combs and trims her hair

    No evidence that it is six decades
    later in this cul de sac filled with light
    like a pint of lemon squash. Not the clothes
(10)   (man in pants and slippers, woman
    in velour robe, dog indifferent furred)
    no autos choking the lane
    only the blue disc of commemory
    pinned to the rustbrick wall.

(15)   There is something in the concentration here
    that man: his dog, that woman, her hair
    that sun: small stopper for the jar
    and me: shooting from the hip

    I pull out my pad. Word sketch.
(20)   And for some reason I make a note
    about nothing I have seen, all of which goes
    unrecorded, except in memory, the reservoir
    of creativity (according to the Joyce
    who lived in Trieste erecting Dublin)
(25)   Instead, there's this:
    the man with an obsession
    is more interesting than
    the moderate balanced man.

Answer Key for Practice Test D
Answers to Multiple-Choice Questions

1.	E	13.	D	25.	A	37.	E	49.	D
2.	C	14.	B	26.	C	38.	C	50.	B
3.	B	15.	D	27.	C	39.	C	51.	D
4.	D	16.	A	28.	D	40.	E	52.	D
5.	C	17.	D	29.	D	41.	A	53.	E
6.	D	18.	D	30.	A	42.	C	54.	A
7.	A	19.	C	31.	B	43.	D	55.	B
8.	D	20.	E	32.	D	44.	D	56.	E
9.	D	21.	A	33.	C	45.	B		
10.	B	22.	C	34.	D	46.	C		
11.	A	23.	B	35.	D	47.	E		
12.	E	24.	D	36.	D	48.	A		

Answer Explanations

1. **E** The poem is a love letter from a man (line 29) to a woman. That the man is married is suggested by line 16: "Others are bound to us, the gentle and the blameless," alluding most likely to the speaker's wife.

2. **C** Conventionally, spring is the season of love. Also, crocuses (line 4) bloom in the spring.

3. **B** The image refers to thoughts of his beloved churning inside him.

4. **D** "Palaver" in this context means the empty, meaningless chatter of everyday life.

5. **C** During a visit, the woman once brought the boys "little wooly birds" (line 21).

6. **D** It takes a powerful imagination to see romance in "two little wooly birds."

7. **A** The color red—the color of blood—often connotes love and passion. It is a "warm" color.

8. **D** When the little boy mentions the woman, the father's yearnings suddenly rise, like the tide.

9. **D** In the end, despite his illicit romance, we sympathize with the speaker, who is "dead set to ignore/The endless repetitions of his own murmurous blood" (lines 29–30). In other words, he is too decent a fellow to act on his passions.

10. **B** Both phrases contain words starting with the same sound. Hence, they are alliterations.

11. **A** The speaker recalls a love relationship that went sour a long time ago.

12. **E** Erosion is the central motif in the poem. Love is the thing that erodes.

13. **D** The speaker is sad (regretful) that the love did not survive. Choices (A), (B), and (C) are too extreme to accurately describe the mood of the poem.

14. B The waves pounded steadily on the Maine lobster town, on the weir (dam), and on the rocks. Taken all together, the sea is regarded as an eroding force.

15. D The image describes an attempt to correct a bad situation—in this case a love going bad.

16. A The speaker recalls that during the height of his passion, the gray rock seemed bluish-purple, the color of iris. Evidently, his vision was distorted, or he viewed the world through the proverbial rose-colored glasses.

17. D The rock withstood the ravages of the sea, despite "flake after flake" being torn away (lines 23–24). The last stanza confirms that the rock remained steadfast while love dissolved.

18. D The speaker reflects on a long-ago time of love. "Remember?" he asks (line 13). "In the end," he adds, "the water [an eroding force] was too cold [read too strong] for us" (lines 31–32).

19. C The poem does not discuss the character traits of seagulls.

20. E The quotation contains a comparison using "like." Therefore, it's a simile.

21. A The woman's complaints, the rain, the approaching darkness, George's responses to his wife—they all contribute to the barren mood of the scene.

22. C The maid knocking on the door indicates that the setting is a hotel. The dialogue in lines 19–23 is in Italian.

23. B Outside there are palm trees and a square illuminated by streetlights.

24. D It gets darker and darker as the wife grows increasingly querulous. Only when the streetlights go on is there a break in the mood. Then, the maid knocks on the door and brings in a cat, easing the tension between husband and wife.

25. A The wife wants something to dote on and to be affectionate with.

26. C A tortoise-shell figurine of a cat indeed falls short of the real thing.

27. C The emptiness of her marriage, indeed her whole life, leads her to yearn for something more.

28. D Events in the passage—directly or by implication—tell readers everything except that the man and woman are infertile.

29. D During the scene, George's words and behavior indicate his self-absorption as well as his indifference toward his wife.

30. A There is no evidence in the passage that she accompanies George to exotic places.

31. B Although an omniscient narrator has an unlimited perspective on the people and places in a story, this narrator sticks fairly close to events that can be observed.

32. D A character without a name is a nonentity. This wife is treated accordingly by her husband.

33. C   We don't know much about the padrone except what the maid says to George and his wife.

34. D   The subject of the passage is announced in the first line.

35. D   Because Shakespeare sets up a contrast with "motion" (line 3), the best interpretation is "stagnation."

36. D   The speaker is referring to life.

37. E   One's view of life after death is usually determined by one's beliefs and culture.

38. C   Our lives ultimately lead us back to the earth, thus, the popular notion of "dust to dust"—and all that.

39. C   Read the word as *de-lighted* (the opposite of *lit up*), for the speaker is hardly delighted by the prospect of death.

40. E   The passage contains no reference or allusion to the so-called Judgment Day.

41. A   The subject matter and emotional color of the piece suggest the speaker's dismay.

42. C   The speaker's uncertainty is made clear in line 1: " . . . and go we know not where . . . ."

43. D   The region must contrast with the "fiery flood" (line 5). Therefore, "thrilling" means "very, very cold."

44. D   The passage is dominated by the sights and sounds of the Pacific, or as the narrator calls it, "the haunting presence of the ocean" (lines 40–41).

45. B   The speaker is on foot (line 16). He views the Monterey peninsula from several perspectives as he moves up the coast toward Santa Cruz (lines 44–59).

46. C   The narrator walks up into nearby hills but does not mention the coastal mountains.

47. E   The description gives an accurate rendering of the topography of Monterey Bay, which includes the shape of the bay, its prominent features, and the effect of the ocean on its shores. Toward the end of the paragraph, however, the writing becomes more impressionistic.

48. A   If nothing else, the images in such phrases enhance the description of the scene.

49. D   General Sherman's comparison is a metaphor. Evidently, Sherman, known for saying "War is Hell," was fond of making metaphors.

50. B   Because the first letters in each phrase make the same sound, the expressions are alliterations.

51. D   The narrator's feelings grow stronger as the passage unfolds. "It would be hard to find a walk . . . more exciting to the mind," the author writes in lines 15–16. Then he adds, "On no other coast . . . shall you enjoy . . . such a spectacle of Ocean's greatness . . . etc." (lines 26–28). He calls the air

"Homeric" (line 28), and in the last paragraph (lines 56–59) details the effects of the area on both his senses and his emotions.

52. D In the last lines of the passage, the narrator's response to the Monterey peninsula is particularly passionate.

53. E Assigning human qualities ("necks") to a place is an example of personification.

54. A The words are the author's attempt to recreate the sounds of the ocean. Therefore, they are onomatopoetic.

55. B Although there is no fixed observation point, the passage is written from a single point of view—the author's.

56. E The narrator focuses on the sights and sounds of the ocean.

Answers to Essay Questions

Answers for essay questions will vary widely, but the following answers identify ideas that could reasonably be included in an essay that responds to each question.

Question 1

The writer articulates a political philosophy that describes three increasingly just forms of government. The first one "must have the sanction and consent of the governed" (line 4). In the second, the State will "recognize the individual as a higher and independent power" (lines 11–12). The third—the ideal form of government—is one that "can afford to be just to all men, and to treat the individual with respect as a neighbor" (lines 14–15).

The author moves through this progression by writing as though he is talking to the reader. This personalization of the discussion reinforces the writer's concern for the individual. Government is not some far-off abstraction, but a neighborly institution that should relate to and respect everyone individually—person-to-person.

Halfway through the passage the author pauses to ask two questions that break the passage into two parts. The first part deals with the government that currently exists, the second with what the author thinks government should be.

Question 2

In essence, the question asks you to discuss what a novel or play has revealed to you about human nature and behavior. Each title on the list offers plenty of material. Were you to write about *Catch-22,* for instance, you might write about war and its consequences for the men and women who fight wars. The whole notion of a "Catch-22," a phrase that is used widely in day-to-day speech even by people who never heard of the book, suggests the lunacy of war. If you chose to write about *The Glass Menagerie,* your essay might contain a discussion of how people tend to delude themselves when they cannot face reality. The play, you may recall, takes place in the 1930s, at about the time Europe is starting its plunge into World War II. Each character in the play finds a way to cope not only with personal defects but with a defective world.

Question 3

The speaker is visiting a literary landmark—the former home of both D.H. Lawrence and the poet Tagore. At the site where immortals once trod, he expects to be awed. But he sees only a man, a woman, and a dog who, ironically, could not care less about the home's former residents. The mundane, everyday images used in this part of the poem reinforce how indifferent these people are to the history of place they occupy. The only evidence that this is hallowed ground is a blue plaque nailed to the wall.

A writer himself, the speaker pulls out a pad, expecting to be inspired by the place. But he writes a sentence that has nothing to do with the site but rather with a man with an obsession—presumably the speaker himself.

Answer Sheet for Practice Test E
Literature and Composition

Multiple-Choice
Questions
Time—1 hour

1. Ⓐ Ⓑ Ⓒ Ⓓ Ⓔ
2. Ⓐ Ⓑ Ⓒ Ⓓ Ⓔ
3. Ⓐ Ⓑ Ⓒ Ⓓ Ⓔ
4. Ⓐ Ⓑ Ⓒ Ⓓ Ⓔ
5. Ⓐ Ⓑ Ⓒ Ⓓ Ⓔ
6. Ⓐ Ⓑ Ⓒ Ⓓ Ⓔ
7. Ⓐ Ⓑ Ⓒ Ⓓ Ⓔ
8. Ⓐ Ⓑ Ⓒ Ⓓ Ⓔ
9. Ⓐ Ⓑ Ⓒ Ⓓ Ⓔ
10. Ⓐ Ⓑ Ⓒ Ⓓ Ⓔ
11. Ⓐ Ⓑ Ⓒ Ⓓ Ⓔ
12. Ⓐ Ⓑ Ⓒ Ⓓ Ⓔ
13. Ⓐ Ⓑ Ⓒ Ⓓ Ⓔ
14. Ⓐ Ⓑ Ⓒ Ⓓ Ⓔ
15. Ⓐ Ⓑ Ⓒ Ⓓ Ⓔ
16. Ⓐ Ⓑ Ⓒ Ⓓ Ⓔ
17. Ⓐ Ⓑ Ⓒ Ⓓ Ⓔ
18. Ⓐ Ⓑ Ⓒ Ⓓ Ⓔ
19. Ⓐ Ⓑ Ⓒ Ⓓ Ⓔ
20. Ⓐ Ⓑ Ⓒ Ⓓ Ⓔ

21. Ⓐ Ⓑ Ⓒ Ⓓ Ⓔ
22. Ⓐ Ⓑ Ⓒ Ⓓ Ⓔ
23. Ⓐ Ⓑ Ⓒ Ⓓ Ⓔ
24. Ⓐ Ⓑ Ⓒ Ⓓ Ⓔ
25. Ⓐ Ⓑ Ⓒ Ⓓ Ⓔ
26. Ⓐ Ⓑ Ⓒ Ⓓ Ⓔ
27. Ⓐ Ⓑ Ⓒ Ⓓ Ⓔ
28. Ⓐ Ⓑ Ⓒ Ⓓ Ⓔ
29. Ⓐ Ⓑ Ⓒ Ⓓ Ⓔ
30. Ⓐ Ⓑ Ⓒ Ⓓ Ⓔ
31. Ⓐ Ⓑ Ⓒ Ⓓ Ⓔ
32. Ⓐ Ⓑ Ⓒ Ⓓ Ⓔ
33. Ⓐ Ⓑ Ⓒ Ⓓ Ⓔ
34. Ⓐ Ⓑ Ⓒ Ⓓ Ⓔ
35. Ⓐ Ⓑ Ⓒ Ⓓ Ⓔ
36. Ⓐ Ⓑ Ⓒ Ⓓ Ⓔ
37. Ⓐ Ⓑ Ⓒ Ⓓ Ⓔ
38. Ⓐ Ⓑ Ⓒ Ⓓ Ⓔ
39. Ⓐ Ⓑ Ⓒ Ⓓ Ⓔ
40. Ⓐ Ⓑ Ⓒ Ⓓ Ⓔ

41. Ⓐ Ⓑ Ⓒ Ⓓ Ⓔ
42. Ⓐ Ⓑ Ⓒ Ⓓ Ⓔ
43. Ⓐ Ⓑ Ⓒ Ⓓ Ⓔ
44. Ⓐ Ⓑ Ⓒ Ⓓ Ⓔ
45. Ⓐ Ⓑ Ⓒ Ⓓ Ⓔ
46. Ⓐ Ⓑ Ⓒ Ⓓ Ⓔ
47. Ⓐ Ⓑ Ⓒ Ⓓ Ⓔ
48. Ⓐ Ⓑ Ⓒ Ⓓ Ⓔ
49. Ⓐ Ⓑ Ⓒ Ⓓ Ⓔ
50. Ⓐ Ⓑ Ⓒ Ⓓ Ⓔ
51. Ⓐ Ⓑ Ⓒ Ⓓ Ⓔ
52. Ⓐ Ⓑ Ⓒ Ⓓ Ⓔ
53. Ⓐ Ⓑ Ⓒ Ⓓ Ⓔ
54. Ⓐ Ⓑ Ⓒ Ⓓ Ⓔ
55. Ⓐ Ⓑ Ⓒ Ⓓ Ⓔ
56. Ⓐ Ⓑ Ⓒ Ⓓ Ⓔ

Three Essay
Questions
Time—2 hours

Write your essays on standard 8½ by 11-inch composition paper. At the exam you will be given a bound booklet containing 12 lined pages.

E Literature and Composition

SECTION I

Total time—1 hour

Read each poem or prose passage carefully, and answer the accompanying questions.

Questions 1–11 refer to the following poem.

THE LIFEGUARD
James Dickey (1923–1997)

> In a stable of boats I lie still,
> From all sleeping children hidden.
> The leap of a fish from its shadow
Line   Makes the whole lake instantly tremble.
(5)   With my foot on the water, I feel
> The moon outside
> Take on the utmost of its power.
> I rise and go through the boats.
> I set my broad sole upon silver,
(10)   On the skin of the sky, on the moonlight,
> Stepping outward from earth onto water
> In quest of the miracle
> This village of children believed
> That I could perform as I dived
(15)   For one who had sunk from my sight.
> I saw his cropped haircut go under.
> I leapt, and my steep body flashed
> Once, in the sun.
> Dark drew all the light from my eyes.
(20)   Like a man who explores his death
> By the pull of his slow-moving shoulders,
> I hung head down in the cold,
> Wide-eyed, contained, and alone
> Among the weeds,
(25)   And my fingertips turned into stone
> From clutching immovable blackness.
> Time after time I leapt upward
> Exploding in breath, and fell back
> From the change in the children's faces
(30)   At my defeat.
> Beneath them, I swam to the boathouse
> With only my life in my arms
> To wait for the lake to shine back
> At the risen moon with such power

(35)   That my steps on the light of the ripples
        Might be sustained.
        Beneath me is nothing but brightness
        Like the ghost of a snow field in summer.
        As I move toward the center of the lake,
(40)   Which is also the center of the moon,
        I am thinking of how I may be
        The savior of one
        Who has already died in my care.
        The dark trees fade from around me.
(45)   The moon's dust hovers together.
        I call softly out, and the child's
        Voice answers through blinding water.
        Patiently, slowly,
        He rises, dilating to break
(50)   The surface of stone with his forehead.
        He is one I do not remember
        Having ever seen in his life.
        The ground that I stand on is trembling
        Upon his smile.
(55)   I wash the black mud from my hands.
        On a light given off by the grave,
        I kneel in the quick of the moon
        At the heart of a distant forest
        And hold in my arms a child
(60)   Of water, water, water.

1. The lifeguard in the poem yearns
    (A)   to forget his cowardice
    (B)   to regain the love of children
    (C)   to relive the events of a happy day
    (D)   to be able to sleep
    (E)   to be a savior

2. The lifeguard dreams that
    (A)   he walks on the lake
    (B)   the children revile him
    (C)   he descends to hell
    (D)   he saves a child
    (E)   he holds a gravestone

3. When, in the lifeguard's dream, the child rises from the water, the lifeguard
    (A)   smiles at his victory over death
    (B)   recognizes the child and is elated
    (C)   does not remember the child
    (D)   falls to his knees in gratitude
    (E)   eventually drowns with the child

4. The subject of this poem is the
   (A) defeat of a lifeguard
   (B) desire of all men to be Christ
   (C) love of children
   (D) heroism of a lifeguard
   (E) cleansing property of water

5. In the poem there is a fusion between
   (A) sea and sky
   (B) sun and moon
   (C) reality and dream
   (D) man and Christ
   (E) stone and grave

6. The sunlit world (lines 13–18) symbolizes
   (A) illusion
   (B) reality
   (C) death
   (D) hope
   (E) faith

7. Because he could not save the child, the lifeguard does all of the following EXCEPT
   (A) hide from the children
   (B) think of suicide
   (C) dream of miracles
   (D) imagine himself kneeling at a grave
   (E) relive the experience of attempted rescue

8. All of the following images appear in the poem EXCEPT
   (A) a moonlit lake
   (B) a lake stirred by leaping fish
   (C) a walk on water
   (D) a gravestone
   (E) a resuscitated child

9. The lifeguard compares diving into the depths of the lake to
   (A) the agile movement of fish
   (B) experiencing resurrection
   (C) learning about death
   (D) challenging death
   (E) being baptized

10. In his dream, the lake seemed to the lifeguard like a
    (A) shimmering ocean
    (B) huge wheatfield
    (C) muddy expanse of earth
    (D) glowing snowfield
    (E) patch of beauty in an ugly earth

11. In the poem water can be considered a symbol of
     (A) failure
     (B) life
     (C) the dark side of man
     (D) resurrection
     (E) heaven

Questions 12–25 refer to the following poem.

THE CONVERGENCE OF THE TWAIN
Thomas Hardy (1840–1928)

1

In a solitude of the sea
Deep from human vanity,
And the Pride of Life that planned her, stilly couches she.

2

Line   Steel chambers, late the pyres
(5)   Of her salamandrine fires,
Cold currents thrid, and turn to rhythmic tidal lyres.

3

Over the mirrors meant
To glass the opulent
The sea worm crawls—grotesque, slimed, dumb, indifferent.

4

(10)   Jewels in joy designed
To ravish the sensuous mind
Lie lightless, all their sparkles bleared and black and blind.

5

Dim moon-eyed fishes near
Gaze at the gilded gear
(15)   And query: "What does this vaingloriousness down here?". . .

6

Well: while was fashioning
This creature of cleaving wing,
The Immanent Will that stirs and urges everything

7

Prepared a sinister mate
(20)   For her—so gaily great—
A Shape of Ice, for the time far and dissociate.

8

And as the smart ship grew
In stature, grace, and hue,
In shadowy silent distance grew the Iceberg too.

9

(25)   Alien they seemed to be:
No mortal eye could see
The intimate welding of their later history.

10
Or sign that they were bent
By paths coincident
(30)   On being anon twin halves of one august event,

11
Till the Spinner of the Years
Said "Now!" And each one hears,
And consummation comes, and jars two hemispheres.

12. The poem states that
    (A) human beings control their destinies
    (B) there is disorder in the universe
    (C) a destiny rules the universe
    (D) a benign power governs man and nature
    (E) a malevolent force controls the world

13. The third line of each stanza
    (A) makes a philosophic comment
    (B) expresses contrasting thoughts or images to those in the first two lines
    (C) introduces a new idea
    (D) makes a satiric comment
    (E) repeats the thoughts expressed in the first two lines

14. All of the following are themes of the poem EXCEPT:
    (A) Man fashioned the ship; nature fashioned the bridegroom for her.
    (B) Fate is a dominant force in the universe.
    (C) Life is ruled by ironies.
    (D) There is a weird beauty in undersea nature.
    (E) Human aspirations are vain.

15. The "Immanent Will" (line 18) is also the
    (A) "Spinner of the Years" (line 31)
    (B) "Pride of Life" (line 3)
    (C) "creature of cleaving wing" (line 17)
    (D) "sensuous mind" (line 11)
    (E) "Shape of Ice" (line 21)

16. The triple rhyme of each stanza reflects the
    (A) destruction of human creations
    (B) monotony of sea waves
    (C) power of nature
    (D) laments of shipwrecked sailors
    (E) inevitability of the meeting of ship and iceberg

17. The use of "vaingloriousness" in line 15 emphasizes the
    (A) hopelessness of human efforts
    (B) pathos of human aspirations
    (C) arrogance of man
    (D) irony in human attempts to excel nature
    (E) unexpectedness of nature's destructiveness

18. All of the following words or phrases suggest the wrecking of the ship as described in the poem EXCEPT
    (A) "consummation"
    (B) "salamandrine fires"
    (C) "intimate welding"
    (D) "twin halves of one august event"
    (E) "prepared a sinister mate"

19. The Spinner of the Years's one-word utterance, "Now!" is an illustration of the poet's dramatic use of
    (A) oxymoron
    (B) hyperbole
    (C) apostrophe
    (D) climax
    (E) controlled emotion

20. In the second stanza the image describes the
    (A) hiss of fire being extinguished as the ship sinks
    (B) sea animals gliding through the passages of the sunken vessel
    (C) sea beating against the ship's hull
    (D) sea flowing through the wreckage of the sunken ship
    (E) slow sinking of the vessel into the depths

21. The poem is divided into two main sections. The first section ends with stanza
    (A) 5
    (B) 10
    (C) 1
    (D) 8
    (E) 4

22. The main themes of the poem are expressed in
    (A) stanzas 1 and 11
    (B) stanzas 1, 6, and 11
    (C) stanza 1
    (D) stanzas 1 and 8
    (E) stanza 11

23. The basic metaphor of the poem is
    (A) destiny
    (B) the power of fate
    (C) the *Titanic*
    (D) marriage
    (E) the iceberg

24. "In shadowy silent distance grew the Iceberg too" (line 24) is an example of
    (A) inversion
    (B) paradox
    (C) apostrophe
    (D) simile
    (E) parody

25. "In shadowy silent distance grew the Iceberg too" (line 24) gives the effect of all of the following EXCEPT
    (A) an inevitable encounter
    (B) preparation for a convergence
    (C) a sense of doom
    (D) an example of the limits of nature
    (E) a portent of disaster

Questions 26–33 refer to the following poem.

THE FORCE THAT THROUGH THE GREEN FUSE DRIVES THE FLOWER
Dylan Thomas (1914–1953)

The force that through the green fuse drives the flower
Drives my green age; that blasts the roots of trees
Is my destroyer.
Line   And I am dumb to tell the crooked rose
(5)   My youth is bent by the same wintry fever.

The force that drives the water through the rocks
Drives my red blood; that dries the mouthing streams
Turns mine to wax.
And I am dumb to mouth unto my veins.
(10)   How at the mountain spring the same mouth sucks.

The hand that whirls the water in the pool
Stirs the quicksand; that ropes the blowing wind
Hauls my shroud sail.
And I am dumb to tell the hanging man
(15)   How of my clay is made the hangman's lime.

The lips of time leech to the fountain head;
Love drips and gathers, but the fallen blood
Shall calm her sores.
And I am dumb to tell a weather's wind
(20)   How time has ticked a heaven round the stars.

And I am dumb to tell the lover's tome
How at my sheet goes the same crooked worm.

26. The speaker in this poem is
    (A) an old man
    (B) a criminal
    (C) a youth
    (D) a ghost
    (E) a shepherd

27. "The force" in the poem is associated with all of the following EXCEPT
    (A) God
    (B) nature
    (C) good
    (D) destruction
    (E) peace

28. A basic theme of the poem is that
    (A) love brings grief
    (B) life and death issue from the same source
    (C) little happiness is to be found in life
    (D) death is a welcome release from life and pain
    (E) beneath the beauties of nature lies unseen ugliness

29. "Wintry fever" (line 5) is an example of
    (A) irony
    (B) a pun
    (C) litotes
    (D) an epithet
    (E) oxymoron

30. In the first stanza the speaker asserts that
    (A) he is subject to the same natural forces which control other living things
    (B) he is in a state of despair because of the onset of old age
    (C) the power of love enables human beings to transcend death
    (D) man is basically unaffected by the natural processes that surround him
    (E) man's uniqueness lies in his ability to communicate his inner feelings

31. The destruction motif in the poem functions as
    (A) a dominant element in the first three stanzas of the poem
    (B) an ironic contrast to the speaker's optimism
    (C) an expression of the beauty of nature in unrest
    (D) a reflection of the poet's concern for the welfare of mankind
    (E) a contradictory and minor echo to the poet's theme

32. All of the following are expressed in the poem EXCEPT:
    (A) Love and beauty are transitory.
    (B) Death and life are continuously inseparable.
    (C) Time is man's enemy.
    (D) There are moments in life when the destructive element pauses.
    (E) A divine force is to blame for transmuting beauty into ugliness.

33. "The hand" in the third stanza does all of the following EXCEPT
    (A) whirls water
    (B) folds in prayer
    (C) checks the wind
    (D) stirs the quicksand
    (E) brings death

Questions 34–45 refer to the following passage.

From RELIGIO MEDICI
(A Doctor's Faith)
Sir Thomas Browne (1605–1682)

. . . if I hold the true anatomy of myself, I am delineated and naturally
framed to such a piece of virtue; for I am a constitution so general that it
consorts and sympathizes with all things. I have no antipathy, or rather
idiosyncrasy, in diet, humour, air, anything . . . . I am no plant that will
Line
(5)   not prosper out of a garden. All places, all airs, make unto me one country; I am in England everywhere, and under any meridian. I have been
shipwrecked, yet am not enemy with the sea or winds; I can study, play,
or sleep in a tempest. In brief, I am averse from nothing; my conscience
would give me the lie if I should say I absolutely detest or hate any
(10)   essence but the Devil, or so at least abhor anything but that we might
come to composition. If there be any among those common objects of
hatred I do contemn and laugh at, it is that great enemy of reason, virtue,
and religion, the multitude: that numerous piece of monstrosity which,
taken asunder, seem men and the reasonable creatures of God, but, con-
(15)   fused together, make but one great beast and a monstrosity more prodigious than Hydra. It is no breach of his good parts. Though the corruption of these times and the bias of present practice wheel another way;
thus it was in the first and primitive commonwealth, and is yet in the
integrity and cradle of well-ordered polities, till corruption getteth
(20)   ground, ruder desires laboring after that which wiser generations contemn, everyone having a liberty to amass and heap up riches, and they a
license or faculty to do or purchase anything. . . .

34. The speaker in this passage presents
     (A) an objective self-portrait
     (B) a view of himself as modest and gregarious
     (C) a view of himself as one of the common herd
     (D) a view of himself as a biological creature
     (E) a view of himself as unique and different from the masses

35. By the expression "delineated and naturally framed" (line 1), the speaker
     means that he
     (A) was created by God
     (B) inherited his personality from his ancestors
     (C) is a product of evolution
     (D) was designed and formed by nature
     (E) owes what he is to no one

36. When the speaker states "I am no plant" (line 4), he is using
     (A) a simile
     (B) a paradox
     (C) a symbol
     (D) an analogy
     (E) a metaphor

37. In this passage, the speaker initially presents many of his virtues
    (A) by bold and positive assertions
    (B) by the use of examples
    (C) with humility
    (D) by means of negative statements
    (E) with humor and self-deprecation

38. In this passage, the speaker sees himself as
    (A) a lover of nature
    (B) an agnostic
    (C) a lover of man but not of men
    (D) a captain of the souls of men
    (E) a model to be emulated

39. The reader may conclude from this passage that the speaker is
    (A) a person with low self-esteem
    (B) an egoist
    (C) a man of eminence
    (D) a man of great piety
    (E) a man who has suffered greatly

40. In this passage, the speaker claims that all of the following represent the kind of person he is NOT, EXCEPT
    (A) one who can readily come to agreement on issues
    (B) one who fusses about the food served him
    (C) one who is ready to forgive those who tolerate evil
    (D) one who is at home nowhere
    (E) one who is dyspeptic and rancorous

41. In the speaker's view, man is *fundamentally*
    (A) savage and evil
    (B) proud, pompous, and egotistical
    (C) lacking in reason
    (D) gullible and superstitious
    (E) noble and virtuous

42. The speaker supports his contention that he is "averse from nothing" (line 8) by citing all of the following examples EXCEPT
    (A) he is not a particularly fussy eater
    (B) he adapts to strange circumstances
    (C) he accepts the ravages of time and nature
    (D) he is calm even in the face of adversity
    (E) he is tolerant of foolish people

43. In this passage, the speaker reveals himself to be all of the following EXCEPT
    (A) a deeply religious man
    (B) a leader of men
    (C) a critic of social evils
    (D) a scholarly man
    (E) a man who has traveled to many places

44. The allusion to Hydra (line 16) is introduced by the speaker to dramatize the tendencies in men of his time to engage in all of the following EXCEPT
(A) enterprises to acquire wealth
(B) exploitation of the weak and poor
(C) corruption of official
(D) sexual freedom
(E) attendance at church services

45. The speaker sees himself as being able to function and to maintain his peace in all of the following EXCEPT
(A) law courts
(B) storms at sea
(C) public demonstrations
(D) slums
(E) crowded streets

Questions 46–56 refer to the following passage.

From THE PUPIL
Henry James (1843–1916)

One sad November day while the wind roared round the old palace and the rain lashed the lagoon, Pemberton, for exercise and even somewhat for warmth—the Moreens were horribly frugal about fires; it was a cause of suffering to their
Line inmate—walked up and down the big bare *sala* with his pupil. The scagliola
(5) floor was cold, the high battered casements shook in the storm, and the stately decay of the place was unrelieved by a particle of furniture. Pemberton's spirits were low, and it came over him that the fortune of the Moreens was now even lower. A blast of desolation, a portent of disgrace and disaster, seemed to draw through the comfortless hall. Mr. Moreen and Ulick were in the Piazza, looking
(10) out for something, strolling drearily, in mackintoshes, under the arcades; but still, in spite of mackintoshes, unmistakable men of the world. Paula and Amy were in bed—it might have been thought they were staying there to keep warm. Pemberton looked askance at the boy at his side, to see to what extent he was conscious of these dark omens. But Morgan, luckily for him, was now mainly
(15) conscious of growing taller and stronger and indeed of being in his fifteenth year. This fact was intensely interesting to him and the basis of a private theory—which, however, he had imparted to his tutor—that in a little while he should stand on his own feet. He considered that the situation would change—that in short he should be "finished," grown up, producible in the world of affairs and
(20) ready to prove himself of sterling ability. Sharply as he was capable at times of analyzing, as he called it, his life, there were happy hours when he remained, as he also called it—and as the name, really, of their right ideal—"jolly" superficial; the proof of which was his fundamental assumption that he should presently go to Oxford, to Pemberton's college, and aided and abetted by Pemberton, do the
(25) most wonderful things. It depressed the young man to see how little in such a project he took account of ways and means; in other connections he mostly kept to the measure. Pemberton tried to imagine the Moreens at Oxford and fortunately failed; yet unless they were to adopt it as a residence there would be no *modus vivendi* for Morgan. How could he live without an allowance, and where was the
(30) allowance to come from? He, Pemberton, might live on Morgan; but how could Morgan live on *him*? What was to become of him anyhow? Somehow the fact that he was a big boy now, with better prospects of health, made the question of his

future more difficult. So long as he was markedly frail the great consideration he inspired seemed enough of an answer to it. But at the bottom of Pemberton's heart (35) was the recognition of his probably being strong enough to live and not yet strong enough to struggle or to thrive. Morgan himself at any rate was in the first flush of the rosiest consciousness of adolescence, so that the beating of the tempest seemed to him after all but the voice of life and the challenge of fate. He had on his shabby little overcoat, with the collar up, but was enjoying his walk.

46. The attitude of the narrator toward the characters in this passage can be described as being all of the following EXCEPT
   (A) impartial
   (B) objective
   (C) psychologically penetrating
   (D) sentimental
   (E) ironic

47. The narrator appears to be one who
   (A) makes clear moral judgments
   (B) knows and records only outward behavior
   (C) controls the behavior of his characters
   (D) is concerned with form in people's behavior
   (E) treats his characters with cold objectivity

48. The expression "men of the world," which the narrator employs to describe Mr. Moreen and Ulick, is used
   (A) ironically
   (B) amusedly
   (C) angrily
   (D) admiringly
   (E) realistically

49. The attitude of Pemberton toward Morgan Moreen embodies all of the following EXCEPT
   (A) admiration of his genius
   (B) fear of becoming too involved
   (C) irritation at his insensitivity
   (D) deep affection
   (E) concern about his health

50. A major problem of Pemberton's in being Morgan's tutor and friend is that Morgan is
   (A) too bright for him
   (B) not physically strong
   (C) not critical of his parents
   (D) aware that Pemberton is working for a pittance
   (E) hoping to live with him

51. According to Pemberton, Morgan's belief that he would go to Oxford was unrealistic for all the following reasons EXCEPT
    (A) Morgan could not live at Oxford without an allowance.
    (B) Morgan was not physically strong enough for intensive study.
    (C) Morgan did not realize what being free of his family would entail.
    (D) Morgan was not adequately prepared for the intellectual demands of study at Oxford.
    (E) Pemberton himself was not ready to undertake the responsibility.

52. In referring to Pemberton's position with the Moreens as that of an "inmate," (line 4) the narrator is telling the reader that Pemberton thought of himself as
    (A) a prisoner of his own lassitude
    (B) weak and unambitious
    (C) unable to escape his responsibilities to Morgan
    (D) fearful of facing responsibility
    (E) a victim who lacked the courage to protest

53. All of the following were dark omens for the future of the Moreens EXCEPT
    (A) The place where they stayed was empty of furniture.
    (B) Mr. Moreen and Ulick were in the Piazza admiring the sights.
    (C) They hadn't the money to heat their dwelling properly.
    (D) Paula and Amy remained late in bed.
    (E) Their surroundings were in a condition of stately decay.

54. In this passage the narrator informs the reader that Pemberton was beginning to see, most of all, that
    (A) working for the Moreens had no future
    (B) Morgan was doomed
    (C) his sacrifices for Morgan would come to naught
    (D) he must get away or be devoured
    (E) he was being moved by a meaningless sentimentality

55. In telling the story of Pemberton, Morgan, and the Moreens, the narrator
    (A) imposes his interpretation of events upon that of his characters
    (B) ignores any psychological explanation for his characters' actions
    (C) presents views similar in all respects to those of Pemberton
    (D) adds the "voices" of Pemberton and Morgan to his own
    (E) expresses solely the point of view of the author

56. The information in this passage foreshadows *any one* of the following outcomes to Pemberton's dilemma EXCEPT:
    (A) Morgan goes to Oxford. Pemberton gets employment to support the two of them there.
    (B) Morgan becomes aware of his parents' love for him and of Pemberton's inability to support his education further.
    (C) Pemberton leaves the Moreens. Morgan continues his education on his own.
    (D) Morgan realizes that his dream of joining Pemberton at Oxford is an impossibility. His illness becomes acute.
    (E) Pemberton stays on with the Moreens in the palace, recognizing that he will enjoy reflected glory.

SECTION II

Total time—2 hours

Question 1

Suggested time—40 minutes

The narrator of the following passage portrays a doctor going about his daily duties. Read the passage carefully and then write an essay that discusses the ambivalent attitudes of the doctor toward his patients and his work. Analyze the techniques used by the narrator to portray the doctor and to reveal his attitudes.

He finished his duties at the surgery as quickly as might be, hastily filling up
the bottles of the waiting people with cheap drugs. Then, in perpetual haste, he
set off again to visit several cases in another part of his round, before teatime. At
Line   all times he preferred to walk if he could, but particularly when he was not well.
(5)   He fancied the motion restored him.
        The afternoon was falling. It was grey, deadened, and wintry, with a slow,
moist, heavy coldness sinking in and deadening all the faculties. But why should
he think or notice? He hastily climbed the hill and turned across the dark green
fields, following the black cinder-track. In the distance, across a shallow dip in
(10)   the country, the small town was clustered like smouldering ash, a tower, a spire,
a heap of low, raw, extinct houses. And on the nearest fringe of the town, sloping
into the dip, was Oldmeadow, the Pervins' house. He could see the stables and
the outbuildings distinctly, as they lay towards him on the slope. Well, he would
not go there many more times! Another resource would be lost to him, another
(15)   place gone: the only company he cared for in the alien, ugly little town he was
losing. Nothing but work, drudgery, constant hastening from dwelling to dwelling among the colliers and the iron-workers. It wore him out, but at the same time
he had a craving for it. It was a stimulant to him to be in the homes of the working
people, moving as it were through the innermost body of their life. His nerves
(20)   were excited and gratified. He could come so near, into the very lives of the
rough, inarticulate, powerfully emotional men and women. He grumbled, he said
he hated the hellish hole. But as a matter of fact it excited him, the contact with
the rough, strongly-feeling people was a stimulant applied direct to his nerves.

Question 2

Suggested time—40 minutes

Some writers use violent external action to reveal and explore the complex personalities of their characters; other writers, in attaining a similar goal, concern themselves more with inward psychological processes.

Select a work of recognized literary merit, one in which the emphasis is on external action or one in which the emphasis is on mental processes. Write a carefully organized essay showing how in each case a character is revealed and explored.

The works below are listed as examples. You may wish to choose from among them or provide your own appropriate example.

Victory   The Assistant
Wuthering Heights   Wide Sargasso Sea
Lord of the Flies   The Great Gatsby
Man's Fate   The Scarlet Letter
Women in Love   Mrs. Dalloway
Portrait of the Artist   Sister Carrie
Great Expectations   The Red Badge of Courage
As I Lay Dying   Madame Bovary
Crime and Punishment   Emma
Look Homeward, Angel   A Farewell to Arms
The Color Purple   The Return of the Native

Question 3

Suggested time—40 minutes

Read the following poem. Then write an essay that discusses how such elements as diction, imagery, structure, and point of view help to convey meaning in the poem.

THE CHIMNEY SWEEPER*
William Blake (1757–1827)

When my mother died I was very young,
And my father sold me while yet my tongue
Could scarcely cry "'weep! 'weep! 'weep!"
So your chimneys I sweep, and in soot I sleep.

(5)   There's little Tom Dacre, who cried when his head,
That curled like a lamb's back, was shaved; so I said,
"Hush, Tom! never mind it, for, when your head's bare,
You know that the soot cannot spoil your white hair."

And so he was quiet, and that very night,
(10)   As Tom was asleeping, he had such a sight!
That thousands of sweepers, Dick, Joe, Ned, and Jack
Were all of them locked up in coffins of black.

And by came an Angel who had a bright key,
And he opened the coffins and let them all free;
(15)   Then down a green plain leaping, laughing, they run,
And wash in a river, and shine in the sun.

Then naked and white, all their bags left behind,
They rise upon clouds and sport in the wind;
And the Angel told Tom, if he'd be a good boy,
(20)   He'd have God for his father, and never want joy.

And so Tom awoke, and we rose in the dark,
And got with our bags and our brushes to work.
Though the morning was cold, Tom was happy and warm;
So if all do their duty they need not fear harm.

_____
*In centuries past, small boys worked as chimney sweeps. Their slender bodies allowed them to climb into narrow chimney flues and collect the soot in bags. Child labor laws, among other things, put an end to the practice.

Answer Key for Practice Exam E
Answers to Multiple-Choice Questions

1.	E	**13.**	B	**25.**	D	**37.**	D	**49.**	C
2.	A	**14.**	D	**26.**	C	**38.**	C	**50.**	E
3.	C	**15.**	A	**27.**	E	**39.**	B	**51.**	D
4.	E	**16.**	E	**28.**	B	**40.**	A	**52.**	C
5.	C	**17.**	D	**29.**	E	**41.**	E	**53.**	B
6.	B	**18.**	B	**30.**	A	**42.**	E	**54.**	C
7.	B	**19.**	D	**31.**	A	**43.**	B	**55.**	D
8.	E	**20.**	D	**32.**	E	**44.**	E	**56.**	D
9.	C	**21.**	A	**33.**	B	**45.**	C		
10.	D	**22.**	B	**34.**	E	**46.**	D		
11.	A	**23.**	D	**35.**	D	**47.**	D		
12.	C	**24.**	A	**36.**	E	**48.**	A		

Answer Explanations

1. E References to walking on water and to bringing a dead child back to life reinforce the speaker's perception of himself as some kind of savior.

2. A The speaker says, "With my foot on the water" (line 5). In line 11, he adds, "Stepping outward from earth onto water." Still later, he alludes to "my steps on the light of the ripples" (line 35).

3. C The lifeguard states, "He is one I do not remember/Having ever seen in his life" (lines 51–52).

4. E In his dream, the lifeguard returns to the water as though to cleanse himself of the despair he feels about being unable to save a drowning child. In the end, water washes the black mud from his hands (line 55).

5. C Throughout the poem it is difficult to distinguish between the dream and the reality.

6. B In this, the third stanza of the poem, the speaker recalls an event that really happened.

7. B In spite of his despondency, the lifeguard never considers doing away with himself.

8. E A resuscitated child does not appear in the poem.

9. C In lines 19–24 the lifeguard feels the sensation of drowning.

10. D The speaker compares the lake to the "ghost of a snowfield in summer" (line 38).

11. A The speaker's inability to save the child haunts him. The water will forever symbolize his failure.

12. C The poet calls destiny "The Immanent Will" (line 18), an allusion to a divine force which "stirs and urges everything."

13. B   Each stanza concludes with an unexpected image or thought. In stanza 8, for example, lines 1 and 2 describe the building of a beautiful ship. Line 3 undercuts the image with an ominous statement about the ship's future.

14. D   Humanity (the human condition), not nature, is the poet's main concern.

15. A   The ship's destiny has been determined by The Spinner of Years, who gives the signal for the collision between the ship and the iceberg.

16. E   When each line rhymes the reader knows what is coming. A certain inevitability occurs.

17. D   The manmade objects, bedecked with jewels and gold, would not be lying at the bottom of the sea unless man had assumed he could excel nature.

18. B   The orange-colored fires referred to are those that burned the coal to drive the ship.

19. D   Every event in the ship's life leads to that one climactic moment.

20. D   "Thrid" is a form of the verb *to thread.* In effect, the sea threaded its way through the rooms and corridors of the ship.

21. A   The first five stanzas are about the sunken ship. The rest of the poem is about the ship's construction and its inevitable doom.

22. B   Stanzas 1, 6, and 11 pertain to the inevitable fate that awaits the ship.

23. D   Such words as "mate" (line 19) and "consummation" (line 33) are associated with marriage.

24. A   The sentence in question inverts the usual word order of subject-verb-object.

25. D   The limits of nature are not implied by line 24.

26. C   The speaker calls his age "green" (line 2), indicating his youthfulness.

27. E   All but "peace" are the forces mentioned—directly or indirectly—in the poem.

28. B   The force that creates (line 1) and the force that destroys (lines 2–5) are the same.

29. E   A verbal contradiction is an *oxymoron.*

30. A   Both the speaker and the things of nature are changed by the same force.

31. A   The "force" turns young things old, dries up fresh-flowing streams, and destroys life. Images to that effect dominate the first three stanzas.

32. E   The poet does not blame the divine force for its destructiveness.

33. B   The hand does not "fold in prayer." Rather, human hands are more likely to fold in prayer to the divine force.

34. E   While he recognizes that he is part of the masses, which he calls "one great beast and a monstrosity" (line 15), the speaker also holds himself apart, realizing that his individual qualities are unique.

35. D   The phrase "naturally framed" indicates that the speaker recognizes from whence he came.

36. E To make the point that he can live anywhere, the speaker uses a metaphor in which he compares himself to a plant.

37. D Such phrases as "no antipathy," "no plant," "not enemy" (lines 3–7) show that he chooses to define himself by saying what he is not, rather than stating what he is.

38. C He condemns, among other things, "the multitude" (line 13), but when the mulitude is separated into individuals, i.e., "taken asunder" (line 13–14), men are "reasonable creatures of God."

39. B The "voice" in the passage suggests that the speaker thinks very highly of himself.

40. A There is no sign of the speaker's conciliatory nature in the passage.

41. E Men are "reasonable creatures of God" (line 14) and have a great many "good parts" (line 16). In addition, the speaker believes that man's essentially virtuous nature has been corrupted by "ruder desires" (line 20).

42. E The speaker does not claim to suffer fools gladly.

43. B The passage contains no evidence that the speaker has been a leader of men.

44. E Hydra is a beast with many heads. Thus, according to the author, men have found many ways to stray from the paths of virtue and righteousness. Going to church is obviously not one of them.

45. C The speaker says he has maintained his equilibrium through many hardships. But he does not include public demonstrations among them.

46. D The narrator's description of the Moreens contains both objective reporting and an ironic point of view (e.g., "unmistakable men of the world"—line 11). It also analyzes the goings-on inside Morgan's head. The narrator doesn't sentimentalize, however.

47. D The narrator is sensitive to the rank of his employers and comments often on their ability to continue the pattern of life to which they are accustomed.

48. A In spite of their clothes, Moreen and Ulick try to keep up the appearance that they are men of the world.

49. C Pemberton is sensitive to the difficulties of being a teenage boy, and a Moreen at that. He understands well that such lads may be insensitive—being so caught up in themselves—but is not at all annoyed by Morgan's behavior.

50. E Pemberton is concerned that Morgan would not have an allowance if the boy were to live with him.

51. D Morgan assumed he could would go to Oxford and continue to be "aided and abetted" (line 24) by his tutor, Pemberton.

52. C Pemberton says that he lives "on Morgan" (line 30). That is, he depends on Morgan for his livelihood. In a way, he is trapped in the situation. "Inmate," therefore, is an apt name for him.

53. B Mr. Moreen and Ulick's stroll through the Piazza cannot be considered a bad omen. Pemberton merely noticed them there, wearing mackintoshes.

54. C Morgan was on the verge of being grown up, almost ready to be "producible in the world of affairs, etc" (lines 19–20). But the down-at-heels financial condition of the family causes Pemberton to suspect that his work with Morgan may come to nothing in the end.

55. D By the end of the passage, having heard from Pemberton and Morgan, we know the feelings and thoughts of both characters.

56. D Although we know that Morgan has not been altogether well physically, there is no evidence or foreshadowing that his health will take a turn for the worse.

Answers to Essay Questions

Answers for essay questions will vary widely, but the following answers identify ideas that could reasonably be included an a essay that responds to the questions.

Question 1

The first half of the passage describes a doctor going through the daily routine of a medical practice. Continually rushed to get various tasks done, he apparently derives no joy from the work. The town seems equally gloomy and joyless. Three adjectives used to describe the afternoon on which we see the doctor making his rounds—"grey, deadened, and wintry" (line 6) apply equally well to the doctor himself. Even the sight of Oldmeadow, the home of his only friends, the Pervins, gives him no pleasure. In fact, he thinks to himself that he won't be going there many more times—for reasons that are not explained in the passage.

Into this bleak picture the author inserts a surprising contrast. We are told that, although the doctor seems worn down by his work, he "had a craving for it" (line 18). He was stimulated by the close contact with the "rough, strongly-feeling people" (line 23) who were his patients. Why this should be so, we can only infer. Perhaps he felt excitement among them because they were "rough, inarticulate, and powerfully emotional" (line 21)—much unlike himself. Because they are so different from him, he may feel irresistibly drawn to them. To keep up appearances, though, he "grumbled" about them and said he "hated the hellish hole" (line 22).

Question 2

In *Crime and Punishment* by Feodor Dostoyevski, the main character, Rodya Raskolnikov, is revealed to us initially through violent external action. Near the beginning of the book, he commits a terrible murder of an elderly pawnbroker and her sister. But the reader does not thoroughly understand his motives until after the murder when the book becomes a psychological exploration of his very unusual and twisted mind.

Rodya endures a long period of mental anguish. He wanders aimlessly through the streets of St. Petersburg, has wild and frightening nightmares, gets physically ill and stays in bed for days at a time. All the while, the reader is given bits and pieces of the theory of the "extraordinary man" that drove Rodya to commit the crime in the first place

The police inspector on the murder case suspects Rodya but lacks the evidence to arrest him. Rather, he plays a psychological cat-and-mouse game that increases Rodya's suffering still more. To rid himself of his guilt, Rodya confesses his crime to Sonya, a young prostitute, who convinces him that in order to redeem himself in his own eyes and in the eyes of God, he must turn himself in.

Question 3

In general, the poem describes social conditions in England during the eighteenth century. More specifically, it is an account of the experience of Tom, a young boy employed as a chimney sweeper. The speaker himself was a chimney sweep, sold at a young age by his parents—so young, in fact that he could scarcely cry "weep!" a word that is meant to mean "sweep!" (the boys called out "sweep" to attract customers) as well as "weep" (the boys lived miserable lives).

One night Tom dreams of escape from his plight. He and his fellow chimney sweeps are locked up in "coffins of black" (line 12) a phrase that can be taken literally or as a metaphor not only for the life that the boys lead (a kind of death in life) but for the confines of the chimneys in which they do their daily work. But an angel, showing them a piece of heaven, delivers them from their plight. Tom and the other boys know that they will earn their reward in heaven provided they do their duty (line 24). Thus, Tom goes to work on a cold morning feeling "happy and warm."

Tom and the other boys, being young and naive, may indeed be convinced that their reward awaits them in heaven.

Answer Sheet for Practice Test F
Literature and Composition

Multiple-Choice Questions Time—1 hour

1. Ⓐ Ⓑ Ⓒ Ⓓ Ⓔ
2. Ⓐ Ⓑ Ⓒ Ⓓ Ⓔ
3. Ⓐ Ⓑ Ⓒ Ⓓ Ⓔ
4. Ⓐ Ⓑ Ⓒ Ⓓ Ⓔ
5. Ⓐ Ⓑ Ⓒ Ⓓ Ⓔ
6. Ⓐ Ⓑ Ⓒ Ⓓ Ⓔ
7. Ⓐ Ⓑ Ⓒ Ⓓ Ⓔ
8. Ⓐ Ⓑ Ⓒ Ⓓ Ⓔ
9. Ⓐ Ⓑ Ⓒ Ⓓ Ⓔ
10. Ⓐ Ⓑ Ⓒ Ⓓ Ⓔ
11. Ⓐ Ⓑ Ⓒ Ⓓ Ⓔ
12. Ⓐ Ⓑ Ⓒ Ⓓ Ⓔ
13. Ⓐ Ⓑ Ⓒ Ⓓ Ⓔ
14. Ⓐ Ⓑ Ⓒ Ⓓ Ⓔ
15. Ⓐ Ⓑ Ⓒ Ⓓ Ⓔ
16. Ⓐ Ⓑ Ⓒ Ⓓ Ⓔ
17. Ⓐ Ⓑ Ⓒ Ⓓ Ⓔ
18. Ⓐ Ⓑ Ⓒ Ⓓ Ⓔ
19. Ⓐ Ⓑ Ⓒ Ⓓ Ⓔ
20. Ⓐ Ⓑ Ⓒ Ⓓ Ⓔ

21. Ⓐ Ⓑ Ⓒ Ⓓ Ⓔ
22. Ⓐ Ⓑ Ⓒ Ⓓ Ⓔ
23. Ⓐ Ⓑ Ⓒ Ⓓ Ⓔ
24. Ⓐ Ⓑ Ⓒ Ⓓ Ⓔ
25. Ⓐ Ⓑ Ⓒ Ⓓ Ⓔ
26. Ⓐ Ⓑ Ⓒ Ⓓ Ⓔ
27. Ⓐ Ⓑ Ⓒ Ⓓ Ⓔ
28. Ⓐ Ⓑ Ⓒ Ⓓ Ⓔ
29. Ⓐ Ⓑ Ⓒ Ⓓ Ⓔ
30. Ⓐ Ⓑ Ⓒ Ⓓ Ⓔ
31. Ⓐ Ⓑ Ⓒ Ⓓ Ⓔ
32. Ⓐ Ⓑ Ⓒ Ⓓ Ⓔ
33. Ⓐ Ⓑ Ⓒ Ⓓ Ⓔ
34. Ⓐ Ⓑ Ⓒ Ⓓ Ⓔ
35. Ⓐ Ⓑ Ⓒ Ⓓ Ⓔ
36. Ⓐ Ⓑ Ⓒ Ⓓ Ⓔ
37. Ⓐ Ⓑ Ⓒ Ⓓ Ⓔ
38. Ⓐ Ⓑ Ⓒ Ⓓ Ⓔ
39. Ⓐ Ⓑ Ⓒ Ⓓ Ⓔ
40. Ⓐ Ⓑ Ⓒ Ⓓ Ⓔ

41. Ⓐ Ⓑ Ⓒ Ⓓ Ⓕ
42. Ⓐ Ⓑ Ⓒ Ⓓ Ⓔ
43. Ⓐ Ⓑ Ⓒ Ⓓ Ⓔ
44. Ⓐ Ⓑ Ⓒ Ⓓ Ⓔ
45. Ⓐ Ⓑ Ⓒ Ⓓ Ⓔ
46. Ⓐ Ⓑ Ⓒ Ⓓ Ⓔ
47. Ⓐ Ⓑ Ⓒ Ⓓ Ⓔ
48. Ⓐ Ⓑ Ⓒ Ⓓ Ⓔ
49. Ⓐ Ⓑ Ⓒ Ⓓ Ⓔ
50. Ⓐ Ⓑ Ⓒ Ⓓ Ⓔ
51. Ⓐ Ⓑ Ⓒ Ⓓ Ⓔ

Three Essay Questions Time—2 hours

Write your essays on standard 8¹/₂ by 11-inch composition paper. At the exam you will be given a bound booklet containing 12 lined pages.

F Literature and Composition

SECTION I

Total time—1 hour

Read each poem or prose passage carefully, and answer the accompanying questions.

Questions 1–15 refer to the following poem.

HAWK ROOSTING
Ted Hughes (1930–1998)

I sit in the top of the wood, my eyes closed.
Inaction, no falsifying dream
Between my hooked head and hooked feet:
Or in sleep rehearse perfect kills and eat.

Line
(5)   The convenience of the high trees!
The air's buoyancy and the sun's ray
Are of advantage to me;
And the earth's face upward for my inspection.

My feet are locked upon the rough bark.
(10)   It took the whole of Creation
To produce my foot, my each feather:
Now I hold Creation in my foot.

Or fly up, and revolve it all slowly—
I kill where I please because it is all mine.
(15)   There is no sophistry in my body:
My manners are tearing off heads—

The allotment of death.
For the one path of my flight is direct
Through the bones of the living.
(20)   No arguments assert my right:

The sun is behind me.
Nothing has changed since I began.
My eye has permitted no change.
I am going to keep things like this.

1. The speaker in the poem is
   (A) a hawk
   (B) the poet
   (C) a tyrant
   (D) the Creator
   (E) an ornithologist

2. The poem is
   (A) the dream of a nature lover
   (B) a paean of praise by a bird fancier
   (C) an assertion of the force of creation
   (D) an internal monologue
   (E) an animal fable

3. In the poem, the hawk is offered as
   (A) a psychological portrait
   (B) a high point in evolution
   (C) a symbol
   (D) a unique creation of God
   (E) an illustration of the wonder of nature

4. All of the following aid the hawk in its pursuit of game EXCEPT
   (A) its hooked head
   (B) its pride
   (C) the high trees
   (D) the buoyancy of the air
   (E) the light of the sun

5. The line "No arguments assert my right" means all of the following EXCEPT:
   (A) My right to kill comes from my power.
   (B) My victims cannot question my right.
   (C) I don't need arguments to justify my right to kill.
   (D) My right to kill is granted me by the Creator.
   (E) My right to kill is not based on any form of legality.

6. The language in the poem can be described as
   (A) dramatic
   (B) economical
   (C) stilted
   (D) labored
   (E) awkward

7. All of the following are true of the hawk EXCEPT that it
   (A) is pleased with itself
   (B) is unafflicted with doubts
   (C) expresses itself in an arrogant way
   (D) offers itself for inspection
   (E) is not troubled by fears or hesitations

8. The hawk believes itself to be all of the following EXCEPT the
   (A) possessor of complete power
   (B) final perfect product of the evolutionary process
   (C) possessor of a strength equal to that of the tree on which it perches
   (D) center of a revolving world
   (E) lord over its earthly subjects

9. This poem is a
    (A) symbolic comment on tyranny
    (B) portrait of motiveless cruelty
    (C) nature study
    (D) criticism of the Creator
    (E) painting in words of an invincible vertebrate

10. The use of the word "manners" in line 16 is
    (A) humorous
    (B) ironic
    (C) allegoric
    (D) euphemistic
    (E) enigmatic

11. The poem deals with all of the following EXCEPT
    (A) the refinements of civilized existence
    (B) satisfaction with an existing condition
    (C) the nature of autocratic power
    (D) an attack on the evil nature of man
    (E) a plea for the preservation of civilized human values

12. The word "sophistry" in line 15 is used in the sense of
    (A) disguise
    (B) sophistication
    (C) defect
    (D) weakness
    (E) deception

13. In the hawk's view his body was shaped by the Creator for all of the following purposes EXCEPT to
    (A) affirm God's creative power
    (B) subdue the animal world to his needs
    (C) destroy life
    (D) maintain his supremacy
    (E) be a model for other of God's creatures

14. By extension, the hawk becomes a symbol for man because man is
    (A) extending his technological powers
    (B) eliminating disease
    (C) throwing satellites into space
    (D) engendering destruction
    (E) restoring fertility to deserts

15. What takes place in the hawk's mind is
    (A) a delight in his surroundings
    (B) an awareness of limited powers
    (C) a challenge to the Creator
    (D) a rehearsal of a kill
    (E) a consciousness of human frailty

Questions 16–31 refer to the following poem and passage.

SONNET 130
William Shakespeare (1564–1616)

My mistress' eyes are nothing like the sun;
Coral is far more red than her lips' red;
If snow be white, why then her breasts are dun;
Line   If hairs be wires, black wires grow on her head.
(5)   I have seen roses damask'd, red and white,
But no such roses see I in her cheeks;
And in some perfumes is there more delight
Than in the breath that from my mistress reeks.
I love to hear her speak,—yet well I know
(10)   That musick hath a far more pleasing sound;
I grant I never saw a goddess go,—
My mistress, when she walks, treads on the
            ground;
        And yet, by heaven, I think my love as rare
        As any she bely'd with false compare.

NORTHANGER ABBEY
Jane Austen (1775–1817)

No one who had ever seen Catherine Morland in her infancy, would
have supposed her born to be an heroine. Her situation in life, the
character of her father and mother, her own person and disposition,
Line   were all equally against her. Her father was a clergyman, without being
(5)   neglected, or poor, and a very respectable man, though his name was
Richard—and he had never been handsome. He had a considerable
independence, besides two good livings—and he was not in the least
addicted to locking up his daughters. Her mother was a woman of
useful plain sense, with a good temper, and, what is more remarkable,
(10)   with a good constitution. She had three sons before Catherine was
born; and instead of dying in bringing the latter into the world, as any
body might expect, she still lived on—lived to have six children
more—to see them growing up around her, and to enjoy excellent
health herself. A family of ten children will be always called a fine
(15)   family, where there are heads and arms and legs enough for the number; but the Morlands had little other right to the word, for they were in
general very plain, and Catherine, for many years of her life, as plain as
any. She had a thin awkward figure, a sallow skin without colour, dark
lank hair, and strong features:—so much for her person;—and not less
(20)   unpropitious for heroism seemed her mind. She was fond of all boys'
plays, and greatly preferred cricket not merely to dolls, but to the more
heroic enjoyments of infancy, nursing a dormouse, feeding a canary-
bird, or watering a rosebush. Indeed she had no taste for a garden; and
if she gathered flowers at all, it was chiefly for the pleasure of mis-
(25)   chief—at least so it was conjectured from her always preferring those
which she was forbidden to take.—Such were her propensities—her
abilities were quite as extraordinary. She never could learn or understand any thing before she was taught; and sometimes not even then,
for she was often inattentive, and occasionally stupid. . . .

(Questions 16–23 are based on Sonnet 130.)

16. Shakespeare's Sonnet 130 is
    (A) a satire on the deficiencies of the speaker's mistress
    (B) a belittling of a loved one for the amusement of friends
    (C) a playful expression of faults to irritate the lady
    (D) a confession of love for a harlot
    (E) a tribute to the uniqueness and beauty of the speaker's mistress

17. The last two lines of the sonnet
    (A) express the true feeling of the speaker
    (B) seem out of place in the poem
    (C) express a love for someone whose beauty is of the spirit
    (D) reveal the speaker as a liar and boor
    (E) are an illustration of hyperbole

18. The first 12 lines of the sonnet are
    (A) an ironic comment on female adornment
    (B) a humorous description of an ugly woman
    (C) a paradoxical evocation of emotion
    (D) a parody of love sonnets
    (E) a play on metaphors

19. By "false compare" (line 14) the speaker means that
    (A) the conventional praises of mistresses by poets are romantic lies
    (B) to win love one must compare the charms of mistresses with the beauties in nature
    (C) love poetry must abound in hyperbole
    (D) the women whom men love must be worshiped as goddesses
    (E) lovers must be privileged to distort truth

20. The true intent of the speaker is revealed best by
    (A) the outrageousness of his metaphors
    (B) the rare words of praise that creep into his descriptions
    (C) his imaginative conceits
    (D) his sense of fun
    (E) the contrast between the first twelve lines and the last two

21. The reader of the sonnet knows that the criticism of the mistress is indeed a form of praise because
    (A) the progression of fault-finding leads to the wrong conclusion
    (B) the fault-finding involves trivial matters
    (C) there are hidden romantic nuances in the judgments
    (D) the sequence of fault-finding eases in lines 9–12
    (E) there are paradoxical hints in the metaphors

22. All of the following are metaphors EXCEPT
   (A) Her eyes are not the sun.
   (B) The hairs on her head are black wires.
   (C) No roses are her cheeks.
   (D) Music has a more pleasing sound than her voice.
   (E) The lady I love is rare.

23. An essential element of this sonnet is
   (A) praise of a mistress
   (B) search for the blemishes in a loved one
   (C) a lover's compromise with reality
   (D) mockery of a convention in love poetry
   (E) ambiguity of intention

(Questions 24–30 are based on the selection from Northanger Abbey.)

24. The third sentence in the selection (lines 4–6) implies all of the following EXCEPT
   (A) despite her father, Catherine was destined for heroic exploits
   (B) Richard, at the time this passage was written, was a pedestrian name
   (C) Catherine is an unlikely heroine
   (D) good looks are important in the society being described
   (E) clergymen were held in high respect

25. By stating the fact that Catherine's father "had never been handsome," the narrator intends the reader to
   (A) be aware that Catherine also was not attractive
   (B) infer that there is a subtle purpose behind mentioning that fact
   (C) know *all* the facts about Catherine's character and appearance
   (D) recognize that clergymen can be successful even if they are not handsome
   (E) notice that non sequiturs are an element of human experience

26. In reading the many facts recorded in this passage, the reader is invited to conclude that the author
   (A) wants to tell everything about her heroine
   (B) has great respect for the family of her heroine
   (C) recognizes that the potential for heroism exists in all people
   (D) is giving tongue-in-cheek descriptions
   (E) exaggerates and distorts the virtues and faults of her characters

27. The technique of the author can be described as one that
   (A) encourages ironic inferences
   (B) is typical in the telling of romantic tales
   (C) is detailed and realistic
   (D) shows affection for the ordinary things of life
   (E) indicates a superior attitude

28. Like Shakespeare's Sonnet 130, this selection can best be described as
    (A) a paradox
    (B) a parody
    (C) realistic
    (D) romantic
    (E) iconoclastic

29. The narrator in *Northanger Abbey* states that Catherine lacked propensities for heroism for all the following reasons EXCEPT
    (A) She was fond of boys' games.
    (B) She was the fourth of ten children.
    (C) She found distasteful the feeding of canary birds.
    (D) She gathered flowers chiefly to be mischievous.
    (E) She preferred activities that were denied her.

30. The expression "for many years of her life" (line 17) suggests that, in the story that is to be told, Catherine will
    (A) suffer untold misery
    (B) not be courted by gentlemen
    (C) develop into a pretty woman
    (D) remain at home to care for her aging parents
    (E) become a lovable maiden aunt

Question 31 is based on the preceding sonnet and prose passage.

31. Both Shakespeare's Sonnet 130 and the selection from *Northanger Abbey*
    (A) ridicule conventional modes of literary expression in their day
    (B) describe the limitations of being human
    (C) show that the authors realized how foolish some people can be
    (D) ridicule fashions in romantic and domestic relationships
    (E) became models for romantic writers

Questions 32–39 refer to the following passage.

From THE PUPIL
Henry James (1843–1916)

For the first time, in this complicated connection, our friend [Pemberton] felt his collar gall him. It was, as he had said to Mrs. Moreen in Venice, *trop fort*—everything was *trop fort*. He could neither really throw off his blighting burden
Line nor find in it the benefit of a pacified conscience or of a rewarded affection. He
(5) had spent all the money accruing to him in England, and he saw his youth going and that he was getting nothing back for it. It was all very well of Morgan to count it for reparation that he should now settle on him permanently—there was an irritating flaw in such a view. He saw what the boy had in his mind; the conception that as his friend had had the generosity to come back he must show
(10) his gratitude by giving him his life. But the poor friend didn't desire the gift— what could he do with Morgan's dreadful little life? Of course, at the same time that Pemberton was irritated he remembered the reason, which was very honourable to Morgan and which dwelt simply in his making one so forget that

(15)   he was no more than a patched urchin. If one dealt with him on a different basis one's misadventures were one's own fault. So Pemberton waited in a queer confusion of yearning and alarm for the catastrophe which was held to hang over the house of Moreen, of which he certainly at moments felt the symptoms brush his cheek and as to which he wondered much in what form it would find its liveliest effect.

32. The narrator uses the image of a "galling collar" (lines 1–2) to inform the reader that Pemberton considered himself
    (A) a sacrificial lamb
    (B) a prisoner of his feelings
    (C) a pawn in the hands of a selfish boy
    (D) an ingrate
    (E) a weakling

33. One may conclude from this passage that all of the following are true of Pemberton EXCEPT:
    (A) He is flattered that Morgan wishes to live with him permanently.
    (B) He dreads the future.
    (C) He finds his situation unbearable.
    (D) He is having a change of heart.
    (E) He is in an emotional dilemma.

34. According to this passage, Pemberton had
    (A) fulfilled his obligations
    (B) once before deserted Morgan
    (C) antagonized Mrs. Morgan
    (D) never beguiled Morgan with false hopes
    (E) been an incompetent tutor

35. Pemberton was disturbingly aware that Morgan
    (A) was still in ill health
    (B) expected Pemberton to take him permanently under his wing
    (C) no longer needed his services
    (D) knew his parents wished to be rid of him
    (E) was manipulating him

36. The expression "Morgan's dreadful little life" reveals all of the following EXCEPT
    (A) an undercurrent of cruelty in Pemberton's character
    (B) the narrator's psychological understanding of Pemberton's character
    (C) that Pemberton was a normal human being, not a saint
    (D) the ambivalence of Pemberton's feelings toward Morgan
    (E) the truth about Morgan's tragic situation

37. The passage foreshadows all of the following EXCEPT
    (A) the social and financial decay of a prominent and wealthy family
    (B) an end to a close relationship
    (C) a resolution of Pemberton's that will free him
    (D) a disastrous outcome to Pemberton's dilemma
    (E) a break between Pemberton and Morgan

38. Morgan believed that offering to join Pemberton permanently was an act of
    (A) generosity
    (B) penance
    (C) self-interest
    (D) retribution
    (E) gratitute

39. One concludes from reading this passage that Morgan was most probably all of the following EXCEPT
    (A) naïve and deluded
    (B) incapable of hating anyone
    (C) devoted to Pemberton
    (D) arrogant and pompous
    (E) unhappy at home

Questions 40–51 refer to the following poem.

THE EBB AND FLOW
Edward Taylor (1645?–1729)

When first thou on me, Lord, wrought'st thy Sweet Print,
    My heart was made thy tinder box.
    My 'ffections were thy tinder in't:
Line   Where fell thy Sparkes by drops.
(5) Those holy Sparks of Heavenly fire that came
Did ever catch and often out would flame.

But now my Heart is made thy Censar trim,
    Full of thy golden Altars fire,
    To offer up Sweet Incense in
(10)   Unto thyselfe intire:
I finde my tinder scarce thy sparks can feel
That drop out from thy Holy flint and Steel.

Hence doubts out bud for feare thy fire in mee
    'S a mocking Ignis Fatuus,
(15)   Or lest thine Altars fore out bee,
       It's hid in ashes thus.
Yet when the bellows of thy Spirit blow
Away mine ashes, then thy fire doth glow.

40. The poem presents a progression from
    (A) ecstasy, to sorrow, to joy
    (B) faith to agnosticism
    (C) grace, to doubt, to hope
    (D) birth, to manhood or womanhood, to death
    (E) love of humanity to love of God

41. The speaker is a man who
    (A) is an apostate
    (B) struggles to control his baser instincts
    (C) is in a state of religious depression
    (D) is deeply religious
    (E) feels alienated from his world

42. In lines 2 and 7 the use of the passive verb highlights the speaker's view of man or woman as a
    (A) mortal being
    (B) sinful creature
    (C) rebellious antagonist questioning God
    (D) dependent person accepting God's supremacy
    (E) creature overwhelmed by doubt and despair

43. The speaker conceives of himself as being
    (A) the child of devout parents
    (B) fashioned by God
    (C) a strong and vibrant personality
    (D) ready to serve God but not mankind
    (E) the center of the life about him

44. The "tinder box," (lines 2–3) as used in this poem, is a metaphor for the
    (A) work accomplished by the speaker
    (B) absence of goodness
    (C) strength to face frustrations
    (D) inspiration to write
    (E) source for a rich religious life

45. By the statement "my tinder scarce thy sparks can feel" (line 11) the speaker means that
    (A) his life lies in disarray
    (B) he lacks the power to respond to God's demands
    (C) life for him has lost its meaning
    (D) he responds to experience in rational rather than spiritual ways
    (E) wisdom lies in free thought

46. The title suggests that in the speaker's view
    (A) life, like the sea, is subject to tidal forces
    (B) men and women are whimsical creatures
    (C) humanity is subject to an inexorable fate
    (D) one's faith may wax and wane over time
    (E) there is no escaping pangs of conscience

47. The speaker is most likely
    (A) a lawyer
    (B) an artisan
    (C) a blacksmith
    (D) a clergyman
    (E) an architect

48. The figure of speech most basic in this poem is
    (A) metonymy
    (B) hyperbole
    (C) apostrophe
    (D) personification
    (E) metaphor

49. The speaker conceives of a human being as
    (A) being worked on by an outside force
    (B) developing a self in time
    (C) being fashioned by conflict
    (D) driven by undefined yearnings
    (E) yearning for freedom

50. The use of harsh sounds in words or phrases such as "tinder box," "Sparkes by drops," "flint and Steel," "mocking Ignis Fatuus," highlight the
    (A) skill of the poet
    (B) ambivalence and doubts of the speaker
    (C) apostasy of the speaker
    (D) futility of faith
    (E) spiritual victory over doubt and sin

51. The rhyme in lines 7 and 9 is an example of
    (A) alliteration
    (B) assonance
    (C) paradox
    (D) irony
    (E) consonance

SECTION II

Total time—2 hours

Question 1

Suggested time—40 minutes

The following passages concern a person who has behaved improperly in some way. Read them carefully and then write an essay that analyzes how the authors establish each speaker's attitude toward the wrongdoing. You may emphasize whatever stylistic devices (e.g., tone, selection of detail, sytax, point of view) you find most significant.

Passage A

The chaplain had sinned, and it was good. Common sense told him that telling lies and defecting from duty were sins. On the other hand, everyone knew that sin was evil and that no good could come from evil. But he did feel good; he felt positively marvelous. Consequently, it followed logically that
Line
(5)   telling lies and defecting from duty could not be sins. The chaplain had mastered in a moment of divine intuition, the handy technique of protective rationalization, and he was exhilarated by his discovery. It was miraculous. It was almost no trick at all to turn vice into virtue and slander into truth,

(10) impotence into abstinence, arrogance into humility, plunder into philanthropy, thievery into honor, blasphemy into wisdom, brutality into patriotism, and sadism into justice. Anybody could do it; it required no brains at all. It merely required no character. With effervescent agility the chaplain ran through the whole gamut of orthodox immoralities. . . .

Passage B

(15) . . . Jim said it made him all over trembly and feverish to be so close to freedom. Well, I can tell you it made me all over trembly and feverish, too, to hear him, because I begun to get it through my head that he was most free—and who was to blame for it? Why, *me,* I couldn't get that off my conscience, no how nor no way. It got to troubling me so I couldn't rest; I couldn't stay still in one place. It hadn't ever come home to me before, what this thing was that I

(20) was doing. But now it did; and it stayed with me, and scorched me more and more. I tried to make out to myself that I warn't to blame, because I didn't run Jim off from his rightful owner; but it warn't no use, conscience up and says, every time, "But you knowed he was running for his freedom, and you could' a' paddled ashore and told somebody." That was so—I couldn't get around that

(25) no way. That is where it pinched. Conscience says to me, "What had poor Miss Watson done to you that you could see her nigger go off right under your eyes and never say one single word? What did that poor woman do to you that you could treat her so mean? Why, she tried to learn you your book, she tried to learn you your manners, she tried to be good to you every way she knowed

(30) how. *That's* what she done."

I got to feeling so mean and so miserable I most wished I was dead. I fidgeted up and down the raft, abusing myself to myself, and Jim was fidgeting up and down past me.

Question 2

Suggested time—40 minutes

Novelists and playwrights frequently introduce supernatural creatures or elements in their works—oracles, witches, fairies, ghosts; symbolic characters or places or objects—to perform various functions such as the following:

1. To create dramatic irony and arouse thereby the sense of tragic fear or comic expectation in the audience.
2. To serve as a stimulus to set the protagonist's nature in motion without determining whether the direction of the motion will be right or wrong.
3. To point out, often in clear and impressive language, the course of the story.

From the works of novelists and playwrights, select one that contains supernatural creatures and/or elements and in a carefully organized essay show how these fulfill any one of the functions enumerated above.

The works below are listed as examples. You may wish to choose from among them or to select another appropriate work of comparable literary excellence.

Plays

Oedipus the King: Sophocles
Agamemnon: Aeschylus
The Tragical History of the Life and Death of Dr. Faustus: Christopher Marlowe
Hamlet: William Shakespeare
Macbeth: William Shakespeare
The Tempest: William Shakespeare
The Wild Duck: Henrik Ibsen
Saint Joan: George Bernard Shaw
Murder in the Cathedral: T. S. Eliot
Death of a Salesman: Arthur Miller
The Glass Menagerie: Tennessee Williams
Waiting for Godot: Samuel Beckett
Rhinoceros: Eugene Ionesco
The Iceman Cometh: Eugene O'Neill
Mother Courage and Her Children: Bertolt Brecht

Novels

The Odyssey: Homer (epic)
Gulliver's Travels: Jonathan Swift
The Scarlet Letter: Nathaniel Hawthorne
Moby Dick: Herman Melville
Wuthering Heights: Emily Brontë
The Turn of the Screw: Henry James
The Picture of Dorian Gray: Oscar Wilde
To the Lighthouse: Virginia Woolf
A Passage to India: E. M. Forster
Brave New World: Aldous Huxley
1984: George Orwell
The Plague: Albert Camus
The Castle: Franz Kafka
Light in August: William Faulkner
One Hundred Years of Solitude: Gabriel García Márquez

Question 3

Suggested time—40 minutes

Read the following poem carefully. Then write an essay in which you discuss how such elements as language, imagery, structure, rhyme, and tone convey the meaning of the poem.

> THE LOVER SHOWETH HOW HE IS FORSAKEN OF SUCH
> AS HE SOMETIME ENJOYED
> *Sir Thomas Wyatt* (1503–1542)
>
> They flee from me, that sometime did me seek,
> With naked food stalking within my chamber.
> Once have I seen them gentle, tame, and meek,

Line   That now are wild, and do not once remember
(5)   That sometime they have put themselves in danger
        To take bread at my hand; and now they range,
        Busily seeking in continual change.

            Thanked be fortune it has been otherwise,
        Twenty times better; but one especial,
(10)   In thin array, after a pleasant guise,
        When her loose gown did from her shoulders fall,
        And she me caught in her arms long and small,
        And therewithal so sweetly did me kiss
        And softly said, Dear heart, how like you this?

(15)   It was no dream, for I lay broad awaking.
        But all is turned now, through my gentleness,
        Into a bitter fashion of forsaking;
        And I have leave to go, of her goodness,
        And she also to use newfangleness.
(20)   But since that I unkindly so am served,
        How like you this? what has she now deserved?

Answer Key for Practice Exam F
Answers to Multiple-Choice Questions

1. A	12. E	23. D	34. B	45. B
2. D	13. E	24. E	35. B	46. D
3. C	14. D	25. B	36. E	47. D
4. B	15. D	26. D	37. A	48. E
5. D	16. E	27. A	38. E	49. A
6. B	17. A	28. B	39. D	50. B
7. D	18. D	29. A	40. C	51. B
8. C	19. A	30. B	41. D	
9. A	20. E	31. C	42. D	
10. B	21. A	32. B	43. B	
11. A	22. E	33. A	44. E	

Answer Explanations

1. **A** The opening lines and much that follows indicate that the speaker is a hawk.

2. **D** Written in first person, the poem is made up of the internal thoughts of the hawk—or at least the poet's version of a hawk's thoughts.

3. **C** Because the poem is about far more than a hawk sitting on a tree, it is symbolic of something larger, more universal.

4. **B** While the hawk is represented as a proud creature, its pride does not contribute to its skill as a hunter.

5. **D** Unlike various monarchs in human history, the hawk does not claim a divine right to do what comes naturally.

6. **B** The sentences are short, the words clear; in all respects the poem is written economically.

7. **D** Nowhere in the poem does the hawk offer itself for inspection.

8. **C** The hawk knows its own strength, but does not go so far as to liken it to the strength of a tree.

9. **A** The hawk thinks and acts the way you'd expect a powerful tyrant to think and act.

10. **B** To call "tearing off heads" a form of "manners" is indeed ironic.

11. **A** Civilization's refinements do not enter the hawk's mind during the poem.

12. **E** The hawk, unlike a fox or other predator, uses no trickery in hunting its prey.

13. **E** The hawk knows that its body was shaped to do what hawks do best. It is a unique creature, just as all creatures are unique.

14. **D** Most of the poem deals with the hawk's ability to hunt and destroy its prey. By extension, then, it is also about man's penchant for destruction.

15. **D** In its mind, the hawk is figuring out the dynamics of the kill.

16. E   Like all of Shakespeare's love sonnets, this one is meant to praise the speaker's beloved.

17. A   In the final couplet the speaker straightforwardly declares his love for his "mistress."

18. D   The speaker pokes fun at many of the conventions of love poetry—finding the color of roses in a woman's cheeks, for example.

19. A   The speaker has little tolerance for the romantic figures of speech found in a great deal of love poetry. They lack sincerity and are used only for effect.

20. E   Don't jump to conclusions about the intent of the poem before reaching the last line. That's where the speaker's purpose is made clear.

21. A   After reading the entire sonnet, you realize that you've been playfully misled.

22. E   All except the last choice are comparisons stated as metaphors. "The lady I love is rare" is a direct statement.

23. D   What makes the sonnet memorable is that it was written not only to praise the lady but to disparage conventional love poetry.

24. E   Clergymen could not assume that they were respected merely because they were clergymen.

25. B   In context, the statement about the father's appearance seems out of place. But the reader may be sure that the reason for mentioning it will eventually become clear.

26. D   The tone of the entire passage is slightly ironic—a family history told with a twinkle in the eye.

27. A   Phrases such as "addicted to locking up his daughters" (line 8) and "her abilities were quite as extraordinary" (lines 26–27) are used ironically.

28. B   Like Shakespeare's Sonnet 130, this passage makes fun of some of the literary conventions of a certain genre, in this case fictional romances. Even without knowing that, however, you can see that author's tongue is lodged firmly in her cheek while she describes the Morland family.

29. A   Catherine's fondness for boys' games is not included in the list of "heroic" pleasures.

30. B   The implication is that Catherine will either be shunned by gentlemen or will not marry until late in life.

31. C   The ironic tone of each selection reveals the authors' awareness that mortals can be fools.

32. B   The image suggests a kind of shackle, like a ball and chain. Pemberton feels trapped in a painful situation.

33. A   That Morgan came to live with him is hateful to Pemberton. He calls it a "blighting burden" (line 3). Dominated by negative feelings, Pemberton is not likely to be flattered.

34. B   According to lines 6–7, Morgan thinks he is owed a reparation, presumably because Pemberton had walked out on him once before.

35. B Line 7 indicates that Pemberton viewed Morgan expected to stay with him permanently.

36. E The phrase does not reveal or imply anything about Morgan's tragic situation.

37. A Pemberton's thoughts throughout the passage dwell on himself and on his relationship with Morgan. The family situation is not mentioned.

38. E Lines 9–10 indicate that Morgan expects Pemberton to show gratitude.

39. D All of the characteristics listed apply to Morgan except "arrogant and pompous."

40. C Each stanza deals with a different phase of the speaker's relationship with God. At first, the grace of God touches him. Then, he feels doubt. Finally, he recognizes the power of God.

41. D The last two lines of the poem reveal the speaker's strong feelings about God. He is a very religious person.

42. D The syntax suggests that the speaker was an object, an empty vessel. He did nothing to receive God's grace. It just came to him.

43. B The first line of the poem indicates that God wrought the speaker:

44. E The tinder box is a metaphor for the speaker's heart. In effect, God placed His love inside the tinder box.

45. B Extending the metaphor of the first stanza, the speaker can no longer feel the light of God within him.

46. D Faith comes and goes like the tides. In the end, it is difficult to permanently cast out doubt concerning one's spiritual beliefs.

47. D Of all the people listed, a clergyman is most likely to reflect on his faith and suffer torment when his faith flags.

48. E The primary conceit in the poem is the tinder box, in which the flame of God is lit.

49. A The changes that the speaker describes occurred unintentionally. He is like an instrument in God's hands.

50. B These hard sounds suggest the struggle endured by the speaker in the poem.

51. B The words in question repeat the same vowel sounds without the repetition of consonants. Hence, they are an example of *assonance.*

Answers to Essay Questions

Answers for essay questions will vary widely, but the following answers identify ideas that could reasonably be included in your responses.

Question 1   Passage A is written in third person but from the point of view of the chaplain. The opening sentences are meant to startle the reader by their incongruity:

Chaplains are not supposed to sin, and if they do, they are certainly not supposed to feel good about it.

Most of the passage explains why the chaplain was so excited by his discovery that sin could be so much fun. Several statements are short and to the point: "It was miraculous" (line 7); "Anybody could do it" (line 11). Each of these terse sentences contains a new discovery by the chaplain. In fact, much of the passage consists of a list of the chaplain's discoveries: "It was almost no trick at all to turn vice into virtue and slander into truth . . . etc" (lines 7–12).

Irony in the passage is created by employing language that a religious figure might ordinarily use to condemn sin. But the chaplain turns the language on its head by the "handy technique of protective rationalization" (line 6–7). He uses logic to prove to himself that sinning was good. And he is gleeful to discover that sinning is so easy. It merely requires no brains and no character (lines 11–12).

In contrast to the chaplain, the sinner in Passage B suffers pangs of conscience for acting improperly. The irony, of course, is that his alleged sin was an act of humanitarian kindness: he aided Jim (a slave) to become free. He puts the "blame" on himself (line 17) for doing a good deed, and despite rationalizing his actions, continues to be "scorched" (line 20) "pinched" (line 25) by guilt. What he feels most acutely is his betrayal of "poor Miss Watson," who never did him any harm. In fact, Miss Watson had tried to teach him to read and to practice good manners. As a result, he feels "mean and miserable" (line 31) about what he has done.

Question 2

Each of the works listed contains an other-worldly, supernatural dimension. Your job is to describe its role in the work. In *Hamlet,* the appearance of the ghost of King Hamlet serves a stimulus for Prince Hamlet's behavior throughout the play. Similarly, in *Macbeth,* the three weird sisters set the play into motion by predicting Macbeth's future. In *Death of a Salesman,* Willy Loman's long-dead brother Ben returns repeatedly to gnaw at Willy's pride and to deepen his sense of failure.

The oracle in *Oedipus the King,* by setting the stage for the inevitable downfall of the main character, arouses the sense of tragic fear in the audience. Likewise, the basic conceit of *The Picture of Dorian Gray*—that a portrait of the protagonist will age over time while Dorian himself will remain young—creates the sense of impending tragedy. Finally, Orwell's *1984* would not work at all without the presence of the Thought Police and Big Brother.

Question 3

The speaker in the poem is something of a Romeo who enjoyed success with women in the past but now has lost his touch. Now, according to the first stanza, women who once offered him "naked food" (line 2) now flee from him. Once these women were "gentle, tame, and meek" (line 3), but now are wild and uncontrollable.

The second stanza recounts an especially memorable liasion in highly sensual language (lines 11–14). The third stanza returns to the speaker's current state of mind and heart: he has been treated unkindly—forsaken by those who used to fawn on him. The concluding line of stanzas two and three ask "How like you this?" Although the words are the same, the pronoun *this* refers to two very different antecedents. In the second stanza, "this" refers to the kiss. The word "this" in the last stanza, however, refers to being jilted by his former paramours.

Glossary

Literary and Rhetorical Words and Phrases

The following list is made up of words and phrases used by scholars, critics, writers, poets—in fact, all literate people—to exchange ideas and information about language. Knowing these terms won't necessarily transform a mediocre reader into a genius, but familiarity with the terminology will certainly help any aspiring scholar to appreciate the rich possibilities of both written and spoken language.

The authors are indebted for many of the definitions that follow to the *Oxford English Dictionary* and to *A Glossary of Literary Terms* by M.H. Abrams based on the original version by Dan S. Norton and Peter Rushton.

abstract   A very brief synopsis of longer work of scholarship or research. The abstract of an entire book may be reduced to a single page.

abstract terms   As opposed to **concrete terms**, abstract terms represent ideas or thoughts—generalities.

adage   A saying or proverb embodying a piece of common wisdom based on experience and often couched in metaphorical language. Examples of adages: *It is always darkest before the dawn. Fools rush in where angels fear to tread. A fool and his money are soon parted.* See also **aphorism** and **maxim.**

aesthetic distance   Similar in meaning to Keats' "Negative Capability"; refers to a total objectivity of a writer wherein his/her view and judgments are withheld in his/her account of human experience. Another conception of the term defines it as the distance between a work of art and its perceiver, the perceiver recognizing that the work of art is pretense and thereby on occasion larger and truer than life.

allegory   The recounting of an unreal series of experiences bearing such close resemblance to reality as to encourage the reader to make the association; an extended metaphor.

alliteration   The repetition of one or more initial sounds, usually consonants, in a group of words or a line from a poem.

allusion   A reference to a person, place, event, or other source meant to create an effect or enrich the meaning of an idea.

ambiguity   Multiple meaning; lack of clarity in a work consciously used as a phase of the author's view of his/her world or characters and reflecting the vagueness of life.

anachronism   The incorporation of an event, scene, or person who does not correspond with the time period portrayed in the work; as Shakespeare's use of a cannon in *King John* or a hat in *Julius Caesar.*

analogy   A comparison that points out similarities between two dissimilar things.

annotation   Notes added to a text that explain, name sources, summarize, or evaluate the text.

antagonist   The character or force in a story that works against the protagonist to produce tension or conflict.

antithesis   The rhetorical opposition or contrast of words, clauses, or sentences, as in the following:
"as action, not words"
"They promised freedom but provided slavery"
"Ask not what your country can do for you, but what you can do for your country."
John F. Kennedy

aphorism   A short, pithy statement of a generally accepted truth or sentiment, such as "The road to Hell is often paved with good intentions." See also **adage** and **maxim.**

Apollonian   As distinguished from Dionysian; refers to the noble qualities of human beings and nature as opposed to the savage and destructive forces.

apostrophe   A locution that addresses a person or personified thing not present. An example: "Oh, you cruel streets of Manhattan, how I detest you!"

archetype   A plot that repeats basic historical or primitive life patterns; from the psychology of Carl Jung.

assonance   The repetition of two or more vowel sounds in a group of words or a line of poetry.

ballad   A simple narrative verse that tells a story that is sung or recited.

bard   In modern usage, a poet. In the past, however, the term referred to poets who related stories of heroes to the accompaniment of a musical instrument such as the harp.

baroque   In a strict sense, refers to an elaborate style of architecture that followed **classicism;** in general usage, however, refers to elaborate and unstructured style.

bathos   The use of ludicrous, commonplace language; anticlimax; the use of insincere or overdone sentimentality.

belles-lettres   A body of literature including drama, poetry, fiction, and criticism that is inherently artistic, as opposed to scientific discourse.

blank verse   Unrhymed lines of iambic pentameter.

bombast   Inflated language; the use of high-sounding language for a trivial subject.

burlesque   A literary composition that aims to provoke laughter by ridiculing serious works; a grotesque imitation of the dignified or pathetic.

cacophony   The use of inharmonious sounds in close conjunction to create an effect. Contrast with **euphony.**

caricature   A grotesque likeness of striking characteristics in persons or things.

carpe diem   "Seize the day"; a **motif** in poetry; refers to the view that one should enjoy life to the fullest while one is able.

catharsis   A cleansing of the spirit of the spectator at a tragedy through experiencing the emotions of pity and terror; as expressed in Aristotle's *Poetics.*

classic   A highly regarded work of literature or other art form that has withstood the test of time.

Many of Shakespeare's plays and many of Dickens' novels are usually considered classics. They will endure for a very long time.

classical, classicism   Deriving from the orderly qualities of ancient Greek and Roman culture; usually implies objectivity and simplicity, restraint and formality.

cliché   An overused or trite expression.

climax   The high point, or turning point, in a story or play.

conceit   A figure of speech in which a striking association is made between two seemingly dissimilar things; an extended metaphor, as in the poetry of John Donne.

concrete terms   As opposed to **abstract terms,** concrete terms refer to things that have actual existence, that can be seen or known.

connotation   The suggested or implied meaning of a word or phrase. Contrast with **denotation.**

consonance   The repetition of two or more consonant sounds in a group of words or a line of poetry.

denotation   The dictionary definition of a word or phrase. Contrast with **connotation.**

dénouement   The final resolution of the strands of plot complications or problems.

deus ex machina   As in Greek theater, the employment of any artificial device or gimmick that the author uses to solve a difficult situation.

diction   The selection of words in oral or written discourse.

Dionysian   As distinguished from **Apollonian;** refers to the sensual, pleasure-seeking qualities of man and nature.

dramatic irony   An inconsistency, known by the audience or reader, between a character's perception of a situation and the truth of the situation.

dramatic monologue   A type of poem or prose piece in which the speaker gives an account of a dramatic moment in his/her life and, in doing so, reveals his/her character.

elegy   A poem or piece of prose lamenting or meditating on the death of a person or pet.

ellipsis, elliptical   Three periods (. . .) indicating the omission of words. A sentence with elliptical structure omits something in the second half, usually the verb in a subject-verb-object sentence, as in "May was hot and June the same." The verb *was* is omitted from "June was the same."

empathy A feeling of association or identification with an object; experiencing its sensations and responding with similar feelings.

epic A narrative poem, often quite long, that tells of the adventures of a hero important to his nation or race.

epigram The ingenious, witty, thoughtful, provocative statement.

euphony The use of pleasant, harmonious words to create an effect. Contrast with **cacophony.**

exegesis A detailed analysis or interpretation of a poem, parable, or other piece of discourse.

Existentialism As expressed in the works of such writers as Kafka, Camus, and Faulkner, a view of life that emphasizes existence as opposed to essence; human beings are presented as unable to solve the basic enigmas of life.

exposé A piece of writing, often journalistic, meant to reveal or expose weakness, faults, frailties, or other shortcomings.

exposition The explanation or analysis of a subject; setting forth the meaning or purpose of an issue or set of facts.

explication The interpretation or analysis of a text.

Expressionism A form of art in which the artist depicts the inner essence of man and projects his view of the world as colored by that essence.

fable A short story designed to teach a useful lesson; its characters are usually animals or inanimate things.

falling action The action in a play or story that occurs after the climax. During this time, conflicts are usually resolved.

fantasy The creation of unreal worlds and people, bearing a relation to the real.

figurative language Figures of speech, among them metaphor, simile, personification, synecdoche, metonymy, allusion, and symbol.

flashback Returning to an earlier time in a story or play for the purpose of clarifying present actions or circumstances.

foreshadowing Providing hints of things to come in a story or play.

free verse A kind of poetry without rhymed lines or regular rhythm.

genre A term used to describe literary forms such as tragedy, comedy, novel, and essay.

haiku A verse form from Japan, in three lines of five, seven, and five syllables, often depicting an image from nature.

hamartia Aristotle's term for the protagonist's tragic flaw or tragic error of judgment.

hubris, hybris Aristotle's term for the pride of the tragic hero that leads him to ignore or overlook warnings of impending disaster or to break moral laws.

humanism In common usage, an attitude that emphasizes human interests; an optimistic view of human potential.

humor The quality in action, speech, or writing that excites amusement; less intellectual than **wit** and having a more sympathetic tone.

hyperbole Overstatement; gross exaggeration for rhetorical effect.

idyll A lyric poem describing a kind of ideal life or place.

imagery The use of words to represent what can be seen, touched, smelled, tasted, or felt—in short, sensory language.

Impressionism In writing, the presentation of the salient features of a scene, event, or person as they appear to the author at the time; a highly personal approach.

invective In satirical writing, the use of denunciatory, angry, and insulting language.

irony A form of expression in which the meaning intended is the opposite from what is stated; also used to define the tragic contrast between the aspirations of human beings and the dark elements of life that frustrate them; in addition, used to describe the view of humanity in which human limitations and posturings are seen as debasing and ridiculous, there is in the ironic view an element of mockery.

lampoon A violent and scurrilous satirical attack against a person or institution.

light verse   A type of poetry meant to entertain or amuse. Some light verse has a serious intent to satirize or parody, for example.

limerick   A form of light verse, often nonsensical, containing five lines and a prescribed rhythm and rhyme scheme. For example:
There was a young lady of Niger
Who smiled as she rode on a tiger:
   They came back from the ride
   With the lady inside
And a smile on the face of the tiger.

litotes   A form of understatement in which the negative of the contrary is used to achieve emphasis and intensity. An example: *He is not a bad dancer.*

loose sentence   A sentence that follows the customary word order of English sentences, *i.e.,* subject verb object. The main idea of the sentence is presented first and is then followed by one or more subordinate clauses. See also **periodic sentence.**

lyric   Subjective, reflective poetry with regular rhyme scheme and meter that reveals the poet's thoughts and feelings to crate a single, unique impression. Some examples of lyric poems are: "Dover Beach" by Matthew Arnold, "Because I Could Not Stop for Death" by Emily Dickinson, and "Out of the Cradle Endlessly Rocking" by Walt Whitman.

maxim   A saying or proverb expressing common wisdom or truth. See also **adage** and **aphorism.**

melodrama   A literary account in which the incidents are sensational, the characters exceptionally noble or evil, the appeal to the emotions extreme; in a melodrama usually all ends well.

metaphor   A figure of speech that compares unlike objects.

metaphysical poetry   The work of poets, particularly those of the seventeenth century, that implies elaborate conceits; such poetry is highly intellectual and expresses life's complexities.

meter   Poetry's rhythm, or its pattern of stressed and unstressed syllables. See pages 110–111 for full discussion of meter.

metonymy   A figure of speech that uses the name of one thing to represent something else with which it is associated. Example: *"The White House says . . ."*

Middle English   The language spoken in England roughly between 1150 and 1500 A.D.

mode   An attribute or quality of a thing; a work of literature may be written in a particular mode.

montage   A quick succession of images or pictures to express an idea; used primarily in films.

mood   The emotional response that a piece of literature stimulates in the reader.

moral   The lesson a reader infers from a story, poem, or other piece of literature. Because unsophisticated readers often assume that literature is "supposed to" contain a moral truth, they equate literary analysis with finding a simplistic lesson hidden in the story as though authors intend to teach their readers the proper way to think and act. Thus, the moral of *Macbeth* might be: Don't be inordinately ambitious. And the moral of *Crime and Punishment:* Crime does not pay.

motif   A device that serves as a unifying agent in conveying a theme.

Muses   The goddesses presiding over the arts; the daughters of Zeus: *Calliope* (epic poetry), *Clio* (history), *Erato* (lyrics and love poetry), *Euterpe* (music), *Melpomene* (tragedy), *Polyhymnia* (sacred poetry), *Terpsichore* (choral dance and song), *Thalia* (comedy), and *Urania* (astronomy).

myth   A solidly conceived, but entirely imaginative world, with beliefs and values, created by an author; a story that forms part of the beliefs of a faith in which people no longer believe.

narrative   A form of verse or prose that tells a story.

nonsequitur   A statement or idea that fails to follow logically from the one before.

ode   A lyric verse usually marked by serious, respectful, and exalted feelings toward the subject.

Old English   The Anglo-Saxon language spoken in what is now England during the years, roughly speaking, 450 to 1150 A.D.

omniscient narrator   A narrator with unlimited awareness, understanding and insight of character, setting, background, and all other elements of the story.

onomatopoeia   The use of words whose sounds suggest their meaning. Example: *bubbling, murmuring brooks.*

ontological criticism A concern by a critic with analysis of a work itself without seeking answers to problems in the biography or milieu of the author or in influences upon him/her; the method of the New Critics.

oxymoron A term made up of contradictory elements brought into juxtaposition to create a paradoxical effect. Examples: *loud silence, jumbo shrimp.*

parable Similar to **allegory,** but shorter; a story in which the author intends that the reader will relate the events of the story to some moral or spiritual truth. Unlike a fable, the parable deals with events that can occur in the real world.

paradox A statement that seems self-contradictory, but is nevertheless true.

parody A satirical imitation of a work for the purpose of ridiculing its style and subject.

pastoral A work of literature dealing with rural life.

pathos That element of literature that stimulates pity or sorrow.

periodic sentence A sentence that departs from the usual word order of English sentences by expressing the main thought only at the end. In other words, the particulars in the sentence are presented ahead of the idea they support. See also **loose sentence.**

persona The role or facade that a character assumes or depicts to a reader, a viewer, or the world at large.

personification A figure of speech in which objects and animals are given human qualities.

plot line A graphic display of the events in a story, including exposition, rising action, climax, falling action, and resolution.

point of view The view, whether limited or omniscient, the reader gets of the action and characters in a story.

protagonist The chief character in a work of literature.

pun A humorous play on words, using similar-sounding or identical words to suggest different meanings. Example:
"I'm glad we are out of Vietnam," she said.
"So am I" he replied. "It was time to let Saigons be Saigons."

realism In literature and art, the depiction of people, things, and experiences as it is believed they really are without idealization or exaggeration; in recent use, it has often been used synonymously with naturalism as depicting events that are unpleasant or sordid.

rhetoric The language of a work and its style; similar to **diction.**

rhyme The repetition of similar sounds at regular intervals, often used in the writing of verse.

Romanticism In literature and in art, the depiction of idealized, fabulous, or fantastic characters and events; the stories abound in dashing, extravagant adventures, characters of extreme virtues or faults, exotic worlds, strong and inflexible loyalties, and idealized love-making.

sarcasm A sharp, caustic expression or remark; a bitter gibe or taunt; different from **irony,** which is more subtle.

satire A literary style used to make fun of or ridicule an idea or human vice or foible, frequently with the intent of changing or altering the subject being attacked. Jonathan Swift's famous essay, "A Modest Proposal," is a classic example of satirical writing.

sentence structure The manner in which grammatical elements are arranged in a sentence. Although there are endless varieties of sentences, each is a variation on one of the three basic structures: *simple, compound,* and *complex.* (1) A *simple* sentence contains a subject and a verb along with modifiers and perhaps an object. (2) A *compound* sentence consists of two or more simple sentences linked by a conjunction such as *and* or *but.* (3) A *complex* sentence is made up of an independent, or main, clause and any number of dependent or subordinate clauses.

sentiment Refined and tender emotion in literature; sometimes used derisively to represent insincerity or mawkishness.

sentimental Used to describe characters' excessive emotional response to experience; describes also insincere and exaggerated emotional displays.

simile A figurative comparison using the words *like* or *as.*

sonnet A fourteen-line verse form, usually consisting of three four-line units called quatrains and a concluding rhymed couplet. Although Shakespeare and Petrarch are the world's master-sonneteers, many other poets have used the form.

stream of consciousness Refers to an attempt on the part of an author to reproduce the unembellished flow of thoughts in the human mind with its feelings, judgments, associations, and memories.

style The manner in which an author uses words, shapes ideas, forms sentences, and creates a structure to convey ideas.

Surrealism In literature and art, an attempt to reproduce and interpret the visions and images of the unconscious mind as manifested in dreams; characterized by an irrational arrangement of bizarre experiences.

symbolism The use of one object to suggest another, hidden, object or idea.

synecdoche A figure of speech in which a part signifies the whole (*fifty masts* for *fifty ships*) or the whole signifies the part (*days* for *life,* as in *"He lived his days under African skies."*) When the name of a material stands for the thing itself as in *pigskin* for *football* that, too, is a synecdoche.

tension Inclusion in poetry of **abstract** and **concrete** meaning; related to **metonymy** in that expression of the particular suggests the universal; presenting the image suggests the idea; term first introduced by critic Allen Tate.

theme The main idea or meaning, often an abstract idea upon which a work of literature is built.

tone The author's attitude toward the subject being written about. The tone is the characteristic emotion that pervades a work or part of a work—the spirit or character that is a work's emotional essence.

tragedy A form of literature in which the hero is destroyed by some character flaw and a set of forces that cause the hero considerable anguish.

Transcendentalism A form of romanticism, largely of a philosophical nature; sponsored by Americans such as Emerson and Thoreau.

trope Words used with a decided change or extension in their literal meaning; the use of a word in a figurative sense.

verbal irony A discrepancy between the true meaning of a situation and the literal meaning of the written or spoken words.

verisimilitude Similar to truth; the quality of **realism** in a work that persuades the reader that he/she is getting a vision of life as it is.

villanelle A French verse form, strictly calculated to appear simple and spontaneous, but consisting of 19 lines and a prescribed rhyme scheme.

voice The real or assumed personality used by a writer or speaker. In grammar, *active voice* and *passive voice* refer to verbs. A verb is in the active voice when it expresses an action performed *by* its subject. A verb is in the passive voice when it expresses an action performed upon its subject or when the subject is the result of the action.
ACTIVE: The crew raked the leaves.
PASSIVE: The leaves were raked by the crew.
Stylistically, the active voice makes for more economical and vigorous writing.

wit The quickness of intellect and the power and talent for saying brilliant things that surprise and delight by their unexpectedness; the power to comment subtly and pointedly on the foibles of the passing scene.

Works Discussed or Analyzed

Conrad Aiken	"Silent Snow, Secret Snow"
Anna Akhmatova	"Pushkin"
Aristophanes	*The Frogs*
Samuel Beckett	*Waiting for Godot*
William Blake	"London"
Jorge Luis Borges	"In Praise of Darkness"
Emily Bronte	*Wuthering Heights*
Robert Browning	"Summum Bonum"
William Congreve	*The Way of the World*
Joseph Conrad	*Lord Jim*
Stephen Crane	"In the Desert"
Countee Cullen	"Any Human to Another"
e. e. cummings	"The Cambridge ladies"
John Donne	Sonnet XIV
	"A Valediction: Forbidding Mourning"
Ralph Ellison	*Invisible Man*
William Faulkner	*As I Lay Dying*
	"The Bear"
Gustave Flaubert	*Madame Bovary*
Robert Frost	"Mending Wall"
Robert Graves	"The Persian Version"
Joseph Heller	*Catch-22*
Ernest Hemingway	"A Clean, Well-Lighted Place"
Gerard Manley Hopkins	"God's Grandeur"
Langston Hughes	"Dream Deferred"
Henrik Ibsen	*The Wild Duck*
James Joyce	"The Dead"
Franz Kafka	"A Country Doctor"
	"Give It Up"
	"The Hunter Gracchus"
John Keats	"La Belle Dame Sans Merci"
D. H. Lawrence	"The Prussian Officer"
Christopher Marlowe	*Doctor Faustus*
Gabriel García Márquez	*One Hundred Years of Solitude*
Toni Morrison	*Beloved*
Pablo Neruda	"Ode to the Americas"
Katherine Anne Porter	"Noon Wine"
Theodore Roethke	"Elegy for Jane"
Siegfried Sassoon	"Base Details"
William Shakespeare	*Hamlet*
	King Lear
	"My Mistress' Eyes Are Nothing Like the Sun"
	Othello
	"Shall I Compare Thee to a Summer's Day?"
Sophocles	*Oedipus the King*
	Antigone
Edmund Spenser	"Long While I Sought"

Wallace Stevens — "Thirteen Ways of Looking at a Blackbird"

Tom Stoppard — *Rosencrantz and Guildenstern Are Dead*

Jonathan Swift — *Gulliver's Travels*

Alfred, Lord Tennyson — "Ulysses"

Dylan Thomas — "Do Not Go Gentle into That Good Night"

Voltaire — *Candide*

Richard Wilbur — "Museum Piece"

William Wordsworth — "Ode: Intimations of Immortality from Recollections of Early Childhood"

"The World Is Too Much with Us"

W. B. Yeats — "Lines Written in Dejection"

Index

Notes

Notes

Notes

Notes

Notes

Notes

Notes